The Nature of History Reader

The question of what the nature of history is, is a key issue for all students of history. It is now recognised by many that the past and history are different phenomena and that the way the past is actively historicised can be highly problematic and contested. Older metaphysical, ontological, epistemological, methodological and ethical assumptions can no longer be taken as read.

In this timely collection, key pieces of writing by leading historians are reproduced and evaluated, with an explanation and critique of their character and assumptions, and how they reflect upon the nature of the history project.

The Nature of History Reader is an informed guide that is reflexive, engaged, critical and innovative. This work points the way to a positive rethinking of history today, and will be of use both to students and to their teachers.

Keith Jenkins is Professor of Historical Theory, University College Chichester. He is the author of five books on historical theory, including *Refiguring History* (2003). **Alun Munslow** is Professor of History and Historical Theory at Staffordshire University. He is the author of four books on historical theory, including *The New History* (2003). He is also UK editor of the Routledge journal *Rethinking History: The Journal of Theory and Practice*.

The Nature of History Reader

Edited by

Keith Jenkins and
Alun Munslow

Routledge
Taylor & Francis Group

LONDON AND NEW YORK

First published 2004
by Routledge
11 New Fetter Lane, London EC4P 4EE

Simultaneously published in the USA and Canada
by Routledge
29 West 35th Street, New York, NY 10001

Routledge is an imprint of the Taylor & Francis Group

Typeset in Perpetua and Bell Gothic by
Florence Production Ltd, Stoodleigh, Devon

Printed and bound in Great Britain by
TJ International Ltd, Padstow, Cornwall

British Library Cataloguing in Publication Data
A catalogue record for this book is available from the British Library

Library of Congress Cataloging in Publication Data
The nature of history reader / edited and introduced by Keith Jenkins and
Alun Munslow.
    p. cm.
Includes bibliographical references and index.
1. History – Philosophy. 2. Postmodernism. 3. Historiography.
4. Historicism. 5. History – Methodology. 6. History – Historiography.
7. Narration (Rhetoric) I. Jenkins, Keith, 1943–   II. Munslow, Alun, 1947–
D16.8.N35 2004
901–dc22   2003021897

ISBN 0–415–24053–0 (hbk)
ISBN 0–415–24054–9 (pbk)

For Sue and Jane

Brief contents

Detailed contents

Acknowledgements

Geoffrey Elton, *Return to Essentials* (1991), pp. 6–11; reprinted by permission of Cambridge University Press, Cambridge. © 1999 from Deborah A. Symonds 'Living in the Scottish Record Office', in Elizabeth Fox-Genovese and Elisabeth Lasch-Quinn *Reconstructing History*, pp. 164–75; reproduced by permission of Routledge/Taylor & Francis Books, Inc., New York. Edward Royle, *Modern Britain: A Social History, 1750–1997*, pp. 120–5; Arnold, London ([1987] 1998); copyright © 1987 Edward Royle, reproduced by permission. *America: A Narrative History*, 5th edition, by George Brown Tindall and David E. Shi, pp. 21–6; © [1984] 1999 by W.W. Norton & Company, Inc., New York, used by permission of W.W. Norton & Company, Inc. *Paul Revere's Ride* by David Hackett Fischer, pp. 138–41; © 1995 by David Hackett Fischer, used by permission of Oxford University Press, Inc., New York. Luigi Albertini, *The Origins of the War of 1914*, pp. 170–5 (translated and edited by Isabella M. Massey) (three volumes, 1952–7); reprinted by permission of Oxford University Press, Oxford. © David Loades ([1979] 1991), *The Reign of Mary Tudor: Politics, Government and Religion in England, 1553–58*, pp. 18–23; reprinted by permission of Pearson Education Ltd, London. *A History of Water in Modern England and Wales*, by John Hassan (1998) pp. 10–12, Manchester University Press, Manchester. © Michael A.R. Graves ([1987] 1996), *Elizabethan Parliaments 1559–1601*, pp. 90–2; reprinted by permission of Pearson Education Ltd, London. Gertrude Himmelfarb (1984), *The Idea of Poverty: England in the Early Industrial Age*, pp. 6–10, Faber & Faber Ltd, London. Peter Charles Hoffer and William W. Stueck, *Reading and Writing American History: An Introduction to the Historian's Craft*, 1st edition, pp. 38–40; © 1994 D. C. Heath & Company, Lexington, MA, used with permission. Eric Hobsbawm (1997) *On History*, pp. 269–72; Orion, London, by permission. © John Tosh ([1984] 2000), *The Pursuit of History: Aims, Methods and New Directions in the Study of Modern History*, pp. 135–7; reprinted by permission of Pearson-Longman, London. *A History of Civilizations* by Fernand Braudel ([1963] 1993), pp. 15–21; translated by Richard Mayne (Allen Lane, The Penguin Press, Harmondsworth); translation copyright Richard Mayne, 1993. *The French Revolution:*

Rethinking the Debate, Gwynne Lewis (1999), pp. 8–11; by permission of Routledge, London. David R. Roediger (1991) *The Wages of Whiteness: Race and the Making of the American Working Class*, pp. 97–100; with permission from Verso, London. *Orientalism: History, Theory and the Arts*, by John M. MacKenzie (1995), pp. 3–7; Manchester University Press, Manchester. Jan P. Nederveen Pieterse (1990) *Empire and Emancipation: Power and Liberation on a World Scale*, pp. 8–11; reprinted by permission of Pluto Press, London. *History and International Relations*, Thomas W. Smith (1999), pp. 1–4; reprinted by permission of Routledge, London. *Understanding the Industrial Revolution*, Charles More (2000), pp. 9–12; reprinted by permission of Routledge, London. Richard F. Bensel, *Yankee Leviathan: The Origins of Central State Authority in America, 1859–1877*, pp. 2–8; reprinted by permission of Cambridge University Press, Cambridge. John Tosh, 'What Should Historians do with Masculinity? Reflections on Nineteenth-Century Britain', *History Workshop Journal*, 38, 1994, pp. 70–2; by permission of Oxford University Press, Oxford. *Reading Witchcraft: Stories of Early English Witches*, Marion Gibson (1999), pp. 4–6; reprinted by permission of Routledge, London. Copyright © Paul Thompson ([1978] 2000); reprinted from *The Voice of the Past: Oral History* by Paul Thompson (3rd edition, 2000), pp. 5–8; by permission of Oxford University Press, Oxford. Mark S.R. Jenner, 'The Great Dog Massacre' from *Fear in Early Modern Society* by William G. Naphy and Penny Roberts (eds) (1997), pp. 52–6; Manchester University Press, Manchester. 'Performing On the Beaches of the Mind: An Essay' by Greg Dening, with permission of *History and Theory*, 41 (1), 2002, pp. 1–22. Walter Benjamin, *The Arcades Project*, pp. 35–41 and 420–3; reprinted by permission of the publisher from *The Arcades Project* by Walter Benjamin, translated by Howard Eiland and Kevin McLaughlin, Cambridge, MA: The Belknap Press of Harvard University Press; © 1999 by the President and Fellows of Harvard College. Richard Price, *First-Time: The Historical Vision of an African American People* ([1983] 2002), pp. xi–xv, 37–40 and 43–53, The University of Chicago Press, Chicago; with permission of the author. Robert A. Rosenstone, *The Man Who Swam Into History* (2002), pp. xi–xvii and 3–27; 1st Books Bloomington, IL, by the kind permission of the author. Hans Ulrich Gumbrecht, *In 1926: Living At The Edge of Time*, pp. vii–xv and 66–73; reprinted by permission of the publisher, Harvard University Press, Cambridge, MA; copyright © 1997 by the President and Fellows of Harvard College. Sven Lindqvist, *A History of Bombing*; copyright © 2000 by Sven Lindqvist; translation © 2001 by The New Press. Dipesh Chakrabarty, *Provincializing Europe: Postcolonial Thought and Historical Difference* (2000), pp. 3–11; © Princeton University Press; reprinted by permission of Princeton University Press, Princeton, NJ. Hayden White, *Figural Realism: Studies in the Mimesis Effect*, pp. 66–86, © 1999, The Johns Hopkins University Press, Baltimore, MD; reprinted with permission of The Johns Hopkins University Press and the author. Iain Chambers, *Culture After Humanism* (2000), pp. 7–19; by kind permission of the author and Routledge, London. Jacques Derrida, 'Deconstructions: The Im-possible'; © 2001 from *French Theory in America* by S. Lotringer and S. Cohen, pp. 13–31; reproduced by permission of Routledge, Inc., New York. David Roberts, *Nothing But History*, © 1995, The Regents of the University of California Press, Berkeley, CA, pp. 1–9, by permission. Carolyn Steedman, 'About Ends: On How the End is Different From an Ending', *Dust* (2001), pp. 142–54; by permission of the author and Manchester University Press, Manchester. Joan Scott, 'After History?', *Common Knowledge*, 5 (3), Winter 1996, pp. 9–12 and 19–26; reproduced by kind permission of the author. Rita Felski, 'Fin de siècle, Fin de sexe: Transsexuality, Postmodernism, and the Death of History', in *New Literary History*, 27 (2), 1996, pp. 337–49; by kind permission of the author and publisher. Elizabeth Deeds Ermarth "Beyond 'The Subject'", in *New Literary History*, 31 (3), 2000, pp. 195 and 200–15; by kind permission of the author and publisher. David Harlan, *The Degradation of American History* (1997), pp. 127–30, 153–7, 209–13; University of Chicago

Press, Chicago, with kind permission of the author and publisher. Dipesh Chakrabarty ''The Death of History? Historical Consciousness and the Culture of Late Capitalism'', in *Public Culture*, 4 (2), pp. 56–65; © 1992, Duke University Press, Durham, NC; all rights reserved, used by permission of the publisher. Jean François Lyotard, *The Postmodern Explained to Children* (1992), pp. 35–47, by kind permission of the publisher, Turnaround PSL, London. 'The End of the Millennium or the Countdown' by Jean Baudrillard, *Economy and Society*, 26 (4), 1997, pp. 447–55; reproduced by permission of Taylor & Francis Group plc (Journals), http://www.tandf.co.uk. Kerwin Lee Klein, 'On The Emergence of Memory in Historical Discourse', © 2000 by The Regents of the University of California, Berkeley, CA; reprinted from *Representations*, 69, Winter 2000, pp. 127–50, by permission.

Note

Every effort has been made to obtain permission to reproduce copyright material. If any proper acknowledgement has not been made, we would invite copyright holders to inform us of the oversight.

The text and/or notes of some contributions have been abridged.

INTRODUCTION

Positionings

In the 1960s a whole series of theoretical developments emerged out of what has since been called European 'continental' philosophy. Some of the particular names that these developments first travelled under have fallen into obscurity, but today, some forty years on, many have become familiar to us: the linguistic turn, deconstructionism, post-structuralism, post-feminism, post-colonialism, post-Marxism, postmodernism, etc. And although these 'postist' phenomena differ from each other in their detail, nevertheless, taken singly or in some form of combination, their effect upon the old modernist 'discipline' of history in its professional, academic forms (let alone its metanarrative forms) has arguably been, and is, devastating. For what these various developments did – and do – was to provide an enormously critical challenge to, and indeed denial of, the still influential but essentially nineteenth-century belief that some sort of empiricism was the only proper basis for the practice of professional historians, and that the result of these practices, the embodiment of the historian's labour – books, chapters, articles, etc. – had the status of an *epistemology*. That is to say, professional historians thought (and generally still think) that they possessed certain empirical methods by which they could have objective and demonstrable *knowledge* of 'the past' both in its generalities and in its particulars. And it is this belief, this epistemological claim, that the coming of the 'postmodern' has rendered problematic.

Accordingly, it is the problematicisation of this type of history – the type of history which has long dominated and in certain variants still dominates academic understandings of what history is and ought to be – that this Reader principally considers, responds to and possibly begins to move beyond. For we think that students who are coming to the study of 'the nature of history' possibly for the first time *ought* to understand – if they are to try to comprehend their 'discourse' (*not* discipline) reflexively and critically – something about this dramatic (and for some historians) traumatic state of affairs. Consequently, it is this that this text tries to accomplish, for, from our perspective, it seems clear that we are living at a moment when the power of 'postist' challenges to professional/academic historians has not only undercut its more 'conservative' and revisionist approaches (what we shall call its 'reconstructionist' and 'constructionist' genres), but has also helped to raise for consideration – not least by the instal- lation of a radical 'deconstructionist' history that has taken the impact of the 'posts' very seriously into account – the possibility that not only have we to rethink 'history as we have known it' along deconstructionist, postmodern lines, but that we may have come to the end of history in all of its current manifestations; that our 'postmodern condition' can perhaps produce its own, non-historical acts of the imagination for us to live by which do not figure in its number any sort of recognisable history at all.

Consequently, what we have tried to do in this text is to provide a collection of readings that we hope is sufficient to allow students of history to reflect upon the way histories are written, taught and thought about today, and possibly how they might be considered tomorrow. The picture which emerges in the following pages reveals history's up-dating from the hard- core, late nineteenth-century Rankean documentarist/'reconstructionist' style of historiography to a more pluralist, perspectival, 'constructionist' genre, its challenge by 'deconstructionist' approaches and, as stated, reflections on the possible demise of this interesting experiment of 'historicising of the past' in both modernist and postmodernist ways. This transitional perspec- tive – the general position held by the editors of this Reader, despite their sometime differences on this or that detail – thus calls into question, at most, the very idea of history and, at least, makes highly problematic some of the dominant ongoing practices we still think are being encouraged in many history departments in many contemporary institutions of higher education.

One of the many consequences of the above problematisation (not only within the discourse of history but in many other areas of contemporary life as well) has been that the mainstream (reconstructionist and constructionist) makers of history have had to come out of their lairs, wherein they have long cherished the opinion that the histories they have produced have effect- ively been written by the past itself as they shyly but insistently pledge their allegiance to the 'sovereignty of the past' while denying the full power of their own interpretive bulk, and talk much more about their theoretical positions and their idiosyncratic methods (for there is no single, definitive, historical method). At which point they have become sometime participants in that culture of confession in which we live, a culture in which it has become the norm for writers to explain that intellectual/ideological place 'they have come from'. Of course, this professing of a position can be invasive or sensationalist, as well as ritualistic, formulaic, empty and thus actually obfuscatory. Nevertheless, while the readings offered here are intended to give a general overview, we expect that it is clear already that this text is itself self- consciously positioned; that it has no pretence of being – this is what we are confessing – some sort of disinterested or neutral 'view from nowhere'. Any text, including this one, stakes out a claim, is inevitably intertextual and partial/partisan, and thus an engagement which is unavoidably *polemical*, for it is impossible today – in fact, strictly speaking it may always have been 'logically' impossible – to write in any other way. And this is because there just is a condition of *polemos* whenever (and this seems to have always been the case) there is no metalanguage or locus of truth or absolute criteria or universal method or transcendental view- point (a god's-eye view) *outside* of the discursive field to act as arbiter between positions, the consequent radical historicising and relativising of the field necessarily 'guaranteeing' multi- plicity and heterogeneity for ever. And so we ourselves perhaps ought to say just a little about what we see as our own 'polemical' position in this text so that readers can, if they wish to, and relative to their own lights, take it into account.

Basic to our position(s), then, and informing this text throughout are, on the one hand, certain anti-post-empiricist and anti-post-epistemological assumptions and, on the other, certain pro-deconstructionist and pro-aesthetic perspectives. We are anti-post-empiricists because we think that the historicising of the past (the turning of what seems to have happened 'before now' into something the 'before now' never actually was – an article, a film, a book, a conference paper – a history), is as much a linguistic undertaking (and especially a narrativisation, an aestheticising and thus a figurative undertaking) as it is an empirical one. To turn (to trope) something that isn't in the form of a narrative – all that has gone on before everywhere – into a narrative (that is, into a linguistic convention, a literary mode of structuration, a genre) is just an act of the imagination. And this imaginative, constitutive element gives history qua history the unavoidable status of being *fictive*. Not, let us note immediately, the status of being a piece of *fiction* – for in fiction the imagined goes 'all the way down' – but fictive in the sense of *fictio*; that is to say, made up, fashioned, created, fabricated, figured. We thus take it as read that histories as such are aesthetic, figurative productions which, while they contain what can be called facts (and which indeed refer, indirectly, via the mediations of a performative language use, to the traces of aspects of a once actuality) are, nevertheless, always more than the sum of their factual/cognitive parts: a sum total that can never actually be total. And this 'fact' – the fact that histories are irreducible to 'the facts' and thus knowledge closures; the fact that histories always contain acts of the creative imagination – means that histories are impossible to close down, because it is impossible to close down the imagination. This openness of the 'before now' to interminable appropriation is further guaranteed on two counts. First, because the 'before now' doesn't have in it a shape of its own, because the 'before now' doesn't have in it 'events' that have, as it were, the shape of narratives, there is nothing against which we can check out our imagined narrative orderings to see if they 'correspond', for there is literally nothing for them to correspond to. Consequently, although objectivity and truth might well operate at the level of the statement in so far as it demonstrably corresponds to a singular piece of 'evidence', no such correspondence can ever be achieved at the level of the text, at the level of a history (and histories are always 'at the level of the text'). Second, all (further) attempts to effect some kind of closure by reference to *context* – historians are always talking about 'putting things into context' – is also impossible epistemologically because no 'context' is ever exhaustive: you can always get another context, always get another (arbitrary) set of circumstances. Consequently, because new contexts are always – in principle and in practice – open to future recontextualisation ad infinitum, so the 'before now' is too. In that sense, while the past is literally behind us, histories are always 'to come'; in other words, the before now is always unstable 'historically' because history cannot, in that sense, die. (This is not to say, incidentally, that we cannot come to the end of history in the sense that the whole discourse of history could become obsolete, forgotten; rather, it is to say that, in so far as the 'before now' remains as something that is 'historically' considered, then *logically* what that consideration results in is never final, never definitive.)

For us this inability ever to secure what are effectively interpretive closures – the continuing *raison d'être* of the vast bulk of the historical profession in even these pluralist days – is not only logically *impossible*, but politically and ethically/morally *desirable*. The fact that the 'before now', both as a whole and in its parts, is so very obviously underdetermining vis-à-vis its innumerable appropriations (one past, an infinity of histories) is to be both celebrated and worked. It is to be celebrated because we think it is a positive democratic value when everybody can (at least potentially) author their own lives reflexively and so create their own intellectual and moral genealogies and thus identities, that there is no credible authoritative or authoritarian historicised past that one has to defer to over one's own personal 'memory', or indeed even to register and/or acknowledge. And it is to be worked because it offers the logically impossible-to-prevent opportunity for those who still have the desire to articulate past-tensed fictive productions under (or beyond) the old name or history, to do so in radical disobedience to what we consider to be the stultifying orthodoxies of mainstream academic histories as epistemologies. And so our anti-post-epistemological position pushes us towards the view that it is wonderful news that historians can never get things right; that histories qua histories are always representational failures. This opens up the 'before now' to endless acts of the creative imagination unshackled by epistemology narrowly construed.

In his essay 'Deconstructions: The Im-possible', Jacques Derrida addresses the question – which he had been asked to address – of estimating the significance of, the impact of, Derridean deconstruction in American academic life over the previous twenty years. Derrida replied that, while to reconstruct that impact could not actually be done, nevertheless, he can offer a certain *emphasis*, an emphasis which, as he puts it,

> would concern a past periodization I don't quite believe in, that lacks rigour in my opinion, but is not totally insignificant. In other words it would possess, without being either rigorously true or rigorously false, a certain appearance in its favour.

'A certain appearance in its favour': here, in just six words is a brilliant encapsulation of the shortfall of the attempted empirical, the attempted epistemological; 'historically speaking', *this is as good as it gets*. Yet whether – especially when yoked to other considerations – it is good enough to keep even historical *emphases* of this kind (that is, of a postmodern, deconstructionist kind) in business is debatable today, a debate that is considered in the Part Four of this Reader.

The reference to Part Four, without having yet strictly mentioned Parts One to Three, obviously needs an immediate explanation, an explanation we will turn to now and which allows us to leave any further comments about our position(s) as we move on to say – relative to our positional assumptions – how we have organised and structured this text.

Structurings

It is not unusual for writers who are about to explain what a text contains and the way that such contents are structured, to begin by saying what has been left out and what sort of organisational structure has *not* been adopted; what context has *not* been chosen. And it may be useful to do this briefly ourselves.

We could have organised the readings which follow by grouping them under types of histories – social, economic, political, cultural, theoretical, feminist, Marxist, post-structuralist, etc. – or by schools; or by methods; or by ideological positions; or clustered around events; or around concepts, etc. And if we had, then 'the nature of history today' would have been different relative to each of the above ways of carving up histories and to the way we ourselves have done so. For we have not used any of the above possibilities. Rather, keeping faith with our view that histories are aesthetic, figurative, positioned, imaginary artefacts – and especially *literary artefacts* – we have adopted the idea of literary genre as our organising principle. That is, we think that it is possible to characterise *all* historical writings as one of three basic types, basic genres. For us, no matter if history texts are written by economic or social or cultural historians; no matter what the period or specialisation; no matter if the writers are Marxist or liberals, feminists or reactionaries; no matter if they are overtly positioned or not, the most insightful and productive way of organising them all is to locate them as belonging to – having an orientation to – one of the following three genres: reconstructionist, constructionist or deconstructionist. Accordingly, it is by this characterisation of the historian's writings that we think we might be able to establish our claim – to make you think it may have 'something in its favour' – that histories get their power to give significant meanings to areas of the 'before now' through their narrative figurings as much as through their empirical content. This is one of the best ways we can think of to express our view that historians today can best be understood as having turned away – whether they know it or not, or like it or not – from privileging the empirical and the epistemological towards the linguistic and the aesthetic and thus the figure: towards *figural realism*. And this reference to figural realism – incidentally, the title of the latest book by the American theorist of history, Hayden White – allows us to line ourselves up alongside White's (in)famous definition of history as being best understood as *a narrative prose discourse the content of which is as much imagined* (the modes of troping, emplotting, arguing) *as found* (the 'facts', etc.).

What we have just outlined thus helps to provide us with a rationale for the organisation of the Reader into three Parts. But, as we have already stated, there are four Parts to the book. So what – to develop a little further what has been merely hinted at thus far – constitutes Part Four?

The answer is that while we think it is useful to locate the *writers of history* examined into the three genres indicated, there are those – historians and others – who think that it is unnecessary to have histories 'as we have known them' or, maybe, even histories at all; that, one way or another, we can look forward to, or be conscious we may be coming to, 'the end of history'. Therefore, the writers who make up Part Four are examined not because they are concerned to write about the 'before now' in a particular kind of way, but rather because they are reflecting much more theoretically, much more philosophically, on the status, the point, the condition and the 'possible possibilities' of history today. So that is why, in a Reader that goes under the title of *The Nature of History Reader*, they are included. For us, they are a crucial dimension in a text that wishes to present a certain kind of picture of what is going on around, about and under the name of 'history today'. This is why this Reader has four Parts.

The three genres and endism

We are arguing that every historian, then, occupies a particular genre position, one that is clearly reflected in the nature of his or her historical narratives. The attitude that historians have towards empiricism, how they perceive the nature and status of facts and their description, how they deploy the explanatory strategies of emplotment, tropology and ideology, and how they view language as the vehicle for their thinking, will lead to their particular genre choice. In effectively blurring the distinction between historian and history that occurs through the act of narrative construction, we are reminded that historians can choose their own genre. It should be clear by now that we believe that this choice is determined by attitudes towards the significance of empiricism in the overall process of creating and writing the history narrative.

It is to accommodate our view that history in general is constituted by the compulsions of empirical data *and* language that allows us to distinguish our three main orientations to the organisation of knowledge about the past. These three history genres share many of the characteristics we would normally associate with literary genres, rather than, as we have suggested, conventionally recognised 'schools', 'varieties' or 'approaches' to history. While the notion of genre categories as the way of describing major orientations towards historical thinking and practice is probably unfamiliar to you, steeped as you may be in conventional epistemological definitions of history, such a redefinition is required in order to acknowledge that history is indeed a narrative, aesthetic and thus fictive creation.

History, conceived on the model of genres, as broad classificatory types of historical composition, is thus an innovative method of evaluating the types or classes of history. Of course, in suggesting our three categories as the main generic history divisions, we are not claiming any originality for thinking about history as a literary genre. While our insistence on defining history as a narrative space may be novel, it has to be acknowledged that historians and philosophers of history have long examined the connections between the historical narrative and genre. But this has tended to be done within the specialist field of biography and life histories, and it now needs to be put to the profession as a whole. We are making the claim that all kinds or forms of written history fall within these genre categories. The question, therefore, is not what mode or specific form of history do you write, but what genre do you choose to work within? It is the answer to that question which determines the meanings it is possible to generate. This recognition of history's composition as a narrative form leads us to acknowledge the typologies of its texts. Yet while we are saying that almost all historians work within one of these three epistemological categories, we are aware that they may not do so all the time. We do not believe it is possible (nor desirable) to attempt to be absolutist here. There are historians whose work will not readily conform to this model. Genre boundaries can be transgressed. However, we believe that such historians are relatively rare and that they do not seriously invalidate our broad conceptions of how historians think and organise their work. As literature has poetry, drama and the novel, so history has 'reconstructionism', 'constructionism' and 'deconstructionism'.

Histories written from a particular 'way of knowing', then, have much in common in spite of surface appearances of different themes and sources, and should be grouped together under broad headings. The benefit of being attentive to these divisions is that they tell us what kind of history text it is we have before us without straying into too rigid a taxonomy. Much of the critical evaluation provided by us through the extracts we shall be using will be directed to providing information about how 'author-historians' elect to compose and configure/prefigure the past in the narrative form. Hence, we have introduced each extract with a short explanation of how the reading fits into the bigger 'doing history' picture, as well as how it fits in with the other works of the historians being considered. As a general rule, then, the historian domesticates 'the past as history' by offering her/his own particular narrative form of explanation – i.e. their preferred notion of what constitutes the 'proper' way to gain historical knowledge and, most importantly, generate historical meaning. So it is our hope that genre categories will demystify the fundamental nature of the overall 'history project'.

In literary studies we are used to thinking of 'content' as what is said, and 'form' the way it is said. For the most part, in literature content and form are indivisible – i.e. how the content is presented/represented cannot be separated into two 'things': there can be no represented (content) without its representation (form). This applies to all realist literature and, of course, includes history. In the case of history, the historian-author chooses a broad conceptual framework as the preferred way of gaining knowledge about the past. Learning about the past is not only to be done according to an empirical-analytical strategy; it is not merely an epistemological matter of 'looking at the evidence' or 'reading the sources'. The kind of history we make depends on what kind of approach to knowledge creation we take – reconstructionist, constructionist or deconstructionist.

What we need to do now is explain the nature of our three genre categories. Before doing that, however, we offer a disclaimer. Instead of trying to replace definitively one canon with another (our genres for schools or varieties of history, for example), we intend only to direct you to the historiographical nature of history and the three major choices within which a variety of approaches or modalities can be deemed to exist. How we describe these thematic modes for the reconstructionist, constructionist or deconstructionist genres is thus very much the function of how we imagine them (and history) to be. Hence, we are happy that the modalities we isolate are far from exhaustive. And, as you will also note shortly, one of the key features of deconstructionist historians is their attempt to challenge the modalities of history writing in the reconstructionist and constructionist genres. You will also note that the writings we call 'endist' are a challenge not only to the other three genre categories, but also a forthright provocation to the very idea of history, to history books and, certainly, to books like this.

Part One: Reconstructionism

We stipulate our definition for this genre as being characterised by an undiluted belief in the power of empiricism to access the past (defined according to its individual events) as it actually was. It is distinguished by its appeal to those historians who endorse what they like to call their 'common-sense', 'realist', 'the-past-as-knowable history' belief; that the 'truth' of the past can somehow be found. It can be discovered in the sources and, hence, *the* true story of the event can be rediscovered and cannot only be, but must be, narrated accurately. Referentiality, inference, the truthful statement, and adequate and accurate representation of people's actions and intentions, along with the primacy of events over social processes and structures, are the touchstones of this epistemological position. In effect, the truth of the past event will emerge when the historian's ontological existence is detached from her/his epistemology. In other words, the past can be 'known' truthfully under the careful and responsible tutelage of the knowledgeable and scrupulous historian who 'stands outside' her/his own existence or situation. This, the conventional view of history writing in the West, has thus been anchored in the correspondence and coherence theories of knowledge which are the foundations of the belief in a realist epistemology.

Reconstructionist history's insistence on dispassionately finding *the* truthful interpretation and *the* story *in* the sources was once described by the British Tudor historian, Geoffrey Elton, as the '... rational, independent and impartial investigation ... of the evidence by the distanced historian observer' (Elton 1991: 6, 77–98). This investigation and the inferences drawn from it (i.e. conclusions inferred about its meaning) could then be written up in a realist and, *by definition*, objective historical narrative. In other words, *the* story can not only be 'found' in the evidence thanks to painstaking archival research and the correspondence and coherence theories of knowledge, but it can be accurately represented in the narrative. What this means, as historians like Geoffrey Roberts, Arthur Marwick and Gertrude Himmelfarb have argued, is that their narrative form is merely a link between description and analysis, rather than the medium through which *both* are created. Reconstructionists tend to see the narrative as simply the vehicle for the truth of the past because the image in the narrative refers (corresponds) to the reality of the past. In so doing, they endorse the idea that *the* story of the past can (with a high degree of probability) be located.

Geoffrey Roberts, in his pursuit of the story of *the* past, has argued in favour of the characteristically reconstructionist principle that what happened can be accurately represented in the narrative. He maintains that historians can tell what the *intentions* of people in the past were because they were basically like us. So, telling *the* story of what they did is largely unproblematic. As he says (our italics):

> telling *the* story, explaining *the* action, and reconstructing *the* experience of people in *the* past is not more difficult than dealing with human happenings from yesterday

> – excluding, that is, problems of evidence, temporality, and cultural context –
> which, of course, is where the special skills, experience, and scholarship of histo-
> rians come into use.
>
> (Roberts 1997: 251)

In what appears to us to be an impossible position to maintain – because history is *a narrative about* the past – Roberts believes '*the* past lives on'. Moreover, Roberts insists that in the
normal course of their job, historians come into contact with that past 'as a real object' which
is found in the action of a past human subject or subjects (ibid.: 254). He concludes that
action '. . . has outcomes ('events') and that it occurs in descriptive settings (the 'facts') but
these do not constitute or define the stories told by narrative historians. The action itself is
the story' (ibid.: 256). The action as found in the data is thus presumed to provide *the* real
story to which the historian's narrative can correspond. This is the essence of reconstructionist
historical analysis. Roberts's conclusion is plain: because stories can be lived, with appropriate
attention to the sources, they can be accurately retold.

Arthur Marwick, another card-carrying reconstructionist writer and legitimist, seems less
interested than Roberts in the idea that it is possible to discover the intention behind the action
of the historical agent which can then be retold in the narrative. Indeed, he seems to regard
narrative as inferior to the other aspects of what it is that historians do. As he says '. . .
straight narrative is the easiest form of historical writing save that it is not very historical'
(Marwick [1970] 1989: 144). It is not very historical, apparently, because it does not permit
either the distinguishing of the relative importance of events, nor the determination of the
underlying structures of change. Although he does not consider (as Roberts does) action as
the primary agent of historical change, like Roberts he seems to accept that *the* story is back
there.

Empiricism, rather than being viewed as just one way among many that is open to historians to address the past, is thus assumed by its supporters to be *the* methodology of that
'proper history' that reconstructionism takes itself to be (Davies 2003). It is 'The Great Story'!
Empiricism is further vindicated as being the only defence against the worst mistake that
historians can apparently make – the fall from objectivity into relativism. Of course, as Geoffrey
Elton and other reconstructionists like Deborah A. Symonds and the realist philosopher Martin
Bunzl have recently argued, objectivity is hard to attain because history is only as good as its
sources. Thus, Symonds claims that

> history, whatever it may become, begins from the materials of history, and that
> it is in confronting these materials that questions of belief, intention, falsification,
> and truth have to be confronted and resolved. Theory comes later, after one has
> decided what one is, in fact, at the most empirical and scientific level, theorising
> about, and how one's own biases dance at the edge of every apparently objective
> pool of light.
>
> (Symonds 1999: 166)

Not dissimilarly, Bunzl has tried to defend the reconstruction of the past – in terms of the
event – by dropping correspondence and arguing that although descriptions of events can
change, the events don't. It does not matter that you have to narrate events and facts – they
still have a knowable reality beyond their description. As he concludes, if information is
missing, it does not mean that it never existed (Bunzl 1997: 111).

As Symonds's comment reveals, by the late 1990s a more temperate reconstructionist
tone, if not 'position', had emerged in an attempt to combat the broad assault on the genre

of reconstructionist history. While still defending the strong possibility of knowing the truth back there through the facts, there is at least some acknowledgement that it is a flawed exercise, albeit because of problems with the sources rather than with any more significant problem of 'knowing'. For us, however, this clearly misses the point, which is that reconstructist history is founded on the belief that historical method is about empiricism first, last and always. Of course, historical 'facts' are constrained by the compulsion of 'reality'. But it is undeniable that they are also narrated in order to create *an* explanation with *an* emplotment. They are also always laden with concepts, theories and ideologies and, ultimately, exist only under the sway of various types of representation. Once we ratchet up from the single factual statement about the event, we enter the universe of judgements, encodations, descriptions, depictions, ethics, values, images, metaphors, decisions, verdicts and interpretations of 'texts'. None of these at this level (that of the creation of meaning) can be verified, validated or confirmed epistemologically relative to a putative 'reality'. This is the fundamental flaw in reconstructionist histories.

In spite of the common reconstructionist notion that historians don't like theory, at the beginning of the twenty-first century it is not a matter of 'to theorise or not to theorise', but which theory to use (Goodman, in Bentley 1997: 795). This is the crux of the epistemological difference between the reconstructionist and constructionist genres. It is the recognition that empiricism without concept, argument and ideology is blind, deaf and dumb. Accordingly, with its anti-theory stance and its belief in 'truth' and accurate representation, the reconstructionist genre is the epistemological point of departure for the other two genres we are using here.

Part Two: Constructionism

It would be wrong to suggest that what we shall characterise as the constructionist genre emerged in response to the problems with reconstructionist approaches to 'knowing things about the past'. In fact, the forerunner to the new 'practical realism' that we associate with the constructionist genre that emerged in the US and Western Europe in the 1960s and which dominates up to the present, had its antecedents in nineteenth-century positivism – itself the first actual intellectual extension of empiricism. As a 'way of knowing' in its own right, positivism was a theory of knowledge developed by the French sociologist Auguste Comte. Essentially, Comte argued a 'stagist' theory of historical development, the final stage of which (in the mid- to late-nineteenth century) is represented by the ability of 'social scientists' to discover and measure the nature of modern industrial society. As such, Comte is credited with inventing what he called 'social physics' or what we call 'sociology'. Based on objective, distanced empirical observation, positivism suggested that it was possible to explain human society in a fashion similar to that of science through the discovery of society's mechanics and the laws of human behaviour.

The implication for history was that it seemed possible to account for human experience by discovering regular patterns of human behaviour which, in the mid-twentieth century, the philosopher of history, Carl Hempel, called 'covering laws'. The identification of such laws of human behaviour allowed historians more accurately to describe and explain the past. This was a very attractive proposition for many historians and, although it was moderated and indeed rejected as too simplistic by many since the high tide of social history in the 1960s and 1970s, it has remained popular. The reason for this is because of its empirical basis (the 'discovery of the facts'), its maintenance of the epistemological gap between observer and observed, and the possibilities of seeking the determining social, political and economic structures beneath the 'surface' of the social. In that sense, then, positivism reinforced some basic reconstructionist principles – namely, that the past was once real and remains so through its traces; that inference is the mechanism for 'discovering' the meaning of the evidence; that it is possible to 'tell the truth' by finding *the* story; that fact and fiction are quite different, and that history and historian occupy different universes.

On the other hand, positivism pushed beyond the description and evaluation of the single event or decision of the historical actor/agent that so preoccupied nineteenth-century reconstructionists. Consequently, the debate among historians moved increasingly (as the constructionist philosopher of history, Patrick Gardiner, said in the early 1950s and reconstructionists like Elton recognised) towards the study of the actions of people in groups. As Gardiner argued, 'The historian is concerned with human activities, and he is principally interested in those activities in so far as they have been found related to one another in social groups' (Gardiner [1952] 1961: 60). Gardiner was influential in maintaining the distinction between science and history, but accepted the key constructionist idea that historians deploy concepts and arguments in order to make generalisations, but not ones that are absolute.

Gardiner thus essayed the theoretical foundations for constructionist history, and it is this constructionist 'empiricism plus concepts' which constitutes the mainstream of historical thinking today. Gardiner concluded that 'The fact that the historian's interest is directed upon particular events rather than upon universal laws is a fact about the purpose of history and not a fact about the type of event with which history deals' (ibid.: 64). As we read Gardiner, what he was saying is that while events may be unique, they can be represented as belonging to categories of events that share certain basic similarities. In other words, Gardiner was arguing that historical explanation is somewhat more complex than reconstructionists imagine if they only concentrate on the unique character of all events and human decisions. This is important because it leads into the debate about the distinction between human agency and structure which came to dominate historical thinking in the second half of the last century, and which has been at the heart of the development of constructionist history.

It is also important to note that the challenge to the legacy of nineteenth-century 'event history' (the modes of which tended to be nationalist, political and diplomatic) came not least with the rise of a new socially conscious, positivist-inspired British leftist history. Initiated by Sidney and Beatrice Webb, J.L. and Barbara Hammond, G.D.H. Cole, Raymond Postgate and R.H. Tawney, it was a tradition that continued from the 1950s to the 1990s, led by Victor Kiernan, E.P. and Dorothy Thompson and several US historians like Phillip Foner and Harvey Kaye. History leaving the politics out (or putting the economics in) marked the shift towards what would later be called 'history from the bottom up'. At least, this was the case according to its major early British practitioner, George Trevelyan, in his path-breaking and appropriately entitled book *English Social History* (1944). Apart from what was seen as undeniable evidence that progress was not the keynote of modern historical development, many early twentieth-century constructionists thus sought out the structural reasons in society for the failure of social justice. This continued as a major theme throughout the rest of the century with the dominance of social history, although it metamorphosed into a much more complex and sophisticated cultural history in the last thirty years or so.

Parallel to these developments in social history in Britain and the US, in France in 1929 Lucien Febvre and Marc Bloch established the *Annales* School as an alternative orientation for the historicisation of the past (they established a journal bearing that title). Although not an alternative genre, it nevertheless stressed a different method in empirically based and structural history. Borrowing from the emergent social sciences (especially sociology, anthropology and geography), the *Annalistes* stressed large-scale thematic and comparative structural change (as opposed to smaller event scale historical change) in an effort to understand the 'totality' of history. The leading successor to the founders of the movement was Fernand Braudel who vigorously pursued the notion of total history in his famous book *The Mediterranean World in the Age of Philip II*, published in 1949.

As this little narrative of our own suggests, then, the last century witnessed a mixed reaction to the genre of reconstructionism in the emergence of a great variety of, not least, social histories. And this multiplication of the modes of constructionist history became ever greater in the second half of the century as the discipline became open to a wider range of practitioners, especially women and historians in the developing world. There was also a number of parallel methodological developments by the 1970s. The last thirty years or so have thus witnessed the growth of cliometrics (the use of statistics in history) and a vast diversity of cultural histories (micro-history, local and regional history, *Altagsgeschichte* (the study of everyday life)), subaltern studies (history from below, with particular reference to the ex-British colonies), social memory, public history, etc.

Constructionism is thus, as suggested, empiricism married to varying levels of social theory and to more or less complex forms of explanatory conceptualisation. Historians writing within this genre accept that the correspondence theory of knowledge is flawed. However, they still maintain their due respect for empiricism, accurately rendered in the historical narrative. Ultimately, what distinguishes the constructionist from the reconstructionist is the belief that history can be 'objective', not simply through source analysis, etc., but when the understanding of them is fostered by appropriate theorisation and through the deployment of various helpful concepts. Constructionists recognise that their historical narratives cannot easily reflect the experience of past reality and that distanced objectivity is a position that is difficult to sustain.

Nevertheless, there is still a parallel with reconstructionist attitudes towards the referentiality of the sources. Constructionists claim that, in using concepts and theories such as race, class, gender, imperialism, nationalism, psychohistory, ethnography, etc., they encompass what are, in effect, non-narrative or narrative-free conceptual or topic organising categories. It is this belief that allows constructionists, such as the social historian John Tosh, to relegate narrative in importance as a mechanism for analysing and understanding the past, while subscribing to the opinion that *the* story in the past can still be found (Tosh [1984] 2000: 96). Unlike reconstructionists, constructionists accept that getting at *the* story is not simply assured by a detailed knowledge of the sources. However, for constructionists, knowing the truth of the past is still feasible in principle precisely because history is constructed through using the tools of sophisticated conceptualisation and social theory; on the other hand, for reconstructionists, empiricism alone is enough.

Hence, the prudent use of concepts and theories of explanation borrowed and adapted from other humanities and social science disciplines is an essential prerequisite to understanding the structures that shaped abstract social processes, as well as the political lives, human intentions and actions of people in the past. For constructionists, conceptual interventionism does not generate false knowledge about the reality of the past because it is regarded as being of a provisional kind; that is, the theory or utility of the concept is tested in the evidence. The constructionist way of approaching history is animated by a complex and self-reflexive, yet still a basically objective, empirical methodology. No matter what ontological assumptions are made about the nature of the past or the historians' experience of the present, constructionist historians share with reconstructionists the desire to maintain the distance between themselves and the past. But, unlike reconstructionists, they do this by viewing the concepts and tools of analysis as serving the evidence rather than as impositions upon it.

In spite of their scepticism about what we can know through the sources, constructionists are realists – in fact, practical realists, as Appleby, Hunt and Jacob describe it (Appleby, *et al.*: 1994). They continue to believe in correspondence, referentiality and the possibilities of accurate representation in language. For a growing minority of post-constructionists (aka deconstructionists), however, history is not a construction in pursuit of the truth of the past; for these historians the 'epistemological gap' does not exist because we exist in a non-epistemological world. History is primarily the figural, narrative creation of the historian in the present. In an ironic echo of reconstructionist thinking, such post-constructionists argue that every social theory, or a concept used in the pursuit of the past, is an unfixing, a desta-bilisation of it. Each and every concept and every operation of presumed laws of human behaviour are impositions of an artificial order on the past by the historian. But there is something more which acts to undermine conventional reconstructionist and constructionist thinking. This is that language is a poor conductor of meaning because of its arbitrary and historicist nature. What this means is that we can only 'know' the past through our concepts which, rather than being constituted out of the evidence, are created through our language use – rhetorical constructionism. It was the incursion of post-structuralist thought into the mainstream of history that heralded this move: the revolution of the linguistic and aesthetic 'turn' from the belief in empiricist epistemology (i.e. *the* epistemology) to the narrativist, and from the reconstructionist and constructionist genres to the deconstructionist.

Part Three: Deconstructionism

From a perspective that assumes that history is as much a narrative-linguistic aesthetic as it is an empirical-analytical activity, deconstructionist historians tackle and go beyond what they believe to be the limited possibilities of reconstructionism and constructionism. Among the assumptions of epistemology they question are: the epistemological principle of empiricism whereby content (the past) must always determine its narrative shape (form); the existence of a discoverable emplotment (that the story exists in the action/intentions of historical agents), and that the ontological separation of knower (historian/being) and known (the past/history) leads to objectivity. Deconstructionists also critique correspondence and coherence theories of knowledge (referentiality); the notion of inference and the truthful statement (explanation to the best fit); the clear distinction between fact and fiction; the subject-object division (objectivity); representationalism (accurate representation), and the idea that the appropriate use of social theory (concept and argument) can generate truth-statements.

On the other hand, deconstructionists do not deny in any way whatsoever the 'actuality' of the past or the existence of its sources, i.e. the 'data-stream' or the factual statement. Deconstructionist historians are not anti-realists. However, being anti-representationalist and anti-epistemological, as the pragmatic philosopher Richard Rorty points out, means not swallowing all the epistemological and methodological baggage of an unthinking empiricism that associates the existence of data with ultimately being able to know what it means with a high degree of certainty. Again, as the Dutch theorist Frank Ankersmit argues, not only are facts essentially events under a description (how else can we know them except when we describe them?), but all the historical interpretations built on them exist only in relation to other interpretations. One of the foundations of the deconstructionist genre is that there is no original or given meaning that history can *discover*; that there is *no* story, *no* narrative, *no* emplotment or argument *in* the past per se and that the past has in it neither rhyme nor reason. Nor is the past per se internally 'historical'; the past has to be made into history by the work(s) of historians. Deconstructionists ask all historians to consider their answer to the question: if historical interpretations can only exist in language, what does this mean for historical understanding? The fact that something happened does not mean that we know or can adequately describe what it *means* – there is *no* entailment from fact(s) to value(s).

While for reconstructionist and constructionist historians the problem is about how we can objectively know the past (i.e. make truthful statements about it), for deconstructionists 'doing history' is the exercise of a literary activity that doubts that empiricism and language are adequate to the task of representation of 'reality' at a fundamentally truthful level when the aim is the recovery of what it *actually* means. Deconstructionists do not share their reconstructionist and constructionist colleagues' belief that the past can be faithfully translated into a truthful historical description. Rather, they choose to follow the anti-representationalist argument that the distinction between appearance and reality cannot be overcome by the traditional methods of empirical research (contextualisation, comparison, verification of evidence, inference and the correspondence theory of knowledge). Deconstructionists do not accept that the constructionist view that the categories we use in our historical narrative necessarily (by dint of the study of the empirical evidence) correspond to the 'meaning' of any past reality.

For deconstructionist historians, then, the idea that objectivity is hard to attain (because history is only as good as its sources and the honesty and ability of its practitioners who will, if they are any good, infer properly what the past means) misses the point of the debate. It is not that objectivity is possible or impossible, but rather how we cope with the fact that, given that the past no longer exists, how can we infer 'true' propositional statements (i.e. facts) from events and then 'truly' narrate them? While the traces of the past remain (documents, newsreels, buildings, paintings, oral testimony), they no longer contain the reproducible functionality of original cause and effect. Most historians work on the remains of the past in the belief that they can mine them for their veins of meaning. But all we end up with are the inferences they draw as to the fixity of meaning they assumed must have once existed. The point at issue for deconstructionists is how can we know the historicised past if we assume there is no knowable truth back there because our only access to it is when we speak it or write it 'historically'? As Ankersmit argues, we can only know the meaning of the represented through its representation – a circular, self-referencing position to be in.

But what of truth? Taking up a similar position to Ankersmit, the American pragmatist philosopher, Richard Rorty, suggests that only our descriptions of the world can be true or false – i.e. we make prepositional constitutive statements about 'the real'. The world itself – past events – do not possess this characteristic. Most historians (working in both the reconstructionist and constructionist genres) would respond not so, for what makes a statement 'true' is the nature of the reality it describes (correspondence). Unfortunately, say deconstructionists, 'the world' of the past no longer exists in the sense that 'the word' refers to an observable reality. How can you accurately describe, let alone confidently infer, the meaning of something that is literally no longer real? Arguably, history is an inferential activity that cannot get back to any original meaning. You can only assume original meaning if you choose to believe that the data-stream of the past contains a true meaning. For deconstructionists who want to 'do history', this is the problem. So how do deconstructionists 'do history'?

For deconstructionist historians, 'doing history' means engaging with the past in ways that are far from traditional because of their anti-epistemological assumptions. Thus, deconstructionists might choose, for example, to explore the consequences of reversing the priority of content over form and thus experimenting with representation. Or by exploring the subjectivity of the historian as an author. Or by addressing the possible consequences of reading the past as one would a text, specifically a text that has no author but is culturally provided and that the literal is only ever accessed through the figurative. Or by recognising that because we know through narrative, we cannot know the past as it once was (facts = events under a description). Or by acknowledging that history is ideological through and through. Or by deconstructing the arguments and theories that deconstructionist historians deploy as they 'do history' (how their creation of history affects the past). Or by asking what are the possible results of the collapse of the distinction between being and knowing in a post-epistemological world.

For Frank Ankersmit and Hayden White, the realist principle that there is a distinction (endorsed by both reconstructionists and constructionists) between language and reality, forfeits its meaning. Language cannot be the mirror of nature as Richard Rorty puts it. The reason is straightforward. Our language is part of the reality being depicted. This means that whenever we think about the past we should start by deconstructing our basic assumptions about it. Take, again, the historical fact. As we have already suggested, facts are not bits of reality lying around in the past waiting to be picked up, polished and displayed. They are propositional statements about the nature of reality (past events under a description): to argue that facts exist in the ontic 'world' is nonsensical. Moreover, is it really good enough, deconstructionists argue, for reconstructionists and constructionists to claim (as they sometimes do) that recognising history as a narrative construction might somehow trivialise the horrors of the Nazi Holocaust or allow its deniers the freedom to peddle their lies? Holocaust deniers, of course, are not deconstructionists; they are reconstructionists and constructionists who choose to be highly selective in selecting their data (usually for fascist ideological reasons).

So while reconstructionist/constructionist historians appear to describe empirical reality by standing apart from it, distanced and detached, they are, of course, directly implicated in it. To use the language, for example, of women's history or the 'post-feminist' is to organise the facts of the past into a preferred reality. There is no actual 'post-feminist' corpus of data. There is no 'post-feminist fact' back there. There is no 'post-feminist' emplotment. The existence of, say, a data-stream is no insurance against historians avoiding the error of the referential illusion that allows them (if they are so inclined) to equate description with reality.

Thinking about the implications of the links between language (the word) and reality (the world) is clearly at the forefront of deconstructionist history. Those working within the deconstructionist genre hold that history is always written from the need (which is prior to the empirical) to engage critically with those languages or discourses through which we set to work with the real world. The deconstructionist objective is to establish how such discourses – like the reconstructionist and constructionist genres – can achieve or fail to achieve their objective of truthful knowing. Deconstructionist history is thus self-reflexive at the basic level of the connection between knowing and telling, and thus very different in its emphasis from the scepticism about 'the sources' of reconstructionists or the social theory experimentation of constructionists. The reconstructionist and constructionist preoccupations with the sources and debates between competing interpretations, or trying to avoid ideology and bias, or understanding the conflicts between agency and structure, or even being aware of the tensions between description, analysis and narrative, is never enough for deconstructionist historians.

In a recent book on 'what is history?' and 'how to do it', two constructionist historians argue that postmodernism threatens the foundations – the epistemological roots – of the discipline (Black and MacRaild [1997] 2000: 161). But it may do more than that. For there is today a group of theorists for whom postmodernism calls into question the very discourse of history as such, including the deconstructionist genre. For today there are those who would move well beyond 'epistemological questions' that reflect upon the need for and utility of empiricism, referentiality, representation and narrative. From what we have said so far, for reconstructionists historical knowledge is referential – i.e. found in the evidence. This suggests that the past can be accurately represented and it can, therefore, be faithfully reconstructed in the historical narrative. For the self-conscious and conceptually sophisticated constructionist historian, history is at a foundational level still made out of the traces of the past. For deconstructionist historians the link between the real and its narration remains so tenuous that they question whether the past can be turned into truthful history, or that any story can be retold, or is, maybe, worth the effort. The fourth position – the endist position – questions and discusses whether there can be any useful historical knowing in the sense of understanding the meaning of a somehow connected series of events and, moreover, mistrusts our cultural need for it. This position can be understood, perhaps, through a long and complicated 'story' of its own, but it is a story that has now been essayed many times so that, here, the following short-ened version can hopefully suffice. It goes as follows.

Part Four: Endisms

Not so long ago in the West, there existed an essentially religious but, in the last two hundred years, a thoroughly secularised belief that the past, history, had in it its own intrinsic value, its own purposeful meaning, an essence which, made manifest in its material effects could, if it were read carefully (hermeneutically), bring history's underlying *raison d'être* to the surface. Almost invariably this perceived history, this unfolding of meaning, was cast in a form of a progressive teleology – i.e. that right from the start history had a direction and destiny in it which, fully realised, would bring it to an end. Like all teleologies, this particular teleology culminated in *closure*, the substance(s) of which, in this instance, was expressed in the idea that the point of history was to bring about emancipated human rights communities in one or two basic forms (with internal inflections): a bourgeois, liberal, capitalist form or a prole-tarian socialist/communist one.

Rooted in, and thus expressive as these aspirational beliefs were of sectional interests within social formations riven with inequalities and class conflicts, it was these respective legit-imations of very different ideas of progress that helped lead towards, to help cause the way that those particular antagonisms, conflicts, revolutions, wars and attempted 'rational means-ends' totalitarianisms that came to plague the twentieth century – turning it into the bloodiest and most genocidal century on record – were played out. It is arguably one of the greatest ironies, arguably one of the greatest tragedies, that the empowering belief in such human rights com-munities which wished to see the harmonious end of the very conflictive conditions that gave it birth was unable to escape these self-same clutches and that this great fable of emancipation was destined to play itself out in the form of the (basically) 'Western' nation state, the most effective killing machine that has ever existed on the face of the earth.

Within those nation states that resisted the drive towards human rights communities prole-tarian style – within those states that have today become 'our' Western democracies, our bourgeois, liberal, capitalist social formations – then 'our' current condition has been reached as a result of a whole series of transformations that have required, to be the transformations they were, their own specific cultural logics of 'social relations'. Fredric Jameson charac-terised the logic of the present-day as 'postmodern'. Although one may not agree in every detail with the kind of analysis implied by the tautologous title of Jameson's now classic text, *Postmodernism, or, The Cultural Logic of Late Capitalism* (1991) (i.e. that postmodernism *is* the cultural logic of late capitalism, that late capitalism's cultural logic *is* postmodernism), the point we want to make is that the *need* for contemporary social formations in general for past/postmodern modes and relations of production (flexible accumulation, flexible labour, flexible production and distribution; for short-term contracts and relationships; for mobile, migratory finance capital and migrant workers; for niche-marketing and venture capitals that spin around the globe), has, by the sheer force of everyday necessity, generated a ubiquitous *relativism* that 'absolutely' nothing has the power to escape from.

Thus, we can see very clearly that *relativism* is inevitable and unavoidable today, for if you get rid of, empty out, every idea that anything has an intrinsic value; if 'goods' – including men, women, ideas, concepts – have only got a market value, an exchange value (as they must have if nothing transcendental has credibility; if no 'use value' escapes exchange), then it is inconceivable that the saturation of the socio-economic with relativism should exclude from its sodden state any other area of life. And so this obviously includes – and the implications of this is what is crucial to note – ethics, morality and the discourse of history per se. Consequently, the only attitude we can have towards any form of absolute ethics, morality and history, is one of incredulity.

Of course, there are some who still think that it is possible to have an ethics, morality and maybe, in some form, a history that stands above and beyond the 'ravages' of relativism. But it is a thought that cannot now be substantiated and, therefore, sustained. And, again, it is easy to isolate what causes relativism to be 'the only game in town', for what the rela- tivising market has done in its everyday divorce of fact and value, in its everyday logical divorce between commodities and their market price/value, is to raise to consciousness as never before the problematic nature of the 'facts of the matter' and what value should be *given*, extrinsically, to them. And it is to raise to the level of consciousness with regard to all histor- ical accounts 'the fact' that, from the facts of the past, the syntax of the past, no value, no semantics are entailed: you can read the past, in its parts or its putative whole, *any way you like*. No necessary meaning, no necessary significance, no necessary emplotment follows; or, to put it this way, 'nothing (necessarily) follows'. In this 'context', it is pertinent to note that Jacques Derrida always talks of the 'non-ethical opening of ethics'; the way in which, although you are always called upon to make a decision about something that *is*, the facts of the matter of what *is* the case *cannot* tell you what you *ought* to do; cannot tell you how you must decide. Consequently, freed up for choice but with no guarantee that you will ever make the 'right choice', Derrida talks about the 'undecidability of the decision'. Although you are always called on to make a decision (for to refuse to make a decision is still yet a decision), the status of the decision is always problematic, interminably open – this is the condition of aporia, of radical undecidability. And so, although it may be foolish to offer to define postmodernism, for us postmodernism might be best considered here as the era of the raising to consciousness of the aporia . . . of the undecidability of the decision and of incredulity towards metanarra- tive, towards metaphysics.

And we think that this definition applies also to professional, academic histories which, although they have no time for metanarratives, nevertheless find it difficult to radically prob- lematicise – as postmodernism so defined radically problematicises – the very idea, the very act of the imagination that is – all the way down – the intellectual experiment of historicising the past, the 'before now'. For if petite narratives as well as metanarratives are undercut by their incredible status and relativised out of any notion of *immanence* (of intrinsicality), then they can no longer make claims – at the level of the text – to truth, objectivity, disinterest, neu- trality, non-present-centredness, science or whatever – i.e. they can make no claims to being *epistemological*. And, let us note, deconstructionist historians are not, unfortunately, immune from harbouring at least part of those delusions, for deconstructionist historians are still, at the end of the day, historians. Of course, their histories are often wondrously different, radical and problematicising; their histories are multi-levelled, multi-perspectival and highly reflexive as they draw attention to the way *their* words on *their* page create *their* intervention in the dis- courses of historicisation. These are histories that are reflexively and thus self-consciously troped, spoken, emplotted, argued for in overtly positioned ways and thus inevitably metaphor- ical/allegorical; bespoke histories, cut and made to measure to suit. *But they are still histories.*

There are some people, though – some of whom appear in Part Four – who have vari- ously given up on history and thus occasioned/contributed to, 'endist' debates. Elizabeth Deeds Ermarth's radical rethinking of not just history but the idea of time(s) is perhaps fundamental here in catching a certain mood; there is a certain unconcerned everydayness about her indifference to whether history continues or not: there are better things to think about. For just as, say, the nineteenth century witnessed the announcement (by F.W. Nietzsche, for example) of the death of God, that announcement pointed to a particular kind of dying. For Nietzsche, it wasn't as if there had once been a God and that that God had died, but that God (and gods) were the products of a particular belief system which, when that belief system had become thoroughly secularised, just dropped out of the (secular) conversation. The very idea of God/gods now looked irrelevant, such that 'His' death was caused by our unconcern; by our neglect; we had other things on our minds. And so, while the working out of the death of God/gods was, for Nietzsche, destined to take place through at least the twentieth and twenty-first centuries, although His shadow would hang over us, the substance of God/gods, had gone. Similarly, Ermarth takes it for granted that, sired and born within modernity, histories as we have come to know them – in metanarrative and professional, academic forms – are now, in postmodernity, also slipping out of our conversations. Although still invoked and still talked about in universities and among academics – just as God is still talked about among, say, Christians – nevertheless, the seminar rooms and the churches are 'empty in their history talk', are 'empty in their God talk'. And so Ermarth doesn't bother to argue for the end of history or pencil in some new historical timing of time befitting time(s) beyond modernity. She is not concerned to apply, say, her idea of rhythmic time to aspects of the eighteenth or nineteenth centuries. Rather, she just forgets histories to talk about things more interesting and urgent, acts of the imagination that rethink time and the 'time of our lives' in ways that are not contaminated by (what she calls) the radioactivity of the old idea(s) of history, ways of producing postmodern acts of the imagination as yet to come. Here, postmodernity gives rise to new births.

Not all those who appear alongside Ermarth in Part Four think as she does. The way that considerations on the 'idea of the end of history' vary widely in the writings of, say, J.F. Lyotard, Jean Baudrillard, Rita Felski, Hayden White, Frank Ankersmit, David Harlan and Joan Scott. And this is to be expected – it's fine, because Part Four is not composed of readings that all agree on the details of the death of – or the moribund condition of – history. Nor are all the extracts in favour of history coming to an end, however construed. No. What all the readings of Part Four do is *address*, from a series of positions taken up relative to modernity/postmodernity, the question of whether postmodernism signals the end of history in some way or not: this is a discussion *about* the idea of, and the practices of, Endism. Accordingly, it is this *engagement* which is considered in Part Four to help bring, when allied to Parts One to Three, the question of 'the nature of history today' into as wide a view as possible.

Concluding thoughts

We think – we hope – that we have now justified the organisation of this Reader on the nature of history today, and that, if you leaf back to the Contents page, you will see the range of historians we have drawn on and who has been categorised as belonging to this or that genre and why; how they have 'been put in their place'. We think we need to make only one final point. You will see from the Contents page that the genre section(s) and the 'endist' section have different numbers of readings in them and that individually, the readings vary in length and 'style' (e.g. some provide footnotes or endnotes, while others do not). These differences can be explained by our saying that we think that, on the whole, the reconstructionist and constructionist extracts will be more familiar to readers than those in the deconstructionist and 'endist' sections. The readings in the latter two categories are thus longer than those in the first two; correspondingly, overall there are fewer of them. The differences in number and length, then, seem justified to us with regard to our intention of producing a useful, workable and hopefully thoughtful text about the nature of this thing called history. Whether we have achieved our intentions we cannot be sure, but we hope – once again *après* Derrida – that you might find in the following pages 'something in their favour'.

References

Appleby, Joyce, Hunt, Lynn and Jacob, Margaret (1994) *Telling the Truth About History*, New York: Norton.

Black, Jeremy and MacRaild, Donald M. ([1997] 2000) *Studying History,* Houndmills: Macmillan.

Bunzl, Martin (1997) *Real History*, London: Routledge.

Davies, Stephen (2003) *Empiricism and History*, Houndmills: Palgrave.

Elton, G.R. (1991) *Return to Essentials,* Cambridge: Cambridge University Press.

Gardiner, Patrick ([1952] 1961) *The Nature of Historical Explanation*, Oxford: Oxford University Press.

Goodman, Jordan (1997) 'History and Anthropology', in Michael Bentley (ed.), *Companion to Historiography,* London: Routledge, pp. 783–804.

Marwick, Arthur (1995) 'Two Approaches to Historical Study: The Metaphysical (including Postmodernism) and the Historical', *Journal of Contemporary History*, 30: 5–36.

Marwick, Arthur (2001) *The New Nature of History*, Houndmills: Palgrave.

Roberts, David D. (1995) *Nothing But History: Reconstruction and Extremity after Metaphysics*, Berkeley, CA: University of California Press.

Roberts, Geoffrey (1997) 'Postmodernism Versus the Standpoint of Action', review of "On 'What is History?'" by Keith Jenkins, *History and Theory*, 36: 249–60.

Symonds, Deborah A. (1999) 'Living in the Scottish Record Office', in Elizabeth Fox-Genovese and Elisabeth Lasch-Quinn, *Reconstructing History*, New York and London: Routledge, pp. 164–75.

Tosh, John ([1984] 2000) *The Pursuit of History*, Harlow: Longman.

White, Hayden (1978) *Tropics of Discourse: Essays in Cultural Criticism*, Baltimore, MD: The Johns Hopkins University Press.

White, Hayden (1987) *The Content of the Form: Narrative Discourse and Historical Representation*, Baltimore, MD: The Johns Hopkins University Press.

PART ONE

Reconstructionism

Texts in the genre of reconstructionism reflect the author's foundational belief in the knowability of the past; that it can be turned into history through the mechanism of the correspondence of sources and their data to meaning – to 'tell the truth about history', as it were, by recovering its 'true narrative'. The meaning or, as it is more usually described, the historian's interpretation, entails engaging with the referential. But, for reconstructionists, the idea that the past might be 'storyless' seems as nonsensical as the constructionists' nomothetic orientation. In other words, the form or shape we 'find' in the past must be the result of its inner or given meaning. If we choose not to believe that the past has an intrinsic shape, then it ceases to be something with which we can meaningfully engage. This is the major preoccupation of the authors of our first extracts.

CHAPTER 1

Geoffrey Elton

RETURN TO ESSENTIALS
(1991)*

Born in Germany, Geoffrey Elton taught at the University of Cambridge, rising to the post of Regius Professor of Modern History. His specialism was the Tudor administrative state. In several well-known books, he re-evaluated the Tudor monarchy and its administrative machine. But he is almost as equally well known for his stout defence of reconstructionist history, particularly in his book *Return to Essentials* (1991). In the following extract he weighs into what he sees as one of the worst excesses of both the constructionist and deconstructionist, as well as those entirely beyond the pale. Elton doubts that the meaning of the past can be derived through an epistemological model based on science. Doing so, he believes, results in the malign practice of calling 'for behavioural laws to be extracted from an inspection of the past'. He associates this with prediction and it has no place in history. So, what makes for change in the past? For Elton, history teaches '. . . a great deal about the existence of free will' or agency. Laws have no place but choice and intentionality do because it is individuals who make history. This does not seem, however, to apply to historians. As Elton insists, the past 'must be understood for itself' and remain uninfluenced by the 'predilections of the present'. Accordingly, historians do not set up theoretical models which they then 'validate or disprove by an "experimental" application of factual detail'. He is especially dismissive of the (arch constructionist) French *Annales* School in this respect. Finally, he rejects all theories that are either ideological or which are, as he sees it, literary and aimed at destroying 'the reality of the past as it had previously emerged from a study of that past's relics'.

A GOOD MANY PEOPLE can see no virtue in history (except perhaps mere enjoyment) unless knowledge of it offers directly usable guidance to the present in its confrontation with the future. As the phrase goes, they wish to learn from history, a desire in which they have too often been encouraged by historians themselves. And they wish this learning to be precise and reliable – like the lessons of science. For them it is not enough to gain some understanding of how people may act and react in given circumstances; they call for behavioural laws to be extracted from an inspection of the past. They like such laws as that the repression of a sector of society that is rising in wealth will lead to subversion and revolution; or that the accumulation of armaments will lead to war; or that only perfect democracy will ensure peaceful relations within society; or that ideological differences will always give way before economic interests (or the other way round). We can certainly find historical examples to illustrate all such generalizations, as well as

---

* Geoffrey Elton (1991) *Return to Essentials*, Cambridge: Cambridge University Press, pp. 6–11.

others to cast doubt. The lawmakers insist that phrases of this sort, the product of particular investigations, must have a normative function – must precisely predict what will happen – and this is where they go wrong. I remember once encountering the statement that when people have exhausted the lands they live on they will move to new lands: in effect that there is a law compelling them to do so. But there is no such law, and they do not always obey its nonexistent force. Generalizations based upon a study of past events may be convincing or contrived; what they can never be is a law of human behaviour. The trouble is that historians cannot make predictions by virtue of their science, though like anybody else they can try to prophesy as human beings, with a barely better chance of success than other people. They cannot claim powers of prediction because the secret of their success as historians lies in hindsight and argument backwards. Historians do not even know what it is they wish to analyse and understand until after it has happened; of necessity, they always reason from the situation they study to its prehistory – from what is to how it came about, not from what is to what may come of it. Thus the hunt for predictive laws contradicts the very essence of our enterprise; we leave such things to the social scientists whose scientifically based ordinances find themselves regularly ignored by disobedient mankind.

Does this mean that the simple hope enshrined in the phrase 'learning from history' is totally misplaced? It does not, but the relationship between the teaching and the learning differs a great deal from the simplicity so often imagined. A knowledge of history offers two uses to the present. It equips the living with a much wider and deeper acquaintance with the possibilities open to human thought and action than people can ever gather from their own limited experience, and it demonstrates the magnificent unpredictability of what human beings may think and do. History teaches a great deal about the existence of free will. Of course, it demonstrates the effects of circumstances, conditioning, interrelationships, but it also demonstrates that even when this scene-setting looks remarkably alike the outcome can and will vary enormously because it arises not from environment alone but from environment used by human beings. If you incline to believe those who would reduce humanity to the mere product of discoverable nature and nurture, the study of history (provided it is free of preconceptions) will soon disabuse you. There are no human beings who do not feel the influence of the setting within which they move, but all of them also transcend their setting and in their turn affect it: what they do both within and to it remains explicable but unpredictable. The call for predictive laws thus deprives mankind of its humanity – of its power for good and evil, its ability to think and choose, its chance to triumph and to suffer. Whatever we may at times feel like, we are not the helpless playthings of a fate reducible to laws, and the variety of experiences inside the given settings – a variety revealed by an open study of the past – shows that this is so. Individuals do make history, a truth denied only by those who would rather not be saddled with the responsibility. For free will does imply a high degree of responsibility: if history teaches that we are not just the products of inescapable circumstance, it also denies us the comfort of blaming laws of behaviour for our misdeeds and false decisions.

However, if we are to absorb that very useful lesson – the lesson that frees mind and spirit from the bondages that the makers of laws are forever trying to impose upon us – we need to escape from the most insidious temptation hiding within the very concept of learning from history. That temptation lies in seeing history as essentially relevant to the present; the technique which operates that temptation is known as present-centred (sometimes presentist) history. This is what Herbert Butterfield notoriously dubbed the 'whig interpretation': it selects from the past those details that seem to take the story along to today's concerns and so reconstructs the past by means of a sieve that discards what the present and time-limited interest determine is irrelevant. The method is totally predictive: it produces the result intended because it is designed to do so. The making of convenient laws receives assistance from such simplifications, but they assuredly ruin the real historical enterprise. Though as a fact of progress through time the present has emerged from the past, it was not the task of the past to create the present, any more than it is our function today to set up a predictable future. If knowledge of the past is to entitle the historian to speak to his own day, it must not be so organized as to satisfy that day's whim; if it is to teach usefully about mankind and the human condition, it must be understood for itself and in all its variety, undetermined by the predilections of the present and unruled by it at a time when the present did not yet exist.

True, this call for an understanding of the past on its own terms has some formidable implications for the working historian confronted by an endless agglomeration of events, of circumstances, of deeds and pronouncements and reflections. How is he to create some order out of such seeming chaos, especially if he is to be barred from just constructing a simple line terminating with today's outcome? The recognition of this difficulty has produced the first great threat to unprejudiced historical study that I shall here consider: the call for a general theory organizing the past. No sense, we are told, can be made of the usual morass of historical evidence unless it is fitted into a theoretical framework: it is this framework, which exists independently of the historical detail, that will create meaning for what without it remains meaningless. Furthermore, so the argument runs, whether the historian thinks he is using such a framework or not he will inevitably be doing so as he selects his facts, makes his connections, sees significance; and it is better to be conscious of the theory employed rather than allow unrecognized predilections to direct the operation. There is weight in this argument: unconscious presuppositions have indeed done much to distort the hunt for truth about the past. What needs to be understood is the fact that recognizing one's preconceptions should enable one to eliminate them, not to surrender to them. However, the historian faces the formidable example of the social scientist who swears by theory. The social sciences tend to arrive at their results by setting up a theoretical model which they then profess to validate or disprove by an 'experimental' application of factual detail. The belief that it is only by such theories that the historian can make sense of history is not new, but it became dominant with the appearance of the French school based on the journal *Annales*. That school deliberately resorted to various theoretical models developed by such social sciences as economics, sociology and social anthropology. The result, we are assured, was to revolutionize the history of France, especially by replacing interest in the evanescent event by the extraction of the long-term structure – a neat concept because it left so much uncontrolled speculation in the hands of the historian. That influence spread after the last World War when progressive thinkers more and more took their inspiration from France, and in the United States today very few historians even question the rightness of the method. More especially they revere the name of Clifford Geertz.

And yet it is wrong, and yet it threatens the virtue of history. I am speaking, you will understand, of the great or general theories, whether or not they can be represented by mathematical models – universal theories within which all historical exposition is to be accommodated. There are, in fact, two kinds of such theories with which historians have been confronted: some are strictly ideological (they impose an overarching interpretation on the past), while others are philosophical and question the whole concept of the study of the past. Today I shall try to deal with the former. Ideological theories have been around for a long time – general interpretative schemes embodying a faith of universal validity, imposed upon the reconstruction of the past rather than derived from it. And it does not matter whether the champions of the faith claim to base it on the study of the past, because in actual fact the faith always precedes that study. In my second lecture I shall turn to some current philosophical schemes, namely the endeavours to use literary theory to destroy the reality of the past as it had previously emerged from a study of that past's relics.

CHAPTER 2

Deborah A. Symonds

'LIVING IN THE SCOTTISH RECORD OFFICE' (1999)*

The next extract is from a chapter by the American historian Deborah A. Symonds called 'Living in the Scottish Record Office', published in *Reconstructing History: The Emergence of a New Historical Society* (1999). The extract is helpful in establishing the basic empiricist epistemological principle of the genre and the reconstructionist attitude of genuflection. Symonds works from the founding canon that to know the past the historian must first know the archive. She then adds the rider that there is '. . . something in the experience of research that defines the historian. It is humbling, refining, and tempering . . .'. This declaration of self-effacement is regularly employed by reconstructionists because of the elevation of the sources as the route to truth and the concomitant removal of the historian-author from the process. Hence, it does not sit well with them to adopt other than an appropriate posture of reverence. Beyond this deference to empiricism, logical reasoning must, of course, apply. As she says, what she is interested in is 'how one verifies and evaluates' the story found in the archive. She concludes with a statement with which all reconstructionist historians would agree: 'We are left . . . to infer what we can from the various testimonies that . . . survive.' The historian reads the runes.

T HERE IS SOMETHING IN the experience of research that defines the historian. It is humbling, refining, and tempering, although not, at least in my experience, as obvious as a conversion. Nonetheless, the effect of the research experience reminds me of a nineteenth-century French popular print in which bad husbands are dropped into

---

* Deborah A. Symonds (1999) 'Living in the Scottish Record Office', in Elizabeth Fox-Genovese and Elisabeth Lasch-Quinn (eds) *Reconstructing History*, New York: Routledge/Taylor & Francis Books, Inc., pp. 164–75.

a large chemical apparatus, coming out the other end quite literally converted to good husbands. This strikes me as an excellent graphic metaphor for the process, which for bad husbands, bad wives, bad partners of all sorts, and historians, takes many years; but for historians, at least, the process does indeed have its roots in the empirical experience of the archive, record office, and library.

In 1974 I was briefly locked into the main library at Edinburgh University one night, a victim of my Yankee unfamiliarity with the late sunlight at that latitude. Engrossed in a card catalog in a library in which everything up to and apparently including the incunabula was in open stacks, I sat hunched over a tall desk until the lights went out, and I slowly understood from the slanting light and utter silence that I was alone. The library, relatively new, had glass walls, and after not too long I caught the attention of a night watchman outside, who let me out. I was sorry to leave, and even after twenty-four years I remember the regret I felt as I made my way down the steps into George Square. Those cards hardly constituted the kind of primary research I intend to write about here, but that was the first time I had been so caught up that I understood that what I was doing was more important to me than my carefully cultivated air of worldliness and competence, the armor of a wet-behind-the-ears graduate student in a new country. I left some of that feigned arrogance behind me as I walked out of the library, shedding it almost absentmindedly.

Ten years later, having turned from literary history and folklore to history, I returned to Edinburgh, a city I have never been able to leave easily since I first set foot in it. Working in Register House until it closed at 4:45, I slowly became accustomed, not to the imposing monumental architecture of the neoclassical Adam building, with its rotunda and its flocks of law clerks and genealogists, but to how quickly I forgot them once my books were delivered. At the risk of arrant romanticization, I am inclined to argue that historians must hold the original documents of whatever they study, look at the paper, and smell everything. Only by coming face to face with surviving documents, seals, letters, maps, accounts, and receipts can one, I believe, fully weigh the meaning of terms like intention, falsification, and truth.

All of them are hard to evaluate, not just truth, which so often comes in for a drubbing these days. A colleague of mine, an earnest and serious scholar, illustrated this current attitude toward truth a year or two ago by saying (as well as I remember) that we in the history department should stop lying to our students, for there is no knowable past, and hence no past within human comprehension. This strikes me as an unbearably sad position to take in relation to the universe and to the past, reeking of a desolation that is more familiar to me in Rimbaud, before World War I, or in Wittgenstein in the 1920s. That this attitude should reappear in the late twentieth century, when the influx of material in history alone, about all sorts and conditions and kinds of men and women suggests quite the opposite—that the past is becoming increasingly knowable, in all its damnable and glorious complexity, and even inanity—strikes me as perverse. And it also suggests that, once the Donation of Constantine was discovered to be a forgery, historians who pondered Laurentius Valla's detective work had no choice but to face the full intricacy and irony of their position. In other words, face value—itself a telling phrase—dissolved a long time ago, but not into nothingness. What lay behind that face was research: more papers, more questions of face value, but ultimately the possibility of corroboration amounting to reasonable proof. To paraphrase Wittgenstein, survivor of the trenches: what we cannot speak about, and must pass over in silence, or contemplate in an agony of theory, seems to me, currently, to be greatly outweighed by what we can, have, and must discover and discuss.

But let me go back to Register House, past the guards and the notices about unattended packages and security, past the cloakroom and the old man with several teeth missing, who for years greeted me every morning with, "Go get 'em, sunshine." The Historical Search Room lies up a cast iron staircase, off a balcony that circles the rotunda, through large double doors that cannot be opened silently. Inside, as in many another archive, are rows of desks, surrounded by bookcases that run up to a high ceiling. Men in uniforms who have worked here for years take slips of paper out of a basket, whisper to each other, and push carts full of bundled papers, bound volumes, and boxes of loose papers in and out of the room. In almost complete silence, papers are distributed to the numbered desks, and you get what you ordered.

For the sake of simplicity, all I will argue here is that history, whatever it may become, begins from the materials of history, and that is in confronting these materials that questions of belief, intention, falsification, and truth have to be confronted and resolved. Theory comes later, after one has decided what one is, in fact, at the most empirical and scientific level, theorizing about, and how one's own biases dance at the edge of every apparently objective pool of light. In this case, to return to the story, what I had ordered was a volume of circuit court records, from the West Circuit, including Glasgow and surrounding counties, covering the period from September 18, 1767, to May 29, 1769. These volumes traveled with the judges from the High Court of Justiciary who rode the circuits, and probably to make travel easier, they were much smaller than the volumes used by the court in Edinburgh. They were carried in saddlebags, and written in, probably often, by bleary-eyed clerks. This particular volume, JC 13/16, is covered in dried leather, and smells of dust and old paper. I dare say that my friends who are more obliged to critical theory might call this description of an old book as "old" a delusion, an imposture, a facade of some sort. I am willing to call it an old book. The cover does not matter much, and my most immediate, personal, and ingrained response to it, because I am allergic to dust, is to sneeze.

What is in JC 13/16, on its unnumbered pages, is much more important. In this instance, I find something I was not looking for, but which holds my attention. Agnes Dugald, widow of a deceased "coallier," or collier from Campsie, is indicted for murder and denies the charge, which is that she had cut the throat of her own young daughter, near a hedge on the banks of the Clyde, a river just west of Glasgow. Several witnesses heard her confess, and although she later denied the charge in court, she was convicted and hanged. This is clearly no great matter of state, and this brief report of the incident might stand as a small footnote to some larger, but perhaps not much larger, matter in social history. But what I want to discuss is not whether this is important, or how, but something simpler—how one verifies and evaluates this story. Working with court records might seem a sort of escape from the problem, given that the testimony is, simply, the testimony on which the jury had to base its decision. But people lie in court, sometimes because lying comes naturally to them, and sometimes because as good lawyers know, ordinary people confuse direct observation with their own presumptions, and tell stories with implicit conclusions that are not proved, but only suggested by what they have observed.

What follows is not only a small part of Agnes Dugald's story, but also a record of how I worked with the case to find these people, corroborate what they said, understand how the court members heard and questioned their testimony, and expand the slender story left on a few pages of paper into something with implications. The first witness called, William Rutherfurd, was an apothecary or druggist in Glasgow, "aged thirty and upwards," and unmarried. He was probably called first by the prosecutor, Cosmo Gordon, because he had seen much of what there had been to see, and because he was respectable, in the sense that he had a profession, and a medical one at that. Rutherfurd said that "time and place libelled [named]" he had been walking along a footpath with Walter Stirling, a merchant from Glasgow. They came across the body of a child lying face down near the path, and one or both of them turned the body over; it was probably Rutherfurd, for he remembered saying to Stirling, after perceiving the wound, that "the Murderer can be at no great distance." Rutherfurd then went to the end of a nearby hedge, found a boy herding cows, and asked if anyone had passed by. The boy "pointed out a Woman at a considerable distance," and added that she "had just murdered a Child." At this point Rutherfurd gives us the first clue to where this has taken place, near a road or path running west of Glasgow, along the northern bank of the Clyde. Members of the court would have known this already, for it would have been part of the indictment presented at the beginning of the trial—but that indictment, contained in a long list of the court's business in that county, the Porteous Roll, was a separate document, which may or may not now survive among the small papers of the court.

In that indictment, the prosecutor, Gordon, would have tried to draw up both an exact and a general description of the crime, clear enough that it would justify, as it was noted in this court journal, taking the case to trial: "Cosmo Gordon . . . [c]raved the Lords would find the Indictment relevant & Remitt the Pannel [accused] & Indict. to the knowledge of an Assize [jury]." But the indictment is not here for us to consider, for, to save time, the court clerk had only written, in the place on the page where the indictment would have been written in by the High Court clerk, had this trial taken place in Edinburgh, "(Here record the Indict)." So we are left, without the Porteous Roll, to infer what we can from the various testimonies that do survive in the document we have in hand.

CHAPTER 3

Edward Royle

MODERN BRITAIN: A SOCIAL HISTORY, 1750–1997 ([1987] 1998)*

Most broad surveys are deliberately cast in simple reconstructionist terms. The next extract, from Edward Royle's *Modern Britain: A Social History, 1750–1997* ([1987] 1998), exemplifies this. We have included the Table of Contents as an indicator of the exhaustive nature of the referentiality of such an enterprise. Royle is a Professor in the Department of History, University

* Edward Royle ([1987] 1998) *Modern Britain: A Social History, 1750–1997*, London: Arnold, pp. 120–5.

of York. In his book he offers an extensive review of the social history of Britain from the Age of Enclosure in 1750 up to the near present. As the Table of Contents reveals, the approach is thematic and chronological (within each theme), as would be expected in this genre. The key themes are typical of recent thinking in reconstructionist social history, being a mix of the physical (The Changing Environment), the human (People), social structure (Class), the distribution of wealth (Poverty and Welfare), cultural pursuits (Life and Leisure), the role of faith and religion (Religion) and education (Education). Comprehensiveness is a key aim. But, as with all texts in this genre, there are inevitable omissions. And questions can always be asked about the balance struck in the narrative in respect of the organisation and significance given to certain aspects of the past (the City of York, for example, has about the same number of index entries as women). In the extract printed here from the section entitled 'The Challenge of Radicalism' from the chapter on class (viewed not as a theory but a given), Royle specifically addresses the reconstruction of radicalism and class conflict between 1800 and 1850. While acknowledging the provisional nature of all interpretations – provisional on the discovery of fresh evidence – the authoritative tone and style is typical of the reconstructionist survey genre. This flows in large part from the assumption that a detailed knowledge of the events of the past will insulate against those who might wish – through prejudice and lack of empirical knowledge – to abuse the past through their ideological prejudices. Cast in the standard survey style, Royle reverses the 'research monograph' approach of 'premise-evidence-inference' by providing the interpretative conclusion, followed by the premise and reference to the evidence. Thus, in the second paragraph he immediately offers the interpretation that the industrial middle classes 'did not at first seek to challenge the political power of the aristocracy . . .', then the evidence 'though there were some early signs of this . . . the first real evidence . . . similar grumblings were heard . . .'. This style marks it as a history which seems trustworthy and dependable, which carries conviction and has the ring of truth.

Tables and Maps
Preface
1 The Changing Environment
   The Countryside
      The Age of Enclosure and Improvement, 1750–1830
      The Victorian Countryside, 1830–1914
      The Twentieth-Century Countryside
   Transportation
      Turnpikes and Canals
      The Railway Age, 1830–1914
      Urban Transport
      Road Transport in the Twentieth Century
      Private Road Transport
      Rail, Sea and Air
   Towns
      The Growth of an Urban Society
      The Urban Environment, 1750–1830
      Urban Development in the Age of the Railway
      The Built Environment

Radicalism and class conflict, 1800–50

IN THE EARLY nineteenth century assumptions about the unity of the productive classes became increasingly difficult to maintain. Small producers were finding themselves excluded not only by the upper class from political power but also by the capitalist middle class from economic power; while for their part middle-class radicals were beginning to doubt the wisdom of extending political power to those who had no substantial property to guarantee their social moderation, and were finding it expedient to distinguish their own position from that of the lower classes. So, while both sections of the excluded were determined to destroy the aristocratic system and needed each other's help to do so, they were also themselves divided by class as their economic interests diverged.

The industrial middle class did not at first seek to challenge the political power of the aristocracy. Their main concern was the prosperity of their businesses, and they came to politics when their economic interests appeared threatened by government policy. Though there were some early signs of this in protests at the ending of the lucrative commercial war in 1763, the first real evidence of a new spirit among the urban manufacturers of the provinces came in 1785 when the General Chamber of Manufactures was formed to protest at Pitt's Irish trade policy. One of the first things the Chamber did was to point out the lack of representatives of the manufacturing interest in Parliament. Similar grumblings were heard over the cost of the French War and the imposition of an Income Tax in 1798, but only towards the end of the long wars in 1811–12 did the extra-parliamentary opposition experience success with its campaigns to end the East India Company's monopoly of the India and China trades and to secure the abolition of the Orders in Council which were damaging British industry and commerce, particularly in the American market. There was always a suspicion, though, that opposition to the government during wartime was unpatriotic, and so the full force of organized middle-class opinion was not felt until 1815 when a campaign was launched against the Income Tax (abolished 1816) and the new Corn Law of 1815 which seemed to guarantee high returns to the landed interest at the expense of the rest of the community.

By this time middle-class opinion was well organized to demand representation in the Commons for major manufacturing cities such as Manchester, Leeds and Birmingham which did not have their own borough members. In the West Riding, the *Leeds Mercury* was acquired by Edward Baines in 1801 and became the mouthpiece of the manufacturing interest; across the Pennines, the *Manchester Guardian* was founded with a similar function in 1821. In London, the Benthamite radicals, especially James Mill and radical master tailor, Francis Place, were urging the necessity of an extension of the suffrage. And likewise in most major centres of population a vocal party was formed to demand an end to the old, closed, oligarchic and aristocratic system of government. But the opportunity for a radical reform of Parliament did not come until 1830, following the temporary division of the governing Tories over the legal emancipation of Roman Catholics which was carried in 1829 against the force of British Protestant opinion. This attack on one of the pillars of the Constitution signalled the end of an era and the beginning of a decade of intense reform. The reforms of the 1830s, though, were carried by aristocratic ministries, not by revolutionaries as in France.

The politicization of the emergent working class also occurred during the period of the Revolutionary and Napoleonic Wars. Here the main issue was the plight of domestic manufacturers in the textile industry, especially during the great economic depression associated with the Orders in Council and the American blockade in 1811–12. There was a long tradition of legislative protection for workers, going back to the reigns of Edward VI and Elizabeth I, but much of this had fallen into neglect. In response to the demand that the law should be enforced on such matters as the ban on gig mills (used to raise the nap on cloth) in the woollen industry, and the apprenticeship clauses of the Statute of Artificers, Parliament proceeded to remove the protective legislation, denied further legislation to protect such groups as the framework knitters who were petitioning Parliament for relief, and made frame-breaking a capital offence. It was quite clear to the leaders of the workers that the law existed to protect the property of the capitalists but not their own sole property – their labour. This was an aspect of that 'abdication on the part of the governors' of which Thomas Carlyle was later to write. Thus in the dreadful winter of 1811–12, when bread prices reached record levels, economic hardships and industrial grievances merged with the remnants of 'Jacobin' radicalism from the 1790s and burst out in the angry name of 'Ned Ludd'.

Of course class was not made by one episode, but by cumulative reactions to events, especially in the years 1815–20, which culminated in the so-called 'Peterloo' massacre of 16 August 1819. This infamous event, when 11 people were killed and hundreds injured at a peaceful reform demonstration, epitomized all the social tensions of the post-war years. The victims were largely domestic textile workers and their families who had marched into Manchester to hear that great exponent of the radical platform, Henry Hunt, advocate the cause of universal suffrage; the assailants were the Yeomanry Cavalry, drawn from the local middle class. Although some leading middle-class Manchester radicals were quick to condemn the authorities for their action, the central government made haste to congratulate the magistrates on their good work. The Manchester massacre entered the mythology of the working class, a symbol of class pride and class hatred.

A further development in the 1820s which emphasized the growing difference between leaders of middle- and working-class opinion was the adoption of anti-capitalist economics by artisans influenced by such lecturers and writers as Thomas Hodgskin, William Thompson and – above all – Robert Owen. Though some followers of the latter were persuaded to seek the co-operative commonwealth by means other than political, the overall effect of the new ideas in the 1820s was to strengthen the identity of a separate working-class radicalism, denouncing not only aristocratic corruption, jobbery and boroughmongering but also dehumanizing, greedy and oppressive capitalism. At the same time, middle-class radicalism was consolidating around the ideology of utility and polit-ical economy. At the time of the Reform Bill crisis in 1831–32, working men in London, Leeds and Manchester formed their own Political Unions to rival those of the middle-classes, and when the Whig Reform Bill was finally carried in 1832 the measure was regarded at best with suspicion and at worst with downright hostility.

The Reform Act of 1832 achieved much in principle, but little in practice. The major new centres of population received separate representation in the Commons, the manu-facturing interest was given political recognition, the wealthier middle-class householders were given the vote, and some of the worst features of boroughmongering were removed. By uniting the propertied classes behind the modified constitution it thus ensured the continued political dominance of the aristocracy, and those middle-class radicals who had hoped for more found themselves outmanoeuvred.

The policy which united property against poverty appeared vindicated over the next 20 years. Whereas on the Continent middle-class liberals, still excluded from political power, provided the leadership for a revolutionary upsurge which experienced partial success in 1848, in Britain the governing class was immeasurably strengthened to with-stand the demands of radical reformers. Meanwhile, in the reformed Parliament Whig legislation inspired by principles of utility and political economy looked to working-class leaders suspiciously like 'class legislation', the first-fruits of the middle class's newly found political power. The most frequently cited examples of this 'class legislation' were the dismissal by Parliament of the Ten Hours factory movement in 1833 and the passing of the Poor Law Amendment Act in 1834.

The factory movement had gathered new pace from 1830, when Richard Oastler took up the cause of the children working in the Bradford worsted mills. During 1831 and 1832 a massive campaign was mounted in the West Riding in which working-class Short Time Committees joined with Tory reformers to condemn their common adversaries, the Whig-Liberal manufacturers led by Edward Baines and the *Leeds Mercury*. Evidence of conditions in the factories was gathered by the working men and presented to a parliamentary Select Committee led by Oastler's friend, Michael Sadler. But the work of the Committee was disrupted by the dissolution of Parliament in 1832, and meanwhile the manufacturers rallied and persuaded a Royal Commission that the laws of sound political economy would not permit the working hours of adults as well as of children to be reduced. The division of opinion was a stark matter of class. On the one side were manufacturers and political economists wedded to the doctrines of free enterprise and *laissez-faire*, abetted by Philosophic Radicals with their coldly rationalized view of humanity and efficiency; on the other were old-fashioned Tory paternalists, suspicious of upstart manufacturers, and working men looking to government to protect them from the cruelties of the 'free' market.

This social division was repeated when in 1834 the main recommendations of the Royal Commission on the Poor Laws were implemented in the Poor Law Amendment Act. What looked to Philosophical Radicals like a sensible reform and to political economists like a necessary withdrawal from interference in the labour market, was denounced as the 'poor man's robbery bill' by working men who feared brutal imprisonment in the proposed new 'bastilles' (workhouses) for the crime of poverty, and resented the removal of the traditional right of the poor to parish assistance in their own homes in time of need. Local communities throughout England responded to the new law with violent protest. In the textile districts, already seething with discontent over the failure of the Ten Hours movement, the new law was openly defied – in some cases for over a year.

The Poor Law Amendment Act illustrates clearly how far the common ground of radicalism had been divided between opposing economic classes, because the Act was in fact one of the most radical administrative measures of the nineteenth century. Taken with the repeal of the Test and Corporation Acts (1828), the Parliamentary Reform Act (1832) and the Municipal Corporations Act (1835) it revolutionized local government in England and Wales. Together these measures effectively broke the power of ancient local oligarchies and introduced the elective principle into local government. And yet, far from being hailed as welcome breaches of the aristocratic system they were seen as new forms of oppression because they did not fundamentally alter the social base of local political control: on the contrary they helped place it even more firmly in the hands of the urban élites which, in the manufacturing districts, meant the industrial middle classes.

Seen from the point of view of certain Tories such as Oastler, Carlyle and Disraeli, the Whig reforms signalled the death of the old, paternalist, aristocratic system of government. Seen through the pages of periodicals aimed at working-class audiences, it was not the Tories but the working classes who were the victims of change. The so-called 'Great Betrayal' of the Whig legislators was powerfully felt; Whigs, Philosophical Radicals, Political Economists and middle-class reformers who in the 1820s had seemed to be supporters of 'the people' in their attack on the aristocratic system, were now reckoned among the bitterest enemies of the working class.

Working-class hatred was reciprocated by middle-class distrust. Since the first decade of the nineteenth century, class positions had been expressed through radical political agitation in a fitful kind of way, but between 1830 and 1850 both the middle and working classes achieved a new sense of identity through separate and conflicting radical organizations: the Anti-Corn Law League was the essence of a middle-class pressure group; Chartism was the voice of the working class, excluded from political and economic power. It was not differences in immediate aims which divided the two organizations: most Chartists wanted the cheap bread and more plentiful employment which repeal of the Corn Laws promised; and the leaders of the Anti-Corn Law League wanted to destroy the aristocratic system and to extend the franchise. The difference between them was one of *class*. To the *Charter* newspaper (not an extreme publication) in 1839, the League was 'a party comprised of avaricious, grasping, money-mongers, great capitalists, and rich manufacturers'. To the *Leeds Mercury* the Chartist leadership of the great strike against manufacturers in the summer of 1842 comprised 'wicked and designing men' who were 'deplorably ignorant' of sound political economy.

CHAPTER 4

George Brown Tindall and David E. Shi

AMERICA: A NARRATIVE HISTORY ([1984] 1999)*

George Brown Tindall and David E. Shi provide the next extract. They are two of America's most distinguished historians. Individually they have published widely in the areas of cultural and regional history of the US. Their textbook *America: A Narrative History* ([1984] 1999) has now run to several editions and is one the leading textbooks of US history used at the college level. Taking one short extract from a book that runs to almost 1,700 pages – which makes this a monumental example of the survey text genre – is, at one level, unfair. But the extracts chosen from early on in the book and entitled 'The Great Biological Exchange' and 'Professional Explorers', reveal the same response to the needs of reconstructionist surveys as we saw in the Royle example (Chapter 3). Once again, the tenor and literary technique is authoritative and full of examples of events and happenings, and deliberately makes few demands on the reading abilities of the audience. The title of the full text – *A Narrative History* – is presumably chosen because of the popular and common association between the concept of a narrative and the telling of a story. The extract reveals the authors' epistemological assumptions that the past has a clearer and more immediate meaning when cast in terms that

---

* George Brown Tindall and David E. Shi ([1984] 1999) *America: A Narrative History*, 5th edition, New York: W.W. Norton & Company, Inc., pp. 21–6.

have a resonance today, as well as also through rational action theory – that is, the tracing of the intentions and work of historical agents. The reference to the 'green revolution' exported from the Americas and how these now make up a third of the world's plants indicates the effort to promote the relevance of the past today. The short yet vivid narrative about the professional explorers emphasises their expertise and specialised skills through the most well-known examples: Columbus, Cabot, de Balboa, da Gama and Magellan. Another important feature of survey texts pervades the extract, which is the sense of inevitability in the veracity of the story being retold. This is how it was and what it means.

The great biological exchange

THE FIRST EUROPEAN contacts with the New World began a diffusion of cultures, an exchange of such magnitude and pace as humanity had never known before. It was in fact more than a diffusion of cultures: it was a diffusion of distinctive biological systems. If anything, the plants and animals of the two worlds were more different than the people and their ways of life. Europeans, for instance, had never seen such creatures as the fearsome (if harmless) iguana, flying squirrels, fish with whiskers like cats, snakes that rattled "castanets," or anything quite like several other species: bison, cougars, armadillos, opossums, sloths, tapirs, anacondas, electric eels, vampire hats, toucans, Andean condors, and hummingbirds. Among the few domesticated animals, they could recognize the dog and the duck, but turkeys, guinea pigs, llamas, and alpacas were all new. Nor did the Native Americans know of horses, cattle, pigs, sheep, goats, and (maybe) chickens, which soon arrived from Europe in abundance. Yet, within a half century, whole islands of the Caribbean would be overrun by pigs, whose ancestors were bred in Spain.

The exchange of plant life worked an even greater change, a revolution in the diets of both hemispheres. Before the Great Discovery three main staples of the modern diet were unknown in the Old World: maize, potatoes (sweet and white), and many kinds of beans (snap, kidney, lima, and others). The white potato, although commonly called "Irish," actually migrated from South America to Europe and only reached North America with the Scotch-Irish immigrants of the 1700s. Other New World food plants included peanuts, squash, peppers, tomatoes, pumpkins, pineapples, sassafras, papayas, guavas, avocados, cacao (the source of chocolate), and chicle (for chewing gum). Europeans in turn soon introduced rice, wheat, barley, oats, wine grapes, melons, coffee, olives, bananas, "Kentucky" bluegrass, daisies, and dandelions to the New World.

The beauty of the exchange was that the food plants were more complementary than competitive. They grew in different soils and climates, or on different schedules. Indian corn, it turned out, could flourish almost anywhere—high or low, hot or cold, wet or dry. It spread quickly throughout the world. Before the end of the 1500s, American maize and sweet potatoes were staple crops in China. The green revolution exported from the Americas thus helped nourish a worldwide population explosion probably greater than any since the invention of agriculture. Plants domesticated by Native Americans now make up about a third of the world's food plants.

Europeans, moreover, adopted many Native American devices: canoes, snowshoes, moccasins, hammocks, kayaks, ponchos, dogsleds, and toboggans. The rubber ball and the game of lacrosse had Indian origins. New words entered the languages of Europeans:

wigwam, teepee, papoose, succotash, hominy, tobacco, moose, skunk, opossum, wood-
chuck, chipmunk, tomahawk, hickory, pecan, raccoon, and hundreds of others—and new
terms in translation: warpath, warpaint, paleface, medicine man, firewater. And the
natives left the map dotted with place names of Indian origin long after they were gone,
from Miami to Yakima, from Penobscot to Yuma.

There were still other New World contributions: tobacco and a number of other
drugs, including coca (for cocaine and novocaine), curare (a muscle relaxant), and cin-
chona bark (for quinine), and one common medical device, the enema tube. But Europeans
also exposed the New World inhabitants to exotic new illnesses they could not handle.
Even minor European diseases such as measles turned killer in the bodies of Indians who
had never encountered them and thus had built up no immunity. Major diseases such as
smallpox and typhus killed all the more speedily. According to an account from the first
English colony, sent by Sir Walter Raleigh on Roanoke Island, within a few days after
Englishmen visited the Indian villages of the neighborhood "people began to die very fast,
and many in short space. . . . The disease also was so strange that they neither knew what
it was, nor how to cure it." Epidemics ravaged the native population. In central Mexico
alone, some 8 million people, perhaps a third of the entire population, died of disease
within a decade after the Spaniards arrived. In what is now Texas, one Spanish explorer
noted, "half the natives died from a disease of the bowels and blamed us."

Professional explorers

Undeterred by new diseases and encouraged by Columbus's discoveries, professional
explorers, mostly Italians, hired themselves out to the highest bidder to look for a western
passage to Asia. They probed the shorelines of America during the early sixteenth century
in the vain search for an opening, and thus increased by leaps and bounds European knowledge of the New World. The first to sight the North American continent was John Cabot,
a Venetian whom Henry VII of England sponsored. Acting on the theory that China was
opposite England, Cabot sailed across the North Atlantic in 1497. His landfall at what
the king called "the new Founde lande" gave England the basis for a later claim to all of
North America. During the early sixteenth century, however, the English grew so preoccupied with internal divisions and conflicts with France that they failed to capitalize on
Cabot's discoveries. Only fishermen exploited the teeming waters of the Grand Banks.
In 1513 the Spaniard Vasco Núñez de Balboa became the first European to sight the Pacific
Ocean, but only after he had crossed the Isthmus of Panama on foot.

The Portuguese, meanwhile, went the other way. In 1498, while Columbus prowled
the Caribbean, Vasco da Gama sailed around Africa and soon set up the trading posts of
a commercial empire stretching from India to the Moluccas (or Spice Islands) of Indonesia.
The Spaniards, however, reasoned that the line of demarcation established by the Treaty
of Tordesillas ran around the other side of the earth as well. Hoping to show that the
Moluccas lay near South America within the Spanish sphere, Ferdinand Magellan, a
haughty Portuguese seaman in the employ of Spain, set out to find a passage through or
around South America. Departing Spain in 1519, he found his way through the dangerous
strait that now bears his name, then moved far to the north. On a journey far longer than
he had anticipated, he touched upon Guam and eventually made a landfall in the
Philippines, where he lost his life in a fight with the natives.

Magellan's remaining crew members made their way to the Moluccas, picked up a cargo of spices, and returned to Spain in 1522. This first voyage around the globe quickened Spanish ambitions for empire in the East, but after some abortive attempts at establishing themselves there, the Spaniards, beset by war with France, sold Portugal their claims to the Moluccas. From 1565, however, Spaniards would begin to penetrate the Philippines, discovered by Magellan and named for the Spanish prince who became Philip II. In the seventeenth century, the English and the Dutch would oust Portugal from most of its empire, but for a century, the East Indies were Portuguese.

CHAPTER 5

David Hackett Fischer

PAUL REVERE'S RIDE (1995)*

Another popular reconstructionist form is 'myth debunking'. This has a particular appeal to those historians who choose to believe that detailed factualism is the antidote to all historical fables. Such fables are, of course, normally the interpretations of previous generations of historians. The celebrated US historian, David Hackett Fischer, is Warren Professor of History at Brandeis University and in his book, *Paul Revere's Ride* (1995), he aims to describe the true story of the ride of Paul Revere, the American Revolutionary patriot, on the night of 18 April 1775. Revere was asked to spread the word that British troops were about to capture a store of the colonist's gunpowder at Concord, just outside Boston. An otherwise unexceptional crossing of the Charles River and ride by horseback from Charlestown to Medford was transformed in the American popular imagination through the patriotic, but factually inaccurate poem 'Paul Revere's Ride' by the poet Henry Wadsworth Longfellow (1861). As Fischer says, the legendary image is a romantic idea, 'but it is not what actually happened'. As a sophisticated reconstructionist, the point that Fischer does not miss, but fails to expand upon, is the way in which the various Revere narratives are told and constructed. Fischer points out (in a historiographical appendix) how the event has been used to create myths for various political and ancestor-worshipping reasons. But Fischer, of course, has his own agenda. His epistemological preference is revealed (in an echo of Brown Tindall and Shi) when he portrays Revere (and the several other similar riders who were abroad that night) as warning 'town leaders and military commanders of their region'. With this description Fischer argues that, in awakening political institutions (as represented by these people), 'human will' and 'individual action' are central to historical explanation. That this is Fischer's epistemological choice is as likely to do with his view of the world (where reality is about choice, accident and human agency and, who knows, individuals 'choosing' the path of destiny), as it is with the historical evidence of the ride. For Fischer it seems that, despite the legendary character of Revere, the essential

---

* David Hackett Fischer (1995) *Paul Revere's Ride*, New York: Oxford University Press, Inc., pp. 138–41.

nature of the event provides the enduring message for all proper history – that it is the actions of individuals that ultimately count in the fall and rise of nations and empires.

———————

It must have been a preconcerted scheme in them.
—British Colonel Francis Smith, April 22, 1775

The men appointed to alarm the country on such occasions . . . took their different routes.
—American leader John Adams, April 19, 1775

IN THE TIME THAT Paul Revere remained a prisoner, his message traveled rapidly across the countryside. To many Americans, the legend of the Lexington alarm conjures up the image of a solitary rider, galloping bravely in the darkness from one lonely farmstead to the next. This romantic idea is etched indelibly upon the national memory, but it is not what actually happened that night. Many other riders helped Paul Revere to carry the alarm. Their participation did not in any way diminish his role, but actually enlarged it. The more we learn about these messengers, the more interesting Paul Revere's part becomes—not merely as a solitary courier, but as an organizer and promoter of a common effort in the cause of freedom.

Earlier that evening, while Paul Revere was making ready for his own midnight ride, he and his Whig friends began the work of dispatching other couriers with news of the British march. While he was still in Charlestown, preparing to travel west to Lexington, arrangements were made for another "express" to gallop north with the news that he had brought from Boston. The identity of this other courier is not known. Many people heard him in the dark, but few actually saw him, and nobody recorded his name. He set out from Charlestown at about the same hour as Paul Revere himself. His route took him north, through the present towns of Medford, Winchester, Woburn, and Wilmington. So swiftly did he gallop on dark and dangerous roads that by two o'clock in the morning he was in the town of Tewksbury on the Merrimack River, twenty-five miles north of Boston.

Whoever he may have been, this messenger knew exactly where he was going, and what he was to do. When he reached Tewksbury, he spurred his horse through the streets of the sleeping village, and rode directly to the farm of Captain John Trull on Stickney Hill, near the town's training field.

Captain Trull was the head of Tewksbury's militia, and a pivotal figure in the alarm system that Whig leaders had organized during the past few months. He was awakened by the courier who told him, "I have alarmed all the towns from Charlestown to here." Trull rose from his bed, and took up his musket. Still in his nightdress, he fired three times from his bedroom window. This was a signal previously arranged with the militia commander in the neighboring town of Dracut, north of Tewksbury on the New Hampshire border.

The sharp report of Captain Trull's alarm gun carried across the Merrimack River, and the militia company of Dracut instantly began to muster. The hour was a little after two o'clock in the morning. At the moment when General Gage's Regulars were still in the marshes of the East Cambridge, the news of their secret mission had traveled thirty miles from Boston to the New Hampshire line. These were 18th-century distances. Thirty miles was normally a long day's journey in that era.

The astonishing speed of this communication did not occur by accident. It was the result of careful preparation, and something else as well. Paul Revere and the other messengers did not spread the alarm merely by knocking on individual farmhouse doors. They also awakened the institutions of New England. The midnight riders went systematically about the task of engaging town leaders and military commanders of their region. They enlisted its churches and ministers, its physicians and lawyers, its family networks and voluntary associations. Paul Revere and his fellow Whigs of Massachusetts understood, more clearly than Americans of later generations, that political institutions are instruments of human will, and amplifiers of individual action. They knew from long experience that successful effort requires sustained planning and careful organization. The way they went about their work made a major difference that night.

While the Tewksbury rider was galloping north, Paul Revere himself was on the road, traveling northeast from Charlestown to Medford. As we have seen, he had not planned to go that way, but once in the village of Medford, he went quickly about the task of awakening that community with remarkable economy of effort. He rode directly to the house of Captain Isaac Hall, commander of Medford's minutemen, who instantly triggered the town's alarm system. A townsman remembered that "repeated gunshots, the beating of drums and the ringing of bells filled the air."

From Medford, Paul Revere's friends started yet another express rider galloping to the northeast. He was Doctor Martin Herrick, a young Harvard graduate who studied in Medford and worked in the town of Lynnfield, fifteen miles to the north. Several Whig messengers that night were physicians. In that far-distant era when American physicians made house-calls, a country doctor was apt to own the best saddle horse in town, and be a highly experienced rider. He also tended to be a "high-toned son of liberty." So it was with Martin Herrick. He carried Paul Revere's message of alarm northeast from Medford to the village of Stoneham, then turned east toward Reading, where he roused the militia officers in the south precinct of that town. From Reading he rode to Lynn End, alarmed the militia company and later joined it as a volunteer on the march—a busy night for young Doctor Herrick.

Within a few hours, Doctor Herrick awakened a large area on the North Shore of Massachusetts Bay. He also set other riders in motion. One "express" was in Lynn by "early morn." Another galloped from Reading fifteen miles east to Danvers. A third rode fourteen miles north to Andover, where militiaman Thomas Boynton noted that "about the sun rising, the Town was alarmed with the News that the Regulars were on their March to Concord." Another resident of Andover, slower to get the word, wrote in his diary, "About seven o'clock we had alarum that the Reegelers was gon to Conkord we gathered at the meting hous & then started for Concord."

Along the North Shore of Massachusetts, church bells began to toll and the heavy beat of drums could be heard for many miles in the night air. Some towns responded to these warnings before a courier reached them. North Reading was awakened by alarm guns before sunrise. The first messenger appeared a little later.

While the alarm was spreading rapidly to the north, Paul Revere and his fellow Whigs started yet another courier in a different direction—east from Medford to the town of Malden. This express rider delivered the alarm to a Whig leader who went to an outcropping called Bell Rock, and rang the town bell. That prearranged signal summoned the men of Maiden with their weapons to a meeting place at Kettell's Tavern. From Maiden, the alarm was carried east to Chelsea on the Atlantic coast.

Meanwhile, Paul Revere himself was carrying the same message west from Medford to the village of Menotomy. There again he started other messengers in motion. This was the part of his journey of which he later wrote, "I alarmed almost every house, till I got to Lexington." From some of those houses men rode north and northwest to the precincts above Cambridge and Menotomy. Captain Ebenezer Stedman, a prominent Whig leader, was awakened at an early hour. He sent an express rider to Captain Joshua Walker and Major Loammi Baldwin in Woburn, north of Menotomy. From Woburn village, Captain Walker sent a messenger riding west to Jonathan Proctor in the second parish, now the town of Burlington. The alarm was also carried to the northwest in the same way. All along Paul Revere's route, town leaders and militia commanders were systematically engaged—a fact of vital importance for the events that followed.

Much of what happened that night was cloaked in secrecy, but repeated evidence indicates that Paul Revere played a unique role. From long association he was acquainted with leaders throughout the province. He knew who they were and where to find them, even in towns that he had not expected to visit. They knew him as well.

CHAPTER 6

Luigi Albertini

THE ORIGINS OF THE WAR OF 1914 (1952–7)*

Diplomatic history was long the staple of reconstructionist history before the rise and rise of social history in the 1960s. Its high point came with the work, from which the present extract is taken, by the Italian historian Luigi Albertini, *The Origins of the War of 1914* (three volumes, 1952–7). Albertini was also a leading journalist, editor, publisher and politician (Italian Senator). The debates over the cause and responsibility for the First World War prompted Albertini to devote several years to painstaking archival research in diplomatic documentary sources. His eventual triple-decker history (in excess of 2,000 pages) was almost universally acclaimed as a 'fair' assessment of the causes of the First World War and where the responsibility for it lay. The Preface to the book (by Louis Magrini) claims that Albertini had that clear-sighted practical common sense that is essential for an objective approach in determining agent intentionality and for penetrating the minds of protagonists in order to lay

---

* Luigi Albertini (1952–7) *The Origins of the War of 1914*, Oxford: Oxford University Press, pp. 170–5.

bare their motives. Albertini's thorough and scrupulous approach to the sources (telegrams, letters, reported conversations, minutes and notes of meetings, and speeches in archives in Berlin and Vienna and through personal correspondence with several still living protagonists), produced an intricate reconstruction of events in the crisis of July 1914. The overall effort was akin to a judicial inquiry. He concluded that no single agent in the process learned much from history, but while they were a mediocre generation of men, they were essentially trapped in a historical situation largely not of their own making. Within the context of Austro-German intentions toward Serbia after the assassination in Sarajevo of the Austrian Archduke Francis Ferdinand (Crown Prince to the thrones of Austria and Hungary) on 28 June 1914, the extract references the retaliation clamoured for in the dual monarchy against Serbia. For Albertini, the evidence was plain: the assassination was to be the pretext for a settling of accounts with Serbia for being an independent Slav state and the centre of attraction for the Croats and Serbs of the monarchy. Although Albertini emphasises the breakdown of diplomacy through his incredibly detailed scrutiny of the crisis of July 1914, he makes it clear that German assertiveness was the key cause of the war.

The laborious process of concocting the terms to be imposed on Serbia

BERCHTOLD'S REMARK AT the Council of Ministers shows that he was now sure of war even if Tisza's suggestions as to procedure were adopted. To Tschirschky he said after the meeting that even if Francis Joseph were to take the standpoint of Tisza that in the first instance definite demands should be made on Serbia, he 'would advise his Sovereign so to formulate these demands that their acceptance appears impossible'.[1] The Council of Ministers discussed the following demands to be presented to Serbia:

1. The punishment and expulsion from the Serbian Army of officers implicated in Pan-Serb propaganda;
2. an apology to be tendered by the Serbian Government for expressions used by Spalaiković, the Serbian Minister at St. Petersburg;
3. an investigation to be held into the circumstances in which the bombs were procured by the conspirators;
4. the dismissal of certain officials implicated in the earlier (Pokrayats) incident;
5. new legislation on the press and proceedings against the newspaper *Piemont*;
6. the revision of the Serbian law of associations;
7. the prohibition in officers' clubs and public places of journals hostile to Austria-Hungary.

These demands did not yet include those which were most burdensome and incompatible with Serbian sovereignty.[2]

Berchtold having put off his visit to the Emperor until the 9th, Conrad called on him on the 8th at 6 p.m. and was told of

the demands which were to be contained in an ultimatum to Serbia with a short time limit of twenty-four or forty-eight hours. It was to be presumed that Serbia would reject the demands so that on the expiry of the time limit mobilization and war would follow.

But Berchtold still had doubts about the whole business:

Berchtold:	'What happens if Serbia lets matters get to the point of mobilization and then capitulates all along the line?'
Conrad:	'Then we invade.'
Berchtold:	'Yes—but if Serbia simply does nothing?'
Conrad:	'Then Serbia remains occupied until the war expenditure is reimbursed.'
Berchtold:	'We shall not send the ultimatum till after harvest and after the close of the Sarajevo inquiry. . . .'
Conrad:	'When is the ultimatum to go off?'
Berchtold:	'In a fortnight's time. On 22 July. It would be a good thing if you and the War Minister would go away on leave for a while, so as to keep up an appearance that nothing is going on. . . .'
Berchtold:	'If we move into Serbia and occupy a sufficient area of territory, what then?'
Conrad:	'The occupation of territory does not settle anything, we should have to go on until we have beaten the Serbian Army.'
Berchtold:	'And if it gives us the slip?'
Conrad:	'Then we insist on its being demobilized and disarmed. When we have reached that point, the rest will come of itself.'
Berchtold:	'On no account take any steps now which might betray us; nothing must be done that might attract attention.'[3]

In order to win Tisza over, Berchtold on the same day (8 July) wrote him a private letter:

> Tschirschky has just left, after having told me that he has received a telegram from Berlin containing instructions from his Imperial master to emphasize here that Berlin expects the Monarchy to take action against Serbia and that Germany would not understand our letting the opportunity slip without striking a blow. . . . Tschirschky's declarations seem to me of such far reaching importance that they might well have some influence on your conclusions. That is why I hasten to communicate them to you and would beg you, if you think advisable, to telegraph (in code) to Bad Ischl where I am to spend to-morrow and could act as exponent of your views to His Majesty.[4]

As we have already seen, some historians deny that the Kaiser ever sent such orders to Tschirschky. But let it here be repeated that, given the intimacy of Tisza's relations with Tschirschky, Berchtold could never have made out to Tisza that Tschirschky told him something if Tschirschky had not done so. He and Tschirschky might, of course, have put their heads together to invent the story. If this were so, it had no effect on Tisza who did not send a telegram to Ischl, where Berchtold in consequence had on 9 July to tell Francis Joseph that there was a difference of opinion between himself and Tisza and explain the two points of view.

Information on what took place at Ischl is given by Conrad, and in a telegram sent by Tschirschky to Berlin on 10 July, Conrad relates:

On 10 July I called on Count Berchtold back from Ischl. He told me that he had found the Emperor very calm and resolute. His Majesty seemed to be in favour of action against Serbia and only had apprehensions about possible unrest in Hungary. Berchtold said that because of Germany, if for no other reason, we could not draw back now. Tisza, he says, is urging prudence, and opposes war; but Baron Burian is in Budapest for discussions with Tisza.[5]

Tschirschky's telegram informed Berlin that when Francis Joseph learnt of the difference of opinion between Berchtold and Tisza he

expressed the opinion that it might be possible to bridge it. But on the whole His Majesty rather leant to the view that concrete demands should be placed before Serbia.[6]

On 12 July Conrad had a talk with Berchtold:

He mentioned that Baron Burian is at Ischl. . . . The French President, Poincaré, he says, is on a visit to the Tsar, so he [Berchtold] wants to wait until Poincaré's departure and postpone the ultimatum to Serbia until 23 July. It would expire on 25 July, and 28 July could therefore be the first day of mobilization.
   I replied, that, if the military chancery agreed, I would go off on leave on 14 July and remain absent until 22 July, and so would the War Minister; but this programme would have to be changed if Serbia were to move troops northward. If that happened the ultimatum would have to be sent at once, because it would be a great advantage to us to cross the river barriers before the Serbs had taken adequate counter-measures. Count Berchtold said he needed this interval to await the end of the inquiry into the outrage and the getting in of the harvest and to carry out the diplomatic preliminaries.[7]

Before departing on 12 July Conrad wrote to Berchtold:

In my capacity as Chief of the General Staff I am only concerned with the exact terms of the decision, whether directly aiming at the outbreak of a war with Serbia or only reckoning with the possibility of a war. The diplomatic handling of either alternative lies, of course, outside my province; I must however again point out, as I explained verbally to Your Excellency with your complete approval, that in the diplomatic field everything must be avoided in the nature of protracted or piecemeal diplomatic action which would afford our adversary time for military measures and place us at a military disadvantage. . . . Hence it would be wise to avoid everything that might prematurely alarm our adversary and lead him to take countermeasures; in all respects a peaceable appearance should be displayed. But once the decision to act has been taken, military considerations demand that it must be carried out in a single move with a short-term ultimatum which, if rejected, should be followed immediately by the mobilization order.[8]

This letter gives the impression that, in spite of Berchtold's assurances, Conrad, because of Tisza's opposition, was not yet fully convinced that matters would come to a head. But Berchtold endeavoured to bring Tisza round by fixing a meeting with him for 14 July. By that day he would have received the full results of the inquiry into Serbian responsibility for the Sarajevo outrage which he needed for the drafting of the final form of the ultimatum. The drafting had been begun some time before. Tschirschky in his telegram of 10 July already, as we shall see, foreshadows some of the stiffest demands. But it was soon realized that more information must be obtained about the guilt of Belgrade. Therefore, on 10 July, Dr. Wiesner, the Legal Counsellor at the Ballplatz, an able and conscientious official, was sent to Sarajevo with instructions to report by telegram in forty-eight hours. On 13 July Wiesner telegraphed that the documents produced by the civil and military authorities gave no indication that the Belgrade Government had encouraged Pan-Serb propaganda but were enough to show that the movement had its origins in Serbia and was fostered by societies with the tolerance of the Belgrade Government.

There is nothing to show the complicity of the Serbian Government in the directing of the assassination or in its preparations or in the supplying of weapons. Nor is there anything to lead one even to conjecture such a thing. On the contrary there is evidence that would appear to show that such complicity is out of the question. . . .

 . . . Depositions of accused place it practically beyond doubt that the outrage was decided in Belgrade and, prepared with the help of the Serbian railway officials Ciganović and Major Tankosić, by both of whom bombs, Brownings, ammunition and cyanide of potassium were procured. . . . Bombs definitely proved to have come from Serbian army stores, but nothing to show that they had been taken out for this express purpose, since they might belong to the supplies of the Comitaji in the war. . . . Hardly room for doubt that Princip, Čabrinović and Grabež . . . secretly smuggled across the frontier by Serbian officials. . . . Other investigations after the outrage open a glimpse into propaganda organization *Narodna Obrana*. Received valuable utilizable material not yet examined, rapid inquiries in progress. If the intentions prevailing at my departure still exist, demands might be extended:

(A)   Suppression of complicity of Serbian Government officials in smuggling persons and material across the frontier.
(B)   Dismissal of Serbian frontier officers at Šabac and Ložnica and implicated customs official.
(C)   Criminal proceedings against Ciganović and Tankosić.[9]

This report was not to the liking of the war party. Potiorek, writing to Conrad from Sarajevo on 14 July declared:

> I regard it as utterly impossible but that at least one or other member of the democratic Government of so small a country as Serbia had knowledge of the preparations for the outrage. . . . It is moreover a fact that alongside of the official Government there is a military rival Government emanating from the army. That Serbian officers on the active list took part in the preparations for the outrage and took a leading part in the whole propaganda . . . is proved.[10]

But General Potiorek, who threatened to resign his command if military action were not taken, had no reason to be alarmed at the mildness of Wiesner's findings. He had both Berchtold and Conrad with him in his demand for stern measures. It seems, however, that right up to the previous day, 13 July, Berchtold continued to show hesitation. It was only on that 13 July that Tschirschky was able definitely to telegraph to Berlin.

> Minister is *now himself convinced that speediest action is imperative* (the words 'now himself convinced' and 'speediest' are twice underlined by the Kaiser). He hopes to-morrow with Tisza to draw up an agreed text of the note to be sent to Serbia, would then submit it on Wednesday 15 July to the Emperor at Ischl, after which without loss of time—perhaps even before Poincaré's departure—the handing over in Belgrade could take place.[11]

Notes

1   DD. I, 19.
2   Roderich Goos: *Das Wiener Kabinett und die Enstehung des Weltkrieges* (Vienna, 1919), pp. 93–4.
3   Conrad, IV, pp. 61–2.
4   Oe-U. VIII, 10145; see pp. 150–1.
5   Conrad, IV, p. 70.
6   DD. 1, 29; see p. 259.
7   Conrad, IV, p. 72.
8   Conrad, IV, p. 78.
9   Oe-U. VIII, 10252–3; KSF., 1925, p. 653.
10 Conrad, IV, pp. 82–5.
11 DD. I, 40.

CHAPTER 7

David Loades

THE REIGN OF MARY TUDOR: POLITICS, GOVERNMENT AND RELIGION IN ENGLAND, 1553–58 ([1979] 1991)*

A staple of reconstructionist history beyond the diplomatic is political and institutional history. Professor David Loades is a sixteenth- and seventeenth-century political and ecclesiastical Tudor specialist who trained in Cambridge under Geoffrey Elton. The book from which the

* David Loades ([1979] 1991) *The Reign of Mary Tudor: Politics, Government and Religion in England, 1553–58*, London: Pearson Education, pp. 18–23.

extract here is taken, *The Reign of Mary Tudor: Politics, Government and Religion in England, 1553–58* ([1979] 1991), is widely acknowledged as a benchmark account of the politics of the five-year reign of Mary Tudor. The extract deploys the foundational reconstructionist heuristic device whereby the author 'speaks through the sources'. At the outset Loades infers what he takes to be his justified belief concerning the broadly popular nature of Mary's support, but especially that of the middling and upper gentry. He does this through his reference to the contemporary account of events by Robert Wingfield. Here again the central argument is advanced through the appeal to source-based knowable agent intentionality. Where the sources are silent (as with the lack of council oaths), Loades resorts to reasoned supposition and conjecture, even though it is founded in the overall context of the available sources. This constitutes a straightforward example of 'explanation to the best fit'.

THE NATURE OF MARY'S victory in July 1553 puzzled and somewhat alarmed foreign observers. They were accustomed to aristocratic faction and to peasant revolt, but this was neither. Robert Wingfield, who wrote his account within a few months of the events, emphasised the spontaneous and popular nature of her support, but his work also makes clear the crucial importance of the middling and upper gentry.[1] It was the 'middling sort' who first rallied to her at Kenninghall and Framlingham, her own affinity and their friends and neighbours, whose swift and resolute action convinced a wavering and uncertain aristocracy where the path of duty lay. This made English politics different and therefore unpredictable from a continental point of view. It also meant that Mary had no 'shadow' council waiting to take over the government (as Elizabeth was to have in 1558) and therefore had to assemble her administration from scratch. From the moment when she proclaimed herself queen she needed the appurtenances of royalty and had no option but to create a council from the material which was immediately to hand.[2] The uncertain nature of her prospects during the previous decade and the strict religious tests which she had herself imposed, had meant that her household as heir apparent had not attracted a very glittering array of talent. Her faithful servants, Robert Rochester, Edward Waldegrave and Sir Francis Englefield, did not make an impressive royal council, but fortunately they were not called upon to sustain that role unaided. By 12 July, when she moved her growing host to Framlingham, she had been joined by Sir John Shelton, Sir Henry Bedingfield and Sir Richard Southwell,[3] and over the following week, as the tide turned decisively in her favour, there arrived the earl of Bath, the earl of Sussex, Lord Wentworth, Sir Thomas Cornwallis, Sir John Mordaunt, Richard Morgan, Thomas Wharton and several other men of substance and experience.[4] By the time that Lord Paget and the earl of Arundel arrived on the 19th to offer the submission of the lords in London, the queen already had a working council of nearly twenty members. She also had a *de facto* secretary in the person of John Bourne, who kept such notes of the business of the Framlingham council as have survived.[5] She did not, however, have the makings of a stable and successful government. Even if we include those who had clearly declared for Mary in other parts of the country, such as the earl of Oxford, Lord Rich, Lord Dacre, Sir Thomas Cheney and Sir John Gage, she could still deploy only a fragmentary assortment of political talent, with little recent experience of high office.

For their part, the London council had never been solidly behind Northumberland. Indeed Lord Paget had been disgraced in 1551 and had been recalled only after the king's death.[6] He had been closely associated with Somerset, but was innocent of any involvement in the plot to crown Jane Grey. The earl of Arundel had also been excluded for opposing the duke and recalled in an attempt to win his support earlier in the summer. He had signed the instrument recognizing Jane, but was not committed to her cause. The same was true of the earl of Pembroke, who had had his own quarrels with Northumberland,[7] and to a lesser extent of the earls of Bedford and Shrewsbury. There was also a conservative group among the less powerful members of Edward's council who had succeeded in avoiding more than a token involvement: Sir Thomas Cheney, Sir William Petre, Sir John Gage, Sir John Mason, Dr Nicholas Wotton and one or two more. On the other side stood Northumberland himself; his faithful but rather ineffectual associate the duke of Suffolk; William Parr, marquis of Northampton; Sir John Gates; and Sir Philip Hoby. Rather more equivocal in their views, but still deeply entangled in the plot, were the earl of Huntingdon; Walter Devereux, Viscount Hereford; Thomas Lord Darcy; Sir William Cecil; and the two ecclesiastics Cranmer and Goodrich. When the crisis came and it became clear that Mary could command and was prepared to use, a far more active support than her opponents had calculated upon, the council split. Arundel, Pembroke and Paget naturally took the lead, since they had the most to hope for and the least to fear in declaring for Mary. After that it was a question of *sauve qui peut* and the queen's main problem was to know how to react to the seasoned and powerful politicians who now hastened to Framlingham to offer their services. Paget and Arundel were promptly received into favour and the latter was immediately given the responsible task of apprehending Northumberland.[8] They may well have been sworn of the council at the same time, since no council oaths are recorded for the Framlingham period and neither appears on any subsequent list. The first record of a councillor's oath is that of Sir Edward Hastings on 28 July.[9] Sir Edmund Peckham, the treasurer of the mint, was sworn on the 29th and thereafter the Edwardian councillors begin to appear: the earl of Bedford on the same day and Sir William Petre and Sir John Mason on the 30th.[10] By the time that Mary entered London on 3 August her council must have numbered about twenty-five, and they were already a somewhat ill-assorted team.

In most cases the queen seems to have shown good sense and discrimination. Northumberland's belated and rather pathetic gesture of proclaiming her at Cambridge on 19 July convinced no one. The duke and all his five sons were rounded up and put on trial. Northampton, Gates, Sir Thomas Palmer and subsequently Cranmer, shared the same fate. Of those closest to Northumberland, only the duke of Suffolk escaped with a brief period of imprisonment.[11] Of the others who were deeply implicated, the earl of Huntingdon was committed to the Tower and the earl of Rutland to the Fleet, Viscount Hereford, Sir William Cecil and Sir John Yorke were similarly imprisoned, while Lord Darcy was placed under house arrest.[12] Northumberland himself, Gates and Palmer died immediately for their part in the conspiracy; Guildford Dudley and Jane Grey the following February. Suffolk was executed for a subsequent treason and Cranmer for heresy.[13]

Notes

1   'The "Vita Mariae Reginae" of Robert Wingfield', ed. D. MacCulloch; *Camden Miscellany*, XXVIII, 184, 188.

2   Mary's initial letter to the council was written from Kenninghall, and it must have been there, or during her flight, that the first meetings of her own embryonic council were held, although nothing was recorded until after her arrival at Framlingham.

3   'Vita', 254–5.

4   The *Chronicle of Queen Jane*, Camden Society, 48 (1850), 5; C. Wriothesley, *A Chronicle of England*, Camden Society, n.s. 11 (1877), II, 87. Wharton and Mordaunt were the sons of the barons of those names.

5   Notes of the Framlingham meetings begin on 14 July, *APC*, IV, 415 *et seq*. The MS containing these notes is among the Cecil Papers at Hatfield House (245/1) and it has been convincingly attributed to Bourne by G.A. Lemasters. Lemasters, 'The Privy Council in the reign of Queen Mary I' (unpublished PhD thesis, Cambridge, 1971), 255–6.

6   Paget actually joined the lords in London only a day or two before their decision to submit and their invitation to him must be seen as a move in that direction. S.R. Gammon, *Statesman and Schemer* (1973), 186–7.

7   Sheyfve had reported friction between them in February. *Cal. Span.*, XI, 13. The marriage of his son, Lord Herbert to Lady Catherine Grey on 25 May was probably an attempt to secure his doubtful loyalty. See also Jordan, *The Threshold of Power*, 526.

8   *Chronicle of Queen Jane*, 10–11.

9   *APC*, IV, 418. By this time Mary was at Newhall.

10   Ibid., 419.

11   Suffolk was committed to the Tower on 27 July and released on 31 July, *Diary of Henry Machyn*, 38. He was pardoned on 27 November for all offences committed before 1 October. *Cal. Pat.*, Philip and Mary, I, 194.

12   *APC*, IV, 306–8.

13   Cranmer was tried for high treason on 13 November and convicted. PRO Baga de Secretis, KB8/23. His attainder was confirmed by parliament the following month and he was never pardoned, but the queen preferred to execute him on what was, to her, the major charge. Loades, *The Oxford Martyrs (OM)*, 120-1.

CHAPTER 8

John Hassan

A HISTORY OF WATER IN MODERN ENGLAND AND WALES (1998)*

That the complexities of non-political history are not solely the preserve of constructionist historians is indicated in the extract from John Hassan, a British historian working in the area of energy and water history. The extract reproduced here from his *A History of Water in Modern England and Wales* (1998) is an example of environmental history, a field that attempts to explore the connections between the natural world and human society. In this extract the early history of the consumption, provision and disposal of water is addressed through the major secondary sources – the historiography. There is no paradox in this, given the reconstructionist fixation with 'the fact of the matter' and 'what actually happened'. Any

* John Hassan (1998) *A History of Water in Modern England and Wales*, Manchester: Manchester University Press, pp. 10–12.

apparent doubts are removed when it is understood the force that this historiographical approach has in demonstrating the reality of the past through coherence and consensus versions of the truth. The enormous benefit of secondary source reference constitutes a powerful reality effect produced by an orientation to what other historians have said. Reconstructionists actually have a great deal of choice when it comes to establishing the veracity of what they say. Correspondence is only the most obvious way to 'get back to reality' (history mirrors the sources), but equally effective is the heavy-duty historiographical approach of Hassan's. Invoking substantial numbers of other historians has the enormous benefit of creating the appearance of widespread agreement as to the real nature of the past.

The consumption, provision and disposal of water

The consumption of water

WATER HAS BEEN described as the '*sine qua non* of the city . . . whether for sustenance, sanitation, fire-fighting or industrial use, water was the original public utility and historically the first urban problem' (Lampard, cited in Hassan 1985: 531). As in France, the nineteenth-century drive to address these needs has been interpreted as the outcome of the recognition that water was a matter of collective, not simply private, concern. Public health anxieties, in particular, were paramount (Hardy 1984: 250; Dupuy 1982: 244–6). Yet the concern of medical and sanitary experts was almost exclusively directed at the moment of human consumption. What animated them, above all, were the adequacy and the safety of drinking water supplies. Human ingenuity in developing this industry concentrated initially on the task of bringing water to the individual consumer. Wider public issues, such as the management of the water cycle on a regionally equitable or environmentally sound basis, received understandably little attention for the time being.

Society, especially middle-class society, according to Hardy (1984: 272), craved greatly improved access to water, for reasons of personal health, convenience, ease and enjoyment. She has stressed the cultural importance of water to the English, in its use in washing, cooking and making beverages: 'Water was also used to make tea – that great British consolation, a luxury which even the very poor deemed essential to everyday life'. In addition, reformers were tireless in their advice to the working-classes to employ water and soap more regularly in order to stave off the threat of disease: 'Among the poor in London there will always be filth, putrefaction, and all the essences of plague and pestilence. . . . To display clean things to a dirty man is to throw pearls to swine, who will certainly trample them in the filth of their stye', it was stated in 1871 (*The Field*, 3 June 1871, quoted in Taylor 1946: 30). But this was not a typical attitude. Much more so was the Royal Sanitary Commission's opinion of that year, that one of the first priorities of a 'civilised social life' was 'the supply of wholesome and sufficient water for drinking and washing' (cited in Hassan 1985: 543).

The main impediment to acting on reformers' good advice was the state of water supplies in the early nineteenth century. Water was so scarce in Liverpool that begging for it was common and, with barely enough for cooking or drinking, it was scarcely surprising that little was used for personal hygiene (Taylor 1976: 145). The local authority provided water free of charge to the poor in Bolton, but it was 'of a nasty green colour', the source polluted by farmland, and generally fit only for street-cleansing (Hassan and Taylor 1996: 13). Well-water was popular with Londoners because of its flavour, but scientific assessment from the 1860s revealed the extent to which it was contaminated by cesspool soakage (Hardy 1993: 158). In Bristol in 1845, 73,443 persons relied wholly on wells which were also liable to cesspool contamination, water from which was delivered by water-carriers to the poor in many parts of the city at expensive rates (BRO, 40619/A/2/b, 1845). The modernisation of the water industry from the 1840s brought better piped supplies to many, but social inequalities remained. The proportion of homes in Manchester with access to water fittings increased from about 50 per cent in 1846 to almost complete coverage by the 1870s, and the proportion with an internal supply increased from 23.4 per cent in 1846 to 79.4 per cent in 1879. Poorer districts were less well provided for, and here reliance on standpipes persisted into the 1870s (Hassan 1984: 35). So inadequate was provision that the first fountain erected by a new philanthropic society in London to supply free, filtered water attracted over 7,000 people daily, after it was opened at St Sepulchre's in 1859 (Davies 1989: 14). Octavia Hill, who managed tenement homes for the poor with the intention of promoting higher domestic standards, provided only cold water to her houses, piped to a communal tap on each floor; this was better than what it replaced, namely a single source for many storeys. Until the 1890s in London, many private homes were without a piped supply of water at all (Hardy 1984: 273). As late as 1913, there were still 43,000 houses in Birmingham without internal fittings, where all water had to be fetched from outside (Reynolds 1943: 99).

Thus, in nineteenth-century England domestic consumption of water was held back by the lack of appropriate installations. In early nineteenth-century America, according to popular sentiment, those who bathed risked dissipation and ill health, but significantly, once waterworks were built demand for water quickly outstripped supply (Wilkie 1986: 649). It is revealing that historians of water-using amenities such as baths and water-closets, often emphasise the behaviour of royalty – a reflection of social imbalances in this area.

The aristocracy and monarchy may have been fashion pace-setters, but there was consumer resistance to the use of water for cleansing, 'dry cleaning' through rubbing down and powdering being preferred, at least up to the seventeenth century, in the belief that washing could provoke all manners of ailments, or even prove lethal (Lanz 1995: 45). French monarchs in the eighteenth century might, on coming to the throne, inherit fabulous *appartements de bains* in their royal palaces, only for the facilities to be demolished or converted to other uses due to indifference. Louis XIII, in the early eighteenth century, made do with a wooden tub for bathing (Wright 1960: 8). When Victoria became Queen in 1837 Buckingham Palace lacked a bathroom (Allen 1976: 30). Similarly, even though the aristocracy pioneered their use, 'rather rare and rude' water-closets were a novelty in great English houses of the eighteenth century (Wright 1960: 103). Nevertheless, innovation in this area of personal hygiene was concentrated in the upper classes. In the eighteenth century, Hepplewhite encased washstands made an appearance, although there was Anglo-Saxon resistance to *bidification*, with its 'aura of Continental impropriety', even in Georgian England (Wright 1960: 115).

Nineteenth-century exhortations to wash as an aid to good health formed a connection with an older hydropathic tradition associating health with regular bathing. Perhaps making a virtue out of a necessity given the virtual absence of hot water, the benefits of the cold bath were extolled in Victorian England (at a time, nevertheless, when the immersion of invalids in winter seas was becoming less fashionable as a cure). Icy-cold plunges were believed to be particularly good for the young. According to Wright (1960: 165): 'Until the end of the century a healthy young man who took his bath hot was thought effeminate.' There was a widespread view in both England and America in the middle decades of the century, justified by spurious pseudo-science, that warm bathing could cause numerous skin or other maladies. Nor, surprisingly, was the use of soap unanimously encouraged. Thus, according to much mid-century advice, 'the typical bath consisted of a cold plunge or sponge unencumbered by the use of soap and taken solely as a prescription for health' (Wilkie 1986: 652). In time the fascination with cold immersions abated and the pleasures of hot bathing were discovered. Attempts to employ gas for these purposes, such as heating cast-iron baths directly by a gas-burner, sometimes had disastrous results for the bather. Subsequently techniques slowly improved.

CHAPTER 9

Michael A.R. Graves

*ELIZABETHAN PARLIAMENTS 1559–1601 ([1987] 1996)**

Reconstructionists, as we have just seen, can work very plausibly through the historiography. *Elizabethan Parliaments, 1559–1601* ([1987] 1996), by Michael A.R. Graves, a teacher at the University of Auckland, New Zealand, reaches its conclusion through a historiographical appraisal. Published in the famous Longman Seminar Series, the text is supported by what are judged to be the key primary documents upon which the historiographical survey is based. Graves's book deals with the political, organisational and functional characteristics of Elizabethan Parliaments between 1559 and 1601. The extract here is from the final section of the book in which Graves summarises the historiography of the Elizabethan Parliaments. He comments how interpretations are very much the reflections of historical circumstances and the influences of major historians, noting the Whiggish interpretation of Pollard and Neale which 'marked them off as men of their times'. This 'political school' emerged during the 1920s to 1950s because they saw Elizabethan Parliaments as odd deviations on the long upward road to the neutralisation of the monarchy. The revisionists (inspired by Elton) chose to examine the Parliaments themselves rather than the bigger issues that surrounded their development. What Graves is demonstrating is that the history you get is largely dependent upon the assumptions you hold and the questions you ask. Even the most unreconstructed of reconstructionists recognise this essential fact of history research and writing: that history is ultimately as much about historiography as it is about the past.

---

* Michael A.R. Graves ([1987] 1996) *Elizabethan Parliaments 1559–1601*, London: Pearson Education, pp. 90–2.

IN HIS STUDY OF *The Evolution of Parliament*, published in 1920, A.F. Pollard identified the consolidation of the House of Commons as the most important development in the parliamentary history of the sixteenth century. It acquired a corporate consciousness, superseded the Lords, and became the focus of parliamentary activity. His pupil and successor, Sir John Neale, elaborated upon this theme, detected a growing, Commons-based opposition to royal authority and postulated the thesis that the origins of the English Civil War were to be found in the Elizabethan parliaments. Thus there was created a coherent, consistent and well-rounded picture of a rising Parliament and, within it, a politically maturing House of Commons which was becoming more disposed and able to criticise, oppose and challenge the Crown. This thesis had a seductive quality because it was consistent with events during the forty years after Elizabeth's death – or at least with the views of early Stuart historians who wrote at the same time as Pollard and Neale. In contrast, the well-established interpretation which they overthrew was certainly not in harmony with either pre- or post-Tudor developments. It can be summarised briefly. The long-term rise of Parliament was interrupted when fifteenth-century Lancastrian constitutionalism gave way to the strong 'New Monarchy' of the Yorkists and Henry VII. Sixteenth-century government was characterised by submissive parliaments and autocratic Tudor rulers. In 1603 this lengthy aberration ended and Parliament resumed its upward progress which culminated in the neutralisation of the monarchy, the political castration of the Lords, adult suffrage and the Commons' supremacy during the nineteenth and twentieth centuries.

The new interpretation fitted neatly into this scheme. Moreover, its adherents were conscious of the need to see the Tudor parliaments in the context of what came before, and especially of what happened afterwards. So Neale searched for the origins of seventeenth-century conflict, whilst Wallace Notestein, an American historian working in the same field, was one of the few (then or since) to produce a parliamentary study which did not stop or start in 1603. There are elements of truth in their thesis of a rising Parliament and they should not be dismissed lightly. The sovereignty of King-in-Parliament and the supremacy of statute were products of the sixteenth century, whilst the monopolies uproar in 1601 demonstrated how a united House of Commons could extract concessions from a Tudor monarch. Nevertheless, their political interpretation has come under serious attack from revisionist historians during the past fifteen years and it is not difficult to see why. Pollard, Neale, Notestein and others fell into the trap of trying to explain seventeenth-century upheavals, instead of studying Tudor parliaments in their own right and not as a mere prologue. They imposed upon their material a preconception, which in turn determined their treatment of parliaments in political terms. Their own historical training reinforced this approach. Pollard's apprenticeship was as a contributor to the *Dictionary of National Biography*, and thereafter his best pieces were the biographical studies of great men. Likewise, Neale won acclaim for his life of Queen Elizabeth I and later he became editor of the Elizabethan volumes of the *History of Parliament*. This was a misnomer, because it consisted of no more than a collection of constituency surveys and biographies of knights and burgesses in the Commons. It was not an institutional study and it excluded the House of Lords. The political-cum-biographical approach to Tudor parliaments, combined with the concentration on the Commons and the concern to relate them to Stuart developments, dictated the priorities of the political school.

The whiggish interpretation of Pollard and Neale marked them off as men of their times. The Tudor revisionists are no less creatures of circumstances, responding to both particular and general contemporary influences such as G.R. Elton's institutional, archival and administrative emphases, and the impact of the human sciences, which first expressed itself in Elizabethan and early Stuart county and urban studies. They have moved away from kings and queens, great politicians and high political drama, and asked new questions: how did the institution of Parliament work? what was its business? and how did it relate to the community in which its members lived? These were questions to which the political school supplied few answers. Much of Neale's supposed institutional study of the House of Commons was devoted to the politics of its elections and biographical information about its members. Although Pollard published articles on the clerical organisation of Parliament, as well as *The Evolution of Parliament*, he was less fluent, often obscure, and at times almost incomprehensible when he turned from biography to the history of an institution.

The revisionists, with their different priorities, have supplied some of the deficiencies of the political school. They have argued persuasively that to examine the politics of an institution without an adequate knowledge of its functions, its business, and how that business was transacted, is to put the cart before the horse. In the process they have rehabilitated the House of Lords a sensible exercise because it was, after all, co-equal with the Commons in law-making. And they have also treated Parliament as representative of the community and reflecting its concerns, rather than as some kind of autonomous creature with a political life of its own. In all of these respects the revisionists' work represents an advance on that of the political school. As yet, however, their approach has been piecemeal rather than comprehensive. They have demolished some aspects of the older interpretation and criticised others without, as yet, providing a coherent alternative, although a number of general interim assessments have appeared in print.

CHAPTER 10

Gertrude Himmelfarb

THE IDEA OF POVERTY: ENGLAND IN THE EARLY INDUSTRIAL AGE (1984)*

Continuing in the social history mode, Gertrude Himmelfarb has been a leading American historian of Victorian England for over fifty years. Of late, she has been particularly well known for her vigorous defence of reconstructionist history and her combative attitude towards postmodern history. In the extract here, taken from *The Idea of Poverty: England in the Early Industrial Age* (1984), Himmelfarb analyses the key feature of her book – how historical agents defined and then tried to solve 'the problem of poverty'. She couches her analysis as a rejection of the rise of the so-called Whig interpretation of history that, she says, sees 'the past as a progressive movement toward a more enlightened future'. As a reconstructionist,

* Gertrude Himmelfarb (1984) *The Idea of Poverty: England in the Early Industrial Age*, London: Faber & Faber, pp. 6–10.

Himmelfarb is generally not in favour of such pattern-seeking in history. Using a quote establishing a long historical perspective going back to the Tudor period, she prefers the metaphor of a pendulum oscillating between regression and progression. But, as she says, even this image 'distorts reality', given the ambiguity, the ambivalence and the unintended consequences of people's actions. Only in the historian's retrospective gaze can a pattern 'of increasing governmental control over every aspect of social life' be detected. In spite of the up-fronting of the record, Himmelfarb's belief that the knowledge of what happened will tell us what it means through the ideas people held at the time is foregrounded. Himmelfarb eventually settles for the characteristically reconstructionist argument: 'to find the meanings they attached to the facts' and 'to try to reconstruct their own interpretation of their experience'. She rightly denies objectivity of the sort that stands 'outside the received opinion', but then happily assumes that what people felt and said is some kind of insulation against the epistemological slippage between past reality and present history. Recognising the 'ideas lurking behind the facts' and placing what happened and what people thought in a context, Himmelfarb seems to believe that this relieves her of the danger of seeing facts as atoms of past reality. She concludes, somewhat dangerously, that the ideas 'deduced from' sources and documents 'reflect the sensibility and consciousness of contemporaries rather than of the historian'. This is the most basic reconstructionist principle as well as the genre's collective call to arms.

THE PERIOD COVERED BY this volume is the century during which England emerged as the "first industrial nation," roughly 1750 to 1850, a time not only of intensive economic and social change but of those social experiments, ideologies, and policies designed to cope, as Tawney put it, with "those of its members who fall by the way." Because of the crucial role of legislation in this national effort—the climactic reform of the poor law in 1834, factory and mine acts regulating the hours and conditions of work of children and women, sanitation and public health acts, education and prison acts—much of the social history of England has been written as a history of social reforms. This kind of history, as Asa Briggs has pointed out, is especially prone to the "Whig interpretation of history," the tendency to read the past as a progressive movement toward a more enlightened future. In this reading of history, the nineteenth century reforms become the "origins" of the welfare state, the first stage in its "evolution" and "development."

A longer historical perspective suggests the inadequacy of this interpretation. If ever there was a corrective to the Whig fallacy, it can be found in the history of social policies going back to Elizabethan times. So far from falling into a linear pattern, an ineluctable line of development culminating in the welfare state (or beyond that, in a socialist state, as some would have it), this history more often resembles a pendulum oscillating between extremes of regression and progression, of punitive, repressive, policies and generous, melioratory ones. Even this image distorts the reality, for it assumes that policies can be clearly identified as regressive or progressive, negative or positive. In fact most policies, if they were not ambivalent in intention, were ambiguous in their effects. Contemporaries were well aware of the "unintended consequences" of their actions, of reforms conceived in the most positive, benevolent spirit which turned out to have the most unfortunate negative results. "Ambiguity" and "ambivalence" also lend themselves to a Whig interpretation, if they express the historian's sense of what was consistent and fitting rather than the contemporary's. The Elizabethans were not "ambivalent" toward the poor when they proposed to punish the able-bodied vagrant and at the same time to give relief to the disabled and the aged; they were deliberately distinguishing between two kinds of poor and devising policies which, as they saw it, dealt appropriately with each. Nor were the nineteenth century reforms all of a piece. From a later perspective they can be made to fit a pattern of increasing governmental control over every aspect of social life. At the time, the process was much more differentiated and the outcome more problematic.

Another approach to the subject of poverty avoids the Whig fallacy by coming to it not from the "solution" side of the equation—policies, reforms, laws, institutions, administrative agencies—but from the "problem" side. The emphasis here is on the economic, technological, social, demographic, urban, and other conditions which helped determine the nature and incidence of poverty at any particular time and place. Intensive archival research and econometric analysis have yielded valuable information about costs and standards of living, wages and employment, infant mortality and life expectancy, housing and literacy, drink and crime, income differentials and social mobility, the opportunities and "disamenities" of urban life compared with those of rural life, if the implications of some of these findings are still being hotly debated, the debate itself has elevated the discussion to a new level of sophistication, making the old standard-of-living question seem primitive and coarse.

Confronted with these "problems" and "solutions," the historian is tempted to look for correlations between the two, for solutions appropriate to the problems. Often what he finds are disjunctions. And not only because of the familiar "social lag," the sheer passage of time required to cope with a problem, so that the solution is always somewhat "out of sync" with the problem (the familiar phenomenon of the general staff fighting the last war), but also because of all the other circumstances which mediate between the perception of a problem and the proposal of a solution. The problem had first to be recognized as a problem requiring solution; different formulations of the problem, reflecting different interests and ideologies, lent themselves to different solutions; and what may now seem to be an obvious, rational solution might have been precluded by any one of a number of economic, legal, administrative, political, or cultural factors.

One of the mediating facts that intervened between problem and solution and played a crucial part in this history was the set of ideas contemporaries brought to it—ideas about how to mitigate or "solve" the problem of poverty, and ideas about what constituted poverty and what made it a problem requiring remedy or solution. This raises a host of questions that are somewhat different from the conventional concerns of the social historian. What was the idea or conception of poverty that elevated it to the status of a problem? How did one conception give way to another, so that the "natural," unproblematic poverty of one age became the urgent social problem of another? Which of the poor were regarded as problematic, and how did the popular image of that group affect the proposals for reform? How were the "unworthy," "undeserving" poor distinguished from the "worthy" and "deserving," and why was it that first the former and then the latter became the primary focus of the social problem? How did the concept of the "deserving poor" become redefined so as to make them eligible for public assistance, when earlier they were thought deserving precisely because they were self-sustaining, hence not in need of assistance? How did the largely undifferentiated poor of earlier times ("the poor" equated with the "lower orders") become highly differentiated, the "dependent" poor being sharply distinguished from the "independent," the "pauper from the laboring poor, the residuum from the respectable poor"? How were these essentially moral categories integrated with the later "objective" definitions of poverty based on income and subsistence? And how did these conceptions, definitions, and categories relate to the prevailing social ethos, the moral and intellectual climate that affected the condition of the poor as well as the disposition of those reformers who took it upon themselves to improve that condition?

None of these questions can be divorced from the familiar issues of "problems" and "solutions." Yet they are a different order of questions and require a different treatment. Even when they draw upon the same materials for their answers, they use those materials in a different way, eliciting from them different kinds of information and meanings. To ask these questions, to address oneself to the "idea" of poverty in this sense, is not to belittle either the problem of poverty or the policies designed to ameliorate it. It is rather an effort to elucidate both by adding another dimension to the social reality.

Nor does a concern with the "idea" of poverty imply any priority or determinacy for ideas in general or for this idea in particular. I would not say, as did R. G. Collingwood, that "all history is the history of thought," or even that the history of thought determines all of history. I do believe, however, that there is a history of thought in all of history, and that the two are often intertwined and interdependent. Even the "hard facts" about poverty—about wages and prices, employment and unemployment, living and working conditions—appeared to contemporaries as facts and functioned as such only as they were mediated by a structure of ideas, values, opinions, beliefs, attitudes, perceptions, and images. This does not mean that nothing was real unless contemporaries thought it to be so. Late eighteenth century reformers, seeking to alleviate the poverty of agricultural laborers, had no clear idea of the extent to which their distress was caused by "under-employment," as we would now say, rather than unemployment, or by structural rather than cyclical changes. If they were ignorant of these distinctions (it may be argued that they were familiar with them under other terms), that itself is a fact of some consequence in shaping the social reality.

History is full of discrepancies between what historians believe to be fact and what contemporaries thought to be such. The famous standard-of-living question is one such instance. The latest econometric evidence may demonstrate that the standard of living was rising at a time when most contemporaries were convinced that it was falling. It is vitally important to have that evidence. But it would distort the historical reality, indeed make much of it unintelligible, if this fact were permitted to displace others—if in the zeal to correct the historical record, the ideas of contemporaries were expunged from the record for no other reason than that they have since been exposed as mistaken. Historians on both sides of this controversy have been at fault: the "optimists," as they are known, who argue so strenuously that the standard of living was rising that they pay little heed to contemporaries who believed otherwise and acted on that belief; and the "pessimists" who maintain that whatever the truth about the material standard of living, the important fact was the decline of the "quality" of life, and who define that quality in terms more appropriate to the sensibilities of a late twentieth century professor than of an early nineteenth century laborer. This is not to disparage the efforts to determine either the material standard of living or the quality of life. It does suggest that an essential part of the reality was what contemporaries took it to be, what they thought was happening to them, how they felt about it, and what they did about it.

John Stuart Mill once rebuked Bentham for being interested only in the question "is it true?" The more significant question, he said, was that posed by Coleridge: "What is the meaning of it?"

> The one [Bentham] took his stand *outside* the received opinion, and surveyed it as an entire stranger to it: the other [Coleridge] looked at it from within, and endeavoured to see it with the eyes of a believer in it; to discover by what apparent facts it was at first suggested, and by what appearance it has ever since been rendered credible—has seemed, to a succession of persons, to be a faithful interpretation of their experience.

The "idea of poverty" is responsive to Coleridge's question. It obliges the historian to take his stand with contemporaries, to look at history from their point of view, to attend to the facts available to them and in the form in which they were available, to find the meanings they attached to those facts, and to try to reconstruct their own "interpretation of their experience." Most historians pride themselves, like Bentham, on standing "outside the received opinion," as if this were a warrant of objectivity and superior insight. But the "received opinion" of contemporaries is a vital part of the historical reality, and the historian's sensitivity to that opinion is the best security for objectivity.

The Coleridgean question "What is the meaning of it?" also alerts us to the danger of taking contemporary documents at face value—taking them as facts rather than meanings, as truth rather than opinion or interpretation. This has been the case with the two major sources for the study of nineteenth century poverty: Henry Mayhew's *London Labour and the London Poor*, published in the middle of the century, and Charles Booth's *Life and Labour of the People in London*, at the end. The latter has been especially seductive, with its carefully delineated classes of "poor" and "very poor," its estimates of the number of people falling into each of these classes, its statistics about earnings and expenditures, employment and housing, drinking habits and religious affiliations. While being critical of Booth's moral judgments and practical recommendations, historians have been insufficiently skeptical about his classifications and statistics. The point is not whether his figures were accurate but how they were ordered and arranged; what conceptions, definitions, and assumptions produced those particular classes and thus the numbers that fell within them; what configuration classes and numbers led him to focus upon a particular class of the poor and a particular kind of poverty; and how that delineation of the "social problem" suggested a particular kind of social policy.

For the purposes of this study, sources such as Mayhew or Booth are less interesting for their manifest content—facts about the conditions of life and work, the incidence and degree of poverty—than for their latent content, the ideas lurking behind the facts. Some of these ideas do appear on the surface, in the form of judgments and opinions voiced by the author or attributed by him to his subjects. Other ideas are implicit in the facts themselves, "facts" that are, in effect, intellectual constructs. In this sense a social document may be read as a literary text to elicit meanings that are not overt—on the condition, however, that it is read in its contemporary context, that the words are given their contemporary connotation, and that the ideas deduced from them reflect the sensibility and consciousness of contemporaries rather than of the historian.

PART TWO

Constructionism

As we know, the genre of constructionism constitutes the large middle ground of historical thinking and practice today. Characterised by its distinctive epistemological position that places agency within larger social, political, economic and cultural structures and groups, constructionism displays a rich variety of conceptual and theoretical approaches, problems and topics. As a description of this epistemological orientation, constructionism encompasses a vast range of histories, but the most significant mode has been that of social history. While reconstructionist history celebrates its idiographic tradition, with the rise of the social sciences with their nomothetic conventions aimed at developing theories and finding empirical support for them (or not, as the case may be), a new fundamental form of history emerged in the early twentieth century, that of social history. Social history rapidly became the dominant form of constructionist history because of the appeal of its key organising concepts – class, feminism, gender and race. Constructionism is keynoted, therefore, by its concept and theory turn.

CHAPTER 11

Peter Charles Hoffer and William W. Stueck

READING AND WRITING AMERICAN HISTORY: AN INTRODUCTION TO THE HISTORIAN'S CRAFT (1994)*

The concept and theory of constructionism are demonstrated in the extract from the text by the American historians Peter Charles Hoffer and William W. Stueck, *Reading and Writing American History: An Introduction to the Historian's Craft* (1994). This is a student primer that (unsurprisingly) reflects the dominant epistemological assumptions of the genre. The extract acknowledges how disputes among historians 'can be disquieting', but the authors defend disagreement, arguing that this does not mean 'historians should indulge their prejudices'. Rather than address the question of epistemology, Hoffer and Stueck choose to point to what they call the 'intergenerational' aptitude of all historians to disagree with 'what previous generations of historians have written'. Although they suggest that historians today are less prejudiced through their training in the 'rules of scholarship' than previous generations, they will no doubt be superseded in their turn. But their final comment backtracks. What seems clear is that Hoffer and Stueck are articulating the modernist idea of progress, specifically of historians standing on the shoulders of their predecessors in their ever more sophisticated pursuit of the reality of the past.

When historians disagree

YOU MAY HAVE NOTED that at times your instructor has disagreed with portions of the textbook. Such disagreements are normal and remind you that no matter how skilled the authors or how comprehensive the coverage in the textbook, there are many other ways the authors could have told their story than the way they chose. The authors know that many subjects in American history are controversial and that historians may not agree about what happened or why it happened. When your professor and your textbook differ, they merely reflect larger differences of opinion within the community of scholars.

Disagreement among historians is like a brush fire in an overgrown woods; it makes room for new growth — new books and articles. Nevertheless, the perpetually unsettled state of historical scholarship can be disquieting. It is a rare event when historians agree that one of their number has written a definitive account. Indeed, accounts that one generation of historians regard as final are often completely revised by a new generation of historians.

---

* Peter Charles Hoffer and William W. Stueck (1994) *Reading and Writing American History: An Introduction to the Historian's Craft*, Lexington, MA: D.C. Heath & Company, pp. 38–40.

With this fact in mind, some historians believe that it is impossible for historical accounts to be objective or neutral. These "relativists" argue that historians are just as much influenced by their time and place as are the people they study. All secondary sources, relativists insist, are subjective accounts colored by the historian's own bias and background. Ironically, such committed relativists still aspire to write persuasive, assured, and reliable books and articles themselves. The relativists may be right, but their claims do not mean that historians should indulge their prejudices. Every historian can afford to be, in the words of intellectual historian Peter Novick, more "self-conscious about the nature of our activity."

Rewriting history

Without taking a position in the quarrel between relativists and their critics, we can state that a good deal of the disagreement among American historians seems to be intergenerational. Each generation of historians seems determined to dispute what previous generations of historians have written. We can gain some perspective on these disagreements by thinking about secondary sources as though they were primary sources. For example, a textbook on early American history written in 1980 can be regarded as a primary source for historians' attitudes in 1980 as well as a secondary source on the colonists' attitudes in 1774. We can then uncover patterns of disagreement among historians by asking the same question about secondary sources that we learned to ask about primary sources: how does the author's work fit into his or her own time and place?

Historians are human and are as influenced by their times as anyone else. Most modern historians are trained in universities to be professional scholars. Part of this training includes recognizing and countering their own prejudices. In earlier periods of our history, historians were not so constrained, and they expressed their points of view more openly. Today, historians still have points of view, and although their differences are muted by professional rules for scholarship, a variety of interpretation is inevitable.

A fairly extended example of historiography the study of historical writing may serve to illustrate how historians are historical actors whose view of the world is influenced by the times in which they live. In broad terms, it is possible to group succeeding generations of historians into "schools" of like-minded individuals who lived and worked in the same era of history.

Leading historians of the **romantic school** wrote in the mid-nineteenth century, an age when history was considered a branch of "letters," or literature. They believed, that the United States was unique and special, and described how men and women in America carried out a mission to bring democracy to the wilderness. These histories feature much the same dramatic plots and florid language that characterized the fictional literature of the age.

Although the romantic historians visited collections of primary sources in the United States and in Europe, these writers were more concerned with sweeping storytelling than precise documentation. In this sense, the members of the romantic school were amateur historians. They did not teach history nor did they have advanced degrees from universities. Most of them came from solid middle-class merchant or ministerial backgrounds, and they saw the country's history mirroring the story of their own families.

Despite their popularity, the authority of the romantic historical writers was challenged by a new school of professional historians in the last decades of the nineteenth century. These younger scholars, trained in German and American universities, drafted long and copiously documented dissertations to obtain doctor of philosophy degrees (Ph.D.'s) in history, and progressed to careers as professors. Influenced by the rise of the physical sciences in Germany, England, and the United States, they regarded history as a science, capable of exacting standards of proof, rather than as a branch of literature. They and their students shared a faith that history could be truly objective. This doctrine is not widely accepted today, but the educational standard that this **scientific school** fashioned for history graduate students entrenched itself in the universities: to become a professional historian, one still has to go to graduate school, obtain a graduate degree, and write a dissertation based on exhaustive research in primary materials.

Despite their foreign travel, historians in the scientific school had a very nationalistic view of history and wrote about the rise and progress of the United States as though the "nation" were a natural, inevitable, and desirable product of every people's historical development. Each nation supposedly was different, and its history reflected the traits of its people. Within this nationalism flourished racist and sexist biases that induced some scientific historians to join the movement to restrict eastern European and Asian immigration to the United States.

When the nationalistic doctrine of historical development fed into the fires of World War I, a number of younger historians broke from the scientific school's creed and sought other explanations for Americans' conduct and beliefs. These founders of the **progressive school** announced that they had discovered the mainsprings of human motivation in economic self-interest. This group of historians committed themselves to political and economic reform as well as reform of historical ideas, and their views dominated the scholarly writing of the 1920s and 1930s.

With the approach of World War II, the cynical and dispassionate analyses of the progressive school came under attack. Some politically conservative critics of the progressive historians claimed that their writings undermined American morale by denying the virtue of the founders of the nation, a particularly damaging charge as the nation geared itself for struggle against dictatorships in Europe and Asia. During and immediately after the war, a younger generation of historians proclaimed that American history was not a tale of many warring economic interests, each seeking only its own benefit, but a story of many groups merging into one nation bound by common ideals and opportunities. These historians stressed the ways in which American consensus built a great nation, and hence have been called the **consensus school**. Although progressive ideas continued to infuse the work of some young historians in the 1940s and 1950s, consensus history dominated these decades.

The rise of the civil-rights movement and increasingly acerbic domestic protest against the Vietnam War in the 1960s influenced yet another generation of historians to seek its own theoretical orientation. In reexamining American history, these scholars found that the travails of many Americans — immigrants, women, African Americans, Native Americans, and the very poor — were minimized in the consensus version of history. The younger historians argued that disfavored groups were the victims of dominant elites, abused in the factories and denied equal treatment in the public arena. The historical writing of this **New Left school** (the Old Left was a handful of radical writers in the previous generation) retains its vitality, and many of the central ideas of the New Left, particularly the need to include minority and women's history in textbooks, have enriched every history survey course.

In recent years, the self-critical momentum of the historical profession has been maintained by feminist historians calling on the profession to recognize the contributions and the separate needs of women throughout our history. In the **feminist school**, contemporary politics and professionalism have once again combined to invigorate historical writing and to prove that historians are historical actors.

The most recent generation of historians does not show the dominance of any one doctrine, however. Indeed, older scholars have recently complained that the historical writing of younger scholars is too fragmented and diverse. One characteristic does shine through this diversity, and that is an attraction to methodological rigor and innovation. Younger historians have embraced interdisciplinary studies and boldly borrow concepts from economics, sociology, anthropology, and literary criticism. Computer printouts of data figure prominently in their work. One might call the proponents of this kind of history a **technocratic school** because its leaders are so concerned with getting the methods and the definitions of the methods right. They do not have an overarching theory of our history; in fact, they attack the very notion of such a theory. Of course, if history is any guide, the next generation of historians will cast aside the technocrats' assumptions and proclaim its own vision of our past.

None of the "schools" of history described is really as uniform or as narrow-minded as we have suggested. In fact, most historians in this country are unwilling to classify themselves or to label their work, much less admit that they belong to a particular school of thought. It is only through the fine-grained textures of their arguments that we can even attempt to categorize the writing of a particular historian as belonging to a distinct school.

CHAPTER 12

Eric Hobsbawm

ON HISTORY (1997)*

In certain respects a very different 'What is History?' book is Eric Hobsbawm's On History (1997). Professor Emeritus at Birkbeck College, London University, as he says in his recent autobiography, he was and remains an 'unrepentant communist'. Among his many books he is perhaps best known for his trilogy: The Age of Revolution (1962), The Age of Capital (1975) and The Age of Empire (1987), as well as his enormously popular Industry and Empire (1968). While Hobsbawm would not fit into the Hoffer and Stueck classifications, he has, like them, an epistemological model at work. At the outset he acknowledges an essential paradox in what it is that historians do – they must discover and record the past, but they also have 'important social and political functions'. As a constructionist of the political left, Hobsbawm accepts that truth must be pursued, while recognising that all pursuits are politically motivated. But, interestingly, he immediately chooses to take a swipe at the idea of 'history as fiction' – postmodernism – before pursuing his belief that a detailed knowledge of the data

---

* Eric Hobsbawm (1997) On History, London: Orion, pp. 269–72.

will allow the historian to dispense with myths – invariably those myths of the political right. His argument against postmodernism is that it is 'profoundly relativist'. He anchors his own leftist history and his antagonism to epistemological scepticism on 'the supremacy of the evidence', citing the existence of the Nazi gas ovens. His conclusion is that, like the law courts, historians can demonstrate the difference between 'historical fact and falsehood' but, most importantly, this procedure is 'not ideological'. The implication is that a detailed knowledge of the evidence, despite ideology and theory, will authenticate the past as history.

T HE PROBLEM FOR professional historians is that their subject has important social and political functions. These depend on their work – who else discovers and records the past but historians? – but at the 'same time they are at odds with their professional standards. This duality is at the core of our subject. The founders of the *Revue Historique* were conscious of it when they stated, in the *avant-propos* to their first number that 'To study the past of France, which will be our main concern, is today a matter of national importance. It will enable us to restore to our country the unity and moral force of which it has need.'

Of course, nothing was further from their confident, positivist minds than serving their nation otherwise than by the search for truth. And yet the non-academics who need and use the commodity which historians produce, and who constitute the largest and politically decisive market for it, are untroubled by the sharp distinction between the 'strictly scientific procedures' and the 'rhetorical constructions' which was so central to the founders of the *Revue*. Their criterion of what is 'good history' is 'history that is good for us' – 'our country', 'our cause', or simply 'our emotional satisfaction'. Whether they like it or not, professional historians produce the raw material for the non-professionals' use or misuse.

That history is inextricably bound to contemporary politics – as the historiography of the French Revolution continues to prove – is probably today not a major difficulty, for the debates of historians, at least in countries of intellectual freedom, are conducted within the rules of the discipline. Besides, many of the most ideologically charged debates among professional historians concern matters about which non-historians know little and care less. However, all human beings, collectivities and institutions need a past, but it is only occasionally the past uncovered by historical research. The standard example of an identity culture which anchors itself to the past by means of myths dressed up as history is nationalism. Of this Ernest Renan observed more than a century ago, 'Forgetting, even getting history wrong, is an essential factor in the formation of a nation, which is why the progress of historical studies is often a danger to nationality.' For nations are historically novel entities pretending to have existed for a very long time. Inevitably the nationalist version of their history consists of anachronism, omission, decontextualization and, in extreme cases, lies. To a lesser extent this is true of all forms of identity history, old or new.

In the pre-academic past there was little to prevent pure historical invention, such as the forgery of historical manuscripts (as in Bohemia), the writing of an ancient, and suitably glorious Scottish national epic (like James Macpherson's 'Ossian'), or the production of an entirely invented piece of public theatre purporting to represent the ancient Bardic rituals, as in Wales. (This still forms the climax of the annual National Eisteddfod or cultural festival of that small country.) Where such inventions have to be submitted to the tests of a large and established scholarly community, this is no longer possible. Much of early historical scholarship consisted of the disproof of such inventions and the deconstruction of the myths built on them. The great English medievalist J. Horace Round made his reputation by a series of merciless dissections of the pedigrees of British noble families whose claim to descent from Norman invaders he showed to be spurious. The tests are not necessarily only historic. The 'Turin shroud', to name a recent example of a holy relic of the kind that made the fortunes of medieval pilgrimage centres, could not resist the test of carbon-B dating to which it had to be submitted.

History as fiction has, however, received an academic reinforcement from an unexpected quarter: the 'growing scepticism concerning the Enlightenment project of rationality'. The fashion for what (at least in Anglo-Saxon academic discourse) is known by the vague term 'postmodernism' has fortunately not gained as much ground among historians as among literary and cultural theorists and social anthropologists, even in the USA, but it is relevant to the question at issue, as it throws doubt on the distinction between fact and fiction, objective reality and conceptual discourse. It is profoundly relativist. If there is no clear distinction between what is true and what I feel to be true, then my own construction of reality is as good as yours or anyone else's, for 'discourse is the maker of this world, not the mirror'. To cite the same author, the object of ethnography, as presumably of any other social and historical enquiry, is to produce a co-operatively evolved text, in which neither subject nor author nor reader, nor indeed anyone, has the exclusive right of 'synoptic transcendence'. If, 'in historical as in literary discourse, even presumably descriptive language *constitutes* what it describes', then no narrative among the many possible ones can be regarded as privileged. It is not fortuitous that these views have appealed particularly to those who see themselves as representing collectivities or milieux marginalized by the hegemonic culture of some group (say, middle-class white heterosexual males of Western education) whose claim to superiority they contest. But it is wrong.

Without entering the theoretical debate on these matters, it is essential for historians to defend the foundation of their discipline: the supremacy of evidence. If their texts are fictions, as in some sense they are, being literary compositions, the raw material of these fictions is verifiable fact. Whether the Nazi gas ovens existed or not can be established by evidence. Because it has been so established, those who deny their existence are not writing history, whatever their narrative techniques. If a novel were to be about the return of the living Napoleon from St Helena, it might be literature but could not be history. If history is an imaginative art, it is one which does not invent but arranges *objets trouvés*. The distinction may appear pedantic and trivial to the non-historian, especially the one who uses historical material for his or her own purposes. What does it matter to the theatrical audience that there is no historical record of a Lady Macbeth urging her husband to kill King Duncan, or of witches' predicting that Macbeth would be king of Scotland, which indeed he became in 1040–57? What did it matter to the (pan-African) founding fathers of West African post-colonial states that they gave their countries the names of medieval African empires which had no obvious connection with the territories of the modern Ghana or Mali? Was it not more important to remind sub-Saharan Africans, after generations of colonialism, that they had a tradition of independent and powerful states somewhere on their continent, if not precisely in the hinterland of Accra?

Indeed, the historians' insistence, once again in the words of the first issue of the *Revue Historique*, on 'strictly scientific procedures, where every statement is accompanied by proofs, source-references and citations', is sometimes pedantic and trivial, especially now that it no longer forms part of a faith in the possibility of a definitive, positivist scientific truth, which lent it a certain simple-minded grandeur. Yet the procedures of the law court, which insist on the supremacy of evidence as much as historical researchers, and often in much the same manner, demonstrate that the difference between historical fact and falsehood is not ideological. It is crucial for many practical purposes of everyday life, if only because life and death, or – what is quantitatively more important – money, depend on it. When an innocent person is tried for, murder, and wishes to prove his or her innocence, what is required is the techniques not of the 'postmodern' theorist, but of the old-fashioned historian.

CHAPTER 13

John Tosh

THE PURSUIT OF HISTORY: AIMS, METHODS AND NEW DIRECTIONS IN THE STUDY OF MODERN HISTORY ([1984] 2000)*

The third extract in the 'What is History?' form of constructionism is taken from *The Pursuit of History: Aims, Methods and New Directions in the Study of Modern History* ([1984] 2000) by the British social historian John Tosh. Tosh is the only historian to have two entries in this section (the other being on masculinity – see Chapter 22, pp. 102–4). In the following extract, Tosh, also a Marxist of a kind, offers us his rationalisation for social theory in history. He argues that there are three reasons for the theoretical nature of 'historical explanation'. First, it is to address the 'enlargement in the scope of historical inquiry'. This is done by supplying a means by which historians can provide 'some theory of the structure of human society in its widest sense'. As a materialist himself, it is not surprising that he notes that the metaphoric analogies often used in this endeavour are drawn from the physical world. The second reason for 'the application of theory' is the nature of historical change. He maintains that historians are often attracted by the notion of revolutionary (economic or demographic in his examples) material change. The final reason for using social theory is to extend beyond historical explanation to determine 'the direction in which all change is moving'. This is to give 'a meaning to history'. Here Tosh is changing historical explanation, while also endeavouring to validate his own materialist position. He ends by acknowledging that some historians (we refer to them in this book as 'reconstructionists') reject the use of theory, arguing that if patterns exist they are unknowable and always speculative. The other reason is that, given poor evidence or a questionable selection, much theory is the refuge for 'mere supposition and wishful thinking'. Tosh recognises that any theory can be 'proved' by gathering enough illustrative material, but it is the testing of theory that counts in the end.

---

* John Tosh ([1984] 2000) *The Pursuit of History: Aims, Methods and New Directions in the Study of Modern History*, London: Pearson-Longman, pp. 135–7.

BROADLY SPEAKING, SOCIAL theories arise from the problems presented by three aspects of historical explanation. There is first the difficulty of grasping the inter-relatedness of every dimension of human experience at a given time. For most historians up to the end of the nineteenth century this was not in practice a major problem since their interest tended to be confined to political and constitutional history; accordingly some notion of the body politic was all the conceptual equipment they required. But during the present century the enlargement in the scope of historical enquiry and in the volume of evidence, together with the pressures towards thematic specialization, have demanded an ever greater capacity to think in terms of abstractions. We saw how easily historians fall into the trap of seeing the past as compartmentalized into 'political', 'economic', 'intellectual' and 'social' history, and how the idea of total history' arose as a corrective. But total history is unattainable without some concept of how the component aspects of human experience are linked together to form a whole – some theory of the structure of human society in its widest sense. Most concepts of this kind depend heavily on analogies with the physical world. Society has been variously conceived as an organism, a mechanism and a structure. Each of these metaphors represents an attempt to go beyond the crude notion that any one sphere determines the rest, and to express the reciprocal or mutually reinforcing relationship between the main categories of human action and thought.

The second problem which invites the application of theory is that of historical change. Historians spend most of their time explaining change – or its absence. This dominant preoccupation inevitably raises the question of whether the major transitions in history display common characteristics. Is historical change driven by a motor, and if so what does the motor consist of? More specifically, does industrialization require adherence to one particular path of economic development? Can one identify in history the essential components of a revolutionary situation? In framing their hypotheses in particular instances historians are often influenced by the attractions of this kind of theory – for example the idea that demography holds the key or that the most durable changes in society arise from the gradualist reforms conceded by paternalistic ruling classes rather than from revolutionary demands articulated from below.

Thirdly, and most ambitiously, there are the theories which seek to explain not merely *how* historical change takes place but the direction in which all change is moving; these theories are concerned to interpret human destiny by ascribing a meaning to history. Medieval writers conceived history as a linear transition from the Creation to the Last judgement, controlled by divine providence. By the eighteenth century that view had been secularized as the idea of progress: history was interpreted as a story of material and intellectual improvement whose outcome in the future would be the triumph of reason and human happiness. Modified versions of that outlook continued to have a powerful hold in the nineteenth century: on the continent history meant the rise of national identities and their political expression in the nation state; for the Whig historians of England it meant the growth of constitutional liberties. Full-blown professions of faith in progress may be rare today, given the trail of destruction which has marked the history of the present century; but theories of progressive change still underpin many historical interpretations in the economic and social sphere, as is shown by the frequency with which historians reach for such words as 'industrialization' and 'modernization'.

Although these three types of historical theory are analytically distinct, they all share an interest in moving from the particular to the general in an effort to make sense of the subject as a whole. It might be supposed that this is a natural progression, shared by all branches of knowledge. A great many historians, however, reject the use of theory completely. They see two possible grounds for doing so. The first argument concedes that there may be patterns and regularities in history, but maintains that they are not accessible to disciplined enquiry. It is hard enough to provide an entirely convincing explanation of any one event in history, but to link them in a series or within an overarching category places the enquirer at an intolerable distance from the verifiable facts. As Peter Mathias (here acting as devil's advocate) concedes:

> The bounty of the past provides individual instances in plenty to support virtually any general proposition. It is only too easy to beat history over the head with the blunt instrument of a hypothesis and leave an impression.

On this view, theoretical history is speculative history and should be left to philosophers and prophets.

The possibility that theory will 'take over' from the facts is certainly not to be made light of. The gaps in the surviving historical record, and especially the lack of clinching evidence in matters of causation, leave a great deal of scope for mere supposition and wishful thinking. At the same time, the range of evidence bearing on many historic problems is so large that selection is unavoidable – and the principles governing that selection may prejudice the result of the enquiry. The record of recent centuries is so voluminous and varied that contradictory results can be obtained simply by asking different questions. In the context of American history Aileen Kraditor puts this point as follows:

> If one historian asks, 'Do the sources provide evidence of militant struggles among workers and slaves?' the sources will reply, 'Certainly'. And if another asks, 'Do the sources provide evidence of widespread acquiescence in the established order among the American population throughout the past two centuries?' the sources will reply, 'Of course.'

Almost any theory can be 'proved' by marshalling an impressive collection of individual instances to fit the desired pattern.

Theory-oriented history is certainly prone to these dangers – but so too it must be recognized, is the work of many historians who reject theory and remain blissfully unaware of the assumptions and values which inform their own selection and interpretation of evidence. The way forward is not to retreat into an untenable empiricism, but to apply much higher standards to the testing of theory. Wishful thinking is more likely to be controlled by historians who approach their enquiries with explicit hypotheses than by those who try to follow where the sources lead. When selection of the evidence cannot be avoided, it must be a representative selection which will reveal both contrary and supporting indicators. A given theory may account for *part* of the evidence relating to the problem in hand, but that is not enough; it must be compatible with the weight of the evidence overall. In Kraditor's words, 'the data omitted must not be essential to the understanding of the data included'. All this assumes a certain detachment on the part of historians towards their theories, and a readiness to change tack in the lack of evidence. But where these controls are neglected, the profession as a whole is vigilant in its defence. Historians are seldom happier than when citing contrary evidence and alternative interpretations to cast doubt on the work of their colleagues – especially those who seem to have a bee in their bonnet.

CHAPTER 14

Fernand Braudel

A HISTORY OF CIVILIZATIONS *([1963] 1993)**

Among the most popular forms of constructionist history is the survey or 'student text'. One of the first and most popular of these, and also one of the most important to the development of the genre, was Fernand Braudel's *A History of Civilizations* ([1963] 1993) from which the extract given here is taken. Braudel was one of the most innovative historians of the last century. Following the policy of the 1929 history journal *Annales d'histoire économique et sociale* (*Annals of Economic and Social History*), Braudel's work was challenging in both its form and content. He rejected conventional political history in favour of the in-depth and longer term study of the social and economic forces that shaped the development of nations. His most famous text, *The Mediterranean and the Mediterranean World in the Age of Philip II*, covered the history of the Mediterranean world from the Renaissance to the sixteenth century in elaborate detail. This involved imaginatively combining underlying structures of change with surface events, actions and intentions of agents. In so doing, Braudel constructed his history according to three forms of change within the three time frames of long-term structures and traditions (*la longue durée*), the in-between conjuncture (of a few generations) and the rapid turnover of events (*l'histoire événementielle*). In the extract reprinted here Braudel works on the principle that the study of civilisations involves all the social sciences. Invoking the anthropologist Claude Lévi-Strauss, he defines the key concept of society as culture, civilisation, towns, the countryside, the structure of economic change, class and (in an echo of Tosh's comments – see Chapter 13) a sense of the direction of his historical explanation. Braudel's history is complex, nuanced and determinedly all-inclusive.

Civilizations as societies

THERE CAN BE NO civilizations without the societies that support them and inspire their tensions and their progress. Hence the first inevitable question: was it necessary to invent the word 'civilization' and encourage its academic use, if it remains merely a synonym for 'society'? Arnold Toynbee continually used the word 'society' in place of 'civilization'. And Marcel Mauss believed that 'the idea of civilization is certainly less clear than that of society, which it presupposes'.

Society and civilization are inseparable: the two ideas refer to the same reality. Or, as Claude Lévi-Strauss put it, 'they do not represent different objects, but two

---

* Fernand Braudel ([1963] 1993) *A History of Civilizations*, Harmondsworth: Allen Lane, The Penguin Press, pp. 15–21.

complementary views of a single object, which can perfectly well be described by either term according to one's point of view.'

The idea of 'society' implies a wealth of content. In this it closely resembles that of civilization, with which it is so often linked. The Western civilization in which we live, for example, depends on the 'industrial society' which is its driving force. It would be easy to characterize Western civilization simply by describing that society and its component parts, its tensions, its moral and intellectual values, its ideals, its habits, its tastes, etc. – in other words by describing the people who embody it and who will pass it on.

If a society stirs and changes, the civilization based on it stirs and changes too. This point is made in a fine book by Lucien Goldmann, *The Hidden God* (*Le Dieu caché*, 1955), which deals with the France of Louis XIV. Every civilization, Goldmann explains, draws its essential insights from the 'view of the world' it adopts. And in every case this view of the world is coloured, if not determined, by social tensions. Civilization simply reflects them like a mirror.

The age of Jansenism, Racine, Pascal, the abbé de Saint-Cyran and the abbé Barcos, whose fascinating letters Goldmann has rediscovered, was as *The Hidden God* shows an impassioned moment in the history of France; and the tragic view of the world that prevailed then had originated with the parliamentary upper middle classes, disillusioned by the monarchy with which they were at odds. The tragedy of their fate, their awareness of it, and their intellectual ascendancy all combined to imbue the period with their own dominant mood.

In a quite different spirit, Claude Lévi-Strauss also identifies civilizations with societies when he argues the difference between primitive and modern societies – or, as most anthropologists put it, between cultures and civilizations. Cultures in this sense are societies

> which produce little disorder – what doctors call 'entropy' – and tend to remain indefinitely as they originally were: which is why they look to us like societies that lack both history and progress. Whereas our societies (those that correspond to modern civilizations) . . . are powered by a difference of electrical pressure, as it were, expressed in various forms of social hierarchy . . . Such societies have managed to establish within them a social imbalance which they use to produce both much greater order – we have societies that work like machines – and much greater disorder, much less entropy, in relations between people.

For Lévi-Strauss, then, primitive cultures are the fruit of egalitarian societies, where relations between groups are settled once and for all and remain constant, whereas civilizations are based on hierarchical societies with wide gaps between groups and hence shifting tensions, social conflicts, political struggles, and continual evolution.

The most obvious external sign of these differences between 'cultures' and 'civilizations' is undoubtedly the presence or absence of towns. Towns proliferate in civilizations: in cultures they remain embryonic. There are of course intermediate stages and degrees. What is Black Africa but a group of traditional societies – of cultures – embarked on the difficult and sometimes cruel process of fostering civilization and modern urban development? African cities, taking their models from abroad in a style now international, remain islands amid the stagnation of the countryside. They prefigure the society and the civilization to come.

The most brilliant societies and civilizations, however, presuppose within their own borders cultures and societies of a more elementary kind. Take, for example, the interplay of town and country, never to be underestimated. In no society have all regions and all parts of the population developed equally. Underdevelopment is common in mountain areas or patches of poverty off the beaten track of modern communications – genuinely primitive societies, true 'cultures' in the midst of a civilization.

The West's first success was certainly the conquest of its countryside – its peasant 'cultures' – by the towns. In the Islamic world, the duality remains more visible than in the West. Islamic towns were quicker to arise – were more precociously urban, so to speak – than in Europe, while the countryside remained more primitive, with vast areas of nomadic life. In the Far East, that contrast is still the general rule: its 'cultures' remain very isolated, living by themselves and on their own resources. Between the most brilliant cities lie tracts of countryside whose way of life is almost self-sufficient, at subsistence level, and sometimes actually barbaric.

Given the close relationship between civilization and society, there is a case for adopting the sociological mode when looking at the long history of civilizations. As historians, however, we should not simply confuse societies with civilizations. We shall explain in the next chapter what we believe the difference to be: in terms of the time-scale, civilization implies and embraces much longer periods than any given social phenomenon. It changes far less rapidly than the societies it supports or involves. But this is not yet the moment to go fully into that question. One thing at a time.

Civilizations as economies

Every society, every civilization, depends on economic, technological, biological and demographic circumstances. Material and biological conditions always help determine the destiny of civilizations. A rise or a fall in the population, health or illness, economic or technological growth or decline – all these deeply affect the cultural as well as the social structure. Political economy in the broadest sense is the study of all these massive problems.

For a long time, people were humanity's only major implement or form of energy – the sole resource for building a civilization by sheer brawn and brain. In principle and in fact, therefore, an increase in the population has always helped the growth of civilization – as in Europe in the thirteenth, sixteenth, eighteenth, nineteenth and twentieth centuries.

Just as regularly, however, when the population grows faster than the economy, what was once an advantage becomes a drawback. Such was the case, undoubtedly, by the end of the sixteenth century, as it is today in most underdeveloped countries. The results in the past were famines, a fall in real earnings, popular uprisings and grim periods of slump: until epidemics and starvation together brutally thinned out the too-serried ranks of human beings. After such biological disasters (like that in Europe in the second half of the fourteenth century, with the Black Death and the epidemics that followed it), the survivors briefly had an easier time and expansion began again, at increasing speed – until the next setback.

Only industrialization, at the end of the eighteenth century and the beginning of the nineteenth, seemed to have broken this vicious circle and made even surplus people valuable again, able to work and live. As the history of Europe showed, the growing value and cost of human labour, and the need to economize on employees, encouraged the development of machines. Classical antiquity, intelligent as it was, had no machines to match is intelligence. It never really tried to acquire them. Its failing was that it possessed slaves, Imperial China, flourishing long before the eighteenth century, very intelligent and technically skilful, nevertheless suffered also: it had too many people. They cost very little, and performed almost all the tasks required by an economy virtually lacking animal power. As a result, although China enjoyed a long lead in matters scientific, it never crossed the threshold of modern science and technology. That privilege, that honour, that profit it left to Europe.

Economic life never ceases to fluctuate, at intervals sometimes long and sometimes short. Good times and bad times succeed each other; and societies and civilizations feel their effects, especially when the upturn or downturn is prolonged. The pessimism and disquiet that were widespread in the late fifteenth century — what Johan Huizinga called *The Waning of the Middle Ages* — reflected a marked recession in the economy of the West. European Romanticism, likewise, coincided with a long economic recession between 1817 and 1852. The expansion in the mid-eighteenth century (from 1733 onwards) saw some setbacks (for instance on the eve of the French Revolution); but in general at that time economic growth placed the intellectual development of the Enlightenment in a context of material well-being, active trade, expanding industry, and growing population.

Whether in boom or slump, economic activity almost always produces a surplus. The expenditure, or squandering, of such surpluses has been one of the indispensable conditions for luxury in civilizations and for certain forms of art. When today we admire architecture, sculpture or portraits we are also contemplating, not always consciously, the calm pride of a city, the vainglorious folly of a prince or the wealth of a *nouveau-riche* merchant banker. In Europe from the sixteenth century onwards (and probably earlier), the ultimate phase of civilization wears the emblem of capitalism and wealth.

So civilization reflects a redistribution of wealth. Civilizations acquire different characteristics, first at the top and then among the mass of the people, according to their way of redistributing wealth, and according to the social and economic machinery which takes from the circulation of wealth whatever is destined for luxury, art or culture. In the seventeenth century, during the very hard times of Louis XIV's reign, there were very few patrons except at Court. Literary and artistic life was confined to this small circle. In the lavish, easy-going economic climate of the eighteenth century, aristocracy and bourgeoisie joined with royalty in spreading culture, science and philosophy.

But luxury, at that time, was still the privilege of a social minority. The civilization underlying it, that of modest workaday life, had very little share in it. And the ground floor of a civilization is often its crucial level. What is freedom — what is an individual's culture — without enough to live on? From this point of view the much-maligned nineteenth century, that boring century of the *nouveaux riches* and the 'triumphant bourgeoisie', was the harbinger (if not yet the exemplar) of a new destiny for civilizations and for the human personality. While the population rapidly increased, more and more of its members were able to enjoy a certain collective civilization. No doubt the social cost of this transformation — unconscious, admittedly — was very heavy. But its advantages were great. The development of education, access to culture, admission to the universities, social progress — these were the achievements of the nineteenth century, already rich, and full of significance for the future.

The great problem for tomorrow, as for today, is to create a mass civilization of high quality. To do so is very costly. It is unthinkable without large surpluses devoted to the service of society, and without the leisure that mechanization will no doubt soon be able to offer us. In the industrialized countries, such a future can be envisaged not too far ahead. The problem is more complex in the world as a whole. For, just as economic growth has made civilization more accessible to some social classes than to others, it has similarly differentiated various countries in the world. Much of the world's population is what one essayist has called 'the foreign proletariat', better known as the Third World – an enormous mass of people, many of whom have yet to earn a bare living before they can enjoy the benefits of their own countries' civilization, which to them is often a closed book. Unless humanity makes the effort to redress these vast inequalities, they could bring civilizations – and civilization to an end.

CHAPTER 15

Gwynne Lewis

THE FRENCH REVOLUTION: RETHINKING THE DEBATE (1999)*

Emeritus Professor of History at the University of Warwick, Gwynne Lewis is the author of several books on the French Revolution. The extract here is taken from *The French Revolution: Rethinking the Debate* (1999). In it Lewis offers a broad survey and introduction to what many, if not most historians think was the key event of the past two hundred years. In contextualising this event, Lewis deliberately connects what he calls 'the high peak of the Enlightenment' with 'considerable economic growth' in France. He also notes population expansion which was 'in all probability' associated with climatic change. Invoking the well-known metaphor of economic 'take-off', Lewis notes how it was aborted in France, but the importance to French industrialisation of the empire in the Caribbean (in an echo of Eric Hobsbawm's thesis in his *Industry and Empire*). He goes on to elaborate a simple two-sided model of the French economy which he then complicates by reference to the rise of French eighteenth-century consumerism (evidenced by the French workers' consumption of *café au lait*) and the emergence of an articulated class system. He concludes that, as 'Professor Sydney Pollard has shown', European industrialisation was not a national but a regional phenomenon and this militated against continued French economic development. Lewis's analysis reveals the Braudelian legacy and the force of Tosh's arguments for social theory and hypothesis testing – the desire for the comprehensive linking of diverse events in one plausible explanatory construction.

---

* Gwynne Lewis (1999) *The French Revolution: Rethinking the Debate*, London: Routledge, pp. 8–11.

I S IT A COINCIDENCE that the high peak of the Enlightenment in the 1750s and 1760s coincided with a period of very considerable economic growth in France? Marxist historians such as Albert Soboul certainly posited an *indirect* relationship between the widely perceived growth of capitalism and the intellectual 'take-off' of the Enlightenment: 'the philosophers explained that man must try to understand nature so that he could more effectively control it and could increase the general wealth of the community'. For *marxisant* scholars, socio-economic change provides the soil in which the seeds of the Enlightenment could germinate. There can be no doubt that the advance of science and technology did encourage new thinking, new *applied* thinking on the relationship between science and society. Most historians would also agree that there was a relationship between population growth – around 7 million more citizens in 1789 than in 1700 – economic success and social crises. And population growth was, in all probability, associated with climatic changes – the need to understand the natural sciences again – involving far less severe winters and fewer catastrophic crop failures, particularly during the middle decades of the century. More mouths to feed, more food to feed them with, more hands to produce manufactured goods; capitalism, in its commercial and nascent industrial forms, was provoking change, occasionally violent protest, in all but the more secluded rural recesses of eighteenth-century French society. It was certainly provoking discord and debate amongst the king's ministers and civil servants in the corridors of Versailles.

Bearing in mind the crucial point that agriculture provided three-quarters of the gross national product – in other words, there were a great many rural recesses in France – economic research, or rather computerisation of old research, indicates that during the eighteenth century French manufacturing and industrial performance was comparable to that of Britain, at least until the late 1770s when the 'take-off' was sustained in the former country, but 'aborted' in the latter. Around this time, textiles accounted for over half of the value of all industrial production. The production of woollen goods increased by almost 150 per cent between the beginning and the end of the eighteenth century; the number of looms producing high-quality articles in the silk capital of the world, Lyon, doubled during the same period. Nîmes, 250 kilometres due south, was producing over one hundred different articles for the cheaper end of the market – silk stockings, handkerchiefs, ribbons to grace the feet, hands and heads of ladies and gentlemen from Paris to Peru. Even in the 'leading sector' of the industrial revolution, cotton, French production increased sharply after the 1740s, recording growth rates of almost 4 per cent per annum. In and around Rouen, 'the Manchester of France', production of cotton goods tripled between 1730 and 1750. To the north-east, towns like Lille were also becoming transformed by the impact of the textile revolution. To the south, reaching its highest levels of output around the middle decades of the century, the woollen industry of Languedoc, centred on towns such as Carcassonne, Clermont-de-Lodève and Sommières, provided work for tens of thousands of peasant-artisans. Even in the heavy industrial sector, France was producing more cast iron than England by the 1780s, and, at around three-quarters of a million *tonnes*, its annual production of coal was starting to look, well, almost respectable, although it was still under a tenth of British coal production.

However, the jewel in France's economic crown was not Lyon, or Rouen, or even Paris, but Saint-Domingue (today known as Haiti), emphasising the remarkable growth of France's overseas trade and the supremacy of commercial over industrial capitalism. The volume of her foreign trade more than doubled in the course of the eighteenth century; trade with her colonies increased tenfold! With its thousands of imported slaves producing cheaper sugar and coffee than the English West Indian islands, Saint-Domingue alone had monopolised three-quarters of France's lucrative colonial trade by the time of the Revolution. The English traveller, Arthur Young, was deeply impressed with the visible and recently acquired wealth of Atlantic ports such as Nantes and Bordeaux: 'we must not name Liverpool in competition with Bordeaux', although, liberal as he was, he fails to relate the joys of merchant wealth to the miseries of the black slaves upon which they were largely based. Henry Swinburne, visiting Marseille in 1776, provides us with the best description of these bustling eighteenth-century ports:

> The commerce of Marseille is divided into a multiplicity of branches, a variety of commodities are fabricated here, or brought from the other ports and inland provinces of France to be exported, and numerous articles of traffic are landed here to be dispersed in this and other kingdoms.

The lustre of France's overseas and colonial trade has led some historians to suggest that there were two distinct types of economies in France: one, thriving until the Revolution, anchored on the great ports and rivers of France, the other, increasingly sluggish after the mid-1770s, based in the France of the small provincial town and its huge, rural hinterland.

This neat division has some merit, not the least of which is its simplicity. The situation was more complicated, however, as the recent emphasis on the development of an eighteenth-century, 'consumerist' society indicates, one which affected most French people, although certainly more immediately in Paris, the major manufacturing towns, like Lyon, Lille and Rouen, and the prosperous ports of the Atlantic and Mediterranean coasts. Symbolic of the advance of this kind of economy was the fact that workers had already taken to the habit of popping into their local bar for a *café au lait* on their way to work, whilst their wives may have been putting on their bonnets to visit the place de Grève, site of public executions on most weekdays, but transformed on Mondays into a second-hand clothes market where women with a few *sous* to spare might haggle for hand-me-downs from the rich merchant's or lawyer's wardrobe. Daniel Roche notes that, during the eighteenth century, the commercial life of Paris was focused increasingly upon the needs of the *classes populaires*, a society which

> had its habits, rhythms, manners, and pitches like the pillars of les Halles, Saint-Esprit, the quai de la Ferraille, quai de l'Ecole, under the Pont-Neuf; they tramped the town, cutting, restitching, taking apart and remaking the ordinary garb of the people.

That acute observer of the social mores of the Parisians on the eve of the Revolution, Louis-Sébastien Mercier, bemoaned the fact that consumerism was beginning to cover up class distinctions, with 'the wife of the petit bourgeois seeking to imitate the wife of the marquis and the duke'. Recent work upon the growth of a 'consumerist society' in France, one which pre-dates the Revolution, reinforces the importance of capitalism, again in its commercial guise, as eroding the bases of the old order.

However, there is overwhelming evidence to suggest that the French economy on the eve of the Revolution was failing to satisfy demand, at the right price, both domestic and foreign. During the late 1770s, France's balance of trade would move into deficit; the huge textile industries of Brittany, Normandy and Languedoc would suffer a serious decline, which, in certain sectors, would prove terminal. In Languedoc, the 'golden age', of the woollen industry had already passed away by the 1760s, whilst the silk trade was severely disadvantaged by the Spanish embargo on French imports after 1778. The growth of capitalism was an international, not a French, phenomenon. As Professor Sidney Pollard has shown, European industrialisation developed on a regional, not a national basis, challenging the old economic structures. The serious downturn which characterised the fortunes of the flourishing wine industry in France during the 1780s – another example of a change in consumption patterns – aggravated the situation: between 1778 and 1788, profits from wine were halved; in the champagne region around Rheims, tax-collectors were speaking of a crisis 'the like of which had not been known for thirty years'. Undoubtedly, a series of poor harvests reduced internal demand in a country which depended so heavily upon agriculture for its gross national product. But there were other reasons, possibly of greater importance. For example, foreign competition, from Prussia, Switzerland, Italy, as well as from Spain and, of course, England, adversely affected the crucial textile sector. When in 1786, the Eden Treaty with England opened up French markets to certain English exports, howls of outrage could be heard from cotton wholesalers and merchant-manufacturers from Rouen to Lille. There were, of course, notable exceptions to the rule of recession: the colonial trade, for example, continued to serve the greater glory of rich merchants in the Atlantic ports.

CHAPTER 16

David R. Roediger

THE WAGES OF WHITENESS: RACE AND THE MAKING OF THE AMERICAN WORKING CLASS (1991)*

While surveys are often national or address major events, there are also histories constructed as explanations of concepts or theories. One such is included here to illustrate what we might call the cultural and intellectual form of constructionist history. The extract is from David R. Roediger, *The Wages of Whiteness: Race and the Making of the American Working Class* (1991). Roediger is a leftist historian at the University of Illinois at Urbana-Champaign, US, who specialises in the history of labour, race relations and the South. Roediger has written

* David R. Roediger (1991) *The Wages of Whiteness: Race and the Making of the American Working Class*, London: Verso, pp. 97–100.

several books, including *Black on White: Black Writers on What it Means to be White* (1998) and *Coloured White: Transcending the Racial Past* (2002). In the following extract, he argues that the language of race reflected changes in class formation. His analysis of the 'coon' image is a study of how language mediates material and especially political change that is not, in this case, at first racial in association. He also uses his study to construct the meanings of 'buck' and 'mose', claiming that they illustrate the 'trajectories that led from white to black'. The intention of his argument is to justify his belief that, in a capitalist economic world, those who could potentially disrupt the system were easier to deal with when signified as black. Roediger calls this 'the concept of projection' which he deploys to account for the 'sense of whiteness among antebellum [pre-Civil War] workers, who profited from racism'. Roediger's history is an illustration of the sophisticated construction of explanations that reflect the onto-logical and ideological commitments of the historian, as much as the dictates of the evidence.

Language in blackface

JUST AS THE LANGUAGE of class that developed in the United States in the early nineteenth century were shaped at every turn by race, so too did racial lan-guage reflect, in a broad sense, changes and tensions associated with class formation. In 1767, a featured Black performer in the first musical to be published in America sang a variation of what was to become 'Yankee-Doodle' as he portrayed a character called Raccoon, an 'old debauchee'. Seventy years later, the white entertainer George Washington Dixon had popularized Zip Coon as the blackface minstrel embodiment of the irrepressible, irresponsible, dandified free Black in the North. Seventy years after that, at the end of the nineteenth century, the 'coon song' craze swept the nation, with individ-ual racist songs selling as many as three million copies in sheet music. Probably the best-known of the 'coon songs', Ernest Hogan's 'All Coons Look Alike to Me', bore a title that suggested how thoroughly dehumanizing racist stage stereotypes could be.

And yet even amidst this lineage of seemingly unrelieved prejudice, the 'coon' image carried a substantial and striking complexity during most of the years between 1767 and 1900. A song like 'All Coons Look Alike to Me' could, quite simply, not have been written before 1848, because human *coons* were typically *white* until that point. It is true that Zip Coon and Raccoon strutted on early American stages, but the word *coon* referred to a white country person, to a sharpster or, in phrases like a *pretty slick coon*, to both.

To complicate matters, the eagerness of the Whig party to identify with rural white common people led it to adopt symbols like Davy Crockett's coonskin cap and, in the 'log cabin and hard cider' presidential campaign of 1840, to nail coonskins to supporters' cabin doors and to use live coons as signs of party loyalty. Thus Whigs also became 'coons', especially in the speech of Democrats, who cursed Whigs in 'coongress' and Whig 'coonventions', Whig 'coonism' and a lack of Whig 'coonsistency'. The Whigs, to New York City Democrats, were a 'Federal Whig Coon Party' – a slur that, though sometimes seen in historical writing as racist, probably had nothing to do with the Whigs' slightly greater tolerance for antislavery. Instead, the accusation was that Whigs were sly political manipulators, posturing in coonskin as friends of the common man.

Only gradually did *coon* emerge as a racial slur, with the first clear case of such usage coming in 1848. That it first found racist use mainly on the minstrel stage suggests that the slur evolved from Zip Coon, and in the context of the many references to coon-hunting and eating coons in blackface songs. An alternative explanation is that *coon* derived from the corruption of *barracoon*, from the Spanish *barracon*, which came into increasing use to describe the 'enclosures in which slaves [were] temporarily enclosed after escape or during travel' in the years just before the Civil War. Whatever the derivation, all coons decidedly did not look alike in the 1850s. Lewis Garrard's *Wah-to-Yah*; or, *The Taos Trail* of 1850, for example, introduces a frontiersman who says of himself, 'This coon . . . had made Injuns go under some.' He quickly adds, 'This child's no nigger.'

The ambiguities of meaning in *coon* were not lost on Herman Melville, who brilliantly explored the mutability and the social construction of race, and even the deleterious effects of whiteness, in such works as *Benito Cereno*, *Moby Dick*, 'Paradise of Bachelors and Tartarus of Maids' and 'The Encantadas'. The racial dimensions of his work have received penetrating treatment from such scholars as Sterling Stuckey, Joshua Leslie and Carolyn Karcher. Karcher particularly observes that Melville's enigmatic masterpiece, *The Confidence-Man* (1857), mocks any firm distinction between black and white. She sees Melville's repeated characterization of the book's most disgusting character as a 'coon' as one key to the racial ambiguities of the novel. The character, an outspoken antiabolitionist and probably a child molester, is of questionable color himself. 'My name is Pitch and I stick to what I say', he says at one point. By calling him a 'coon' Melville emphasizes the uncertainty as to his race. If we add to Karcher's analysis the knowledge that *coon* itself was racially ambiguous in the 1850s and that it could in fact refer to a rural white or to a white confidence man, the layers of Melville's playfulness and seriousness become clearer.

Other racial slurs had similar histories. *Buck*, for example, was used to mean a 'dashing, young, virile man', presumably white, at the time of the American Revolution. As the nineteenth century wore on, buck came to signify a 'dandy' and a 'self-proclaimed fascinator of women'. Only in 1835 does the first recorded usage of 'buck nigger' appear, and it is seven years later before *buck* is unambiguously cited as used as a noun to refer to a Black man. Paul Beale's *Dictionary of Slang* directs readers to see '*masher*, *dude* and *swell*' for a sense of British usages. The term also found some antebellum applications to Indian men – as did *coon* in at least one instance – and gradually became a racial slur. By the early twentieth century, *Dialect Notes* would write of *buck*: 'Formerly a fop; now applied [almost] exclusively to male negroes.'

Likewise possessed of a checkered past was the name Mose, which originally denoted the most interesting white male character type on the American stage. Mose was, in the late antebellum period, synonymous with the character of the 'B'hoy', the Irish and urban street pronunciation of *boy*, and one that denoted a particular type of tough, rowdy and often dandified urban white youth. A low-comedy representative of young urban maleness – a fighter and a lover – Mose was typically an unemployed or apprentice artisan and a member of the volunteer fire departments whose disorderly behavior provoked the wrath of city fathers before the Civil War. When Mose appeared in 1848, according to one contemporary account, 'pit and galleries joined in the outcry' as many recognized themselves in his performance. He quickly became an American urban hero, a 'tough melon but sweet at the core', gracing the parades of artisan-based volunteer fire departments even in an outlying city like Nashville by the early 1850s.

But by the time white Mose had made his way to Nashville, a blackface Mose was appearing in New York City. As early as 1852 the permanent minstrel companies there were performing the song 'Wake Up, Mose', in which the racial identity of the black-faced hero changed from verse to verse. Tunes like 'De Darkey Fireman's Song' continued the confusion. The minstrel show's 'end men', coming into prominence during the last antebellum years, were, as Alexander Saxton has shown, part Zip Coon but also part Mose. 'White Mose enjoyed a striking, but relatively brief, popularity. Scholars have blamed the steam engine and the professionalization of fire fighting for his demise. But Mose in blackface proved quite durable, incarnated as both an urban dandy and as a fatherly Southern Black. He became Aunt Jemima's husband in the ragdoll and salt-and-pepper shaker families of the twentieth century.

Such words as *coon*, *buck* and *Mose* had more than ambiguous or multiple meanings: they had trajectories that led from white to black. More than that, each of them went from describing particular kinds of whites who had not internalized capitalist work discipline and whose places in the new world of wage labor were problematic to stereotyping Blacks. Rustics and con-men, fops and 'fascinators of women', brawlers and 'sentinels of the new army of the unemployed' – all of these proved easier to discuss when blacked up. Such an evolution of language suggests that some use of the concept of projection is necessary to understand the growth of a sense of whiteness among antebellum workers, who profited from racism in part because it enabled them to displace anxieties within the white population onto Blacks. But the process of projection was not abstract. It took place largely within the context of, working class formation and addressed the specific anxieties of those caught up in that process.

CHAPTER 17

John M. MacKenzie

ORIENTALISM: HISTORY, THEORY AND THE ARTS (1995)*

One of the most popular and mature forms of constructionist history is the body of work that deals with the nature of imperialism. As one of the central concepts used in history today, there are as many definitions of imperialism as one could wish for. Consequently, the next extract has been chosen because it addresses one of the central debates around the meaning of just one of imperialism's most intriguing features, Orientalism. John M. MacKenzie is Professor of Imperial History at the University of Lancaster and author of several books on the social, cultural and environmental history of the British Empire. In this extract from his *Orientalism: History, Theory and the Arts* (1995), MacKenzie describes how the Palestinian critic Edward Said redefined Orientalism by combining and adapting 'two influential

* John M. MacKenzie (1995) *Orientalism: History, Theory and the Arts*, Manchester: Manchester University Press, pp. 3–7.

theoretical constructs of the twentieth century' (in Said's books called *Orientalism* and *Culture and Imperialism*). The first theoretical construct Said used to produce his new definition of Orientalism was the French historian Michel Foucault's notion of discourse. This was Foucault's idea of the linguistic form through which the 'articulation of knowledge becomes an expression of power'. The second construct linked occidental imperialism to the concept of cultural hegemony by the early twentieth-century Marxist, Antonio Gramsci. Said connected the concept not to the power of intellectuals and economic class as Gramsci did, but to race. Said's construction transformed Orientalism into a set of myths about the Orient that he claims was deliberately engineered by the West. MacKenzie is highly critical of Said's work, seeing it as essentially a repackaging of what most historians of imperialism know and, at worst, the product of anti-Zionist rage. MacKenzie concludes in this extract by declaring Said as being 'situated at the watershed of the modernist-postmodernist debate'. He is, however, unable to determine exactly where he is in relation to postmodernism's antagonism to master narratives. What this extract reveals is the constructionist's self-consciousness about other construction-ists and the multiple levels of concept and theory that characterises this genre of historical practice. This is perhaps why so much mainstream history today is concerned with historians critiquing each other. The question is whether the method has got in the way of the message.

T**HE VALUATION OF THE** words 'Orientalism' and 'Orientalist' and the activities which they described came, of course, from within the cultures that had spawned them. The transformation in their meaning and use came from outside, from the world of comparative literature in a post-colonial and post-nationalist context. Edward Said combined and adapted two influential theoretical constructs of the twentieth century to produce his major revaluation of Orientalism. He took Michel Foucault's concept of the discourse, the linguistic apparatus through which the articulation of knowledge becomes an expression of power, and linked it to Antonio Gramsci's notion of cultural hegemony through which elite control is maintained over the masses. But whereas Foucault was often more interested in the internal topography of his apparatus, Said was concerned to apply it to a large body of heterogeneous texts. And where Gramsci dealt with class in a European context, Said transferred his hegemonic principles to racial rep-resentation and control in an imperial frame. Said's work is thus strikingly eclectic, both in philosophical and theoretical terms as well as in his use of a mixture of literary and non-canonical sources. It transformed 'Orientalism', in which the Orient is appropriated by the Occident by being turned into a structure of myth prefabricated for western use, into one of the most ideologically charged words in modern scholarship. Moreover, its seem-ingly wide-ranging character and the power and freshness of its message prompted responses from a number of disciplines in both the humanities and the social sciences.

Indeed, few books have at the same time stimulated so much controversy or influ-enced so many studies. Colonial literary theory, anthropology, women's studies, art his-tory, theatre history, media and communications studies, the history of philology, historical geography, even the modish study of 'heritage' and tourism have all come under its sway. Not only has it become almost impossible to consider the relationship between West and East without grappling with its insights, but its method has also been applied to Europe's relationship with other parts of the globe. Yet, with a few rare exceptions, the conventional study of history, even that concerned with the highly relevant examination of travel in the Mediterranean, North Africa and the Levant has been notably absent from this list. Moreover, historians of imperialism, for whom Said seems to have the clearest messages, have paid it relatively little attention. It is one of the purposes of this chapter and the next to consider why this should be so.

Like most books that acquire 'epochal' status, *Orientalism* has been seen, both as merely enshrining a great truth and as constituting a major polemic. While Said has castigated the literary–cultural establishment in both *Orientalism* and his more recent *Culture and Imperialism* (1993) for having 'declared the serious study of imperialism and culture' as being 'off limits', imperial historians have been concerned with the culture of imperialism for more than twenty years. Indeed, since the early 1980s it has become a major historical preoccupation. Most historians have little difficulty in seeing texts as 'worldly', as 'to some degree events' in their own right, as 'a part of the social world, human life, and of course the historical moments in which they are located and interpreted'. For them 'rubbing culture's nose in the mud of politics' is a perfectly conventional rather than iconoclastic activity. Yet, as we shall see, historians continue to have problems both with *Orientalism* and, more particularly, with some of the work inspired by it, for, like Marx and Freud, Said has spawned followers (Saidians or Saidists), producing work both subtle and crude, some of which the master might wish to disown. However, if *Orientalism* at times conveyed the seductive ring of the codification of the obvious, *Culture and Imperialism* [. . .] presents far greater problems for historians as well as literary critics.

But if Said's intellectual influence on a number of related disciplines in the humanities and the social sciences has been considerable, his work has also been seen as both highly polemical and distinctly schizophrenic. A large proportion of Said's examples are drawn from the Middle East and he is concerned, as he has insisted in a later commentary on *Orientalism*, not to defend Arabs or Islam, but to show that these terms exist as

> 'communities of interpretation' which gave them existence, and that, like the Orient itself, each designation represented interests, claims, projects, ambitions and rhetorics that were not only in violent disagreement, but were in a situation of open warfare. So saturated with meanings, so overdetermined by history, religion and politics are labels like 'Arab' or 'Muslim' as subdivisions of 'the Orient' that no one today can use them without some attention to the formidable polemical mediations that screen the objects, if they exist at all, that the labels designate.

Given that this is indeed his starting-point, it is not surprising that his work has been seen as a product of rage, the anti-western and by extension anti-Zionist tract of a dispossessed Palestinian. It might reasonably be objected that other religious and ethnic designations are equally overdetermined and saturated with meanings, not only in the Orient, but also in other continents and the West itself. Indeed, it may be that Said himself contributes to this saturation by occidentalising the West, by 'essentialising' (describing by means of essences or stereotypes) the characteristics of European powers no less than they 'essentialised' the East. Moreover, 'Jew' and 'Zionist' are clearly overburdened terms, and it is, perhaps, inevitable that some of the most powerful critiques of Said have come from scholars of Jewish heritage. One proclaimed himself as 'tired of the Said phenomenon'. Another became embroiled in a bitter correspondence in the *Times Literary Supplement* after a particularly hostile review of *Culture and Imperialism*. Yet another, writing within Israel, has used the viewpoint of women's studies to deliver a powerful, if largely implicit critique of *Orientalism*. For conventional literary critics, Said has had the audacity to attempt to implicate the literature of sensibility, the Leavisite great tradition, in the squalor and brutality of imperialism, while scholars imbued in western liberal humanism, have seen the Enlightenment-tradition, the scholarly explorations celebrated by the writers of the British Council pamphlets, arraigned as the accomplices of colonialism.

Yet herein lies the schizophrenia. Said has declared himself to react to the word 'humanist' with 'contradictory feelings of affection and revulsion'. He seeks to expose the humanistic tradition, while essentially writing within it himself. His works are a collective plea for a new kind of liberal humanity, which Ernest Gellner, in a magisterial review, found an unexceptional truism. He is steeped in the western musical tradition, but finds it compromised by its political context. He admires the art of Kipling, valuing it above that of the more ambivalent Forster, for example, while loathing its imperialist assumptions. Thus, though he has toyed with the language of base and superstructure, while he has been a member of the Palestine National Council, he writes outside Marxist or revolutionary traditions. Indeed, it is a characteristic of his work that neither economics nor class plays a particularly central role if indeed any role at all. He has said that he finds Marxism 'more limiting than enabling' and that he is more interested in an ethic of individualism than class-consciousness. He is atheistic in religion, agnostic in politics and has no general intellectual attachment beyond a respect for an anarcho-syndicalism. Thus, influenced though he is by Gramsci and Foucault, he stands beyond any scholarly collective, his political objectives (except perhaps Palestinian freedom – though not through partition, which he decries – and wider global understanding) largely undefined.

Further, Said is situated at the watershed of the modernist–postmodernist debate. In *Orientalism* he identifies an imperial totalising project, a 'master narrative' of western power. But his is of course a Whiggism in reverse. He exposes these constant leitmotifs of intercultural relations to condemn rather than to celebrate. Instead of 'progress' or an ineluctable historical dialectic, his master narrative is regressive, a tool of dominance which survives the end of formal imperialism to continue its destructive role in the world of today. As he has put it, decolonisation is an unfinished project. Thus he totalises for the purpose of demolition. But his trade mark is continuity: his Orientalist programme has had continuous showings from at least the eighteenth century to the present day. It prepared the way for full-blown imperial rule and survives as the cultural and ideological superstructure of neo-colonialism, particularly America's self-satisfied and culturally blinkered role (as he sees it) as imperial world policeman in the late twentieth century.

Yet he profoundly distrusts all other 'metanarratives' as interpretative tools. Instead of the 'theorization of the whole', he prefers a 'more unbuttoned, unfixed, and mobile mode' which he has dubbed (in a direct allusion to his own exiled status) nomadic and unhoused. He is also disturbed by the cultural guerrillas which beset the fringes of the master narrative. These he has identified as 'nativism' (which extols the virtues of and seeks to resurrect individual indigenous cultures), 'nationalism' (which asserts the political creed of contesting nations) and 'fundamentalism' (which seeks to restore religious purity as a rallying cry of resistance). Each is concerned to subdivide and separate, by cultural, political or religious means, in order to escape the western coils, and in doing so contributes to a reorientalisation by appearing to confirm the irrational, the divisive, the aberrant character of the West's Orient.

CHAPTER 18

Jan P. Nederveen Pieterse

EMPIRE AND EMANCIPATION: POWER AND LIBERATION ON A WORLD SCALE (1990)*

Jan P. Nederveen Pieterse is Associate Professor of Sociology at the Institute of Social Studies in The Hague. He has written extensively on imperialism and most recently on the theory of development, raising questions about the links between development and globalisation and the nature of economic inequality between nations. The extract reprinted here is from his *Empire and Emancipation: Power and Liberation on a World Scale* (1990). That constructionism as a genre of history constantly moves into the social sciences is evident in the extract that follows. In it Pieterse offers a detailed assessment of the characteristic features of empires and how they are vanquished, noting especially the work of Lenin and Marx. Paving the way for post-colonial studies, the book itself focuses on liberation themes of empire that, in the late 1980s, rarely gained the attention they have today, such as Irish nationalism, the position of Native Americans and the African diaspora. Interdisciplinary in form, it integrates concepts and theoretical scaffolding taken from social sciences, including anthropology, law, political science, economics and sociology, as well as cross-disciplinary areas, such as gender, public administration and environmental sciences. In Braudelian fashion, the topics covered recognise the interaction between macro- and micro-level development strategies, structures and processes.

L ENIN'S THEORY, WHILE making a particular case of economic imperialism, is also defined by the cases it does *not* make, by the dimensions and actors of imperialism which are marginalized and obscured in this perspective: the role of strategic objectives and the military, the international states system with its own dynamics and players, the role of nationalism, the cultural dimensions of imperialism, the role of race, the role of religion. Most conspicuously it is the role of the *state*, the actual imperialist agent itself in most instances, that is underplayed in this perspective. Generally the assumption is simply that the state operates as an instrument of capitalist interests: 'The state is a reflection of the economic infrastructure'. A simplification in its own right, this is also contradicted by many data. Moreover, it lags behind developments in Marxist thinking on the state over the past two decades, although these theoretical developments have been mainly concerned with the relationship between the state and society, the state and domestic

---

* Jan P. Nederveen Pieterse (1990) *Empire and Emancipation: Power and Liberation on a World Scale*, London: Pluto Press, pp. 8–11.

classes, not with the state and international relations. The references in Poulantzas' work to the 'imperialist chain' only paraphrase Lenin's metaphor. The work of James Petras is exceptional in that it provides a developed theory of the *imperial state*: 'It is time that we discard the notion that imperialism is an "economic phenomenon" that can be analyzed by looking merely at the flow of capital and corporate behavior. The literature on the multi-nationals, as unsystematic and rich in detail as it may be, tends to forget the institution that created the universe in which they function: the imperial states'.

While a thought-provoking and multifaceted theory, it is still conceived within the same theoretical tradition of defining imperialism in terms of capitalism, for example: 'The U.S. imperial state can be defined as those executive bodies or agencies within the "government" that are charged with promoting and protecting the expansion of capital across state boundaries by the multinational corporate community headquartered in the imperial center'. Does this or does this not include the Central Intelligence Agency? Axiomatic statements drive the point home: 'The imperial state embodies the present and future collective interests of the most dynamic sector of capital'. The lack of congruence between specific actions of the imperial state and capitalist interests is addressed by Petras and Morley by differentiating levels of consciousness: enterprise consciousness, industry consciousness, and class consciousness—a formulation which at least makes it possible to conceptualize certain problems. The element of tautology comes in with terms such as the 'imperial capitalist class'. The notion of the autonomy of the imperial state is rejected as an illusion: 'To exaggerate the relative autonomy of the state is to miss the all-inclusive manner in which the decision makers are immersed in the symbols and substance of capitalist power'. But the term 'capitalist power' itself is the result of a combination of discourses. In contrast with other Marxist formulations which float in an ocean of woolliness, this perspective at least is sharply formulated such that it is possible to pinpoint areas of testing: 'The more important the region or social formation to imperial expansion, the greater the coincidence of interest between capital and state, and the more directly will imperial state policy be an expression of class interests'. If this held or holds in the case of Chile, Brazil, Indonesia, Iran, and the Caribbean, is it tenable also for Indochina, Central America, Angola, South Africa, and Libya? Extraneous considerations are introduced to account for actual imperial undertakings: 'Indo-China was an area of symbolic/tactical interest to the United States', that is, considerations which do not follow directly from capitalist class interest, unless one accepts the postulate that the capitalist class considers imperial growth and its strategic imperatives necessary to the pursuance of its interests, which again leads to tautology. Other specific situations, not mentioned in this essay, further stretch the plausibility of this approach: 'If economic rather than cold-war, ideological/moral, or domestic considerations dominated foreign policy, the United States stance in the Arab-Israeli crisis would have been very different over the last three decades'. In all these instances, postulates of identity of interests of capital and imperial expansion are not substitutes for analysis and obscure the discrepancies and conflicts of interest which do exist; strengthening ideological coherence, they weaken analytical capacity. Finally the argument ends up swallowing its own tail: 'The imperial state provided a protective nest within which U.S. capital operated in a manner *not* conducive to developing a competitive edge'. In other words, in the beginning the imperial state is defined in terms of its capacity to facilitate U.S. capital accumulation and in the end it is shown that U.S. capital accumulation has declined *because* of the imperial state and the political and military cost of maintaining the imperial system. It follows that either the theory is invalid or its implementation has been wrong. In effect, the theory is one not of factual conditions (on an empirical level the congruence between imperial state interests and capitalist class interests does not obtain with any degree of consistency) but of relations between *states of consciousness*, namely imperial consciousness and class consciousness. This congruence of consciousness, the theory's ultimate resort, itself cannot be demonstrated or validated and resolves in a paradox: 'Thus the apparent paradox that the consciousness of class interests of the imperialist classes are normally far more concentrated in the imperial state than in the individual class members themselves'. A consensus which does not in fact exist then turns out to be the foundation of a convergence of interests of imperial state and multinational capital which does not in fact exist either.

Earlier, in 1970, Petras wrote, 'Imperialism is a multidimensional phenomenon whose components are in dynamic interplay'. This understanding has been put into practice in the theory of the imperial state, but only in the sense of a *multidimensional elaboration* of a *monocausal* perspective, in which a multiplicity of dimensions is used to preserve the postulate of a *single* set of organizing principles (i.e., capital accumulation). This is about as convincing as the use of subatomic physics to prove a geocentric theory of the universe. If imperialism is really conceived as *multidimensional*, then theories of a 'prime mover' character are out of place, epistemologically anachronistic, and analytically blunt.

Dependency theory, another perspective within the general tradition of Lenin's theoretical framework, is a theory primarily concerned with the problem of underdevelopment rather than imperialism as such. A restatement of the theses of monopoly capitalism, it argues, in addition, that 'peripheral capitalism' is different in its dynamics from metropolitan capitalism and makes for the 'development of underdevelopment'. While this perspective has deepened our understanding of the economic and political impact of the expansion of capitalism, although it has also overstated its case, as a theory of imperialism it has simply reproduced the postulate of identity of imperialism and capitalism. Moreover, capitalism, in the formulation of Andre Gunder Frank, has been redefined in terms of the sphere of exchange, such that precapitalist production relations are regarded as 'capitalist' if they are involved in exchange relations in the world market; this raises the question of 'where to draw the line between imperialism properly so called and market relationships between countries of 'different economic potential'.

Among the criticisms of dependency theory, the critique of Bill Warren has been cast in the form of a polemic against Lenin's theory of monopoly capitalism. Warren notes that 'the bulk of current Marxist analyses of and propaganda about imperialism actually reverse the views of the founders of Marxism, who held that the expansion of capitalism into pre-capitalist areas of the world was desirable and progressive'. This reversal began with Lenin's theory which redefined capitalism, in its monopolistic stage, as a reactionary, parasitic force and in this respect dependency theory is a postwar version of Lenin's view. Warren seeks to reestablish the original Marxist evaluation of capitalism and restates in effect Marx's views on capital's 'civilizing mission'. Underdevelopment in the Third World is a fiction: *development* has taken place and this 'has been the direct result of the impact of the West, of imperialism'. While rejecting the theory of monopoly capitalism (and in this respect Warren is not alone in the Marxist tradition), Warren follows the larger Marxist framework, defining imperialism as 'the penetration and spread of the capitalist system into non-capitalist or primitive capitalist areas of the world'. Again, a politics of expansion and control is equated with the dynamics of capitalist expansion. On the one hand, in Warren's view, imperialism is the pioneer of capitalism and as such a progressive force, and on the other, 'imperialism declines as capitalism grows.' The political implications of this equation cum reevaluation are bizarre: Apparently, imperialism must be welcomed; and it is expected to decline as with the growth of capitalism the development gap narrows. Aside from the merits of the thesis of underdevelopment, which cannot be gone into here, when development in the Third World is represented as 'the direct result of the impact of the West, of imperialism', as if a simple process of transfer, this is no different from standard modernization theory: What is entirely overlooked are the dialectics in the process, the role of resistance, of Third World nationalism in building the political and economic bases of 'autocentric development'. A return to Marx, it is also a return to the narrowest Europocentrism of Marx. If there is room for reappraisals of the theses of dependent capitalism, at the same time this shows the error—analytically and politically—of equating capitalism with imperialism.

CHAPTER 19

Thomas W. Smith

HISTORY AND INTERNATIONAL RELATIONS (1999)*

While few examples of constructionist history have been directly influenced by recent developments in the postmodern deconstruction of history, occasionally some historians do acknowledge its impact. One such is Thomas W. Smith in his book *History and International Relations* (1999) that surveys the field of international relations, history and politics. Smith's aim is to challenge scientific approaches to international history. His self-proclaimed scepticism picks out the contingency and the moral choices of both historical agents and historians. In the extract, Smith highlights what he views as the key problems in international relations and history: epistemology, ideology and sociology. He makes the very important point that, epistemologically, 'history turns out to be an indispensable, but fickle, research partner'. History, he explains, is less an archival puzzle to be solved than 'a patchwork of often incongruous facts and more or less plausible inferences, interpretations, and impressions'. Smith continues by arguing that this is particularly so as the historian 'moves into the realm of meaning and causality', concluding that numerous diverse readings of the agreed past are possible. In a sense, he is acknowledging that the essence of constructionism is 'imaginative reconstruction' and that, ideologically, history is often subject to the confusion of evidence and advocacy. He also sees how constructionism, especially of an extreme sociological kind, can descend into a positivist-inspired hypotheses testing, rather than the self-reflexive process that it should be. He concludes by signalling several of the challenges that confront history

* Thomas W. Smith (1999) *History and International Relations*, London: Routledge, pp. 1–4.

today. These include bias in evidence selection, anecdotalism, an ahistoricism that empties interpretation of its content and context, perverse choices of theory, and what he calls 'cathedrals of clay', by which he means that researchers too often can assume that their data reflects the past as it actually was. However, in Smith's plea for scepticism there is no rejection of the epistemological position. He ends up arguing that historians should simply tread more carefully with their model-making and testing, and that empiricists (reconstructionists) need to be more self-conscious.

––––––––––––

Out of our conceptions of the past, we make a future.

Hobbes (1994: 32)

"**T**HE PAST,**"** the great skeptic of British philosophy Michael Oakeshott once noted, is "a field in which we exercise our moral and political opinions, like whippets in a meadow on a Sunday afternoon" (Oakeshott 1962: 166). Prompted by Oakeshott's critique of history-as-ideology, this study scrutinizes international relations theory and research across the methodological spectrum from classical realism to quantitative and postmodernist work. Perhaps because it is a child of history, international relations, as it has developed, has tried to distance itself from historical discourse, through methodological and theoretical innovations seeking general knowledge about international and global politics. In this flight from the old ways of history, researchers have tended to downplay the historical content of their own work, and, at times, to embrace an easy historical empiricism. This uncritical view of the past has contributed to an often licentious historical method, with history serving less as an independent body of evidence than as a trove to be plundered, and which in the discipline's most scientific work saddles history with more certainty than it can bear.

The historical problem is to some extent inherent in the material. As Hans Morgenthau noted in an opening passage of *Politics Among Nations* (1948):

> The most formidable difficulty facing a scientific inquiry into the nature and ways of international politics is the ambiguity of the material with which the observer has to deal . . . The first lesson the student of international politics must learn and never forget is that the complexities of international affairs make simple solutions and trustworthy prophecies impossible. It is here that the scholar and the charlatan part company . . . In every political situation contradictory tendencies are at play . . . which tendency actually will prevail is anybody's guess. The best the scholar can do, then, is to trace the different tendencies which, as potentialities, are inherent in a certain international situation.
>
> (Morgenthau 1948: 4–6)

Quincy Wright, an early advocate of the quantitative study of international politics and one of the field's greatest interdisciplinarians, had especially kind words for history. He noted that "in their emphasis on contingency [historians] provide a healthy antidote to the overenthusiastic social scientist," and that an appreciation of history lent the student of war a balanced sense of continuity and change, of uniqueness and repetition, of causation and contingency, and of choice and standards. He can better realize the complexity and uncertainty of human affairs, the many factors to be considered in making judgments, the dangers of abstraction, of dogmatism, of prediction, of action, and of inaction. He can better understand the abundance and variability of human values and the opportunities as well as the insecurities of any situation.

(Wright 1955: 87, 89)

Now more frequently cast in the mold of political science, students of international politics have largely abandoned these earlier ideas about the nature of history and the limits that history suggests for social science research. Today, "rigorous," often grand, historical models are the norm, as is routine disregard for the problems of historical discourse.

The historical problem: an overview

In its most basic outline, the historical problem in the field of international relations comprises epistemology, ideology, and sociology. Epistemologically, history turns out to be an indispensable, but fickle, research partner. It is decidedly not the independent body of evidence touted by Leopold von Ranke (1874: vii) as history "as it really was" (*wie es eigentlich gewesen ist*). If getting history right is "like nailing jelly to the wall," as Peter Novick suggests in his highly controversial, meticulously documented *That Noble Dream: The "Objectivity Question" and the American Historical Profession* (1988: 1), then the use of history in social science is no less challenging. Plunging into the historical literature, the researcher is quickly enmeshed in lively debate over description and explanation. History turns out to be not so much an archival puzzle, whose parts eventually fall neatly into place, than a patchwork of often incongruous facts and more or less plausible inferences, interpretations, and impressions. This is particularly the case as the historian moves into the realm of meaning and causality. As Stanley Hoffmann has argued (1987: 455), "many different readings of the same reality are possible. Even if all historians agreed on the facts, they would still disagree on the respective weight of those facts; in the act of 'imaginative reconstruction' that any causal analysis performs, assessments of motivation and causal efficiency vary considerably."

Ideologically, history is ripe for partisan selection and interpretation. As the theorist constructs and reconstructs histories, allying inquiry with one interpretive school and carefully ignoring others, the findings risk being dictated or distorted by individual ideological or intellectual commitments. In place of searching historical inquiry, we get a lawyer's brief that confuses evidence and advocacy. In terms of sociology, the customs and conventions of international relations have increasingly fostered a kind of heedlessness toward historical questions. It has become standard practice to brandish easy anecdotes and analogies, pursue ahistorical, stand-alone theory, or else to approach the "history" part of the enterprise as merely a formal testing stage on the road to theory. This is symptomatic of a broader affliction in the field. Yosef Lapid (1989: 249–50) suggests that, for many years, international relations has held "the dubious honor of being among the least self-reflexive of the Western social sciences." Most debate in the discipline takes place within a "positivist" framework; it is assumed that rationally justified assertions about the "essential" nature of politics can be scientifically verified by observing its historical manifestations. Critics of theory and history generally respond with theory and history of their own, in what often becomes an all-or-nothing contest of evidence and ideas. Rarer are examinations of the field's underlying assumptions and methods, particularly regarding the historical evidence itself, or the field's roots in social science.

Most of the historical challenges described in this study fall within the following categories:

Selection bias: as the title of Barbara Geddes's article (1990) states, "the cases you choose affect the answers you get." This is the overarching problem in historical usage across the social sciences. Selection bias can be systematic, resulting from shoddy research; or it can be instrumental, aimed at promoting a particular theoretical position. Partisan selection bias is usually accompanied by the sin of omission of studiously avoiding unhelpful history. In all social science research, potential alternative explanations often reside in sources not enlisted or data not collected.

Anecdotalism generalizes from carefully chosen particulars. This is often more of a didactic tool than a research method, as the theorist airily presents hand-picked events and narratives in order to corroborate his/her ideas. Analogies may be anecdotal as well, as the scholar or policymaker sees current dilemmas closely mirrored in the past. Although it is a sub-set of selection bias, the anecdotal fallacy is so prevalent as to warrant special mention.

Ahistoricism promotes political theory emptied of content and context, often in an effort to sidestep the idiosyncrasies of political choice and the processes of change. Theorists may also be ahistorical in failing to recognize the impact of *moment et milieu* on their own research, thus presenting historically-contingent constructs as timeless laws of politics. The field is ahistorical as well in its focus on contemporary history and policy issues (Buzan and Little 1994: 233–4), and in its tendency to read the present back into the past.

Theoretical filtering interprets history through one's theoretical lens. This practice is to some degree unavoidable: history needs theory to lend it coherence. At the extreme, theoretical filtering produces tautological research, undermining history's role as an independent source of corroboration or falsification, as the case may be. Theoretical filtering is related to the quantitative fallacy as well, which arises when statistical methods propel research in a particular substantive direction. In postmodern work, a fixation on diversity and difference may prove so fine a filter that any similarities across historical periods or event are lost, thus walling off the past from the present.

Cathedrals of clay: here one constructs theories of painstaking precision as though the medium of research were Carrara marble rather than the softer stuff of history. This fallacy is common among quantitative researchers, who assume a tight affinity between historical data and history as it really was. Statistical methods allow for a great deal of sophistication and precision in research and theory, yet this precision may overstep the archival and historiographic evidence on which quantitative data are based.

CHAPTER 20

Charles More

*UNDERSTANDING THE INDUSTRIAL REVOLUTION (2000)**

A historian at the University of Gloucestershire, Charles More is a modern European historian interested in British economic and social history. His books include *Understanding the Industrial Revolution* (2000) from which the extract here is taken. In this he describes some models of the British Industrial Revolution. In classic constructionist terms, More defines a model as providing 'a schematic outline which maps the broad sweep of reality – or of what the deviser of the model thinks is reality'. Behind all models are theories and, as More acknowledges, this is one reason why historians of economic growth disagree. Another reason for disagreement is the complexity that can be built into the model. More concludes that these are two good reasons 'why it is so difficult to achieve consensus about the Industrial Revolution'. He then elaborates on the definitions of the various factors of production that go into all such models: land, labour and capital, and how their productivity can be increased. As he points out, the historical interpretation is dependent on the definitions provided for each factor and the emphasis placed on each one. He concludes that the factors of production and their changing levels of productivity are the 'building blocks of the growth models of economists and historians'. The implication is clear. How the building blocks are put together determines the utility and explanatory power of the models. With economic history we have the clearest example of the historian's assumptions turning the past into history.

Land, labour and capital

THE VARIOUS ATTEMPTS to explain the Industrial Revolution can be described as 'models'. An historical/economic 'model' is a simplified way of representing a set of economic processes – in this case, those processes which brought about the Industrial Revolution. The model provides a schematic outline which maps the broad sweep of reality – or of what the deviser of the model thinks is reality. Behind the models there are economic theories which explain why the processes outlined in the model should lead to economic growth. Theories differ, however, which is one reason for disagreement between writers on economic growth; another is the schematic nature of models, which means that it is difficult to construct a model which is simple, but is also a sufficient representation of reality. These two potential reasons for disagreement help to explain why it is so difficult to achieve consensus about the Industrial Revolution.

---

* Charles More (2000) *Understanding the Industrial Revolution*, London: Routledge, pp. 9–12.

Underlying all the models is the concept of factors of production: land, labour and capital. Land appears self-explanatory as the essential medium for agricultural output. But the economist's land also includes the minerals below the earth's surface, and the latent power of wind and water; paradoxically, it also includes the fruits of the sea. In effect, 'land' to economists is shorthand for all the products of the natural world. Labour is more straightforward, since we all understand what work is; but there are complexities because workers can be more or less skilled. Capital has a dual meaning, as the funds which are used to finance some productive asset, and the asset itself. Capital assets include buildings to house machinery, the machinery itself, mines and other expensive items; and also such less obvious assets as the craftsman's tools, the farmer's seedcorn, and the factory owner's stocks of raw cotton.

Simple economic growth, without industrialisation, can be achieved by adding inputs of one or more of these different factors. Most economists would agree that such simple addition of factors is also necessary for industrialisation, but they would add that something else is needed: more efficient use of one or more of the factors. There are various ways in which this may be achieved.

It can be achieved through the advantages of size, usually known as economies of scale or increasing returns. For instance, as ships increase in size, their cargo capacity grows at a faster rate than their weight, and so the capital cost of building a bigger ship does not rise as fast as its cargo capacity. Nor does its crew size, and therefore the labour of the crew is used more efficiently and crew costs per tonne carried will be smaller. In economists' jargon, capital productivity and labour productivity will both be raised. In the same sort of way, as roads become more intensively used, the capital cost of building them is spread over more vehicles; and if tolls are charged on the road, the tollgate keeper opens the gate more often, rather than just hanging about waiting for the occasional cart. Again, capital and labour productivity are both increased. If the new road also enables the land nearby to be cultivated more intensively because the produce is cheaper to take to market, then land productivity will be increased too. These examples could be multiplied over almost every industry and activity.

Economies of scale do not apply only to individual capital assets such as ships and roads. In a growing economy, there will be more economic transactions between individuals and firms. As the number of transactions multiplies, all sorts of savings enable assets and labour to be used more effectively. For instance, ships will spend less time waiting in port for a cargo as traffic grows; more letters will be written and it becomes worth establishing a postal service, which cuts the cost of exchanging commercial information. The reduction in transaction costs, of which transport costs are an important part, is a significant economy arising from growth. Postal services are examples of the beneficial civic activities that a larger economy makes possible. Others are the provision of lighthouses and charts to aid navigation, and of effective military forces to discourage unfriendly foreign powers or pirates. Sometimes these activities can only be financed by taxation and have to be left to the government, in which case they are known as public goods. Reductions in transaction costs, public goods and other benefits which are external to the firm are collectively known as external economies or beneficial externalities.

Another way in which factors can be used more effectively is summed up in the phrase 'gains from trade'. At its simplest, this expresses the principle that if two partners, each producing a different product more cheaply than the other, exchange those products, both partners will gain so long as transaction costs are lower than the saving in production costs. Such gains can occur through internal and foreign trade. Thus if Lancashire produces cotton cloth and uses resources economically to do so, and East Anglia produces wheat with similar efficiency, they will exchange these goods and each will benefit. The theory of comparative advantage develops the analysis by showing that different partners will maximise income by specialising in products in which they have the greatest relative, or comparative, advantage. Thus even if Britain produced both cotton cloth and wheat using fewer factors of production than France, it would suit Britain to concentrate on producing the one in which its efficiency advantage over France was greatest. If that was cotton cloth, then irrespective of its efficiency advantage in both commodities, Britain would specialise in cloth and exchange it for wheat.

Greater efficiency in factor use can also be achieved by innovation – the adoption of a change which yields a more effective use of resources or provides some new service or item of consumption. Resources might be used more effectively because of a newly-invented machine or through an improvement in organisation. An example of the second is the spread in the eighteenth century of institutions known as turnpike trusts. These levied tolls on roads, enabling more money to be spent on maintenance and new building: thus vehicles could be heavier and go faster, and as a result, the productivity of carriages and wagons (capital), and that of their drivers (labour), increased. Improvement is often achieved through 'learning-by-doing': a simple name which describes exactly what is meant. A machine or a process might have its efficiency improved not by any sort of physical change or new type of organisation, but just by incremental improvement of what is already there. For instance, as engineers in textile mills gained experience they found they could work their steam engines harder and so drive more machinery with the same engine. There was no new technology and no investment was required: it is an example of pure learning-by-doing. (It is possible to distinguish different types of learning-by-doing – for instance, learning-by-making and learning-by-using – but to avoid complexity these will be subsumed under learning-by-doing.)

All the above types of change could be described as process innovations. Product innovation is also important. A new product might appeal to consumers – as did cotton clothing when it was introduced – or it might be a product which is primarily of commercial or industrial importance. New types of insurance, for example, might reduce the risks of foreign trade and thus its cost. It is important to stress the wide nature of innovation. The headlines about the Industrial Revolution have been made by the great inventions – Watt's steam engine, the various textile machines, and so on. The term innovation encompasses the adoption of these, but also the other less spectacular types of change mentioned above.

The factors of production, and the concept that their productivity can be increased, are the main building blocks of the growth models of economists and historians. The models put the blocks together in various ways and sometimes add other components, and it is these various combinations which are described below.

CHAPTER 21

Richard F. Bensel

YANKEE LEVIATHAN: THE ORIGINS OF CENTRAL STATE AUTHORITY IN AMERICA, 1859–1877 (1991)*

The American historian and Professor of Government at Cornell University, Richard F. Bensel, provides a sophisticated model of the role of the state in economic and social change in the US in the mid-nineteenth century. In three books – *Sectionalism and American Political Development* (1984), *Yankee Leviathan: The Origins of Central State Authority in America, 1859–1877* (1991) and *The Political Economy of American Industrialisation, 1877–1900* (2000) – Bensel is writing history that combines several forms of change over time: social, economic and political. As this extract from the middle book in the trilogy indicates, his intention is to construct and test a historical model that will explain historical change – essentially the nature of the American modernisation process – on a national scale. To do this he believes that he is justified in linking together developments in the US party political system, government/public policy decisions and the social/cultural bases of American politics. In the extract that follows, Bensel tries to explain the connections between the Civil War, the process of modernisation and the development of the American state. His chosen methodology is to construct a three-stage model. According to this, the Republican Party first captured political power at the expense of the southern plantation elite and then oversaw an explosive expansion of central state authority by allying itself with other groups. Finally, with the re-entry of the South into the political system, the Republican Party had to compromise its control. Unsurprisingly, given its form, Bensel's model-making is infused with often arcane social science language such as 'nascent nationalism', 'balance of power', 'statism' and 'pluralistic nationalism'. Bensel tests his model against 'more conventional theories of modernization', some of which he relegates to his heavy-duty references. The point of this exercise, one must assume, is to reveal how his model, being more complex, accounts for more variables in the data and, therefore, is more 'realistic' as history. His primary source – votes in both the Confederate and US Congresses – he evaluates with a quantitative methodology with the objective of, presumably, producing both an unambiguous and persuasive argument.

The Civil War and the American state

The Civil War and Reconstruction periods encompassed three stages by which a starkly defined and exclusive political coalition captured the nascent American state, infused that

* Richard F. Bensel (1991) *Yankee Leviathan: The Origins of Central State Authority in America, 1859–1877*, Cambridge: Cambridge University Press, pp. 2–8.

state with vast powers to remake, the national political economy, and, finally, was compelled by internal contradictions within the alliance to compromise its own control of the state apparatus. The first of these stages entailed *capture*: the ascent to power of a cohesive political-economic alliance (the Republican party) combined with the exit of its major opponent (the southern plantation elite). Up to the point of capture, the American state had been little more than an arena in which contending forces and coalitions in the national political economy competed over decisions related to continental settlement and foreign policy. The secession of the South and the decision of the North to attempt military reunification produced an *explosive expansion* of central state authority within the framework of the Republican alliance. Part of this explosive expansion can be attributed to the enactment and implementation of the political economic agenda of the groups allied within the Republican party. The secession of the South in effect broke the logjam behind which this agenda had languished in the years just prior to the Civil War and a major portion of state expansion was composed of policies that had been proposed and debated in the prewar period.[1] The mobilization of the northern political economy for war, however, both provided the major impetus for state expansion and reshaped the antebellum agenda. The war had an even greater impact on the structure and substantive policies of the emergent southern Confederacy.

Prosecution of the war, implementation of the major elements on the northern agenda, and the reentry of the South into the political system all combined to *compromise control* of the central state by the Republican party and allow the development of internal contradictions within the alliance to halt expansion. As an increasing divergence of interest within the alliance spawned factional conflict within the Republican party, support for reconstruction of the southern political economy withered away. With the return of former Confederate nationalists to Congress, the Democrats became a competitive alternative to the Republicans in national politics. All of these factors – Republican factionalism, the return of former Confederates, and Democratic competition – brought the Civil War party-state to an end. The Civil War and Reconstruction period thus encapsulated several stages in which a starkly defined and exclusive party coalition captured the nascent American state, infused the central government with vast powers to remake the national political economy, and, finally, was compelled by internal contradictions within its alliance to compromise its own control of the state apparatus. The process delineated by these three stages produced the context for the Compromise of 1877 – the resolution of the Hayes–Tilden presidential election in the Republican's favor and the associated withdrawal of Union troops from the South. This, in turn, slowed the pace of post-Reconstruction state development. Once it became possible for the "rebel" South to participate in a winning presidential coalition, the state bureaucracy became a potential balance-wheel between rival political-economic coalitions. With that possibility of a balance-of-power position in national politics and the emergence of civil service protection from partisan influence, the state could at last begin to develop a "statist" sensibility, an identity and interest apart from any class or partisan interest.[2]

From 1861 to 1877, the American state and the Republican party were essentially the same thing; the federal government was simply the vehicle of common interests in economic development associated with northern finance, industry, and free soil agriculture.[3] By 1877, party and state had become dissociated to such an extent that the individual factions of the Republican party, particularly finance capital and western agrarians, could entertain alliances with the Democratic party and the general interests of state sovereignty and expansion were no longer the exclusive province of northern Republicans. From a statist perspective, this dissociation might be viewed as the silver lining that accompanied Reconstruction's failure. While we can easily exaggerate this transition from unmediated party rule to state-centered pluralistic nationalism (which, in any case, occurred slowly), the transition from a revolutionary party-state to state-centered pluralism is still significant, and possibly generalizable as an historical process.[4] This process can be profitably contrasted with more conventional theories of modernization.

Modernization and American state development

Samuel Huntington and others have argued that political modernization has involved three elements. The first of these has been the rationalization of authority throughout the nation – which is accomplished by the destruction of decentralized institutions which might resist the extension of that authority. The second has been the differentiation of new political functions and the development of specialized institutions to perform those functions. The last factor in modernization has been the broadening of political participation, primarily through the emergence of mass-based political parties. In most European societies, modernization occurred in that order: first, the extension and consolidation of central state power; second, bureaucratic specialization; and, last, popular political participation. In America the order was reversed, and it is said that the early emergence of broad political participation in the form of manhood suffrage was premature because it aborted the development of the specialized and politically insulated bureaucracies necessary to a strong central government.[5] The nineteenth-century patronage-based party system was characterized by issueless competition and retarded the growth of a strong state because it allowed constantly shifting public opinion to sweep unhindered through the structure of government, preventing the erection of stable, insulated, and self-conscious bureaucratic forms. From this perspective, the late nineteenth century was a period in which the nascent institutions of a modern state groped blindly through a whirlwind of patronage, corruption, and sloganeering in an attempt to "recast" (Stephen Skowronek's word) the basis of American government.

Modernization itself "involves such basic changes in the structure a society as rapid economic development, urbanization, industrialization, the creation of an integrated national economic and political structure, and generally, the spread of market-oriented capitalist economic relations and of mental attitudes viewing continuous social change as natural and desirable." From this perspective, the American Civil War was a part of the process by which the "modernizing" North integrated the "premodern" South into the national political and economic system. Painted in even broader strokes, the American Civil War appears as but one of many conflicts in the nineteenth-century world economy by which industrializing regions and nations successfully penetrated and reorganized the socioeconomic bases of less-developed, usually agrarian societies.[6]

While generally sympathetic to the modernization school, the theoretical perspective of this book parts company with some of the assumptions and conclusions of that approach. First, the connection between modernization and state development is more complicated than many of these scholars suggest. In one formulation of the thesis, state expansion in the late nineteenth century was the indicated response to two developmental imperatives:

the emergence of inter- and intraclass conflict that accompanied rapid growth in the capitalist economy and a general, equally rapid increase in social complexity. These imperatives provided the context, even the necessity, for the emergence of a "modern" American state in the sense that quasi-autonomous administrative structures would have made the management of class conflict and the coordination of complex social functions possible.[7] Recognition of these objective requirements by influential elements of the national elite, it is argued, will (and did) move the state forward on a modernizing trajectory even in cases, such as the American one, where the statist response was painfully slow and often inadequate.

Without exception, scholars associated with the developmental school have viewed the industrializing, urban North as the bearer of American modernization and the Civil War as presenting one of the most important administrative challenges of the nineteenth century. On the basis of these two facts, it could be argued that the response of the modernizing North to the requirements of the American Civil War should have been much more state-centered and administratively advanced than that of the comparatively underdeveloped South. In fact, however, many features of the Confederate war mobilization were far more statist and modern than their counterparts in the Union (see Chapter 3). This appraisal does not in itself vitiate a connection between modernization and state development. For example, the theoretical framework could be amended by interpreting war mobilizations as statist responses driven more by the battlefield challenge presented by the enemy than by the domestic consequences of economic development, thus excepting war from the normal course of state development. Even so, proper recognition and correct implementation of the statist response to such challenges requires a modern sensibility not often attributed to the southern plantation elite. On these grounds alone, we might conclude that the (already contingent) connection between modernization and state development in the nineteenth century was somewhat looser than has been suggested.

A second problem with the thesis as applied to the American case arises out of the tendency to assume a "unitary" society in the sense that modernization policies advance the development of the entire society or are a response to external challenges arising out of increased participation in the world system.[8] On both counts, the reality was very different in the United States in the nineteenth century. In the United States, central state policies promoted modernization primarily in the North and, to a lesser extent, the West. Economic development took place in those regions at the expense of the southern periphery, which fell further and further behind the remainder of the nation throughout the late nineteenth century (see Chapter 7).[9] State-sponsored modernization in the South (such as the replacement of slavery with more market-oriented versions of peonage) was carried out only incidentally, if at all, for national developmental reasons.[10] The primary purpose and impact of such policies was a weakening of the political economic base of the southern plantation elite, not the promotion of social efficiencies arising out of free market allocation of the southern labor supply.

Notes

1. See, for example, David M. Potter, *The Impending Crisis: 1848–1861* (New York: Harper Torchbooks, 1976), pp. 390–1.
2. With appropriate caveats, the developments of this period correspond to one of Michael Mann's conditions for the emergence of state autonomy: the creation of "a certain 'space'

. . . in which a state elite could manoeuvre, play off classes against war factions and other states, and so stake out an area and degree of power autonomy for itself." See Michael Mann, "The Autonomous Power of the State: Its Origins, Mechanisms and Results," *Archives Europeennes de Sociologie* 25 (1984), pp. 186–7.

3. As C. Vann Woodward put it, "the Republican party had . . . become the conservative party, spokesman of vested interests and big business, defender of an elaborate system of tariffs, subsidies, currency laws, privileged banks, railroads, and corporations. . . . The old Whig element of the North that had combined with the Free-Soil Democrats and Abolitionists in the fifties to form the Republican party was on top in 1876 and had written its antebellum economic program into law." *Reunion and Reaction: The Compromise of 1877 and the End of Reconstruction* (Boston: Little, Brown, 1966), p. 35.

4. Within the scope of this book, "unmediated party rule" and "state-centered pluralistic nationalism" can be viewed as polar opposites. Unmediated party rule describes a regime that meets three criteria: (1) a political system in which a single party dominates all other contenders for power; (2) the dominant party coalition excludes important groups and classes in the national political economy from almost all participation in government decision making; and (3) membership in the dominant party is the most important single qualification for office holding within the state bureaucracy. In contrast, state-centered pluralism describes a political system in which two or more parties are serious contenders for power, the social bases of competing political parties contain at least a fraction of all important groups and classes in the national political economy, and party membership is not a qualification for bureaucratic service.

5. Samuel P. Huntington, *Political Order in Changing Societies* (New Haven, Conn.: Yale University Press, 1968), pp. 93–139. Huntington also accepts Cyril Black's argument that Union victory in the American Civil War marked the "consolidation of modernizing leadership" in the United States (p. 46). Also see Stephen Skowronek, *Building a New American State: The Expansion of National Administrative Capacities 1877–1920* (Cambridge: Cambridge University Press, 1982), pp. 6–8, 39–40; Gianfranco Poggi, *The Development of the Modern State* (Stanford, Calif.: Stanford University Press, 1978), p. 93; Charles C. Bright, "The State in the United States during the Nineteenth Century," in Charles Bright and Susan Harding, eds., *Statemaking and Social Movements: Essays in History and Theory* (Ann Arbor: University of Michigan Press, 1984), pp. 123–4.

6. The quotation is from Eric Foner, *Politics and Ideology in the Age of the Civil War* (New York: Oxford University Press, 1980), p. 20; also see S. N. Eisenstadt, *Modernization: Protest and Change* (Englewood Cliffs, N.J.: Prentice-Hall, 1966); and George Fredrickson, ed., *A Nation Divided: Problems and Issues of the Civil War and Reconstruction* (Minneapolis: Burgess, 1978); Raimondo Luraghi, "The Civil War and the Modernization of American Society: Social Structure and Industrial Revolution in the Old South before and during the War," *Civil War History* 18 (September 1972): 230–50; Barrington Moore, Jr., *Social Origins of Dictatorship and Democracy: Lord and Peasant in the Making of the Modern World* (Boston: Beacon Press, 1967), ch. 3; Richard D. Brown, *Modernization: The Transformation of American Life, 1600–1865* (New York: Hill and Wang, 1976), ch. 7; and C. E. Black, *The Dynamics of Modernization: A Study in Comparative History* (New York: Harper & Row, 1966), p. 111.

7. Skowronek, *Building a New American State*, p. 11. Also see Bright, "The State in the United States during the Nineteenth Century," pp. 121–58.

8. This preoccupation with national destiny led Barrington Moore to pose, as a counterfactual possibility, "what would have happened had the Southern plantation system been able to establish itself in the West by the middle of the nineteenth century and surrounded the Northeast. Then the United States would have been in the position of some modernizing countries today, with a latifundia economy, a dominant antidemocratic aristocracy, and a weak and dependent commercial and industrial class, unable and unwilling to push forward toward political democracy." *Social Origins of Dictatorship and Democracy*, p. 153. Given the

climatic constraints on the territorial expansion of the southern plantation economy and the fact that antebellum southern political systems were, with few exceptions, as fully democratic as any in the North and more democratic than any contemporary European system, the historical possibility of this counterfactual faces major theoretical and empirical difficulties. The point, however, is not to criticize Moore's vision but, instead, to suggest a reason why he chose to project a southern-dominated United States rather than the much more plausible separation of the South into a new nation. Moore's "unitary" counterfactual was chosen over southern independence, I would argue, because he wanted to compare the American experience with the unitary histories of Britain, France, and Japan. In the process, however, he implicitly confused a hypothetical contest over control of the national political economy with a struggle for separate national existence. An exception to the mainstream emphasis on *national* modernization is David F. Good, "Uneven Development in the Nineteenth Century: A Comparison of the Habsburg Empire and the United States," *Journal of Economic History* 46 (March 1986): 137–51.

9. See, for example, Richard A. Easterlin, "Regional Income Trends, 1840–1950," in S. E. Harris, ed., *American Economic History* (New York: McGraw-Hill, 1961); and Easterlin, "Interregional Differences in Per Capita Income, Population, and Total Income, 1840–1950," in *Trends in the American Economy in the Nineteenth Century* (Princeton, N.J.: Princeton University Press, 1960), pp. 85–9. Though this book will take the position that the Civil War on the whole contributed to the modernization of the American nation, that contention is subject to a number of important qualifications and is even susceptible to repudiation in terms of national economic growth. See, for example, Thomas C. Cochran, "Did the Civil War Retard Industrialization?" and Stanley L. Engerman, "The Economic Impact of the Civil War," in Ralph Andreano, ed., *The Economic Impact of the American Civil War* (Cambridge, Mass.: Schenkman, 1967), pp. 167–79, 188–209.

10. The most general form of the modernization thesis maintains that the replacement of slavery with some form of labor market and the removal of plantation-elite opposition in national politics were necessary steps for the economic development of the United States and says little or nothing about their impact upon the South. In fact, the combination of these two alterations in the national political economy produced an environment in which representatives of southern plantation and subsistence agriculture could not resist the massive redistribution of wealth and resources to the northern economy that enables American industrialization to proceed. For that reason alone, the Civil War can be interpreted as a modernizing event for the northern industrial system and, plausibly, for the nation. Just as certainly, however, the policies of the federal government during the Civil War and Reconstruction retarded southern economic development by systematically redistributing wealth to the North. Secondary consequences of this redistribution of wealth include strong southern opposition to central state expansion and progressive disfranchisement of blacks and poor whites in the last decades of the nineteenth century. A complete account of the demodernizing influence of the Civil War upon the American South would include references to all three impacts: retardation of economic development, resistance to central state expansion, and a retreat from mass-based political participation. See, for example, J. Morgan Kousser, *The Shaping of Southern Politics: Suffrage Restriction and the Establishment of the One-Party South, 1880–1910* (New Haven, Conn.: Yale University Press, 1974) for an account of disfranchisement; and Richard Bensel, *Sectionalism and American Political Development, 1880–1980* (Madison: University of Wisconsin Press, 1984), ch. 3, for a description of southern opposition to expansion of the central state in the late nineteenth century.

CHAPTER 22

John Tosh

'WHAT SHOULD HISTORIANS DO WITH MASCULINITY? REFLECTIONS ON NINETEENTH-CENTURY BRITAIN' (1994)*

The following extract is the second one in this Reader by John Tosh, the author of several books on masculinity and African history, in addition to *The Pursuit of History: Aims, Methods and New Directions in the Study of Modern History* (see pp. 69–71). The extract is from his article 'What Should Historians do with Masculinity? Reflections on Nineteenth-Century Britain', published in *History Workshop Journal* (1994), in which the form of constructionism is that of gender history. Tosh wants to make the claim that the character of 'masculine formation' in the middle years of the nineteenth century was 'largely determined' by the 'balance struck' between the three key components in the lives of men: home, work and their male associations. His aim is to decouple the category of masculinity from other categories of analysis. He dismisses the old interpretation of 'separate spheres', basing his explanation on his concept of a 'linked system'. While this is 'characterized . . . by contradiction and instability', he still thinks of it as being one of the 'most promising ways of pinning down the social dynamics of masculinity'. The extract illustrates how the notion of provisionality is almost always built into constructionist forms of history. The intention is to systematically whittle away at this provisionality through the fitting of the evidence into a coherent, systematic and plausible explanatory model which, in this case, is to construct the category of masculinity. Tosh then starts the process by employing a simple two-class model to evidence the unstable nature of masculinity (later he notes how gender status cannot be reduced to class status by acknowledging the work of agency). The extract clearly indicates that the pleasure for readers of much constructionist history is not to learn about the true nature of the past as it is, but to see how the historian formulates it and puts it together. In this case, it is the fabrication of an architecture of balance and contradiction designed by its author.

I N D W E L L I N G O N T H E importance of home, work and association as minimal components of masculine identity, I have doubtless laboured the obvious. My reason for doing so is that I have wanted to prepare the ground for the more interesting claim that the precise character of masculine formation at any time is largely determined by the

---

* John Tosh (1994) 'What Should Historians do with Masculinity? Reflections on Nineteenth-Century Britain', *History Workshop Journal*, 38, Oxford: Oxford University Press, pp. 70–2.

balance struck *between* these three components. I think it's now widely recognized that constant emphasis on the 'separation of spheres' is misleading, partly because men's privileged ability to pass freely between the public and the private was integral to the social order. And some notion of complementarity is always implied by that key nineteenth-century indicator of masculinity achieved, 'independence', combining as it did dignified work, sole maintenance of the family, and free association on terms of equality with other men. But it's much rarer to see these elements considered as any such system must be, by contradiction and instability. Yet this, it seems to, me, is one of the most promising ways of pinning down the social dynamics of masculinity.

Consider, first of all, the Victorian middle class. Any notion of a solid bourgeois masculinity is not tenable. The balance between my three components was inherently unstable and often gave visible signs of strain. Essentially this was because the ideology of domesticity raised the profile of home life far beyond its traditional place in men's lives, and hence posed in an acute form the conflict between the private and public constituents of masculinity. Already in Cobbett's writings one can see the tensions between family life and 'the gabble and balderdash of a club or pot-house company'. By mid-century, when middle-class mores placed the tavern off-limits, this conflict was less stark. The decorous entertainment of lectures and concerts, not to mention collective action in the public interest, appeared to be in less conflict with domestic values, though real devotees of domestic comfort had to be reminded that duty in the public sphere might require some personal sacrifice. More fundamental was the clash between work and home. In which sphere was a man really himself? The implications of the work ethic, in its unyielding Victorian form, were clear, and in spelling them out Carlyle had immense and enduring influence. But there was a strong current running the other way. The adage 'an Englishman's home is his castle', which enjoyed wide currency by the 1850s, conveyed a double meaning of possession against all comers, and of refuge or retreat from the world beyond. This second meaning spoke with special force to those middle-class men who experienced the world of work as alienating or morally undermining. From Froude through Dickens to William Hale White, Victorian fiction propounds the notion that only at home can a man be truly himself; as Froude put it in *The Nemesis of Faith* (1849), 'we lay aside our mask and drop our tools, and are no longer lawyers, sailors, soldiers, statesmen, clergymen, but only men'. And, lest you should suppose that historians were above this alienation, Coventry Patmore (writing in the same vein) specifically included the scholar 'wearying his wits over arid parchments'. By the 1880s the balance had shifted. For the professional classes at least, domesticity was increasingly associated with ennui, routine and feminine constraint. The result was a higher rate of male celibacy, rising club membership, and a vogue for 'adventure' – both in the real-life hazards of mountaineering and the rougher sports, and in what Sir Arthur Conan Doyle admiringly called 'the modern masculine novel' of Robert Louis Stevenson and Rider Haggard. For middle-class men at the turn of the century the respective pulls of home and the homosocial world were much more evenly matched than they had been for their grandfathers. Perhaps no clearer evidence could be found than the enormous appeal of Scouting to boys and scoutmasters alike: the camp-fire was all that the domestic hearth was not.

In the working class men's commitment to home was more problematic still. In most cases there was of course far less to hold the working man there. If his home served also as a workshop it was unlikely to boast the modicum of amenities which might draw him to his own fireside. If he was an employee on average earnings or less, his wife's work at home combined with domestic overcrowding were likely to increase the attractions of the pub. There were plenty of people within the working class who deplored this state of affairs. Anna Clark has drawn attention to that strand within Chartism which advocated a domesticated manhood, like the London Working Men's Association which denied 'the attributes and characters of *men*' to those who were forgetful of their duties as fathers and husbands. By the 1870s the claim to a dignified home life was part of the stock-in-trade of trade union leaders. It seems clear that in the late Victorian period there was a growing minority of comparatively well-paid skilled workers who entirely supported the household and spent much of their leisure-time there. Yet the reality could be very different outside this privileged group. Both Ellen Ross and Carl Chinn describe an urban working-class world from which private patriarchy had almost disappeared. The husband was often made to feel a bull-in-a-china-shop, excluded from the emotional currents of the family. More likely than not, as a boy he would have developed domestic and nurturing skills, but an important part of his growing up to manhood was to 'forget' these skills. The wife, on the other hand, was the one who maintained vital neighbourhood support, who negotiated with landlords and welfare workers, and who supervised the children's schooling. Even moving house was often her decision. London magistrates sometimes spoke of the wife's 'headship of the home'. This was in the context of domestic assault – surely a symptom of the acute masculine ambivalence experienced by men married to women who so effectively controlled the domestic sphere? One can argue whether working men's attachment to convivial drinking was cause or effect of their discomfort in the home, but cutting a figure in the pub was clearly a far less equivocal sign of masculine status than presiding over the home. Charting the ebb and flow of men's commitment to domestic life, whether in the working class or the bourgeoisie has much to reveal about the dynamics of masculinity – then and now.

CHAPTER 23

Marion Gibson

READING WITCHCRAFT: STORIES OF EARLY ENGLISH WITCHES (1999)*

Although technically not a card-carrying historian but a lecturer in English at the University of Exeter, Marion Gibson represents a new generation of constructionist 'historians' who have broken down conventional disciplinary boundaries. In her study *Reading Witchcraft: Stories of Early English Witches* (1999) she challenges the view that scholars can use primary sources, such as pamphlet accounts and legal records about witchcraft, as straightforward foundations

---

* Marion Gibson (1999) *Reading Witchcraft: Stories of Early English Witches*, London: Routledge, pp. 4–6.

of 'truth'. In the following extract she seems to be saying that, as the form of the story changes, so does its content. She casts doubt on both the records and the stories constructed from them as being windows 'through which we can view early modern life'. She insists that historians should be more circumspect and tentative in their assertions concerning the trajectory of source to discourse. Unusually, she begins by dismantling the concept of 'truth', 'reality' and 'fact'. She asks how can historians know the truth – what she defines as a 'truthful story' – about the 'impossible crime' of being a witch? Inevitably, she begins with the event that was alleged at the time to be connected with magic. While she notes the possibility of truthful stories defined as that version of reality that satisfies an audience, she soon falls back on the notion 'that we are trying to reconstruct a once tangible reality, also called "the truth"'. The representation that we think we are justified in believing has, she argues, to be based 'on internal evidence'. She maintains that we must compare and contrast accounts, and that even our subjectivity 'can be both informed and reasoned'. She concludes with the observation that historians can construct 'tentative hierarchies of the truthfulness of accounts – a genealogy of witchcraft . . . following multiple and diverging branches of inquiry back from a point once accepted as stable'. Here again, even the sophisticated constructionist – one who is fully aware of the problems associated with representation and narrative making – must feel that, like the novice swimmer, she must keep a toe on the bottom.

RECENT CHALLENGES TO this view have emphasised different aspects of early modern conflict (over trade, local politics or female power, for example) but basically all accept that it is relatively safe to reconstruct real events in early modern England from pamphlet accounts of witchcraft, or from the legal records or eyewitness stories on which they were so often based. In this way modern scholars and writers on witchcraft have responded to stories of witchcraft in exactly the same way as the sixteenth- and early seventeenth-century authorities did: they have synthesised the stories, looked for patterns in them that would allow coherent interpretation of supposedly 'real' events, and treated the stories about witchcraft as if they were almost transparent, a window through which we can view early modern life and see, vividly, witches and their victims interacting. While good historians like Alan Macfarlane, Keith Thomas, J.A. Sharpe and Clive Holmes do not believe in magic, they often believe that other activities or occurrences described in witchcraft pamphlets are factual. This book sets out to question this assumption, and to turn it into a far more tentative assertion. It is important to explore the truthfulness of stories of witchcraft, looking at who told them and why, how they were recorded, how they might have been distorted or stereotyped, and at factors which shape their presentation in print.

Before beginning, it is important to define what is meant by 'truth', 'reality', 'fact' and other such terms. If we are questioning the truthfulness of stories, then what would we wish to define as a 'true' story about witchcraft? This would depend in part on what we believe 'witchcraft' to be. In simplified terms, this book proceeds on the basis that magic does not work, but that some 'witches' may have believed both that it did, and that they used it. Equally, it seems likely that some 'witches' had no experience of magical practices beyond the beliefs and stories current in their communities – that, when prosecuted, they were accused of a crime which they had never even tried to commit. All these people would have been, in modern terms, 'innocent' victims of a misconception about the possibilities of human and diabolic power. A 'witch', for the purposes of this discussion, is thus a person defined as such by his or her society, and has no intrinsic, essential qualities which would make the label an objective one. Diane Purkiss calls such a person a 'blank screen' on to which fantasies were projected. I would add that the 'witch' may choose to accept the label, and may even court it or create it, but this book concentrates on the moment when the community codifies its identification of the person as a witch in a legal document or printed story, and on what happens during and after that process and because of it. The definition of witchcraft and of what it is to be a witch would thus depend in part on stereotypes rather than individual 'realities'. Stereotypes are defined here as agreed patterns used by communities and members of those communities to identify individual events or people as connected with the impossible crime of witchcraft. The stereotype may or may not reflect the actual form and sequence of events, or the features of an individual's life, but whether it reflects these or not it is recognisable chiefly by its ubiquity. It is unconnected with reality but follows its features closely. Thus, this book does not seek to identify real objects at the heart of the definition of 'witchcraft' and 'a witch': in textual terms – in pamphlets, particularly – both ideas are definable only from the outside, since any central reality is inaccessible. One is left with only a husk of representation, which suggests the shape of a reality which is missing, but also highlights its absence.

How then, can one define a truthful story about this impossible crime? I would suggest that by 'truth' or 'accuracy' we should mean 'closeness to events'. Events such as the speaking of curses or incantations, arrests, begging, illness and neighbourly quarrels happened tangibly in early modern England and were recorded, and although we can have no access to these events beyond the accounts given by those who recorded them, we can be fairly certain that at the centre of each cluster of accounts is some event, or string of events, which were perceived by contemporary observers to be connected with alleged magic – however distorted, mistaken or multinatured the accounts of these events may appear to us to be. Given this definition of truth, it is up to individual readers of accounts to decide what is true – which account is closest to inaccessible tangibilities or 'reality'. Malcolm Gaskill suggests that 'truth is no more than a version of reality which satisfies an audience, or which cannot either be proved or disproved more conclusively', but it is also the case that we are trying to reconstruct a once tangible reality, also called 'the truth'. Our decision about which version to accept as the best representation of this, our accepted 'truth', usually has to be based on internal evidence: on our trust of the teller of each event, which we might assess by (among other factors) an examination of his or her tone, level of access to the reported events, and possible reasons for perceiving them in a certain way and telling the story in a particular form. We can also compare accounts of events, looking for consensus or difference, and add to our judgement – which will always be subjective – other evidence such as records of unrelated aspects of the lives of the storytellers or their communities. Subjectivity is inevitable in any assessment of such hotly contested and unfamiliar material, but this should not prevent inquiry while we await an impossibly objective methodology, since subjectivity can be both informed and reasoned, and therefore useful to the scholar. By using the above definitions, and by recourse to the means described above, we can produce some tentative hierarchies of the truthfulness of accounts, although individual versions of the hierarchies might differ substantially. This book does not pretend to find a grand unifying theory of the relative truthfulness of accounts of witchcraft, but it attempts to make readers aware of both the necessity for creating such hierarchies of truthfulness and of the occasionally insoluble difficulties of constructing it. It is a kind of empirically based 'genealogy' of witchcraft in the Foucauldian sense, following multiple and diverging branches of inquiry back from a point once accepted as stable: the definition of witchcraft, our knowledge of what witchcraft was.

CHAPTER 24

Paul Thompson

THE VOICE OF THE PAST: ORAL HISTORY ([1978] 2000)*

Oral history necessarily confronts many of the basic epistemological issues that most constructionists avoid. Notable among these is that the sources may take the historian beyond the archive often to locate wholly unknown written documents, photographs, etc., which can place extra pressure on their model-making and testing. This is recognised at the start of the next extract. Research Professor in the Department of Sociology at the University of Essex, Paul Thompson has long been associated with the development of life and oral history researched and written within the disciplines of sociology and social history. The author of several books, in the extract reprinted here from *The Voice of the Past: Oral History* ([1978] 2000), Thompson turns this necessity into a virtue. Anchored to the epistemological model, he argues that having first-hand testimony from the 'rank and file' means there 'can be no doubt that this should make for a more realistic reconstruction of the past'. His choice of the term 'reconstruction' is revealing of his desire for the truth of reality, although, as he acknowledges, it is 'complex and many-sided'. Much more significantly than this, however, is the fact that oral history meets head-on one of the most awkward of epistemological problems. This is the collapse of the distinction between subject and object. Thompson does not fully appreciate this, even though he acknowledges that 'the social message' of the historian 'is usually present'. In fact, he tries to make out a case that oral history ('evidence from the underside') is more of a safeguard against this aberration than any other form of source. He notes that once historians 'start to interview [them] they find themselves inevitably working with others'. The conclusion he reaches, however, is that finding themselves 'off their desks' and 'sharing experience on a human level' is somehow a better way to get at the truth.

* Paul Thompson ([1978] 2000) *The Voice of the Past: Oral History*, Oxford: Oxford University Press, pp. 5–8.

FOR MOST EXISTING KINDS of history, probably the critical effect of this new approach is to allow evidence from a new direction. The historian of working-class politics can juxtapose the statements of the government or the trade union headquarters with the voice of the rank and file—both apathetic and militant. There can be no doubt that this should make for a more realistic reconstruction of the past. Reality is complex and many-sided; and it is a primary merit of oral history that to a much greater extent than most sources it allows the original multiplicity of standpoints to be recreated. But this advantage is important not just for the writing of history. Most historians make implicit or explicit judgements—quite properly, since the social purpose of history demands an understanding of the past which relates directly or indirectly to the present. Modern professional historians are less open with their social message than Macaulay or Marx, since scholarly standards are seen to conflict with declared bias. But the social message is usually present, however obscured. It is quite easy for a historian to give most of his attention and quotations to those social leaders whom he admires, without giving any direct opinion of his own. Since the nature of most existing records is to reflect the standpoint of authority, it is not surprising that the judgement of history has more often than not vindicated the wisdom of the powers that be. Oral history by contrast makes a much fairer trial possible: witnesses can now also be called from the under-classes, the unprivileged, and the defeated. It provides a more realistic and fair reconstruction of the past, a challenge to the established account. In so doing, oral history has radical implication for the social message of history as a whole.

At the same time oral history implies for most kinds of history some shift of focus. Thus the educational historian becomes concerned with the experiences of children and students as well as the problems of teachers and administrators. The military and naval historian can look beyond command level strategy and equipment to the conditions, recreations, and morale of other ranks and the lower deck. The social historian can turn from bureaucrats and politicians to poverty itself, and learn how the poor saw the relieving officer and how they survived his refusals. The political historian can approach the voter at home and at work; and can hope to understand even the working-class conservative, who produced no newspapers or organizations for investigation. The economist can watch both employer and worker as social beings and at their ordinary work, and so come closer to understanding the typical economic process, and its successes and contradictions.

In some fields, oral history can result not merely in a shift in focus, but also in the opening up of important new areas of inquiry. Labour historians, for example, are enabled for the first time to undertake effective studies of the ill-unionized majority of male workers, of women workers, and of the normal experience of work and its impact on the family and the community. They are no longer confined to those trades which were unionized, or those which gained contemporary publicity and investigation because of strikes or extreme poverty. Urban historians similarly can turn from well-explored problem areas like the slums to look at other typical forms of urban social life: the small industrial or market town, for example, or the middle-class surburb, constructing the local patterns of social distinctions, mutual help between neighbours and kin, leisure and work. They can even approach from the inside the history of immigrant groups—a kind of history which is certain to become more important in Britain, and is mainly documented only from outside as a social problem. These opportunities—and many others—are shared by social historians: the study of working-class leisure and culture, for example; or of crime from the point of view of the ordinary, often undetected and socially semi-tolerated poacher, shoplifter, or work-pilferer.

Perhaps the most striking feature of all, however, is the transforming impact of oral history upon the history of the family. Without its evidence, the historian can discover very little indeed about either the ordinary family's contacts with neighbours and kin, or its internal relationships. The roles of husband and wife, the upbringing of girls and boys, emotional and material conflicts and dependence, the struggle of youth for independence, courtship, sexual behaviour within and outside marriage, contraception and abortion—all these were effectively secret areas. The only clues were to be gleaned from aggregate statistics, and from a few—usually partial—observers. The historical paucity which results is well summed up in Michael Anderson's brilliant, speculative, but abstract study of *Family Structure in Nineteenth-Century Lancashire* (1971): a lop-sided, empty frame. With the use of interviewing, it is now possible to develop a much fuller history of the family over the last ninety years, and to establish its main patterns and changes over time, and from place to place, during the life cycle and between the sexes. The history of childhood as a whole becomes practicable for the first time. And given the dominance of the family through housework, domestic service, and motherhood in the lives of most women, an almost equivalent broadening of scope is brought to the history of women.

In all these fields of history, by introducing new evidence from the underside, by shifting the focus and opening new areas of inquiry, by challenging some of the assumptions and accepted judgements of historians, by bringing recognition to substantial groups of people who had been ignored, a cumulative process of transformation is set in motion. The scope of historical writing itself is enlarged and enriched; and at the same time its social message changes. History becomes, to put it simply, more democratic. The chronicle of kings has taken into its concern the life experience of ordinary people. But there is another dimension to this change, of equal importance. The process of writing history changes along with the content. The use of oral evidence breaks through the barriers between the chroniclers and their audience; between the educational institution and the outside world.

This change springs from the essentially creative and co-operative nature of the oral history method. Of course oral evidence once recorded can be used by lone scholars in libraries just like any other type of documentary source. But to be content with this is to lose a key advantage of the method: its flexibility, the ability to pin down evidence just where it is needed. Once historians start to interview they find themselves inevitably working with others—at the least, with their informants. And to be a successful interviewer a new set of skills is needed, including an understanding of human relationships. Some people can find these skills almost immediately, others need to learn them; but in contrast to the cumulative process of learning and amassing information which gives such advantage in documentary analysis and interpretation to the professional historian well on in life, it is possible to learn quite quickly to become an effective interviewer. Hence historians as field-workers, while in important respects retaining the advantages of professional knowledge, also find themselves off their desks, sharing experience on a human level.

CHAPTER 25

Mark S.R. Jenner

'THE GREAT DOG MASSACRE' (1997)*

Finally, in another form of constructionism that leans heavily on anthropology, ethnography and the notion of literary representation and critical thinking, Mark S.R. Jenner, who teaches history at the University of York, has examined the nature of canine regulation and slaughter during periods of epidemic. In the following extract taken from 'The Great Dog Massacre' in William G. Naphy and Penny Roberts (eds), *Fear in Early Modern Society* (1997), Jenner briefly explores how social order was maintained in early modern towns. He describes the ways in which dogs mediated human conduct and were generally 'privileged creatures'. Invoking the description of dogs by the leading French anthropologist of the last century, Claude Lévi-Strauss, as 'metonymical humans', Jenner explores how dogs were easily transformed into culprits when plague appeared and what this represented for the overturn of established practices of public order. Jenner uses such acts as a metaphor through which to explain the reinstatement of authority and the 'repression of human bestiality at a time when sinfulness was being punished'. Dogs also became the representation of social status as certain bourgeois pooches were spared the cull, and how the wandering dog was viewed as a representation of the dangers of unregulated social intercourse. It seems that not all constructionism is only hard-core social science; some of it can be mixed with literary constructionism as well.

IN AND AROUND CITIES dogs were used for guarding the house and for work turning spits in large kitchens. Butchers in particular kept large and fierce dogs, sometimes for baiting animals before slaughter. However, it is likely that many urban dogs were not particularly closely tied to one household. Certainly nineteenth-century commentators complained that the dogs of the poor were turned out to fend for themselves for much of the day; few labouring households could afford to feed an animal when it could scavenge at least part of its own living.

Consequently English towns regulated dogs from the Middle Ages, if not before. In medieval Winchester, for instance, butchers' dogs were to be chained up for much of the day. During the late fourteenth and fifteenth centuries mayors of London issued proclamations against permitting dogs to wander the streets without a guard; similar provisions were general in early modern towns. Such regulations were not without foundation. Sessions records contain a fair number of prosecutions for anti-social dogs. In 1612, for instance, the Middlesex justices had to deal with one Ann Fisher of Saffron Hill, 'for not reforminge of a Curste Mastie Dogge wch hath thrice bitten one Thomas Dallyn . . . who goeth . . . in greete danger of the said dogge'.

---

* Mark S.R. Jenner (1997) 'The Great Dog Massacre', *Fear in Early Modern Society* by William Naphy and Penny Roberts (eds), Manchester: Manchester University Press, pp. 52–6.

Canine slaughter in time of epidemic was in part an extension of this habitual regulation. As we have seen, the London plague orders particularly singled out for death dogs which howled or otherwise annoyed their neighbours. In other words, without the slightest contemporary medical justification, those dogs deemed a nuisance were also treated as the likeliest to spread the infection. The slaughter policy thus at one level marked an intensification of household regulation and of the norms of good neighbourliness. Just as Robert Darnton demonstrated that a story about the killing and torture of cats could be a rich cultural historical source with which to explore the psychodynamics of the eighteenth-century bourgeois household, so the slaughter of dogs can illuminate the maintenance of order in early modern towns, for, to adapt the axioms of Lévi-Strauss and S. J. Tambiah, dogs in early modern England were good to think with and good to prohibit.

For dogs were not just ubiquitous, they also carried an extraordinary variety of emphatically anthropocentric meanings. M. P. Tilley records 113 proverbial uses of 'dog' in sixteenth- and seventeenth-century England. As Jean-Claude Schmitt demonstrated, in folklore and popular culture hounds could epitomise suprahuman loyalty, selflessness and obedience. Within learned culture the *Odyssey* memorialised the faithfulness of Ulysses' dog, Argus, which alone recognised and greeted his master after his long absence before expiring. As Pope rendered it in the early eighteenth century,

> When wise *Ulysses*, from his native coast
> Long kept by wars, and long by tempests tost,
> Arriv'd at last, poor, old, disguis'd, alone,
> To all his friends, and ev'n his Queen unknown . . .
> Scorn'd by those slaves his former bounty fed,
> Forgot of all his own domestic crew;
> The faithful Dog alone his rightful Master knew!

The extent to which dogs provided metaphors for aspects of human conduct and character, even before the English began figuring themselves as the Bulldog, indicates just how far they were privileged creatures. They lived close to human beings and often carried human names; they were, in Lévi-Strauss's formulation, metonymical humans. Despite Vesalius' polemical juxtaposition of a canine and a human skull in illustrations of *De Humani Corporis Fabrica*, in order to show how Galenic anatomy had incorrectly used a dog as the basis for human anatomy, in many experiments during the seventeenth and early eighteenth centuries canine bodies acted in the place of human ones.

In part, precisely this privileged status with regard to humans meant that they were easily understood to share diseases with humans. They shared human spaces, food and names; they could thus readily be imagined as the means by which infection was communicated. When Alderman Micklethwaite and his son were commanded to remain in their home in York because their servants used to visit the house of a suspected plague victim, they were also ordered to kill their dogs and cats as part of this household isolation. Furthermore, animals had widely acknowledged therapeutic uses in early modern England. Unlike contemporary medical teaching, which suggests that pets reduce stress and thus heart disease, early modern doctors believed in the possibility of a more direct physical exchange between animal and human. The humanist physician, John Caius, noted when discussing small spaniels in his *Of Englishe Dogges* (a development of Gesner's natural history) that we find that these litle dogs are good to asswage the sicknesse of the stomacke being oftentimes thereunto applyed as a plaster preservative, or borne in the bosom of the diseased . . . person, which effect is performed by theyr moderate heate. Moreover the disease . . . chaungeth his place and entreth (though it be not precisely marcked) into the dogge, which be no untruthe, experience can testify, for these kinde of dogges sometimes fall sicke, and somtime die, without any harme outwardly inforced, which is an argument that the disease of the . . . owner . . . entreth into the dogge by operation of heate intermingled and infected.

The possibility that infection could pass from human to other animal through the operation of heat underpinned that (to modern eyes) most bizarre of therapies found in medical texts from Dioscorides onwards – the application of live animals to the body of the plague victim. The College of Physicians, for instance, recommended that one should take a live cockerel, hen or pigeon, hold it firmly by the beak and remove its tail feathers. Then one should press the bird 'hard to the Blotch or swelling, and so keepe them at that part untill they die, and by this meanes draw out the poison'.

But the slaughter of dogs also articulated a reordering of society in time of plague. As is well known, aristocratic and royal portraiture, such as Titian's portrait of the Emperor Charles V and many Van Dyck portraits of Caroline courtiers, regularly displayed the magisterial character of the subject by representing them with a masterful hand upon the head of a well-disciplined and obedient hound.

Plague challenged precisely these uncomplicated lines of authority. Colin Jones has recently noted the paradoxical parallels between a plague-stricken city and one in carnival – both with the conventional hierarchies of good order and government overturned. The slaughter of dogs represented a ferocious reinstation of magisterial authority, whereby the hand resting upon the canine head has become a club beating out its brains. To put it another way, the slaughter of dogs was also an acting-out of the necessary repression of human bestiality at a time when sinfulness was being punished. For canine qualities were not always painted as positively as Pope represented Argus. One was 'as greedy as a dog', 'as idle as a dog'. Dogs symbolised lust – in one London ecclesiastical court case a woman was said to be 'worse than anie salte bitche which the dogge followethe up and downe the streete'. In an image taken from the book of Proverbs, a life of repeated sin was often characterised as resembling a dog returning to its vomit. In his *Dictionary*, Samuel Johnson developed these anthropocentric and anti-canine sentiments. As Ronald Paulson has put it, 'Johnson's dog is simply part of man, his baser or less fortunate . . . aspect.' Dogs thus symbolised the beastly aspects of human nature which religion and civil government sought to train, master and control.

Moreover, crucially it was *dogs* that they slaughtered, not other members of the canine commonwealth. Ladies' lap-dogs and the hounds of the gentry were specifically excluded from these regulations. When the aldermen of London sent the dog-killers into action in 1590 they excepted 'greyhounds, spanyelles and hounds' from the cull. Social difference and monetary value was thus respected and their difference was alleged also to be expressed in a superior character. As Katherine Philips wrote of the Irish Greyhound, a lion amongst dogs,

> This Dog hath so himself subdu'd,
> That hunger cannot make him rude:

And his behaviour does confess
True Courage dwells with Gentleness.

Dogs, curs, the less valuable and less restrained creatures of the middling and lower sort were not seen in such a positive light. They lived a liminal lifestyle, regularly traversing the threshold between the domestic interior of house and shop and the more public world of the street. The dog-whippers employed in many urban churches and cathedrals sought to control the problem posed by large numbers of these creatures literally transgressing the boundaries of human or sacred space. Like the *cureuses* of Geneva discussed by Naphy, in the eyes of civic authorities they were incompletely integrated into the fabric of society. Like the sale of second-hand clothes, the movement of dogs and other semi-domestic animals such as pigs or cats thus provided a way of understanding the social exchanges which spread the plague. Such creatures were a *visible* source of disorder in a way that rodents and lap-dogs were not.

This anxiety about the wandering dog was part of a wider anxiety about relationships consequent upon epidemic. Within medical and civic discourse all interaction was dangerous; unregulated social intercourse, especially through unknown media such as hackney carriages, water-bearers or itinerants (human or canine) was especially to be feared. This anxiety was articulated in a variety of ways. Some medical commentators suggested that dogs and cats could carry the disease because their fur attracted the sticky miasma from which it originated. Others attributed it to canine diet. One anonymous plague pamphlet warned the reader to

> suffer no Dogs nor Cats to come into your houses, nor to keepe any your selves, (except you dwell in some open place of the Ayre) for they be very dangerous, and most apt (of any kind of thing) to take infection of sicknesse, and to bring it home to their maisters house; by reason that they run from place to place and from one house to another, continually feeding upon the uncleanest things that are cast forth into the streets.

The language in which this concern was expressed echoed the frequent precepts against beggars and vagrants that were said to 'wander up and downe the streets' and whose expulsion from the city was a regular theme of plague regulations. As William Empson noted, late sixteenth- and early seventeenth-century texts often used canine metaphors to describe vagrants. In Harman's *Caveat for Common Cursitors*, for instance, the rogue was said to rise in the morning and to shake his ears, while upright-men (another variety of rogue) and their harlots were said to shelter in barns 'where they couch comely together, and it were dog and bitch'. Householders were similarly ordered to ensure that servants and apprentices were kept within doors on holidays, to ensure that they did not 'wander abroade in the streetes'. The slaughter of dogs was thus more than an extension of the policy of household isolation that played so important a part in the response to plague. Dogs in streets were not simply breaking sanitary regulations. They were quite literally masterless. In London in 1563 and 1584–86 they were allowed out so long as they were on a leash and thus visibly and physically fixed within a particular social relationship. Their slaughter was a symbolic warning to the rest of the population.

In August 1665, at the height of the plague in London, Samuel Pepys mused in his diary that the epidemic was 'making us more cruel to one another then we are [to] dogs'.

This chapter develops this parallel. For although English national and local government never enforced its plague policy with regard to humans with quite the sanguinary enthusiasm that they displayed towards wayward canines, considerable force was required to sustain the deeply unpopular policies of household isolation and segregation which were the keystone of their response to the plague. It is to this overall context of the coercive exercise of authority and of social differentiation that we should look when we try to understand these dog massacres. They were not based upon simple ignorance, nor were they the febrile panic reactions of a terrified generation unable to control their environment. Rather, they articulated a variety of fears about human relationships with each other, with the bestial aspects of humankind and with the wider world.

PART THREE

Deconstructionism

Texts in the genre of deconstruction are texts which undercut the idea of the narrator as nobody and stress the author's creative role. Dispensing with linear narratives in favour of multi-voiced, multi-perspectival, multi-levelled, fragmented arrangements, such writing plays with the possibility of creating new ways of representing and figuring 'the before now'. This writing is thus often experimental and stylistically innovative, the negative aspects of deconstruction opening up the possibility of positive re-articulations often informed by overtly expressed positions.

CHAPTER 26

Greg Dening

'PERFORMING ON THE BEACHES OF THE MIND: AN ESSAY' (2002)*

The first extract in *Part Three* is 'Performing On the Beaches of the Mind: An Essay', published in *History and Theory* in 2002. In it Greg Dening, Adjunct Professor at the Centre for Cross-Cultural Research, the Australian National University, Canberra, and the author of several books which blend the theories and practices of anthropology and history (for example *Mr Bligh's Bad Language* (Cambridge: Cambridge University Press, 1992), *The Death of William Gooch* (Melbourne: Melbourne University Press, 1995) and *Performances* (Chicago: Chicago University Press, 1996), reflects upon the way that history ('the past transformed into words or paint or dance or play') is always a performance. Accepting that we live in postmodernity – but by no means a self-confessed postmodernist – Dening's writings mix the past and the present, subject and object, the speaker and the spoken, discourse and poetry, giving a highly reflexive and multi-perspectival impression (performance) that undercuts the single authorial voice – the 'true story' – in favour of an interminable multiplicity of renditions that create, in their dissonance, a movement that manifests itself in a lyrically expressed 'harmony of differences'. Invited a few years ago by the journal *Rethinking History* to write in their 'Invitation to Historians' feature, Dening – as the American Editor of the journal, Robert Rosenstone wrote – subverted the idea of writing an expected professional autobiography by creating a new piece of history ('a rumination of past, present and future ... his, ours, that of the Marqueses islanders – that better than any direct explanation, demonstrates the reasons for the kind of history he has long been producing') (*Rethinking History*, 2 (2), 1998: 140). And, in many ways, this is the same approach that Dening uses in the *History and Theory* essay reproduced here. The reprinting of this particular essay was thus the result of a difficult decision on our part, since his two recent autobiographical pieces admirably illustrate both his views on 'the nature of history after modernity' and his style – a style that readers can consider at length in the books mentioned above and, especially perhaps, in his now 'Mutiny on the Bounty' classic, *Mr Bligh's Bad Language*.

History — the past transformed into words or paint or dance or play — is always a performance. An everyday performance as we present our selective narratives about what has happened at the kitchen table, to the courts, to the taxman, at the graveside. A quite staged performance when we present it to our examiners, to the collegiality of our disciplines, whenever we play the role of "historian." History is theater, a place of *thea* (in the Greek, a place of seeing).

---

* Greg Dening (2002) 'Performing On the Beaches of the Mind: An Essay', *History and Theory*, 41(1): 1–22.

The complexities of living are seen in story. Rigidity, patter, and "spin" will always destroy the theater in our history performances. That is because we are postmodern. The novelists, the painters, the composers, the filmmakers give us the tropes of our day, alert us to the fictions in our non-fiction, and give us our freedoms.

How do I persuade anyone that the above theory is true? By *thea*, by seeing its truth. By performing. I have a true story to tell about beaches and those who cross them — Paul Gauguin, Herman Melville, and I.

I. The flight of the yolla

EVERY YEAR IN LATE September, if I am lucky, I can look down from the desk where I do much of my writing, across the tops of eucalyptus trees, over the beach and rocky coastline, and see for hours a long black procession of birds snaking its way south around the headlands and into bays.

"Kaoha!" I say to them. "Welcome home!" They are the yolla — the shearwaters, the "short-tailed shearwaters," "slender billed puffins," *Puffinus tenuirostris*, "moon-birds," "mutton-birds." They are on the last leg of their 30,000-km circuit of the Pacific. Their line ripples and rolls as one living body. In their hundreds of thousands, they look to be in direct, determined, and undistracted flight. They are flying home to nest where they nested last year, and who knows how many years before that.

I see hundreds of thousands of yolla in a stream maybe ten meters deep and fifty meters wide. Matthew Flinders from the thirty-three-foot longboat, *Norfolk*, in which he charted these southern Australian waters in 1798, calculated that he saw a 100 to 150 million of them in a stream fifty to eighty meters deep and 300 meters or more wide. Civilization hasn't been kind, at least in the last 200 years of the perhaps two million years that the yolla have been making this journey. The birds sustained convict settlements in their starving needs, and were killed off in uncontrolled frenzy. They had sustained, in more controlled ways, for forty thousand years at least, the first people in Tasmania and along this Victorian coast where the yolla are my neighbors.

James Cook saw these yolla in the cold waters of the Bering Sea in the northern summer on the last voyage of his life. William Ellis, his artist, gives us our first images of these "short-tailed," "slender-billed" dark birds. We have Ellis's exquisite drawings of them in the British Museum of Natural History. Their stiffwinged shearing, arcing flight is the yolla's grace. Into the troughs of the sea and up the weather side of the waves, independent and intense in their search for food, they are as part of the grey north seascape as foam and cloud is of a Turner painting. But they are not really northerners, just visitors, restless visitors. As the summer warms the northern waters a little, they cluster at the cold upswells that bring to the surface the krill, crustaceans, and small fish on which they feed.

Cook had first seen the yolla at the other ends of the earth, in the *Endeavour*, as she approached the coast of what Cook would call New South Wales. It was April. The yolla were on the start of their voyage. The autumn southwest winds will drive them northeast above the North Island of Aotearoa (New Zealand) for the first leg. There they will veer to the northwest between Fiji and the Solomons and drive north to the Japan Sea, curving east after that to the Bering Sea, as far north as 71°. If all conditions are right, they will have flown 10,000 km in little over a month, more than 300 km a day. They will feed themselves as they fly, skimming, diving. The warm tropical waters will be their greatest obstacle. It will force a fast on them. The return flight down the northwest coast of North America and across the vast Pacific east of the Tuamotus will be more life threatening. In the years in which the cool waters of the Humboldt Current up the west coast of South America do not reach out into the Pacific — during El Niño — the yolla are likely to falter and die in huge numbers.

These remarkable birds soar and scythe and knife their way over a vast space of sea and islands. They have time and space imprinted in their bodies. They have ways of interpreting signs that they have never seen before, in ways I cannot explain to you, nor science to us all.

I will call that vast space they circuit "Oceania." It has had other names these past four hundred years — "South Seas," "Pacific," and currently "Sea of Islands." The peoples who lived on its islands for the two thousand years before that would call the great ocean in their different dialects "Moana."

I'll keep to the name Oceania. Oceania is a lived-in space as much as a natural vastness. It is a tracked-on space. The wakes of ships and canoes that have crossed it have left no permanent mark on its waters. But if we voyaged in a *New 20,000 Leagues under the Sea*, looking up to the canopy of the sea's surface above us and had a sort of time-exposure vision, we would find the tracks a closely woven tapestry of lines. Very few of these lines would be random. They are all directed in some way by systems of knowledge: of stars, of time, of distance — and of purpose: of trade, of empire, of science, of way-finding. There are many other tracks, too, of whales in seasonal migration, of tuna, of birds. These too, more mysteriously, are directed by systems of knowledge.

I call this enveloping of space with knowledge, "encompassing." Encompassing is imprinting this island-seascape with spirit and life — human, animal, vegetable. For nearly fifty years now, I have dreamed of Encompassing Oceania. It is my current project, my current performance. I want to see, hear, write, and reflect the double space and time of Oceania. The flight of the yolla is my metaphor for encompassing Oceania. The yolla encompass Oceania every year in their twelve-year life span. I would like to do it just once in my mind.

II. Performing

The past I visit — the two-hundred-year past that I visit — is on paper. Mostly. Sometimes it is in things with human creativity encapsulated in them — ships, ornaments, art, buildings, landscape. A two-hundred-year past is beyond experience and memory, though, and beyond the radar of our various electronic recording systems. There are no voices from two hundred years ago, no smells, no touches, no movement.

No, the two-hundred-years past I visit is stilled onto paper, millions of pieces of paper. Written-on paper. One-off pieces of paper, mostly without copy. Not printed paper. Hand-written paper. Script. The first mark of my history is always a pen's or a pencil's. My first performance as a historian is to be a reader. And those first readings I make are always shaped by the transience of the moment in which they were made. The hand that writes them is still trembling with anger or fear or sorrow. Or it is scribbled in a hurry. Or it is flourished with power. It is stained or burnt on its edges, or blotted. It is corrected and erased. It belongs to times that are as long or short or broken or continuous as the human experience that sustains it.

To visit my two-hundred-year past, I read. I read to write. Actually, I read to live. Reading for me is life. I love the dance on the beaches of the mind that reading is. I read fast and slow. I slow-read poetry. I slow-read the sacred texts in my life. I soak up the timelessness of their words. These sacred texts look like they are bound to time but they are not. Their meaning stretches out to me beyond the meanings their writers ever had. I easily fly over their contradictions and errors and know what truth they hold for me.

I read fast most of the time. That is because reading books, as distinct from reading the written-on pages of my two-hundred-year past — reading books is my conversation with the world. My eyes are ahead of my mind when I read fast. I gobble sentences, paragraphs, pages whole. There is a white noise in the back of my mind as I read. It is the babble of worldwide conversations that affect my thinking. I'm in conversation with novelists, philosophers, anthropologists, historians, critics in this sort of reading. It is full of erotic, ecstatic moments when I think that what they are saying is what I myself am just about to say. But I'm going to say it better!

So I agree with a reader like Michel de Certeau, a writer who makes such challenging reflections in *The Practice of Everyday Life* (1988).

Reading, in his view, is a creative act "full of detours and drifts across the page, imaginary or meditative flights taking off from a few words, overlapping paragraph on paragraph, page on page, short-lived dances of the eye and mind."

My performance as a reader is also pro-active, creative. It is in no way passive, a mirror to someone else's thoughts. My eyes might be attached to the page, but my mind is soaring.

I am an observer in my reading. Observing is my performance, too. I observe the past. I read to write true stories, history. My cultural antennae are at their peak when I am observing. I cannot afford to be a spectator, an outsider, divorced from what I see and hear. It is my cultural humanity that joins me to everything I observe. I recognize, I understand, I see difference from within myself first. There is not a word that I read that does not have many meanings — for the occasions in which it is used, for the relationships among its users, for the trope of which it is a part. Nothing I observe is so trivial or particular that it is not larger than itself in some way, not interconnected with everything else, not suffused with system or structure. Nothing is so boxed in my theoretical or disciplinary vision that it doesn't jump out of that box into another box — nothing economic that is not also psychological, that is not also gendered, that is not also . . . whatever.

I read to write true stories, I say. All stories need to be true, perhaps you will respond. Stories need to be honest to the realities of living, experiential, recognizably human. Even the most maverick, bizarre, or eccentric behavior has to be recognizably human. Stories don't need to be specifically accurate, but they need to be generically true.

My true stories are something else. There is a heavy obligation that I owe the past. If I claim to represent it — if I claim to re-present it — I owe it something, its own independence. I owe it a gift of itself, unique in time and space. The history I write will always be mine and something more than the past, but there is a part of it that is never mine. It is the part that actually happened, independently of my knowing that or how it happened. My true stories are ruled by my belief that I have always something to learn.

I write to give back to the past its own present moments. There is no better place to catch that tenuous, trembling moment than when the pen is just put to paper. I am a pilgrim and initiate when I want to read that piece of paper. That piece of paper never comes to me like a book does. I must go to it where it is housed. Wherever it is housed, it is cared for. It is precious, and there are rules to be obeyed to read it — gloves to be put on, pencils to be used rather than ink, logs to be signed in and out of, silence to be kept.

There is always theater and performance in the archives and Rare Books and Manuscript Rooms. Humbling, self-effacing roles to be played before steelyeyed librarians. Dissembling roles to hide one's ignorance. Brazen in-your-face roles sharpening pencils on a noisy pencil sharpener. Outraged "I've come 10,000 miles to see this" roles when denied access to critical material. There's plenty of theater in the archives.

Our performance in the archives is marked by two characteristics, I think. The one is our sense of "being there." The other is our performance consciousness.

"Being there" is that feeling for the past that can only be matched by the hours, the days, the weeks, the months, the years I sit at the tables in the archives. It is an assurance that my extravagance with time here is rewarded with a sensitivity that comes in no other way. It is an overlaying of images one on the other. It is a realization that knowledge of the past is cumulative and kaleidoscopic, extravagantly wasteful of my energy.

The name of our game is persuasion, not domination. Our performance is to let others perform. The extravagance of our engagement in the archives will always give our language richness, our images color and sharpness, our arguments conviction, our examples pertinence, our selection an informed boldness. "Being there" where the past leaves itself most particularly is our signature gesture in research performance. Without it we are just literary critics.

There are delusions in "being there." Of course there are. The discipline of anthropology knows them only too well. "Being there" can too often be a claim on an experience that can't be checked or even shared. A claim of "being there" is blind arrogance if it is not accompanied by performance consciousness.

There is a double quality in performance. Performance is always to somebody, an audience, a reader, self. In the loneliness of research and writing that somebody else might only be oneself. But when there are others, it is always also to oneself. In performance we research and write in stereo consciousness. In performance we are theater critics in the foyer of our minds. We are measuring the effectiveness of what we are doing against the reception in the audience. We are always measuring what we do against the ideals and ambitions we have for doing it. In performance, we know our own tricks to hide what we don't know. We know the masks (the *persona*) of our own person. That stereo consciousness is our strength. It is our realism in a postmodern world.

I'm a storyteller. A true storyteller. You are true storytellers, too, That's our performance, true storytelling. Sometimes, our performance is live. And shared. An exchanged performance. The audience performs to me, the storyteller, as much as I to them. They perform with their silences and their fidgets, with their polite-but-not-yet-committed seminar faces. I read their signals in their performance. I calibrate their silences — engaged silences, disapproving silences, sleeping silences. I measure the spontaneity of their responses. I adjust my rhythms and speed to them, I'll move from my text. I'll catch their eye. I'll infuse energy into my voice to stop their attention slipping away.

This is our performance as true storytellers, as makers of history. We speak to one another, not randomly, but in disciplined discourse. We hear in company. We read for ourselves. We write for others. We travel. We lock ourselves in libraries and archives. We observe. We reflect. We claim authority, but have no other power than to persuade. We make theater about trivial and everyday things, and about awful and cruel realities. Maybe we write to change the world in some way.

We tell our stories, but there is never any closure to them. There is always another sentence to be added to the conversation that we have joined. There is always another slant on the story that we have just told. We live by our creativity and originality. That's our pledge: "This work is mine." But we couldn't, if we tried, plumb the depths of our own intellectual and cultural plagiarism. Plato, Jesus Christ, Karl Marx, Sigmund Freud, and so many others are in our minds somewhere.

So is our postmodernity, whether we like it or not. We know — because our everyday living performances are never separated from our academic performing — how liberated we have been by the painters, dancers, composers, film directors, novelists, and poets on our cultural horizon. Just by being everyday cultural performers in our own times we know that performance art engages the whole body, all the senses, all the emotions. Not just the mind, not just rationality. Performance art has given us a multitude of narrative strategies for our stories. We know that formulaic monotone won't do what we want it to do — persuade, convince, change, enter into somebody else's consciousness in a meaningful way. We have to be artful. We must take out the cliché, not just from our concepts and words, but from the very structure of our presentations. We are mouthing soundlessly, like goldfish in a bowl, unless we display our postmodernity. Not our postmodernism. Our contemporaneity to the tropes of our times.

There is art and science in delicate mix in this performance of ours. Catharsis for our readers, their enlightenment, their seeing the plot in our plays, aren't at all certain products of our performance, at least in ways that we anticipate. We've learned enough about paradigm, episteme, discourse, and language these past twenty years to know that the forms and expressions of our performances cannot be divorced from their content and logic. Our performances cannot be all style anymore than they can be all argument. We all wait in our examiner's reports and our reviews for the "but" that follows praise for our expression and style. "He or she writes well, but . . ." Persuasion by our art is always linked with our science-in the exhaustiveness of our research, a display of our control over not only our discipline but of the disciplines on the edge of ours, an openness about the degrees of our certainties and uncertainties, a show of our adversarial skills.

We know some things about performing, though, don't we? That is because we are constantly observers of other performers. We know what bores us. We know what confuses us. We know when jargonistic language cuts us off from understanding. We know that the enemy of an effective performance is formalistic ritualism. Rigidity and patter will always deny the creativity of the moment. So we know when we have heard a story told well, and when we have heard a story told badly. Perhaps the most important thing that we know is that we are least persuaded by overpowering knowledge preoccupied with itself. Roland Barthes called this preoccupation a peppering of our writing with "reality effects" — extraneous, uncontexted facts that become an end to themselves. The last things we want to know are all the reality effects that are in another performer's head. What we really want to know is how the other performer is joining a conversation we are already having in our own heads.

Victor Turner, with that linguistic tricksterism that he loved to play, reminded us that the *per* in words like "experience" and "performance" comes from an Indo-European root phrase meaning "to risk," "to venture." There is always a gamble in performance. There is a commitment which cannot be taken back once the performance has begun, once we step onto the page, once we give our dissertation to the examiners, our book to the reviewers. If only we had another rehearsal, if only we had 10,000 more words, if only we had another deadline . . . No, there is never perfection in performance. We have to gamble on what we do in the conditions in which we do it. The search for perfection only strikes us dumb, only gives us stage fright.

Our gaze at the moment is on "Past Performances." There is an ambiguity in the phrase. Are these past performances *in* the past? Or are they our performances *of* the past? I would like to think that they are both.

All my academic teaching life, I taught the past by asking my students first to describe something of their present. It wasn't a surrender to presentism. It was a method of teaching my students to recognize what performances in the past might be. "Ethnogging," they used to call it with affectionate disrespect. I used to ask them to "emplot," in Aristotle's word of the theater (*mythos*), something different in their daily living. The different could be large — across languages, across beliefs, across disabilities, across the ways people ritualize their lives. Mostly the different was ordinary — across gender, across age, across class.

Difference is always hard to see. It always requires a little giving — young to old, old to young; black to white, white to black; male to female, female to male. Seeing difference always requires entering somebody else's metaphors. It always requires catching the interconnectedness between the different parts of living. To understand difference, you have to see the system in it.

If difference is hard to see, it is even more difficult to describe. I wasn't too particular about the ways that my students described difference. They could write a poem about it, or a play. They could paint it, video it, make a tape about it. But whatever they did, they had to make theater of it, and by prologue or epilogue, put what they thought they were doing into words.

I used to say to them that culture is in the end talk. Talk in all the ways in which meanings are symbolized — in gesture, in color, in style, in spaces. Culture is talk in all its symbolized ways, but mostly the talk is in words.

Difference in words is usually in the silence of words, the things that words don't say. The "ethnoggers" real problem is a problem of translation of these silences. How do they do that? They must use their imaginations. Not their fantasies, their imaginations. Imagination is finding a word that someone will hear, a metaphor that someone will see. Imagination is taking the cliché out of something that has been said over and over again. Imagination is working the fictions in our non-fictions the better to be read.

Their ethnographies must be art. There is no art in multiplying the reifications. Art is the dismantling of reifications. In art there is one cultural miracle. Every difference has a sameness. Every smallness a largeness. Every shape, every color, every gesture has a theory. In art we need the directness of a novelist, the choosiness of a poet, the discontinuity of a filmmaker, the engagement of a violinist.

If culture is talk, it is not all stream of consciousness. It has rhythms. It has dramatics. It has theater. When my students came to make art of this theater, when they came to inscribe not only what they had experienced in their observing, but also what they had experienced more vicariously in their reading, they had to realize that they would be least convincing when they spout theory. They needed to understand that no one learns the truth by being told it. Everyone needs to experience truth in some way. Their readers would not need all their protestations about what they meant. Their readers would demand of their writing the same theater that life is itself. Their readers will demand that their writing be art. It will have to dance and sing. It will have to be a performance.

We are in conference mode to unravel the ambiguities of the phrase "Past Performances." We have put boundaries of space and time around ourselves so that we might share each other's creativity. We ask ourselves to share what John Dewey would have called "an" experience. Experience is not just stream of consciousness. Experience is something reflected upon, something pulled out of the flow of things. We humans are very ingenious in creating a hedged-around space and time to have our experiences. It is an in-between space and in-between time — in-between ordinary living, in-between everyday relationships, in-between other conversations, in-between other performances. We sometimes called this hedged-around space ritual, sometimes theater. I'd like to call it, here, limen, threshold, or in a metaphor that, has occupied my attention through many years, a beach.

I want to say that to perform the past we must cross a beach in some way. I want to say that in performing the past I want to be a beachcomber to the past.

III. Beaches

Beaches. My life with all its memories is filled with them. My books are all written beside a beach or overlooking one or within the sound of one's waves. As I write now, the combers on the beach below my window roll into a continuous rush of sound. It is the white noise that separates my mind from my body and lets me think to write.

There is hardly a week that I don't walk a beach. These days I can't walk their soft white sand. There is too much pain and reminders of mortality in that. A dune to cross to reach a beach drains energy and resolve. The beach I walk is the hard wet sand at the sea's edge. It is an edge that moves with the tide and each wave in the tide, of course. So, unless it is barefoot, the walk meanders just beyond the reach of the largest wave in a set — always the ninth, don't the fishermen say?

This glistening strand between high and low tide is my freedom trail. I lose myself as I walk. I write in my mind. The waves are my worry beads. It is an in-between space in an in-between space. The last reach of the sea soaks into the sand. On one side, colonies of gulls and terns dry themselves on the white sand. On the other, the sea side, gannets dive into the troughs between breakers. Occasionally dolphins are to be seen surfing in the green transparencies of the waves. In the soak of the sea, life stirs almost immediately as the crab holes bubble. Worms and pipi wander just below the surface, sucking life from the brine seeping into their world. Sandpipers ballet after the retreating waves.

This wet stretch between land and sea is the true beach, the true in-between space. Among the peoples of Oceania about whom I write — the *maohi* of Tahiti, the *enata* of the Marquesas, the *kamaiana* of Hawai'i — it is a sacred, a *tapu*, space, an unresolved space where things can happen, where things can be made to happen. It is a space of transformation. It is a space of crossings.

Yesterday, when I felt the need to reflect on what it meant to write that the beach is a "space of transformation," "a space of crossings," I went for a walk on my favorite beach. It was the first day of the southern hemisphere summer. The tide was low. The soak of the sea was a glistening twenty yards wide. The beach curves for five miles in the shelter of hills just a road-width back. There is a fishing harbor at one end behind a rock groyne. Squid boats shelter there. I see their lights at night like UFOs on the horizon of the sea. At the other end of the curve, the beach ends, as so many Australian beaches end, with a small stream riding against a rocky headland. That stream is always my walking goal.

This first day of summer was brilliant. Pale blue sky, deep blue sea. Miles of white, white foam. Oceanographers tell us that at any one time 2% of the earth's surface is under sea foam. That is pretty in-between. The breeze beats against the green, green hills. The spring rains still hold their effect. It is a steady breeze, just right for the hang-gliders who float above my head. That is an in-between space that I haven't dared try.

I'm thinking beaches, of course, as I walk. And crossings. A very rewarding thing happened to me in this last year. Fenuaenata, The People of the Land, the Marquesans, through their Association Eo' Enata, published a French translation of Islands and Beaches in a splendid edition. It was a great honor for me. I was humbled to be giving these sad and silent islands a history that they could never before read.

Islands and Beaches (1980) was an important book for me. Forty-five years ago I made a discovery that changed my life. I discovered that I wanted to write the history of Oceania in a double-visioned way. I wanted to write the history of Pacific islands from both sides of the beach. I began to read the voyagers — Cook, Bougainville, Bligh, Vancouver, La Pérouse — then the whalers' logs, missionary letters, beachcombers' journals, not so much to tell their stories as to see what their unseeing eyes were seeing, life on the other side of the beach as the islanders actually lived it, not as it was framed in the mind-galleries of outsiders. What attracted me most of all were the beachcombers, those who left their ships and "went native," those who crossed beaches.

Beachcombers. There were hundreds of them in the years I was interested in — the mutineers of the *Bounty*, among them. They were a peculiar breed. They were as varied as humanity itself, and as good and as evil. They were always a scandal to the societies they left, deemed traitors to it. They took freedoms that other men (there were no women among them in these years) didn't dare or want to take. They soon found that their beaches were dangerous places. If they were wise, they did not bring any material goods with them. These would be taken from them, with their lives if they resisted. What they couldn't bring with them was all the cultural and social support, including language, that made them who they were. To survive, they had to enter into native society in some way, its language first of all. They had to bow to the realities of politics and social relationships. They had to be good mimics and actors. They had to be able to read gestures and understand the ways in which power and class and gender can be in a color or a shape or a look.

So for me, who wanted to see across the beach, the beachcombers' eyes saw more than most. I began to "see" the Land, Fenua, the Marquesas, through a beachcomber's eyes, Edward Robarts and a lone nineteen-year-old missionary beachcomber, William Pascoe Crook. They both wrote long manuscripts of their experiences in the Land. *Islands and Beaches* grew out of that seeing.

Islands and Beaches freed me in many ways. It gave me courage to take risks in the theater of cross-cultural writing. The metaphors "islands" and "beaches" allowed me to escape the tunnel vision of an island topic and to discover the many ways in which there are liminal spaces and boundaries in life. I experimented structurally in the book, balancing the two requirements of the historical endeavor, narrative and reflection, in a quite explicit way. I gained a freedom especially by giving back to Enata — The People — of Fenua — The Land — something of their own identity in how they named themselves and their islands. But more importantly, how they structured their identity in the opposition of native (*enata*) and stranger (*haoe*). It was a first and small step in inverting the priorities of our cross-cultural gaze.

"Life is a Beach," the tee-shirts in every seaside resort proclaim. Yes, life is a beach, though the truth of that is not as hedonistic as the tee-shirts are meant to imply. Life is the marginal space between two unknowables — its befores and its afters. All of living is a crossing. Living is all the crossings within one crossing.

It is the process in these crossings that intrigues me. The process, not so much the change. Not essences and polarities that never were, but creative unfolding. How does one catch creative unfolding, movement, in words? Music might catch the flow of things, and so might painting. But there is stasis in a word that describes the world as *things*. "To arrest the meaning of words, that is what the Terror wants," Jean-François Lyotard once wrote. And Herbert Marcuse put his slant on the idea: "All reification is a process of forgetting. Art fights reification by making the petrified world speak, sing, perhaps dance." I want to write history that avoids both the Terror and the forgetting.

Poetry might keep my words alive, make them dance. It wouldn't shame me to tell my stories in poetry, or at least to write my prose poetically. Let me be more ambitious than that, though. Let me represent all the crossings that are in even one beach crossing. They are all there — yours, mine — whether we know it or not, whether we like it or not.

All living is in flow, but our cultural living is sentenced, paragraphed, chaptered. In all the passage moments, in all the crossing moments, of our cultural life — in becoming adult, or married, or healthy, or educated — in all the specifying moments of roles-gender, age, status, kin — the normal times of living are interrupted by times of defining, moments of marking, occasions of abnormality. We sometimes call these marking and abnormal times ritual. They are always theater: moments of in-between, moments of seeing, moments of reflection. Beaches. Let me be a storyteller of beach crossings of others and catch the flow of living and telling on the beaches of my own mind.

There is no beach without sea, no sea without sky, no sky without the earth's curve. In the view from the beach, the forefront is all detail and movement, all history, one is tempted to say. But the ordered restlessness of the waves diffracts the gaze, dissolves attention into reflection. From a beach, things loom in the gum of the horizon and in the shimmer of the mind's eye. From a beach, it is possible to see beyond one's horizons, Beaches breed expansiveness. My beaches do, anyway.

IV. Herman Melville and I

I am flying over an immense ocean. Not shearing, arcing and knifing like the yolla to be sure. I am sitting nervously behind two gesticulating French pilots. They point to every button on their instrument panel as if it is the subject of some great philosophical or mechanical crisis. It is December 1974. We have just taken off from Tahiti's Faa airport in a wet-season storm. We are flying on a northeast tack over 1500 km of open sea to Fenuaenata, the Land of the Native People. I would not have then called the people Enata or their islands Fenua at that time. My visit would give me the cultural courtesy and the academic courage to call them what they called themselves and their land. I would have called them in 1974 what the Spanish outsiders called them 400 years ago, the Marquesas.

I am apprehensive. The Land and its Natives have already changed my life. But I have been to the Land and met its Natives only in libraries and archives. I know that I am Stranger to them, and I know the cost of every Stranger's intrusion. The sadness of their story has affected me ever since I began to learn it. Inevitably I come with a sense of trespass. Their terrible story and my knowledge of it has been the capital of my life. The rewards of twenty years study of them to this time in 1974 have been great. I bring to them in my luggage the pride of my academic life to this time, my first book about them. I know all my shortcuts in that book. I know all its tricks of camouflage for my ignorance. Early in my studies of the Land, I had read Frantz Fanon's *The Wretched of the Earth* (1961). It had shaken me to my core. In a world of victims, he wrote, there are no innocents. No one can write two-sided history who in some way benefits by the power of the victors. No one can mediate between the disempowered living and the voiceless dead. All of us writing in a history so terrible as that of the Pacific — or of the Americas or of Africa for that matter — have had to resolve that dilemma for ourselves. No doubt we all do it differently. For me, giving the dead a voice has been reason enough for my history. I am with Karl Marx, too. The function of my history is not so much to understand the world as to change it. If my history by story and reflection disturbs the moral lethargy of the living to change in their present the consequences of their past, then it fulfills a need. I have not silenced any voice by adding mine.

It was a near miraculous moment for me when we discovered through a break in the clouds that we were above the island and the very valley to which I had been thousands of time in my mind. We touched down on something like the deck of an aircraft carrier on the island of Hiva Oa.

I remember my emotions as we approached Vaitahu down the straits between the islands of Hiva Oa and Tahuata, and saw the winds rushing down the valley to ruffle the waters of the bay. I don't know how many times I have noted that wind in my notes and how a whaler or a naval vessel dragged its anchors before it. I stood in sad awe at the place where the Spaniards after celebrating high mass had recreated a Golgotha scene by placing the bodies of those they had killed on three stakes and piercing their dead hearts with a spear. I walked about the hill where the French in 1842 had built their fort from which they had slaughtered those who had resisted their prostituting the women and enslaving the men and killing hundreds with their lack of hygiene.

There is a triviality about these places where terrible things have happened that is mystifying. A place of a massacre becomes a caravan park, a place of suicidal flight becomes a barbecue site. I don't know how one puts history into these sites, let alone memory, but I am confident that history and social memory will come to them.

An old man, Teifitu, gave us hospitality. He was a direct descendant of the *haka'iki*, or chiefs of the valley. An ancestor of his had been killed by James Cook's men because he had stolen a halfpenny nail. Another had looked after the beachcombers I had come to know. Just three generations before, others had scrawled their signs on the documents giving away their land. The French *Ministre de la Marine* insisted the documents should be in triplicate. I had held all three copies in my own hands in the archives in Paris. I would sit with Teifitu into the night and in my poor French and poorer Marquesan tried to translate what Edward Robarts, the beachcomber whose journal I had edited, said to him of his past. I still have the names he wrote in my field notebook that joined Teifitu to those I knew.

I learned much about crossing cultures from Teifltu on the beach at Vaitahu. One thing was that I learned to hear the silences within myself. Another thing was that I learned to discern the continuities that outlive all the discontinuity of cultural change.

Paul Gauguin lived the last years of his life, 1901–1903, in Fenuaenata. On the black sand beach at Atuona on the island of Hiva Oa, he had painted *Riders on the Beach*. Two hooded riders — death on horseback — lead the other horsemen to an endless horizon.

There is nothing "real" in the painting, no black sand, no dark tumbling rocks, no closed bay. Differences are sponged out in his consuming effort to make mythic and universal this art by the last savage of the last savages. Gauguin doesn't write his beach. He paints it out of his crazy imagination, filled with his own native myths, shaped by all the art history that flows through his fingers.

My first ambition on Hiva Oa was to walk the black sand beach at Atuona. Death had been frequent on that beach. The bay was called Traitors' Bay, from the boat crews that had been cut off there. But death had come more usually for Enata from canoes of their enemies as they came "fishing" for victims. In times of social crisis or in celebration of some sacred moment in their lives, Enata went fishing (e ika) for victims, heana. They would go raiding other islands, other valleys. They snatched their victims where they could, off the shore, from their houses. These heana were brought back, sometimes alive, sometimes dead, but always in the fashion in which fishermen brought back a catch of their most tapu fish. They were strung on poles, with large hooks in their mouths, baskets of bait attached to their limbs. When the victims had been killed, their corpses were mocked and played with and parts of bodies were ceremonially eaten. Then they were strung up with other sacrifices in the me'ae, the sacred spaces of the gods.

Back from the beach — over Gauguin's shoulders as he painted — we walked the dusty roads and up the trails among the silent stone remains. Here and there a tiki head had been incorporated into a fence. The massive statues had long gone from this valley. You can see them in the museums of the world staring wide-eyed and meaningless at the bored crowds. I liked the tiki in the fences better than all the tiki in the exhibition halls. The tiki in the fences had a modest dignity. Shadows and flowers gave them a life that spotlights and pedestals took away.

Everywhere in the valley of Atuona are empty stone remains. They were stone platforms on which houses once stood, or stone stages on which people had once danced and feasted, or stone altars in sacred places where sacrifices had been placed. They were scattered among the trees, overgrown and silent, all through the valley. They were relics of populations wiped out in the few short years of their encounter with Euro-American strangers. Diseases for which the people had no immunity killed most; but they died more horribly than that. In a cultural paroxysm in the 1860s, they killed themselves. When they had no explanation of why they were dying in such horrific numbers, they turned to killing one another for the machinations and sorcery they presumed was among them.

The missionaries, early in the nineteenth century, hopeless in their efforts at conversion, had focused on destruction of the tapu system, which they believed was the key to native heathenism. They promised that the native dying would stop if the evil of the tapu was broken. They evolved a series of rituals by which the native gods were challenged to punish broken tapu. Men were asked to walk under women's most intimate clothing. Women were asked to walk over the most sacred objects. The effect was not so much change as emptiness and listless hopelessness. Enata were numb for a while, with liquor as much as cultural anomie.

Then in the 1860s, here in the valley of Atuoria, there was a terrible revival of an old tapu custom, e ika, fishing for victims. In the cultural hopelessness of the 1860s, any rebirth of custom would be bastard. The revival of e ika was monstrous. Whatever balancing principles there had been to the death and violence of the old ways were now gone. This time, the killings had no ritual. They were not across islands and valleys. They were internecine, familial even, and orgiastic. In a population depleted in fifty years to three thousand from a hundred thousand, they now killed one another by the hundreds.

The death throes of this valley of Atuona were awful. It was and is today a place of extraordinary beauty, the sort of wild beauty that Gauguin ached to find. The peak of Temetiu dominates it. The wide sweeping southern arm of its bay bends out into the straits towards the neighboring island of Tahuata. Its black sand beach collects the waves coming in on the southeast winds. Its river sparkles over a bed of stones. But its silence clings.

Among the silent stones, Gauguin's imagination does not seem so crazy. Nor does his playing with the real seem so irresponsible. His cowled riders of death have a monkish feel, enough to remind us how much death those who preached eternal life had brought. The wash of his colors reminds us that any re-presentation of the past will have a dream-like quality. The past has its own silences that never will be voiced.

We paid Gauguin honor. We walked up the hill of Hueakihi to the cemetery. His grave is easily seen. Amid white cement tombs open to the sun, his is of reddish rocks and shaded by a frangipani tree. Seventy-five years after his death one of Gauguin's final wishes was granted. The cast of a favorite work, a ceramic sculpture he had called *Oviri*, was placed on his grave. *Oviri* was a favorite of Picasso, too, and inspired him. Gauguin had sculpted *Oviri* in Brittany on his return to France after his first trip to Tahiti, just before that terrible brawl that left him with a wounded leg for life. Gauguin thought it his finest work of art. He knew it was enigmatic, mysterious. "Oviri" in Tahitian means "wild," "savage." The woman of the statue is indeed wild, a mixture of incompatible lore. She has the head of a mummified Marquesan skull. She crushes a wolf under her feet, just as those most unwild statues of the Virgin crush a serpent. Gauguin put his customary signature on the statue, "PGO." That reads as "pego." It is sailors' slang for "prick." *Oviri's* wildness creates a disturbing restlessness over the grave. One cannot think that Gauguin's bones rest in peace.

We went on to Nukuhiva, a hundred miles to the north, on a World War II landing craft. Herman Melville had called his three weeks beachcombing on Nukuhiva *Typee. A Narrative of Four Months Residence among the Natives of a Valley in the Marquesas Islands; or, A Peep at Polynesian Life*. We came along the sheer, dark cliffs, passed Taipivai, Melville's valley, looking for the white line of crystalline rock that had been the sign for hundreds of sailing vessels of the passage into Taiohae Bay. Then we were through.

November 14, 1851 is a special day for Herman Melville. It is the official publication date of *Moby Dick*. On that day Melville drives his horse and dray from his home in Pittsfield in the Berkshire Mountains to nearby Lenox to have dinner with Nathaniel Hawthorne at the Curtis Hotel. Hawthorne has just finished *The House of the Seven Gables*. Melville had dedicated *Moby Dick* to Hawthorne. "In token of my admiration of his genius." The two friends talked about writing. "From my twenty-fifth year I date my life," Melville tells Hawthorne. "Three weeks have scarcely passed at anytime between then and now that I have not unfolded within myself."

Over the previous seven years Melville had written *Typee* and its near sequel *Omoo*. He had felt the genius within himself and wrote *Mardi* to prove it — not for the money that the public was prepared to pay, but for all his ambitions for American literature. *Mardi* was a commercial and literary disaster. In disgust he set himself to write something that the public would buy. He wrote *Redburn* in three weeks; *White Jacket* in twenty sittings.

Then having done his duty and now quite determined to be the self that had unfolded within him, he wrote *Moby Dick*, or "The Whale," which was its original title. Now, at the Curtis Hotel, Hawthorne and Melville were talking of their deep-down ambitions, away from publishers and reviewers, away from that terrible culture of envy of the literary world. It is "the happiest day of Melville's life," his biographer, Hershel Parker, writes.

In his twenty-fifth year, in November 1844 to be precise, in a cold, most untropical winter, in his lawyer brother's Manhattan Nassau St. office, on pieces of paper whose every space he scrimpingly fills, Herman Melville becomes a writer. He begins his first draft of *Typee*.

He began to unfold the life that was in him. "Unfold." It is the right metaphor. The writer in him is unfolding the layers of experience within him: of ships — the *St. Lawrence* (a New York to Liverpool packet ship), the *Acushnet* (a Fairhaven whaler), the *Lucy Ann* (a Sydney whaler), the *Charles and Henry* (a Nantucket whaler), the *United States* (a US naval frigate); of captains — Oliver P. Brown (a Swede), Vincent Pease (Nantucketeer), Henry Ventome (English), John B. Coleman (Dartmouth, Nova Scotia, Nantucketeer), Thomas ap Catesby Jones (a fiery Virginian and violently contentious commodore); of beaches — Nukuhiva, Tahiti, Maui, Oahu.

Unfolded, too, were all the stories that had dramatized these experiences. Stories told to him in fo'c'sles, on decks, in the yards, in Seamen's Bethels, in jails. Stories he told himself — in messes, parlors, at the family table. Stories whose fictions and dramatics got shaped with every telling. Stories whose audiences dictated their tone. Stories to entertain, stories to tease, stories to excuse. Stories honed in their telling, in their performance.

Folded, too, into his own life experiences were all sorts of vicarious lives from his readings. As he sat down to describe his arrival in his "cannibal islands" in June 1842, he knew that he had been there in his mind's eye, sixteen years before as a nine-year-old boy. That year he had a happy holiday with his eleven-year-old cousin, "Langs." "Langs" was named for Georg Heinrich von Langsdorf, a friend of Langs's father and Herman's uncle, Captain John D'Wolf. Von Langsdorff had visited the Marquesas with the Russian expedition of 1803–1806. Langsdorff's book about that visit, *Voyages and Travels in Various Parts of the World* (London: Henry Colburn 1813) was in Captain D'Wolf's library.

Langsdorff's story is all of tattoos, cannibals, taboos, and language, and about two beachcombers, Edward Robarts and Jean Cabris, who were his informants. The first thing the two boys would have seen in Langsdorff's book was an engraving of one of these beachcombers, Jean Cabris. They had only to turn the pages and there were engravings that caught the tattooed cannibals of the Marquesas forever, front and back, every space on their bodies inscribed with marks, as full as a later Melvilles scrimping pages.

Pahutiki, Enata called their fully tattooed bodies. "Wrapped in Images." Neither the nine-year-old nor the twenty-five-year-old Melville would have seen the tattoos as anything other than exotic ornamentation of the body. Melville could never enter the life- and myth-cycle the images represented. These began with a diagonal line Melville would have seen running across Cabris's face. *Pi'i'e*, "running shit," it was called. It came with a "rubbish name" that the first tattoo brought. Here was the shit of the gods and the shit of the *haka'iki*, chief, who sponsored the first tattoos. From that moment, at every occasion of personal and communal special experience — war, peace, sacrifice, marriage, first skills learned — the tattoos would be added to till there was no part of the skin not tattooed. Not the eyelids, not the lips. The body would be all *paka* ("crust"), *tufa* ("lid"), *po'o* ("skeleton"). The skin would then be like a crab shell, like a tortoise shell over the soft, boundaryless water-life within. Mythic story, told in a glance, enclosed that life. Lightning struck out of the eyespots in the warrior's armpits when he raised his spear to throw, his club to strike. Eyes flashed on his forearm. A filigree of half people that his mythical carers would make whole was an army on his body. When death came, women with their own right hand tattooed with power would begin to rub his images away with oils and ointments, filter them off and consume them. When the body was cleaned of all its images and their power consumed, it was ready to start its journey into freedom. *Pahutiki* was now unwrapped, free flowing water-life. *Pahutiki* was *opou hou*, "conceived for the first time" again.

So at nine years old, Herman Melville met and didn't meet his tattooed cannibals, and his beachcombers as well. Langsdorff's book, forever on its shelf, is in the before and after of Melville's beachcombing experience.

Reading is a dance on the beaches of the mind. Recognition, transformation, future looks, backward glances, flits of understanding and memory are its steps. No beach in reading is pristine. A beach is always marked by the footsteps in the sand of the befores, the wet soaking edginess of the now, and the vague future shapes beyond the dunes. It is difficult to cross a beach by just reading, though.

Most of the crew are on the *Acushnet's* deck as she edges along the southern coast of Nukuhiva. They are a motley, ragged lot after eighteen months at sea from their home port of Fairhaven, Massachusetts. Four "Gees" or Portuguese from the Azores, five blacks and mulattoes, Irishmen, Scots, New Yorkers, Bostonians, Philadelphians. And there is one twenty-one-year-old 5'9½" — what *shall* we say? Albany-Dutch-New-Yorker? Failed, debt-laden Bostonian scribe? Herman Melville.

The *Acushnet* has 700 barrels of whale-oil in her hold, and had sent back another 175 barrels by another whaler. At a guess, that is perhaps fifteen whales at sixty barrels a whale. At a guess again, that is forty-five frenetic days of chase, capture, cutting, boiling, cleaning up. The other 500 days were search — in the South Atlantic, up the west coast of South America, around the Galapagos and along the equatorial line. Days of boredom in which men tested their sufferance of one another, and the limits of the power and authority over them. Days of ugly labor, engulfed in greasy black smoke, covered in the blood and slime of death. Days careless of obligations to family and society. Days that would make men loners, owing nothing, owed nothing. The generosity of others is always a surprise for them. Generosity of others will be the first surprise of their beach.

The Acushnets come with "strangely jumbled expectations," the only writer among them says. Their "gams" — their meetings with other whalers; there had been twenty-two of them — their "gams" had filled their ears with yarns that gave an extravagance to everything about the beach they were about to visit — its dangers, its pleasures, its otherness.

These anticipations became even more strangely jumbled the moment the *Acushnet* turned into Taiohae bay and lost her way in the protected waters. They were not alone. In that vast volcanic cauldron on their starboard side as they entered were the ships of a French expeditionary force. Admiral Abel Dupetit-Thouars on his madcap venture of taking possession of the Marquesas for France and Louis-Napoleon had arrived at Taiohae on May 31 1842, just three weeks before the *Acushnet*.

1,800 sailors, two infantry and artillery companies, and 400 troops had made their mark in that short time. The land in the eastern part of the bay was scoured of all vegetation to the end of the treeline on the slopes. They had forgotten to bring tents and hammocks. Those ashore were tormented by the mosquitoes and the curse of the island, the *noni*, a biting gnat. The smoke of constantly lit fires was their only repellent. Behind a deep trench, palm-leafed barracks and tiled warehouses for provisions and gunpowder were beginning to appear.

A small hillock jutted out into the waters of the bay. Its top was shaved flat and scarred with earthworks. Seven cannons dominated the scene. Fort Collet, the French called it. Fort Collet divided the bay between a native (*enata*) west and a foreign (*haoe*) east. The natives called themselves Teii. "*Ma foi! Oui! Oui!,*" they heard the French exclaim, and called these foreigners *mafaui* for it.

Captain Pease of the *Acushnet*, no doubt realizing that 2,500 *ma-foi-oui-oujs* in the bay meant that supplies would be hard to obtain and expensive, anchored the *Acushnet* on the west, or native side. The whaler *Potomac* was already anchored there; they were only the latest whalers of more than forty to have anchored at Taiohae in the previous twelve months. There would have been none of that Dionysiac welcoming that had become one of the myths about arrival in the Marquesas. Melville had Dionysiac memories, but he was in a time-bubble in which somebody else's yesterday experiences had become his own of today.

Probably some young girls and some older women swam out to the *Acushnet* and plied their trade. But that trade had become more ugly and violent over the years. The rapes and kidnappings had become too ordinary, the diseases of the sailors too public, the brutal transience of the whaler's visits too obvious for the scene to have much charm. There were politics too. They could not see it from the decks of the *Acushnet*, but the beach before them seethed with politics. The beach was divided over what the intrusion of so many strangers meant and what it did to native life, and how it was to be managed, if not controlled.

The *Acushnet* anchored at the extreme western end of the bay, opposite a collection of open sheds that housed a dozen or more canoes. There were war canoes, with their distinctive Marquesan washstrake and breakwaters. There were smaller outrigger fishing canoes as well. They belonged to a man called Vaheketou who was the *tuhuna avaiki*, the actual and ceremonial fisherman of the valley. He was to be killed accidentally in the days Melville was on the island. Melville would feel, unknowingly, the ripple effect of that death in far away Taipivai. The people of the valley would go "fishing," as they called it, for human sacrifices. No death in a land so disturbed in all its ordinariness by the intrusion of strangers and their diseases was ever "accidental." Sorcerers were always thought to be pointing their finger at those who would succumb.

Across the bow of the *Acushnet* — for more than two hundred years sailors have advised one another to anchor fore and aft looking north in Taiohae — the crew could see an idyllic enough scene. A screen of trees — breadfruit, hibiscus, gardenia, coconut, and myrtle stood behind a beach of smooth stones rolling in the waves.

There was a huge banyan tree, fifty meters across. It was alive with birds — the noisy yellow warbler (*komako*), green parrots (*kuku*), blue lorikeets (*pihiti*), flycatchers, king-fishers, pipers, and seabirds, whirling, crying. Perhaps Melville did not see the birds though. The French officers, under all sorts of delusions about their length of stay and tropical plenty, already moped over their rancid lard and vinegared wine. To cope, they had blasted every bird out of the sky in three weeks.

On the foreshore, midway between the canoe sheds and the banyan tree, stood the most obvious structure in the valley. It was a bastard of a house, an architectural icon of the littered spaces of a beach. It was an "English" house, it was said. A door and two windows and divided rooms were the mark of its Englishness. Scavenged materiel from ships and past intrusions were its makings. There was a flagpole waiting for its flag, which the French were happy to give it.

It was Temoana's house. Temoana was *haka'iki* of Taiohae. If Temoana had a beach of a house, Temoana also had a beach of a soul. He used to display it each evening for the "Acushnets" and anyone else to see. He used to ride the foreshore on a white stallion that the French had lent him in a red colonel's uniform that the French had given him. The French had already given him much champagne and 1,800 francs for the pieces of land on which they were building their barracks and fort. They were offering him 2,000 francs per annum stipend if he would be their "king" and sign their deeds of possession. He was playing hard to get. He wanted them to get back his wife first.

Captain Pease had decided that the *Acushnet* would leave Taiohae on July 11. Melville was given shore leave with the rest of the starboard watch on July 9. He knew the opprobrium of "running away." But he knew as well that someone's "runaway" would easily become someone else's replacement crew. The turnover in places like the Marquesas was quick. There were eighteen "runaways" at Taiohae alone in 1842. Melville would lose his "lay," his share of whaling profits, but he probably owed the ship something too. Pease wouldn't just let him go. There was a beachcomber, Jim Fitch — "Irish Jimmy" — policing the beach for the French and the whalers. He would return any "runaways" to the ship. Melville, if he wished to run away from the *Acushnet*, would have to find some way of leaving Taiohae.

May through September were Nukuhiva's wet months. The *Acushnet's* starboard watch spent a wet shore leave under the canoe hangers. No orgies, no romance, not much joy. Melville and his mate, Toby Greene, slipped easily away, some ship's bread, tobacco, and a bolt of cloth for gifts in the folds of their frock shirts. They would have known that it would have been dangerous to come with anything else. It was safer for a "runaway" to come near naked to the beach.

Melville and Greene could not follow the four or five paths that led back from the beach to the interior of the valley and up the slopes to the mountain ridges around. They went directly up to the ridge behind the canoe hangar and thus had to move all around the horseshoe ridge to get to the path to a safe valley next to Taiohae. They missed this in the darkness and rain, and ended up by mistake in the one valley they feared to enter, Taipivai.

Melville did not have to romance the dangerous, slippery trek in the dark on the edges of the high cliffs, uncertain as they were of where they were going, and what awaited them when they arrived. An ulcerated tropical sore on his leg added to the distress of it. His first steps across his beach heighten his fears of otherness, but hunger, pain, discomfort, and disorientation condition his mind and body to some surrender of self in gratitude to those supposed savages who save him.

Melville spends fourteen days among the Taipi, a week of them alone. The Taipi already had a savage reputation among Melville's future American readers. Lt. David Porter, commander of the USS *Essex*, had felt insulted by them in 1814 when he made a claim for the first overseas possession of an American empire on Nukuhiva, precisely where the French made a claim for theirs. Porter was defeated by the Taipi ambush and guerrilla tactics when he raided their valley to punish them. But he returned with a "search and destroy" exercise 150 years ahead of its time, burnt every house of the 2,000-strong population of the Taipi and killed whom he could. Melville didn't have to elaborate the otherness of the Taipi. For American readers the "Typee" had the otherness of a native enemy already known.

Fourteen days of native food, native habitation, native dress, native material goods. Fourteen days to enter the day and night cycle of native living. Fourteen days to catch something of the cycle of life and death, of dance and ceremony, of worship and government. These fourteen days are enough to pepper his story with reality effects, made the more real as a writer in his brother's Nassau St. office where he can go back to Langsdorff and even David Porter.

His memory of his beach is like the line drawings of a coloring book. His reading to write gives him the brush to color them in.

Melville has had important experiences of otherness, nonetheless. One was that difference is a translation. The hospitality, care, and comfort he receives from these savages is civilization in another dress. It isn't an entry into other people's metaphors — not by a long way — but it is a first step in a sense of the relativity of things.

Another realization for Melville is that if there is civilization on both sides of the beach, there is also savagery on both sides. He sees the savagery in the French. He will see it later in missionaries He sees it in himself. Here is how he describes his escape from the Taipi.

> Even at the moment I felt horror at the act I was about to commit [Melville was escaping in a whale-boat; Mow-Mow, his perceived captor, was swimming after him] but it was no time for pity or compunction, and with a true aim, and exerting all my strength, I dashed the boat-hook at him. It struck him just below the throat, and forced him downwards. I had no time to repeat my blow, but I saw him rise to the surface in the wake of the boat, and never shall I forget the ferocious expression of his countenance.

It was the sort of violence, I have to say, that was a daily occurrence on these beaches. It is Melville's surprise that he looks at the otherness of his beach and sees his own violence mirrored in the reflection.

That's my short true story. Since the purpose of our relationship is didactic — here we are meant to learn from one another — let me play Everyman to my theater. Let me pull aside the curtains, step out onto the proscenium, and in an Epilogue tell you what I think you have just read.

Representing the past — re-presenting the past — is always a challenge to perform cross-culturally. It always means crossing a beach. It means seeing otherness, hearing silences with the same generosity and fluency of spirit, and the same fullness of experience, that we have in our reading dances. Our performance will always be reflective. We always will be mirrored in the otherness, but it will always be an enlarged self that is reflected, and the more authoritative because there will be no reflection at all if we have not given something of ourselves to see and hear otherness. Our performance will always be artful, something other than the past that we present. Our creativity will always be obliged by the ideals of truthfulness. Why that should be so, I cannot say. Perhaps I should end with that declaration and witness. The ultimate performance for a historian is truthfulness.

CHAPTER 27

Walter Benjamin

THE ARCADES PROJECT (1999)*

Walter Benjamin's *The Arcades Project* – a translation of his *Das Passagen-Werk* which first appeared in 1982 (published by Suhrkamp Verlag as Volume 5 of his *Gesammelteschriften*) – occupied Benjamin at regular intervals for the thirteen years between 1927 and his early death in 1940. He considered it to be his masterpiece. Benjamin hoped that he would be able to express in the work 'the materialist philosophy of the nineteenth century'. In his excellent essay that appears between pages 929 and 945 of *The Arcades Project*, the translator from the German, Rolf Tiedemann, explains the aims that Benjamin had for his 'project' – its method of construction and its legacy. Readers of this volume should start here for a fuller and extremely insightful understanding of the work. Unfinished in 1940, the work, which is made up of several parts (*Exposés*, on nineteenth-century 'Paris in Europe'; *Convolutes*, which offer details of the Parisian arcades and 'Paris'; *First Sketches*, further impressions of the arcades as a microcosm of the nature of the nineteenth- century bourgeoisie, and *Addenda*, containing an exposé of 1935 (early version), materials for the 1935 exposé and for the arcades), allows Benjamin to articulate, clothe and wed his (Marxist) philosophy of history through, very precisely, his collection of 'impressions' of the Parisian arcades. In the long main section of the work (*Convolutes*) – a section divided into 36 subsections with titles such as Fashion, Baudelaire, The Flâneur, Mirrors, Modes of Lighting and Social Movement – within which there are dozens of observations (generally in single paragraphs or 'fragments') that adhere to no linear sequence, Benjamin, to quote Tiedemann, attempted to 'bring together theory and materials, quotations and interpretations, in a new constellation compared to contemporary modes of representation'. This bringing together would help Benjamin to isolate – and solve through 'montage' – what he saw as the 'central problem of historical materialism' which he himself put thus:

> In what way is it possible to conjoin a heightened graphicness to the realization of the Marxist Method? The first stage of this understanding will be to carry over the principle of montage into history. That is, to assemble large-scale constructions out of the smallest and precisely cut components. Indeed, to discover in the analysis of the small individual movement the crystal of the total event.

———————

The magic columns of these palaces
Show to the amateur on all sides,
In the objects their porticos display,
That industry is the rival of the arts.
　　　　　—"Chanson nouvelle," cited in *Nouveaux Tableaux de Paris, ou*
　　　　　Observations sur les moeurs et usages des Parisiens au commencement
　　　　　du XIX siècle (Paris, 1828), vol. 1, p. 27

* Walter Benjamin (1999) *The Arcades Project*, Cambridge, MA: The Belknap Press of Harvard University Press, pp. 35–41 and 420–3.

For sale the bodies, the voices, the tremendous unquestionable wealth, what
will never be sold.

—Rimbaud

"IN SPEAKING OF THE** inner boulevards," says the *Illustrated Guide to
Paris*, a complete picture of the city on the Seine and its environs from the year
1852, "we have made mention again and again of the arcades which open onto them. These
arcades, a recent invention of industrial luxury; are glass-roofed, marble-paneled corridors extending through whole blocks of buildings, whose owners have joined together for
such enterprises. Lining both sides of these corridors, which get their light from above,
are the most elegant shops, so that the arcade is a city, a world in miniature Flâneur, in
which customers will find everything they need. During sudden rainshowers, the arcades
are a place of refuge for the unprepared, to whom they offer a secure, if restricted, prom-
enade—one from which the merchants also benefit." Weather.

This passage is the locus classicus for the presentation of the arcades; for not only do
the divagations on the flâneur and the weather develop out of it, but, also, what there is
to be said about the construction of the arcades, in an economic and architectural vein,
would have a place here.

> Names of *magasins de nouveautés*: La Fille d'Honneur, La Vestale, Le Page
> Inconstant, Le Masque de Fer <The Iron Mask>, Le Petit Chaperon Rouge
> <Little Red Riding Hood>, Petite Nanette, La Chaumière allemande <The
> German Cottage>, Au Mamelouk, Le Coin de la Rue <On the Streetcorner>
> —names that mostly come from successful vaudevilles. Mythology A glover:
> Au Ci-Devant Jeune Homme. A confectioner: Aux Armes de Werther.

Years of reckless financial speculation under Louis XVIII. With the dramatic signage of
the *magasins de nouveautés*, art enters the service of the businessman.

> "After the Passage de Panoramas, which went back to the year 1800 and which
> had an established reputation in society, there was, by way of example, the
> gallery that was opened in 1826 by the butchers Véro and Dodat and that was
> pictured in the 1832 lithograph by Arnout. After 1800 we must go all the
> way to 1822 to meet with a new arcade: it is between this date and 1834 that
> the majority of these singular passageways are constructed. The most
> important of them are grouped in an area bounded by the Rue Croix-des-
> Petits-Champs to the south, the Rue de la Grange-Batelière to the north, the
> Boulevard de Sébastopol to the east, and the Rue Ventadour to the west."
> Marcel Poëte, *Une vie de cité* (Paris, 1925), pp. 373–374.

[. . .]

The regime of specialties furnishes also—this said in passing—the historical-materialist key
to the flourishing (if not the inception) of genre painting in the Forties of the previous century. With the growing interest of the bourgeoisie in matters of art, this type of painting
diversified; but in conformity with the meager artistic appreciation initially displayed by
this class, it did so in terms of the content, in terms of the objects represented. There
appeared historical scenes, animal studies, scenes of childhood, scenes from the life of
monks, the life of the family, the life of the village—all as sharply defined genres.

The influence of commercial affairs on Lautréamont and Rimbaud should be looked into!

"Another characteristic deriving chiefly from the Directory [presumably until around 1830??] would be the lightness of fabrics; on even the coldest days, one was seen only rarely in furs or warm overcoats. At the risk of losing their skin, women clothed themselves as though the harshness of winter no longer existed, as though nature had suddenly been transformed into an eternal paradise." <John> Grand-Carteret, *Les Eléances de la toilette* (Paris), p. xxxiv.

In other respects as well, the theater in those days provided the vocabulary for articles of fashion. Hats á la Tarare, á la Théodore, á la Figaro, á la Grande-Prêtresse, á la Iphigénie, á la Calprenade, á la Victoire. The same *niaiserie* that seeks in ballet the origin of the real betrays itself when—around 1830—a newspaper takes the name *Le Sylphe*.

Alexandre Dumas at a dinner party given by Princess Mathilde. The verse is aimed at Napoleon III.

> In their imperial splendor,
> The uncle and nephew are equal:
> The uncle seized the capitals,
> The nephew seizes our capital.

Icy silence followed. Reported in *Mémoires du comte Horace de Viel-Castel sur le règne de Napoléon III*, vol. 2 (Paris, 1883), p. 185.

"The *coulisse* guaranteed the ongoing life of the Stock Exchange. Here there was never closing time; there was almost never night. When the Café Tortoni finally closed its doors, the column of stock jobbers would head across the adjacent boulevards and meander up and down there, collecting in front of the Passage de l'Opéra." Julius Rodenberg, *Paris bei Sonnenschein und Lampenlicht* (Leipzig, 1867), p. 97.

Speculation in railroad stocks under Louis Philippe.

[. . .]

"The Passage du Caire is highly reminiscent, on a smaller scale, of the Passage du Saumon, which in the past existed on the Rue Montmartre, on the site of the present-day Rue Bachaumont." Paul Léautaud, "Vieux Paris," *Mercure de France* (October 15, 1927), p. 503.

"Shops on the old model, devoted to trades found nowhere else, surmounted by a small, old-fashioned mezzanine with windows that each bear a number, on an escutcheon, corresponding to a particular shop. From time to time, a doorway giving onto a corridor; at the end of the corridor, a small stairway leading to these mezzanines. Near the knob of one of these doors, this handwritten sign:

> The worker next door
> would be obliged if,
> in closing the door,
> you refrained from slamming it.

Another sign is cited in the same place (Léautaud, "Vieux Paris," *Mercure de France* [1927], pp. 502–503):

> ANGELA
> 2ⁿᵈ floor, to the right

Old name for department stores: *docks á bon marché*—that is, "discount docks." <Sigfried> Giedion, *Bauen in Frankreich* <Leipzig and Berlin, 1928>, p. 31.

Evolution of the department store from the shop that was housed in arcades. Principle of the department store: "The floors form a single space. They can be taken in, so to speak, 'at a glance'" Giedion, *Bauen in Frankreich*, p. 34.

Giedion shows (in *Bauen in Frankreich*, p. 35) how the axiom, "Welcome the crowd and keep it seduced" (*Science et l'industrie*, 143 [1925], p. 6), leads to corrupt architectural practices in the construction of the department store Au Printemps (1881–1889). Function of commodity capital!

"Even women, who were forbidden to enter the Stock Exchange, assembled at the door in order to glean same indications of market prices and to relay their orders to brokers through the iron grating." *La Transformation de Paris sous le Second Empire* (authors Poëte, Clouzot, Henriot) <Paris, 1910>, on the occasion of the exhibition of the library and the historical works of the city of Paris, p. 66.

"We have no specialty"—this is what the well-known dealer in secondhand goods, Frémin, "the man with the head of gray," had written on the signboard advertising his wares in the Place des Abbesses. Here, in antique bric-à-brac, reemerges the old physiognomy of trade that, in the first decades of the previous century, began to be supplanted by the rule of the *spécialité*. This "superior scrap-yard" was called *Au Philosophe* by its proprietor. What a demonstration and demolition of stoicism! On his placard were the words: "Maidens, do not dally under the leaves!" And: "Purchase nothing by moonlight."

Evidently people smoked in the arcades at a time when it was not yet customary to smoke in the street. "I must say a word here about life in the arcades, favored haunt of strollers and smokers, theater of operations for every kind of small business. In each arcade there is at least one cleaning establishment. In a salon that is as elegantly furnished as its intended use permits, gentlemen sit upon high stools and comfortably peruse a newspaper while someone busily brushes time dirt off their clothing and boots." Ferdinand Von Gall, *Paris and seine Salons*, vol. 2 <Oldenburg, 1845>, pp. 22–23.

A first winter garden—a glassed-in space with flower beds, espaliers, and fountains, in part underground—on the spot where, in the garden of the Palais-Royal in 1864 (and today as well?), the reservoir was located. Laid out in 1788.

"It is at the end of the Restoration that we see the first *magasins de nouveautés*: Les Vêpres Siciliennes, Le Solitaire, La Fille Mal Gardée, Le Soldat Laboureur, Les Deux Magots, Le Petit Saint-Thomas, Le Gagne-Denier <Penny Winnings>." <Lucien> Dubech and <Pierre> d'Espezel, *Histoire de Paris* (Paris, 1926), p. 360.

"In 1820 . . . the Passage Viollet and the Passage des Deux Pavilions were opened. These arcades were among the novelties of their day. The result of private initiative, they were covered galleries housing shops that fashion made prosperous. The most famous was the Passage des Panoramas, which flourished from 1823 to 1831. 'On Sundays,' observed Musset, one went en masse 'to the Panoramas or else to the boulevards.' it was also private initiative that created, somewhat haphazardly, the housing developments known as

cités, the short streets or dead ends built at shared expense by a syndicate of property own-ers." Lucien Dubech and Pierre d'Espezel, *Histoire de Paris* (Paris, 1926), pp. 355–356.
    [. . .]

The Flâneur

The attitude of the flâneur—epitome of the political attitude of the middle classes during the Second Empire.

    With the steady increase in traffic on the streets, it was only the macadamization of the roadways that made it possible in the end to have a conversation on the terrace of a café without shouting in the other person's ear.

    The laissez-faire of the flâneur has its counterpart even in the revolutionary philosophemes of the period. "We smile at the chimerical pretension [of a Saint-Simon] to trace all physical and moral phenomena back to the law of universal attraction. But we forget too easily that this pretension was not in itself isolated; under the influence of the revolutionizing natural laws of mechanics, there could arise a current of natural philoso-phy which saw in the mechanism of nature the proof of just such a mechanism of social life and of events generally." <Willy> Spuhler, *Der Saint-Simonismus* (Zurich, 1926), p. 29.

    Dialectic of flânerie: on one side, the man who feels himself viewed by all and sundry as a true suspect and, on the other side, the man who is utterly undiscoverable, the hidden man. Presumably, it is this dialectic that is developed in "The Man of the Crowd?"

    "Theory of the transformation of the city into countryside: this was . . . the main theme of my unfinished work on Maupassant . . . At issue was the city as hunting ground, and in general the concept of the hunter played a major role (as in the theory of the uniform: all hunters look alike)." Letter from Wiesengrund, June 5, 1935.

    The principle of flânerie in Proust: "Then, quite apart from all those literary preoc-cupations, and without definite attachment to anything, suddenly a roof, a gleam of sunlight reflected from a stone, the smell of a road would make me stop still, to enjoy the special pleasure that each of them gave me, and also because they appeared to be concealing, beneath what my eyes could see, something which they invited me to approach and take from them, but which, despite all my efforts, I never managed to discover?" *Du Côté de chez Swann* <(Paris, 1939), vol. 1, p. 256.>—This passage shows very clearly how the old Romantic sentiment for landscape dissolves and a new Romantic conception of landscape emerges—of landscape that seems, rather, to be a cityscape, if it is true that the city is the properly sacred ground of flânerie. In this passage, at any rate, it would be presented as such for the first time since Baudelaire (whose work does not yet portray the arcades, though they were so numerous in his day).

    So the flâneur goes for a walk in his room: "When Johannes sometimes asked for permission to go out, it was usually denied him. But on occasion his father proposed, as a substitute, that they walk up and down the room hand in hand. This seemed at first a poor substitute, but in fact . . . something quite novel awaited him. The proposal was accepted, and it was left entirely to Johannes to decide where they should go. Off they went, then, right out the front entrance, out to a neighboring estate or to the seashore, or simply through the streets, exactly as Johannes could have wished; for his father managed everything. While they strolled in this way up and down the floor of his room, his father told him of all they saw. They greeted other pedestrians; passing wagons made a din around them and drowned out his father's voice; the comfits in the pastry shop were more inviting than ever." An early work by Kierkegaard, cited in Eduard Geismar, *Sören Kierkegaard* (Göttingen, 1929), pp. 12–13. Here is the key to the schema of *Voyage autour de ma chambre.*

"The manufacturer passes over the asphalt conscious of its quality; the old man searches it carefully, follows it just as long as he can, happily taps his cane so the wood resonates, and recalls with pride that he personally witnessed the laying of the first sidewalks; the poet . . . walks on it pensive and unconcerned, muttering lines of verse; the stockbroker hurries past, calculating the advantages of the last rise in wheat; and the madcap slides across." Alexis Martin, "Physiologie de l'asplhalte," *Le Bohême*, 1, no. 3, (April 15, 1855)—Charles Pradier, editor in chief.

On the Parisians' technique of *inhabiting* their streets: "Returning by the Rue Saint-Honoré, we met with an eloquent example of that Parisian street industry which can make use of anything. Men were at work repairing the pavement and laying pipeline, and, as a result, in the middle of the street there was an area which was blocked off but which was embanked and covered with stones. On this spot street vendors had immediately installed themselves, and five or six were selling writing implements and notebooks, cutlery, lampshades, garters, embroidered collars, and all sorts of trinkets. Even a dealer in secondhand goods had opened a branch office here and was displaying on the stones his bric-a-brac of old cups, plates, glasses, and so forth, so that business was profiting, instead of suffering, from the brief disturbance. They are simply wizards at making a virtue of necessity." Adolf Stahr, *Nach fünf Jahren* (Oldenburg, 1857), vol. 1, p. 29.

Seventy years later, I had the same experience at the corner of the Boulevard Saint-Germain and the Boulevard Raspail. Parisians make the street an interior.

"It is wonderful that in Paris itself one can actually wander through countryside." Karl Gutzkow, *Briefe aus Paris* (Leipzig, 1842), vol. 1, p. 61. The other side of the motif is thus touched on. For if flânerie can transform Paris into one great interior—a house whose rooms are the *quartiers*, no less clearly demarcated by thresholds than are real rooms—then, on the other hand, the city can appear to someone walking through it to be without thresholds: a landscape in the round.

But in the final analysis, only the revolution creates an open space for the city. Fresh air doctrine of revolutions. Revolution disenchants the city. Commune in *L'Education sentimentale*. Image of the street in civil war.

Street as domestic interior. Concerning the Passage du Pont-Neuf (between the Rue Guénégaud and the Rue de Seine): "the shops resemble closets." *Nouveaux Tableaux de Paris, ou Observations sur les mœurs et usages des Parisiens au commencement du XIXᵉ siècle* (Paris, 1828), vol. 1, p. 34.

The courtyard of the Tuileries: "immense savannah planted with lampposts instead of banana trees." Paul-Ernest de Rattier, *Paris n'existe pas* (Paris, 1857).

Passage Colbert. "The gas lamp illuminating it looks like a coconut palm in the middle of a savannah." *Le Livre des cent-et-un* (Paris, 1833), vol. 10, p. 57 (Amédée Kermel, "Les Passages de Paris").

Lighting in the Passage Colbert: "I admire the regular series of those crystal globes, which give off a light both vivid and gentle. Couldn't the same be said of comets in battle formation, awaiting the signal for departure to go vagabonding through space?" *Le Livre des cent-et-un*, vol. 10, p. 57. Compare this transformation of the city into an astral world with Grandville's *Un Autre Monde*.

In 1839 it was considered elegant to take a tortoise out walking. This gives us an idea of the tempo of flânerie in the arcades.

Gustave Claudin is supposed to have said: "On the day when a filet ceases to be a filet and becomes a 'chateaubriand,' when a mutton stew is called an 'Irish stew,' or when the waiter cries out, '*Moniteur*, clock!' to indicate that this newspaper was requested by the customer sitting under the clock—on that day, Paris will have been truly dethroned!" Jules Claretie, *La Vie á Paris 1896* (Paris, 1897), p. 100.

"There—on the Avenue des Champs-Elysées—it has stood since 1845: the Jardin d'Hiver, a colossal greenhouse with a great many rooms for social occasions, for balls and concerts, although, since its doors are open in summer too, it hardly deserves the name of winter garden." When the sphere of planning creates such entanglements of closed room and airy nature, then it serves in this way to meet the deep human need for daydreaming—a propensity that perhaps proves the true efficacy of idleness in human affairs. Woldemar Seyffarth, *Wahrnehmungen in Paris 1853 und 1854* (Gotha, 1855), p. 130.

The menu at Les Trois Frères Provençaux: "Thirty-six pages for food, four pages for drink—but very long pages, in small folio, with closely packed text and numerous annotations in fine print." The booklet is bound in velvet. Twenty hors d'oeuvres and thirty-three soups. "Forty-six beef dishes, among which are seven different beefsteaks and eight filets?' "Thirty-four preparations of game, forty-seven dishes of vegetables, and seventy-one varieties of compote?" Julius Rodenberg, *Paris bei Sonnenschein und Lampenlicht* (Leipzig, 1867), pp. 43–44. Flânerie through the bill of fare.

The best way, while dreaming, to catch the afternoon in the net of evening is to make plans. The flâneur in planning.

"Le Corbusier's houses depend on neither spatial nor plastic articulation: the air passes through them! Air becomes a constitutive factor! What matters, therefore, is neither spatiality per se nor plasticity per se but only relation and interfusion. There is but one indivisible space. The Integuments separating inside from outside fall away." Sigfried Giedion, *Bauen in Frankreich* <Berlin, 1928>, p. 85.

Streets are the dwelling place of the collective. The collective is an eternally unquiet, eternally agitated being that—in the space between the building fronts—experiences, learns, understands, and invents as much as individuals do within the privacy of their own four walls. For this collective, glossy enameled shop signs are a wall decoration as good as, if not better than, an oil painting in the drawing room of a bourgeois; walls with their "Post No Bills" are its writing desk, newspaper stands its libraries, mailboxes its bronze busts, benches its bedroom furniture, and the café terrace is the balcony from which it looks down on its household. The section of railing where road workers hang their jackets is the vestibule, and the gateway which leads from the row of courtyards out into the open is the long corridor that daunts the bourgeois, being for the courtyards the entry to the chambers of the city. Among these latter, the arcade was the drawing room. More than anywhere else, the street reveals itself in the arcade as the furnished and familiar interior of the masses.

CHAPTER 28

Richard Price

FIRST-TIME: THE HISTORICAL VISION OF AN AFRICAN AMERICAN PEOPLE ([1983] 2002)*

In Richard Price's *First-Time: The Historical Vision of an African American People* (first published in 1983, with a second edition in 2002 from which this extract is taken), the author (the Diane A. and Virginia S. Dittman Professor of American Studies, Anthropology and History at the College of William and Mary, Virginia) examines the *shape* 'of historical thought among peoples who had previously been denied any history at all' – namely, the sense of history held by the Saramaka, one of six Maroon (or Bush Negro) tribes in Suriname in French Guinea, South America, that currently constitutes some 10 per cent of the total population and whose ancestors were among those Africans who were sold into slavery in the late seventeenth/early eighteenth centuries and who, having intermittently fought for their freedom for over one hundred years were, in 1762 – a further century before the general emancipation of slaves in Suriname – emancipated.

In his text Price presents, on the top part of the page, direct transcripts of 'oral histories' told by living Saramaka about their ancestors, providing on the lower part of the page commentaries that place the oral remembrances into broader intellectual and 'historical contexts'. Although, like Dening, not by his own account a 'postmodernist', he has nevertheless attracted the label ('Price', says Lucy Lippard, 'practices what a lot of postmodernists preach [with] the book's graceful writing and innovative form tossing the reader back and forth in time and space': there is no linearity, no smoothness, no 'getting the story *straight*').

The following extract from *First-Time* is in three parts. In the first part (Preface), Price reflects upon his own intellectual genealogy and his theoretical and interconnected political position. In the second ('On Reading Saramaka History'), he explains the content of the book and its form(s). In the third ('The Events – The Heroic Years 1685–1748'), he juxtaposes oral and documentary sources with his own personal/historical contextualisations which he blends together with mediations on the role of histories – not least his own – and their relationship(s) to meanings.

This is not the only text in which Price has experimented with anthropological/historical representations in 'postist' ways. Following *First-Time* – which Price himself describes as being concerned to represent partial truths through alternative/alternating narratives and multifaceted voices – he wrote perhaps his best known book, *Alabi's World* (Baltimore, MD: The Johns Hopkins University Press, 1990) (in which he used four different typefaces to emphasise the inevitable perspectivalism of his various sources (voices), this in turn being followed by other major works. Thus, his *The Convict and the Colonel* (Boston, MA: Beacon Press, 1998) (a history of twentieth-century Martinique written, as he puts it, 'from widely eccentric perspectives, focussing on marginal incidents and marginal characters – including myself – to tell the story') runs alongside several other equally 'disturbing' historical texts while, with his wife,

---

* Richard Price ([1983] 2002) *First-Time*, Chicago: The University of Chicago Press, pp. xi–xv, 37–40 and 43–53.

he has written 'historically' in the form of a screenplay (*Two Evenings in Saramaka*, Chicago: University of Chicago Press, 1991), in the form of a diary (*Equatoria*, New York: Routledge, 1992) and, in a discussion of their joint ethnographical research, a novel (*Enigma Variations*, Cambridge, MA: Harvard University Press).

Richard Price's work is, to say the least, unusual among both anthropologists and historians. Formally highly innovative, lyrical in expression and tantalising in the telling of many tales that discordantly harmonise, Price has also (again, rare among historians) talked and written in highly reflexive ways about his work(s), methods and intentions. Thus, readers interested in the deconstructionist *genre* would do well to start with Price's autobiographical sketch, 'Practices of Historical Narrative', in *Rethinking History* (5 (3), 2001: 357–65).

PREFACE

BY THE TIME I CAME along to graduate school in the early 1960s, anthropological monographs had long adhered to a fairly uniform and apparently natural format (despite minor differences between the British and American versions). In the words of James Boon, there was a strong "stylistic taboo on authorial viewpoint . . . Its order of contents was physical surroundings firmly first, religion vaguely last, kinship and social organization determiningly at the core" (1982:14). At the tail end of the period that George Stocking calls "the classic period of Anthropology," which he places between 1925 and 1965 (1992:357), my classmates and I were still being trained to do Social Science. Narrative, hermeneutics, and history-among-non-literate-peoples were pretty much off everyone's radar screens.

For reasons that remain somewhat mysterious, many of us went off for a couple of years to what anthropologists still called "the field" (usually deepest, darkest somewhere-or-other), returned to the academy, and discovered, apparently independently, that the kind of encyclopedic social science monograph we had been trained to write (and to think) was simply no longer possible. So each of us—Renato Rosaldo, Paul Rabinow, Greg Dening, and a host of others—began writing books that didn't look or feel at all like the monographs we had grown up with. The 1970s and early 1980s witnessed a transformation in ethnography, marked in a symbolic sense by the appearance of the collective work *Writing Culture* (Clifford and Marcus 1986), in which a group of anthropologists of my generation took stock and boldly declared that anthropology not only had a politics but also a poetics. What came to be called "the literary turn" was in full swing.

One of our collective godfathers, Clifford Geertz, commented aptly on these new challenges, which came both from within and beyond the discipline. There had been a "transformation," he wrote, "of the people anthropologists mostly write about, from colonial subject to sovereign citizens," which had "altered entirely the moral context within which the ethnographical act takes place" and which perforce "leaves contemporary anthropologists in some uncertainty as to rhetorical aim." "Who," Geertz asked, "is now to be persuaded? Africanists or Africans? Americanists or American Indians? Japanologists or Japanese? And of what: Factual accuracy? Theoretical sweep? Imaginative grasp? Moral depth?" (1988:132–33). But at the same time as the moral foundations of ethnography had been shaken, its epistemological foundations, he noted, had also been cracked by general questions raised in other disciplines about the nature of representation. To the anthropologists' worry, "Is it decent?," there was now added "Is it possible?"—a concern, he said, "they are even less well prepared to deal with" (1988:135). Geertz concluded his overview by arguing that what anthropologists needed was effective *art*: "If there is any way to counter the conception of ethnography as an iniquitous act or an unplayable game, it would seem to involve owning up to the fact that, like quantum mechanics or the Italian opera, it is a work of the imagination" (1988:140).

With the wisdom of hindsight, one can now discern, during the early 1980s, the gradual, emergence of a new kind of ethnographic history. Along with books by Renato Rosaldo (1980, on Ilongot headhunters) and Marshall Sahlins (1985, on the native peoples of Hawaii), *First-Time* has been classed among the triumvirate of works that helped shift the attention of anthropologists and historians to the shape of historical thought among peoples who had previously been denied any history at all (Krech 1991). (I would add Cohen 1977 and Dening 1980 to the list.)

At the same time, that book formed part of the search for new ways of "writing culture," for new forms of ethnographic and historical *écriture*. In this regard, James Clifford, struck by its insistence on what he called "partial truths," argued that "*First-Time* is evidence of the fact that acute political and epistemological self-consciousness need not lead to ethnographic self-absorption" (1986:7). John Szwed focused on another aspect of the book's form in suggesting that "by balancing and reconciling the multiple Saramaka accounts with those of Europeans, the author has produced a dialogically reticulated history which properly mimes its subject, the development of a distinctive, isolated Afro-American culture nonetheless bounded by European attempts at control and domination" (1985:227).

First-Time, then, has been read by anthropologists and historians as a work that gives voice to people previously kept mute and as an experiment in forms of historical and ethnographic representation.

The book has also been the subject of a different anthropological reading and critique, relating to the construction of a distinctively Afro-American anthropology. Jamaican anthropologist David Scott takes the classic works of Melville Herskovits and *First-Time* as exemplars of two stages in what he views as a unitary anthropological quest, noting in both "a deep, humanist inclination toward a story about continuities [that] embraces the earnest task of demonstrating the integrity and the intactness of the old in the new, and of the past in the present" (1991:262). In this narrative, he argues, "Africa" and "slavery" form the essential points of reference: "In the discursive or narrative economy of this anthropological problematic, *slavery* and '*Africa*' function as virtually interchangeable terms, or, to put it in another way, slavery in the work of Price comes to perform the same rhetorical-conceptual labor as Africa in the work of Herskovits" (1991:263). "Both," he continues, "turn on a distinctive attempt to place the 'cultures' of the ex-African/ex-slave in relation to what we might call an authentic past, that is, an anthropologically identifiable, ethnologically recoverable, and textually re-presentable past" (1991:263). From Scott's 1990s postcolonial perspective, such an attempt is fundamentally misguided (1991, 1999).

This is not the place for me to engage Scott's critique (for that, see R. Price 2001), but it may be worth noting that his programme for reorienting Afro-American anthropology away from a "sustained preoccupation with the corroboration or verification of authentic pasts" and toward a more exclusive focus on "discourse" goes rather farther than I was willing to venture when I wrote *First-Time*—or am willing to go today. I am not enough of a postmodernist—nor so afraid of essentializing—to be willing to discard, say, the facts of slave-trade demography or colonial statutes or accounts of tortures meted out to recaptured Maroons. All of these, I believe, have *effects*, and not just on discourse, in the present. I believe that we must first embrace the written, oral, and artifactual traces left us by the past in all their epistemological complications (and fully accept their constructedness) and then do our level best to re-present them honestly. For me, Saramakas are far more than an "anthropological metonym . . . providing the exemplary arena in which to argue out certain anthropological claims" (Scott 1991:269). They are at once socially and politically marginalized African Americans who have heroic Maroon traditions, who have against all odds created a vibrant culture, and whose lives (and way of life) are as threatened today as they have been at any moment since the end of the colonial wars two and a half centuries ago. I feel a deep responsibility, as anthropologist and friend, to continue to help Saramakas tell their story, in part as a means of self-defense against severe ongoing repression (see R. Price 1995, 1998a, R. and S. Price 2001).

On the level of theory (for what it's worth), I would argue that rather than apotheo-sizing discourse—which runs real risks—Afro-Americanists must embrace both discourse and event, figuring out imaginative representational strategies to handle them together. (In this regard, Michel-Rolph Trouillot warns that "As social theory becomes more discourse-oriented, the distance between data and claims . . . increases. Historical circumstances fall further into a hazy background of ideological preferences" [1998:15].) One strategy, which I used extensively in *First-Time*, is to hold both discourse and event in mind but to treat them, alternatively, as figure and ground. (Several of the essays in Trouillot's *Silencing the Past* [1995] constitute admirable attempts to achieve similar ends for Haiti in the revolutionary period.) *Alabi's World* (R. Price 1990), which picks up chronologically where *First-Time* leaves off, relates Saramaka history as seen by Saramakas, Moravian missionaries, and Dutch administrators, into the early nineteenth century; multivocal and set in four typefaces, that book expands the methodological experiment begun here. Two subsequent experiments' with representing Saramaka and other Maroon realities may be worth noting—*Equatoria* (R. and S. Price 1992), which, on the recto pages, takes the form of a field diary of a museum-collecting expedition and, on the versos, that of a collection of ethnographic memorabilia (a miscellany of literary citations and line drawings), and *Enigma Variations: A Novel* (R. and S. Price 1995), which is fictionalized account of adventures in art forgery and ethnography where questions of "authenticity" predominate. My most recent foray into Afro-Caribbean historical consciousness, *The Convict and the Colonel* (R. Price 1998b). plays perhaps most radically with voice, time, and other aspects of narrative to explore the changing shape of historical thought among postcolonial Martiniquans, but the questions raised by *First-Time* about discourse and event, history and memory, continue to fuel the endeavor.

In the 1960s, when I began my Saramaka fieldwork, the six Maroon peoples of Suriname and French Guiana were still being referred to by anthropologists as "tribes" which functioned as "states within a state." Running their own political and judicial affairs under the authority of paramount chiefs and village captains, they were known to outsiders for such exotic practices as polygyny, oracular divination, spirit possession, body scarifi-cation, and ancestor worship, as well as distinctive styles of music, dance, plastic arts, and countless other aspects of daily life that reflected their uncompromised heritage of independence and their radical difference from the other peoples of Suriname and French Guiana. Maroons felt tremendous pride in the accomplishments of their heroic ancestors and, on the whole, remained masters of their forest realm.

Since national independence in 1975, Suriname has been pursuing an increasingly militant and destructive policy against Maroons, stripping them of their rights to land and its potential riches and endangering their right to exist as distinctive peoples. In 1980, the army seized power in a coup d'etat, and the country began a downward spiral from which it has never recovered—a plummeting economy, a massive brain drain, and a notable increase in poverty, drugs, and crime. In 1986, civil war broke out between Maroons and the national Creole-run military, sending thousands of Maroons fleeing across the border into French Guiana—some 10,000 Ndyuka Maroons as recognized refugees, confined to camps enclosed by barbed wire, and countless others (mainly Saramakas) as clandestines attempting to build a new life while remaining invisible to French authorities charged with their expulsion. The fighting that raged from 1986 to 1992 pitted Maroons against the national army of Suriname, bringing back to life many of the horrors of their early ancestors' struggles for freedom. African medicine bundles that had lain buried for two hundred years were unearthed and carried into battle. Maroon men and boys, often armed with shotguns, confronted the army's automatic weapons, tanks, and helicopter gunships dropping napalm. Whole villages, particularly in the Cottica Ndyuka region, were razed, as soldiers killed hundreds of women and children with machetes and bullets. And some Saramaka warriors, members of the Jungle Commando, are reported to have carried copies of *First-Time* (which they could not read but the message of which they well knew) with them into battle.

Post-civil war Maroon life in Suriname has been transformed, perhaps irreparably, with rampant poverty and malnutrition, severe degradation of educational and medical resources, and the spread of AIDS and prostitution. The official restoration of peace in 1992 came at a price, as the Maroons were pushed into signing a treaty largely focused on rights to land, minerals, and other natural resources—all of which are now claimed by the Suriname state. The government has embarked on a rigorous program aimed at the legal unification, uniformization, and ultimately appropriation of its Maroon (as well as Amerindian) minorities, insisting that under Suriname law, neither Maroons nor indigenous peoples hold any special rights and that the interests of the total development of the country—which increasingly means the private interests of government officials and their cronies—must prevail (R. Price 1998a). Much of the forest for which the ancestors of the Maroons spilled their blood is being auctioned off by the national government to Indonesian, Malaysian, Chinese, Australian, Canadian, U.S., and Brazilian timber and mining corporations. The eighteenth-century treaties made by the Saramakas (and, separately, by other Maroon peoples) with the Dutch crown, which recognized their autonomy and territory, have unilaterally been declared null and void by the Suriname state. Saramakas, and other Maroons, are valiantly trying to protect themselves legally— and the deeds recounted in *First-Time* continue to form the basis of their claims—but the practical outcome is far from certain (Kambel and MacKay 2000, R. and S. Price 2001).

Suriname is now routinely described by foreign journalists as a "narcocracy," where shady business interests in collusion with the army fly light planes across the forest to exchange arms for drugs with Colombian guerrilla groups, and then ship the drugs to Europe. The 1999 conviction-in-absentia by a Dutch court of Desi Bouterse, Suriname's former president and commander-in-chief who led the 1980 coup d'etat, for international drug trafficking, and his sentence to 16 years in prison and a fine of $2.3 million, have had little effect on the country's general malaise.

The overall decline in the prosperity of Suriname during the past twenty years has had strong trickle-down effects on Saramakas and other Maroons. State services in Maroon territories—clinics, hospitals schools—scarcely function. (The state currently pays five U.S. cents per student per year for the maintenance of school buildings and educational materials in the interior of the country.) Medical facilities and other essential services are consistently far below even the deteriorating standards on the coast.

Today, the Saramaka population—some 20,000 at the end of the 1970s—is closer to 50,000, with nearly a third living (mainly clandestinely) in French Guiana, a significant number in and around Suriname's capital, and something over half in the "traditional" villages of the interior. These latter people are not taking the ongoing assaults of multinationals and the state lying down. In the early 1990s, Saramakas won a major case before the Inter-American Court for Human Rights (R. Price 1995), and in 2001, the Association of Saramaka Captains filed a petition against the state of Suriname with the Inter-American Commission on Human Rights to reassert claims to the territory their ancestors had fought for, their case is under active consideration as this new edition goes to press. Of all the books I have written, *First-Time*—for reasons that would have been absolutely impossible to foresee twenty years ago when it was published — has mattered most to Saramakas. (A partial listing of subsequent books that have appeared about Saramakas includes R. Price 1990, R. and S. Price 1988, 1991, 1992a, 1992b, 1994, 1995, S. Price 1984, S. and R. Price 1999.)

In July 2001, on our latest visit to French Guiana (where many Saramakas work at the European Space Center), we saw the French edition of *First-Time* being painstakingly read by schoolboys to their nonliterate fathers and we were frequently asked to recount particular events, which were then hotly debated by the older men. For many Saramakas, *First-Time* knowledge, even in the most modernistic settings, remains the common currency of identity and selfhood.

I would like to dedicate this new edition to the memory of those eighteenth-century Saramakas and other Maroons who staked their lives on the attainment of freedom, justice, and peace. And to those Saramaka historians who shared their precious knowledge with me. And finally to all their present-day descendants who, though living in significantly changed circumstances, adamantly refuse to forget.

ON READING SARAMAKA HISTORY

The Saramaka—about twenty thousand people—live in the heavily forested interior of the Republic of Suriname in northeastern South America. Their ancestors were among those Africans who were sold into slavery in the late seventeenth and early eighteenth centuries to work Suriname's sugar, timber, and coffee plantations. They soon escaped into the dense rain forest—individually, in small groups, sometimes in great collective rebellions—where for over one hundred years they fought a war of liberation. In 1762, a full century before the general emancipation of slaves in Suriname, they won their freedom. The remainder of this book is divided into two parts, running simultaneously across two channels that divide each page horizontally. The upper channel, set in Garamond Book type, carries the texts' The lower channel, set in Garamond Light type, carries my 'commentaries."

The texts present discrete fragments of Saramaka knowledge, organized in such a way as to describe the development through time of various social groups. Each fragment is, set off by an identifying number, and its source indicated. Regarding these texts, my translating and editing procedures have been aimed at preserving a Saramaka perspective. I often delete repetitive rhetorical features such as "well," "now," or "but"; I delete the conventional second-person contrapuntal interjections; and I am sometimes guilty of concretizing an elliptical or vague referent in a text to make it intelligible to someone who has less background knowledge than the person for whom the fragment was originally spoken. Except when intelligibility is threatened, however, my translations tend toward the literal. I strive to avoid romanticism and sentimentality when it is not intended by Saramakas, yet to render their poetic metaphors with something of their inherent power. Like the other Saramaka translations in which I have had a hand (see, for example, Price and Price 1980:82–83, 184–87, *passim*), those in this book tend to be rather direct.

There is considerable variation in the depth of my knowledge about the events reported in the texts. Some, such as the exploits of Kwasimukámba, I have explored quite fully, with many men, on many different occasions. A few I have heard only as a single fragment, unconfirmed by other speakers. Whenever possible, I try in my commentaries to indicate something of the status of my knowledge about each. In cases when my knowledge of an event, based on oral fragments, is particularly rich, the problem of presentation becomes especially complex. As a matter of principle, I eschew composite versions, even when they would be more richly textured and dramatically satisfying than the words of a single man spoken at a particular moment. For example, I present Otjútju's version of Lánu's initial escape without interlarding it with fragments I have heard from Tebini or others because it better preserves a single vision or perspective on the event, When wish to present full, contrastive versions. I do so separately, seriatim, using a single title to group together fragments that relate to a single event.

A series of texts that strictly replicated Saramaka modes of presentation would be largely impenetrable for the average reader, even with explanatory notes. In the opening section, I tried to give some idea of the general features of Saramaka ways of talking about First-Time, and I continue to give examples intermittently throughout the book; but my interest in organizing this book as I have is to remain faithful to the Saramaka conceptual organization of the past on a more general level. It is I who order the diverse texts, deriving the chronology from internal indicators matched with documented dates (see Cohen 1977:166–86 for a detailed discussion of such techniques). I do so, however, within a framework of ideas about time and history that is a fundamental aspect of Saramaka thought.

In this same vein, I should stress that the clan-based organization of these texts rests on a partial anachronism—justifiable, however, as part of my conscious efforts to maintain a Saramaka perspective. The modern members of a clan, looking backward, tend to assume a perfect fit between modern clans and the significant units of First-Time social interaction; but in fact there has been some redefinition of clan boundaries, shifts in group identities, and additions of new personnel. Indeed, hardly any of the current clans had taken on their full shape before the Peace, and their current designations in some cases (for example, "Awaná") did not yet exist. Although I defer the detailed analysis of processes of group formation to another book (Price 1990), in the present work I consistently draw upon my latest understanding of the actual composition of particular eighteenth-century groups. And, as appropriate. I mention these realities in my commentaries in discussing the nature of Saramaka selectivity about their distant past.

My commentaries in the bottom channel of each page are intended to serve several functions. First, I use them to explain those unfamiliar Saramaka assumptions or concepts that seem minimally necessary to make sense of the particular text. This is always a very partial endeavor; to understand any text fully would presume an ethnographic knowledge—including metaphysical concepts, political ideas, and so on—far beyond the means of this book to provide. Here, I try simply to indicate the most directly useful information at the moment it becomes relevant. Second, I try to spell out something of the special meaning of each fragment to those Saramakas who preserve it, discussing why it is told in the form(s) it is by these particular people. And third, I introduce information from contemporary written sources—chronology, geography, and other facts-to help work toward a picture of "what really happened" against which we can measure and grasp the complex processes of selection used by Saramakas in regard to their distant past.

The available written sources from the first half of the eighteenth century pose problems not unlike my oral materials, in their fragmentation, incompleteness, and obscurity. Rather than providing a solid made-by-colonists whole-cloth backdrop against which we can consider Saramaka selectivity, they permit only intermittent, if vivid, glimpses of the way the colonists regarded Saramakas, and the measures they took to foil them. The reasons are several and worth spelling out. A large portion of the materials in the Algemeen Rijksarchief dating from this period are in woeful condition, and many volumes have been permanently sealed. Other once-available archives of central importance to Saramaka history (for example, those pertaining to the eighteenth-century Portuguese Jewish community) have disappeared forever. And the major historical works published during the eighteenth century that are based on documentary sources raise as many doubts as they settle, as they are either explicit polemics (for example, Nassy's 1788 defense of the Suriname Jewish community) or quite generally uncritical of their sources (for example, Hartsinck's standard 1770 history of the colony, based on official correspondence received in the Netherlands). The fact that even the available archives are truly voluminous, very largely unindexed, and often in archaic Dutch written in difficult handwriting further complicates the task. I often find myself in the frustrating position of having a half-dozen scraps of written evidence about an event (a raid by Saramakas, a military expedition against them) without being able to consult the main report about it, which is contained in a sealed archival volume, or is simply "missing."

Under these circumstances, matching Saramaka memories of a particular battle or raid with archival accounts can be a daunting task. I have found archival records of more than fifty major military expeditions against Saramakas between 1710 and 1762; and this does not include the countless small commandos that were sent out after Saramaka raids or mass escapes from plantations. Likewise, I have historical records of more than one hundred plantation uprisings and Saramaka raids on plantations during this period. (Nevertheless, my archival research is quite incomplete, because of insufficient time, difficulties with handwriting, sealed volumes, and so on.) The detailed maps that routinely accompanied the reports of military expeditions against Saramakas have been removed from the archives and, apparently, lost forever. Moreover, much of the available information about village moves and composition and about internal Saramaka events in general, as reported in the archives, turns out upon inspection to be deliberately falsified. Close study of the information held by the government about Saramaka activities during the mid-eighteenth century reveals that much of it was "planted" by Saramaka secret agents. It was common for Saramakas to send spies to be deliberately captured by the whites, in order to reveal information under "interrogation" (and often just before being executed). In this way, for example, the whites learned (falsely) in 1751 that the Saramakas had moved their villages by four days' march since the military expedition of the previous year and, in a separate interrogation, that the three white men who had been sent out as emissaries (whom the Saramakas had in fact killed) were still alive and being held prisoner. The eighteenth-century historian Hartsinck, who drew solely on such documents—the correspondence of the governors, interrogations at the Court of policy, and so on—tended to accept these accounts at face value.[1] Hence all subsequent histories based on his work (and this includes almost all published historical work on Suriname including the historical portions of Stedman 1796, and much of Wolbers 1861) must be read with more than usual caution.

In my commentaries I tend not to dwell on such historiographical problems regarding the written records, rather presenting my best-considered conclusions based on the evidence as I have been able to weigh it. Nevertheless, the reader should be aware that behind the identification of, say, the 1738–39 raid led by members of the Nasí clan on the plantation of the Jew Peyreyra lies far more than a correspondence between one or two bits of information (a plantation name, a geographical location); in all such cases, I have carefully considered a complicated bundle of evidence, often including apparently contrary facts (for example, from a late eighteenth-century writer), which I am ultimately able to dismiss by critical consideration of the sources.

My separate but simultaneous presentation of texts and commentaries represents a carefully conceived experiment. In principle, a person could read only the upper (Saramaka text) portion of each page, from the beginning of the next section right through to the end of the book, without once referring to the commentaries. I hope, however, that most readers will be sufficiently patient to try out the following procedure, for which the presentation was designed. First, read a text (or bundle of texts) indicated by a single title, for example, "Lánu's Escape." Then turn back and read the commentary indicated by that same title. And finally, reread the text with the commentary in mind before going on to the next text and continuing the process.

Why this complex procedure? One goal is to preserve the integrity of the Saramaka texts—which means avoiding constant interruptive footnotes or comments. Moreover, each commentary takes on meaning only after certain features of the particular text have become familiar; and likewise, any text becomes fully intelligible only with the help of its commentary. With a goal of helping the reader enjoy, appreciate, and more fully understand the Saramaka vision of their distant past, I have chosen this presentation as the most promising of several possible solutions. The texts are sufficiently brief so that the recommended double reading should not prove burdensome. And the second time around, I hope they will be seen through new eyes, focused on a vision that more closely approximates what the Saramaka elder who is speaking the fragment or singing the song would have expected from his listener.

THE EVENTS—THE HEROIC YEARS 1685–1748

Matjáu beginnings, 1685–1735

Because the bulk of my time in Saramaka has been spent living with Matjáus, my information on their early years is richer than for other groups and probably represents a fuller proportion of the knowledge they collectively possess about their own beginnings. Nevertheless, the past fifty years have undoubtedly witnessed a major loss of sharpness and detail concerning their First-Time ancestors: with the early twentieth-century demise of the cults devoted to the great Matjáu fighting and healing *Obias*, the single major context for the transmission of stories about these people disappeared. Yet key aspects of their memory are kept alive because these people and events of two and three centuries ago remain firmly woven into the fabric of ongoing Matjáu life, in terms of everything from local land tenure and interclan political relations to proverbial speech. And occasional rituals specifically devoted to the earliest ancestors maintain particular aspects of their identities through drum rhythms, songs, and dances. Nevertheless, an intense aura of danger and power continues to surround these figures and their exploits, and mention of them tends to be both highly elliptical and brief.

Matjáus conceive of their collective identity as having originated in a tiny band of escaped slaves who lived for some time just outside the bounds of the cultivated plantation area, on the creek now called by them Matjáu Creek [. . .]. The name of their first great leader, Lánu, is considered so powerful that it is rarely spoken; indeed, it is most unusual for a non-Matjáu, no matter how knowledgeable historically, ever to have heard it, and most Matjáus would not know who he was. In references to Lánu—whether in ritual or historical discussion—another name is almost always substituted, normally the teknonym of Lánu's younger brother Ayakô, "DabItatá" (Dabi's father), who was the leading Saramaka chief during the final years of the war against the whites, in the middle of the eighteenth century. Here is Peléki, telling me how his "mother's brother," the late Captain Gidé, used to "interrupt" accounts of early Matjáu history:

> He would say, 'Man, Matjáus did not used to speak Ayakô's name. And one never says Lánu's name on the Pikilio. Those two people. Their names cannot be spoken. They were First-Time people, so 'ripe' [*lépi* = ritually powerful] that their names can't be called. If you speak their names, war will come or who knows what will happen." So, we call him [Ayakô] "Dabitatá. "If someone [Lánu] did something, they'll say it was 'Dabitatá." Because they're so afraid of Lánu's name that it can't be spoken.

Because of such name substitution and masking, Matjáu historians themselves in many cases no longer know which of these men is supposed to have performed a particular act. Indeed, in discussions of these early years, the names of still-more-junior relatives are often substituted because a person considers it too dangerous even to say "Dabitatá," still further confusing identities for posterity.

Eighteenth-century Saramakas understood that death held very different meanings for them and for their enemies. Lane is said to have instructed his brother not to tell the whites when he died (5), and eighteenth-century documents make clear that the deaths of wartime leaders were in fact routinely masked from outsiders. In addition, Saramakas believed that their African-born leaders did not exactly "die—they disappeared, in their familiar form, but continued to play a central role in the lives of the living. Today Saramakas claim that their most powerful early ancestors were not buried at all. Otjútju, for example, described how "one day Lánu entered the forest, and they never saw him again. They didn't find him to bury." Likewise, Captain Gòme, speaking of the Awana clan's equivalent figure, said, "No one knows where Vumà went." They didn't find him to bury. Perhaps he went back to Africa. We simply don't know. He just disappeared." (Since Vumá, like certain other African-born Saramakas, could fly, the possibility of his returning to Africa was considered quite matter-of-factly.)

The rhetorical device of name substitution, then, stems both from desires to confuse the enemy and from complex aspects of the belief system. The danger surrounding the speaking of First-Time people's names (and the related avoidance of referring directly to

First-Time events) became a major source of "noise" in the transmission and learning of knowledge about the Matjáu (and other Saramaka) past.

Lánu's escape

1. His wife—I don't know if she was a girlfriend or a real wife—worked in the white man's house. Once, she gave her husband a drink of water. ([whispering: But they tell me that it was really sugar cane juice, because that was the "water" the white man normally drank.) Well, they saw that and said, "The woman gave Lánu sugar cane juice!" and they whipped her. They beat the woman until she was dead. Then they carried her to him and said, "Look at your wife here." Then they whipped Lánu until he lost consciousness, and they left him lying on the ground. Then, the spirit of his wife came into his head, and he arose suddenly and ran into the forest. The white man, seeing this, said, "Lánu's gone!" But his men said, "He won't live; he's as good as dead already."

When Lánu went into the forest, he ran this way and that, calling out to his wife, trying to find her. This woman was from Dahomey; they called her Osíma of Dahomey. Well, he kept calling out and calling out until he got deep into the forest. Finally, the forest spirit [apúku] named Wámba called out in reply. And Wámba came into Lánu's head, and brought him directly to where some Indians lived. These Indians welcomed him, took care of him, and gave him food. And he lived with them there. (Otjútju 13 August 1976)

Lánu's escape (1)

This fragment was told me by Otjútju, whose personal history is intimately and intricately bound up with the protagonists of the event. Saramakas believe that every person has a nêséki (normally an ancestor, but I know cases involving forest spirits or even deceased hunting dogs) who, like the mother and father, contributes at the moment of conception to that person's fundamental character (see Price 1975 51–52). Otjútju's nêséki, Bôò (his mother's mother's mother's mother, who died shortly before his birth), had as her own nêséki Lukéinsi (the daughter of Adjágbò), who served as the late-eighteenth-century medium for the forest spirit Wámba. Bôò's life was strongly influenced by her relationship—through her nêséki—to Wámba; and her association with the forest spirit has been relevant at several key junctures when she has been credited with intervention in the life of Otjitju. His own knowledge of Lánu's exploits has been built up very gradually, over the full course of his lifetime, by hearing fragments of information spoken or sung by a variety of people during those rituals for his own well-being that were addressed to his nêséki (and to her own nêséki's forest spirit). During such rites, there would have been frequent incidental and elliptical references to Wámba's role as a special protector and advisor of the fledgling Matjáu group.

This Matjáu fragment, incidentally, preserves the memory of a plantation 'law' that seems to have held, in the eyes of both masters and slaves, an extraordinarily heavy symbolic significance—the prohibition on slaves tasting the sweet product of their labors. As Stedman wrote of Suriname slaves during the eighteenth century:

> The other danger is that should a Negro Slave dare to taste that Sugar which he produces by the Sweat of his Brow, he would run the hazard of paying the

expense by some hundred lashes, if not by the breaking out of all his teeth
. . . [later in the book.] As to the Breaking out of their *Teeth* for Tasting the
Sugar Cane Cultivated by themselves, or Slitting up their nose & Cutting off
theyr Ears from private Peek, these are Look'd upon as Laughable Trifles, not
Worth so much as to be Mention'd. (1988:257, 532)

The severity of Osima's and Lánu's punishments, as preserved by Matjáus, conforms to
scores of examples recorded by European observers of plantation slavery in Suriname.

Ayakô's flight

2. [Lánu's younger brother] Ayakô had a sister [called Sééi] on the same plantation.
One day she was at work, with her infant son tied to her back. The child began crying,
but the white man didn't want her to sit down to nurse it. But it kept on crying. She kept
working. The child kept crying. Then the white man called her. "Bring the child here and
I'll hold it for you." So she took the child off her back, handed it to him, and returned to
work. He grasped the child upside down by the legs and lowered its head into a bucket of
water until he saw that it was dead. Then he called the woman and said [gruffly], "Come
take the child and tie it on your back." So she did so. She returned to work until evening,
when they released the slaves from work. The child was dead, stiff as a board.

Well, Dabítatá [Ayakô] saw this and said, 'What sadness! My family is finished. My sister has only one child left, and when she goes to work tomorrow, if the child cries, the
white man will do the same thing again. I'll be witness to the final destruction of
my family. [At this point in his narrative, Kála began pouring a libation of rum; and he then
prayed to the ancestors for several minutes to ask indulgence for speaking to me
of these events before taking up where he had left off.] Now when I was in Africa, I wasn't
a nobody. I will make a special effort, and see if since I left there what [power]
I had has been spoiled." Then he prepared himself [ritually] until he was completely
set. And he escaped. He ran off with his sister and her baby daughter. ([Whispering, to me:]
It was not considered humanly possible to escape from those slave quarters, but he did it!)

When he got to the edge of the forest, he called out his praise name: "I'm the one!
Okúndo bi okúndo. The largest of all animals. I may not have iron [tools] but I can still raise
my family!" Then he entered the forest and continued till evening. All he carried was the
[great *óbia*] Lámba gourd. Whenever they were hungry, they simply ate from that gourd.
That was our food in those days. Lámba fed us. (Kála 5 July 1978)

3. Ayakô was made overseer of Plantation Waterland. He was in charge of all the
slaves. It was at the time they were marching the slaves each day to dig the canal at Para.
The work was too heavy. It was there that they couldn't take it any more. So they made
a plan and escaped. (Tebini 11 July 1978)

[. . .]

Ayakô's flight

While Lánu is something of a shadowy figure in current Matjáu historiography (partly
because for so long he has been considered too powerful to talk about), his younger
brother Ayakô remains known as a rather full person (though knowledge of his exploits
and character is also carefully protected and masked).

The first paragraph of 2 has been grafted by the teller onto the more usual Matjáus account; I have never heard it from another Saramaka. Other Matjáus, when queried, denied it had anything to do with Ayakô, noting that it was a popular slavery story among coastal Afro-Surinamers, and not a specifically Saramaka story at all. This, then, is a nice example of creative embellishment of an important historical event by making use of folk-loric materials. (Stedman describes a similar incident as fact, citing the name of the child-murderer [1988: 267–68].)

Fragment 2, like many others I have heard, stresses the importance of family in the Matjáu conception of their original forebears—Ayakô is depicted as escaping with his sister and her child, having been explicitly motivated by wanting to preserve the nascent matrilineage. And it commemorates the supportive role played during those early days in the forest by the Matjáu "great óbia" known as Mása Lámba. Lámba was part of a complex of Matjáu war óbias (including the great agó óbia Akwádja, closely associated with the forest spirit Wámba) that were transferred by the Matjáus to the Kasitú clan, their collective "children," at the end of the eighteenth century, in an act that helped cement the special relationship of the two groups. Though largely inactive today, Mása Lámba is remembered and praised in part because of the importance of this political relationship. Its distinctive drum rhythms, however, are also played and danced by Matjáus today at (rarely held) rites for their original collective ancestors at the Dángogó shrine of Awónêngè, to commemorate the óbia's role in confusing the enemy and making them-selves unfindable. During the wars, it is said, the whites would hear the Matjáus drums and follow, but always in the wrong direction. I was told also that within the memory of living people, whenever rites were held in honor of Mása Lámba at its shrine outside the Kasitu village of Palúbásu, a deer would appear out of the forest as a sign that Mása Lámba was content.

Fragment 3, like several of my other Matjáu accounts, reports that Ayakô served as plantation overseer, or driver. The praise name attributed to him in 2 leads support to this tradition okúndo bi okúndo is the verbal form of the drum slogan played on the apírti (talking) drum to summon to council meetings the important village officials known as gaán ("big") basiá, a title that derives etymologically from Sranan (coastal Suriname) basya, the term for "black overseer," or "slave driver," on plantations (see Voorhoeve and Lichtveld 1975:169). The heaviness of canal-building labor is cited as the specific motive for escape in the traditions of several Saramaka clans, though various actual coastal canals are mentioned, even within the traditions of any such group. (This fact, plus the frequency with which documentary sources attest to major canal-building protects during the colony's first half-century, reduces the possibility of using such construction dates for purposes of establishing the chronology of escapes.) These widespread stories stand as collective witness to the perception by slaves that this particular form of supervised gang labor—moving tons of waterlogged clay with shovels—was the most backbreaking of the tasks they were called upon to accomplish (see also Rodney 1981:2–4). It is worth noting that the great majority of escape accounts give a specific provocation, most often the imposition of a particularly onerous physical task or the wanton cruelty of the master (or his staff), usually practiced upon a kinsman of the person who then escapes. The formu-laic Saramaccan phrase used in capping the telling of such an incident translates laconically as: "They couldn't bear the punishment any more. So they escaped."

Several already familiar themes appear in 4–6 [excluded from this extract]; the fraternal relationship of Ayakô and Lánu, the extraordinary ritual powers of Lánu (who was supported by the forest spirit Wámba). Lánu's absolute hatred of whites, with whom his enmity was sworn to be eternal, and the supportive role of the Indians who harbored them. Matjáus are well aware that Indians and Africans were plantation slaves together. Indeed, I have been told that "the Indians escaped first and then since they knew the forest, they came back and liberated the Africans." With certain individual exceptions, the relationship between early runaways and those Indians who led relatively near the coastal area is depicted by Matjáus as solidary. The final fragment also includes first mention of the mysterious African Kwémayón, who played an important role as advisor to the Matjáus during their first decades in the forest. The image of the great leader warrior (himself possessed of vast powers) traveling with his personal ritual specialist (in this case Ayakô and Kwémayón) appears again in the historical accounts of other groups the [. . .] leader Kaási had his Indian *óbiama*. Piyái, and the famous late-eighteenth-century rebel leader of the Boni Okilifu had his own special *óbiama*, Djaki Atoomboti Alúkus.

Note

1   Nor was Hartsinck overly concerned with his details regarding Saramakas. He describes how "Claas"—an important Saramaka chief—had three villages in 1730 (1770:761–62), while Lavaux, who had himself visited the area, had depicted five on his famous and widely available map; he simply deleted (possibly to strengthen his own arguments, the important fifteenth article from the supposedly complete printing of the 1762 treaty in his book (1770:809; compare R. Price 1983:document 11); and so on.

CHAPTER 29

Robert A. Rosenstone

THE MAN WHO SWAM INTO HISTORY (2002)*

Robert A. Rosenstone, Professor of History, California Institute of Technology, is the author of a series of highly innovative deconstructionist texts: *Romantic Revolutionary: A Biography of John Reed*, his classic *Mirror in the Shrine: American Encounters in Meiji Japan* (a multi-levelled, multi-voiced text about American sojourners in nineteenth-century Japan), and *Crusaders of the Left* (on Americans fighting in the Spanish Civil War). Rosenstone is also a

* Robert A. Rosenstone (2002) *The Man Who Swam Into History*, Bloomington, IL: 1st Books, pp. xi–xvii and 3–27.

prolific writer on, and advocate of, cinematic representations of 'the before now'; thus, for example, his *Visions of the Past: The Challenge of Film to Our Idea of History* (Harvard University Press: Cambridge, MA, 1995).

The following reading, however, is from none of the above, but rather from his latest book, *The Man Who Swam Into History* (2002), a recounting of family stories – his own family's stories – across three generations and several continents. For years, writes Rosenstone in his Introduction, he had attempted to compose the fragments that were available for him to write his own history into a smooth narrative articulated as a single, unified voice, but when he did 'they stopped speaking'. The result is a book wherein that (impossible) dream is absent; here is a book of unsmooth, rough-cut stories of, as he puts it,

> sequences, windows, moments and fragments resurrected from the lives of my two parental families set in five countries and two continents over a period of over a century . . . my aim here is to do no more than seize and render certain moments and experiences . . . [feeling] it unnecessary to tell yet another immigrant family saga because by now we know the story too well: about how foreigners, spat upon and reviled, overcame horrendous obstacles to become good Americans. The role of my family – of every immigrant family – has already been written.

But few history books are like this one. Self-consciously fabricated by a high visibility author (photograph included); written evocatively with a mixture of pathos, restrained nostalgia and joyous humour, the work has inscribed within it both a philosophy of history and a philosophy – perhaps they are inseparable – of life. Anyone who has done historical research, Rosenstone concludes,

> knows that it takes more than original sources to create a true and meaningful past. The reality of that past – national, personal, familial – does not lie in an assemblage of data but in a field of stories – a place where fact, truth, fiction, invention, forgetting and myth are so entangled that they cannot be separated. Ultimately it is not the facts that make us what we are, but the stories we have been told and the stories we believe.

The extracts reproduced here are from Rosenstone's Introduction, The Prologue and Chapter One.

INTRODUCTION

O N T H E M O R N I N G O F May 9, 1997, the day I was to deliver an evening lecture to the British Academy entitled *Looking at the Past in a Postliterate Age, or Is Oliver Stone a Historian?* I decided to visit the synagogue in which my maternal grandparents had been married ninety-five years before. My reasons for doing so were at once senti-mental and instrumental. The manuscript of the work you hold was almost complete, but I was searching for an introduction that would hold together this collection about my family. A visit to the synagogue held out a vague promise: I would touch the past, see what my grandparents had seen, feel what they felt, and the result would be one of those moments which leads to insight and creativity—and to an introduction.

The telephone directory did not list a Stepney Green synagogue. A helpful woman who answered the telephone at the social service agency, Jewish Meals on Wheels, explained why. A decade ago it had closed because there were not enough Jews in the neighborhood to make a congregation, but the building was still standing and it was still possible to view it from the outside. Following her detailed directions, my wife and I left the Stepney Green tube station in the East End and were confronted with a sense both of historical continuity and irony: as in my grandparents's day, this was still a neighborhood of immigrants, only now the majority were obviously Muslim—dark skinned men, some of them in djellabah's, carrying worry beads; women with scarves over their heads, a few completely covered from head to toe in flowing chadours.

The synagogue was neither tiny, as I had imagined fitting for my impoverished forbears. Nor was it empty. In front of us stood an imposing four-story structure surrounded by the temporary fence of a building site, its walls masked by scaffolding. Through the large, arched main door, workmen carried wallboard, wiring, paint buckets and brushes, loads of lumber, and copper pipes. The explanation came from a gray haired man who introduced himself as The Builder. They were renovating the synagogue, cutting it into apartments. A shame, yes, but it was the only way of saving the structure from being vandalized. As a Registered Building, nothing major could be altered. The stained glass, the abstract mosaics, the Biblical quotations in Hebrew and English in the main hallway and within the apartments—all this would remain. Taking a shower you might comfort yourself with words from Leviticus.

The hour I spent there snapping photos, stumbling over wires, slipping on wet spots, sticking my elbow into fresh paint, and ducking workers carrying tools and materials, did not add up to my imagined period of quiet contemplation. But we have to take our metaphors where we can find them. To save the synagogue, they had to alter the structure, change it, fragment it into spaces that had little or nothing to do with the original purposes of the building or the ceremonies that had taken place there during its century as a religious center. To save the synagogue, they had to hide away some things, subtract others, highlight still others. Gone was the carved wooden balcony where the women had looked down on the services; gone was the alter and the niche for the sacred scrolls. The pillars that once stood free now rose through kitchens and living rooms; the circular stained glass just beneath the ceiling and the tablets with the ten commandments which may have been lost in the broad vistas of the original structure were now the focal point of the three-story open central hallway.

Stepney Green Synagogue was, in short, like any work of history. To save the past— as biographer, autobiographer, memoirist, or historian—we translate the remaining traces of it into language and forms of writing, which necessarily alter and fragment things, highlight some moments and erase others. In writing history we describe and interpret moments and events which participants experienced and interpreted in far different ways. This is to say that, as with the synagogue, we are always altering the remains of the past for our own needs in the present. With words (or images, or sounds) we attempt to simulate a lost world, but the life we bestow upon the dead is not one they would recognize as their own.

The origins of this work lie in a single sentence that more than a decade ago entered my mind one morning when I was jogging on the beach: *There is a man who comes swimming into history.* That man, my father's father, had died thirty years before my own birth. All I knew about him was that single fact, presented in family lore as unique and heroic, a mark of the rare qualities of our lineage. My grandfather had swum the roaring and dangerous Pruth River to get to Romania and escape the military draft in Russia. Only later did I learn that almost every grandfather of every Jewish Romanian claimed the same athletic feat.

When the sentence came to me, I was already a professor of history who was in that dangerous period called midlife. The two major books I had so far published and the third that I was then completing were works that stressed biography rather than the more impersonal forces of history such as social class, nationalism, economic development, or technological change—all of which never seem quite as real to me as people's lives. For two decades my research had focused on marginal characters, people torn between two cultures—American bohemians and radicals of the early twentieth century (*Romantic Revolutionary. A Biography of John Reed*), Communists of the nineteen-thirties and forties (*Crusade of the Left: the Lincoln Battalion and the Spanish Civil War*) and American sojourners in late nineteenth century Japan (*Mirror in the Shrine: American Encounters with Meiji Japan*). I had always thought these topics had arisen largely from personal experiences—college newspaper editor campaigning against racial discrimination in the Fifties, would-be novelist living in the Latin Quarter, graduate student supporting the Free Speech Movement, activist in the Movement against the Viet Nam war, professor teaching American studies at Kyushu University in Japan. It never occurred to me that my choices might also connect to my heritage. That if you are born into an immigrant family with parents from two cultures as different and conflicting in values as those of Latvia and Romania (the German and the Latin), a family in which racketeers and Communists and extra marital love affairs were unremarkable, you might have a tendency to take an interest in characters torn between the values and beliefs of different worlds.

Like many children of immigrants of that era, I had (unconsciously) spent a good part of my life becoming an American. In the Fifties, when I went to high school and college, this meant adapting to a certain kind of conservative speech, dress, and values. For someone born in Canada, this was easy. My parents might sound and look as if their origins lay in some other continent, but not me. And yet at the same time, in school I was always plagued (unconsciously) by the need to prove something—something that must have had to do, though I would never feel this, with being the child of Jewish immigrants. This meant believing and acting differently from those social leaders, the people who belonged to clubs, fraternities, and sororities. It meant taking to heart the core ideals of America—freedom, equality, and justice for all—and attempting to make sure that people and political leaders lived up to them.

This desire to be the same and yet different seems to have emerged in many of my academic and personal choices. Undergraduate major: English, with a focus on American literature. Graduate major: American history. First wife: American lineage back to the seventeenth century. Topics for books: John Reed, the quintessential WASP radical, the Harvard man who becomes the Golden Boy of Bohemia, then chronicles the Mexican and Bolshevik Revolutions, founds the Communist Party and ends up buried in the Kremlin wall. Those nineteenth century sojourners in Japan, mostly New Englanders who are intent upon carrying the values of Christianity and Western civilization to the natives, but who stay long enough to learn the natives are quite civilized already. Even my work on the International Brigades in Spain did not deal with the volunteers as the Jews that so many were, but focused (as did the Lincoln Brigaders themselves) on the struggle to defend the traditional values of Western civilization: democracy, republicanism, free speech, the secular state.

Midlife is a time of reckoning. My parents were rapidly aging, my father having the heart attacks and strokes that would eventually lead to an institution, my mother the first bouts of forgetfulness—not yet named Alzheimer's—that would leave her unable to speak anything other than poetic gibberish. Part of the reckoning is a growing self-consciousness, one which for this professional historian raised the question: how do I fit into History, the history I live as opposed to the one I chronicle. The question obviously extends to include one's family, even if they don't wish to be included. Like so many immigrants of their generation, my mother and father never wanted to talk about the Old Country and I, self-centered young (naturalized) American, had never been interested enough to raise the issue. Now in my mid-forties, as their lives become important to me, I began to press them to talk about their childhoods, their own parents, their memories of schools, journeys, occupations, other relatives, important family events.

The shards of memory, the moments and tales shared by parents and then by other relatives over the next decade (and some were already there, in my consciousness, long before I knew I was hearing them or interested in what they were) eventually grew into this book. The words with which I evoke the past are a mixture of their voices and other voices that began to speak in my head, sometimes in the first person, sometimes in the second, sometimes in the third. For years I attempted to smooth the narrative and turn them into one coherent, unified voice, but when I tried to do so, they stopped speaking. The result is a book told from a variety of points of view and in a variety of styles, a book of stories, sequences, windows, moments, and fragments resurrected from the lives of three generations in my two parental families, set in five countries on two continents over the period of almost a century. Each segment of the work can, I think, stand on its own, though taken together they suggest a larger story.

Putting together these pieces, I felt it unnecessary to tell yet another complete immigrant family saga, because by now we know that story all too well: how poor foreigners, spat upon and reviled, overcome horrendous obstacles to become good Americans. The tale of my family—of every immigrant family—is a story that has already been written. My aim here is to do no more than to seize and render certain moments and experiences that can provide a different perspective on that larger story we already know. In its mixture of genres and styles, this work lies somewhere between history, memoir, and autobiography—the multi-voiced story of a lineage which includes (as any such work must) the life of the teller of the tale. It begins with my grandparents and concludes with yours truly in college, at an age when the great family secrets—racketeers on one side, communists on the other, love affairs on both—are at last revealed. Each section focuses on one or two characters, trying to locate and capture an event or an action or a relationship that defines a larger sense of life's possibilities and meanings. The same characters reappear in other sections, with the result that the work is perhaps closer in form to a collage or a mosaic than to a linear narrative. The narrator of the work tells his tale sometimes in the first and sometimes in the third person: he is Rabin, the historian, yours truly, the all seeing I.

Family stories are fashionable these days. A sign of the times, a signal that History may be returning to its roots in history, that we—historians and non academics alike—are interested in the world of large events only as they have impacted upon our own small lives and helped to shape us. Once upon a time, family stories were tales of rags to riches. More recently they have become woeful accounts of abuse and victimization. The themes of any work, as any historian knows, depend less on the subject matter than on the way you tell the story, less upon the events than on your attitude towards them. Struggle, triumph, and victimization, rags and riches, are all part of my family, but what interests me are the moments of daily life, the memories and secrets by which we mark our days, the quirks, oddities, pains, and joys of simple survival. How people, whatever their circumstances, make choices that change their lives and then have to live with the consequences of those choices.

Any work like this is in part based upon time spent in archives and libraries, in homes and garages, poring over diaries, letters, photos, newspaper clippings and other stuff pasted into family albums, and on lengthy interviews with often recalcitrant or forgetful relatives. To give the reader a taste of the kind of sources used and the ways in which I have attempted to use them, one document and one photo are included in each chapter. This kind of source is necessary but not sufficient to evoke the past. Anyone who has done historical research knows that it takes more than original sources to create a truthful or meaningful past. The reality of the past—national, personal, familial—does not lie in an assemblage of data but in a field of stories—a place where fact, truth, fiction, invention, forgetting, and myth are so entangled that they cannot be separated. Ultimately it is not the facts that make us what we are, but the stories we have been told and the stories we believe.

THE PROLOGUE

In the early nineteen-forties there was a restaurant in Montreal where the only record in the jukebox was a song named Romania. At least it was the only record that could be heard on those crowded Sunday nights when, even with wartime gas rationing, it was difficult to find a parking place on the side streets off of Main near the basement bagel factory where men worked stripped to the waist and the flavor of the bagels seemed to have something to do with the quality of sweat rolling down their glistening bodies. The restaurant was named Moishe's. It was reached up a long, dark, steep and rather evil-smelling flight of stairs that frightened a small child as he climbed to the second floor, where hordes of people humped and pushed and where, if you were not a Romanian who had known Moishe for a long time, and preferably during days in the old country, you might have to wait forever to get a table. The dinner was always the same, steaks much too thick to be anything but black market and much too delicious to be kosher, and marvelously soggy, oily french fried potatoes. But the best dish, even to a child, came first—Moishe's special platter of chopped liver and thin, crisp, fried onions, which you mashed together, salted generously and devoured in an instant.

The dining room had a tiny, wooden dance floor, unused because the ill-lit room was always too jammed with waiters and table-hopping customers. Besides how could you dance to a song named Romania? It was such a sad and serious song that it always made you want to laugh. A male voice began by shrieking, Romania, Romania, Romania, Romania, Romania, until it drooped into sobbing Romania, Romania, Romania, Romania, then it lilted away into mellower tears, Romania, Romania, Romania . . ., until you could not hear it any more because the restaurant was far too noisy. In an occasional rare moment, when the din lessened, a word that was not Romania might enter through one small ear into consciousness. If you asked an adult who had been born in that country what was being said, the answer was always definitive: It's about Romania.

There was something profound about exposure to Moishe's jukebox. Take a child on wartime Sunday nights when hunger has made his stomach and brain equally susceptible to outside influence, and you may mark him for life. Hearing Romania year in, year out in that setting leaves you with a feeling that can never be shaken or altered by later facts or experiences: namely that there was and is and always will be something inherently odd, off-kilter, lopsided, humorous, warped, untidy, even ridiculous about Romania. Later information only confirms this attitude. The spelling, for instance. Nobody, least of all anyone who had actually lived there, could ever tell a bright child if it was Rumania or Romania or Roumania, and if you became insistent, they either said who cares? or told you to go chop a teakettle. Or the history. Was Carol a proper name for a king? And what was his queen's name, then — George? (Very funny among nine-year-olds waiting at Moishe's.) College history courses only made it worse. In any other country did military officers wear corsets and rouge and just a touch of pale lipstick, darling?

One long-range result is this: You can stand before Trajan's column in Rome, ignore the tabby cats cringing beneath crumbling brick walls, the water leaking through a hole in your umbrella and coldly trickling down your neck, your wet woolen socks and fears that you won't be able to find enough vitamin C in the Eternal City to cure the eternal cold which is about to descend with all the ferocity of ancient legionnaires; you can stand outside the iron picket fence while Fiats and Alfas squish past, and like Gibbon brood over the immense, symbolic questions raised by a structure that has been standing erect for almost two millennia. But later, leafing through an art book, when you see closeups of the frieze winding upward around the column and learn that the story carved into rock tells of Trajan's greatest triumph, the conquest of the Dacians, these nobles in odd-looking, brimless hats, unknowing and no doubt unwilling ancestors of modern Romanians, somehow the column begins to shrink, dwindle, diminish in the winter rain. The next time in Rome you visit the Arch of Titus, with its frieze recording that emperor's triumphant victory over the King of Judah.

CHAPTER ONE

The Jews, who are to be found in all Rumanian provinces and have big communities in Bessarabia and the Bukovina, have always been a persecuted and oppressed minority. The brand of anti-Semitism encouraged by almost all Rumanian governments resembles that of Tsarist Russia. Whenever something went wrong in politics or economics the Jews were blamed for it and pogroms were organized, sometimes surpassing in violence those of the Tsarist regime. This traditional anti-Semitism has its roots in the period when wealthy Rumanian absentee landlords let their estates to Jewish agents for management and tax-collection. This was a convenient means of laying the blame for exploitation at the door of the Jews, whilst the *boiars* pocketed the taxes and rents. Jewish influence in Rumanian finance and trade has been very great, as was their share in introducing modern industries into the country. Many Jewish families, especially in Moldavia and Wallachia, can trace their association with Rumania back to the early Phanariots. Others have lived for many years in the Bukovina, in Bessarabia in the Transylvania. The majority has, however, immigrated during the last century. Restrictions on their personal freedom, an almost complete denial of political rights, and organized and government-

> sponsored pogroms are familiar devices which have been used by most
> Rumanian regimes. These measures are supported by the ruling circles and cer-
> tain intellectuals in order to divert the attention of the people from the real
> causes and the real culprits whenever the country passes through a crisis.
>
> From *Rumania* by C. Kormos (Cambridge 1944)

There is a man who comes swimming into history. He first appears in the water of the Pruth River during the last quarter of the nineteenth century. The exact date is impossible to determine, but it is in the late Victorian period, though he knows nothing about that sort of label. Before he plunges headlong into the waters, or gingerly steps into the waters, there is little to know about him, little that can ever be discovered. He kept no diary and told no tales that his children would ever remember. The waters of the river cleansed him, washed away his past. Like some version of the Venus myth, he arises naked and full grown, innocent of history. His wisdom, if any, is water wisdom, the wisdom of currents and sea foam. He is not quite self-made, but he is more than the creation of some God's imagination.

For twenty-five, perhaps thirty years, the man-who-swims-into-history lives in Moldavia. His tongue, trained to the disparate sounds of Yiddish, Russian, and Hebrew, can never quite adjust to the soft, Latin vocal of the native language. The wife he acquires is fluent in Polish. Their children, the three boys and four girls who live to maturity, grow up speaking Romanian. If he must communicate with natives through a heavy accent and an impoverished vocabulary, it does not matter. Even in the Yiddish shared with the family, he has little to say. There may be words in him, but they are not the kind spoken with the mouth. They are voiced with the language of the body, the bowels, the eyes.

His means of communication is the scissors and sewing machine, part of a language that also crossed the river. He is a skilled tailor, far different from most small town practitioners who patch together the threadbare remains of worried lives. His hands, capable of creating new suits, know the feel of fine cloth, woven in far-off English mills; they understand that the cut of a jacket, drape of a coat, turn of a lapel and angled fall of trousers make even a poor man feel, on a day of a wedding, bar mitzvah or other holiness, like a king. In any religious theory, a man should not take pride in the ephemera of outward appearance. But his hands know the wisdom of this world, the instinctive blessing that exists outside the pages of any sacred text.

Life in Romania all those years is quiet, regular, tuned to an unvarying pattern of seasons, holidays. Flights of birds, the sowing of corn, clouds rumbling into rain, the annual festival of grapes, the visit of gypsies—year after year. The man who swims into history fits into the cycle. He is quiet, too, perhaps timid. His only vice is gambling. Never is he known to question the customs and laws that circumscribe his days. He takes part in the ceremonies of the small Jewish community of his town, but never with much enthusiasm or faith. His children never see him as angry, upset, authoritarian, but they do feel his emotional wires are somehow crossed. When it is time to discipline a youngster, he smiles sheepishly and disappears, leaving the task to the strong forearm of his wife. In moments of tragedy or death, he unaccountably grins, sometimes breaks into soft laughter. Then, as if ashamed at the response, he vanishes from the house.

After the swim, he never travels much. Business can take him to the regional center of Bacau, but there is no evidence of visits to the former Moldavian capital, Jassy, or of journeys to Bucharest, less than two hundred miles away. His decision around the turn of the century to leave for America is as much of a surprise to the familiy as to neighbors.

He goes by boat, no doubt from the port of Constanza into the Black Sea. The view from steerage is not very good. A glimpse of domes and minarets, draped across Constantinople's seven hills, or of the massive rock that preserved the Mediterranean for the English sovereign. His voyage consists mainly of dark water, dark bulkheads, dark food, and the dark breath of fellow passengers. At Ellis Island he is turned away, either because he does not have enough money (the version told by his first son, Moishe) or because he is mistaken for an anarchist or some other radical with the same name (the version told by his second son, Lazar). A ship drops him in a French port, and for a year he lives and works in Paris. Rarely does he write letters home. Perhaps he doesn't know how to write.

Some years later there is money for the whole family to go. Lazar will remember but a single incident from the trip. Passing on a train or in a streetcar, or stopped in station in either France or England, the family is assaulted with the violent, incomprehensible words of street urchins, who hurl clods of dung along with insults. The future becomes a lottery spun by some god of the shipping lines and lanes. Their money gone, they decide to take the next ship out, whether it goes to Canada or to Argentina. They land in a city buried in white snowbanks higher than the tallest mid-teen child. By the time the sky melts into blue and bright flowers spring out all over the mountain that rises in the middle of the island of Montreal, home is a dim apartment off the Main. Mother is, as always, in the kitchen much of the time, but the children have no garden to tend, no chickens or goats to feed, no cow to milk. The boys scatter into the streets, and the sounds of English are becoming familiar in their mouths. The girls feel a sweet tender swelling as they hang by the iron stairways that curve gracefully from second story duplexes to the sidewalk. They look past their brothers to catch the eyes of other men.

The man-who-swims-into-history remains silent. He speaks neither of Russia, Romania or the New World, says nothing about past or future, never discusses the Pruth River, the Black Sea, the Atlantic Ocean, the Seine or the St. Lawrence. In the garment shop where he works with many other men whose language he cannot understand, his hands seem less graceful, agile, expressive than before. It is tempting to believe that in this silence he is preparing a message for his children, and the grandchildren and great-grandchildren of all immigrants. Such words cannot come easily or quickly. First there is the matter of a lump on his head, an old companion that has made every journey with him. The operation is routine. Less than a year after arriving in Canada, he leaves his family for a single night in a huge, modern hospital of a kind none of them had seen in Romania. Once the lump has been removed and a bandage wrapped tightly around his head, he never seems quite well. At home and work he is dizzy, vague, tired. A few days after the surgery he returns from the shop, goes to bed and never gets up again. With the family gathered around, his last words are simple: *Take care of your mother*. Then the man-who-swims-into-history floats out of history without leaving any message for his descendants. Perhaps we must look for any message back there in the waters of the Pruth, in the Black Sea and the Mediterranean, in the storms of the English Channel and the hurricanes that sweep the Atlantic seaboard, in breakers off the coast of California and typhoons that slam out of the South Pacific onto the islands of Japan. For a man who swims into it, history must exist in water or not at all.

His name was Chaim Baer and he was walking. The roads were dusty, the day hot. There were vineyards and cornfields. The towns were small, wooden, sagging, each with a church, implacable, arrogant, alien. This is what he would be leaving. He would be leaving nothing. Less than nothing. Family. Yes, family. But the family was not his, was not him.

There was a tie, but there was not a tie, and there were no words to explain this. He did not belong to anyone. Maybe not even himself. The road felt good underfoot. Each step was taking him somewhere. Going somewhere, this is what he had wanted for a long time. Being on a road, going past blue vineyards, feeling the summer sun hot on the back of his neck, feeling the dust of travel, knowing there was somewhere else. He had a feeling that there was somewhere else. But when he tried to share it with friends, they could not understand. Looking down to the harbor, the gray bulk of ships from all over the world, most people turned their eyes to home. They did not want to see where the ships came from. They did not understand his itch to move, if he did not belong here, he did not belong anywhere. He did not belong anywhere. Right now he belonged to the road, to his legs beginning to ache and his dusty shoes, to the pain in his neck from the pack slung at an angle across his shoulder, to the sagging wooden villages, the crippled dogs hiding in the shade of droopy porches, the blank-eyed peasants staring through him, and the churches, always the churches, dark and ramshackle or sunny white, straight lines soaring towards heaven, topped with a golden onion dome.

Arrogant towers, arrogant gold. And always next to graveyards where we cannot be buried. Nor they in ours, and who would want them? These churches, this soil, the dust of the graveyard, the crumbling crosses. Not ours, never could be ours. Decrees stamped by the Czar, his ministers, locked away in St. Petersburg's tomb-like vaults. And if we could make it ours, it would be no use. It would be a game, a deception. Then we would be like them. The land is not to own. It is not ours. Not theirs. It's His. Yet He probably does not exist. Or does He look down and laugh when I think that? Let Him laugh. If He's such a big shot He'd let us know about Him, let us see sometimes. Why does He speak in books, why must we learn to read to understand His words? That's to keep jobs for the rabbis, smart types all their lives with eyes white on the pages of a book.

Chaim Baer put his hand to his face, touched the newly-smooth cheeks, the one tuft of hair sprouting from the chin. It is like being a boy again, a *bar mitzvah* boy with this smoothness. His hair shows the joke of life. Red, a tiny red beard on the chin. Everyone will notice and comment on the contrast from my dark hair. Young ladies, won't they be interested? They'll think I am one of them, maybe, a red beard and these blue eyes. Strange eyes, my mother said, the eyes of my father. Such a strange story. In each generation, one male in the family with blue eyes. Is it a special sign? Or sometime in the past did a *muhjik* or a strange tribesman lie with a woman in the family? A horseback warrior would be better. On a horse you are always going somewhere. On foot I am going somewhere, only it takes longer.

The road goes on through nights and days. Blanket roll in a cornfield, beneath a moon asking questions that are not answered by the stars. Moving towards a horizon, one step at a time through dust of hot afternoons. Gulp cold water at a stream, sneak from the road to pick grapes, snatch unripe corn and gobble it uncooked, raw white. At twilight, frogs sing in ditches; at night, crickets; in the pale hours before dawn, birds whose names he did not know. Sometimes the thought: this has been done before. I am doing it, me walking, but it is someone else with blue eyes and a red goatee. It is a strange feeling, standing by the side of a road in a dust cloud raised by an ox-pulled cart, choking a little, tickling in the nose, to know it is someone else standing there, holding a finger to the nose to keep from sneezing. At night in a bedroll in a vineyard, crickets cheering a moon higher into the sky, you feel you are riot alone. He knew this had been done before. He knew it would be done again. On foot, on horseback, on a river boat. Some other way that was no different, always the same. In each generation there was one son with blue eyes. In each generation there was one son with an itch. It had to be someone on horseback, from Central Asia or the lands beyond. One pair of blue eyes, one horse and one itch. That was the thought he held onto every night when the moon sang him to sleep.

It is a little noted fact of history that the rivers of Eastern Europe were jammed with swimmers in the last quarter of the nineteenth century. Not one grandfather but a whole generation of grandfathers sidling, walking, waddling, hurrying, moseying, lurching, striding, flinging, leaping, jumping, tiptoeing, plunging, screaming themselves into previously empty waters. They were not yet grandfathers, but somehow the image is of aged men, dressed fully in black, yarmulkes affixed firmly to their scalps, long white beards floating miraculously and gently on the surface as they flash towards far-off shores. Are they not praying as they swim, prayer shawls around their shoulders, voices raised to the lord to drown the fearful beating of their hearts. In later years, none of these grandfathers were ever known to go near the water. None ever could teach his sons how to swim, any more than they could teach them how to play baseball, steal a bagel or make love to a woman, all skills more apparently necessary in the New World than the Old. Decades later they were full of foolish tales, babbled in languages that grandsons neither understood nor cared much about. But each grandfather had this one moment of undisputed triumph that would quietly resonate through future generations.

Romania, Rumania, Roumania—but what is Rumania? Modern historians of the late, unlamented People's Republic of Romania seemed unclear about the nature of their country. When leading scholars in 1970 issued a multi-author work as part of a national History Series, they entitled it *Istoria Popurului Roman*, which translates as *History of the Rumanian People* and suggests that the nation itself may be a figment of somebody's imagination. Numerous peoples are mentioned in the more than six hundred pages of the book—Scythians, Avars, Ionians, Dorians, Dacians, Geto-Dacians, Cimmerians, Thracians, Celts, Bastarnians, Samatians, Goths, Visigoths, Ostrogoths, Bulgars, Huns and Pechenegs. Jews (Hebrews) receive but a few passing nods. Nowhere does this work mention that close to a million descendants of the children of Israel once lived within the borders of modern Romania or that they constituted five percent of the population and a social problem that turned the heads of more than a single statesman gray.

Romania in the late nineteenth century was a new name for an old idea. An idea linked to three provinces, but Transylvania, with its tales of vampires and population of Hungarians, did not count for much. The two other regions, Moldavia and Wallachia, had for four hundred years been part of that geographic sprawl known as the Ottoman Empire. In Constantinople the Sultans had come to prefer opium, sweets, and belly dancers to running a government, and who could blame them? Rather than bother with the insoluble problems assailing infidel peasants, they in the late eighteenth century began to subcontract these dreary provinces to clever Greek merchants who lived in the Phanar district of Constantinople. Greeks were infidels too, but infidels capable of coming up with large sums of gold which proved useful in satisfying the rulers' unceasing appetite for young girls. Sought all over the Sultan's domains, which stretched from the Atlantic Coast of Africa to the eastern boundary of the Anatolian Plateau.

Greek merchants cared little about opium, sweets, or belly dancers. Their aesthetic sense responded to the sight of the painted hulls and clean, white sails of vessels from the Mediterranean, Atlantic and even far-off Indian Ocean ports, bobbing in the murky waters of the Golden Horn, and their religious impulse was fulfilled by the satisfying clatter of coins across a polished counter. Moldavia and Wallachia might contain endless dismal collections of hovels, swimming in seas of mud, and be located at the end of the universe, but there was no shortage of volunteers to govern them. Each ruler—they called themselves *Phanariot Princes*, but everyone knew they were only Greeks—arrived at his new post burdened by two problems; one was the vast debt incurred in buying the throne; the other, the knowledge that a more affluent merchant might quickly buy it out from under him.

Greeks seeking gifts proved more than equal to the task. As they liked to point out, their ancestors had, after all, invented democratic government more than two thousand years before. This, apparently, is what allowed them to use the public treasury to pay nonexistent workers to build mythical public works. They forbade certain imports, then put smugglers on the payroll and opened stores to fence their goods. They sold administrative, judicial, and ecclesiastical offices to the highest bidder, and appropriated church revenues for themselves to keep temptation from being placed before the eyes of those who serve the Lord. When peasants began to burn their own houses and slaughter their sheep and cattle to avoid the property and the livestock taxes, the princes seized the furniture and livestock. Actions like this are bound to leave scar tissue on a national psyche. All historians agree that Phanariot rule had an effect on future Romanian social, political and cultural institutions. But historians are a cautious, unimaginative lot, unwilling to specify exactly what such effects were. So here is one suggestion: in the 1940s in Montreal the first joke that any Rumanian man told his eldest born son was the following:

Do you know how to make a Romanian omelette?
No,
Well, first you steal two eggs.

By the time Chaim Baer drags soggily onto the Moldavian shore of the Pruth, Phanariot princes have long vanished and the Turkish Sultan himself no longer exercises any authority over the region. Since the early nineteenth century the Balkans had been boiling with independence movements and bloody uprisings. Troops of Czars named Nicholas and Alexander had fought victorious battles against the Sultan, an entire Russian army had taken a six-year vacation in Bucharest, six hundred nearsighted British cavalrymen had swept to a glorious death at Balaclava and statesmen in frock coats and whiskers had conferred in Paris, signed treaties in Berlin. With two major results of all this. One was an independent Romania. The other was the necessity for Chaim Baer's grandson, Rabin, as a fourth grade student in Montreal to learn by heart a poem beginning *Half a league, half league, half league onward.*

Romania was not only an independent nation, it was also a kingdom. But the king was not Romanian. No Romanian was qualified for such a job. In truth, the king did not even speak Romanian, but his German was excellent and his French not bad. His name was Charles of Hohenzollern-Sigmaringen, but the locals called him King Carol. Selected in a plebiscite by an official margin of 685,969 to 224. Since Carol was a Prussian, which meant that the Habsburgs of Austria-Hungary were not much impressed with his credentials and more than a little suspicious over the lopsided results of the election. Someone in the entourage of Emperor Franz Joseph spread rumors in European court circles that the new ruler would be arrested by Austrian police on the way to his coronation. Carol was undeterred; he was a Hohenzollern after all. He traveled through Austria-Hungary carrying the heavy bags of a traveling salesman and wearing bright blue goggles, took a second-class cabin on a Danube steamer out of Vienna and arrived safely in his new home town. A slight hernia was a small price to pay to become king of the Dacians.

The king might never learn to speak the native tongue, but the citizens of his land were touchy about their prerogatives and, as people who claimed descent from Roman legions, inordinately proud of their heritage. Scratch a Romanian and he was sure to point how his unique ancestry, so different from his rude Slav, Bulgar and Magyar neighbors, made him fit to run an Empire. How appalling it was to learn that, at the Congress of Berlin in 1878, which guaranteed Rumanian independence, the Great Powers insisted on a treaty article requiring Roumania to return to her Jewish residents the civil rights which had been denied them in the 1866 constitution. Manfully, eloquently, passionately, the leaders of the new nation fought the proposal. It was a crime to deny the sovereign right of a nation with a glorious heritage to persecute, disfranchise and otherwise abuse some (or, for that matter, all) of its residents. Such arguments fell on deaf ears. The solemn will of Prussia, Austria-Hungary, France and Great Britain prevailed. At least on paper.

Between the southern bank of the Pruth and the village of Tetscani there is a blank, more of time than space. Chaim Baer acquires a wife, a business, a house, a vegetable garden, a cow, then a second cow. Seven children arrive, bracketed by the considerable number of stillbirths and miscarriages that were normal for that era, that region of the world. Life might be as routine as in any peasant community, but for the diversion thoughtfully provided by the government. It is the mayor who comes to the house to explain. Chaim Baer offers him a cup of tea, listens quietly, patiently, nodding his head. The mayor is a fellow card-player. He has no desire to perform his official duty, but it is not his fault that the time has come for Chaim Baer's family to leave Tetscani. When the tea cups are empty, the two men stand up, shake hands, part. There are no harsh words, no regrets, no deep sadness. Each understands that life is what life is.

The family loads its possessions in a cart and leaves Tetscani for Moinesti, some kilometers away. A few months, or a year or two later, they make the same journey in the opposite direction. These periodic moves partake of a mystery. Official government policy prevents Jews from becoming citizens and from owning land. But nothing is said in historical studies, constitutions, available decrees and statutes to indicate that there is a time limit on Jews residing in small towns or rural areas. Was it officially unofficial, carefully concealed from European statesmen, not even committed to paper so that foreign politicians with special constituencies or certain banking houses that might be persuaded to invest in Romanian development would not know? Was it local custom in Moldavia, sanctioned by decades or centuries of repetition? To Chaim Baer, his wife and children, reasons would have made little difference. The upset and confusion of packing, hauling, setting up in Moinesti were an unsought diversion. There is evidence enough that Chaim Baer was the sort of man who understood the spiritual benefits of an occasional change of scenery.

For Chaim Baer's children, Romania would always be Tetscani. Moinesti is a dim memory, fragments of cobblestones, tall two and three story buildings, crowds in paved streets, butcher shops where the boys worked briefly. Tetscani was where life became real, but only the occasional event or fragment of daily life would remain in the minds of Chaim Baer's children half a century later. These moments throw an unusual light over Tetscani. We imagine the normal color of Eastern Europe to be brown, the sepia tones of picture books on suburban coffee tables in the last third of the twentieth century. Tetscani is saturated with raw color: green of corn glowing in the summer sun; hillsides speckled with bright wildflowers; the purple feet of children and adults after a dance on the grapes; white bodies in icegreen streams where youngsters learn how to swim. The *shtetl* is dun faces full of suffering, acceptance, pain, wonder; invisible bodies clad in coats, hats, dresses long and weighty, dark and confining, personal prisons that reinforce a mentality, a way of life. Tetscani has no rabbis in black, no pale, stooped yeshiva students, no bulky synagogue brooding over the community. Weekly services for the six Jewish families take place in a room behind a store. Religion is quiet, humble, personal, a time for talking directly to Him or meditating softly on His absence.

Days, months, years vanish quickly behind the wispy membrane of consciousness we call the universe. Chaim Baer works at the sewing machine, the children milk the cows and tend the garden, his wife, Sarah, bakes fresh bread in a wood-burning oven, and covers her eyes when she lights candles every Friday night at sundown. Saturday, after the Sabbath ends, is the time for indulgence. Chaim Baer loves the noisy camaraderie of the gaming table, where religion and faith ride heavily on the size of a bet, the chance turn of a card. Summer days may find him spending afternoons with his youngsters, seven of them tumbling along cornfield rows, climbing into hilly vineyards surrounding the gray-walled estates of local nobles. In the autumn everyone—peasants, townspeople, relatives from far-off, even Jews—are welcome in the fields and courtyards of the stone chateau owned by the Rossettis. They haul grapes, lift them into barrels, stomp them with clean feet, then gather amidst pigs and chickens at long trestle tables in the courtyard to sing songs, drink the fresh juice and sample last year's vintage, then roar home, men, women and children, and before the dry throats and sharp headaches of the morrow, try a quick moment of love where the nimble ankles and firm calves of peasant girls mingle with the slow movements of a heavy body you know too well.

Once a year gypsies arrive to camp, barter, gamble, entertain, tell fortunes. Like all the children of Tetscani, Chaim Baer's kids hang around the high-wheeled caravans, regarding the visitors with expressions that seem to equate dark skin, cracked teeth and golden earrings with worlds of wonder. Adults are more cynical. Each year when the nomads depart, villagers complain to each other about all the items, large and small, that have mysteriously vanished from their households. Chaim Baer does not join in such talk. This is no identification of underdogs, no equation of Jew and gypsy as outsiders. It is temperament. He is not a critical sort, not even of men with rings in their ears who begin by losing and invariably end up winning at any evening of cards they are invited to enter.

There is a good story about Chaim Baer and a gypsy. The man came to the house one year and wheedled the tailor into letting him try on a half-finished suit. Perhaps he had played cards with Chaim Baer and found him an easy mark. Once clad in the garment, his own clothing lying in a damp heap on the floor of the front room that doubled as a workshop, the gypsy smiled, announced he would take the suit and began to walk toward the door without offering to pay. We can imagine Chaim Baer's reaction—if not anger, at least consternation. He must have tried to block the door, so the gypsy stood there and began to expose the hairy recesses of his body and to pluck, for the tailor's inspection, a few of the tenacious, hardy creatures who resided in them. Politely his visitor explained that of course the suit could not be sold now, for he was prepared to let everyone know that he had worn it. While he talked, the gypsy cracked lice between his teeth and spat them on the floor like grape seeds. When Chaim Baer absorbed the logic and force of his argument, he stepped away from the door while the gypsy covered his head with a battered hat, touched his fingers to the brim and vanished.

There is no way of knowing if this incident affected Chaim Baer's behavior, viewpoint or attitudes about gypsies. Every image of him is that of a tolerant, accepting man. Except for the hints of dislike for his wife's sister, but who knows what is lost or gained in the distorting effect of a half-century's events? She lived in Bucharest and, regularly arrived in Tetscani to grace the family with her presence. Rich by marriage to a business man, her clothing, accent, manners, air and interests reeked with the scent of city life—with contempt for peasants, land, countryside, cows and people evidently too dumb or unambitious to live in Bucharest. Chaim Baer's children loved her. The visits were like holidays, a time of excitement, food treats, presents. Ever after they would remember her smell of good soap and perfume, and her clothing, the silken dresses that the girls liked to touch, and on her feet, beneath her gowns, thin soled, immaculate highheeled shoes unlike anything ever seen before in the muddy roads of Tetscani.

Her arrival meant that Chaim Baer and his wife were forced out of their bedroom. During the days of her visit the sound of female voices jabbering in Polish rode through the hum of the sewing machine. The tailor left the house for solitary walks. Was it only his imagination that his normally docile wife became distracted and testy during such visits, and that this mood hung on for days after her sister's departure. In front of the children his demeanor did not change, but decades later the second son, Lazar, recalled how often Chaim Baer would speak to them with an uncharacteristic mixture of pride and joy of the misfortune that befell their aunt. Her husband had made his money as a building contractor. This was Romania, where every contract was sealed with a payoff that led to another contract. At last he was awarded a huge job that would secure his fortune, one that involved paving the streets of a substantial section of Bucharest. The night before work was to begin, all was ready and in place—piles of sand, rocks, shovels, picks, heaps of necessary tools and equipment. A freak windstorm—hurricane, typhoon, tornado—roared through the city that night, tearing roofs off houses, demolishing shacks, scattering sand, rocks, tools. Chaim Baer's brother-in-law was ruined. His wife never again came to Tetscani. Perhaps they moved to another country. For the children their aunt simply vanished, to be recalled only at certain seasons by scents and memories of the past.

Everyone remembers Chaim Baer as a kind father; some people thought him indulgent to the point of foolishness. The arrival of the first automobile is a good example. News had come through in advance: Danger! Clear the streets! Children were packed into houses, doors were locked, faces peered through curtains as if awaiting a glimpse of doomsday. And there were Chaim Baer and the seven children, crowded together on the tiny front step behind the sagging wooden fence that separated the front yard from the dirt of the main street. No doubt the tailor was more nervous than he admitted. He pulled the children close, held the two babies in his arms. Worries about the wisdom of his actions were underscored by the angry whispers of his wife through the closed front door, demanding he bring at least the infants back inside. Bravado triumphed over common sense. Noise, dust, a metal contraption and two pale figures blew past. Later they all walked down to the main square. The machine was parked in front of Tetscani's single inn. Adults spoke in hushed tones while the children reached hands out to the shiny, black metal, eyes full of more wonder than gypsy carts could evoke.

In all stories the children emerge as far more important to Chaim Baer than his wife. This is more than selective memory—it is heritage. The man could not only swim broad rivers and brave speeding machines, he could defy tradition in more fundamental ways. Such as when sickness struck the two eldest boys, a frightening palsy, a nervous disease, a terrible twitching and shaking. They could not sleep or keep food down, and two small bodies were beginning to waste away. The doctor from Moinesti could make no diagnosis. A rabbi promised prayers. Chaim Baer found a peasant woman who practiced either folk medicine or witchcraft. Perhaps he was the first Jew ever to request her services. The remedy was simple: dig into the earth under the bed where the boys slept until you found some coal-like rocks. Grind them into powder, mix with cow's milk and have the boys drink the mixture. Chaim Baer dug. The rocks were there. The mixture was prepared. It looked awful. It tasted awful. The twitching and shaking ended quickly. When sometime later Lazar came down with a very high fever and his mind wandered into delirium, there were no calls for doctors or rabbis. The tailor went directly to the old woman and followed her advice to wrap the youngster in the skin of a pig. For three days the boy sweated and moaned and rolled on his bed and yelled aloud, and on the fourth day he arose, cool and healthy once again.

More than seventy years later, when childhood was far clearer than his morning's breakfast, Lazar would tell his own son this story more than once, wondrously, disbelievingly, incapable of understanding how such a cure had worked, perhaps hoping that another such cure would be brought to him again. After months in modern hospitals, his mind was so blitzed by medical technology that he could no longer understand the truth of his own experience—memory was a legend he could neither accept nor disbelieve.

Sitting and smelling the ripeness of damp earth and winds blowing before rainstorms. Was there time on afternoons while clouds piled up over the Carpathian Mountains, over the irregular quilt of wheat fields crumpled into foothills, over the limp, brown tassels of cornstalks, the twisted vines where pregnant grapes swelled beneath tight purple skills, was there time to wonder in those hours locked between past and future? Behind pale blue eyes, speaking through them, was a heritage of more than books, the bright impatience of the nomad, a gleam of some tribe that had boiled out of Asia a millennia before. Thoughts came in nouns, without verbs. Restlessness, some unspoken question amidst the noise of swiftly-growing children. With surprise, the same surprise that would fill the innocent eyes of his second son almost eighty years later when death still eluded him after strokes, massive heart attacks and pleurisy. Lazar would tell about the brass band parade, led by the Pope, which had crashed through the parking lot of Cedars-Sinai Hospital the night before. And the Pope, with his golden robes and silver crown, had called up through the sealed window on the sixth floor, called in a powerful voice amplified by no megaphone or loudspeaker, called in fluent Yiddish, *It's time, it's time. Come along, it's time.* Because Chaim Baer's son was tied to the bed—*poseyed* in the language of hospitals—he was unable to rise, to follow the parade, to follow the Pope, and he had to call back, *Next time, maybe next time.* Pain and quick tears scarred the innocence of his eyes as he told the story—then asked *Do you think they'll return?*

It was the same with Chaim Baer's eyes, waiting for the storms from beyond the mountains, accepting the darkness dropping on Moldavia. Innocent blue had seen it before, fields and churches and rivers, home and friends and parents alter, change, disappear. Sometimes when clouds blew over the mountains, driving down on Tetscani with darkness and wind and the violent slosh of rain, Chaim Baer felt again that strange itch that could not be scratched. There is no reason to believe he had much imagination. In his mind, no images of tropic islands with dusky maidens, of deserts to track or empty mountains to climb. No hunger for the delights of bright boulevards, cafes, concert halls, glittering city scenes he could not even picture. Just the noise of rainstorms, that was enough. Trees swaying in gray winds, mud oozing to the ankles, soiling trousers, and a longing in the soles of the feet. Two decades, maybe more—for who could number the years?—since he had swum the Pruth. Now one century was ending or another beginning. The difference was the same. It was time to be moving.

CHAPTER 30

Hans Ulrich Gumbrecht

IN 1926: LIVING AT THE EDGE
OF TIME (1997)*

The following reading is taken from Hans Ulrich Gumbrecht's *In 1926: Living At The Edge of Time* (1997). In it Gumbrecht (Albert Guérard Professor of History, Stanford University) conducts an experiment in historical writing – representation. Eschewing conventional narratives and argumentation (for narratives suggest meaningful beginnings, middles and ends, and arguments suggest an inherent meaning that the historian sets out to discover and convey), what Gumbrecht's book offers is a collection of fragments that illuminate the facets of the year 1926. Gumbrecht's focus is just one year, a year in which nothing significant seems to have happened ('it seems to be one of the very few years in the twentieth century to which no historian has ever attributed specific hermeneutic relevance'), such that his task is simply to evoke what living in 1926 might have been like. Thus, Gumbrecht's text is organised in five parts. In the first (User's Manual) Gumbrecht sketches his 'guide' to the text: 'Do not try "too start from the beginning" for this book has no beginning . . . Start with any of the fifty-one entries in any of the three sections . . . [and a] web of cross-references will take you to other, related entries . . .'. These fifty-one entries are then organised into the following three parts – Arrays, Codes and Codes Collapsed – within which the entries (generally about eight pages long and on such phenomena as Airplanes, Boxing, Gramophones, Roof Gardens, Telephones; on Centre *v* Periphery, Present *v* Past, Silence *v* Noise; on Action = Impotence, Individity = Collectivity . . .), swirl and rub shoulders with one another, abruptly connecting and disconnecting: 'Adolph Hitler bumps up against John Barrymore ("Movie Palaces"); Fritz Lang rubs shoulders with Jack Dempsey ("Elevators")'. These snippets swirl together as though in a kaleidoscope, forming momentary patterns and then dispersing. It's hard for the reader to know what to do with them. The knowledge that Gumbrecht presents is, literally, 'useless' (Marybeth Hamilton, *Rethinking History*, 4 (1), 2000: 102). This pointlessness – criticised by Hamilton – is, of course, the point. For 1926, is, in and for itself, literally pointless until it is sealed within envelopes of meaning which are as personal to the reader/writer as the contents of letters always are: the past awaits temporary/temporal signification. And this – or something like this – is discussed by Gumbrecht in the fifth part of his text (Frames) wherein his essay on 'the Nature of History' ('After Learning From History') allows him to extend certain thoughts that he first aired in the last section of the User's Manual entitled 'Purpose': 'The book's main intention is best captured in the phrase that was its original subtitle: "an essay on historical simultaneity"'. Gumbrecht thus asks to what extent and to what cost it is possible to make present again, in a text, works that existed before the author was born:

> Although the book shares some of the leitmotifs of what can be called "post-modern philosophy" (the unwillingness to think history as a homogeneous,

* Hans Ulrich Gumbrecht (1997) *In 1926: Living at the Edge of Time*, Cambridge, MA: Harvard University Press, pp. vii–xv and 66–73.

totalizing movement, the argument in favor of a "weak" conception of subjectivity, the fascination with material surfaces), there is, the author thinks, only one reason that it should be recognized as "postmodern" and this is a negative reason. The author believes that the academico-ideological battle for the preservation of "modern" and "modernist" (i.e., nonpostmodern) is a lost cause.

The extracts here are taken from Gumbrecht's User's Manual and from one of his snippets of 1926: Dancing.

CONTENTS

USER'S MANUAL

Where to start

DO NOT TRY "to start from the beginning," for this book has no beginning in the sense that narratives or arguments have beginnings. Start with any of the fifty-one entries in any of the three sections entitled "Arrays," "Codes," and "Codes Collapsed" (the alphabetical order of the subheadings shows that there isn't any hierarchy among them). Simply start with an entry that particularly interests you. From each entry a web of cross-references will take you to other, related entries. Read as far as your interest carries you (and as long as your schedule allows). You'll thus establish your individual reading path. Just as there is no obligatory beginning, there also is no obligatory or definitive end to the reading process. Regardless of where you enter or exit, any reading sequence of some length should produce the effect to which the book's title alludes: you should feel "in 1926." The more immediate and sensual this illusion becomes, the more your reading will fulfill the book's chief aim. Note: you can, if you like, experience this effect *without* reading the last two chapters, "After Learning from History" and "Being-in-the-Worlds of 1926."

Mode(s)

In the sections "Arrays," "Codes," and "Codes Collapsed," the writing aims at being strictly descriptive. This discourse is meant to bring out dominant surface perceptions as they were offered by certain material phenomena, and dominant world views as they were produced by certain concepts during the year 1926. Each entry refrains as far as possible from "expressing" the author's individual "voice," from in-depth interpretations, and from diachronic contextualizations through the evocation of phenomena and world views that occurred "before" and "after" 1926. Each entry is thus supposed to reach maximum surface-focus and concreteness. If possible at all, the style and the structure of the entries would be determined by the individual phenomena that each of them thematizes. In their convergence and divergence, finally, the entries do not seek to produce any specific "mood" (or *Stimmung*). Should some readers discover, for example, a certain "Heideggerian temper" in this book, such an impression would have to be explained as a symptom of the impact that the year 1926 had on Heidegger, rather than as a symptom of the author's ambition to imitate Heidegger's style. In contrast to the fifty-one entries, "After Learning from History" and "Being-in-the-Worlds of 1926" are written in the author's current academic prose (which he did not take as a license for trying to frustrate nonspecialized readers).

Stakes

To make at least some readers forget, during the reading process, that they are *not* living in 1926. In other words: to conjure some of the worlds of 1926, to re-present them, in the sense of making them present again. To do this with the greatest possible immediacy achievable through a historiographic text (as opposed to, say, photographs, sound-documents, or material objects). Although the author had to invent a specific textual form for each entry, the success of this book as a whole depends on the claim that it was *not* "invented" (i.e., on the claim that its content is completely referential). The effect of conjuring the past is based on this more or less "ontological" implication. A historical novel (if the author were at all capable of writing fiction) would not have done the job—at least, it would not have done the same job. And what is *not* at stake? The author's tenure, he hopes; his financial situation, he fears; as well as any attempt at interpreting or understanding the worlds of 1926 (either intrinsically or from what preceded and followed it). Finally, the author would not be disappointed if he learned that the worlds of 1925 or 1927 (and so forth) were not much different from those worlds that he reconstructed for 1926. His book is not about producing an individual description of the year 1926; it is about making present a historical environment of which we know (nothing more than) that it existed in some places during the year 1926.

Question

This is not necessarily and "hermeneutically" the sole question that a reader needs in order to understand this book; rather, it is the question that the author thinks pushed him to write: What can we do with our knowledge about the past once we have given up the hope of "learning from history" regardless of means and cost? This—by now lost—didactic function of history (at least, a certain conception of this didactic function) seems to be closely related to the habit of thinking and representing history as a narrative. If this is true, then a postdidactic attitude vis-à-vis our knowledge about the past must imply the quest for nonnarrative forms of historiographic representation. But the argument that begins with these steps is already too "streamlined." The real question behind the question of what to do with our knowledge about the past is not only the—more or less technical—question of how to write or represent history. It is above all the question of what we imagine the past "to be" (the question about the past as "raw material"), before we even begin to think about possible forms of its representation.

Theses

Since we do not know what to do with our vast and rapidly accumulating knowledge about the past (history no longer having any obvious pragmatic function), we should examine the more or less preconscious impulses that may motivate our fascination with history. This book presupposes that a specific desire is at work here: a desire "to speak to the dead"—in other words, a desire for first-hand experience of worlds that existed before our birth. In catering to this desire, the book brings forth—more implicitly than explicitly—certain features of what "we" (educated people within the Western culture of 1997) imagine "history" to be. We all seem to agree that we no longer think history as a "unilinear" and "totalizing" dynamic of "development." Beyond this negation, however, there is no single dominant form of imagining and representing history. If we imagine and represent it synchronically, as this book does, we realize that the elements of such a synchrony do not converge into a coherent and homogeneous picture. Nevertheless, and perhaps paradoxically, this book suggests the existence of a "web" or "field" of (not only discursive) realities that strongly shaped the behavior and interactions of 1926. So strong indeed is this impression that, at least implicitly, this book makes a plea against any claims for subjective or collective agency. And how could a book concerned with historical simultaneity *not* arrive at this very conclusion? After all, there are no concepts of action and agency that do not require sequentiality as their frame of reference. Yet this is exactly the one form of thinking history with which the idea of historical simultaneity is incompatible.

Context

We cannot avoid the impression that the current intellectual situation in the humanities—at least when seen from the present—marks a comparatively weak moment. (Of course, such an impression may change in retrospect; it also may suffer from the usual problems of self-reflexive assessments.) At any rate, the present appears to be a moment of great sophistication when it comes to affirming that some certainties and assumptions "no longer work"—and of even greater reluctance when it comes to filling the gaps that the vanished certainties and assumptions have left. The present moment seems to correspond to the "end of metaphysics," as Derrida describes it in *Of Grammatology*: we are beyond metaphysics but will never really leave metaphysics behind us. We also lack strong alternatives to options that no longer seem viable. Marxism is but a nostalgic or embarrassing memory, especially in its more recent resurrections and reembodiments (good intentions will not fix an outdated epistemology!). Deconstruction has either turned sour and sectarian (there's an air of Latter-Day-Saintliness about some of today's deconstructors in their black apparel), or has been absorbed by the general interpretative and hermeneutic mood. The charm (and the punch) of New Historicism has withered all too rapidly. And so on. To make matters worse, the author feels that a great deal of pressure is being brought to bear upon his generation to come up with something new, something not exclusively skeptical; but he thinks that he is not particularly good at programmatic writing—i.e., at the genre of writing that, undoubtedly, is required here. Still, he feels that he and the scholars of his generation should become for the scholars of the next generation what Reinhart Koselleck, Nikias Luhmann, Jean-François Lyotard, Richard Rorty, Hayden White, and Paul Zumthor (a purely male kinship, he admits with contrition) have been for him. The possibility of failure notwithstanding, this book is, for the moment, the best he can offer as a reaction to this self-imposed expectation.

"Help"

"Help," in the sense offered by our computer screens, can be found in the chapters "After Learning from History" and "Being-in-the-Worlds of 1926." Especially for readers with a professional interest, these chapters provide a double contextualization of the book as belonging to a specific intellectual and academic situation. "After Learning from History," on the one hand, describes contemporary concepts and contemporary uses of "history," and is meant to show how both the experiment that constitutes this book and the structure in which it is realized are reactions to the specific status of "history" in our present. The chapter also explains why the author chose a random year as the topic of his book—though he does not go so far as to claim, in the end, that this year has a particular (but hitherto hidden) importance. "Being-in-the-Worlds of 1926," on the other hand, suggests how this book can be used for things other than making present the worlds of 1926. The test cases are intensely historical readings of three texts—readings performed in the context of the "worlds of 1926" as they are presented in the fifty-one entries. The texts of reference are Martin Heidegger's *Sein und Zeit*, Hans Friedrich Blunck's *Kampf der Gestirne*, and Carl Van Vechten's *Nigger Heaven*.

Purpose

The author never intended this book to contain anything edifying, either morally or polit-ically. But sometimes, as we all know, our best intentions fail to protect us against our most embarrassing urges. The author likewise had no strong investment in being orig-inal, being witty, producing stylistic beauty, and so on. The book's main intention is best captured in the phrase that was its original subtitle: "an essay on historical simultaneity." The book asks to what extent and at what cost it is possible to make present again, in a text, worlds that existed before its author was born—and the author is fully aware that such an undertaking is impossible. Although the book shares some of the leitmotifs of what can be called "postmodern philosophy" (the unwillingness to think History as a homogeneous, totalizing movement, the argument in favor of a "weak" conception of subjectivity, the fascination with material surfaces), there is, the author thinks, only one reason that it should be recognized as "postmodern," and this is a negative reason. The author believes that the academico-ideological battle for the preservation of "modern" and "modernist" (i.e., "nonpostmodern") values is a lost cause. But who's interested in the author's answer to a question that nobody asked him? If the book has no political or ethical message, should readers perhaps take its form as "the message"? This would imply that the author is hoping many scholars will pick up, imitate, and develop the discourse he "invented." The truth is, however, that he would feel almost guilty if his book ever created such a fashion (which does not seem to be a very serious threat anyway). For, needless to say, there is no dearth of academic trends or schools. Perhaps the problem is that, as things now stand, everything is doomed to remain an experiment.

DANCING

As the only artist of the American dance and music show *La Revue nègre*, the nineteen-year-old Josephine Baker, who within a few weeks has become the darling of the Parisian public, receives a contract to appear at the Folies Bergères. During the winter months, however, she gives two daily performances (at 8:30 P.M. and 11:15 P.M.) at Berlin's Nelson Theater. It is in Berlin that her dancing begins to fascinate the intellectuals of the Old World. Max Reinhardt, who dominates the German-speaking theater scene with his productions in Berlin, Vienna, and Salzburg, tries to persuade Baker to make a "serious" career on the stage: "The expressive control of the whole body, the spontaneity of motion, the rhythm, the bright emotional color: these are your treasures—no, not yours alone— these are American treasures. With such control of the body, such pantomime, I believe I could portray emotion as it has never before been portrayed" (Rose, 85).

There is a certain ambiguity in Reinhardt's reaction to Josephine Baker's dancing. On the one hand, he is impressed with its sheer form and its sensual presence ("the spon-taneity of motion, the rhythm, the bright emotional color"). But on the other hand, he wants to see it as an "expression" or as a "portrait"—i.e., as a signifier for something "deep" (Reinhardt speaks of "emotions") that comes to the surface. [see **Authenticity vs. Artificiality**] Full of enthusiasm, Reinhardt phones his influential friend Harry Graf Kessler late in the evening on Saturday, February 13, and invites him to meet Baker at the apartment of the playwright Karl Gustav Vollmüller. The entry in Kessler's diary referring to this occasion shows an oscillation similar to Reinhardt's: "Baker danced with extreme grotesqueness and purity of style, like an Egyptian or an archaic figure that performs acrobatics without ever losing its style. The dancers of Salamo and Tutankhamen must have danced this way. She does this for hours, apparently without getting tired, always finding new forms, as if in a game, like a playful child. Her body does not get warm; rather, her skin maintains its fresh, cool dryness. A charming creature, but almost completely unerotic" (Kessler, 455). [see **Mummies**] It remains unclear what exactly Kessler and Reinhardt see Baker expressing. The signified of which they "read" her body as a signifier is something vaguely archaic, something authentic, something more real perhaps than the reality of the contemporary world. At the same time, however, Kessler describes Baker's dancing as a pure surface phenomenon, consisting of endless varieties of form. This makes it into the movement of a body that has no more erotic appeal than the body of a child, a body whose skin remains cool and impenetrable. [see **Gomina**]

Or could this view simply be a reaction on the part of Kessler's offended masculinity? He is shocked to see the nude Baker tightly embracing a young woman in a tuxedo: "Between Reinhardt, Vollmüller, and myself lay Baker and Landshoff, wrapped around each other like a pair of beautiful young lovers" (Kessler, 456). [see **Male = Female (Gender Trouble)**] Since there is no easy way out of his confusion, Kessler goes to see Baker's show at the Nelson Theater the following week. But the only certainty he can find lies in the feeling that she stands for something that is stronger than his own culture. This something, he writes in his diary, is both "ultraprimitive and ultramodern": "Went again to the Negro revue at the Nelson in the evening (Josephine Baker). They are somewhere between the jungle and the skyscraper. The same is true of her music, jazz, in its color and rhythm. It is ultraprimitive and ultramodern. Their tension generates their forceful style; the same is true of the Russians. By comparison, our own culture is tame—without inner tension and therefore without style, like a limp bow string" (458, February 17). [see **Roof Gardens, Authenticity = Artificiality (Life)**]

At their very first meeting with Baker, Kessler, Reinhardt, and Vollmüller form the project of writing a ballet for her, "taken half from jazz, half from oriental music, perhaps from Richard Strauss" (Kessler, 456). [see **jazz**] The script they end up writing is hopelessly trivial. Baker is supposed to play a dancer whose nude body awakens the young King Salomo's desire. But the more gifts she receives from the king, the less she is willing to yield to his advances. Then, in a final movement, her young lover appears—in a black tuxedo (460ff.). Baker still ignores this text, but she feels strongly inspired by an "expressionist" sculpture from Kessler's art collection: "Then she began to move, strongly and with grotesque expressions, in front of the grand Maillol sculpture. Clearly she entered into a dialogue with it. She looked long at it, imitating it position, unimpressed by the uncanny rigidity and force of its expression. A childlike priestess imparting movement to her body and her goddess One could see Maillol was much more interesting and alive for her than men such as Max Reinhardt, Vollmüller, and myself" (461, February 24). For many weeks, Baker is undecided about whether to return to Paris and fulfill her contract with the Folies Bergères or to accept Reinhardt's offer and stay in Germany. What finally persuades her that the world of cabaret rather than the serious world of German theater offers the appropriate environment for her dancing is the news that the composer Irving Berlin has been hired for her show in Paris: "Herr Reinhardt hadn't mentioned Irving Berlin" (Rose, 89). The project of integrating Josephine Baker's body into the space of theatrical representation has failed.

Dancing is a synchronization of the rhythm of music with the rhythm of body movement. Rhythm is movement as form, form reconciled with the dimension of temporality, which is inherent in any kind of movement. At first glance, the temporality of movement seems to resist the stability of form (Gumbrecht, 717ff.). [see **Present vs. Past**] But movement can become form through the repetition of basic sequential patterns. Repetition makes the recurrence of such sequential patterns predictable, and it is thus that the form of certain sequential patterns becomes associated with the movement they are constituting. Their form makes this movement recognizable among movements that are based on different patterns, as well as among movements without form. Since rhythm creates form through recurrence, a given rhythm cannot produce anything new (although it may allow for variation within certain basic patterns). As soon as the sequential patterns underlying a rhythm begin to change, it ceases to exist. This is why rhythm inevitably exists in tension with the dual-level nature of signification and meaning, where different forms can stand for the same content (Gumbrecht, 720ff.). Fascination with rhythm points to a fascination with the separation between the human body, which is capable of incarnating (that is, of becoming and being) a rhythm, and the human mind, which, as source of the dual-level relation between signifiers and signified, is never fully compatible with rhythm, because it cannot help associating becoming and being with meanings (Goiston). Putting a body under the sway of musical rhythm therefore sets this body apart from the mind. In *A Vision*, William Butler Yeats has one of the participants in a conversation on poetry complain about a loss of "rhythmical speech," which (he believes) results from realism's fixation on representation: "You will remember that a few years before the Great War the realists drove the last remnants of rhythmical speech out of the theatre" (33). A conception of art that focuses exclusively on meaning-constitution and world-reference must neglect the sensual qualities of its material surfaces: "The realists turn our words into gravel, but the musicians and the singers turn them into honey and oil" (34). For Michael Robartes, another protagonist of Yeats's fictional colloquium, this very insight comes from a paradoxical love relationship with a ballet dancer: "I went to Rome and there fell violently in love with a ballet-dancer who had not an idea in her head. All might have been well had I been content to take what came; had I understood that her coldness and cruelty became in the transfiguration of the body an inhuman majesty; that I adored in her body what I hated in her will" (37).

"Transfiguration," not "expression," is the key concept in Yeats's reflections. The relation that he sees between the "body" and the "will" of the dancer is not a relation that follows the binary logic of the signifier and the signified. It is a transfiguration of one substance into a different substance. On the multiple social levels of Yeats's, Baker's, and Reinhardt's cultures, and in a wide variety of forms, dancing responds to this very distinction between a mode of convergence and a mode of divergence in thinking the mind/body relationship. This distinction also dominates the debate about *Ausdruckstanz*, or "expressive dancing," in Weimar Germany (von Soden and Schmidt, 152ff.), For a select intellectual public, Mary Wigman, who stands at the center of this movement, dances the "expression" of elementary emotions (such as passion, grief, mourning) and of elementary existential situations (such as idolatry, prayer, witchcraft). Often she combines her dancing with the recitation of classical texts—and there is a good chance that Max Reinhardt's insistence on "reading" the movements of Josephine Baker's body as "expressions" goes back to Wigman's widely admired style. In contrast, Valeska Gert, Wigman's main competitor on the Berlin dance scene, is a star of the cabaret stage. Instead of expressing meanings which are supposed to come from an "archaic depth," she strives to become a part of the contemporary world's "concrete reality" by portraying prostitutes, go-betweens, and circus girls. [see **Uncertainty vs. Reality**] It is thus no accident that the press associates Valeska Gert's dancing with Josephine Baker's (von Soden and Schmidt, 158).

The contrast between dancing as expression and dancing as body rhythm mirrors the central antinomy within the political world. The Italian novelist Mario Puccini sees the fox-trot, together with a number of other imported American dances (often called "jazz dances") as an obstacle to the development of Fascist art as an art of expression: "The coming of a Fascist art (that is, an art which improves the race and at the same time expresses it) is impossible so long as thousands and thousands of young people read short stories and novels—you know the ones I mean—that are set in nightclubs or theaters, and full of disreputable operettas and even more disreputable fox-trots" (Puccini, 258). At the opposite end of the political spectrum, the Communist poet Johannes R. Becher, while dutifully attacking the moral decadence of nightclubs and prostitution (Becher, 93, 99), consistently uses dancing as a metaphor for social and individual emancipation: "Oh, dance yourself out of / Your splintering thighs, / Tuschka!" (61ff.). The generations are distinguished by their preference for different styles of dancing, even more than by their preference for different political and social groups. [see **Present vs. Past**] In Thomas Mann's story "Unordnung und frühes Leid" ("Disorder and Early Sorrow"), Professor Cornelius fails to bridge the gap between his own taste and that of his teenaged children—and his reaction to a dance party which they organize at his house becomes even more negative when he sees what a strong emotional impact these modern rhythms have on his beloved four-year-old daughter [see **Gramophones**]:

> The young people dance eagerly—so far as one can it call dancing, this move-
> ment that they perform with such quiet devotion. Indeed, they move in
> strange embraces and in a new style, propelling their lower body by moving
> their shoulders and swaying their hips. They dance slowly around the floor,
> obeying obscure rules, never growing tired, because one can't grow tired this
> way. No heaving breasts, no blushing. Here and there two girls dance
> together, sometimes even two boys; it's all the same to them. So they follow
> the exotic noises of the gramophone, which rotates under the sturdiest of
> needles to make the sound of the shimmies, fox-trots, and one-steps as loud
> as possible. The Double Fox, the African Shimmy, Java Dances, and Polka
> Creoles—wild, perfumed steps, now languid, now military style, with foreign
> rhythms, monotones with orchestral ornamentation, drums thumping and
> snapping, spewing out Negro amusement. (Mann, 514)

The younger generation is eager to assimilate the new rhythms of the fox-trot and the shimmy, the Charleston and the blackbottom. What many of them have learned in their professions comes out in their dancing: they let their bodies be coupled to rhythms imposed from outside. [see **Assembly Lines, Employees**] So tight is this coupling that the dancers relinquish all control over their bodies and continue moving until the point of total exhaustion. [see **Endurance**] So immediate is the connection of their individual bodies to the rhythm of the music that they need no longer be guided through coordination with a partner. Some contemporary observers hail this change as a new peak of gender emancipation. [see **Male = Female (Gender Trouble)**] Yet while the new dances certainly have a gender-neutralizing effect, they do not really foster individual

freedom of choice; rather, they promote a shift from dependence on a partner to dependence on an external rhythm. Instead of a site of domination and surrender, the body of
the dance partner becomes a site—or, rather, a point of reference—for association and
coordination. This is the "deindividualizing" principle (Jelavich, 179ff.) of the kick-lines
which conquer the revue stages, transforming the individual bodies of the "girls" into
complex systems of well-coordinated limbs. [see **Revues**] This is also why the role of
the gigolo does not turn into a role of surrender and therefore hardly ever humiliates
male gender-pride. And, finally, this is why the new dancing bodies are so often perceived
as pure, unerotic surface.

The erotic excitement of the interaction with a dance partner is replaced by the
excitement of continually changing fashions in rhythm. Dance schools therefore empha-
size the variety and novelty of the dances they teach: "To become an *exceptional*
dancer—not merely a 'walkaround'—this is your opportunity to learn all of the latest
Valencia, Fox Trot, Waltz, Tango, and Charleston steps for almost nothing! While
becoming the very best dancer in your crowd, you will enjoy learning in a few private
lessons and in a class of congenial people" (*New York Times*, September 22). Among the
dances mentioned in this advertisement, the tango has a specific status, for two reasons.
Together with the Valencia, and unlike the Charleston, it connotes, first, the "authenticity" of Spanish and Latin-American culture, which is the only current alternative to the
"authenticity" generally attributed to the African and African-American worlds. [see
Bullfighting, Center vs. Periphery] Second, among the dances performed by a
couple, the tango is the only one that does not prescribe complementarity between the
movements of the man and woman. Tango dancers look and act as if they did not see
each other, and their bodies are supposed to follow the rhythm of the music independently from each other. Unlike the preestablished harmony of the traditional
partner-dances, the harmony of the tango couple is staged either as emerging out of a
free collaboration or as the—often violent—resolution of a potential conflict: "Not
rounded, but broken, the rotation produces no center of gravity between the partners
but oscillates from one to the other. If they stay at distance they lose each other, and will
never come together" (Eisner and Müller, 318).

With its proliferation of old and new steps, dancing becomes assimilated
to virtually every other form of entertainment. [see **Bars**] More than half the
advertisements on the back page of the Berlin daily *8 Uhr-Abendblatt* invite the readers to
dance events. With a slogan that seems inspired by the fashion for nonsense poetry, the
Weidenhof, "Berlin's most spectacular dance palace," emphasizes the contrast between
dull everydayness and the pleasure of moving one's body to the rhythm of the music:
"When things become too lousy, come over to the Weidenhof" (October 19). Besides
the "five-o'clock tea dance" with two orchestras, the Weidenhof offers, at 8 P.M. and for
a public of spectators rather than dancers, a show by "Mme. Salome and her beautiful
ballet. Twenty ladies of overwhelming grace and beauty." The Tanz-Cabaret Valencia
features "five-o'clock tea dance, restaurant, bar, attractions," and a "lighted floor" which
makes the dancers feel that they have found some other terrain than the stable ground of
everyday reality. [see **Uncertainty vs. Reality**]

Such forms of light amusement, however, exist side-by-side with the seriousness of
Ausdruckstanz. The premiere on Tuesday, December 14, of Arnold Fanck's film *Der Heilige
Berg*, which marks Leni Riefenstahl's screen debut, is inaugurated by a young actress
dancing to the music of Schubert's Unfinished Symphony (Riefenstahl, 59). [see

Mountaineering] Next to the daily ad for the Nelson Theater, where Josephine Baker's German career has begun, the *8 Uhr-Abendblatt* announces, on October 19, a performance by Katjana Barbakoff, conjuring various ancient and exotic worlds: "Among the new dance styles: Majeftas Asiatika back to nature, a treasure preserved from the No Period" (October 19). The organizers of a ballroom event try to appeal to the older generation by launching, in Gothic letters, the "Senior Competition of the Berlin Blue-Orange Club, followed by a show under the auspices of the National Ballroom Dancing Association"; yet they also view children as potential customers of the dance palaces: "Parents who love their children take them to the world's first children's revue: 'All Puppets Dance.' A fairytale play in thirty scenes. Admiral Palace Theater" (October 22). The blurring of boundaries between the genders and among the various forms of participation in the dance world is epitomized by an advertisement for an establishment called Steinmeier am Bahnhof, Friedrichstraße 96, in the heart of Berlin's lesbian district (von Soden and Schmidt, 160). Under the heading "Täglich Tanz der schönen Frauen" ("Daily Dance of Beautiful Women"), it shows two women with haircuts *à la garçonne* dancing in a close embrace—with two smiling men gazing at them (October 2). [see **Male Female (Gender Trouble)**]

Related Entries

Assembly Lines, Bars, Bullfighting, Employees, Endurance, Gomina, Gramophones, Jazz, Mountaineering, Mummies, Revues, Roof Gardens, Authenticity vs. Artificiality, Center vs. Periphery, Present vs. Past, Uncertainty vs. Reality, Authenticity = Artificiality (Life), Male = Female (Gender Trouble)

References

8 Uhr—Ahendblatt.
Johannes R. Becher, *Maschinenrhythmen.* Berlin.
Monika Eisner and Thomas Müller, "Das Ich und sein Körper: Europa im Tango-Fieber." In Manfred Pfister, ed., *Die Modern isierung des Ich.* Passau, 1989.
Michael Goiston, "'Tm Anfang war der Rhythmus': Rhythmic Incubations in Discourses of Mind, Body, and Race from 1850 to 1944." *Stanford Humanities Review* 5, supplement (1996): 1–24.
Hans Ulrich Gumbrecht, "Rhythmus und Sinn." In Hans Ulrich Gumbrecht and K. Ludwig Pfeiffer, eds., *Materialität der Kommunikation.* Frankfurt, 1988.
Peter Jelavich, *Berlin Cabaret.* Cambridge, Mass., 1993.
Harry Graf Kessler, *Tagebücher,* 1918–1937. Frankfurt, 1961.
Thomas Mann, "Unordnung und frühes Leid" (1926). In Mann, *Sämtliche Erzählungen.* Frankfurt, 1961.
New York Times.
Mario Puccini, "Text from *Critica Fascista*" (1926). In Stanford *Italian Review* (1990): 257–260.
Phyllis Rose, *Jazz Cleopatra: Josephine Baker in Her Time.* New York, 1989.
Leni Riefenstahl, *A Memoir.* New York, 1992.
Kristine von Soden and Maruta Schmidt, eds., *Neue Frauen: Die zwanziger Jahre.* Berlin, 1988.
W. B. Yeats, *A Vision* (1926). New York, 1961.

CHAPTER 31

Sven Lindqvist

A HISTORY OF BOMBING (2000)*

Extracts from *A History of Bombing* (2000) by the Swedish journalist, Sven Lindqvist, forms the next reading. It has received a mixed reception from its reviewers. Thus, in *English Historical Review* (June 2002, pp. 257–8), Simon Bull has dismissed it out of hand. Arguing that the form of Lindqvist's text is based upon children's 'dungeons and dragons' comic books, readers-players pick their way through a choice of 399 numbered paragraphs in no particular sequence; these are not meant to be read in linear style but by way of the reader's own (arbitrary) decisions. As a result, readers-players can plot and re-plot their adventure in almost inexhaustible ways, thus disrupting a single (linear) narrative structure. Yet, just as in 'dungeons and dragons' there is, ultimately, one final 'paragraph', one 'real' end to the story, so that there is one motif running throughout Lindqvist's text; namely, that bombing was the most important legacy – one of its 'facilitatory factors' – of the nineteenth-century's genocidal imperialism; of that 'global violence that is the hard core of our existence'. Well, maybe it is, admits Bull, but 'historically speaking', Lindqvist hardly demonstrates this. In fact, Bull claims, in the end – 'as one might expect in a book whose form was modelled on a series of adventures for boys' – this is a 'puerile work'.

Although Benjamin Noys's review (*Rethinking History*, 6 (2), 2002, pp. 242–6) recognises that Lindqvist's book rests on connecting up Western colonialism, imperialism and an endemic/institutionalised racism to bombing, any thoughts of this being a puerile text is rejected. For Noys, Lindqvist's book can be added to that smallish number of actual postmodern histories – though not one without its tensions. For whilst, on the one hand, the fragmentation of the text is supposed to reflect in its 'chaos' the reality of a chaotic 'actual history' (i.e. that for Lindqvist history actually *is* chaos . . . an ontological claim about its 'real nature'), nevertheless, Noys also detects the strong sense of a single, guiding and thus fixing thesis – namely, the genocidal nature of the West (another ontological claim), of which bombing was but an ethnic/racist expression. The tension, then, says Noys, is thus between this ontological chaos and another – that of a single comprehensive/comprehending thesis. And yet this may be all right, even expected. For maybe that tension is precisely the main characteristic of postmodern histories; a tension between chaos (the postmodern) and order (the modern). Consequently, if postmodern histories have sometimes suggested a leap into a new, purely postmodern writing and their empirical opponents (e.g. Bull) have called for a return to (or a staying with) a traditional empirical/epistemological history, Noys suggests 'we' work within this 'opposition', just as Lindqvist has perhaps had to do. This allows for the possibility of new ways of reading the past and new modes of making/reading it. Reproduced here is Lindqvist's 'Ways into the Book', 'Chronology', and 22 exemplary gobbets.

---

* Sven Lindqvist (2000) *A History of Bombing*, The New Press.

HOW TO READ THIS BOOK

THIS **BOOK IS A** labyrinth with twenty-two entrances and no exit. Each entrance opens into a narrative or an argument, which you then follow by going from text according to the arrow (➤) indicating the number of the section where the narrative is continued. So from entrance 1 you proceed to section 166 and continue reading section by section until you come to 173, where another arrow takes you back to entrance 2.

If you get lost, you can find your way again with the assistance of the table of entrances (Ways into the Book) at the beginning of the book.

In order to move through time, you also have to move through the book, often forward, but sometimes backwards. Wherever you are in the text, events and thoughts from that same period surround you, but they belong to narratives other than the one you happen to be following. That's the intention. That way the text emerges as what it is – one of many possible paths through the chaos of history.

So welcome to the labyrinth! Follow the threads, put together the horrifying puzzle, and, once you have seen my century, build one of your own from other pieces.

WAYS INTO THE BOOK

Numbers refer to section numbers.
Bang, You're Dead: 1, 166–173
In the Beginning Was the Bomb: 2, 24–25, 28–29, 32–33, 62, 65–68
The History of the Future: 3, 46, 55–57, 59–60, 72–73
Death Comes Flying: 4, 76–78, 85, 135, 80–84
What is Permissible in War?: 5, 26–27, 30–31, 35, 45, 40, 43–44, 48–49, 53–54, 58, 64, 75, 79, 39, 41–42, 47, 50
Bombing the Savages: 6, 74, 100–102, 106–108, 112, 23, 113–114, 118, 123, 146–153
Bombed into Savagery: 7, 109–110, 126, 139, 141–143, 155
The Law and the Prophets: 8, 93–96, 103–104, 111, 124–125, 105, 115–117, 133–134, 140, 144–145
From Chechaouen to Guernica: 9, 119, 389, 120–122, 390, 156–164, 293, 399
The Splendid Decision: 10, 178–180, 174–175, 177, 181–182, 190–194, 196
Hamburg, Auschwitz, Dresden: 11, 391, 200–211, 213–218
Tokyo: 12, 197–198, 219–222, 165, 223–228, 231, 137–138, 176, 189, 187–188, 199, 232–234
Hiroshima: 14, 371–374, 235–236, 241–242, 249–250, 326–327, 351, 364–365, 375–377
Living with the Superweapon: 15, 246–248, 251, 254–255, 262–266
Bombs Against Independence: 16, 97–98, 184, 229–230, 243, 256, 259–261, 282–286, 305–309
Korea: 17, 267, 269–272, 237–238, 244–245, 268, 273–275, 366, 276
Massive Retaliation: 18, 36–37, 61, 277–281, 287–292, 296–299, 301–303, 312–320
Flexible Retaliation: 19, 322–325, 328–333, 34, 88, 185, 334–338, 340, 344–346
Surgical Precision: 20, 38, 51–52, 63, 86, 99, 129–130, 136, 154, 195, 212, 253, 257–258, 347–350, 352, 357–358
The Bomb on Trial: 21, 239–240, 252, 294–295, 300, 304, 310–311, 321, 339, 341, 356, 359–361, 378, 380–388
Nothing Human: 22, 367–369, 392, 342, 370, 343, 393, 353–355, 379, 362–363, 394–398

CHRONOLOGY

The following chronology shows which sections correspond to the years indicated.

YEAR	SECTIONS
762–1910	23–74
1911–1939	75–176
1940–1945	177–245
1946–1955	246–291
1956–1965	292–327
1966–1975	328–351
1976–1985	352–365
1986–1995	365–380
1996–1999	381–399

1   BANG, YOU'RE DEAD

"Bang, you're dead!" we said. "I got you!" we said. When we played, it was always war. A bunch of us together, one-on-one, or in solitary fantasies – always war, always death.

"Don't play like that," our parents said, "you could grow up that way." Some threat – there was no way we would rather be. We didn't need war toys. Any old stick became a weapon in our hands, and pinecones were bombs. I cannot recall taking a single piss during my childhood, whether outside or at home in the outhouse, when I didn't choose a target and bomb it. At five years of age I was already a seasoned bombardier.

"If everyone plays war," said my mother, "there will be war." And she was quite right – there was.   ➤ 166

2   IN THE BEGINNING WAS THE BOMB

In the beginning was the bomb. It consisted of a pipe, like a bamboo pipe of the type abundant in China, filled with an explosive, like gunpowder, which the Chinese had discovered as early as the ninth century. If one closed this pipe at both ends, it became a bomb.

When the pipe was opened at one end, it was blown forward by the explosion. The bomb then became a rocket. It soon developed into a two-stage rocket – a large rocket that rose into the air and released a shower of small rockets over the enemy. The Chinese used rockets of this type in their defense of Kaifeng in 1232. The rocket weapon spread via the Arabs and Indians to Europe around 1250 – but it was forgotten again until the English rediscovered it at the beginning of the 19th century.

If the rocket was opened at the other end the bomb became a gun or a cannon. The explosion blew out whatever had been tamped into the pipe, like a bullet or another, smaller bomb, called a shell. Both the gun and the cannon had been fully developed in China by 1280, and they reached Europe thirty years later.   ➤ 24

3   THE HISTORY OF THE FUTURE 1880–1910

Good morning! My name is Meister. Professor Meister. I will be lecturing today on the history of the future as depicted in *Three Hundred Years Hence* by William D. Hay. When this book came out in 1881, my time lay three hundred years ahead of the reader's. Today the society of United Man, in which I live, has drawn much closer to you. But my situation as narrator is essentially unchanged. I am speaking of your future, which for me is history. I know what is going to happen to you, since for me it has already happened.

➤ 46

4   DEATH COMES FLYING

The first bomb dropped from an airplane exploded in an oasis outside Tripoli on November *Dagens Nyheter* the next day. "One of the aviators successfully released several bombs in the camp of the enemy, with good results."

It was Lieutenant Giulio Cavotti who leaned out of his delicate monoplane and dropped the bomb – a Danish Haasen hand grenade – on the North African oasis Tagiura, near Tripoli. Several moments later, he attacked the oasis Ain Zara. Four bombs in total, each weighing two kilos, were dropped during this first air attack. ➤ 76

5   WHAT IS PERMISSIBLE IN WAR?

The laws of war have always answered two questions: When may one wage war? What is permissible in war?

And international law was always given two completely different answers to 'these questions, depending on who the enemy is. The laws of war protect enemies of the same race, class, and culture. The laws of war leave the foreign and the alien without protection.

When is one allowed to wage war against savages and barbarians? Answer: always. What is permissible in wars against savages and barbarians? Answer: anything. ➤ 26

6   BOMBING THE SAVAGES

In an illustration in Jules Verne's *The Flight of Engineer Robur* (1886), the airship glides majestically over Paris, the capital of Europe. Powerful searchlights shine on the waters of the Seine, over the quays, bridges, and façades. Astonished but unperturbed, the people gaze up into the sky, amazed at the unusual sight but without fear, without feeling the need to seek cover. In the next illustration the airship floats just as majestically and inaccessibly over Africa, But here it is not a matter merely of illumination, Here the engineer intervenes in the events on the ground. With the natural authority assumed by the civilized to police the savage, he stops a crime from taking place. The airship's weapons come into play, and death and destruction rain down on the black criminals, who, screaming in terror, try to escape the murderous fire. ➤ 74

7   BOMBED INTO SAVAGERY
                                     THE HISTORY OF THE FUTURE (2)

Jeremy Tuft is an overprotected, middle-aged, middle-class man, helpless without his
privileges. In Edward Shanks's novel of the future, *People of the Ruins* (1920), his London
is bombed and gassed. When Jeremy miraculously comes to life in the ruins, he finds
himself in a new Middle Ages. The English have become savages who live among the ruins
of the 20th century, a civilization incomprehensible to them.

8   THE LAW AND THE PROPHETS

The First World War killed ten million people and wounded twenty million. Was it a
crime against humanity? Or was it quite all right, as long as the dead and wounded were
young, armed men?

    An unknown number of children and the elderly died of hunger and disease as a
consequence of the British naval blockade against Germany. Was that a crime against
humanity? Or was it quite all right, since the English couldn't help the fact that the
Germans sent the little food they had to the front, letting the children and elderly starve?

    The slaughter at the front seemed meaningless even as it was going on. The war had
dug in and got stuck, and the military looked desperately for a new, more mobile way
to wage war. Aerial combat seemed to offer the most obvious solution; attacks against
the civilian population would force rapid results and ultimate victories.

    But "the colonial shortcut" was forbidden in Europe. Here it was a crime against
humanity to save the lives of soldiers by bombing women, children, and old people.
Human rights seemed to forbid what military necessity seemed to demand – a contradiction that has colored the entire 20th century.   ➤ 93

9   FROM CHECHAOUEN TO GUERNICA

Everyone in Chechaouen knows about Guernica. In Guernica no one has ever heard of
Chechaouen. And yet they are sister cities. Two small cities, clinging to mountainsides,
a few miles from the northern coasts of Spain and Morocco, respectively. Both of them
are very old – Guernica was founded in 1366, and Chechaouen in 1471. Both are holy
places – Guernica has the sacred oak of the Basque people, and Chechaouen has Moulay
Abdessalam Ben Mohich's sacred grave. Both are capitals – Guernica for the Basques, and
Chechaouen for the Jibala people. Both had populations of about 6,000 when they were
bombed, Guernica in 1937 and Chechaouen in 1925. Both were bombed by legionnaires
– Guernica by Germans serving under Franco, and Chechaouen by Americans under
French command, serving the interests of the Spanish colonial power. Both had their turn
to be "discovered" by a London *Times* correspondent – Guernica by George Steer,
Chechaouen by Walter Harris, who wrote: ➤ 119

10   THE SPLENDID DECISION

On May 10, 1940, Churchill became Prime Minister of England. On May 11, he gave
the order to bomb Germany.

"It was a splendid decision," writes J. M. Spaight, expert on international law and Secretary of the British Air Ministry. Thanks to that decision, the English today can walk with their heads held high. When Churchill began to bomb Germany, he knew that the Germans did not want a bombing war. Their air force, unlike that of the British, was not made for heavy bombs. Churchill went on bombing, even though he knew that reprisals were unavoidable. [. . .]

| 11 | HAMBURG, AUSCHWTZ, DRESDEN |

During the summer of 1948 I lived with a working-class family in St. Albans, outside London. It was a cold summer, and when we sat and drank tea in the evenings we often lit the electric heater, which was made to look like a glowing heap of coal. Somehow may thoughts flew to the burned-out cities of Germany, and I told them how on my trip across the country the train had struggled, hour after hour, to make its way through the blackened ruins of what were once the homes of human beings.

"We were bombing the military transports on the railways," my host family said. If some houses by the side of the railway were damaged it was unfortunate but unavoidable. "It was war you know."

"This is not a question of 'a few houses,'" I said "Hamburg was razed by British bombs. This was the third time I've traveled through the city, and I have seen nothing but ruins."

"That must have been the Americans," said my host. "The British bombers never attacked civilians."

"I am sorry to contradict you, but it was the other way around. The Americans bombed the industries by day, and the British the residential areas by night. That was the general pattern, I'm afraid."

"I am not going to listen to any more German war propaganda in my house," my host said, cutting me short. "The British bombers attacked military targets, period."   ➤ 391

| 12 | TOKYO |

In the spring of 1941, a series of mysterious explosions occurred at a DuPont factory for the production of synthetic dyes. The Harvard chemist Louis Fieser was assigned to investigate the cause and he found, more or less by chance, that when burned, the fluid divinylacetylene converted into to a sticky goo with an unusually strong adhesive power. It occurred to him that such a liquid, if it were enclosed in a bomb, could be spread in the form of burning, sticky lumps that would cling to buildings and people and could be neither extinguished nor removed.   ➤ 197

| 13 | THE DREAM OF A SUPERWEAPON |
| | THE HISTORY OF THE FUTURE (3) |

On December 10, 1903 (a week before the first airplane left the ground), the Curies accepted the Nobel Prize for Physics. They had shown that radioactive material could release enormous amounts of energy.

The series of discoveries had unfolded at a dizzying speed. The radiation that Röntgen had discovered by chance in 1895 led Becquerel to the discovery of radioactivity in uranium the very next year, then to Thomson's discovery of the "planets" around the nucleus of the atom – the electrons – and finally in 1898 to Marie Curie's discovery of radium and polonium. And in 1903, the future Nobel laureate in physics Frederick Soddy was already giving a talk before the Royal Corps of Engineers on atomic power as the superweapon of the future. The idea of an atomic weapon seems not to have been particularly frightening since weapons in general were something used primarily in the colonies, and thus posed no threat to ordinary well-behaved European citizens. An imagination unworried by fear could play with the idea.   ➤ 69

14   HIROSHIMA

The Smithsonian Institution is the collective name of a group of museums that constitute the national memory of the United States, The most beloved of these is the National Air and Space Museum in Washington, D.C. About 8,000,000 people visit it each year, making it the world's most visited museum.

The only possible rival is the famous Shinto temple Yasukuni and its museum in Tokyo. There, too, about 8,000,000 people come each year. And Yasukuni, too, serves as the memory of a nation or more precisely, the Japanese nation's memory of its wars. ➤ 371

15   LIVING WITH THE SUPERWEAPON
THE HISTORY OF THE FUTURE (4)

"In Hiroshima, everything was over in a second. But the bomb itself is not over. It is still here, awaiting its next opportunity," says Faos Cheeror, an Eastern European refugee whom South African writer Horace Rose met in London, late in the summer of 1945.

"Truman says that atomic power is much too terrible to be unleashed in a lawless world."

"Truman said that after he had already unleashed it."

"He used the bomb to shorten the war and save lives."

"You belong to a nation of hypocrites, my friend," says Faos. "I am thinking of the victims of the bomb in all those future wars, the wars that have already begun in the dreams of maniacs."

In *The Maniac's Dream, A Novel of the Atomic Bomb* (1946) we are allowed a look into those dreams, and we see the atom bomb destroy New York and London. But actually it is not the Londoners the Maniac hates and reviles, but the blacks of his own country. They are subhuman apes, whose existence is justified only by their service to whites. To attribute human desires and feelings to them would be ridiculous. When they rise up against their oppressors, he doesn't hesitate for a moment to let the atom bomb destroy them.

"A land which had been brilliantly alive with colour, movement and activity was utterly and completely motionless, utterly and completely dumb."   ➤ 246

16   BOMBS AGAINST INDEPENDENCE

While everyone's attention was diverted by the superweapon and the necessity of
avoiding total destruction, bombing took up its old role of securing European colonial
power. The same old bombs were dropped, the same old villages burned. The wars were
reported as "police actions" to "reinstate order" or fight "terrorists." Only slowly and
reluctantly did Europe admit that these wars were wars and concerned the right to independence.   ➤ 97

17   KOREA

On June 25, 1950, I found myself in the gallery at the United Nations Security Council.
I was a year away from high-school graduation and was going to enter compulsory military service the following fall. I had received a scholarship to study "international
relations." That was why I was sitting there listening as the Security Council decided to
intervene in the Korean War.
      What would Sweden's position be? Strong forces demanded that we should partici-
pate. I was constantly asked about it in New York. Suddenly international relations were
no longer something that concerned only adults, way above my head. The demand was
being made of me. It was I, personally, who would have to shoot and bomb. I, who at this
point, at the beginning of the war, had scarcely heard of Korea.
      I sat down in the U.N. library and tried to figure out why I should kill or be
killed.   ➤ 267

18   MASSIVE RETALIATION
                                              THE HISTORY OF THE FUTURE (5)

On January 27, 1796, the young researcher Charles Cuvier gave his first public lecture
at the Institute de France in Paris. Before a deeply shocked audience he proved that the
species created by God were not eternal. They could, he said, "become extinct" in a kind
of "revolution of the earth." And we, the new tribes that have taken their place, could
ourselves be destroyed one day, and replaced by others.   ➤ 36

19   FLEXIBLE RETALIATION
                                             MEIDIGUOZHUYI SHI QUAN SHIJIE
                                             RENMINDE ZUI XIONGEDE DIREN

Those were the first words I had to learn when I was studying Chinese at Peking University
in the winter of 1961. The phrase was terribly difficult, partially because I considered the
statement false. "American imperialism is the most evil enemy of all the world's people."
I found myself constantly protesting the Chinese government's distorted image of
American policies.
      "Throughout its history, the U.S. has defended the right of peoples to self-determi-
nation," I said. "That will be the case in Vietnam, as well."

"You underestimate the free press in America," I said. "The facts always come out, sooner or later. You can't overrule public opinion in a democracy. You won't get reelected that way."

"Only Congress can declare war," I explained to my Chinese hosts. Do you think that Congress, only ten years after Korea, will send its constituents and their children to die in a new Asian war? Never. It will never happen. There will be no war in Vietnam. ➤ 322

20   SURGICAL PRECISION

Once upon a time there were a Frenchman, an American, and a German. The Frenchman wanted to prove that the world turns. The American wanted to fly to Mars in a spaceship. The German wanted to go to the North Pole in a submarine. Along with some other monomaniac dreamers, they created an instrument that could aim a rocket out into space and get it to deliver a dozen hydrogen bombs, each to its own separate address on the other side of the globe, more accurately than the postal service, faster than flight, and with the proverbial surgical precision. ➤ 38

21   THE BOMB ON TRIAL

If the dum-dum bullet is forbidden by the rules of war on account of the unnecessary pain it causes (it has been and it continues to be), how can the hydrogen bomb be legal? If the rules of war forbid weapons that do not distinguish between noncombatants and combatants, how could weapons that spread uncontainable radioactivity over large areas be legal? How could military strategies that cold-bloodedly calculate tens or hundreds of millions of civilian victims be legal?

And if through the use of precise weapon systems one could reduce the number of victims in the first round to just a few million while holding the enemies' big cities hostage – would the weapons become more legal? If the "surgical" attacks then escalated to a general atomic war that destroyed all of humankind – could those who made the decisions declare with good conscience that they had, in any case, remained within the bounds of the law? ➤ 239

22   NOTHING HUMAN
THE HISTORY OF THE FUTURE (6)

"War," said the great military theoretician Karl von Clausewitz, "is nothing but a duel on a larger scale."

That was at the beginning of the 19th century. Today we are no longer dueling. That two grown men would believe their honor demanded that they meet at dawn in order to give one of them the opportunity to murder the other in a ceremonial ritual – the mere thought has become absurd, even ridiculous.

And war? Will it one day be equally absurd? ➤ 376

To the reader who has come this far without entering one of the narratives: now you have seen the beginning of them all.

Nothing can prevent you from continuing to read the book page after page as if it were a normal book. That will work, too.

But this is not a normal book. I am trying to give you a new kind of reading experience and therefore ask you to turn back. Choose one of the entrances and read on to the section in which that narrative is taken up again – for example, from entrance 1 to section 166.

CHAPTER 32

Dipesh Chakrabarty

PROVINCIALIZING EUROPE: POSTCOLONIAL THOUGHT AND HISTORICAL DIFFERENCE (2000)*

The next reading is taken from Dipesh Chakrabarty's *Provincializing Europe: Postcolonial Thought and Historical Difference* (2000), in which Chakrabarty (Professor of History at the University of Chicago and the author of the classic *Rethinking Working Class History: Bengal 1890–1940*) argues for 'a history that does not yet exist, a history that is a history alright but not one dominated by "Western European" theories and theorised practices'. By 'Europe' one must understand, then, not a mere region of the world (for that Europe, Chakrabarty argues, has already been marginalised and decentred by the 'forces of change' themselves), but rather an insidious way of looking at things, a legacy of concepts and categories such that any thinking of the phenomenon of political modernity – the rule by modern institutions of the state, bureaucracy and capitalist enterprise – 'is impossible to think of anywhere in the world' without theorisations that are contaminated throughout by that legacy:

> Concepts such as citizenship, the state, civil society, public sphere, human rights, equality before the law, the individual, distinction between public and private, the idea of the subject, democracy, popular sovereignty, social justice, scientific rationality and so on all bear the burden of European thought . . . one simply cannot think . . . without these and other related concepts . . . formed in the course of the European Enlightenment of the nineteenth century.

Consequently, provincialising Europe is, for Chakrabarty, the task of thinking through such a legacy; the question is something like this: what would a history look like if it was properly 'past the modern'; past the theoretical shibboleths of the modern: a post-modern history? What could, both 'here and there', travel under such a name? In the following extract, taken from the Introduction, Chakrabarty looks at all of this rethinking.

> Europe . . . since 1914 has become provincialized, . . . only the natural sciences are able to call forth a quick international echo.
>
> *(Hans-Georg Gadamer, 1977)*

---

* Dipesh Chakrabarty (2000) *Provincializing Europe: Postcolonial Thought and Historical Difference*, Princeton, NJ: Princeton University Press, pp. 3–11.

The West is a name for a subject which gathers itself in discourse but is also an object constituted discursively; it is, evidently, a name always associating itself with those regions, communities, and peoples that appear politically or economically superior to other regions, communities, and peoples. Basically, it is just like the name "Japan," . . . it claims that it is capable of sustaining, if not actually transcending, an impulse to transcend all the particularizations.

(Naoki Sakai, 1998)

PROVINCIALIZING Europe is not a book about the region of the world we call "Europe." That Europe, one could say, has already been provincialized by history itself. Historians have long acknowledged that the so-called "European age" in modern history began to yield place to other regional and global configurations toward the middle of the twentieth century. European history is no longer seen as embodying anything like a "universal human history." No major Western thinker, for instance; has publicly shared Francis Fukuyama's "vulgarized Hegelian historicism" that saw in the fall of the Berlin wall a common end for the history of all human beings. The contrast with the past seems sharp when one remembers the cautious but warm note of approval with which Kant once detected in the French Revolution a "moral disposition in the human race" or Hegel saw the imprimatur of the "world spirit" in the momentousness of that event.

I am by training a historian of modern South Asia, which forms my archive and is my site of analysis. The Europe I seek to provincialize or decenter is an imaginary figure that remains deeply embedded in *clichéd and shorthand forms* in some everyday habits of thought that invariably subtend attempts in the social sciences to address questions of political modernity in South Asia. The phenomenon of "political modernity"—namely, the rule by modern institutions of the state, bureaucracy, and capitalist enterprise—is impossible to *think* of anywhere in the world without invoking certain categories and concepts, the genealogies of which go deep into the intellectual and even theological traditions of Europe. Concepts such as citizenship, the state, civil society, public sphere, human rights, equality before the law, the individual, distinctions between public and private, the idea of the subject, democracy, popular sovereignty, social justice, scientific rationality, and so on all bear the burden of European thought and history. One simply cannot think of political modernity without these and other related concepts that found a climactic form in the course of the European Enlightenment and the nineteenth century.

These concepts entail an unavoidable—and in a sense indispensable—universal and secular vision of the human. The European colonizer of the nineteenth century both preached this Enlightenment humanism at the colonized and at the same time denied it in practice. But the vision has been powerful in its effects. It has historically provided a strong foundation on which to erect—both in Europe and outside—critiques of socially unjust practices. Marxist and liberal thought are legatees of this intellectual heritage. This heritage is now global. The modern Bengali educated middle classes—to which I belong and fragments of whose history I recount later in the book—have been characterized by Tapan Raychaudhuri as the "the first Asian social group of any size whose mental world was transformed through its interactions with the West." A long series of illustrious members of this social group—from Raja Rammohun Roy, sometimes called "the father of modern India," to Manabendranath Roy, who argued with Lenin in the Comintern—warmly embraced the themes of rationalism, science, equality, and human rights that the European Enlightenment promulgated. Modern social critiques of caste, oppressions of women, the lack of rights for laboring and subaltern classes in India, and so on—and, in fact, the very critique of colonialism itself—are unthinkable except as a legacy, partially, of how Enlightenment Europe was appropriated in the subcontinent. The Indian constitution tellingly begins by repeating certain universal Enlightenment themes celebrated, say, in the American constitution. And it is salutary to remember that the writings of the most trenchant critic of the institution of "untouchability" in British India refer us back to some originally European ideas about liberty and human equality.

I too write from within this inheritance. Postcolonial scholarship is committed, almost by definition, to engaging the universals—such as the abstract figure of the human or that of Reason—that were forged in eighteenth-century Europe and that underlie the human sciences. This engagement marks, for instance, the writing of the Tunisian philosopher and historian Hichem Djait, who accuses imperialist Europe of "deny[ing] its own vision of man." Fanon's struggle to hold on to the Enlightenment idea of the human—even when he knew that European imperialism had reduced that idea to the figure of the settler-colonial white man—is now itself a part of the global heritage of all postcolonial thinkers. The struggle ensues because there is no easy way of dispensing with these universals in the condition of political modernity. Without them there would be no social science that addresses issues of modern social justice.

This engagement with European thought is also called forth by the fact that today the so-called European intellectual tradition is the only one alive in the social science departments of most, if not all, modern universities. I use the word "alive" in a particular sense. It is only within some very particular traditions of thinking that we treat fundamental thinkers who are long dead and gone not only as people belonging to their own times but also as though they were our own contemporaries. In the social sciences, these are invariably thinkers one encounters within the tradition that has come to call itself "European" or "Western." I am aware that an entity called "the European intellectual tradition" stretching back to the ancient Greeks is a fabrication of relatively recent European history. Martin Bernal, Samir Amin, and others have justly criticized the claim of European thinkers that such an unbroken tradition ever existed or that it could even properly he called "European." The point, however, is that, fabrication or not, this is the genealogy of thought in which social scientists find themselves inserted. Faced with the task of analyzing developments or social practices in modern India, few if any Indian social scientists or social scientists of India would argue seriously with, say, the thirteenth-century logician Gangesa or with the grammarian and linguistic philosopher Bartrihari (fifth to sixth centuries), or with the tenth- or eleventh-century aesthetician Abhinavagupta. Sad though it is, one result of European colonial rule in South Asia is that the intellectual traditions once unbroken and alive in Sanskrit or Persian or Arabic are now only matters of historical research for most—perhaps all—modern social scientists in the region. They treat these traditions as truly dead, as history. Although categories that were once subject to detailed theoretical contemplation and inquiry now exist as practical concepts, bereft of any theoretical lineage, embedded in quotidian practices in South Asia, contemporary social scientists of South Asia seldom have the training that would enable them to make these concepts into resources for critical thought for the present. And yet past European thinkers and their categories are never quite dead for us in the same way. South Asian(ist) social scientists would argue passionately with a Marx or a Weber without feeling any need to historicize them or to place them in their European intellectual contexts. Sometimes—though this is rather rare—they would even argue with the ancient or medieval or early-modern predecessors of these European theorists.

Yet the very history of politicization of the population, or the coming of political modernity, in countries outside of the Western capitalist democracies of the world produces a deep irony in the history of the political. This history challenges us to rethink two conceptual gifts of nineteenth-century Europe, concepts integral to the idea of modernity. One is historicism—the idea that to understand anything it has to be seen both as a unity and in its historical development—and the other is the very idea of the political. What historically enables a project such as that of "provincializing Europe" is the experience of political modernity in a country like India. European thought has a contradictory relationship to such an instance of political modernity. It is both indispensable and inadequate in helping us to think through the various life practices that constitute the political and the historical in India. Exploring—on both theoretical and factual registers—this simultaneous indispensability and inadequacy of social science thought is the task this book has set itself.

The politics of historicism

Writings by poststructuralist philosophers such as Michel Foucault have undoubtedly given a fillip to global critiques of historicism. But it would be wrong to think of postcolonial critiques of historicism (or of the political) as simply deriving from critiques already elaborated by postmodern and poststructuralist thinkers of the West. In fact, to think this way would itself be to practice historicism, for such a thought would merely repeat the temporal structure of the statement, "first in the West, and then elsewhere." In saying this, I do not mean to take away from the recent discussions of historicism by critics who see its decline in the West as resulting from what Jameson has imaginatively named "the cultural logic of late-capitalism." The cultural studies scholar Lawrence Grossberg has pointedly questioned whether history itself is not endangered by consumerist practices of contemporary capitalism. How do you produce historical observation and analysis, Grossberg asks, "when every event is potentially evidence, potentially determining, and at the same time, changing too quickly to allow the comfortable leisure of academic criticism?" But these arguments, although valuable, still bypass the histories of political modernity in the third world. From Mandel to Jameson, nobody sees "late capitalism" as a system whose driving engine may be in the third world. The word "late" has very different connotations when applied to the developed countries and to those seen as still "developing." "Late capitalism" is properly the name of a phenomenon that is understood as belonging primarily to the developed capitalist world, though its impact on the rest of the globe is never denied.

Western critiques of historicism that base themselves on some characterization of "late capitalism" overlook the deep ties that bind together historicism as a mode of thought and the formation of political modernity in the erstwhile European colonies. Historicism enabled European domination of the world in the nineteenth century. Crudely, one might say that it was one important form that the ideology of progress or "development" took from the nineteenth century on. Historicism is what made modernity or capitalism look not simply global but rather as something that became global *over time*, by originating in one place (Europe) and then spreading outside it. This "first in Europe, then elsewhere" structure of global historical time was historicist; different non-Western nationalisms would later produce local versions of the same narrative, replacing "Europe" by some locally constructed center. It was historicism that allowed Marx to say that the "country that is more developed industrially only shows, to the less developed, the image of its own future." It is also what leads prominent historians such as Phyllis Deane to describe the coming of industries in England as the *first* industrial revolution. Historicism thus posited historical time as a measure of the cultural distance (at least in institutional development) that was assumed to exist between the West and the non-West. In the colonies, it legitimated the idea of civilization. In Europe itself, it made possible completely internalist histories of Europe in which Europe was described as the site of the first occurrence of capitalism, modernity, or Enlightenment. These "events" in turn are all explained mainly with respect to "events" within the geographical confines of Europe (however fuzzy its exact boundaries may have been). The inhabitants of the colonies, on the other hand, were assigned a place "elsewhere" in the "first in Europe and then elsewhere" structure of time. This move of historicism is what Johannes Fabian has called "the denial of coevalness."

Historicism—and even the modern, European idea of history—one might say, came to non-European peoples in the nineteenth century as somebody's way of saying "not yet" to somebody else. Consider the classic liberal but historicist essays by John Stuart Mill, "On Liberty" and "On Representative Government," both of which proclaimed self-rule as the highest form of government and yet argued against giving Indians or Africans self-rule on grounds that were indeed historicist. According to Mill, Indians or Africans were *not yet* civilized enough to rule themselves. Some historical time of development and civilization (colonial rule and education, to be precise) had to elapse before they could be considered prepared for such a task. Mill's historicist argument thus consigned Indians, Africans, and other "rude" nations to an imaginary waiting room of history. In doing so, it converted history itself into a version of this waiting room. We were all headed for the same destination, Mill averred, but some people were to arrive earlier than others. That was what historicist consciousness was: recommendation to the colonized to wait. Acquiring a historical consciousness, acquiring the public spirit that Mill thought absolutely necessary for the art of self-government, was also to learn this art of waiting. This waiting was the realization of the "not yet" of historicism.

Twentieth-century anticolonial democratic demands for self-rule, on the contrary, harped insistently on a "now" as the temporal horizon of action. From about the time of First World War to the decolonization movements of the fifties and sixties, anticolonial nationalisms were predicated on this urgency of the "now." Historicism has not disappeared from the world, but its "not yet" exists today in tension with this global insistence on the "now" that marks all popular movements toward democracy. This had to be so, for in their search for a mass base, anticolonial nationalist movements introduced classes and groups into the sphere of the political that, by the standards of nineteenth century European liberalism, could only look ever so unprepared to assume the political responsibility of self-government. These were the peasants, tribals, semi- or unskilled industrial workers in non-Western cities, men and women from the subordinate social groups—in short, the subaltern classes of the third world.

A critique of historicism therefore goes to the heart of the question of political modernity in non-Western societies. As I shall argue in more detail later, it was through recourse to some version of a stagist theory of history—ranging from simple evolutionary schemas to sophisticated understandings of "uneven development"—that European political and social thought made room for the political modernity of the subaltern classes. This was not, as such, an unreasonable theoretical claim. If "political modernity" was to be a bounded and definable phenomenon, it was not unreasonable to use its definition as a measuring rod for social progress. Within this thought, it could always be said with reason that some people were less modern than others, and that the former needed a period of preparation and waiting before they could be recognized as full participants in political modernity. But this was precisely the argument of the colonizer—the "not yet" to which the colonized nationalist opposed his or her "now." The achievement of political modernity in the third world could only take place through a contradictory relationship to European social and political thought. It is true that nationalist elites often rehearsed to their own subaltern classes—and still do if and when the political structures permit—the stagist theory of history on which European ideas of political modernity were based. However, there were two necessary developments in nationalist struggles that would produce at least a practical, if not theoretical, rejection of any stagist, historicist distinctions between the premodern or the nonmodern and the modern. One was the nationalist elite's own rejection of the "waiting-room" version of history when faced with the Europeans' use of it as a justification for denial of "self-government" to the colonized. The other was the twentieth-century phenomenon of the peasant as full participant in the political life of the nation (that is, first in the nationalist movement and then as a citizen of the independent nation), long before he or she could be formally educated into the doctrinal or conceptual aspects of citizenship.

A dramatic example of this nationalist rejection of historicist history is the Indian decision taken immediately after the attainment of independence to base Indian democracy on universal adult franchise. This was directly in violation of Mill's prescription. "Universal teaching," Mill said in the essay "On Representative Government," "must precede universal enfranchisement." Even the Indian Franchise Committee of 1931, which had several Indian members, stuck to a position that was a modified version of Mill's argument. The members of the committee agreed that although universal adult franchise would be the ideal goal for India, the general lack of literacy in the country posed a very large obstacle to its implementation. And yet in less than two decades, India opted for universal adult suffrage for a population that was still predominantly nonliterate. In defending the new constitution and the idea of "popular sovereignty" before the nation's Constituent Assembly on the eve of formal independence, Sarvepalli Radhakrishnan, later to be the first vice president of India, argued against the idea that Indians as a people were not yet ready to rule themselves. As far as he was concerned, Indians, literate or illiterate, were always suited for self-rule. He said: "We cannot say that the republican tradition is foreign to the genius of this country. We have had it from the beginning of our history." What else was this position if not a national gesture of abolishing the imaginary waiting room in which Indians had been placed by European historicist thought? Needless to say, historicism remains alive and strong today in the all the developmentalist practices and imaginations of the Indian state. Much of the institutional activity of governing in India is premised on a day-to-day practice of historicism; there is a strong sense in which the peasant is still being educated and developed into the citizen. But every time there is a populist/political mobilization of the people on the streets of the country and a version of "mass democracy" becomes visible in India, historicist time is put in temporary suspension. And once every five years—or more frequently, as seems to be the case these days—the nation produces a political performance of electoral democracy that sets aside all assumptions of the historicist imagination of time. On the day of the election, every Indian adult is treated practically and theoretically as someone already endowed with the skills of a making major citizenly choice, education or no education.

The history and nature of political modernity in an ex-colonial country such as India thus generates a tension between the two aspects of the subaltern or peasant as citizen. One is the peasant who has to be educated into the citizen and who therefore belongs to the time of historicism; the other is the peasant who, despite his or her lack of formal education, is already a citizen. This tension is akin to the tension between the two aspects of nationalism that Homi Bhabha has usefully identified as the pedagogic and the performative. Nationalist historiography in the pedagogic mode portrays the peasant's world, with its emphasis on kinship, gods, and the so-called supernatural, as anachronistic. But the "nation" and the political are also *performed* in the carnivalesque aspects of democracy: in rebellions, protest marches, sporting events, and in universal adult franchise. The question is: How do we *think* the political at these moments when the peasant or the subaltern emerges in the modern sphere of politics, in his or her own right, as a member of the nationalist movement against British rule or as a full-fledged member of the body politic, without having had to do any "preparatory" work in order to qualify as the "bourgeois-citizen"?

I should clarify that in my usage the word "peasant" refers to more than the sociologist's figure of the peasant. I intend that particular meaning, but I load the word with an extended meaning as well. The "peasant" acts here as a shorthand for all the seemingly nonmodern, rural, nonsecular relationships and life practices that constantly leave their imprint on the lives of even the elites in India and on their institutions of government. The peasant stands for all that is not bourgeois (in a European sense) in Indian capitalism and modernity. The next section elaborates on this idea.

CHAPTER 33

Hayden White

FIGURAL REALISM: STUDIES IN THE MIMESIS EFFECT (1999)*

Hayden White, Emeritus Professor of History at the University of California, Santa Cruz, and lately Professor of Comparative Literature, Stanford University, is perhaps the *bête noir* of traditional empirical/epistemological historians. Although admired by some constructionists for his 'sometime contribution' to this type of reflexivity, for most of them – and for all reconstructionists – his deconstruction of historical orthodoxies is a deconstruction too far.

---

* Hayden White (1999) *Figural Realism: Studies in the Mimesis Effect*, Baltimore, MD: The Johns Hopkins University Press, pp. 66–86.

Rejected or admired, however, it would be difficult to overestimate the influence of White on thinking about the nature of history such that, for us, there is 'no going back'. In a series of essays collected in three volumes (*Tropics of Discourse*, Baltimore, MD: The Johns Hopkins University Press, 1978), *The Content of the Form* (Baltimore: The Johns Hopkins University Press, 1987) and *Figural Realism: Studies in the Mimesis Effect* (Baltimore, MD: The Johns Hopkins University Press, 1999), White has developed, deepened and reflected upon a whole series of themes first essayed in his seminal text, *Metahistory*, published in 1973 (Baltimore, MD: The Johns Hopkins University Press). Almost single-handedly, White – although sometimes aided and abetted by his brilliant European counterpart Frank Ankersmit – has redrawn (for those who care to listen) our understanding of what is involved in attempting to historicise the past – i.e. to attempt to make something that is not remotely historical – and which certainly doesn't have history *in* it – the past, into history. Arguing that history has to be understood as what it manifestly is – a literary artefact, a narrative prose discourse, the content of which is as much imagined (the modes of figurative emplotments, metaphorical tropologies, argumentative devices, ideological positioning) as found (the evidential facts) – empirical/epistemological history, in whatever *genre* is forever undercut.

White (and Ankersmit) are, of course, widely regarded as being the bearers of the bad tidings to historians of the 'linguistic turn', but actually that turn should be somewhat more accurately described as the 'aesthetic turn'; the turn to regarding history 'at the level of the text' as a figure which cannot be subjected to the tribunal of truth claims. Some of the arguments to this effect appeared in our general introduction and there is no need to rehearse them in detail here. However, it might be worth repeating somewhat differently a couple of points before you go on – perhaps immediately – to read the extract from White, so enabling them to be kept in mind.

So imagine a spectrum. Towards one 'endless end' let us imagine the archive. Here lie some of the traces of the once actual part. And some of these traces can become, if historians are interested in them, sources. And some of these, if historians are interested in them relative to the story/argument they wish to tell (after their exposure to and work in the extant secondary literature) become 'the facts', facts to be used *in* evidence for (*as* evidence for) aspects of the tale to be told. Here, at this level, it is possible to interrogate the always positioned facts from an always positioned position vis-à-vis their truth status; here, at the level of the singular statements there is a possibility of some sort of correspondence between the factual statement and its referent such that one can make knowledge claims – epistemological claims – for this or that or the other. So, although such claims are always ultimately metaphorical and ultimately always relative to the way they have been put under a description, there is an epistemological element here.

But now start from toward the other 'end' of the spectrum, with the finished history – a text. And here you will find in it things that are in no conceivable archive: a story, an emplotment, a narrative structure, tropological figurings, foregrounding or backgrounding arguments, and the positional and positional thesis. How have they got there? Not from the 'past', for 'the before now' has no emplotments/arguments/thesis in it. Thus, isn't the resultant text as much (at least as much) imagined by the historian as found, and isn't this declared by the historian when s/he privileges the text with his or her own signature? All histories bear witness, carry the names of their creators: the historian. As such these texts are, in the figures they are, as the acts of the imagination they are, no longer epistemologies but, precisely, literary artefacts: fabricated, fashioned, figured out and thus aesthetic products. Consequently, it makes no sense to keep posing to aestheticisations of 'the past' epistemological questions simply because the difference between them is not a difference in *degree* but in *kind*; it is an ontological and therefore unbridgeable difference.

The fact that most historians don't get the implications of the aesthetic nature of histo-ries – this shift from epistemology to aesthetics, from truth to metaphor – is evidenced by Mary Fulbrook's *Historical Theory* (New York and London: Routledge, 2002) which is, according to Fulbrook herself, a highly theoretical text of – although this she doesn't add – the constructionist *genre*. Thus, at the end of her text, having failed throughout to see that aesthetic history cannot be brought to heel, truth-style, she writes as follows:

> I have tried to show that, within given parameters and when adhering to certain rather general tenets – to do with honesty, openness and willingness to revise con-ceptual, interpretative and explanatory frameworks in the light of new evidence, however theoretically contaminated all such evidence inevitably will be – it is pos-sible to say that historical knowledge is of a different order from that of fiction, myth and ideology. (p. 196)

And maybe it is. But here's the rub, a rub that comes home to roost in the above quotation – namely, that philosophically 'history'/historians can never clearly make that demarcation from fiction, myth and ideology because history can never be what it must be if such a demarcation is to work. The problematic for Fulbrook (the problematic of all non-deconstructionist, aes-thetic discourse) is that history can never have the status of an epistemology. And if Fulbrook had seen this, she could never have written her book. Accordingly, it is this 'aesthetic fact' that deconstructs it, or which points to the way her 'blindness' has deconstructed it for her.

The reading from White is his 'The Modernist Event', an essay wherein he deconstructs one of the basic building blocks of reconstructionist/constructionist histories, the idea of the event. For, as White writes, the dissolution of the event – the basic building block of traditional history – undermines the very concept of epistemological facticity and, at this level, therefore the distinction between realistic and merely imaginative narratives: 'the denial of the reality of the event undermines the very notion of fact informing traditional realism [thus] the taboo against mixing fact with fiction except in manifestly imaginative discourses is abolished'.

History does not break down into stories but into images.

— Walter Benjamin

The coming extinction of art is prefigured in the increasing impossibility of representing historical events.

— Theodor Adorno

IT IS A COMMONPLACE of contemporary criticism that modernist liter-ature and, by extension, modernist art in general dissolves the trinity of event, char-acter, and plot which still provided the staple both of the nineteenth-century realist novel and of that historiography from which nineteenth-century literature derived its model of realism. But the tendency of modernist literature to dissolve the event has especially important implications for understanding the ways in which contemporary Western cul-ture construes the relationship between literature and history. Modern historical research and writing could get by without the notions of character and plot, as the invention of a subjectless and plotless historiography in the twentieth century has amply demonstrated. But the dissolution of the event as a basic unit of temporal occurrence and building block of history undermines the very concept of factuality and threatens therewith the distinction between realistic and merely imaginary discourse. The dissolution of the event undermines a founding presupposition of Western realism: the opposition between fact and fiction. Modernism resolves the problems posed by traditional realism, namely, how to represent reality realistically, by simply abandoning the ground on which realism is construed in terms of an opposition between fact and fiction. The denial of the reality of the event undermines the very notion of fact informing traditional realism. Therewith, the taboo against mixing fact with fiction except in manifestly imaginative discourse is abolished. And, as current critical opinion suggests, the very notion of fiction is set aside in the conceptualization of literature as a mode of writing which abandons both the referential and poetic functions of language use.

It is this aspect of modernism that informs the creation of the new genres of post-modernist parahistorical representation, in both written and visual form, called variously *docudrama, faction, infotainment, the fiction of fact, historical metafiction*, and the like. These genres are represented by books such as Capote's *In Cold Blood*, Mailer's *Executioner's Song*, Doctorow's *Ragtime*, Thomas's *White Hotel*, De Lillo's *Libra*, and Reed's *Flight to Canada*; the television versions of *Holocaust* and *Roots*; films such as *The Night Porter* (Cavani), *The Damned* (Visconti), *Hitler: A Film from Germany* (Syberberg), *The Return of Martin Guerre* (Tavernier), and, more recently, Oliver Stone's *JFK* and Spielberg's *Schindler's List*. All deal with historical phenomena, and all of them appear to fictionalize, to a greater or lesser degree, the historical events and characters that serve as their referents in history.

These works, however, differ crucially from those of their generic prototype, the nineteenth-century historical novel. That genre was born of the inscription within and interference between an imaginary tale of romance and a set of real historical events. The interference had the effect of endowing the imaginary events with the concreteness of reality while at the same time endowing the historical events with the magical aura peculiar to the romance. However, the relationship between the historical novel and its projected readership was mediated by a distinctive contract: its intended effects depended upon the presumed capacity of the reader to distinguish between real and imaginary events, between fact and fiction, and therefore between life and literature. Without this capacity, the affect in which the familiar (the reader's own reveries) was rendered exotic while the exotic (the historical past or the lives of the great) was rendered familiar could not have been produced.

What happens in the postmodernist docudrama or historical metafiction is not so much the reversal of this relationship (such that real events are given the marks of imaginary ones while imaginary events are endowed with reality) as the placing in abeyance of the distinction between the real and the imaginary. Everything is presented as if it were of the same ontological order, both real and imaginary – realistically imaginary or imaginarily real, with the result that the referential function of the images of events is etiolated. Thus, the contract that originally mediated the relationship between the nineteenth-century (bourgeois?) reader and the author of the historical novel has been dissolved. And what you get, as Gertrude Himmelfarb tells us, is "history as you like it" representations of history in which anything goes – to the detriment of both truth and moral responsibility, in her view. It is exactly the sort of thing of which Oliver Stone has been so often accused since the appearance of *JFK* (1991).

Stone was criticized by journalists, historians, politicians, and political pundits for his treatment of the events surrounding the assassination of President John F. Kennedy. In part, this was a result of the "content" of his film. He was accused, among other things, of fostering paranoia by suggesting that President Kennedy's assassination was a result of a conspiracy involving highly placed persons in the United States government. But also – and for some critics even more seriously – Stone's film seemed to blur the distinction between fact and fiction by treating a historical event as if there were no limits on what could legitimately be said about it, and thereby bringing under question the very principle of objectivity on the basis of which one might discriminate between truth, on the one side, and myth, ideology, illusion, and lie, on the other.

Thus, in a review of *JFK* that appeared in the *Times Literary Supplement* entitled "Movie Madness?" Richard Grenier wrote:

> And so Oliver Stone romps through the assassination of John Kennedy, inventing evidence that supports his thesis [of conspiracy], suppressing all evidence that conflicts with it, directing his film in a pummelling style, a left to the jaw, a right to the solar plexus, flashing forward, flashing backward, crosscutting relentlessly, shooting "in tight" (in close), blurring, obfuscating, bludgeoning the viewer until Stone wins, he hopes, by a TKO.

Note that Grenier objects to the ways in which Stone slants evidence concerning the assassination, but he is especially offended by the form of Stone's presentation, his "pummelling" and "bludgeoning" style, which apparently distorts even those events whose occurrence can be established on the basis of historical evidence. This style is treated as if it were a violation of the spectator's powers of perception.

So, too, another film critic, David Armstrong, was as much irked by the form as he was by the content of Stone's movie. He excoriated what he called Stone's "appropriation of TV car commercial quick-cutting" and reported that, for him, "watching *JFK* was like watching three hours of MTV without the music?" But Armstrong disliked "the film as a film" for other reasons as well, reasons more moral than artistic. "I am troubled, . . . by Stone's mix'n'match of recreated scenes and archival footage," because "young viewers to whom [Stone] dedicates the film could take his far-reaching conjectures as literal truth." Armstrong suggests, then, that Stone's editing techniques might destroy the capacity of young viewers to distinguish between a real and a merely imaginary event. All of the events depicted in the film – whether attested by historical evidence, based on conjecture, or simply made up in order to help the plot along or to lend credence to Stone's paranoid fantasies – are presented as if they were equally historical, which is to say, equally real, or as if they had really happened. And this in spite of the fact that Stone is on record as professing not to know the difference between history and something that people make up, in other words, as viewing all events as equally imaginary, at least insofar as they are *represented* events.

Issues such as these arise within the context of the experience, memory, or awareness of events that not only could not possibly have occurred before the twentieth century but whose nature, scope, and implications no prior age could even have imagined. Some of these events – such as the two world wars, a growth in world population hitherto unimaginable, poverty and hunger on a scale never before experienced, pollution of the ecosphere by nuclear explosions and the indiscriminate disposal of contaminants, programs of genocide undertaken by societies utilizing scientific technology and rationalized procedures of governance and warfare (of which the German genocide of six million

European Jews is paradigmatic) – function in the consciousness of certain social groups exactly as infantile traumas are conceived to function in the psyche of neurotic individuals. This means that they cannot be simply forgotten and put out of mind or, conversely, adequately remembered, which is to say, clearly and unambiguously identified as to their meaning and contextualized in the group memory in such a way as to reduce the shadow they cast over the group's capacities to go into its present and envision a future free of their debilitating effects.

The suggestion that, for the groups most immediately affected by or fixated upon these events, their meanings remain ambiguous and their consignment to the past difficult to effectuate should not be taken to imply in any way that such events never happened. On the contrary, not only are their occurrences amply attested, but also, their continuing effects on current societies and generations that had no direct experience of them are readily documentable. But among those effects must be listed the difficulty felt by present generations of arriving at some agreement as to their meaning – by which I mean what the facts established about such events can possibly tell us about the nature of our own current social and cultural endowment and what attitude we ought to take with respect to them as we make plans for our own future. In other words, what is at issue here is not the facts of the matter regarding such events but the different possible meanings that such facts can be construed as bearing.

The distinction between facts and meanings is usually taken to be a basis of historical relativism. This is because, in conventional historical inquiry, the facts established about a specific event are taken to *be* the meaning of that event. Facts are supposed to provide the basis for arbitrating among the variety of different meanings that different groups can assign to an event for different ideological or political reasons. But the facts are a function of the meaning assigned to events, not some primitive data that determine what meanings an event can have. It is the anomalous nature of modernist events – their resistance to inherited categories and conventions for assigning meanings to events – that undermine not only the status of facts in relation to events but also the status of the event in general.

But to consider the issue of historical objectivity in terms of an opposition of real to imaginary events, on which the opposition of fact to fiction is in turn based, obscures an important development in Western culture which distinguishes modernism in the arts from all previous forms of realism. Indeed, it seems as difficult to conceive of a treatment of historical reality that would not use fictional techniques in the representation of events as it is to conceive of a serious fiction that did not in some way or at some level make claims about the nature and meaning of history. And this for a number of quite obvious reasons. First, the twentieth century is marked by the occurrence of certain "holocaustal" events (two world wars, the Great Depression, nuclear weapons and communications technology, the population explosion, the mutilation of the zoosphere, famine, genocide as a policy consciously undertaken by "modernized" regimes, etc.) that bear little similarity to what earlier historians conventionally took as their objects of study and do not, therefore, lend themselves to understanding by the commonsensical techniques utilized in conventional historical inquiry nor even to representation by the techniques of writing typically favored by historians from Herodotus to Arthur Schlesinger. Nor does any of several varieties of quantitative analysis, of the kind practiced in the social sciences, capture the novelty of such events. Moreover, these kinds of event do not lend themselves to explanation in terms of the categories underwritten by traditional humanistic historiography, which features the activity of human agents conceived to be in some way fully conscious and morally responsible for their actions and capable of discriminating clearly between the causes of historical events and their effects over the long as well as the short run in relatively commonsensical ways – in other words, agents who are presumed to understand history in much the same way as professional historians do.

But beyond that, the historical event, by which one used to mean something like "the assassination of the thirty-fifth president of the United States," has been dissolved as an object of a respectably scientific knowledge. Such events can serve as the contents of bodies of information; but as possible objects of a knowledge of history that might lay claim to the status of scientific lore, they are of interest only as elements of a statistical series. Indeed, such singular events as the assassination of a head of state are worthy of study only as a hypothetical presupposition necessary to the constitution of a documentary record whose inconsistencies, contradictions, gaps, and distortions of the event presumed to be their common referent itself moves to the fore as the principal object of investigation. As for such singular events of the past, the only thing that can be said about them is that they occurred at particular times and places.

An event such as the assassination of President John F. Kennedy will inevitably continue to generate the interest of history buffs and even of professional historians as long as it can be made to seem relevant to current concerns, political, ideological, or group- or individual-psychological, as the case may be. However, any attempt to provide an objective account of the event, either by breaking it up into a mass of its details or by setting it within its context, must conjure with two circumstances: one is that the number of details identifiable in any singular event is potentially infinite; and the other is that the context of any singular event is infinitely extensive or at least is not objectively determinable. Moreover, the historical event, traditionally conceived as an event that was not only observable but also observed, is by definition an event that is no longer observable, and hence it cannot serve as an object of a knowledge as certain as that about present events that can still be observed. This is why it is perfectly respectable to fall back upon the time-honored tradition of representing such singular events as the assassination of the thirty-fifth president of the United States as a story and to try to explain it by narrativizing (fabulating) it – as Oliver Stone did in *JFK*.

But this is where the distinction between the fact as against the event of modernism must be addressed. The notion of the historical event has undergone radical transformation as a result of the occurrence in our century of events of a scope, scale, and depth unimaginable by earlier historians and the dismantling of the concept of the event as an object of a specifically scientific kind of knowledge. So too, however, for the notion of the story; it has suffered tremendous fraying and at least potential dissolution as a result of that revolution in representational practices known as cultural modernism and the technologies of representation made possible by the electronic revolution.

On this last point, we can consider profitably the power of the modern media to represent events in such a way as to render them not only impervious to every effort to explain them but also resistant to any attempt to represent them in a story form. The modern electronic media can manipulate recorded images so as literally to explode events before the eyes of viewers. The uses made in courtroom presentations of television images of Los Angeles police beating a black man (Rodney King) had the effect of making this seemingly unambiguously documented event virtually unintelligible as an event. The very precision and detail of the imagistic representation of the event are what threw it open to a wide variety of interpretations of "what was really going on" in the scene depicted. The contingency of the videographic recording of the event (the videographer happened to be within sight of the scene with camcorder available, loaded, functioning, etc.) precluded the fiction that the events recorded followed a specific scenario, script, or plot line. It is no accident, as it used to be said, that accidents have traditionally served as the very archetype of what historians formerly thought of as events, but the accidents in question were always of a certain kind, namely, the sort that yielded to the imperatives of storytelling and followed the rules of narrativization.

But not only are modern postindustrial accidents more incomprehensible than anything earlier generations could possibly have imagined (think of Chernobyl), but the photo and video documentation of such accidents is so full that it is difficult to work them up as elements of a single objective story. Moreover, in many instances, the documentation of such events is so manipulable as to discourage the effort to derive explanations of the occurrences of which the documentation is supposed to be a recorded image. "It is no accident," then, that discussions of the modernist event tend in the direction of an aesthetics of the sublime-and-the-disgusting rather than that of the beautiful-and-the-ugly.

An example of what I have in mind is provided by an article in the periodical *I-800*. Here Michael Turits analyzed the hermeneutic gymnastics inspired by media coverage of two amply documented techno-air disasters: the collision of three Italian MB 339A (*Frecce tricolori*) jet planes in an air show over Ramstein, Germany, in August 1988, killing 50 and injuring 360; and the explosion in 1986 of the NASA *Challenger* space shuttle, just after lift-off in full view of a live audience and millions of television viewers. In his analysis of the media's presentations of these events, Turits likens the impact of their endless re-presentations on TV to the ambiguating effects of those televised replays of crucial events in sporting contests. Turits observes that, "when the [*Challenger*] blew up and the *Frecce tricolori* collided, . . . the optical geometries yielded by endless replays far outran the capacities of the network techno-refs to make a call?" What had been promised as a clarification of what happened actually produced widespread cognitive disorientation, not to say a despair at ever being able to identify the elements of the events in order to render possible an objective analysis of their causes and consequences. Thus, Turits notes:

> Like an out-of-control computer virus somehow lodged in the network's video editing desks, the Ramstein collision and the Challenger explosion could do nothing but frantically play themselves over and over. . . . The frame-by-frame re-runs that followed [the *Challenger* explosion] for months served the same purpose as the media's obsession with the deep-sea recovery of the shuttle and astronaut remains − to reconstruct the too brief event as *a visually intelligible* accident.

The networks played the tapes of the *Challenger* explosion over and over. In response to the question of why they had done so, the news commentator Tom Brokaw said: "What else could we do? People wanted answers." But, as Turits remarks, the tapes certainly provided no answers. All that the "morphing" technology used to re-present the event provided was a sense of its evanescence. It appeared impossible to tell any single authoritative story about what really happened − which meant that one could tell any number of possible stories about it.

And this is why the issues raised in the controversy over *JFK* could be profitably set within a more recent phase of the debate over the relation of historical fact to fiction peculiar to the discussion of the relation between modernism and postmodernism. For literary (and, for that matter, filmic) modernism (whatever else it may be) marks the end of storytelling – understood in Walter Benjamin's sense of "the tale" by which the lore, wisdom, and commonplaces of a culture are transmitted from one generation to another in the form of the followable story. After modernism, when it comes to the task of story-telling, whether in historical or in literary writing, the traditional techniques of narration become unusable – except in parody. Modernist literary practice effectively explodes the notion of those characters who had formerly served as the subjects of stories or at least as representatives of possible perspectives on the events of the story; and it resists the temptation to emplot events and the actions of the characters so as to produce the meaning-effect derived by demonstrating how one's end may be contained in one's beginning. Modernism thereby effects what Fredric Jameson calls the derealization of the event itself. And it does this by consistently voiding the event of its traditional narrativistic function of indexing the irruption of fate, destiny, grace, fortune, providence, and even of history itself into a life (or at least into some lives) "in order to pull the sting of novelty" and give the life thus affected at worst a semblance of pattern and at best an actual, transsocial, and transhistorical significance.

Jameson shows how Sartre, in a typically modernist work like *Nausea*, thematizes the experience of time as a series of instants that either fail to take on the form of a story or fall apart into sherds and fragments of existence. The thematization takes the form of a representation of the ineradicable differences – indeed, the opposition – between ordinary life and a putatively adventurous one. Thus, in a scene analyzed by Jameson, the protagonist Roquentin reflects to himself:

> I have never had adventures. Things have happened to me, events, incidents, anything you like. But no adventures. . . . I had imagined that at certain times my life could take on a rare and precious quality. There was no need for extraordinary circumstances: all I asked for was a little precision. . . . From time to time, for example, when they play music in the cafés, I look back and tell myself: in the old days, in London, Meknes, Tokyo, I have known great moments, I have had adventures. Now I am deprived of this. I have suddenly learned, without any apparent reason, that I have been lying to myself for ten years. And naturally, everything they tell about in books can happen in real life, but not in the same way. It is to this way of happening that I clung so tightly. (53–55)

Roquentin's problem is that, to him, in order for an event to have the meaning of an adventure, it would have to resemble the kinds of event met with in adventure stories. Events would have to be narratable. Here is how Sartre represents Roquentin's desire for story-events:

> This is what I thought: for the most banal event to become an adventure, you must (and this is enough) begin to recount it. This is what fools people: a man is always a teller of tales, he lives somehow surrounded by his stories and the

stories of others, he sees everything that happens to him through them; and he tries to live his own life as if he were telling a story.

But you have to choose: live or tell.

Roquentin's melancholy stems from his realization that:

Nothing *happens* while you live. The scenery changes, people come and go out, that's all. There are no *beginnings*. Days are tacked on to days without rhyme or reason, an interminable, monotonous addition. . . . That's living. But everything changes when you tell about life; it's a change no one notices: the proof is that *people talk about true stories*. As if there could possibly be true stories; things happen one way and we tell about them in the opposite sense. You seem to start at the beginning: "It was a fine autumn evening in 1922. I was a notary's clerk in Marommes." And in reality you have started at the end. It was there, invisible and present, it is the one which gives to words the pomp and value of a beginning. . . . I wanted the moments of my life to follow and offer themselves like those of a life remembered [as in Proust!]. You might as well try to catch time by the tail. (56–58 passim; my emphases)

And this realization leads him to conclude:

This feeling of adventure definitely does not come from events: I have proved it. It's rather the way in which the moments are linked together. I think this is what happens: you suddenly feel time is passing, that each instant leads to another, this one to another one, and so on; that each instant is annihilated, and that it isn't worth while to hold it back, etc., etc. And then you attribute this property to events which appear to you in the instants: *what belongs to the form you carry over to the content*. You talk a lot about this amazing flow of time but you hardly see it. . . . (79; my emphasis)

If I remember correctly, they call that the irreversibility of time. The feeling of adventure would simply be that of the irreversibility of time. But why don't we always have it? Is it that time is not always irreversible? There are moments when you have the impression that you can do what you want, go forward or backward, that it has no importance; and then other times when you might say, that the links have been tightened and, in that case, its not a question of missing your turn because you could never start again. (80)

These passages from Sartre today seem dated, melodramatic, even hackneyed – as the recent past always does – but they usefully point up the bases of a distinctively modernist apprehension that the meaning, form, or coherence of events, whether real or imaginary ones, is a function of their narrativization. Jameson concludes that the modernist derealization of the event amounts to a rejection of the historicity of all events and that this is what throws the modernist sensibility open to the attractions of myth (the myths of Oedipus, Ulysses, Finnegan, and so on) or the extravagances of melodrama (typically institutionalized in the genre of the detective, spy, crime, or extraterrestrial alien story). In the former case, the meaning of otherwise unimaginable events is seen to reside in their resemblance to timeless archetypal stories – like the death of the young hero-leader, JFK. In the latter case, meaning is rendered spectral, seeming to consist solely in the spatial dispersion of the phenomena that had originally seemed to have converged only in order to indicate the occurrence of an event.

Sartre's treatment of the event is a representation (*Vorstellung*) of a thought about it, rather than a presentation (*Darstellung*) of the event itself. A typically modernist presentation of the event is found in a passage from Virginia Woolf's last novel, *Between the Acts*. The title itself indicates a typical concern of high modernism, namely, an interest in what, if anything, goes on in the intervals between those rare instants in our lives in which something eventful seems to be happening. But the story thematizes the insubstantiality not only of the intervals between events but also of those events whose seeming occurrence renders possible the apprehension of what comes between them as an interval.

In *Between the Acts*, the life of the Oliver family seems to be as orderly as the pageant that is to be performed by the villagers on the family estate on that single "day in June in 1939" which frames the nonaction of the story. The pageant is depicted, however, as differing from the real world by its possession of a discernible plot; its intervals mark the acts which themselves represent identifiable periods of English history from the Middle Ages to the present. In the intervals between the acts of the pageant, the members of the Oliver family and their guests disperse and recombine in moments of what always turn out to he failed epiphanies, so that in reality the events that might have served to mark out a plot in their lives never quite occur. What happens "between the acts" is nothing at all, indeed the difference between the acts and the intervals between them is progressively smudged and finally erased. The principal difference we are left with is that between the pageant, with all its acts marked by events, and the real life of the spectators, in which no events whatsoever occur. An eventful instant of time would have been one that would have collected and condensed the vagrant events that are experienced more as intervals than as occurrences and endowed them with pattern and cohesion, if only for a moment. But there are no such events in this story. All of the events that take place before, during, between, and after the acts of the pageant itself are shown to have been as insubstantial as what takes place between the individual frames of a movie film and as fictitious as those historical events depicted in the pageant.

The passage I referred to as exemplifying the typically modernist approach to the representation of an event appears in the second scene of the story (there are no chapter designations). The central figure of the novel, Isabella (Mrs. Giles) Oliver, has just entered the library of the family house, located "in a remote village in the very heart of England," on the morning of the pageant. Her father-in-law, Bart Oliver, a retired civil servant, is already there, reading the newspaper. As she enters, she recalls a phrase uttered by a woman visitor to the library some years earlier.

> "The library's always the nicest room in the house," she quoted, and ran her eyes along the books. "The mirror of the soul," books were. . . . *The Fairie Queene* and Kinglake's *Crimea*; Keats and *The Kreutzer Sonata*. There they were, reflecting. What? What remedy was there for her at her age – the age of the century, thirty-nine – in books? Book-shy she was, like the rest of her generation; and gun-shy, too. Yet as a person with a raging tooth runs her eye in a chemist shop over green bottles with gilt scrolls on them lest one of them may contain a cure, she considered: Keats and Shelley; Yeats and Donne. Or perhaps not a poem; a life. The life of Garibaldi. The life of Lord Palmerston.

Or perhaps not a person's life; a county's. *The Antiquities of Durham; The Proceedings of the Archaeological Society of Nottingham.* Or not a life at all, but science – Eddington, Darwin, Jeans.

None of them stopped her toothache. For her generation the newspaper was a book; and, as her father-in-law dropped the *Times*, she took it and read: "A horse with a green tail . . ." which was fantastic. Next, "The guard at Whitehall . . ." which was romantic and then, building word upon word, she read: "The troopers told her the horse had a green tail; but she found it was just an ordinary horse. And they dragged her up to the barrack room where she was thrown upon a bed. Then one of the troopers removed part of her clothing, and she screamed and hit him about the face . . ."

That was real; so real that on the mahogany door panels she saw the Arch in Whitehall; through the Arch the barrack room; in the barrack room the bed, and on the bed the girl was screaming and hitting him about the face, when the door (for in fact it was a door) opened and in came Mrs. Swithin carrying a hammer.

She advanced, sidling, as if the floor were fluid under her shabby garden shoes, and, advancing, pursed her lips and smiled, sidelong, at her brother. Not a word passed between them as she went to the cupboard in the corner and replaced the hammer, which she had taken without asking leave; together – she unclosed her fist – with a handful of nails. (19–20)

Notice that quite a few (and for the most part mundane) events are registered here: Isabella peruses the bookshelves for a possible remedy for the ills that afflict her generation – significantly marked by a date: 1939. She considers poetry, biography, history, science and turns away from them all, to the newspaper where she reads an account of an event, a rape, an event so surreal that she sees it "on the . . . panels" of the library door. But the image of the event, which happened in the past, metamorphoses, without a break in grammar or syntax, into that of Mrs. Swithin, Bait's sister, entering the library in the fictive present: and "on the bed the girl was screaming and hitting him about the face, when the door (for in fact it was a door) opened and in came Mrs. Swithin carrying a hammer."

The image of the girl being raped leaks into that of the quite ordinary event of Mrs. Swithin entering the library and contaminates it, endowing it with a sinister, phantasmagoric aspect: Mrs. Swithin "*advanced, sidling*, as if the floor were *fluid* under her *shabby* garden shoes, and, *advancing, pursed her lips* and *smiled, sidelong*, at her brother. Not a word passed between them as she went to the cupboard in the corner and replaced the hammer, which she had taken without asking leave; together – she unclosed her fist – with a handful of nails" (my emphases). The two events, the rape of the girl and the entrance of Mrs. Swithin into the library, are endowed with an equal measure of significance or, rather, of ambiguity of meaning. There is no way of distinguishing between their respective phenomenal aspects or their different significances. Both events flow out of their outlines. And flow out of the narrative as well. The effect of the representation is to endow all events with spectral qualities. Mrs. Swithin's replacement of the hammer leads to an exchange between herself and her brother which Isabella recognizes – uncannily – as having taken place every summer for the last seven years.

> Every summer, for seven summers now, Isa had heard the same words; about
> the hammer and the nails; the pageant and the weather. Every year they said,
> would it be wet or fine; and every year it was – one or the other. The same
> chime [of the clock] followed the same chime, only this year beneath the chime
> she heard: "The girl screamed and hit him about the face with a hammer." (22)

The outside of events, their phenomenal aspects, and their insides, their possible meanings or significances, have been collapsed and fused. The meaning of events remains
indistinguishable from their occurrence, but their occurrence is unstable, fluid, phantasmagoric – as phantasmagoric as the slow motion, reverse angle, zoom, and rerun of the
video representations of the *Challenger* explosion. This is not to say that such events are
not representable, only that techniques of representation somewhat different from those
developed at the height of artistic realism may be called for.

Contemporary discussions of the ethics and aesthetics of representing the Holocaust
of the European Jews – what I take to be the paradigmatic modernist event in Western
European history – provide insights into the modernist view of the relationship between
history and fiction. With respect to the question of how most responsibly to represent
the Holocaust, the most extreme position is *not* that of the so-called revisionists, who
deny that this event ever happened; but, rather, that of those who hold that this event is
of such a kind as to escape the grasp of *any* language even to describe it and of *any* medium
– verbal, visual, oral, or gestural – to represent it, much less of any merely historical
account adequately to explain it. This position is represented in George Steiner's oft
quoted remark, "The world of Auschwitz lies outside speech as it lies outside reason."
Or that of the philosopher Emile Fackenheim: "The Holocaust . . . resists explanation –
the historical kind that seeks causes, and the theological kind that seeks meaning and
purpose. . . . The Holocaust, it would appear, is a qualitatively unique event, different
in kind even from other instances of genocide. One cannot comprehend [the Holocaust]
but only confront and object."

The historian Christopher R. Browning addresses questions and assertions such as
these in a remarkably subtle reflection on the difficulties he had to face in his efforts to
reconstruct, represent, and explain a massacre of some 1,500 Jews – women, children,
elders, and young men – by German Army Reserve Battalion 101 on 13 July 1942 in the
woods outside the Polish village of Jozefów. Browning has spent years pondering the documents that attest to the facts of this event and interviewed 125 members of the battalion
who, neither regular soldiers nor members of the SS, took on the role of professional
killers in the course of their service as anonymous executors of the genocidal policy
conceived and implemented by their Nazi leaders. Browning's aim was to write the history
of one day in the life of the "little men" who were the perpetrators of specific crimes
against specific people at a specific time and place in a past that is rapidly receding from
living memory and passing into history. And in his report on his research, Browning asks:

> Can the history of such men ever he written? Not just the social, organiza-
> tional, and institutional history of the units they belonged to. And not just the
> ideological and decision-making history of the policies they carried out. Can
> one recapture the experiential history of these killers – the choices they faced,
> the emotions they felt, the coping mechanisms they employed, the changes
> they, underwent?

He concludes that such an "experiential history" of this event, all too typical of all too many events of the Holocaust, is virtually impossible to conceive. The Holocaust, he reminds us, "was not an abstraction. It was a real event in which more than five million Jews were murdered, most in a manner so violent and on a scale so vast that historians and others trying to write about these events have experienced nothing in their personal lives that remotely compares." And he goes on to assert that "historians of the Holocaust, in short, know nothing – in an experiential sense – about their subject." This kind of "experiential shortcoming," Browning points out, "is quite different from their not having experienced, for example, the Constitutional Convention in Philadelphia or Caesar's conquest of Gaul. Indeed, a recurring theme of witnesses [to the Holocaust] is how 'unbelievable' [that event] was to them even as they lived through it."

The shortcoming in question pertains to the nature of the events under scrutiny; these events seem to resist the traditional historian's effort at the kind of empathy which would permit one to see them, as it were, from the inside, in this case, from the perpetrators' perspective. And the difficulty, Browning argues, is not methodological. It is a question not of establishing the facts of the matter but of representing the events established as facts in such a way as to make those events believable to readers who have no more experience of such events than the historian himself.

Browning, in short, draws back from suggesting what appears to me to be the obvious conclusion one might derive from this problem. Which is that the problem is indeed not one of method but, rather, one of representation and that this problem, that of representing the events of the Holocaust, requires the full exploitation of modernist as well as premodernist artistic techniques for its resolution. He draws back from this possibility because, like Saul Friedlander and other experts in the study of representations of the Holocaust, whether in writing, film, photography, monuments, or anything else, he fears the effects of any aestheticization of this event. And especially by making it into the subject matter of a narrative, a story that, by its possible "humanization" of the perpetrators, might enfable the event – render it fit therefore for investment by fantasies of intactness, wholeness, and health which the very occurrence of the event denies.

According to Eric Santner, the danger of yielding to the impulse to tell the story of the Holocaust – and, by extension, any other traumatic event – opens the investigator of it to the danger of "narrative fetishism:" which is, on his view, a "strategy of undoing, in fantasy, the need for mourning by simulating a condition of intactness, typically by situating the site and origin of loss elsewhere." In short, the threat posed by the representation of such events as the Holocaust, the Nazi Final Solution, the assassination of a charismatic leader such as Kennedy or Martin Luther King or Gandhi, an event, such as the destruction of the *Challenger*, which had been symbolically orchestrated to represent the aspirations of a whole community, this threat is nothing other than that of turning them into the subject matter of a narrative. Telling a story, however truthful, about such traumatic events might very well provide a kind of intellectual mastery of the anxiety that memory of their occurrence may incite in an individual or a community. But precisely insofar as the story is identifiable as a story, it can provide no lasting psychic mastery of such events.

And this is why it seems to me that the kinds of antinarrative nonstories produced by literary modernism offer the only prospect for adequate representations of the kind of "unnatural" events – including the Holocaust – that mark our era and distinguish it absolutely from all of the history that has come before it. In other words, what Jameson calls the psychopathologies of modernist writings and film, which he lists as "their artificial closures, the blockage of narrative, [their] deformation and formal compensations, the dissociation or splitting of narrative functions, including the repression of certain of them, and so forth," – it is these very psychopathological techniques, which explode the conventions of the traditional tale (the passing of which was lamented and at the same time justified by Benjamin in his famous essay "The Storyteller"), that offer the possibility of representing such traumatic events as those produced by the monstrous growth and expansion of technological modernity (of which Nazism and the Holocaust are manifestations) in a manner less fetishizing than any traditional representation of them would necessarily be.

What I am suggesting is that the stylistic innovations of modernism, born as they were of an effort to come to terms with the anticipated loss of the peculiar sense of history which modernism is ritually criticized for not possessing, may provide better instruments for representing modernist events (and premodernist events in which we have a typically modernist interest) than the storytelling techniques traditionally utilized by historians for the representation of the events of the past that are supposed to be crucial to the development of their communities' identity. Modernist techniques of representation provide the possibility of defetishizing both events and the fantasy accounts of them which deny the threat they pose in the very process of pretending to represent them realistically and clear the way for that process of mourning which alone can relieve the burden of history and make a more if not totally realistic perception of current problems possible.

It is fortunate, therefore, that we have in the work of one of the greatest of modernist writers a theorization of this problem of representing events in the narrative. In four lectures entitled *Narration*, delivered at the University of Chicago in 1936, Gertrude Stein reflected on the unreality of the event in contrast to "things which have really existed?" An event, she suggested, was only an "outside without an inside:" whereas a thing that has existed has its outside inside itself. When "the outside is outside:" she said, "it is not begun and when it is outside it is not ended and when it is neither begun nor ended it is not either a thing which has existed it is simply an event." She went on to contrast both journalistic and historical treatments of events with a specifically modernist artistic treatment of them, on the basis of the failure of the former kind to put "the outside inside?"

> In real life that is if you like in the newspapers which are not real life but real life with the reality left out, the reality being the inside and the newspapers being the outside and never is the outside inside and never is the inside outside except in the rare and peculiar cases when the outside breaks through to be inside because the outside is so part of some inside that even a description of the outside cannot completely relieve the outside of the inside.
>
> And so in the newspapers you like to know the answer in crime stories in reading crime and in written crime stories knowing the answer spoils it. After all in the written thing the answer is a let down from the interest and that is so every time that is what spoils most crime stories unless another mystery crops up during the crime and that mystery remains.
>
> And then there is another very peculiar thing in the newspaper thing it is the crime in the story it is the detective that is the thing.
>
> Now do you begin to see the difference between the inside and the outside.
>
> In the newspaper thing it is the crime it is the criminal that is interesting, in the story it is the story about the crime that is interesting. (59)

As for historical representation, she has this to say:

> Anyone can see that there is more confusion that is to say perhaps not more confusion but that it is a more difficult thing to write history to make it anything than to make anything that is anything be anything because in history you have everything, you have the newspapers and the conversations and letter writing and the mystery stories and audience and in every direction an audience that fits anything in every way in which an audience can fit itself to be anything, and there is of course as I have been saying so much to trouble any one about any one of any of these things. (54)

It was, Stein argued – or rather poetized – because of the specifically modern awareness of the exteriority of events that their narrative treatment was so difficult.

> We talked a great deal all this time how hard it is to tell anything anything that has been anything that is, and that makes a narrative and that makes history and that makes literature and is history literary.
> Well how far have we come.
> Can history be literature when it has such a burden a burden of everything, a burden of so many days which are days one after the other and each has its happening and still as in the newspaper what can make it matter it is is not happening to-day, the best thing that can happen about that happening is that it can happen again. And that makes the comfort of history to a historian that history repeats itself, that is really the only comfort that a historian can have from anything happening and really and truly it does not happen again not as it used to happen again because now we know really know so much that has happened that really we do not know that what has happened does not happen again and so that for poor comfort has been taken away from the historian.
> What I mean is this, history has gotten to be so that anybody can if they go on know that everything that happened is what happened and as it all did happen it is a very serious thing that so much was happening. Very well then. What would be the addition to anything if everything is happening, look out of any window, any window nowadays is on a high building if it happens right and see what is happening. Well enough said, it is not necessary to go on with recognition, but soon you do know anybody can know, that it is all real enough. It is all real enough, not only real enough but and that is where it is a difficult thing not real enough for writing, real enough for seeing, almost real enough for remembering but remembering in itself is not really an important enough thing to really, need recalling, insofar as it is not seeing, but remembering is seeing and so anything is an important enough thing for seeing but it is not an important enough thing for writing, it is an important enough thing for talking but not an important enough thing for telling.
> That is really the trouble with what history is, it is important enough for seeing but not important enough for writing, it is important enough for talking but not important enough for telling. And that is what makes everybody so troubled about it all about what history is, because after all it ought to be important enough for telling for writing and not only important enough for

talking and seeing, it really ought to be, it really ought to be, but can it be. Cannot it really be. (59)

Now the same thing is true when the newspaper tells about any real thing, the real thing having happened it is completed and being completed can not be remembered because the thing in its essence being completed can not be remembered because the thing in its essence being completed there is no emotion in remembering it, it is a fact like any other and having been done it is for the purposes of memory a thing having no vitality. While anything which is a relief and in a made up situation as it gets more and more exciting when the exciting rises to being really exciting then it is a relief then it is a thing that has emotion when that thing is a remembered thing.

Now you must see how true this is about the crime story and the actual crime. The actual crime is a crime that is a fact and it having been done that in itself is a completion and so for purposes of memory with very rare exceptions where a personality connected with it is overpowering there is no memory to bother any one. Completion is completion, a thing done is a thing done so it has in it no quality of ending or beginning. Therefore in real life it is the crime and as the newspaper has to feel about it as if it were in the act of seeing or doing it, they cannot really take on detecting they can only take on the crime, they cannot take on anything that takes on beginning and ending and in the detecting end of detective stories there is nothing but going on beginning and ending. Anybody does naturally feel that that a detective is just that that a detective is just that that it is a continuity of beginning and ending and reality nothing but that. (42)

I will resist the impulse to comment on this passage since it is composed in such a way as to collapse the distinction between its form and its semantic content on which the possibility of commentary pretending to clarify what the passage "means" is based. But as I was first revising this essay, the newspapers were filled with accounts of another "trial of the century," in this case, preliminary hearings in the case of a famous African American athlete and movie personality, O. J. Simpson, suspected of brutally murdering his (white) wife (mother of his two children) and her male companion (a male model and aspiring actor, white and Jewish). These court proceedings were themselves preceded by a bizarre incident in which Simpson, apparently contemplating escape from the country, led police on a slow-moving "chase" on the freeways of Los Angeles to the accompaniment of television cameras, nationwide radio and TV coverage, and the same kind of commentary as that which attended the explosion of the *Challenger* or the very athletic events in which Simpson had made his fortune. Few events of such notoriety have been so amply documented as this chase, which featured live spectators who had rushed to the route of the flight to cheer Simpson, thereby being transformed into actors in the scene by the television camera's eye.

What is the inside and what the outside of this event? What the beginning and what the end? Although the trial of Simpson was intended to determine the specific role played by him in the commission of the crime of double murder, it is evident that this trial was another event rather than a continuation of the event that occasioned it. Interestingly, the prosecuting attorneys announced that they would not seek the death penalty for Simpson if he were convicted of the crime, indicating that, given the American public's affection for this hero, any effort to seek the death penalty would prejudice the possibility of a jury's convicting him. The crime-event was already being detached from the trial-event, almost as if to suggest that they belonged to different universes of occurrence. In fact, the trial had the purpose of providing a scenario compatible with a commonplace of the discourse of justice, namely, that everyone is equal under the law but that the law of the rich and famous is one thing and that of the poor and obscure quite another.

CHAPTER 34

Iain Chambers

CULTURE AFTER HUMANISM (2000)*

The following extract is taken from 'A Question of History', in Iain Chambers's *Culture After Humanism* (2000). Chambers, who is Professor in the Faculty of Arts and Philosophy at the Istutio Universitario Orientale, Naples, and the author of several previous works where the nature of history is considered *inter alia* with wider, cultural concerns – *Border Dialogues: Journeys in Postmodernity; Migrancy, Culture and Identity*, and *The Post-Colonial Question* – reflects in this extract on the possibility of rewriting history ad infinitum as exemplified in microcosm by his recasting of a specific moment in the history of Naples. In 1799 a revolution in Naples led to the seizure of power by the local intelligentsia and the abandonment of the city by the Bourbon monarchy. The new state lasted for five months before it was crushed by local forces, aided by the naval presence of Horatio Nelson and the British Fleet. How is '1799' to be read? As an attempt to gain liberty relative to just one reading of the French revolutionary 'model'? From the perspective of Nelson, sent to the Mediterranean in the war against France, is 1799 part of that history too? Or can it best be seen from the perspective of revolutionary Europe and North America; here, is not Naples a part of a genealogy of modern revolts and revolutions from 1776 and thus part of a genealogy that includes the revolutionary efforts of the Black Jacobins – the slave revolt of Saint-Domingue which established the first black republic in Haiti in 1804? In this extract, Naples is linked to the rest of the world by a colonial system sustained by black slaves exported from Africa. And so on and so on. Chambers multiplies his readings of 1799 such that it becomes the focus of disturbing questions that interrogate any manner of fixing the past definitively; certainly to rethink the time and place of Naples is to dislocate that historiography which has predominantly directed the culture and history of Naples such that it now becomes forever open to multifarious modalities of narration.

* Iain Chambers (2000) *Culture After Humanism*, London: Routledge, pp. 7–19.

Knowledge, viewed as a transitive process, has no foundation – only a structure in time.

Roy Bhaskar

From a flagship

THE BAY OF NAPLES, 1799. In the early months of the year a revolution had led to the seizure of power by the local liberal intelligentsia and the abandonment of the city by the Bourbon monarchy. The new state lasted a hectic five months before being crushed by the peasant army of Cardinal Ruffo, aided and abetted by the naval presence of Horatio Nelson and the British fleet. Many of the leaders were publicly executed in Piazza del Mercato: decapitation for the aristocrats, hanging for the bourgeoisie. Directly inspired by the French Revolution, the short-lived Republic of 1799 is still today lived by many Neapolitans as an open wound whose spilt blood stains the formation of the contemporary city. In this vision of the past, '1799' represents a lost moment, and subsequent history the testimony of the brutal negation of its possibilities. This historical, and historicist, explanation is considered to evoke a singular event – the sole independent republic in modern Italian history – that sets the history of Naples apart from the rest of the peninsula. Beyond the confines of an often numbing idealisation, there nevertheless emerges an important proximity between 1799 and, say 1999, when that specific history comes to be inscribed in a more extensive charting of occidental modernity. Perhaps the manner in which to appreciate this proximity lies not so much in once again investigating 1799 as a peerless historical affair, but rather in listening to the questions that emerge from that particular moment; questions that query the eventual conception and representation of both then and now.

I could begin with a simple scene, borrowed from the work of the American critic and writer Susan Sontag, *The Volcano Lover* (1992). There is a British warship anchored in the Bay of Naples that offers a view of the city from the sea. From the ship, orders are issued for the suppression of the fledgling republic. On board there is Nelson, Sir William and Lady Hamilton. Sir William is a lover of Vesuvius, a founder of the new science of vulcanology and a member of the Royal Society. Nelson, Lady Hamilton's lover, is admiral of the fleet sent by London to sustain the Mediterranean front in the war against France. The previous year he had destroyed the French fleet in Egyptian waters at the battle of Aboukir. In the meantime republican France was on the verge of transforming itself into the Napoleonic state. The local Neapolitan revolution and subsequent republic were also part of this history.

This telescopic view encourages the insertion of the local history of Naples in a European, even global, perspective, and invites me to consider the events of 1799 under other eyes. Here, for example, Naples finds itself located in a genealogy of modern revolts and revolutions. This particular narrative commences in 1776 with the revolt of the British colonies in North America, which, in turn, lent inspiration to the most famous: the French Revolution of 1789. But the longest and most bloody was the revolt of the 'Black Jacobins' – the slaves of Saint-Domingue led by Toussaint L'Ouverture and directly influenced by the events in France. After thirteen years of combat against the British, Spanish and, above all, the French, the revolt resulted in the establishment of the first black republic of Haiti in 1804. In the year previous to the founding of the Neapolitan Republic, the Catholic–Protestant alliance of Wolfe Tone's 'United Irishmen' fought for

Irish independence before being vanquished in blood. In the following twenty years all of Latin America was shaken by a series of revolts as the colonies violently seceded from the Spanish Crown. In the diversified contestation of authoritarian, centralised and non-representative powers (frequently in order to ensure local interests and oligarchies), it becomes possible in hindsight to identify the transit towards a modernity characterised by the uneven acquisition of mass politics, mass democracy and mass culture.

To return to the Bay of Naples, to Nelson's ship. This warship, like all those of the British Navy, with 30 per cent of the crew composed of black sailors, had its decks painted red in order to hide the blood of those who fell in action. This ship, this fleet, represented the brutal pragmatism of an imperialism in which the Mediterranean, like the Caribbean, the Atlantic, the Indian Ocean and recently colonised Australia, were pieces of a global political economy. The question is whether this perspective represents only a view of Naples seen from a British warship and dictated by the Foreign Ministry in London, or whether this other point of view permits the emergence of a wider prospect? I would suggest, just as the presence of a Japanese project that presently dominates the architectural skyline of Naples, that the view that arrives from elsewhere offers, whatever the eventual verdict, an opening that interrupts the official consensus of a local picture. Transferring the history of the Neapolitan Republic on to a less provincial and more worldly map, the events represented by the five months of life of the republic are able to acquire a wider ethical resonance and enter a more extensive political and historical configuration.

Before a wider horizon, the presence of France in this particular history, beyond the symbolic force of 1789 and the physical presence and support of French troops in the early days of the republic's constitution, reveals a series of concerns and conditions as difficult to explain as the presence of the British fleet in the Bay of Naples a few months later. The hesitancy of the Paris Directory in recognising the Neapolitan Republic, like its equal reluctance to accept the demand for the abolition of slavery in the richest island of its colonial empire (Saint-Domingue), exposes a policy dictated more by the political and economical needs of the metropolitan centre than by requests for local liberties. In this perspective there emerges a Naples as both the object of more powerful European interests and a particular European city caught up in the complexities of wider, global concerns.

One of the principal chains, largely invisible to its inhabitants, that linked the specific locality of Naples to the rest of the world in this historical period was a colonial system sustained by the labour of black slaves imported from Africa into the Americas. The recognition of the centrality of that economy to the cultural and political formation of modernity draws attention to subaltern histories narrated from elsewhere; in this case, to the 'Black Atlantic', as Paul Gilroy's important study eloquently suggests. Returning that discourse to our initial locality, and restricting it to gastronomy, coffee, chocolate, tomatoes, chillies, potatoes and sugar were all goods and tastes that developed in the wake of colonial expansion, sustained by the same political economy that provided the basis for the demand for new political rights. New World 'discoveries' also inaugurated the new world of post-feudal political demands that came to a head in events as the English Civil War, the French Revolution and the Neapolitan Republic. It is to this paradoxical development that Jaurès referred when insisting that slavery and the slave trade were the economic bases of the French Revolution: 'The fortunes created at Bordeaux, at Nantes, by the slave trade, gave to the bourgeoisie that pride which needed liberty and contributed to human emancipation'. Occidental modernity, whether evidenced in Georgian London or Bourbon Naples, were part of that shared picture.

Using a fictitious account in order to approach the question of the Neapolitan Republic, and thereby extract further dimensions from the story, might seem a rather oblique appropriation (illegitimate, subversive?) of the historical archive. Still, beyond the rhetorical play of different points of view, such an approach is fundamentally connected to a sought-for reconfiguration of the contemporary sense of 'knowledge' and 'truth'. In the historical account, in the accounting of the past, I am here invited to consider, as Paul Ricoeur insists, that 'sense' does not arrive from nude 'facts' and isolated 'events', but is something that emerges within the temporality of the narrative, in the telling of time. So, where and how does the distinction of the narration of '1799' proposed in the historical representation of Benedetto Croce and the careful research exposed in all its historical details in *The Volcano Lover* lie? On what bases are such distinctions established? In narrating the world, from where are the protocols drawn? In the constellation of narratives that orbit around '1799', suspended in writing, in the language of representation, where does fiction conclude and 'reality' commence? Even if it were possible to return to the past and collate the 'facts', that reality would still have to be transmitted in the logics and languages of representation: public documents, private diaries, statistical data, the testimony of costume and the arts; elements that all require re-elaboration in order to become legible in a structure organised by writing. Here we are on the threshold of a debate in which the tropes of historiography, as Hayden White has consistently argued, become objects of analysis in their own right.

To put the discipline of historiography in question implies a reconfiguration of its language, transferring it from the abstract regime of 'truth', guaranteed by the neutral 'scientificity' of 'facts', to a site in which language itself becomes the factor of temporal meaning. Historiography itself becomes history. At this point, and given the symbolic weight that 1799 has for the history and culture of present-day Naples, perhaps a more adequate manner to honour the sacrifice of those who died in its name lies not so much in a narrative of heroes and victims but rather in the elaboration of a mourning that opens up a living space in the languages that represent both that historical moment and our present selves. Considered in this light, the return to, and of, 1799 could be experienced as a disturbing question that interrogates our manner of using, understanding and constructing the past.

When a revolt and revolution becomes part of the official history of a city, of a culture, it is almost inevitably authorised in a narration of the past that contributes to the conservation of the hegemonic configuration of the present. In this use, and abuse, of history it is possible to read the betrayal of the historical constellation of 1799. Concentrated in a restricted historical–cultural specificity, the light that the Neapolitan Republic might throw on the present state of the city is actually obscured. In order to allow the emergence of another history of the Republic, a history of a European city involved in a complex global scenario, and thus a history with political, historical and ethical resonances close to the contemporary world, it becomes necessary to undo and rewrite the version that holds sway. This calls for a critique of the culture that constructed and conserved that particular history. At this point, prior to entering into any attempt at a socio-historical and cultural explanation of the particular formation of Neapolitan society, it is necessary to consider the institutional structure of 'scientific' and historiographical 'knowledge', which, as Michel Foucault insisted, is always a structure of power, through which the particular manner of representing '1799' is established and diffused.

The vulnerability of interpretation

In the case of Naples this is to confront an approach to history identified with the premises (the ideology?) of historicism. To rethink the time and place of Naples is to dislocate the historicism that has directed the culture and the history of this city, and to open up that 'history' to a distinction between the closed consolation of the already determined and the vulnerability of a history susceptible to other modalities of narration. If historicism narrates the continuity of the winners, secured in a homogenous understanding of time and knowledge, a critical, open and vulnerable history might, on the contrary, be conceived as a narration, an account, suspended between inclusion and exclusion, between representation and repression, in which the final word never arrives. This would be a history that lies beyond the grand design of historical destiny. It would equally be a history irreducible to empiricist representation and the discursive tyranny of a purportedly objective realism. This would not be a history of the past 'as it actually was', but a history of the present shot through with the interrogations of the past, a mutual confrontation and configuration in which both past and present become sites of temporal transit, cultural translation, and ethical inquiry. This would be to abandon the impossible task of a neutral or 'objective' account of the past for the altogether more imperative terms of taking responsibility for the accounting of time, bearing testimony to past generations in a language open to judgement in every instance. This, clearly, has:

> nothing in common with the self-effacing posture of the historicist, who fondly imagines that he can abstract from the conditions of his existence and who himself, as a result, turns into a bloodless shade. For Benjamin, as for Nietzsche, such selfless objectivity is in fact 'empathy' with the 'victor'. Historicism is thus far from disinterested; but the interests it represents are far from its own. The 'methodological' bracketing-out of the present, coupled with the contrary enthronement of the present as the sole presiding, sole surviving judge of the past – this constitutes the basic contradiction of historicism.

If empiricism offers the incontestable authority of facts and artefacts, historicism proposes the assurance of a coherence that is impermeable to questioning, for it relies on a rhetoric that is oblivious to the ontological question of language and the unstable co-ordinates of narration. Where does the account commence; how, why and for whom? Where does it conclude? As Hans Kellner points out, 'the source of the assumption that the past is in some sense continuous is a literary one'. If empiricism appeals to the non-mediated facticity of the world, historicism evokes the perennial structure of a unique temporality marching out of the past into the future. For both, historical truth lies not in the languages that provide us with our sense of inhabiting and making sense of the world but elsewhere, in the 'facts' and 'truth' revealed by reason. In particular, for historicism, intellectual coherence is guaranteed by the continuum in which history and reason mirror one another, resulting indivisible and unique. Here the historian is not so much one who returns to the past to revisit, represent and rewrite it, but is rather the custodian of the growing archive of human knowledge; an archive that remains stable in its form, fundamentally unalterable in its premises. This is a vision of the past destined to produce only 'victims': all is explained in the unfolding of the historical process itself. In a technical lexicon this is teleology, in more immediate terms it is 'destiny'. It is in this light, as

Walter Benjamin announced in the 1930s, before the then triumphant storm of fascism, that historicism reveals an empathy with the version of the past proposed and imposed by the victors.

That historical time may be both crossed, constructed and contested by, and in, language; that it can only be apprehended and interpreted in the framings of cultural transit that precede and exceed all appeals to the stability of meaning, poses an irrefutable challenge. Perhaps, instead of merely testifying to the official memory of the Neapolitan Republic as if it were now a closed event, buried in its defeat, it might be the case of seeking to extract from that historical and critical event the energies to crease, bend and fold the present in order to contest a destiny seemingly imposed by 'history'. This would mean to see in the events of 1799, in its specific details and complexities, not the arrest of a process that was expected to open up a direct passage leading the city to modernity and the realisation of 'progress', but an altogether more disturbing sign: Naples as an allegory of the precariousness of modernity. Here the city would be transferred from a site where a determined continuity is reaffirmed and celebrated in a folkloric identity to become a disturbing place where it constantly confronts itself in the unfinished business of worldly modernity.

This is to think of the world I inhabit as a product of time. To think of time, and of my being in the time dubbed modernity, is to consider the categories that render this earthly transit comprehensible. However, to consider such categories is also to register the mutable configuration of time; it is to appreciate the cultural construction of how time comes to be represented the languages and limits of what we usually refer to as history. If all that passes away is destined for the domain of history it is equally the case that not all that passes comes to be registered as history. The history of *time* is also the *history* of time. Diverse conceptions of temporality, and diverse configurations of its social and semantic organisation, have come to be historically hegemonised in the ascendancy of occidental modernity by a linear temporality. Here the representation of the past is subordinated to the insistence of progress. Whether conceived directly in causal terms, or in the contradictory developments of dialectical movement, historical time is presumed to reveal a teleological purpose. But whose particular time and definition is this? Can time be treated as the homogeneous transmitter of our desires and actions? Does time respond only to the linear imperative, to an abstract public identity that never dies? Such metaphysical speculations seem impossible to respond to until we remember the proposed premise that time, what we instinctively register in a heart beat, the lines of a face, and what is officially custodised in monuments, museums and institutional archives, is always received, transmitted and understood in the languages, that is, in the cultural and historical formation, in which we emerge and make sense of our lives.

Such a history that does not lie outside each of us, as though an independent object to be investigated and explained, but is a history in which each of us is in-corporated and, as it were, 'spoken' and articulated. We make history under conditions not of our own choosing, Karl Marx rightly reminds us. History itself emerges from the act of incorporation that we might better grasp as the act of interpretation. In a television interview in 1969, Martin Heidegger deliberately glossed Marx's famous insistence in the *Theses of Feuerbach* that philosophy has only interpreted the world when the question is to transform it by suggestively rendering proximate the apparent opposition between transformation and interpretation. The transformation of the world, he argued presupposes the *representation* of the world that is dependent upon *interpretation*. To which Salman

Rushdie's more recent words can be added: 'it is clear that redescribing a world is the necessary first step towards changing it'. Marx's denouncement reveals a critical, philosophical announcement.

History is an interpretative act that presents itself in natural guise. Realism, as the privileged modality of historical narration, reinforces and extends this disposition until the limits of the historical discourse become the limits of the world. Out of the presumed division between imaginary and realistic accounts of the world emerge the modern disciplines of 'literature' and 'history'. Both disciplines are nevertheless bound to an underlying matrix that limits the epistemological pretensions of 'history' to explain 'what happened'. Both proffer accounts of the world in the world. Both are sustained and verified in language, where language is not merely the technical support of linguistics and print culture but the ontological sustenance of making sense. That history is considered the bedrock of explanation and literature its imaginary embroidery, is itself a form of narration, a social articulation, that speaks of the history of a particular cultural formation.

History otherwise

Still, such a knowledge of the past, and the present, given its contemporary hegemony, and despite subaltern, counter-vailing, instances, cannot simply be cancelled. Its limits, what institutional 'history' itself represents and represses, can, however, be acknowledged and inscribed into further and contesting configurations of time. This would imply wresting modernity away from the tyranny of an omnipotent rationality and the universalism of a single, linear, point of view, in order to set its terms, languages, understandings and desires in a more open terrain, and there to move in a world irreducible to its identity. In the mourning light of a positivist and self-assured modernity, there here emerges not the expression of grief for the lost figures of certitude but a necessary burying of the dead in order 'to reinvest the world and the self with symbolic significance'. Such a mourning issues in a cultural and political constellation attentive to mortality and modesty, to limits. This is not to give up the dream, to abandon the utopic, but to transform it into a contemporary act, that is, into an ethics attendant upon the uncertain historical configuration in which it speaks and which permits it to speak.

But what, exactly, is this configuration? Where does it arise, and what does it respond to? To begin to answer that question is inevitably to acknowledge a differentiation of cultural and historical place that is increasingly dependent upon a largely unacknowledged global structure that has been evolving since the inception of occidental modernity five centuries ago. In the mutual complexities of the westernising of the world and the worlding of the West, each and every history bears witness to its particular worldly location, and the manner in which that has come to be represented and . . . repressed. So, in speaking from somewhere the voice that testifies to a particular past and present increasingly resonates in the channels of global amplification. This, however, is not merely to cast a particular history and location into the pluralist cacophony of disparate voices seeking to tell a story; it is, rather, to brush a sense of narrative, a testimony of time, of life, up against the structural powers that frame us in different and unequal fashion.

The United Nations Programme for Development, published in 1997, speaks of 18 per cent of the world's population (circa 800 million) enjoying 83 per cent of its income, while 82 per cent (circa 5 billion) have 17 per cent of its income at its disposal. The same publication suggests that extreme poverty could be eliminated by spending each year less than the patrimony of the seven richest people in the world. In the United States 1 per cent of the population owns 40 per cent of the wealth, another 20 per cent own 40 per cent, while the remaining 71 per cent is left with 20 per cent. It is foreseen that by 2010 in the state of California one child in four will suffer malnutrition. The United States simultaneously houses 25 per cent of the world's incarcerated. Such statistics speak of a profoundly undemocratic framing of the political resources and responsibilities of everyday life, most acutely signalled in the 'First' world in the United States where appeal to law and the unquestioned status of the Constitution – 'a plan of government drawn up by a group of merchants and slave owners at the dawn of the modern era' – invariably takes precedence over justice and democratic process.

In Bulawayo, stepping between the cars, a casually smart black youth with a multi-coloured Star Tac™ Motorola cellular phone hooked to his belt crosses by the lights. Yet the south of the world, with its unstable mix of global signs and local realities, remains the south of the world. Investments, standards of living and life prospects remain so dramatically diverse that even the drone of statistics cannot mute the tragedy they embody. In Zimbabwe, average life expectancy has dropped by 30 years in the wake of the HIV epidemic. No US airline flies to any city in Africa, and that includes Cairo and Johannesburg. In a continent in which power appears to be sustained more by patronage than by profit or development, to speak of Africa as being in a neo-colonial relationship to the West has little sense in economic terms when its share in world trade was only 1.9 per cent in 1990 (it was 5.2 per cent in 1950), and returns on investments in the continent have dropped from 30.7 per cent in the 1960s to 2.5 per cent in the 1980s. The scene is one of almost total disinvestment, with external, private, commercial investment totalling only $504 million in 1992, 'or 1.6 per cent of the total investment in Africa, Asia and Central and South America as a whole'. The gross national product (GNP) of the whole of sub-Saharan Africa in 1992, at $270 billion, was less than that of the Netherlands. Sub-Sahara Africa includes South Africa. Put bluntly, 'the continent is slipping out of the Third World into its own bleak category of the nth world'. This is the part of the world where the 60 per cent of the world's population who have never made a phone call in their lives is concentrated. There are, Zillah Eisenstein reminds us, more telephone lines in Manhattan than in all of sub-Saharan Africa.

In the global calculus a continent – Africa – has simply gone missing. The World Bank predicts that one-third of all food required will have to be imported by 2000. Between 1961 and 1995, Africa's food production per person decreased by 11.6 per cent (by comparison Latin America's increased by 31.4 per cent and Asia's by 70.6 per cent). In this scenario the state is a 'neo-patrimonial' structure in which it is not development but staying in power that is the main issue:

> Staying in power is the main objective. The army must be kept happy, urban masses must be fed, conflicting interests of political coalitions must be balanced. To this end every aspect of the economy becomes an instrument of patronage. Quotas, tariffs, subsidies, import licences, the over-valued currency and so on become channels of enrichment, through rent-seeking activity. The privileges of the elite depend on the monopoly of power within a society, and not on the productivity of society as a whole, much less on any feelgood factor permeating the population at large. In the short term at least,

a successful programme of economic development conflicts with that. The political and economic exigencies of personal rule follow their own logic. Mismanagement actually has a rationale with the neo-patrimonial system.

This, too, is a central part of the complex historical inheritance and contemporary configuration of modernity. It is not a peripheral idiosyncrasy but a structural component of that history, that modernity.

Out of the past

How, in this light, might the past, the pasts, be narrated? Of course, the coherence of established accounts cannot be matched by an alternative coherence. After all, it is precisely the sense of coherence, leading to the conclusive nature of rational finitude, that is the problem: a finitude, like subject-centred perspective, that is ultimately infinite in its pretensions. Perhaps, the Baroque motif of the 'ruin' is more appropriate here. The established edifice of occidental historiography is not swept away, it persists and lives on, but it is now haunted by a series of interrogations, its structure fractured by unforeseen cultural movement and shaken by the accommodation of new, previously unacknowledged, historical inhabitants. The history that emerges from this building no longer offers the revelation of an abstract destiny, nor neatly corresponds to the articulation of verifiable socio-economic structures: it now houses a more unruly temporality produced by the social production of a location in time. All of this is to speak of a multiple modernity in which past and present are conjoined and mutually interrogated. For in such a contemporary affiliation a sense of the present, and its associated 'progress', finds itself in debt to the questions that come to meet it from the past.

So, the past erupts into the present not only announcing the other, repressed, side of modernity but also seeding a more unruly disturbance. Modernity does not merely become more complex through the addition of the unacknowledged, it remains irretrievably undone by the questions it can no longer contain. The archaic, presumed to lie back there in the mist of time, appears in the midst of modernity bearing another sense, another direction. An absence, the 'lost' world of the past against which the present measures its 'progress', unexpectedly returns to haunt modernity. Rational certitude confronts a ghost that bears witness to the return of the apparently timeless economy of the 'archaic' and the 'primitive': 'a rumor of words that vanish no sooner than they are uttered, and which are therefore lost forever. For the potent traces of such lost languages, of diverse cultural configurations of time and place – prehistoric rock paintings in South Africa and Zimbabwe, pre-Colombian cities in the jungles and deserts of the Americas, song lines in the Australian bush, prayer flags in Asian mountain passes – can prise open the present to interrogate its all-inclusive manner of knowing. The tourist 'exotic' can unexpectedly testify to a deeper testament when an absence of immediate meaning can open up a rift in time.

The disturbance of the idea of stable cultural formations located in the mythic time of 'primitive' societies comes to be countered by the evidence of austral Africa and north America (not to speak of the evidence of perpetual Pacific and Asian migrations): historical spaces traversed by migrations, movements and shifting territorial claims and confines, both before and after 'first contact' with Europeans. The pressure of the Iroquois

Confederacy from the Eastern Seaboard to the Great Lakes stretched out into the eastern prairie as it pushed other nations, including the Sioux or Lakota further west. Eight hundred years ago a part of the Athabascan linguistic group migrated out of northwest Canada into the present south-west of the United States; in the process they became Navahos and Apaches. In southern Africa, there was the early-nineteenth-century movement of the Ndebele out of Natal into southern Zimbabwe (itself probably induced by coastal slavery in Mozambique), putting military and territorial pressure on the Shona and the San peoples of that area prior to the direct usurpation of that space by Anglo-Boer colonisation. The land as mythic point of origin, as the constant horizon of identity and the testimony of tradition, is, despite appearances, never timeless. It is cultivated by language and, if transformed by myth into a constant referent, is not immune to a new inscription, a new telling. This is to insist on the historical nature of the 'archaic' introducing a temporality that disturbs the unilateral assumptions of occidental 'progress' and its historiography, but which, nevertheless, remains a temporality that registers historical being and cultural transformation in its own terms.

The maintenance of temporal and cultural distance, both by instrumental rationality and the transcendental certitudes of historicism, can be confounded not only by historical evidence but also by the contemporary traces of the archaic announced in the human transit traced on a rock face, in a hieroglyphic narrative whose mystery and magic resists the imperatives of teleology and instrumental transparency. In the presence of another language, and associated forms of knowledge, there emerges an unsuspected dynamism that sunders the sharp distinction between the presumably natural and static universe of the 'primitive' and the perpetual cultural movement of the 'modern'. A logocentric linearity that insists on the passage from the pre-historic to the historical, from nature to culture, from orality to writing, dissolves into something less reassuring. For if writing enters into the archaic, fracturing any illusion of recovering that world 'as it was', the archaic also re-emerges to become a contemporary instance of the writing that seeks to represent and circumscribe it. A world as 'it was' is lost forever, what remains are the remnants of representation. Such traces, however, are not dead objects, waiting to be classified and explained in a universal logic, but living interrogations that ghost my understanding with other stories, with others. The archaic, as Pier Paolo Pasolini's cinema, for example, strives to suggest, is not simply and safely back there, before my time, but is also a disturbing presence that proposes a new configuration of my present. Such scenes do not represent modernity's 'exotica' so much as its interrogation, its interruption: an invitation to reconceptualise and reconfigure modernity itself. In *Oedipus Rex* (1967) mythical Greece and contemporary North Africa are temporal, cultural, physical and psychic peripheries that Pasolini renders disturbingly proximate. The 'aboriginal', the 'native' and the 'primitive' suddenly become contemporary, part of the modernity that structurally excludes them.' This is to draw upon other orders of sense – archaic, mythical, unconscious, poetical – in order to re-write the world, to set stories to another rhythm and there seek to render the mundane magical. To insist upon the archaic as a strategic narrative that interrogates the presumptions, rationalisations, repressions and negations of modernity is not to seek the recovery of a lost innocence, but is rather to propose a critical research on how to narrate, how to eroticise the real.

Against this possibility', the spatialisation of knowledge seeks to insure the distinction between centre and periphery, that is, the perspective between subject and object. This permits the realisation of a controlled plane over which the subsequent narrative can unfold in a continual reaffirmation of the narrator. Such distancing permits a recognition of the other always and only in terms of the subject:

> A part, of the world which appeared to be entirely other is brought back to the same by a displacement that throws alterity out of skew in order to turn it into an exteriority behind which an interiority, the unique definition of man, can be recognised.

CHAPTER 35

Jacques Derrida

'DECONSTRUCTIONS: THE IM-POSSIBLE' (2001)*

The final reading on deconstructionism is an extract from Jacques Derrida's essay, 'Deconstructions: The Im-possible'. Jacques Derrida, Professor at the *Ecole des Hautes Etudes en Sciences Sociale*, Paris, is one of the best-known philosophers in the world, a prolific writer of over seventy books and hundreds of articles and reviews, such that he is at the centre of what one might call the 'Derrida industry' (for a list of works by and on Derrida, along with where to go to find even fuller bibliographies, see Nicholas Royle's *Jacques Derrida* (London: Routledge, 2003)).

Yet although Derrida has written continuously on the history of philosophy, has ranged up and down the phallo-logocentric 'Western tradition' that he has effectively taken apart (deconstructed); has written on odd occasions – albeit briefly – on history per se; has considered aspects of the past under such terms as 'inheritance' and has, in *Specters of Marx* (New York: Routledge, 1994), examined the idea of 'the end of history via, not least, attention paid to the works of Francis Fukeyama, nevertheless, the academic discipline of history is something he has given little direct attention to, although he did discuss it briefly in, for example, *Positions*.

The extract featured here has been selected for two reasons. First, 'Deconstructions: The Im-possible', was given as a paper at a conference which was considering the impact of deconstruction in America over 'the last 20 years', a paper in which Derrida addressed – as he had been asked to address – his own reading of that impact. In other words, Derrida had been asked to consider the *history* of deconstruction in America – had been asked *to be* a historian. And what is interesting in his response is his understanding not only of the status of his own attempt at a history but, by implication, any historian's historicisation of anything. Asked to account directly for deconstruction's impact, Derrida replies that he cannot – and nor can

* Jacques Derrida (2001) 'Deconstructions: The Im-possible', from *French Theory in America* by S. Lotringer and S. Cohen, New York: Routledge, Inc., pp. 13–21.

anyone else – 'reconstruct' all the topoi and movements of such an impact, but that he will only be able to suggest at best (and then 'hypothetically') an 'emphasis'. This emphasis (and here we quote words already quoted in a different context in the Introduction) would, he writes,

> concern a past periodization that I don't quite believe in, that lacks rigour in my opinion, but is not totally insignificant. In other words, it would possess, without being rigorously either true or false, a certain appearance in its favour, and an appearance we should take account of.

A proposal, in other words, which says,

> try reading things this way, try thinking of things as I've suggested and, if you think it has something in its favour like I, Jacques Derrida, does, then think of adopting this way of seeing, but in ways fully aware of its epistemological frailty (knowing it is neither rigorously true or false) and knowing its figurative nature (its topoi, its figuring, shaping emphases).

This, to repeat something said earlier, is 'as good as it gets'; this, arguably, is the status of all historicisations of 'the before now'.

Second, in the middle of his paper, where Derrida considers several examples of the aporia, one is not only immersed immediately into the notion of 'the undecidability of the decision' that historians always have to live with and which thus saturate the discourse of even the most hard-boiled reconstructionist (know it or not, like it or not), but, through his 'examples' of the aporetic nature of 'the gift', 'the invention', 'the promise', is ushered into the way Derrida mobilises the aporia to metaphysically underpin (it acts as a quasi-transcendental) the very idea of an unavoidable undecidability. Derrida's paper is therefore a fitting 'end' to this part entitled Deconstructionism, and thus the opening up (for there is, in this sense, no end at all) to the next, to that part of the Reader we have called Endisms.

PERHAPS THIS TIME I WILL add an English subtitle to my French title, which Tom Bishop just pronounced for this conference whose posters have advertised, with a remarkable painting by Mark Tansey, that it would be given in French. The English subtitle will be the following. I pronounce it as best I can and you will understand it how you will: *Falls*. Or to return to French at its most untranslatable: *comment tirer un trait*.

It is autumn. Autumn for me is the season of the gracious hospitality of NYU, which always welcomes me "in the fall" and always welcomes a visitor immersed in his own gratitude. Last spring, in Paris, once again in friendship, Tom Bishop extended an invitation to attend a conference here, and he made it clear that my proposal, whatever freedom he would grant me, as he always so generously does, should be inscribed within a series of retrospective, if not melancholy, reflections on so-called French theory in America over the last twenty years. This is the theory that has, and I quote, "massively penetrated the American university and the American art-world"—thus runs the beautifully illustrated poster that I will shortly say a few words about. Well, last spring, before I answered Tom, I must have said to myself, someone in me must have instantly said: *impossible*. I will not talk on this impossible subject, whether because it is not feasible in an hour, or because, in a thousand different ways, here and there, and here often enough, we have already said so much about it. This inexhaustible subject has exhausted even us. It is becoming more than a *topos* or a common place: it is becoming a genre. It has its rites, its theater, its unavoidable characters, its laws, its law of genre. And since we mention law of genre and French theory over the last twenty years, allow me to remind Tom, and myself, that twenty years ago, in 1979, I think, the first conference that I attended here was entitled "The Law of Genre." Already there was a superb poster, which you can admire in the French department. At that time, the poster did not yet show me in the process of getting ready for a fall, on the point of sinking into some abyss, mimicking a scene from the well-known detective novel *The Death of Sherlock Holmes:* Moriarty connected by some dance to a well-known partner, "Derrida queries de Man," whom I am dragging or who is dragging me toward, toward what? The falls, precisely, in the fall. But a fall at the edge of a waterfall, a torrent. Falls. A fall at the edge of falls in the fall. As you have noticed, the landscape, the rocks are saturated with inscriptions, letters, hieroglyphs, a sort of text in stone: a somber and autumnal landscape, waterfalls like Niagara Falls. All of that is falls, false. This is the subtitle that I would give to the painting. Falls in the fall of the falls which remain at the edge of the falls, thus at the edge of itself, transfixed, photographed as in freeze-frame, in the imminence of a fall that does not come to an end, that in the end does not take place. Falls. Thus the fall will not take place, you see, there it is still. In any case, by all appearances, we are surely at the edge of the fall, as ever, as we have been from the beginning, but gripping the edge just enough to provoke the impatience, or the desire mixed with concern, of those observing this bizarre ballet, a dangerous *pas de deux*, and who no longer even know what they want. Like graffiti on the wall, this painting remains unreadable, somber as an autumn night, blue, blue-black, in the fall, For if in the end we ended up falling, things might fall out right. And no one knows who might get the upper hand, indeed raise himself up in the fall, from the very fall. Falls. I do not know what Mark Tansey meant to tell us; perhaps he himself does not know, and the only time we met, during a breakfast at the French Embassy, we hardly said a word to one another; I forgot to ask him what he meant to say, what he expected from all these Frenchmen that he puts on stage. In the shadow of this painting, next to Barthes, another representative of French theory, who they will talk to you about on October 27—next to Barthes I appear on this other painting entitled *Mont Sainte Victoire*. Because of this title and, to be sure, because of the fact that I find myself between Barthes and a bearded French veteran of the last war, we are in the French memory of Cézanne; the word *victoire* belongs to a landscape of war, but a war of the past, the First World War, and this surpassed war of the past, this victory both archived and pregnant with catastrophes to come, from the Treaty of Versaille to the Second World War, is perhaps an allegory of French theory in America. A victory pregnant with a menacing future. In any case, already or once again in *Mont Sainte Victoire*, whose reproduction you have just seen, I am put or see myself put on stage at the edge of an abyss, but this time a little like a tree at the edge of a river or lake, a reflective watery surface, wherein my image seems to have fallen to reflect itself before me, while I remain still on the edge, like a tree whose branches continue to grow. But the image that is reflecting me in the water is deformed, deforming: I am an other. You see, I would have preferred to run away or to talk around Tom Bishop's impossible proposition. And instead of talking to you about French theory in America over the last twenty years, I would have preferred to spend more than an hour reflecting on the desire and the work of Mark Tansey, who has me either dancing dangerously at the edge of a waterfall, or growing like a tree, but still at the edge of somber and menacing water, to the bottom of which, in the autumn, in the fall, I could sink. In the fall, into the falls, falling down into the false. Of course I will not do so, I mean, I will not speak of these simulacra any longer.

I could have, because this painting—seen in a certain light, of course—these paintings say everything, metonymically, that there is in my opinion to say, think, interpret, or overinterpret, about French theory in America over the last twenty years, at the edge of which all the equivocations and ambivalences can transfix or immobilize themselves as in a freeze-frame. Naturally, when I foolishly proposed the title in the plural, "Deconstructions: The Im-possible," I did not just let speak, like a symptom, the spontaneous recoil that the program inspired in me: talk on this subject, pretend to talk on it? Again no, impossible. Rather, I meant something else that I will try to explain.

After the fact, thus after having improvised this title, "Deconstructions: The Impossible," in my proposal to Tom Bishop, I realized that—so as not to play, not to deceive, once again at the edge—I had inscribed the word *deconstruction* in a title, undoubtedly for the first time in my life, in more than thirty years. And for the first time I had announced that I was going to talk, without subterfuge, about this thing and this name, this name in the plural of course, and in quotation marks, mentioning the name rather than using it, referring to it: to the effects of this name rather than to some improbable thing itself. Deconstruction in the singular does not exist and has never presented itself as such in the present, and the plural signifies first and foremost this: the open set of effects that one can, here or there, in the world and in America, associate *with*, invest *in*, love or hate to death under this name. The impossible is already this: identifying in the singular something that may present itself, that may be accessible as deconstruction. But I thought that, out of courtesy and a taste for hospitality and gratitude, I should talk as directly as possible, straightforward without ruse or subterfuge, about this word *deconstruction* and what has happened to it, what has happened through it, with it, in spite of it, in this country and, above all, over the last twenty years.

First, allow me another preliminary reflection on this number, this sequence: twenty years. Why not thirty years, why not ten? I take this number quite seriously. Why twenty years? Twenty years ago the massive penetration that the poster mentions had already begun. It had been going on already for at least ten years. Ten years of penetration before twenty more years of penetration, that is a long time. It is long for a pleasure or for a suffering, or for a suffering at the edge of pleasure, or the opposite, and yet it is indisputable. Things had begun around October 1966, in the autumn, the fall, the date that classic historiographers generally record. In October 1966, the marker, the quasi-event, would be, would have been the famous autumnal conference in Baltimore at Johns Hopkins University that some have interpreted as the end of structuralism and the birth of poststructuralism, a purely American notion, moreover, as you well know, which I do not care for, and which I am eager to maintain as suspect and problematic; nevertheless, more than thirty years ago, the symbolic or symptomatic moment of this conference of 1966, in which I had the privilege of participating with my elders—Hyppolite, Lacan, Barthes, Vernant, Goldman, et cetera—will have marked the beginning of what some will call, depending on the figure, the desired trope: penetration, invasion, reception, welcome, alliance, assimilation, incorporation, injection, grafting: the transformation in America of this thing come from France and for which one created the name and the concept of "theory," yet another purely American word and concept. In France, theory does not have an accredited conceptual equivalent any more than poststructuralism does.

So why point out this difference of a decade between the thirty years I have just recalled and the twenty years alluded to in the title of this series, French theory over the last twenty years? Because from the beginning of the nineteen seventies, as far as deconstruction in the plural is concerned, they were already beginning the prognosis, indeed the diagnosis of the fall, its decadence and decline. They were already saying that it was damaged, that it was going over the dam. Falls, falling down, dead. The word they used was *waning*, on the wane. This was the mantra or the wishful thinking of the times. Falls: is that not the fall, decadence from the start, already in the nineteen seventies? In German *fall* means "case." Fall, such is the case. Make no mistake. It is over.

The end is approaching, the time of the end keeps approaching, but that was already yesterday. And it has not stopped. This diagno-prognosis has not stopped resounding and echoing. I could give you a thousand examples, exhibit an entire dossier of references, but we do not have the time, and what is the point? In any case, it was and still is for me a source of astonishment and endless entertainment, as well as a subject for historical reflection, from at least two points of view: that of the diagno-prognosis, that is, the death notice, and from the point of view of the thing whose fall and then death one announces.

First, from the point of view of the diagnosis and prognosis. What happens when a fall does not stop? Falls and falls and falls in the falls from the beginning. Isn't this just like an inaugural fall or an original sin? The origin of sin or evil begins with the fall. And what happens when a death notice is rehearsed day after day for the same death in the same newspaper? Even for Diana it did not last so long, a week, two weeks (already an exception), and then it's over. What is dead is dead. The fall takes place once, and it's over. But when it comes to the end of deconstruction, of French theory, the fall lasts, it repeats itself, it keeps insisting, it keeps multiplying. Falls. Perhaps it is this suspended imminence, this suspense of the fall, the fall into the falls, that Tansey wanted to represent or immobilize or transfix in his painting. Like an instrument panel, perhaps he wanted to register the fall or the imminence of the fall, or the desire for the fall, in the spectator. It lasts and lasts endlessly. And the spectator, the one who watches without exerting any effort, and who grows impatient, who would like to get on with it, who wants it finally to fall, will say to himself: How long can this last! And the longer it endures, the harder the fall. But it lasts too long, it's not possible, it's intolerable, unbearable. It's impossible.

Secondly, from the point of view of the thing one is talking about, for example, a moribund deconstruction, we can ask ourselves what it means to begin, when all is said and done, from the very start by declining and deceasing, by wearing the joyful color of mourning, mourning for oneself, as the best protection against aging, even to the point of appearing invulnerable to the usual rites of fashion, the rites of passing, that the sociologist and historian of ideas or intellectual fads know so well. Regarding the question of fashion, longevity, or death, the question of an originary fall, I was saying to myself a little while ago as I came here that perhaps I envied the few French compatriots who have recently been shelved and swiftly classed in what one calls "the new French thought." You know, the incredible artifact, editorial or academic, that they swiftly immortalize on the market after having announced in advance that this *bricollage* was *new* in order to ensure that the advertisement escape no one. At all costs, this novelty should become the new fashion. Well, I confess, I envy the ins and outs of this new French thought, for I am just about sure, and I am ready to bet on it, that they would not announce, that they will never announce the death of some new French thought. It will have been born immortal, deprived of any possibility of dying from its very first day. So, what can this mean: to be

immortal from birth? You can perhaps guess. It is quite the opposite of the decomposi-
tions that would threaten the French theory associated with the deconstructions that I
would like to speak to you about this evening.

Perhaps it is a certain impatience with the rebounding longevity of this thing that
does not cease to fall and fall out so well, perhaps a feeling of impatience or resentment,
that makes so many academic spectators sigh, so many idle passersby, feeling annoyed,
say: This is not possible. There, again, impossible. But it is these people who are impossible. That would thus be one possible sense of the word *impossible*, but it does not interest
me very much, and as you suspect, it is something else that I have in mind by the title
"Deconstructions" in the plural and "the Im-possible" as two words.

I fear that I will disappoint those who in reading the title may have come, mouth
watering, to see someone contritely admit to the failure of a whole project, a whole lifetime, and confess with a tear in his eye:, "Contrary to what I had thought or tried to
make others think, I must recognize that deconstruction is impossible. Please forgive me,
that was a faux pas." I just asked for a grand pardon, and now I must beg your pardon
for not begging pardon.

I thus arrive at my subject. And instead of yielding to the temptation, a legitimate one,
moreover, of a history, a sociology of ideas or currents or modes, I still have the desire to
work and to speak to you about what is at work, hard work, about what endures, in the
way of deconstructions, and about what works deconstructions through and through, in
the very body, at the very brink, of the impossible—or through the impossible. The preceding remarks were not intended to speculate in specular or narcissistic fashion, self-
indulgently, in a watery mirror, on the indefatigable longevity of deconstruction, which I
never did believe in. I believe only in death and in death precisely as impossible, for which
reason I am obsessed with, curious about, and convinced of mortality. Rather, it was a
matter of preparing a reading of this dash that I thought it necessary to draw right in the
middle of the word "im-possible," of the im-possible. Perhaps there we find the reason for
signing this autumn evening with the word *falls*, and of giving to a painting as blue as the
falling of water its true title, *falls*. It is not a question of crossing out deconstruction with
one stroke, nor of finding in deconstruction or deconstructions features tired and drawn
from a too long career, over the course of which one would have taken too much pleasure in penetrating a culture. Rather, it is a question of doing justice to a trait, a hyphen,
a joining and thus a separation, a dash drawn in the heart of the impossible. In other words,
this im-possible is everything but impossible; in any case, it calls for an other reflection on
what possible, power, potentiality, dynamic, *dynamis*, "I can," "I can be," and "maybe" all
mean. And the entire business of deconstruction seems to me more and more concerned
precisely with deconstructing, with all its consequences, this semantics of the possible
inherited from Greco-Christian, indeed biblical, thinking: the possible opposed to the
impossible, the possible as virtual opposed to the actual or the act, the possible versus
the real, *dynamis* opposed to *energeia*, and so on. There you go, and so now I begin, and
since I have been invited to, I will improvise a historical periodization.

From the beginning, from the first decade, of which I spoke a little while ago, there
existed a certain Americanization of a certain deconstruction, the one in any case that I
was trying to put to work by that name. By Americanization I mean a certain appropriation: a domestication, an institutionalization, chiefly academic, that took place elsewhere
in other forms as well, but here in a massively visible fashion, I mean, in this country.
What they asked me to speak about tonight is this Americanization. From the first decade,

it rested on the supposition of what I would call the becoming-possible of that which was already taking the form of the impossible. What does this mean? That often, here and there, most notably in the domain of literary theory and literature departments preoccupied in the first place with the concerns of reading and interpretation with the method and epistemology of literary criticism, in all these places critics took pleasure in drawing on these texts or discourses that had apparently come from France and were identified as examples or paradigms of deconstruction—in drawing from these texts, borrowing from them, translating, transporting *possibilities* and *powers*. That is to say, organized bodies of rules, of procedures and techniques, in a word, *methods*, know-how applicable in a recurrent fashion. One could even formulate or formalize (and I applied myself in this way at first) a certain consistency in these laws which made possible reading processes at once critical and critical of the idea of critique, processes of close reading, which could reassure those who in or outside the wake of new criticism or some other formalism who felt it necessary to legitimize this ethics of close reading or internal reading. And among the examples of these procedural and formalizing formulae that I had proposed, and which were circulating precisely as possibilities, new possibilities offered by deconstruction, there was the reversal of a hierarchy. After having reversed a binary opposition, whatever it may be—speech/writing man/woman, spirit/matter, signifier/signified, signified/signifier, master/slave, and so on—and after having liberated the subjugated and submissive term, one then proceeded to the generalization of this latter in new traits, producing a different concept, for example, another concept of writing such as trace, *différence*, gramme, text, and so on. Or to take another example: the privilege granted to the self-contradictions or the performative contradictions of a discourse, contradictions that could furnish a strategic lever in the consideration of marginalia, a minor text, a brief essay, a bizarre footnote, a symptomatic phrase or word, in order to dislocate and destabilize the auto interpretive authority of a major canonical text. For example, Rousseau's *Essay on the Origin of Language*, or the word *pharmakon*, the "supplement," "hymen," or a minor text of Kant such as the *Parergon*. Although I am the last to find this useless, illegitimate, or contingent, I would say, nevertheless—I was already saying—that this slightly instrumentalizing implementation tended to reduce the impetus or the languages, the desire, the arrival so to speak, the future, of deconstructions, and might well arrest them at the possible: that is, at a body of possibilities, of faculties, indeed of facilities, in a word, a body of easily reproducible means, methods, and technical procedures, hence useful, utilizable; a body of rules and knowledge; a body of theoretical, methodological, epistemological knowledge; a body of powerful know-how that would be at once understandable and offered for didactic transmission, susceptible of acquiring the academic status and dignity of a quasi-interdisciplinary discipline. For deconstructions migrate, hence the plurality, from philosophy to literary theory, law, architecture, et cetera. From this standpoint, although this movement, contrary to what its enemies have always claimed, remained in the minority and under attack, deconstruction was becoming or risked becoming not only possible in the sense of "feasible" but practical: a practical theory, a practical praxis, giving rise to instructions, evaluations, legitimizations, and to signs of recognition. *Possible*, deconstruction was becoming not only an act, an activity, a praxis, but it was becoming practicable, and, as they say in French, practical, in the sense of easy, convenient, and even salable as a commodity, as merchandise. Editors and university presses never spat on it, even at the most difficult moments, even at the most reactionary universities such as Cambridge, where an entire pack of dons, foaming at the mouth, spat on the deconstructionists; moreover, the word *deconstructionist*, yet another American invention, designates precisely this adaptation of deconstructions to a possible praxis, a quasi-doctrine that is teachable, institutionalizable and reproducible. And that is the case most often made against deconstruction, either from the point of view of a frightened conservatism, or from the point of view of a leftist activism that had an interest, to be sure, in leaving a certain political code undisturbed. The paradox of this situation or this phase that began, I repeat, after the first decade, is that what we were then trying to appropriate by making it possible, that is, functional and productive, was in any case that which had already shown itself explicitly as impossible, as the im-possible, in discourse, writing, or teaching that interested me personally and in which I found myself involved. I could show you, but I can develop this topic no further on account of time constraints and because I want to get beyond this phase we have come to.

Here are three brief and schematic arguments on the topic of this phase, which was more than a phase and which was already resistant to periodizations. First, very quickly, it was shown that *deconstruction*, if this word has a sense that does not let itself be appropriated, was indissociable from a process and a law of expropriation or ex-appropriation proper that resists in the last instance, in order to challenge it, every subjective movement of appropriation of the following sort: *I* deconstruct, or *we* deconstruct, or we have the *power* and the *method* that make it possible. Deconstruction, if there be such a thing, happens; it is what happens, and this is what happens: it deconstructs itself, and it can become neither the power nor the possibility of an "I can." I insist here on the "it happens" because what I would like to make clear later on is this affirmation of the event, of the arrival or the future at the beating heart of a reflection on the im-possible.

Second, early on, all the motifs that we tried to possibilize or make possible, but only to a certain point, and this success is not negative—all these motifs became reading techniques or techniques of interpretation, such as *différance*, the undecidable, the supplement, the pharmakon, the parergon, and so on. These are not only names, but if we wanted to nominalize them, there would be fifty or so of them. All these motifs became possible and made many decodings and many texts possible. But these motifs also mark, precisely, the impossible the limit of the possible. And this appeared quite clearly from the beginning. All quasi-concepts or quasi-transcendentals at work in deconstruction are inconceivable impossibilities, inconceivable concepts of neither/nor: the trace is neither present nor absent, the specter (which appears much earlier than *Specters of Marx*) is what is neither living nor dead, the parergon that is neither sensible nor intelligible neither/nor, etcetera.

Third: already, from this quasi first decade, it is often literally a question of the conditions of possibility as conditions of impossibility. A law of contamination compromises and renders impure, without absolute rigor, the very thing that it makes possible. It is everywhere insistent, particularly in *Signature, Event, Context*, or in *Limited Inc.* concerning the performative. What makes a performative possible, what makes it successful or felicitous, as they say in the language of speech act theory, what makes the performative possible is that which threatens it, which threatens its possibility, and thus which renders its purity impossible. And the risk of the unfortunate case, of infelicity, a risk that must remain always open, this is what makes possible and gives the performative event a chance, but instantly renders its purity and its pure presence as performative impossible. This schema was in fact already generalized, but I cannot develop it further here for lack of time. This recurrent expression of the conditions of possibility as conditions of impossibility did not fail to signal some major stakes, namely the shock delivered to hardly calculable consequences. Naturally it is a question here of the calculable and the incalculable. Shock, indeed a trauma, which it is necessary to register within the classical philosophical concept of possibility, in the style of the Kantian transcendental critique devoted to the search for the conditions of possibility, in the canonical expression of Kant. For all these reasons, what thus was happening in the so-called first decade should or should have resisted, did resist in fact, a sort of possibilization, this facilitating practice which was a certain, particularly American, institutionalization. Luckily, in this country and elsewhere, there were studies that measured up to this resistance, and in paying them tribute I would very much like to avoid reducing, simplifying, or homogenizing them as their detractors have all too often done.

I am now going to try to deal more directly with my subject and take up the sequence of the last twenty years from the point of view of this possibility of the impossible. It just so happens, and this is no coincidence, that all my work these last two decades have made of the impossible their privileged theme, and of the very experience of the event—the sense of possible, experience and event being different, having evidently changed—the very focus of their formalization. Since I cannot here reconstruct all the *topoi* and movements of these demonstrations over the last twenty years, you will allow me to propose, hypothetically, an emphasis and a taxonomy. The emphasis would concern a past periodization that I don't quite believe in, that lacks rigor in my opinion, but is not totally insignificant. In other words, it would possess, without being rigorously either true or false, or false, a certain appearance in its favor, and an appearance that we should take account of. It just so happens that what some—not myself, above all not myself—have thought to fix or actively identify by the name of "ethical or political turn" in deconstructions in fact dates from the time when this thematics of the impossible became preponderant or massively insistent. The timing of this supposed, presumed turning point is not by accident and should give us pause. Now of course I do not believe, and I explained why, that there ever existed such an ethical, political turn: in the first place, because what others find reassuring in texts thus designated (e.g., but allow me not to list them all here: *Force of Law, Ethics of Discussion, Other Heading, Specters of Marx, Politics of Friendship*) had been in the works for a very long time; in the second place, these texts that people like so much to read and think about, and the concepts therein of responsibility, decision, justice that organize them, are anything but reassuring to those who wish to reassure themselves in ethics and politics. That said, it is not entirely false, if it is not true either, that the explanation with these classical figures of ethics, law, politics, responsibility, decision, and so on begins to gain a kind of immediate visibility, a kind of pedagogical insistence, that they did not before possess to the same degree. Above all, and here are the principal stakes of the conference I have been wanting to get at, this ethico-politico-juridical, indeed religious, phenomenality, this opening is indissociable from its key, namely the urgency to reflect otherwise on the impossible. There you have it as for the emphasis or periodization.

As far as the taxonomy is concerned, the classification of themes and concepts, I am going once again to pretend to paint them before your eyes and to disentangle them from each another when they are inexplicably intertwined and in motion: they are just so many figures of the impossible. There you have the essence of what I wanted to say tonight: figures. These figures, I give them a few names, about a half-dozen names, in a list by definition open-ended. They are the figures of invention, the event, the gift, the pardon, the aporia of decision, and the "perhaps."

In the brief analysis that follows I will content myself with running along the edge that forms the union and the separation of the possible and the impossible, the dash between them—the im-possible as possible or the possible as im-possible—a hyphen, an impossible that is not simply negative and that questions the *as*, the phenomenological *als*, possible as impossible.

I begin with invention, invention in art, in literature, as well as technical invention, technoscientific invention or the invention of the other. For it is by working through this terribly equivocal concept of invention that I attempted more than fifteen years ago, to formulate this intriguing intrigue between deconstruction and the possible as im-possible. The only quotation I will allow myself this evening comes from an essay on invention, "Psyche or the Inventions of the Other," and reads as follows:

> Deconstruction at its most rigorous has never presented itself as a stranger to literature nor, above all, as something that is possible. It loses nothing in admitting itself to be impossible, and those who would too quickly rejoice over it lose nothing for waiting. The danger in the task of deconstruction would rather be its possibility, the danger of becoming an available body of regimented procedures, of practical methods, of accessible paths. The interest of deconstruction, of its force and its desire [and I underline the word *desire* for reasons which will become apparent later], if it possesses any, is a certain experience of the impossible, experience of the other as invention of the impossible, in other words, as the only possible invention.

What is the aporia here in its driest, most abstract form? Well, in whatever domain it may be, an invention that could only invent what it is possible to invent would invent nothing. Let's suppose the historical analysis of a paradigm in the sense of Kuhn or an episteme in the sense of Foucault, some "themata," or as they say, an historical analysis of givens, a configuration that explains that at a certain moment an invention was made possible, that it became practicable under certain conditions. technical, economic, social, psychological, scientific, et cetera. According to this analysis that I hold to be necessary and, to be sure, legitimate, and which we must push as far as possible, the invention of this possible will have done nothing but make explicit, reveal, deploy that which was already there, potentially, programmatically in reserve. And of course what then appears as an invention whose responsibility and initiative are attributed to the creativity of the inventor or inventors, this "invention" will have invented nothing. In other words, for an invention worthy of its name to be possible, it must invent the impossible, that which appears as impossible. And to invent the impossible, it must do otherwise than deploy the potentialities that a subject or a community of subjects could posit as properly their own: their powers their know-how, their force, their *Vermögen*, their *Möglichkeit* proper. I use these German words because I would like to come back to them at the end. Hence the conclusion I thought it necessary to draw in "Psyche or the inventions of the Other," namely that invention, if there be such a thing, must always be invention of the other; a double genitive. That invention may not be possible except as impossible and come from the other, indeed from the other irreducibly other than myself, does not mean that the aporia prohibits invention and that there does not exist such an event worthy of its name. To the contrary, this means that the event of invention, if there be such a thing, can never present itself as such to a theoretical or observing judgment, to a historical judgment of the observing sort, a determining judgment, permitting itself to say: invention exists, it presents itself, it falls to this subject, to this community of subjects capable of claiming it as their own, of reappropriating it for themselves. Invention as the invention of the other is not possible except as impossible, as exceeding the observing reappropriation of whoever would be tempted to say: I, we, have invented this or that. And to paraphrase what I was at that time trying to show, I would say that if invention is of course still possible, if it is the invention of the possible, then invention would conform to its concept, to the dominant traits of its concept and word, only insofar as invention, paradoxically, invents nothing: when the other does not appear in it, when nothing comes to the other and from the other. For the other is not the possible. It would thus be necessary to say that the only possible invention would be the invention of the impossible. "But the invention of the impossible is impossible," objects another. Indeed. But it is the only thing possible, it is the only possibility. An invention must announce itself as the invention of what did not seem possible, without which it does nothing but make explicit a program of the possible, in the economy of the same.

In the seminars or texts that began exactly twenty years ago in 1978, even if some of them were not published until later, I had tried to formulate an analogous aporia on the topic of the impossible possibility of the gift or the pardon. To put it once again in the driest, most formal, most economical way possible, a gift must break precisely with every economy to be impossible. It must remove itself from every horizon of exchange, restitution, and retribution, and even from any recognition, any gratitude. Which means that if the gift appears, if it is determined as gift, whether from the side of the receiver or the side of the giver, if it presents itself phenomenologically as gift, as such, it is instantly destroyed. For then, no matter how symbolically, it is dragged into the circle of exchange, into compensation, reciprocity, et cetera. Thus the gift can never be possible as present. There is never anything that can represent itself as gift to consciousness, to the determining judgment or some such teleology. This does not mean, as some have too hastily concluded, that I do not believe that gift giving ever takes place. I say only that these events, if they take place, must appear as impossible, must exceed in any case any possibility of appearing and of presenting itself in the present as such to a consciousness or even to an unconscious. In other words, here we see the introduction to an unparalleled aporia, an aporia of logic rather than a logical aporia; here we see an impasse of the undecidable through which a decision cannot not pass, through which a responsibility must pass, and which, far from paralyzing this new thinking of the possible as impossible, rather puts it into motion. This aporia ensures it its rhythm and breathing, systole/diastole, syncopation, pulse of the possible/impossible of the impossible as condition of the possible. And from the very heart of the impossible, one would thus hear the pulsing drive of what is called deconstruction. The condition of possibility would thus give one chance as possible but by depriving it of its purity. And the law of this spectral contamination the impure law of this impurity, is what one must never cease reelaborating.

For example, a promise must be able not to be kept. And this in the end concerns the means of the performative, too — well, the possibility of failure, of infelicity, is not only inscribed in the preliminary risk, not only in the condition of possibility of the success of a performative (and the gift is also a kind of performative). A promise must threaten not to be kept, to become a threat even to be a free promise and even to be successful; it must continue to mark the event, even when it succeeds, as the trace of an impossibility, sometimes its memory and always its haunting. This impossibility is not the simple contrary of the possible. It supposes and also gives itself over to possibility, traverses it, and leaves in it the trace of its removal. There is nothing fortuitous about the fact that this discourse on the conditions of possibility, at the very place where its claims are haunted or tormented by impossibility, can spread to all the places where performativity, indeed pure factual history (beyond every performativity or performative power), would be at work: the event, invention, the gift, the pardon, hospitality, friendship, the promise, the experience of death, et cetera. By contagion, and without limit, it contaminates in the end every concept and undoubtedly the concept of concept.

To give without the hope of knowing, recognizing, seeing my gift recognized or reciprocated by some sign of recognition or gratitude, I must do the impossible without knowing it, without knowing, beyond all knowing. The event, this event here, if there be such a thing, is not the actualization of a possible, a simple passing to the act, a realization, an effectualization. It is more than a performative. The event must announce itself as impossible or its possibility must be threatened.

When I say *must* it is meant to indicate that there exists here as well a necessity, a law. We must rethink this relationship, this hyphen or union between the possible and the impossible. You have seen that this impossibility of the gift is not negative. In spite of its terrifying aporia, it seems to prohibit any gift from presenting itself or appearing possible, to give itself up to be known; well, the desire of the gift, the thinking of the gift, beyond the knowing of the gift, does not give up, and does not give up on the impossible. It is the experience of the impossible that makes it so that I never give, that I can never say with assurance or complacency: I give, it is I who am giving. But what I give is in a way given always as the event of which I spoke a moment ago: in the name of the other, as the gift of the other. And I am trying at this very moment to deploy the same logic on the topic of the pardon, which moreover it is already a question of at the end of *Given Time: Counterfeit Money* concerning Baudelaire.

I purposely more than once underlined the word *aporia* in the exposition of the two examples I just gave: invention as event, the gift. I did so for several reasons: first to indicate, I cannot do more here, that this thinking of the aporia, the nonpassive endurance of the aporia—which I systematize, recall and also project in the book bearing the title *Aporias*—shows the affinity between the possible and the impossible, the principle of ruin and chance, a chance that is given, but also the forms and the political stakes of this aporia. Second, this reflection on the aporia is very different, to say the least, from that of Paul de Man who often uses the word *aporia* and predicament, but in a space much more linguistic or rhetorical than I do myself: the reflection on the aporia as aporetical experience of the event that I propose remains marked by this questioning of logocentrism, liguisticism, and rhetoricism, which was the ABC of deconstruction thirty years ago. I mark this difference from Paul de Man and do so today mostly because I did not want to do so at a time when it would have been indecent and overinterpreted by de Man's pack of enemies that I wanted nothing to do with. Finally, the choice of Tansey's painting, *Derrida Queries de Man*, marks an apostrophe of this genre on the edge of the abyss. And if the aporia was not circumscribable as an effect of language or rhetoric, the same question, the same query could he addressed to Lacan precisely on the topic of the impossible, of what he himself calls the impossible. The book that bears the title *Aporias* extends the possible as impossible also to love, friendship, the gift, the other, witnessing, hospitality, and so on.

In recalling its many stages, it is undoubtedly here that the logical trajectory of this deconstruction of the possible is assembled or formalized in the most explicit fashion. But in questioning the Heideggerian discourse on death, on its possibility as (*als*) impossibility, this trajectory is closest to a meditation of death. Thus Heidegger defines death: the possibility of an impossibility. The analysis then leads one to call into question the phenomenological authority of the *as such*, precisely, concerning the possible *as impossible*. The as, the *als*, signifies that possibility is *at the same time* unveiled and penetrated by the impossible. This is not merely paradoxical possibility, a possibility of the impossible: it is possibility as impossibility. This possibility as impossibility, this death as the most proper possibility of Heidegger's *Dasein* as much as its most proper impossibility, there we see it at the same time "unveiled' and unveiled by Heideggers penetrating advance.

But here at least we have the schema for a possible/impossible question. What difference is there between, on the one hand, the possibility of appearing as such of the possibility of an impossibility and, on the other, the impossibility of appearing as such of the same possibility? And it is in the aporetical logic of this necessity that we thus come to think a kind of law of impossibility. For example, if one must endure the aporia, if such is the law of every decision, of every responsibility, of every duty without obligation, then the aporia cannot ever be simply endured *as such*. The ultimate aporia I would say, is the impossibility of the aporia *as such*, the impossibility for it to appear *as such*, phenomenologically. And the reserves of this statement appear incalculable: it is uttered and reckoned with the incalculable itself.

I come now to our last theme, decision, without which indeed there would be neither responsibility nor ethics, neither rights nor politics—with or without an ethical or political turn. The aporia of which I am speaking, the non-passive endurance of this aporia—well, not only is it not negative, not only is it being in paralysis at an impasse (for the etymological figure of *aporia* seems to say "dead end," "nonpath"), but it is, when understood in a certain way, the condition of possibility of everything it seems to make impossible. How does one schematize the possible decision impossible, such as I try to elaborate it in diverse places and above all in *Specters of Marx, Politics of Friendship*, most notably against the decisionism of Carl Schmitt? A decision, as its name indicates, must interrupt, cut, rend a continuity; the fabric or the ordinary course of history. To be free and responsible, it must do other and more than deploy or reveal a truth already potentially present, indeed a power or a possibility, an existent force. I cannot decide except when this decision does more and other than manifest my possibilities, my power, my capacity-to-be, the predicates that define me. As paradoxical as it may seem, it is thus necessary for me to receive from the other, in a kind of passivity without parallel, the very decision whose responsibility I assume. What I decide for the other, he decides as much for me, and this singular substitution of two or more than two irreplaceable singularities seems at the same time impossible and necessary. This is the sole condition of possibility of a decision worth its name, if ever there were such a thing: a strangely passive decision that does not in the least exonerate me of responsibility. Quite the opposite.

And you have undoubtedly noticed that for all these "impossibles"—invention, the event, the gift, decision, responsibility, et cetera.—I always cautiously say, "if there be such a thing." Not that I doubt that there ever were such a thing, nor do I affirm that it does not exist, simply if there be—this is why I say *if there be* such a thing—it cannot become the object of an assertive judgment, nor of an observing knowledge, of an assured, founded certainty, nor of a theorem, if you like, nor a theory. There is no theory on this topic. It cannot give rise to a theoretical proof, to a philosophical act of the cognitive sort, but only to testimonies that imply a kind of act of faith, indeed an act of "perhaps." Perhaps. Nietzsche says, and I quote him in *Politics of Friendship*, that the philosophers of the future will be the thinkers of the "dangerous perhaps." Philosophy, in its Hegelian form, has always tried to disdain or ridicule the category of "perhaps." The perhaps would be for the classical philosopher an empirical and approximate modality that the philosopher should begin by being right about. It would be incompatible with the thinking of the necessary and the law. Now without wanting to *rehabilitate* this category or this modality of "perhaps"—I say *perhaps* rather than *maybe* in order, precisely, to liberate this reference to the event, the happening, from the thinking of being—I would be tempted to see in it only the element itself in which a possible/impossible decision always takes place, if it takes place. A decision must be exceptional and incalculable; it must make an exception; a decision that does not make an exception, that does nothing but repeat or apply the rule, would not be a decision. And perhaps the haunting of the incalculable exception could here indicate the passage, if not the way out. I say *the haunting* because the spectral structure is here the law both of the possible and of the impossible, and of their strange intertwining. The exception is always required. And the same goes perhaps for this stubborn "perhaps" in its modality, which is elusive but irreducible to any other, fragile and yet indestructible. Reflecting on the perhaps, a reflection on the perhaps, perhaps gets under way the only possible reflection on the event.

When the impossible is made possible, the event takes place—possibility of the impossible—and here it is, incontestably, the paradoxical form of the event. If an event is possible, that is, if it inscribes itself within the conditions of possibility, if it does nothing but make explicit, unveil, reveal, accomplish what is already possible, then it is not an event. For an event to take place, for it to be possible, as event, as invention, it must be the arrival of the impossible. There we see a poor proof, an evidence that is nothing less than evident. It is this evidence that will have never left off guiding us here between the possible and the impossible, and that often drove us to speak of conditions of impossibility.

Without concluding, I conclude on a note that might seem slightly theological if one lends his guard to it, but which is intended here to call upon, for thinking, the impossible possible and the more than impossible, and more than a language. Already the word *fall*, *Fall*, resonated in more than one language, and deconstruction has always been defined precisely in its irreducible plurality—"Deconstructions: The Im-possible"—as more than a language. I recall having said one day that if, God forbid, I had to provide a minimal definition of deconstruction, it would be "more than a language"; that is, several languages, more than one language, more than language. However, how can the "more than a language," more than language, resonate here with the more than impossible impossible? In German, *Mögen* means to love, to desire, before it means to be able and before *Möglichkeit* means possibility. And that's why I emphasized the word desire a little while ago. In his "Letter on Humanism" and elsewhere, Heidegger adopts this meaning of *Mögen* as desire and love rather than as possible, the possible traditionally opposed to the real, or to the act, the actual, just as the virtual or a dynamic is opposed to its realization, to the *energeia*, the energy of the act. A total rereading of Heidegger's thinking on *Mögen* and *Vermögen* becomes necessary—which I should try to connect one day to what I have often analyzed in the work of Heidegger: the rapport between *Möglichkeit* and *Unmöglichkeit*, particularly in the aporia concerning death. With that in mind, let me recommend to you my friend Richard Kerney's book, which goes back to 1984, entitled

Poetics of the Possible, which takes a keen interest in the story behind this *Mögen*. Here one should reinterpret the propositions in the "Letter on Humanism" that situate the *Mögen* as love or desire, not as power before being or before essence, beyond the being and essence that precisely desire gives rise to, and gives to the other, where being is not or not yet is. For lack of enough time to do this work here, I will simply cite a few words from Heidegger's "Letter on Humanism," some sentences that I had not previously given my full attention but deserve a closer look. Heidegger says the following: "to take charge [*abnehmen*] of a 'thing' or a 'person,' *das heisst sie lieben, sie mögen*." That means to love them, to desire them. He goes on: "This *Mögen*, if one takes it more originarily [*bedeutet ursprüglicher gedacht*], means *das Wesen schenken*, to make a present of the essence." We have to reread the entire passage, and I will quickly reread it in translation:

> The power of desire and that thanks to which something properly has the power of being, this power is properly the possible, that which the senses propose in desire. Through this desire, being can think that something, desire makes it possible. Being as desire which accomplishes itself in power is the possible [*Mögen*]. Insofar as it is the element, the quiet force of loving-power, i.e. the possible. Under the sway of logic and metaphysics, our words possible and possibility, actually, are only thought in opposition to reality, that is, through an interpretation which is determined metaphysically, a metaphysical interpretation of being conceived as *actus et potentia*, an opposition which we identify as the one between *existentia* and essence, and *essentia*. When I speak of the quiet force of the possible [*die stille Kraft des Möglichen*], I no more mean the possible as *possibilitas* than I do *potentia as essentia*. I do not mean the possible as only a represented *possibilitas* of an *actus of existentia*, but rather the being itself which, desiring, has power over thinking and thereby over the essence of man, i.e. over the relation of man to being, etc. To be capable of doing a thing here means to keep it in its essence, to maintain it in its element.

I would have to say much more to follow and question this text by Heidegger, but I simply wanted to quote it here as a way of pointing out its necessity. For the moment, what I would like to keep in mind about this other way of thinking of the possible is that emphasizing the affinity between the possible and desire or love according to a desire to give, and to give what is, according to a giving which does not have and is not that which gives and cannot present itself as such, this does not amount to the act of a subject. Indeed the thinking of such a possible is inseparable from an experience of the impossible, of that which is not possible. What is not is not possible as an act, a reality, or a present object of knowledge possible according to the classic philosophical determination of the word *possible*. Such a possible gift must therefore endure every aporia of the impossible evoked earlier. Henceforth, the im-possible—there you see the dash I wanted to draw, the stroke I wanted to make—the impossible is no longer the negative of the possible, dialectical or nondialectical, but it is at the same time more impossible than the one we discussed and nevertheless possible as the more than impossible. More than one language is more impossible, more than impossible.

Angelus Silenus says this very well in German in his "Cherubim Pilgrim" when he names God, in any case when he names the impossible or the more than possible. He writes, "*Das Überunmöglichste ist möglich*." He says it as much of God as of nothing. Becoming God as becoming nothing. I quote: "*Nicht wer den ist Gott werden*." To become nothing is to become God, it is God-becoming. In a recent text, I tried once again to join a thinking of the possible impossible, more than impossible, to the strange adventure in thought or in Western mysticism that others call in such a problematic way "negative theology." Without coming back here on the political perspective that I suggested for this Greco-Christian theology and its limits, I will rather conclude this evening by emphasizing how this becoming nothing as God-becoming, which seems in fact impossible, is more than impossible, the most impossible possible, possible because more impossible than the impossible, if the impossible is simple negative modality. This seems strangely familiar to what we call deconstructions. These are not methods or techniques, not programs or procedures deploying powers or possibilities, but the very experience of what happens, of what arrives as event in the figures of the impossible possibility of impossibility: in the gift, the pardon, the yes, decision, witnessing, hospitality, et cetera. And perhaps death. Perhaps.

With regard to the "perhaps," moreover, there exists a theological vein, in the work of Böhme, Bruno, Nicholas of Cusa, that defines God not as being—and precisely for which fact they break with what Heidegger calls the "ontotheological tradition"—but defines God as "before" and outside of being, *without being*. They define God as "perhaps." God is the perhaps. According to a potentiality or a *dynamis*, a *posse* they call it—the word is theirs—a *posse* that no longer depends on the metaphysical definition of the possible, a *posse* that is "before" being and that no longer is what a dominant tradition in philosophy calls the possible. A *posse*. God as perhaps. Then the becoming nothing, the becoming other than being as becoming God, becoming (*werden*) as engendering or invention of the other, from the other, there you see what according to Silenus Angelus is possible but as still more impossible than the impossible. And here the more, *über, Das Überunmöglichste ist möglich*, this *über* is over and beyond, and signifies an absolute heterogeneity between two qualities of the possible. That which is possible as impossible is not so according to the same region, the same regime of the possible. There it stands as an interruption in the traditional sense of the word possible. There is a changing of gear in the thinking on the experience of the possible, the traditional sense of possible, which nonetheless continues to signify within us, as we think, "possible." And in the three verses which I will read aloud and translate to finish up, the *über* of *überunmöglichste* signifies, can signify, perhaps "the most" as well as "more than," more impossible and more than impossible, otherwise than impossible. The most impossible becomes more than impossible, otherwise than impossible.

> Das überunmöglichste ist möglich
> Du kannst mit deinem Pfeil die Sonne erreichen
> Ich kann mit meinem wohl die heilige Sonne bestreichen

> The most or the more than impossible is possible
> You cannot with your arrow reach the sun
> But with my own at the eternal sun I take aim

The arrow of the possible impossible, this arrow that takes the sun in its aim, will they say that it must fall back to earth, that it desires the fall? In any case, this arrow to the sun, this arrow lights up a whole other landscape in a whole other light than that of autumn or the falls. And that is what I called, in my French title, drawing a dash or an arrow.

PART FOUR

Endisms

The texts in this Part are all concerned, either positively or negatively, with the question of the coming to the end of history in both metanarrative and lower case (reconstructionist, constructionist and deconstructionist) forms. By now, the plausibility of metanarratives has gone – towards them we can only have an attitude of incredulity. But the deconstruction of metanarratives has impacted upon academic history too, especially at the level of epistemology, and it is this that has problematicised reconstructionist, constructionist and even deconstructionist genres. As Frank Ankersmit has recently put it, although modernist histories are epistemologically driven and deconstructionist texts are aesthetic, figurative representations, the latter are still histories. The question raised in this Part is whether this shift is enough to preserve – in the medium and longer term – the discourse of history in any form. The readings in this Part engage with this situation.

CHAPTER 36

David Roberts

NOTHING BUT HISTORY (1995)*

The first reading in Part Four is taken from David Roberts's *Nothing But History* (1995) in which he examines the condition of history – and especially, though not exclusively academic history, – in the twentieth century, a century he considers to be 'postmetaphysical'. Roberts, who is Professor of History at the University of Georgia, believes that the erosion and collapse of foundational metaphysics has affected discourses right across 'our' Western cultural formations – from philosophy to science, from literature to politics, from epistemology to ethics – turning their once certainties into the problematical fabrications they have always actually been, but which they have tried, with much success, to disavow. And the fabricated discourse of history has not escaped this anti-post-foundationalism. Today, nobody in our relativistic culture could plausibly maintain that we have not come to the end of the great metanarratives, those great historical fables that were bequeathed to the inhabitants of the twentieth and twenty-first centuries, and equally nobody could think that professional, academic histories had been able to remain unscathed: there are not, at any level, epistemological foundations for 'history as we have known it'. Thus, we seem to have come to the end – if not of history in all its possible (future) guises – of at least histories epistemologically styled. This is not to say – to repeat points made in the Introduction – that 'time' has ended or that there never was 'a before now'. Rather, the point is that we may well have come to the end of particular modernist ways (especially reconstructionist and constructionist ways) of plausibly organising 'the before now' as 'history'; the bankruptcy of a particular way of thinking about how to historicise things in ways that were held to have the status of 'real' knowledge.

It is in ways loosely associated with the above arguments that Roberts, then, thinks that we have been left with 'nothing but history'. Of course, at first glance it may appear that Roberts is contradicting the above; being left with 'nothing but history' means, does it not, that history continues? But Roberts's phrase – and his understanding of history – must be understood to mean that, bereft of histories of a putative foundational/epistemological kind, we 'individuals' are left with nothing more 'real' than our own personal histories which, of course, are not really histories at all but 'memories' . . . such that the recent growth in the popularity of 'memory studies', of 'personal testimony' and 'personal witnessing', may be a symptom not of the continued vitality of history, but its decline and possible 'temporary' replacement – as we shall see in some of the final chapters in this Part. In that sense, we are thus 'witnessing' the possible end of the hegemony of history as the main way of publicly rooting our identities, our senses of self as explanatory outgrowths of 'the before now'. Bereft, therefore, of anything that is bigger, better, more commanding and more demanding, more objective or truer than our own personal memories, we have 'nothing but memory' ('nothing but history', as Roberts phrases it) by which to make ourselves feel at home in the world.

This argument constitutes the drift of the following extract and is the leitmotif of Roberts's text. Yet although this is indeed Roberts's drift, he himself is not prepared to give up totally

---

* David Roberts (1995) *Nothing But History*, Berkeley, CA: The Regents of the California Press, pp. 1–9.

on a public history – albeit one that is more modest in its knowledge claims and more circumspect about academic historians' shibboleths: a 'weak history'. Drawing on the works of theorists such as Nietzsche, Croce, Foucault, Derrida and Rorty, Roberts argues that it might still be possible 'to stake out the terrain of postmetaphysical [postmodern] history and to assess the possibilities within it'. Thus, opines Roberts, 'I will be concerned especially to identify the elements that might serve as a moderate alternative [and] . . . to show how such a moderate strand [weak history] entails a continued role for historical understanding. Not completely 'writing off' history, then, Roberts's engagement with 'endism' is, nevertheless, a suggestive and thoughtful beginning to this Part wherein historians consider the problematical status of various histories and their possible life – and death.

A difficult adjustment

O VER THE PAST century or so, cultural changes centering on the erosion of foundationalist metaphysics have called forth an ever more explicit effort to specify the contours of a postmetaphysical culture. That effort has encompassed earlier thinkers like Friedrich Nietzsche, Benedetto Croce, and Marlin Heidegger, and it has brought hermeneutics, deconstruction, and neopragmatism to center stage in recent decades. All the strands in our culture, from philosophy and science to literature and politics, have been at issue in this discussion, but the place of "history" has been central—and especially elusive. Sometimes explicitly, often only implicitly, thinkers prominent in this cultural reassessment have thought anew about what is historical and about the role of historical inquiry and understanding. Taking for granted the waning of metaphysics, this study examines its implications for the place of history, as one competing cultural strand.

As Richard Rorty has emphasized, the foundationalist assumptions of our tradition have been gradually eroding for the last one hundred fifty years, as philosophers have chipped away at such notions as "self-validating truth," "transcendental argument," and "principle of the ultimate foundation of all possible knowledge."[1] After Nietzsche, Heidegger, John Dewey, Ludwig Wittgenstein, W. V. Quine, and Donald Davidson, there are few foundationalists to be found on either side of the notorious divide between Continental and Anglo-American philosophy. And because our whole philosophical tradition has been *fundamentally metaphysical*, what is apparently unraveling is not simply a delimited philosophical genre but also epistemology and any possibility of privileged methods or decision procedures affording access to certain, suprahistorical truth. But what is left, and how do we make our way in the world that remains to us?

This change in the intellectual landscape has had implications for history in both its customary senses—as *res gestae*, the past, the stuff that historical inquiry seeks to apprehend, and as *historia rerum gestarum*, the past as related or conveyed, the historical account. At issue, in fact, have been broad questions about the human relationship to a world that sometimes seems fundamentally historical in a new, radically post-Hegelian sense. But whereas some of the answers seem to portend an expanded cultural role for history, others seem to undermine even the role—modest by some measures, grandiose by others—that history came to play by the late nineteenth century. Indeed, assaults on "history" have been central to a number of the cultural responses to the eclipse of metaphysics, and history itself is sometimes assumed to be-ending along with foundationalist philosophy.

Even the terminology surrounding history has become ever more complex and uncertain as the wider intellectual framework has changed. The term "historicisin" has remained central to humanistic discussion, even taking on yet another lease on life by the latter 1980s as "the new historicism" became a catchphrase in literary studies, then spilled over to influence historiography. What historicism might entail proves crucial to any effort to assess the status of history after metaphysics, yet even within the same intellectual camp, some refer to it approvingly, others disparagingly.[2] Those seeking to place our situation in historical perspective often refer to an earlier "crisis of historicism," yet they do not seem to understand the crisis in the same way, or even to date it at the same time.

Among thinkers responding to the waning of metaphysics, the now-familiar sequence of Nietzsche, Heidegger, Michel Foucault, and Jacques Derrida has been especially influential. Their efforts, taken together, constitute a culture of extremity, as Allan Megill showed in his influential *Prophets of Extremity*, published in 1995. Although some found the extremes nihilistic in implication, many embraced them as liberating from the authoritarianism of our metaphysical tradition. Also prominent, by the 1980s, was a more general aestheticism that similarly contested metaphysically grounded approaches, though its relationship with the extremes was complex. This aestheticism affected readings of Nietzsche and Heidegger, gave a certain spin to deconstruction, and led to a particular recasting of the hermeneutic and pragmatist strands within our tradition.[3] The understanding of postmetaphysical possibilities that resulted from the combination of extremity and aestheticism seemed to have unfavorable implications for history.

However, some who welcomed the postmetaphysical turn sought an alternative response, though their efforts were disparate and their alternative hard to characterize. In one sense, it was to be "moderate"—no longer metaphysical, and thus not "authoritarian," yet eschewing the extremes at the same time. But though moderate in this sense, such an alternative might prove more radical than the extremes, which, despite their apocalyptic quality, seemed to some to undermine the scope for any politically significant radicalism. At the same time, those seeking this moderate alternative were leery of aestheticist tendencies and clung to the scope for truth. Rather than accent personal edification, they played up the human role in the ongoing reconstruction of the world in history. And the approach they envisioned seemed to entail an enhanced cultural role for empirical historiography.

The outcome of the waning of metaphysics has so far been a kind of field of forces, including an array of extreme responses, not all of them compatible, a generically aestheticist tendency, and a quest for a moderate, constructive alternative. In my view, there is value, or at least plausibility, to a great many of these impulses, including extremes that some find merely nihilistic. But the sources of these diverse responses, their implications and the connections among them, have not been well understood. Moreover, uncertainty regarding the baggage that "history" must carry has produced confusion and excess. As a result, our understanding of postmetaphysical cultural possibilities has been prejudicial and limiting.

Dissolving and inflating the historical

The status of history was already in question before the waning of metaphysics forced the more insistent reconsideration of cultural priorities that has marked the period since about

1960. Indeed, it has long been a commonplace that the break into twentieth-century culture was bound up with a retreat from the premium on historical approaches that marked "the great age of history" in the nineteenth century.[4] Somehow the sphere of public, objective history, which had seemed deeply meaningful, grew blurry, and the focus shifted to subjective temporal experience or, at most, to one's own personal history. The advent of Freudian psychoanalysis has frequently been cited as the most significant example.[5] In addition, the modernist use of simultaneity and collage seemed to challenge the notion of linear time and thus to undermine the confidence in linear narrative that was apparently essential to any historical approach.[6]

At the same time, the cataclysmic events of the twentieth century seem to have constituted such a rupture that history, with its connotations of continuity, coherence, and intelligibility, must surely diminish as a cultural component. In his widely admired *The Great War and Modern Memory*, Paul Fussell notes World War I "was perhaps the last to be conceived as taking place within a seamless, purposeful 'history' involving a coherent stream of time running from past through present to future."[7] Especially insofar as "history" necessary carries this particular baggage, it seems to have been undermined by the events of history itself, in the twentieth century. Some insist that only literature, even if still in narrative form, can get at the real, lived reality of what is commonly taken as a historical experience or event, such as the First World War.[8]

Indeed, changes in the cultural situation seemed to thrust a new kind of leadership on the literary culture, even responsibility for what once seemed part of the historians' domain. The distinguished critic Harold Bloom noted this tendency with a certain grim resignation in the early 1970s, when he pondered the special difficulties we have come to encounter in conceiving the relationship between our present experience and our tradition or history:

> The teacher of literature now in America, far more than the teacher of history or philosophy or religion. is condemned to teach the presentness of the past, because history, philosophy and religion have withdrawn as agents from the Scene of Instruction, leaving the bewildered teacher of literature alone at the altar, terrifiedly wondering whether he is to be sacrifice or priest. If he evades his burden by attempting to teach only the supposed presence of the present, he will find himself teaching only some simplistic, partial reduction that wholly obliterates the present in the name of one or another historicizing formula, or past injustice, or dead faith, whether secular or not. Yet how is he to teach a tradition now grown so wealthy and so heavy that to accommodate it demands more strength than any single consciousness can provide, short of the parodistic Kabbalism of a Pynchon?[9]

Only one chunk of the cultural terrain is at issue in this passage, and for Bloom responsibility for it fails to the literary culture by default, not as the booty of confident imperialist conquest. But the notion that literature must assume responsibility for a historical world grown too overwhelming for the competence of historians was central to the overall rethinking of cultural priorities.

If history was still to contribute to the wider culture, it seemed to need major recasting in light of the twentieth-century experience. Writing in 1966, Hayden White argued that "the historian serves no one well by constructing a specious continuity between the present world and that which preceded it. On the contrary, we require a history that will educate us to discontinuity more than ever before: for discontinuity, disruption and chaos is our lot."[10] But as even categories ancillary to historiography, such as continuity, chronology, and narrative, became suspect, the notion that "history" is ending, along with God, metaphysics, and the true world became widespread in humanistic discussion.

Poststructuralists like Foucault and Derrida were widely assumed to have shown "that there really is no such thing as 'history.'"[11] All we can do is think instead in terms of sheer becoming, or mere flux, or slippage, or the play of differences. Throughout his *Radical Hermeneutics*, John D. Caputo falls back on the notion of "flux," which he takes to be a kind of neutral, premetaphysical category capable of withstanding even the postmodernist critical onslaught.[12] It comes to seem that in shaping the formless ooze into "recorded history," we are simply seeking an antidote to "the primitive terror" we feel in the face of the real nothingness of the flux.[13]

Tainted with metaphysical prejudices, historical-mindedness came to seem but another Western pretense, even a form of domination by the winners, who enforce remembrance of the course of the actual and forgetting of all the rest. If story is always written by the victors, and victory conflates with domination and exclusion.[14] From this perspective, any premium on historical thinking is inherently conservative, since it justifies the present power configuration by affording privilege to the course of the actual and thus the status quo.

However, another body of evidence suggests that what ends with the erosion of metaphysics is not history writ large but simply a certain approach to history—and a certain way of understanding our own place within our particular history. Our idea of history had indeed come to carry a good deal of metaphysical baggage, but to jettison that baggage may force us to take history seriously in ways inconceivable before.[15]

Recent antihistorical thinking often simply assumes that *any* notion of history must carry such baggage. There is a tendency to conflate the coherence and continuity that do seem necessary, if we are to speak of "history" at all, with the progressivism and even teleology that may not be. Indeed, postmetaphysical discussions of history persistently slip in G. W. F. Hegel at key junctures, as if a cultural emphasis on history necessarily entails Hegelian assumptions.[16]

The metaphysical tradition rested on the belief that, on some level, things are a certain way we might discover, that there are stable, suprahistorical foundations or essences, origins or purposes, "firsts" or "ends." In one form or another, metaphysics seemed to specify a kind of container for all the variable and contingent stuff of history. For Rorty, in fact, traditional philosophy was fundamentally "an attempt to escape from history—an attempt to find nonhistorical conditions of any possible historical development."[17] But if so, then something like history might seem what remains as, with the end of metaphysics, we recognize that any such suprahistorical realm is inaccessible, even inconceivable.

In one sense, the modern subjectivism that began with René Descartes was a new, more radical attempt at a suprahistorical metaphysics in the face of Renaissance skepticism. With the Cartesian recasting of Western philosophy, subjectivity or consciousness became the bedrock, that which could not be doubted. Taking form as the self or ego, subjectivity was a priori and somehow transcendent, capable of seeing the world whole, even mastering it.

In some of our accounts, to be sure, we accent the sense in which modern subjectivism was itself postmetaphysical. As the old metaphysics no longer seemed to hold, a new kind of humanism emerged, accenting the scope for human beings to make their own world on earth. Thus the Enlightenment project and the several political strands that followed from it; thus, eventually, the idea of progress and the particular relationship to history that it entailed, in this sense, the departure from antihistorical metaphysics involved embracing history as meaningful—as the arena for making the world, thereby creating or revealing ourselves. But even insofar as modern subjectivism entailed this premium on action in history, the ahistorical core of that tradition remained in place. The metaphysical tradition led us still to posit a universal rational standard, a congruence between mind and reality, and a direction, even a telos, to history itself.

What happens when "modernity," combining still-metaphysical assumptions with one brand of historical consciousness, loses its aura? Most basically, the subjective ego or consciousness no longer seems a priori and transcendent but is "thrown" into some particular context. And this means not only that individual subjectivity is always historically specific but also that my selfhood emerges only through the larger historical happening into which I am thrown. My self-understanding begins in a past I did not create and is projected into a future I cannot control.[18] But it is equally crucial that with the waning of metaphysics, we cannot conceive this history as an overarching process of human self-realization, of "becoming what we are." Because there is no a priori human essence, there is no scope fulfilling ourselves by overcoming some fragmentation or alienation.

So the subject is neither transcendent nor in process of self-realization but is rather bound up with some specific situation that is historical in a non-Hegelian sense. It would seem, then, that a post-Hegelian form of historical inquiry might replace subjectivity or consciousness as the key to self-understanding.

From within the modern framework, "modern" was an honorific term expressing our sense of ourselves as the privileged culmination of a benign historical process. The West was superior, and Western modernity was the culmination of human development, because scientific reason afforded a privileged access to the truth of things—and thus an increasing technological mastery of the world. But on this level, too, we come to seem more significantly bound up with history as our modern world comes to seem merely a contingent historical resultant, "modern" in no more than a neutral chronological sense and certainly not metaphysically privileged. As modernity loses its aura, we become postmodern, relating to our earlier pretensions in a newly self-conscious way, perhaps through parody or nostalgia.[19] But the res gestae, the stuff history deals with, still may be sufficiently coherent to make possible historical inquiry, and such inquiry may have deeper cultural import precisely insofar as history is *not* progressive, with an a priori frame.

For over a century, those assaulting the metaphysical tradition have found themselves face-to-face with something like history—but not the history that nineteenth-century advocates of a historical approach had in mind. Even as he deplored the implications of the hypertrophy of one kind of historical consciousness, Nietzsche reduced reality to perpetual becoming and emphasized the contingent constructedness of the worlds we fashion for ourselves. By the first decade of the century, Croce was submerging philosophy within history as he sought to posit an absolute historicism. Heidegger thought through first the centrality of historicity to human living, then the particularity of our world as a purely historical resultant. By midcentury, Wittgenstein had reacted against his earlier attempt to provide a suprahistorical map of language and was suggesting that. on every level, we may alter or devise the rules as we go along, subject to the historically specific form of life in which we find ourselves. A bit later. Thomas Kuhn modestly proposed "a role for history" even in the self-understanding of the natural sciences, thereby initiating one of the most fruitful discussions, of the century. By the 1980s, Robert C. Solomon was offering a strikingly contemporary Hegel whose "closing" telos proves the empty yet liberating awareness that the world is perpetually incomplete; Michael Ryan was suggesting that "history" is another name for the undecidability that Derrida allots us; and Richard Rorty, underscoring the historical contingency of what once seemed the inevitable philosophical problems, was proposing that history affords the only therapy when we find ourselves intellectually befuddled. More recently still, Brook Thomas concluded that, with the end of all we have encompassed under the term "metaphysics," ours is "a historically contingent world" in which "there are only historical ways of knowing."[20]

Examples could be multiplied, and, though disparate, they have a significant family resemblance. For a hundred years, some have suggested that as we cease to believe in foundations, essences, or "metanarratives," we are left with a world that is particular and provisional, endlessly differing, forever incomplete; ever more of reality seems but a contingent historical resultant. A kind of "inflation of history" or "reduction to history" seems to have been at work. With the dissolution of metaphysics, history could no longer be understood simply as the mundane testing ground, specified in our religion, tradition, or as the revelation or dramatization of truths, principles or values already there, or as the path to goal given beforehand. Rather, history was left standing alone, naked, for the first time—as all there is.

But whether what is left can usefully be termed "history" obviously depends on the baggage the term must carry. Perhaps, to avoid metaphysic[s], we must settle for empty becoming, or, with Caputo, mere flux. However, it is possible that we must understand the world more fully as "historical" than ever before, but "historical" in a new, "weak" way in the absence of metaphysical buttressing.[21] Even if we find ourselves doing so, however, it is not obvious how the human relationship to such a world is to be conceived. Nor is it clear how we might respond to a purely historical world. A simple dichotomy between pro- and antihistory does not seem sufficient to sort out the cultural directions that have opened in response to this inflation of history.

At this point, it is enough simply to grasp the overall line of questioning that these preliminaries suggest. If our conventional ways of understanding history prove to rest on outmoded metaphysical assumptions, are we left with sheer becoming mere flux, or the play of differences, or can we make new sense of history, both as a conception of what "there is" and as a mode of inquiry and understanding? If our world seems to reduce to nothing but history, what is the range of plausible responses? Does the mix of extremity and aestheticism rest on a fair reading of the possibilities, or has there been something prejudicial about the way the alternatives have been sorted out? What is the scope for a moderate, constructive orientation toward history within a post-metaphysical culture, and how would any such orientation relate to the extremes?

Notes

1   Richard Rorty, *Essays on Heidegger and Others* (Cambridge: Cambridge University Press, 1991), 109–110.
2   For a good assessment of the term and its recent uses, see Georg G. Iggers, "Historicism: The History and Meaning of the Term." *Journal of the History of Ideas* 56, no. 1 (January 1995), 129–152.

3   "Aestheticism" is central to Allan Megill's account in *Prophets of Extremity: Nietzsche, Heidegger, Foucault, Derrida* (Berkeley, Los Angeles, and London: University of California Press, 1985). See also Alexander Nehamas's aestheticist reading of Nietzsche in *Nietzsche: Life as Literature* (Cambridge: Harvard University Press, 1985); and Richard Rorty's discussion of the category in *Contingency, Irony, and Solidarity* (Cambridge: Cambridge University Press, 1989), 119n.

4   Introducing the pioneering modernism of Vienna, Carl Schorske refers to "our century's ahistorical culture" almost in passing. See Carl E. Schorske, *Fin-de-Siècle Vienna: Politics and Culture* (New York: Random House, Vintage, 1981), xviii.

5   Stephen Kern *The Culture of Time and Space, 1880–1918* (Cambridge: Harvard University Press, 1983), p. 63. Schorske, *Fin-de-Siècle Vienna*, chap 4.

6   See, for example, Eugene Dunn's lucid discussion of this direction, especially as represented by Brecht and resisted by Lukács, in *Marxism and Modernism: An Historical Study of Lukács, Brecht Benjamin and Adorno* (Berkeley, Los Angeles, and London: University of California Press, 1982), 48–55, 121–124. See also Gianni Vattimo, *La fine della modernita* (Milan: Garzanti, 1985), 18, for a comparable argument about the impact of the modern media, especially television, in dehistoricizing our experience through simultaneity.

7   Paul Russell. *The Great War and Modern Memory* (London: Oxford University Press, 1975), 21.

8   Modris Ekstems, in *Rites of Spring: The Great War and the Birth of the Modern Age* (Boston: Houghton Mifflin, 1989), 290–291, 296, argues explicitly that literary writers proved better able than historians to get at the reality of World War I. The war itself had undermined the historical imagination, so that history could not make sense of the experience.

9   Harold Bloom, *A Map of Misreading* (Oxford: Oxford University Press, 1975), 39.

10 Hayden V. White, "The Burden of History," reprinted in his *Tropics of Discourse: Essay's in Cultural Criticism* (Baltimore: Johns Hopkins University Press, 1978), 50.

11 David Hoy, "Jacques Derrida." in *The Return of Grand Theory in the Human Sciences*, ed. Quentin Skinner (Cambridge: Cambridge University Press, 1985), 48–49, referring to the stance of Foucault, Derrida, and "other modern Nietzscheans." See also pp. 59–60, and, in the same volume, Mark Philp, "Michel Foucault," 78–79, for further indications that any premium on continuity or tradition has come to seem conservative, limiting, even authoritarian.

12 John D. Caputo, *Radical Hermeneutics: Repetition, Deconstruction, and the Hermeneutic Project* (Bloomington: Indiana University Press, 1987); see, for example, pp. 97–98.

13 See T. S. Eliot, "The Dry Salvages," in *Four Quartets* (San Diego: Harcourt Brace Jovanovich, 1971; orig pub. 1943), 39, lines 96–103. See also Hans Kellner's way of making the point in his "Beautifying the Nightmare: The Aesthetics of Postmodern History," *Strategies* 4–5 (1991): 292–293.

14 See especially Walter Benjamin, "Theses on the Philosophy of History," in *Illuminations*, ed. Hannah Arendt, trans. Harry Zohn (New York: Schocken, 1969). 253–264. See also Vàclav Havel, *Disturbing the Peace; A Conversation with Karel Hvizdala*, trans. Paul Wilson (New York: Random House, Vintage, 1991), 166–167, for a more recent example of this tendency.

15 What it means to take history seriously" is crucial. See David Couzens Hoy's way of framing the issue in 'Taking History Seriously: Foucault, Gadamer, Habermas," *Union Seminary Quarterly Review* 34, no. 2 (Winter 1979): 85–95.

16 For Michel Foucault, "our age . . . is attempting to flee Hegel." See "The Discourse on Language" (1970), published with *The Archaeology of Knowledge*, trans. A. M. Sheridan Smith (New York Harper and Row, Colophon, 1976), 235. See also Megill, *Prophets of Extremity*, 186–187, on Foucault's enduring preoccupation with Hegel; and Vattimo, *La fine delta modernita*, 10–17, on the effort to escape Hegel in Nietzsche and Heidegger. In questioning the Hegelian legacy, Jacques Derrida, like Vattimo, worried plausibly about the notion of *Aufhebung*, or "overcoming," but a sense that the ghost of Hegel lurked everywhere may have led these thinkers to load certain categories with unnecessary baggage. See especially Jacques Derrida, *Of Grammatology*, trans. Gayatri Chakravorty Spivak (Baltimore: Johns Hopkins University Press, 1976), 25.

17   Richard Rorty, *Philosophy and the Mirror of Nature* (Princeton: Princeton University Press 1979).

18   Georgia Warnke makes the point nicely in specifying the central Heideggerian insight influencing Hans-Georg Gadamer. See her *Gadamer: Hermeneutics, Tradition and Reason* (Stanford: Stanford University Press, 1987), 40.

19   Jean-François Lyotard's *The Postmodern Condition A Report on Knowledge*, trans. Geoff Bennington and Brian Massumi (Minneapolis. University of Minnesota Press, 1984; orig. French edn 1979) focused attention on these possibilities within the postmodern discussion.

20   Robert C. Solomon, *In the Spirit of Hegel* (New York: Oxford University Press, 1983) 14–16, 636–637. Ludwig Wittgenstein, *Philosophical Investigations*, trans. G.E.M. Anscombe, 3rd edn (New York Macmillan, n.d.), no. 83 (p. 39e): Michael Ryan, *Marxism and Deconstruction: A Critical Articulation* (Baltimore: Johns Hopkins University Press, 1982), 21: Brook Thomas, *The New Historicism and Other Old-Fashioned Topics* (Princeton: Princeton University Press. 1991), 215–216. I discuss Rorty in chap. 10.

21   The notion of "weakness" in recent humanistic discussion is associated especially with the Italian Gianni Vattimo, whose thinking derives from his innovative and illuminating synthesis of Nietzsche and Heidegger. For a good brief introduction, see his "Dialettica, differenza, pensiero debole," in *Il pensiero debole*, ed. Gianni Vattimo and Pier Aldo Rovatti (Milan Feltrinelli, 1983), 12–28. In English, see Gianni Vattimo, *The End of Modernity: Nihilism and Hermeneutics in Postmodern Culture*, trans. Jon R. Snyder (Baltimore: Johns Hopkins University Press, 1988, orig. Italian edn 1985). Although I am indebted to Vattimo's work, I depart from his position in accenting the divergence between Nietzsche and Heidegger within the postmetaphysical space, as well as the scope for a constructive alternative between the extremes they were the first to establish. Thus my use of the term "weak" is not precisely congruent with Vattimo's.

CHAPTER 37

Carolyn Steedman

DUST (2001)*

The next reading is taken from Carolyn Steedman's chapter, 'About Ends: On How the End is Different From an Ending', which appears in her book *Dust* (2001). In the extract, Steedman, who is Professor of History at the University of Warwick, argues that while poems and novels (while literature) have an end ('at the end of the novel, no matter how arbitrary and strange that ending may be, you know that there has been someone there all along, who knew the story, all of it, from beginning to end, and was able to bring you to this place, this ending, now'), and while histories do indeed reach conclusions, they also have inscribed within

---

* Carolyn Steedman (2001) 'About Ends: On How the End is Different From an Ending', *Dust*, Manchester: Manchester University Press, pp. 142–54.

them the understanding – sometimes raised to the surface of the text – that 'things are not over, that the story isn't finished, and that it can't ever be completed. For some new item of information may always come along to alter the account as it has been given. (And also because – the most obvious of points – we have not yet come to the end of it.)' All historians, as Steedman puts it, 'including even the most purblind empiricists, recognise this in their acts of writing: they are *telling the only story that has no end*'.

If endings are what historians deal in, and if these must be arbitrarily drawn, then so is every beginning too. Nothing in 'the before now' tells us when and where to start, or tells us of significant beginnings. Consequently, for Steedman the historian's 'real' verb tense is not the conventional past historic of 'English-speaking historians', but the syntax of the fairytale . . . 'once upon a time', 'long ago . . .'. Thus, in this simple, disarming way, Steedman problematicises the objectivist/empiricist/epistemological ambitions of histories. Yet there is more to Steedman than this, for in the last pages of her essay she argues for a 'double nothingness' in the writing of historians. Where, she asks, exists the historian's 'real referent'; where exactly is the past thing which historians refer to? Initially, using arguments from Maurice Mandelbaum, Steedman argues that historians, that histories, do not refer to the archive in general, nor to specific documents therein contained. Nor, she goes on, is the 'historical referent' any existing work of history. No, what historians refer to in their texts are what she terms 'anterior entities' which the historian assumes stand behind (or exist before) the archival sources: the historian's referents are thus 'previous' structures, processes, happenings, occurrences, whose once existence can only be *inferred* and never shown precisely because such existences are, precisely, inferences (abductions). Here Steedman makes the 'double absence' point in her own concluding words:

> Mandelbaum seems to suggest that the historian's statements are not inventive, not creative, but rather that the history they write makes references to history – to something that has a prior, pre-textual existence. [But] We should probably go beyond this by allowing that it is, in fact, the historian who makes the stuff of the past (Everything) into a structure or event, a happening or a thing, through the activities of thought and writing: that they were never actually *there*, once, in the first place; or at least, not in the same way that the nutmeg grater once was, and certainly not in the many ways in which they have been told. So there is a double-nothingness in the writing of history, and in the analysis of it: it is about something that never did happen in the way it comes to be represented (the happening exists in the telling, in the text); and it is made of materials that aren't there, in an archive or anywhere else . . . The search for the historian's nostalgia for origins and original referents cannot be performed because there is actually nothing there: she is not looking for anything: only silence, the space shaped by what once was; and now is no more.

———————

. . . but we, at haphazard
And unseasonably, are brought face to face
By ones, Clio, with your silence. After that
Nothing is easy.

(W.H. Auden, 'Homage to Clio', 1948–57)

Y OU CAN NEVER BE quite sure whether Auden has seen something of very profound importance, or whether what you have before you is simply an extraordinarily moving string of phonemes; but perhaps it doesn't really matter which, as we are given his Clio anyway, figured as the most mysterious of the Muses (though mysterious, as it turns out in the end, only because she has absolutely nothing to say). Indeed the poet wrote to a friend telling her that in his view, his Clio was actually the Virgin Mary.

'What icon/Have the arts for you?' the poet asks, 'Who look like any/Girl one has not noticed and show no special/Affinity with a beast?'

He continues:

> . . . I have seen
> Your photo. I think, in the papers, nursing
> A baby or mourning a corpse; each time
> You had nothing to say, and did not, one could see,
> Observe where you were, Muse of the unique
> Historical fact, defending with silence
> Some world of your beholding.

It must be Clio's silence that is her most important attribute here, for the poem deals with reversals, with a disturbance of the taken-for-granted view of history as a *telling* of the past. Then a moment later, there is the grander and more striking reversal of the ordinary relationship between Memory and History (which we have already noted being observed by other commentators) when the poet entreats the Muse to 'teach us our recollections'.

But the silence is the more provoking, for what is left to us if Clio does not speak, if history is not to be something that is told about what has happened, – if really, Clio has nothing to say?

> . . . but we, at haphazard
> And unseasonably, are brought face to face
> By ones, Clio, with your silence. After that
> Nothing is easy.

The recent linguistic turn in historical studies came – as most of Clio's turns do – from outside the field, as the echo of an attention paid to history as a form of language by philosophers, literary theorists and cultural critics. However, over the thirty years the turn took, while the question of telling – of narrative – was endlessly discussed, the dizzying proposal of Clio's silence seems never to have been contemplated. Slow turn, endless discussion . . . In 1986, for example, David Carr was concerned to answer the charge of narratologists and philosophers, that in the historical enterprise, narrative is no more than a kind of window dressing or packaging, something incidental to our knowledge of the past'. He referred in particular to the work of Louis Mink, and Mink's judgement that stories are not things that are lived, so much as told; that what comes to be told about the past is not *part of* the events that are narrated: that telling is always something different from *what happened* (whatever that was). Indeed, in this period of discussion, Hayden White thought that anyone who believed that 'sequences of real events possess the formal attributes of the stories we tell about imaginary events', was living in a fantasy, or daydreaming. Paul Ricoeur had long paid attention to narrative as a kind of semantic innovation; to the way in which something new is brought into the world by language – the words that tell; to the ways in which narrative does not so much describe the world as redescribe – or re-make – it. In the accounts of the 1970s that Carr attempted to displace, the function of narrative was seen to be the way it attaches to the real world a shape and form that it does not intrinsically possess.

In *Time, Narrative and History*, Carr brought his understanding of an *event* to bear on the early orthodoxies. In his account, events are something so wrapped up in and with time that it cannot be denied. Time-consciousness pervades our very existence; narrative is thus not a clothing for something else but, rather, is the very structure of human existence and action. Time-consciousness is rooted in the apprehension of now, of each and every moment of being; time is a structure that inheres in the very phenomena being narrated. Indeed, to 'exist humanly' is not just to be *in* time, but rather is to 'encompass it or "take it in" as our gaze takes in our surroundings'. For Carr, all narratives – historical narratives and all sorts of narrative – are made out of this experience of time. Counter arguments (like those of Ricoeur and Mink) were probably less to do with the phenomenology of time, and more to do with the ways in which historical narratives have borrowed from other forms of mimesis and representation. Ricoeur believed this experience of temporality to be 'mute', for poetry and plot had the power to reconfigure confused and inchoate experience, but plot and poetry were the creative work of historians and other narrators, never actually *there* in the first place.

In these opposing accounts, then, Clio had a very great deal to *say*, though most commentators had very severe doubts about her capacity to explain what it was she told. Ricoeur in particular emphasised the borrowed plots she used, pointing to the way in which historical narratives easily incorporated generalities, or theoretical and causal explanations that came from outside: 'every historical explanation is looking for an explanation to incorporate into itself because it has failed to explain itself'.

Yet Clio *writes* Auden pays attention to her silence, and the discussants of the linguistic turn endlessly debated her deficiencies as a narrator, because they forgot her typical stance, pen in hand, foot on the ground, glancing up from the page, momentarily *looking at you* as she writes. (Or maybe – we must just briefly consider this – the silence Auden hears comes from her not being Clio at all; it is possible that she really is – as he believed – the Virgin Mary.) But in the *Homage to Clio* collection, Auden encounters her again, in 'Makers of History' where he is utterly clear that she is the historian – the historian of the *miserabilis personae* – who cannot care for 'Greatness', the Kings, Senators and Generals who are the Names of History; rather:

> Clio loves those who bred them better horses,
> Found answers to their questions, made their things

Clio may have nothing to say, but she has everything to write. The historian's massive authority as a writer derives from two factors: the ways archives *are*, and the conventional rhetoric of history-writing, which always asserts (though the footnotes, through the casual reference to PT S2/1/1 . . .) that you *know* because you have been there. There is story put about that the authority comes from the documents themselves, and the historian's obeisance to the limits they impose on any account that employs them. But really, it comes from *having been there* (the train to the distant city, the call number, the bundle opened, the dust . . .) so that then, and only then, can you present yourself as moved and dictated to by those sources, telling a story the way it has to be told. Thus the authority of the historian's seemingly modest 'No; it wasn't quite like that . . . .'

History (the work of historians; history writing) could not (can not) operate differently. There is everything, or Everything, the great undifferentiated past, all of it, which is not history, but just stuff. The smallest fragment of its representation (nearly always in some kind of written language) ends up in various kinds of archive and record office (and also in the vastly expanded data banks that Derrida refers to in 'Archive Fever'). From that, you make history, which is never what *was* there, once upon a time. (There was only stuff, Everything, dust . . .) 'There is history', says Jacques Rancière, after his long contemplation of Michelet,

> because there is the past and a specific passion for the past. And there is history because there is an absence . . . The status of history depends on the treatment of this twofold absence of the 'thing itself' that is *no longer there* – that is in the past; and that never was – because it never was *such it was told*.

It seems probable that history cannot work as either cognition or narrative without the assumption on the part of the writer and the reader of it that there is somewhere the great story, that contains everything there is and ever has been – 'visits home, heartbeats, a first kiss, the jump of an electron from one orbital position to another', as well as the desolate battlefield, the ruined village – from which the smaller story, the one before your eyes now, has simply been extracted. This form of thinking and imagining – the way history is – was formalised by Robert F. Berkhofer as 'The Great Story'. He remarks that 'Although historians may be wary of Great Stories . . . it seems they cannot do without them. Their histories need the larger and largest contexts that Great Stories provide, especially if the Great Past is conceived of as the Great(est) Context of all stories, small and Great.'

However, as Louis Mink told us in 1981, stories are only truly narrativised when they take on the same meaning for the listener as the teller: and they come to an end when there is no more to be said, when teller and audience both understand that the point that has been reached, this end-place, this conclusion, was implicit in the beginning: was there all along. Considered in this light, all stories, no matter what their content, take part in the art of fiction. At the end of the novel, no matter how arbitrary and strange that ending might be, you know that there has been someone there all along, who knew the story, all of it, from beginning to end, and was able to bring you to this place, this ending, now. *This* extraordinary turn of thought and temporality hidden by the labels 'the development of print culture', 'the rise of the novel' has been explored, notably by Benedict Anderson and Franco Moretti. In the spoken or written life-story there is in operation a simple variant of this narrative rule. The man or woman, standing up against the bar (in a public house, or a court of law), is the embodiment of something completed. That end, the finished place, is the human being, a body in time and space, telling a story, a story that brings the listener or the reader to the here and now, or to this rounded and finished character in the pages of the book. Written autobiography ends in the figure of the writer, and the narrative closure of biography is the figure that has been created through the pages of the book.

In narrative terms like this, these forms of writing – biography and autography – must always remain in conflict with the writing of history, which does indeed come to conclusions and reach ends, but which actually moves forward through the implicit understanding that *things are not over*, that the story isn't finished, can't ever be completed, for some new item of information may alter the account as it has been given. (And also because – the most obvious of points – we have not yet come to the end of it: the Great Story, Everything . . .) At the centre of the written history lies this recognition of temporariness and impermanence. And all historians, even the most purblind empiricists, recognise this in their acts of writing: they are *telling the only story that has no end*. Indeed, this was quite conventionally recognised when the modern profession established itself on a positivistic high in the middle years of the nineteenth century. It was understood for example, that history would never be able to furnish its own inductive laws, for to be sound, 'an induction must take in, actually or virtually, all the facts. But history is unlike all other studies, in this, that she can never have actually or virtually all the factors in front of her. What is past, she knows in part.'

The apostles of 'scientific' history, Claude Langlois and Charles Seignobos, looked back to the 1850s from the 1890s to reflect on how every modern work of history needed to be 'continually recast, revised, brought up to date', for each one of them has superseded earlier works and would be 'sooner or later, superseded in their turn'. Closures have to be made, in order to finish arguments and get manuscripts to publishers; but the story can't be finished because historians have as their stated objective exhaustiveness (finding out again and again, more and more about some thing, event or person), and they proceed upon the path of refutation by pointing to exceptions and to the possibility of exception. The practice of historical inquiry and historical writing acknowledges its own contingency (it will not last), and in this way is a quite different literary form from that of the life-story in both its modes – the fictional and the biographical – which presents momentarily a completeness, a completeness which lies in the figure of the writer or the teller, in the here and now, saying: that's how it was; or, that's how I believe it to have been. At the centre of the written history, on the other hand, lies a recognition of temporariness and impermanence.

History is not about ends. We have seen David Carr counter Ricoeur and Mink and Hayden White and their claims about stories being told things rather than lived things, about the power of narrative to attach to the real world an order and form it does not intrinsically possess. We could abandon this discussion about whether or not narrativity exists in the real world with the observation that Carr may be right, and Ricoeur (for example) may be wrong, but they all fail to take enough account of writing, and the extraordinary specificity of history as a written form. Whether it is life itself that has narrativeness embedded in it, or not whether action, life and history have narrative form because they acquire it in some way by borrowing from other cultural artifacts, particularly literary ones (the novel again), or not – history does something most peculiar (as writing) and unique (as cognition): it turns what possesses narrative coherence into something without an end, possessing only an ending.

The question of biography complicates the question even more. At the end of a 300-year process of ideation it is difficult indeed to think outside the biographical mode, the telling of all stories *as if they were a life*. The figure of *personification* may offer more than a description of the way in which human shape has been given to abstract ideas and notions; it can point to the way in which new information about human bodies, their workings, their finitude, came to function as the representation of all events, happenings and plots, observed throughout the whole of the natural world. Biography gives a name and a face to the subject that is its reference; history gives a habitation and a name to all the fragments, traces — all the inchoate stuff — that has ended up in the archive. History and biography came into being together as modes of perception and ways of thinking; the life is the analogy of history, for historians want ends, quite as much as anybody else. They, though, are the only narrators who cannot have what they want. And here is a problem: history and biography came into being together, make constant reference to each other, make us see the one in the other, make us think in the same way; but one is about the end, and the other can only ever be about endings.

If endings are what History deals in, then its mode of beginning always suggests a wayward arbitrariness: 'once upon a time' is the rhetorical mode: the unspoken starting point of the written history. The grammatical tense of the archive is not then, the future perfect, not the conventional past historic of English-speaking historians, nor even the *présent historique* of the French, but the syntax of the fairy tale . . . 'once, there was', 'in April 1751' . . . 'once *upon* a time . . . in the summer of 1995'. And then there is the content of these tales: the release of muffled and occluded voice, 'the whispers of the souls who had suffered so long ago and who were smothered now in the past' — the voice of the People — has been the injunction laid on social historians for nearly two centuries now. This is what we do, or what we believe we do: we make the dead speak, we rescue the handloom-weavers of Tipton and Freshitt from the enormous indifference of the present. We have always, then, written in the mode of magical realism. In strictly formal and stylistic terms, a text of social history is very closely connected to those novels in which a girl flies, a mountain moves, the clocks run backwards, and where (this is our particular contribution) the dead walk among the living. If the Archive is a place of dreams, it permits this one, above all others, the one that Michelet dreamed first, of making the dead walk and talk.

The archive gives rise to particular practices of readings. If you are a historian, you nearly always read something that was not intended for your eyes: you are the reader impossible-to-be-imagined by Philip Ward keeping his justice's notebook as aide memoire (quite different from the way that Henry Fielding, who had a good deal of horrifying fun with what went on in the justice room, *did* imagine you, a reader, with *Joseph Andrews* in your hands, reading the novel he wanted someone to read). The vestry man recording an allowance of 6d. a week in bread to a poor woman, the merchant manufacturer's wife listing the payments-in-kind to her serving maid (silk ribbons, a pair of stays, a hat-box!) in Howarth 1794, had nothing; like you in mind at all. Productive and extraordinary as is Derrida's concept of the *carte postale* (the idea of the relationship between language and truth that 'La Carte postale' explores), of messages gone astray, messages not sent in the first place, or unread because you can't see them for looking at them, as in Poe's 'Purloined Letter', none of it gives insight (indeed, it was not meant to) into the message that was never a message to start with, never sent, and never sent to the historian: was just an entry in a ledger, a name on a list. Moreover, historians read for what is *not there*: the silences and the absences of the documents always speak to us. They spoke of course, to Jules Michelet (he was actually after the silence, the whisper, the unrecorded dead: what wasn't there at all, in the Archives Nationales); and they spoke to post-Second World War social and labour historians whose particular task it was to rescue and retrieve the life and experience of working-class people from the official documents that occlude them. An absence speaks; the nameless watchmaker's apprentice is important *because* he is nameless: we give his namelessness meaning, make it matter. Indeed, Rancière claims that it was Michelet who first formulated the proper subject of history: all the numberless unnoticed *miserabiles personae*, who had lived and died, as mute in the grave as they had been in life. According to Rancière, Michelet's modern reputation, as mere Romantic – indeed, sentimental – rescuer of 'the People', serves to repress both his startling originality as a historian, and History's proper topic. Of course, Michelet was wrong, about the Dust, and about the life he believed he gave back to the People, by breathing it in. His dead were not there, or, not the dead he wanted, for they really had never really existed. He inhaled the dust of the animals and plants that provided material for the documents he untied and read; the dust of all the workers whose trials and tribulations in labour formed their paper and parchment. He did indeed, breathe in the People, giving them life by the processes of incorporation that resulted in his terrible headaches, his Archive Fever, but they were not the People he named in his histories.

On several occasions during the 1980s, it was very sensibly suggested by Christopher Norris that it was best for historians to have nothing to do with the manner of reading texts most closely connected with Derrida's name, best for them not to mess with deconstruction because, as a method devised for the interrogation of philosophical texts, its power lies solely in that particular terrain (and that of literature). Norris made this point for political purposes, when an extreme relativism wedded to a form of deconstruction allowed some historians (and others, using works of history as their evidence) to deny that certain past events had actually taken place. They are presumably the historians Derrida had in mind when he raised questions about 'débats autour de tous les "révisionisms" . . . [les] séismes de l'historiographie' (debates about all the 'revisionisms' . . . seismic shifts in historiography) (and which questions force one to ask whether it is not historians and the history they write that he has in his sights, rather than the archives that he names as the trouble in *Mal d'archive*).

What is clearer seven years on is that it was not historians who needed warning off by Norris, but rather a number of cultural critics and theorists who wanted to address the question of history, or historicity, or merely have something to say about its relationship to deconstructive practice. It was the question, or problem of diachronicity (in the realm of synchronic analysis and thinking) that was being raised. Or the problem of pastness, *tout court*. It was the urgency with which Norris needed to make his strictures against revisionist historians that perhaps prevented him from looking at what happens when the traffic goes the other way, and deconstruction considers historians and the history they write. It has long been noted that when literary theorists alert historians to the fact that they write in the tragic mode, or as ironists; tell them that they emplot their stories in particular ways, and thus that they may produce meanings that work against overt and stated arguments – that all of this makes absolutely no difference at all to your dogged and daily performance of positivism. The text that is usually taken to stand in for the whole deconstructive endeavour (as far as historians are concerned) when observations like these are made, is Hayden White's *Metahistory*, a work now almost thirty years old. With Hayden White's work in view, it has been suggested that one of the reasons for the absence of meaning that deconstruction has for history, for the way in which deconstructive readings slither around the written history (or more plainly: do not touch it; cannot affect it) is that their analyses do not have reference in mind. History-writing, says Maurice Mandelbaum, does not refer to the Archive (nor to archives), nor to the documents they contain. Neither is the point of reference any existing account of those documents in already-existing works of history. Rather, says Mandelbaum, what is referred to are anterior entities: past structure, processes and happenings. The writings of historians 'refer to past occurrences whose existence is only known through inferences drawn from surviving documents; but it is not to those documents themselves, but to what they indicate concerning the past, that the historian's statements actually refer'.

Mandelbaum seems to suggest that the historian's statements are not inventive, nor creative, but rather that the history they write makes reference to History – to something that has a prior, pre-textual existence. We should probably go beyond this, by allowing that it is, in fact, the historian who makes the stuff of the past (Everything) into a structure or event, a happening or a thing, through the activities of thought and writing: that they were never actually *there*, once, in the first place; or at least, not in the same way that a nutmeg grater actually once was, and certainly not as the many ways in which they 'have been told'. So there is a double nothingness in the writing of history and in the analysis of it: it is about something; that never did happen in the way it comes to be represented (the happening exists in the telling or the text); and it is made out of materials that aren't there, in an archive or anywhere else. We should be entirely unsurprised that deconstruction made no difference to this kind of writing. The search for the historian's nostalgia for origins and original referents cannot be performed, because there is actually *nothing there*: she is not looking for anything: only silence, the space shaped by what once was; and now is no more.

CHAPTER 38

Joan Scott

'AFTER HISTORY?' (1996)*

The following extract is taken from Joan Scott's article 'After History?' which appeared in the journal *Common Knowledge* (5 (3), 1996). One of the leading feminist historians in the world (Scott is Professor of Social Science at The Institute for Advanced Studies, Princeton University), her article is an interesting engagement with various arguments vis-à-vis the possible end of history, and her ultimate rejection of them. Much paraphrased, the skeleton of her argument might be put as follows.

Despite the fact that at the very heart of the status of historical knowledge there is an absolutely unavoidable paradox that undercuts its empirically based epistemological claims ('This discourse is doubtless . . . one in which the referent is addressed as external to the discourse though without it ever being possible to reach it outside of this discourse'), historians, rather than admitting this, have sought to disavow it as they have dismissively ignored 'mere theory' and 'practically pressed on – regardless'. And yet, as with all disavowals, the repressed has constantly returned to haunt them, a haunting which, at the present moment

* Joan Scott (1996) 'After History?', *Common Knowledge*, 5 (3): 9–12 and 19–26.

has lost its merely spectral 'presence' to become actualised in that mongrel-mix of 'postist' theorists and theorisations that are constitutive of postmodernism. Searching for ways still to validate their grail-like quest for historical truth via such notions as objectivity, reality, experience, authenticity and the like, their lack of success has caused history to enter a crisis of such critical power that even the end of history has loomed up as a possibility: 'when the "reality effect" is either dispensed with entirely or offered as incontestable truth, we have reached the end of history'.

But have we? Can't we conjurors, we makers of something out of nothing (to recall Carolyn Steedman's point in the previous reading) pull yet another trick out of the hat? What if the 'end of history' is only the end of a certain conceptualisation of ways of historicising the past; what if there are other ways of treating that debilitating paradox, this time not by disavowing it but by making it constitutive of a new sort of history? A new phoenix from the ashes? Is it possible? Yes it is, says Scott.

The way that 'yes' might work is the concern of most of Scott's remaining pages. Her 'yes' has three component parts; three replacements for a tired and near-moribund history 'reconstructionist/constructionist style'. First, for history to become 'effective' (a concept borrowed from Michel Foucault), Scott suggests replacing discontinuity for teleology; second, that processes of differentiation would supersede processes confirming identities, and third, a thorough-going historicisation of history would replace any idea that history had some kind of essence which, if it were to be deemed non-existent, then the whole discourse would collapse. In these ways, says Scott, an 'effective' history rooted inescapably in discourse would mean that, emptied of its old significations, the name of history – now the bearer of newness – could remain revitalised – alive, not dead. Consequently, although there is an end to a certain concept of (modernist) histories, postmodernist histories of a type that have not yet been, embody a life after death. And so Scott's final line: 'After history? History'.

HISTORY IS IN THE paradoxical position of creating the objects it claims only to discover. By creating, I do not mean making things up, but rather constructing them as legitimate and coherent objects of knowledge. Construction is a complex process that takes place according to standards of coherence and intelligibility that are widely diffused and usually unarticulated (they function as a kind of disciplinary "common sense") except in moments of crisis. In these moments—when intense conflict breaks consensus, when change threatens or is accomplished, when public scrutiny intensifies—historians feel called upon to justify their standards, not always an easy task.

The paradoxical position of history has long been acknowledged by historians, even when they write history *as if* it existed "as it was" in the form they recount it. Leaving aside the abundant observations of philosophers of history (who, because of their penchant for systematic thinking and abstraction, were placed outside the domain of the discipline at its inception in the late nineteenth century), there is no absence of commentary by historians themselves about this aspect of their craft. In 1954 the *Harvard Guide to American History* warned against a simple belief in objectivity this way: "If a time machine were available to carry the historian back through the past at will, he would confront, on stepping off the machine, the very problems of interpretation he thought he left behind."[1] Earlier, Crane Brinton rejected the "metaphysical overtones" of the belief in "a reality that lay altogether outside . . . thinking." "We can now admit," he wrote in 1939, "that the past . . . is forever lost to us; that the historian must relate his facts to a pattern, a conceptual scheme of which he can require only that it prove useful."[2] More recently, Neil Harris, reflecting on the Enola Gay controversy at the Smithsonian Institution, dismissed the idea that a once value-free history had been only recently corrupted. "It was all interpretive," he said—by which we might say he meant "always already" interpretive.[3] The futility of separating fact from interpretation was captured by the wry definition that Merle Curti offered to his graduate seminars at the University of Wisconsin in the 1960's. You knew it was a fact, he told them, when there were identical accounts from two independent witnesses not self-deceived.

In a recent paper, historian of science Peter Galison has tracked the changing definition of the concept of objectivity among scientists, and his work reminds us that the terms I have been using—history, reality, interpretation, objectivity—must themselves be historicized. (Galison shows that objectivity in the early nineteenth century dealt not with human perception, but with the mechanical transmission of images. Later, when objectivity referred to the activity of scientists, it included, first, qualities of morality and, then, the training of Judgment.)[4] I think Galison's project is one we could undertake in relation to history; rather than treating the "objectivity question" as a static question whose meaning was fixed once it was posed, it would be interesting to analyze the changing meanings historians have attributed to terms such as objectivity. That, however, is not my purpose here.

Instead, I want to remind us of the fact that there is a paradox at the heart of the historian's practice: the reality to which the historian's interpretation refers is produced by that interpretation, yet the legitimacy of the interpretation is said to rest on its faithfulness to a reality that lies outside, or exists prior to, interpretation. History functions through an inextricable connection between reality and interpretation that is nonetheless denied by positing reality and interpretation as separate and separable entities. The historian's inevitable dilemma consists in the need simultaneously to avow interpretation and to disavow the productive role interpretation plays in the construction of knowledge. This dilemma is not a new discovery, neither the product of the ravings of radical relativists nor the by-product of some nihilistic "deconstructionism"; it inheres in the practice of history itself.

To say that historical reality is produced by the interpretive practice called history is not to deny the seriousness or the usefulness of the enterprise. It just calls analytic attention to the interpretive operations of the discipline, to the various ways it achieves its authority. I find Roland Barthes' structuralist dissection of some of these operations extremely useful; it is unsurpassed in its clarity and constructiveness and so provides me with a framework for thinking about our contemporary debates on these issues. Barthes points out that historical discourse claims merely to report what, in fact, it constructs and it does this in a number of ways. It suppresses the subjective or emotive presence of the historian, substituting for him (or her) an "objective" person; then, since there is no "sign referring to the sender of the historical message, history seems to *tell itself*."[5] This Barthes calls the "referential illusion" because it establishes the (false) impression that what is being referred to exists entirely apart from the story being told about it: "[F]act never has any but a linguistic existence (as the term of discourse), yet everything happens as if this linguistic existence were merely a pure and simple 'copy' of *another* existence, situated in an extra-structural field, the 'real'". Not only must the voice of the historian be rendered neutral or silent to achieve this effect, his writing also employs a "two-term semantic schema" that equates referent and signified. In this way the troubling intervention of language (the presence of the signified) in the representation of the real is denied. The signifier is taken as a faithful reflection of the referent; signified and referent thus become one: "[I]n 'objective' history, the 'real' is never anything but an unformulated signified, sheltered behind the apparent omnipotence of the referent. This situation defines what we might call the *reality effect*".

Barthes' use of the terms "referential illusion" and "reality effect" have often been taken as debunking measures, aimed at undermining history's authority to tell us what happened in the past. But this negative impact would be so only if we took the naïve philosophical position that external reality has the power to imprint itself directly on the human mind. If we do not believe that that is the case, then we cannot avoid the questions Barthes poses about representation and signification. By problematizing the ways in which signification shapes the past, we can critically examine the knowledge we are being given and the knowledge we ourselves produce.

But there is more to it than that. Barthes' analysis of historical discourse has the virtue, for me at least, of describing not only how historical knowledge is produced and how it achieves its authority, but also why reinterpretation and revision are such troubling, vital, and contested issues: what is at stake is "reality itself":

> The extrusion of the signified outside the 'objective' discourse, letting the "real" and its expression apparently confront each other, does not fail to produce a new meaning, so true is it, once more, that within a system any absence of an element is itself a signification. This new meaning—extensive to all historical discourse and ultimately defining its pertinence—is reality itself. . . .

One of the assets of this process is its openness to change: the pursuit of an ever-elusive "real" leads to new objects of knowledge and new interpretations that reorganize reality. The reorganization alters not only our understanding of the past, but our sense of possibility for the future. (This is surely the import of the adage, "every generation writes its own history.") If the opening to the future is an asset, it is also a liability because it exposes the instability of reality, its dependence, finally, on the discourse that signifies it. Even when change comes in "scientific" form with the discovery of new evidence or with the introduction of new documentation to support a new interpretation, the fact that historical knowledge can be revised is unsettling. How much evidence is required to challenge a prevailing understanding of the past? What is the test of validity that will prove the superiority of the new story? There are no ready answers to these questions. What then is the appeal against false revisionism and misinterpretation? The answers given by some historians—[. . .] are not definitive; they recognize the complexity involved in establishing facts; they live with plausibility instead of truth; they make judgments according to changing disciplinary standards of procedure and coherence.

But complexity of this kind is not easy to live with at moments of heated political debate about the past and the future. At those moments—and we are in one of them now—the quest for truth becomes a way to banish the paradox at the heart of historical knowledge. In response to the paradox that cannot be resolved ("This discourse is doubtless the only one in which the referent is addressed as external to the discourse though without its ever being possible to reach it outside this discourse"), some historians have sought ways to install truth—in its many guises as objectivity, reality, experience, authenticity, human nature, or transcendent morality—as the guarantor of the knowledge they in fact produce. This effort not only does violence to historical practice by repressing the interpretation that makes sense of the past and links it to a future we might have a hand in making, it also substitutes dogma for open-ended inquiry. When the "reality effect" is either dispensed with entirely or offered as incontestable truth, we have reached the end of history.

[. . .]

Is there history after the "end of history"?

Much has been written lately about history after the "linguistic turn"—can it exist without foundations? Are the referents really real? In these debates, historians have spent a good deal of time fruitlessly trying to sever the inseparable connection between reality and interpretation by defending truth, facticity, and objectivity, or seeking to specify limits to interpretation. The far more troubling question—about the practice of history after the "end of history"—has been given decidedly less play. Perhaps that is because there has been no shortage of demand for the services of historians as providers of birth certificates and titles of ownership for politicized identities. Perhaps that is because the heightened public interest in history (theme parks, specialized magazines, museums, local societies, a television cable channel, and even the debates about interpretation and ownership) has been misread as a confirmation of the vitality of a history that still looks to the future. Perhaps it is simply because we have taken every invocation of "history" to mean the same thing.

What would it mean to think about our practice in the face of the declared "end of history"? How might we rescue time (and so some sense of futurity) without reintroducing teleology? How can we argue for the validity of one account over another? How can we work with the "referential illusion" without repressing interpretation in the name of truth? There have been answers offered to these questions, but because they make interpretation (the production of knowledge and its categories) the object of historical inquiry, they have often been rejected as themselves causing the end of history. I want to argue a contrary proposition: it is precisely by reconceptualizing the object of historical inquiry that we can maintain (in the current discursive context) the connection between history and time.

There are at least three aspects to such a reconceptualization. The first takes *discontinuity*, not continuity or linear development, to be the operative principle of history. The second is concerned not with lineages for difference, but with *processes of differentiation*. And the third *historicizes interpretation*, understanding it not as a shameful distortion of objectivity, but as the very source of knowledge itself.

Discontinuity

If teleology implies an "end of history," discontinuity keeps it forever open. The present is understood to have resulted from its break with the past (however many elements or traces of the past are sedimented into contemporary actions and behaviors). Historical investigation locates the breaks, describes them as the deviations they are from established norms, and attempts to account for their emergence—not in terms of general principles of development, but in terms of the specificity of their occurrence. This is what Foucault called "effective history":

> "Effective" history . . . deals with events in terms of their most unique characteristics, their most acute manifestations. An event, consequently, is not a decision, a treaty, a reign, or a battle, but the reversal of a relationship of forces, the usurpation of power, the appropriation of a vocabulary turned against those who had once used it, a feeble domination that poisons itself as it grows lax, the entry of a masked "other." The forces operating in history are not controlled by destiny or regulative mechanisms, but respond to haphazard conflicts. They do not manifest the successive forms of a primordial intention and their attraction is not that of a conclusion, for they always appear through the singular randomness of events.[18]

For Foucault, "randomness" is a replacement for determination; it introduces contingency into history: "We want historians to confirm our belief that the present rests upon profound intentions and immutable necessities. But the true historical sense confirms our existence among countless lost events, without a landmark or a point of reference". The absence of inherent meanings does not plunge us into an abyss; rather, it makes the production of meaning a human, albeit historically variable and contested, activity. If there is nothing inevitable about the direction of change, it nonetheless happens and it does so because of human intervention, understood not as an assertion of autonomous will, but as a discursively situated challenge to prevailing rules and as a disruption of existing hierarchies. If there are no inherent landmarks or points of reference, this has not prevented humans from establishing them. Indeed the "lesson of history" is that human agency consists in imposing sense, differently and mutably, upon our worlds.

Discontinuity posits fundamental ruptures and, therefore, profound differences between present and past. These are not differences that function (as do any relations of contrast) simply to establish the present as a distinctive time. They are more decisive, more disruptive differences. There is no continuous transmission imagined from the past to the present—whether of identity, ancestors, or humanness: "'Effective' history differs from traditional history in being without constants. Nothing in man—not even his body—is sufficiently stable to serve as the basis for self-recognition or for understanding other men". Foucault's histories showed that differences in the knowledges of madness, illness, sexuality, and illegality made for differences in the phenomena themselves, as they were perceived by observers and subjectively experienced. The madmen and delinquents of the past had nothing (but a name, perhaps) in common with those of the present. By depriving us of the comfort of self-recognition, "effective" history not only establishes the difference of the past, its remove in time, it also severs its connection—as direct antecedent or precedent—to the present. That which we take most for granted loses its universal or transcendent dimension. It depends only on current time. In this way, the present is historicized.

This historicizing of the present opens the way for a future. Not one that is foreordained or whose dimensions are predictable, but one that will exceed—in undetermined and contingent ways—the limits of the present. The difference of the past challenges the certainty of the present (its understanding of itself as the culmination of evolution, for example) and so introduces the possibility of change. If neither sentiments, nor instincts, nor bodies have always been as we believe them to be now, then Fukuyama's claim to know "man as man" cannot be sustained as a universal insight. It must be read instead as a political gesture taking place at a particular time. "Effective" history's insistence on the temporality of our conceptual categories denies the totalizing power of any system of thought, any regime of truth. The result does not guarantee progress; but it does support belief in futurity.

Certeau ties such a belief to history's ethical project, a project in which time establishes the difference not only between past and present, present and future, but also between "what is and what ought to be":

> My analysis of historiography (that is, of history writing or historical practice) must be situated in the context of a question too broad to be treated fully here, namely the antimony between ethics and what, for lack of a better word, I will call dogmatism. Ethics is articulated through effective operations, and it defines a distance between what is and what ought to be. This distance designates a space where we have something to do. On the other hand, dogmatism is authorized by a reality that it claims to represent and in the name of this reality, it imposes law. Historiography functions midway between these two poles: but whenever it attempts to break away from ethics, it returns toward dogmatism. ("HSF," 199)

To get from "what is to what ought to be" does not require that we equate history with inevitable progress, but that we understand that limits and rules (in all conceptual spheres: political, economic, aesthetic, religious, sexual, etc.) have always been, and still are, susceptible to change. From this perspective, "discontent" is not (as Fukuyama wanted to treat it) a distraction; it is, as he also recognized, a sign that motion in space (time) is still possible, that, in other words, history has not come to an end.

Processes of differentiation

In contrast to histories that establish the roots of politicized identities in their distinctive cultures and experiences and so essentialize those identities, I am suggesting we produce histories that focus on the production of identity as a process both of homogenization and differentiation.

Although such a focus most obviously applies to marginalized groups, it also pertains to the study of dominant identities, including national identities. To assume that Americanness or Frenchness consists only in an enduring set of traits or beliefs established (say) in 1776 or 1789 is to accept the ideological terms of national identity rather than to write the history of the repeated and changing ways in which the imagined community was consolidated. With the first approach, historians collude in a nationalist project by abstracting the Nation from the processes that continually produce and reproduce it; with the second approach, they demystify national identity and expose the various differences it has been used to balance and contain.

In the case of so-called marginal groups, history has been used to mobilize protest, but it has often had an effect analogous to celebrational national histories: it makes identity static and invests it in the past. In these histories of marginal groups, the pain of the present is shown to be long-standing, hence that much more intense, that much more immoral. Their demands become more legitimate in the light of their long history. At the same time, past and present are conflated and identity is reified as a universal, ahistorical story of exclusion and suffering. When identity becomes synonymous with exclusion and suffering, inclusion and the end of suffering portend the end of identity. From this perspective, the future is unimaginable. Brown describes the operations of contemporary identity politics this way:

> In its emergence as a protest against marginalization or subordination, politicized identity thus becomes attached to its own exclusion. . . . [I] installs its pain over its unredeemed history in the very foundation of its political claim, in its demand for recognition as identity . . . Politicized identity . . . enunciates itself, makes claims for itself, only by entrenching, restating, dramatizing, and inscribing its pain in politics; it can hold out no future—for itself or others—that triumphs over this pain. The loss of historical direction, and with it the loss of futurity characteristic of the late modern age, is thus homologically refigured in the structure of desire of the dominant political expression of the age: identity politics. (SI, 73–74)

To the extent that histories of different groups both produce and reflect contemporary identity politics, they contribute to what Brown calls a politics of resentment (in which the expression of victims' anger substitutes for strategic interventions aimed at structural reform) and also to the "end of history." Of course, these histories, importantly, give enormous visibility to the diversity and difference we associate with multiculturalism. But they also naturalize differences, making them appear to have always existed in the way they do now, depriving them as well of their specific political significance. Jacques Rancière offers an alternative to this naturalizing of difference by calling for histories that attend to the enunciation of social subjects, to the specificity of their political expression:

> The identity of social combatant is . . . not the expression of the "culture" of some group or subgroup. It is the invention of a name for the picking up of several speech-acts that affirm or challenge a symbolic configuration of relations between the order of discourse and the order of states of affairs. (NOH, 97)

Rancière suggests that the alternative to the universalization of difference (in the culture of a group or subgroup) is the historicization of identity. If instead of asking how women were treated in some former time, we ask how and in what circumstances the difference of their sex came to matter in their treatment, then we have provided the basis for an analysis of "women" that is not a rediscovery of ourselves in the past.[19] The examples can be multiplied. If we ask not how African Americans—as a universal category—were treated under slavery, but how and under what circumstances race came to justify forced labor, we understand the oppression of slaves but have to ask different questions about how racism constructs black identity today. Or if we document not the long history of homophobia, but the ways and times and terms in which certain sexual practices were pathologized and others normalized, we historicize rather than naturalize both homosexuality and heterosexuality. Or, to take up the question of national identity again, if we ask not what it means to be an American, but how Americanness has been defined—and by whom—over time, we can write the history of the United States not as the realization of an essence, but as the story of ongoing political contestation around terms and practices that are at once durable and changeable.

This kind of history requires a certain *dis*identification with the objects of our inquiry, a deliberate effort to separate ourselves from others who seem to be like us. The relationship between identity and identification changes. Making identity a contingent, historical event, not a fixed property, creates analytic distance not only between ourselves and our objects, but also on our own sense of self: "History becomes 'effective' to the degree that it introduces discontinuity into our very being. . . . It will uproot its traditional foundations and relentlessly disrupt its pretended continuity" ("NGH," 154). Identity, in other words, is not a fixed set of attributes into which one is born; rather, it has multiple and contradictory aspects that are contextually articulated and that change. And this reconceptualization of identity problematizes the question of identification by complicating the terms of (self-)recognition. If "women" have not always been the same, what aspects of myself can I find in "women" of the past?

The analysis of processes of differentiation is not a matter of applying a predetermined grid to events of the past—not a matter of assuming that the differences (national, ethnic, racial, religious, class, sexual, etc.) that order our social relationships always have been or will be the same. For this reason, it is necessary to historicize the terms of difference themselves. This historicization refers us back to the question of discontinuity (of the different meanings of apparently similar words) and it brings us to the question of interpretation. For if the historical analysis of differentiation I am proposing is premised on discontinuity, it takes interpretation as one of its objects. Interpretation is the means by which we participate in shaping reality.

Historicizing interpretation

What if instead of thinking of interpretation as something historians (and others) do to the facts of history, we thought of interpretation as a fact of history? By this I do not mean simply that no fact can be known without interpretation (that, to put it in other terms, historians produce knowledge), but that interpretation inheres in social phenomena—in institutions, relationships, political systems, markets, as well as in various forms of written texts. The study of the history of these phenomena is, at its most profound, an analysis of changing interpretations. As Foucault puts it:

> If interpretation were the slow exposure of the meaning hidden in an origin, then only metaphysics could interpret the development of humanity. But if interpretation is the violent or surreptitious appropriation of a system of rules, which in itself has no essential meaning, in order to impose a direction, to bend it to a new will, to force its participation in a different game, and to subject it to secondary rules, then the development of humanity is a series of interpretations. The role of genealogy is to record its history: the history of morals, ideals, and metaphysical concepts, the history of the concept of liberty or of the ascetic life; as they stand for the emergence of different interpretations, they must be made to appear as events on the stage of historical process. ("NGH," 151–52)

This kind of history understands facts to be objects of knowledge brought into view or granted importance in a conceptual system; they are the data that provide insight into particular interpretive operations. Of course, the insight gained from "genealogical" analysis is no more fixed than any other. Nor does it dispense with the "reality effect" since interpretations are treated as "facts" of history, even as they produce other kinds of facts. There will also continue to be debates about how systems of knowledge are to be read as well as about their causes and effects. Making interpretation an object of inquiry precludes neither judgment nor the need for standards of evaluation; the discipline will continue to have to furnish ways to distinguish persuasive from unpersuasive readings. The shift of focus to interpretation does, however, entail at least two other consequences. It means that attention to "facts" involves attention to signification as the means by which subjects and their objects of knowledge are constituted. (I will return to this point later.) It also makes visible historians' interpretations, for we cannot read for conceptual differences without distinguishing them from our own.

Historical consciousness is in this approach always double; it is a process of confrontation between or among interpretations. It recognizes that recounting the "facts" of another age without analyzing the systems of knowledge that produced them either reproduces (and naturalizes) past ideologies or dehistoricizes them by imposing present categories. It recognizes that the "discovery" of new materials is actually an interpretive intervention that exposes the terms of inclusion and exclusion in the knowledges of the past. (Women's history, from this perspective, is not the simple addition of information previously ignored, not an empirical correction of the record, but an analysis of the effects of dominant understandings of gender in the past, a critical reading that itself has the effect of producing another "reality.")

Historical consciousness takes responsibility for its interpretations, for the place from which it speaks. "Connecting history to a place is the condition of possibility for any social analysis," writes Certeau.[20] And by that he means less an avowal of the individual political commitments of a historian than an examination of the social (or discursive) relationships of the production of history in which he or she is enmeshed. These relationships determine not the immediate political impact of interpretations (are they good or bad for some constituency or another?), but how they do or do not serve to protect time from ideological foreclosure and thus keep open possibilities for change. For Certeau, a history that loses the dimension of time is no history at all. And a history committed to time is necessarily a critical history:

> [T]aking [the historian's] place seriously is the condition that allows something to be stated that is neither legendary (or "edifying") nor atopical (lacking relevance). Denial of the specificity of the place being the very principle of ideology, all theory is excluded. Even more, by moving discourse into a non-place, ideology forbids history from speaking of society and of death—in other words, from being history.

Assuming responsibility for one's interpretations also means acknowledging their place in evaluations of other interpretations, other histories with which one does or does not agree. I do not mean here applying a test of political correctness, but recognizing the part that interpretation (according to systems of knowledge, standards of coherence) plays in assessment. This recognition makes it no harder than before to refuse revisionist claims about the nonexistence of the Holocaust even if it does not make knowledge dependent upon truth. Instead, accuracy is established in accord with agreed-upon historical procedures. And there can then be a critical reading of the ideological investments of revisionists, a set of questions about the discursive sites of their interpretations and the effects they seek to produce. Similarly, Mississippi civil rights workers can contest the effects of accounts that give heroic agency to government operatives, offering their own readings of what happened, without claiming sole possession. If this means historical accounts are forever contestable, so be it. The alternative (to return to the comment from Certeau I cited earlier) is dogmatism. Only a history that is both the study and prac- tice of interpretation enables the "effective operations" Certeau called "ethics": "It defines a distance between what is and what ought to be. This distance designates a space where we have something to do" ("HSF," 102–3).

The historicizing of interpretation is necessarily the historicizing of signification, and this is the link back to discontinuity and differentiation. For it is through attention to sig- nification that historians practice history, that they bring past, present, and future into being as functions of time. In his recent critique of cultural history and of the *Annales* school in particular, Rancière offers "poetics" as the alternative to the "scientist belief" he asso- ciates with the "end of history." He recommends that history become interested in

> the exploration of the multiple paths at the unforeseen intersections by which one may apprehend the forms of experience of the visible and the utterable, which constitute the uniqueness of the democratic age and also allow the rethinking of other ages. It becomes interested in the forms of writing that render it intelligible in the interlacing of its times, in the combination of numbers and images, of words and emblems. To do this it consents to its own fragility, to the power it holds from its shameful kinship with the makers of histories and the tellers of stories. (NOH, 102–3)

In response to those who fear an invasion of literary techniques into history's domain, Rancière replies in terms more eloquent than any I could supply as an end for this column. I will therefore give him the last word:

> [N]othing threatens history except its own lassitude with regard to the time that has made it or its fear before that which makes its material sensitive to its object—time, words, and death. History doesn't have to protect itself from any foreign invasion. It only needs to reconcile itself with its own name. (NOH, 103)

After history? History!

Notes

1   Robert F. Berkhofer, Jr., *Beyond the Great Story: History as Text and Discourse* (Cambridge: Harvard University Press, 1995), 64.
2   Peter Novick, *That Noble Dream: The "Objectivity Question" and the American Historical Profession* (Cambridge: Cambridge University Press, 1988), 141.
3   *New York Times*, 11 February 1996, sec. 2, 26.
4   Peter Galison, "Judgment Against Objectivity," unpublished paper, June 1995.

5   Roland Barthes, "The Discourse of History," *The Rustle of Language*, trans. Richard Howard (New York: Hill and Wang, 1986), 131.

[. . .]

18   Michel Foucault, "Nietzsche, Genealogy, History" in *Language, Counter-Memory, Practice: Selected Essays and Interviews* , ed. Donald F. Bouchard (New York: Cornell University Press, 1977), 154 thereafter cited as NGH").

19   This is the project of Denise Riley, *"Am I That Name?" Feminism and the Category of 'Women" in History* (London: Macmillan, 1988). See also Riley, "A Short History of Some Preoccupations," in Butler and Scott, *Feminists Theorize the Political*, 121–29.

20   Certeau, *The Writing of History*, trans. Tom Conley (New York Columbia University Press, 1988), 69.

[Wendy Brown, *States of Injury*, Princeton: Princeton University Press, 1995, cited as "SI." Michel de Certeau, "History, Science and Fiction," in *Heterologies: Discourse on the Other*, trans. Brian Massumi, Minneapolis: University of Minnesota Press, 1996, cited as "HSF."

Jacques Roucière, *The Names of History*, Minneapolis: University of Minnesota Press, 1994, cited as "NOH."]

CHAPTER 39

Rita Felski

'FIN DE SIÈCLE, FIN DE SEXE: TRANSSEXUALITY, POSTMODERNISM AND THE DEATH OF HISTORY' (1996)*

In her essay, 'Fin de siècle, Fin de sexe: Transsexuality, Postmodernism and the Death of History' (1996), Rita Felski, who is Professor of English at the University of Virginia, engages with the 'end of history' only to recoil from its implications, not least because of feminist concerns.

Felski's essay starts provocatively: when exactly, she asks, did history die? After Auschwitz? After the plausibility of metanarratives had collapsed? After postmodern arguments that our sense of time has become flattened so that we all live in a synchronic, presentist world? And how, no matter how caused, does our sometime sense of the loss of historical timings of time relate to changing perceptions of gender and sexual differences? Felski begins to answer these questions tentatively by essaying what she sees as the relationship – which may not be immediately obvious even to those who have been paying attention – between the idea of the end of history and sex through the now ubiquitous notion of transsexuality – i.e. we live with the idea that we are, today, all transsexuals, 'not in an anatomical sense but

* Rita Felski (1996) 'Fin de Siècle, Fin de sexe: Transsexuality, Postmodernism and the Death of History', *New Literary History*, 27(2): 337–49.

rather in the more general sense of transvestitism, of playing with the commutability of the signs of sex': things that have been kept apart, things that made us really different, are now in the process of elision. Boundaries mutate and become fuzzy, edges are blurred, the inside and outside interpenetrate; relativism rules. And, 'historically speaking', the sense of the (historicised) past as distinct from the present collapses, is reduced to presentist productions. 'History' is no longer back there, different from us, but is constituted by us: the historicised past is just us, back there. It is no longer obvious where once reality ends and representations begin . . . and vice versa. Transsexism, transhistoricisations, ideologisations and mythologisations mingle without clear methods of demarcation: all that was once solid has now indeed 'melted into air'.

Of course, these are just claims (claims that are symptomatic of the above condition; of being unable to say anything certain in matters such as these); ways of figuring things out that are, as Felski says, not open to 'proof': 'the end of history is clearly not a thesis that is amenable to empirical adjudication'. Rather, she says, in her essay she wishes only to comment about who is making the running here, what is implied in such talk and the extent to which feminists should 'affirm or question the thesis of the end of history and the end of sex'.

Felski's answers to these questions – via analyses of Jean Baudrillard, Gianni Vattimo and Donna Haraway – form main part of the extract offered here. In her conclusion she states that, so far as she is concerned, feminists cannot afford to lose the idea of history (or sexuality) completely. For history (and sexuality) have more than one referent; logically, anything can live under its name. Just because there is no longer one (or two) 'true' histories, doesn't mean that the name of history is totally dead. Rather, reinvested with 'postist'-type meanings, such meanings can rise from the ashes. In the end, Felski's engagement with the end of history is an engagement that saves the name. In this she is like Roberts, Scott and – to a lesser degree maybe – Steedman. But her views are different from those of Elizabeth Deeds Ermarth, Jean François Lyotard and Jean Baudrillard who feature in the next three readings.

WHEN AND HOW DID history die? Was its passing a climactic and catastrophic one, tied to the unspeakable horrors of Auschwitz and Hiroshima which shattered, once and for all, any lingering belief in the redemptive power of Western myths of progress? Or did it dissolve slowly and invisibly into a phantasmagoria of media images, into glossy simulations of a rapidly receding, ever more unknowable past? At what point in time did the idea of history itself become history, did it become possible to say, "that was then, this is now?" And how does this perception of a temporal gulf between "then" and "now," between the era of past history and *posthistoire*, tally with the claim that we no longer possess a historical consciousness? Is it history that has died, or merely the philosophy of history, and is there a difference? And finally, and most importantly for my present purposes, what is the connection between discourses of the end of history and the end of sex? How do our cultural imaginings of historical time relate to changing perceptions of the meaning and nature of gender difference?

I begin some tentative responses to these questions by noting the pervasiveness of images of transsexuality within much postmodern and poststructuralist thought. For example, in *The Transparency of Evil*, Jean Baudrillard writes, "the sexual body has now been assigned an artificial fate. This fate is transsexuality—transsexual not in any anatomical sense but rather in the more general sense of transvestism, of playing with the commutability of the signs of sex . . . we are all transsexuals."[1] Here transsexuality, or perhaps more accurately, transgenderism, serves as an overarching metaphor to describe the dissolution of once stable polarities of male and female, the transfiguration of sexual nature into the artifice of those who play with the sartorial, morphological, or gestural signs of sex. The media visibility of such celebrities as Madonna, Michael Jackson, and La Cicciolina becomes symptomatic for Baudrillard of a fascination with the exaggeration, parody, and inversion of signifiers of sexual difference which pervades the entirety of contemporary Western culture. Contemporary critical theory itself both echoes and intensifies such practices of gender bending and blending in its sustained conceptual challenge to the ontological stability of the male/female divide. While male theorists like Derrida, Deleuze, and Baudrillard himself profess their desire to "become woman" by aligning themselves with a feminine principle of undecidability and masquerade, so feminists are in turn increasingly appealing to metaphors of transvestism to describe the mutability and plasticity of the sexed body. Two of the most influential feminist theorists of recent times, Donna Haraway and Judith Butler, have both sought in different ways to break out of the prisonhouse of gender by reconceptualizing masculinity and femininity as performative, unstable, and multiply determined practices.

"Fin de siècle, fin de sexe": the epigram coined by the French artist Jean Lorrain to describe the symbolic affinity of gender confusion and historical exhaustion in the late nineteenth century seems even more apt for our own moment.[2] An existing repertoire of fin-de-siècle tropes of decadence, apocalypse, and sexual crisis is reappropriated through self-conscious citation, yet simultaneously replenished with new meaning, as gender emerges as a privileged symbolic field for the articulation of diverse fashionings of history and time within postmodern thought. Thus the destabilization of the male/female divide is seen to bring with it a waning of temporality, teleology, and grand narrative; the end of sex echoes and affirms the end of history, defined as the pathological legacy and symptom of the trajectory of Western modernity. Ineluctably intertwined in symbiotic relationship, phallocentrism, modernity, and history await their only too timely end, as a hierarchical logic of binary identity and narrative totalization gives way to an altogether more ambiguous and indeterminate condition. Indeed, this idea that history has come to an end has become perhaps the most ubiquitous and least questioned commonplace of postmodern thought, even as particular expressions of this motif vary in register from the nostalgic to the celebratory.

My aim in this paper is not to prove or disprove such claims—the end of history is clearly not a thesis that is amenable to empirical ajudication—but to investigate further the rhetorical mechanisms of their deployment and their varying political agendas. What does it mean exactly to talk about the death of history? To what extent does such a claim tacitly reinscribe the very logic of temporality that it seeks to negate? And to what extent does a perspective sensitive to gender issues either affirm or complicate the thesis of the end of history and the end of sex? Through a brief discussion of the work of Baudrillard and Haraway, two of the most influential diagnosticians of the postmodern moment, I will suggest that their writings are in fact imbued with large-scale visions of historical time which are in turn allied to their diverging views of the transgendered subject as either apocalyptic or redemptive metaphor. I then turn to the work of Italian philosopher Gianni Vattimo, which usefully explores the inevitable historicity of postmodern thought, though I will also argue that it fails to address adequately the different meanings and political valencies accruing to particular manifestations of this historicity. Finally, I will consider the significance of discourses of the end of history and the end of sex from the standpoint of feminist theory.

(Trans)gendered histories: Baudrillard and Haraway

Baudrillard's relentless polemic against the pathology of Western culture depicts a world overflowing with meaning and thus empty of it, a teeming promiscuity of information/communication that is obscene in its total transparency. Media saturation, computerization, the imperatives of consumerist and cybernetic logics conspire to create a hallucinatory limbo of the hyperreal which has no exteriority, no point outside the network. Notions of history, reality, and linear time live on only as exo-skeletal traces, fossilized remains endlessly replayed on the screens of our video terminals. Post 1968, politics has been revealed as a self-delusory project; all forms of liberation—sexual, political, aesthetic—engender only an escalation of networks of simulation which subsume, neutralize, or dissolve all meaning. Increasingly, the model of the code gives way in Baudrillard's work to that of the virus, signaling the invasive yet invisible multiplication of contagious signifiers engaged in constant proliferation.

In Baudrillard's later work, questions of gender and sexuality centrally define this nightmarish vision of an epidemic of signification. *The Transparency of Evil* mourns the reduction of sexuality to "the undifferentiated circulation of the signs of sex" (*TE* 12) as the erotic falls prey to the logic of simulation through its own ubiquitous presence as spectacle. "After the demise of desire," Baudrillard writes, "a pell-mell diffusion of erotic simulacra in every guise, of transsexual kitsch in all its glory" (*TE* 22). In Baudrillard's relentlessly heterosexual and sexist universe, this loss of desire is attributed to the disappearance of sexual difference; we have become "indifferent and undifferentiated beings, androgynous and hermaphroditic" (*TE* 25), creatures without gender and hence without sex. Biotechnological research heralds a brave new world of cloning and parthogenesis, of serial reproduction by celibate machines replicating like protozoa. Feminists in turn accelerate this confusion of gender categories by reducing the once inescapable destiny of being male or female to a matter of preference and rights. The figure of transsexuality thus becomes for Baudrillard a privileged metaphor of a general social process of implosion and de-differentiation which renders all terms commutable and indeterminate. The end of sex echoes and affirms the end of history, understood both as a problem of agency (the eclipse of the subject by the sovereignty of the object) and also of knowledge (the impossibility of imputing any meaning or direction to temporal processes).

Yet, even as he insists that narrative has become impossible, Baudrillard's writings inscribe a metahistorical fiction of the first order, articulating a powerfully nostalgic narrative of the fall. Harking back to an imagined era of referential plenitude, they emplot an exemplary parable of the decline of Western civilization from the standpoint of the latecomer, the one who comes after. At one point, Baudrillard writes, "we are merely epigones. . . . The highest level of intensity lies behind us. The lowest level of passion and intellectual illumination lies ahead of us."[3] Such a melancholic vision of cultural decadence is of course a recurring trope within the modern, the faithful and constant shadow of the overarching myth of historical progress. On the one hand, Baudrillard denies the possibility of a meaningful future, claiming that linear and progressive time no longer exist in an imploding universe where history turns back on itself in a necrophilic spiral of infinite regression. In the mythic no-time of TV that we all inhabit, history is flattened out into a smorgasbord of endlessly recycled images of the past. On the other hand, this very diagnosis explicitly posits a history that once *was* and is no more, expressing a profoundly historical sense of the current impossibility of history. Even as he insists that linear time has been replaced by reversibility and repetition, Baudrillard reinscribes a temporal schema structured around the triadic relation of a disappearing present, an absent future, and an authentically self-present, if no longer knowable past.

This point can be highlighted by considering Donna Haraway's very different emplotment of historical time. Like Baudrillard, Haraway insists on the radical transformation of social relations engendered by cybernetic systems, biotechnological innovation, and an all-pervasive dissemination of media networks. She too argues that old oppositions of masculine and feminine, along with their corollary distinctions of private versus public, mind versus body, culture versus nature, no longer hold in the new world system that she entitles the informatics of domination. In this context she introduces her resonant symbol of the postmodern cyborg, a hybrid blend of male and female, organism and machine, that emblematizes the contemporary fusion and intermingling of previously distinct categories. We are all cyborgs now, she states; "the cyborg is our ontology, it gives us our politics."[4] Haraway's transgendered cyborg, however, bears little kinship to Baudrillard's transsexual subject. An ironic and polyvalent symbol of both matrices of domination and possibilities of resistance, it gestures resolutely toward the future rather than gazing toward the past. Instead of demonizing technology and taking refuge in a nostalgic vision of an organic feminine, Haraway argues, feminists need to explore the new possibilities, pleasures, and politics made possible by transgressed boundaries and fragmented selves. The cyborg serves as a feminist icon for the postmodern era, an unruly child of technological systems that it simultaneously exploits and contests.

How, then, do cyborgs embody or subvert existing patterns of historical time? Haraway explicitly refuses the redemptive frame of Western progress narratives as well as the organicist myth of the fall. The cyborg, she declares, is outside salvation history and has no origin story; it rejects the seductions of vanguard politics and teleological notions of agency. Yet even as it weaves its way among multiple perspectives, Haraway's manifesto (a quintessentially modernist genre which her text both ironizes and reproduces) expresses a deeply historical awareness of the irreversible and linear nature of time. Drawing upon Fredric Jameson's tripartite scheme of capitalist development, her argument insists on both the distinctiveness of our own epoch and the impossibility of returning to an earlier moment. "We cannot go back ideologically or materially," she writes; "it's not just that 'god' is dead, so is the 'goddess'" (204). The "Manifesto for Cyborgs" is a text permeated by a strong sense of its own temporality, of the irrevocable historical transformation of our material and conceptual universe by cybernetic and biotechnological logics which have definitively severed us from our own past. Without minimizing the logics of domination shaping our own era, Haraway seeks nonetheless to recuperate both political agency and the redemptive promise of the future. Coding the transgendered subject of the postmodern as liberating icon rather than nightmarish catastrophe, she sees new and unimagined possibilities in hybrid gender identities and complex fusions of previously distinct realities. In its expectant and hopeful gesturing toward a "not yet" that may liberate women from the naturalized oppressions and dichotomies of the past, Haraway thus carves a resolutely utopian, forward-looking temporality out of social conditions often identified with the dwindling of political possibilities. The texts of Baudrillard and Haraway, then, exemplify two very different political and philosophical responses to the de-differentiation of sexual difference as postmodern trope. Transsexuality, as Sandy Stone observes, currently functions as a hotly contested site of cultural inscription; this contestation expresses itself not simply in ongoing disputes between doctors, feminists, and transsexuals themselves, as Stone argues, but also in the more general cultural appropriations of the figure of transsexuality as a semiotically dense emblem in the rhetoric of fin de millenium.[5] Interpreted as historical symptom or philosophical symbol, this figure inspires a multiplicity of claims and counterclaims regarding its liberatory or catastrophic meanings. Nowhere is this more apparent than in two recent anthologies on gender and the postmodern body edited by Arthur and Marilouise Kroker, *Body Invaders* and *The Last Sex*.[6] Here celebrations of transsexuality as perverse artifice couched in the vocabulary of postmodern feminism and queer theory are juxtaposed alongside dark apocalyptic imaginings of docile bodies completely inscribed by intersecting grids of commodification and biotechnological control. While *Body Invaders* inclines toward a more pessimistic reading of the aestheticized body as a dystopian symbol of the omnipresent tyranny of simulation, *The Last Sex* euphorically celebrates this same free-floating aestheticism as the necessary precondition for a future transgender liberation and the emergence of a third sex. Thus the editors rhapsodically gesture toward a "new sexual horizon" that is "post-male and post-female"; their goal, they write, is to achieve the indeterminate state of "female, yet male, organisms occupying an ironic, ambivalent and paradoxical state of sexual identity."[7] If ends of centuries serve as privileged cultural moments for articulating highly charged myths of death and rebirth, senescence and renewal, in our own era such hopes and anxieties are writ large across proliferating representations of the transgendered body.

The paradox of historicity: Gianni Vattimo

What interests me in these various writings, then, is not just the weighty yet conflicting meanings assigned to transsexuality in recent theories of the postmodern, but also the paradoxical reinscription of historicity in the very act of its disavowal. Even as they subvert conventional structures of sociological realism and philosophical narrative through fragmented and multiperspectival forms, the texts I have discussed simultaneously reveal a profound sense of locatedness in time, positioning themselves in relation to past and future histories that are richly endowed with both redemptive and dystopian meanings. This paradox is explored in some detail by a contemporary theorist of the condition of *posthistoire*, Gianni Vattimo. According to Vattimo, the defining feature of the modern is its narrative structuring of time as the progressive realization of an ideal of human emancipation; modernity is epitomized by a project of Hegelian overcoming which assumes the emancipator)' value of the new as a means of transcending the errors of the past. Vattimo thus agrees with Lyotard and others that postmodernity signals the dissolution of such a unilinear narrative of history with its corollary notions of progress and overcoming. What has come to an end, Vattirno insists, is not simply a certain set of ideas about history, but history itself, insofar as history is inseparable from its rhetorical articulation as a metaphysically driven narrative.[8]

Yet Vattimo also recognizes the contradictory nature of such a claim; the elevation of the postmodern over the modern reproduces precisely that same gesture of historical overcoming, the valorization of the new and the now over the inauthentic past, that is endemic to the logic of the modern itself. The critique of history and modernity thereby reveals itself to be inexorably enmeshed within the very Enlightenment narrative that it seeks to contest. As many writers have noted, the announcement of the end of metanarratives thus becomes another metanarrative, which assigns an ontological reality to history in the very act of its negation. Here Vattimo takes Lyotard to task for seeking to ground his own account of the postmodern through unproblematic procedures of historical legitimation. To argue that Auschwitz, or the terrors of Stalinism, have irrevocably dissolved the project of modernity is to endow such events with world-historical significance and hence to reaffirm the very philosophy of history that is ostensibly being called into question.[9] Vattimo's aim here is not to minimize the tragic and unspeakable events of the twentieth century, but merely to note that they cannot in themselves prove or disprove a progress narrative without recourse to a competing account, such as a view of the modern as exemplifying a historical logic of escalating domination. Similarly, Lyotard's insistence on the unrepresentability and singularity of Auschwitz as signaling the definitive dissolution of Western progress narratives would itself be seen by Vattimo as a profoundly historical affirmation of the irreversible change of consciousness brought about by a particular event. These events, in turn, never speak to us in their raw actuality, but always involve multilayered processes of mediation, interpretation, and emplotment.

According to Vattimo, then, the heritage of history and modernity cannot simply be transcended, because any such project of going beyond history must remain trapped in the very logic of overcoming that it seeks to contest. While archaism and progressivism, the idealization of the past and of the future, are both revealed as philosophically bankrupt positions, Vattimo simultaneously insists that we cannot transcend metaphysics but can at best begin to recover from it as if from a sickness. Thus he advocates an alternative of Heideggerian *Verwindung*, a resigned and self-conscious acceptance of one's own necessary implication within historicism which thereby seeks to deflect much of its force. Yet Vattimo is himself, I would argue, insufficiently self-conscious in his philosophical emplotment of the *Bildung* of a metahistorical subject which has lost its previous unconditional belief in the universal truth of history. First of all, such a sweeping narrative ignores alternative voices and traditions within the history of modernity itself; one might consider, for example, the ambiguous yet often contestatory relationship of nineteenth-century feminist discourses to dominant male-centered philosophies of history.[10] The repeated inscription of a single linear trajectory from modern totality to postmodern plurality within much contemporary theory simply reaffirms a reified and ultimately problematic construction of the homogeneity of the past. Secondly, this same narrative is in turn insufficiently attuned to the nonsynchronous relations of various social groups to the condition of historicity in our own time. Thus the present explosion of women's texts exploring issues of memory, temporality, tradition, and change seemingly contradicts the bland assertion that "we" no longer live historically. To assume that because history is not pure event it can only be defined philosophically, to reduce the question of history to a problem in the self-critique of Western metaphysics, is surely to fall prey to a disabling theoreticism unable to address the multiple discursive sites at which the category of the historical is constituted as a social and pragmatic concern. Indeed, from a sociological perspective, one might speak not of the death of grand narratives but the proliferation of them, as ever more subordinate groups identify themselves as historical actors in the public domain.

Thus second-wave feminism, for example, has given rise to diverse and conflictual fashionings of historical time. One of its most familiar stories emplots the historical *Bildung* of the female subject as she liberates herself from the manacles of tradition and the constraints of the past in order to enter and transform the world as an autonomous, self-determining, modern individual. An opposed and equally influential feminist narrative appropriates and rewrites the myth of the fall, situating an authentic femininity in a nondifferentiated prelapsarian condition (nature, the organic, the pre-Oedipal) prior to the alienating subject-object split of modernity. Both of these competing stories have come to appear increasingly problematic in their construction of a historical metanarrative grounded in a normative ideal of femininity, as poststructuralist feminists have been eager to point out. Yet, as my discussion of Haraway suggests, such critiques in turn engender their own developmental stories and binary oppositions in describing how the naive essentialisms and binarisms of early feminist thought have given way to the more enlightened, sophisticated, and theoretically self-conscious perspectives of the present. Indeed, as M. J. Devaney has recently argued, the discourse of legitimation of much postmodernist thought often invokes a relatively uncomplicated idea of progress in its claims to refute the past errors of a univocal and monolithic entity variously defined as modernity/Enlightenment thinking/the Western metaphysical tradition.[11]

Rather than seeking simply to "transcend" narrative or teleology, then, feminism can perhaps more usefully acknowledge both its own inevitable enmeshment within rhetorics of emplotment and their changing forms, meanings, and effects. To argue that the evident failure of Western myths of progress renders any further appeal to history terroristic and totalizing is surely to remain trapped within a logic of identity which subsumes the changing uses and elaborations of a particular paradigm within the binary logic of either/or: *either* metanarrative and hence a reactionary because totalizing politics, *or* linguistic fragmentation and (by questionable analogy) social freedom. One might insist at this point that Western feminist metanarratives, however problematic in certain respects, *mean* differently from those of liberalism or Marxism, because of their own historically particular and relatively fragile relationship to institutional power and authority.[12] The politics of big historical stories is not, after all, given in their form, but depends upon the specific mechanisms of their deployment, circulation, and institutionalization. Such stories may, for example, help to engender symbolic solidarities and affiliations within disadvantaged groups eager for enabling myths of origin or inspiratory utopias, even as they may in turn become regulatory mechanisms of exclusion and totalization. Which of these will turn out to be the case can surely only be answered in contingent rather than absolute terms.

In his recent work, Vattimo both acknowledges yet minimizes the force of such oppositional voices in noting that the new visibility of social movements and minorities has irrevocably pluralized, and hence dissolved, the category of history. For Vattimo, like Baudrillard, the proliferation of histories signals the death of history, leaving only multiple images of the past projected from different points of view.[13] Yet this is surely to construct an over-simple relationship between the universal and the particular, as if the histories being written by women or postcolonial peoples, to take just two examples, comprised nothing more than a random plurality of local narratives, whose various truth claims remained inaccessible to meaningful ajudication. Yet many of these histories seek to contest and transform our view of the past by discovering its exclusions, oppressions, and hidden triumphs, to rewrite and extend, rather than negate, history. The discourses of contemporary social movements such as feminism often seem in this respect to blur the clarity of the ubiquitous distinction between *grands* and *petits récits*. As narratives engendered by a profound sense of exclusion from conventional Oedipal genealogies, they question rather than affirm the notion of a universal subject of history; yet they also seek to reconfigure our understanding of both past and present in a manner that transcends the local. From the perspective of those whose view of historical knowledge is indissolubly linked to the pragmatics of everyday life and contestatory politics in the public arena, Vattimo's own metatheoretical pronouncements may speak more eloquently of the European philosopher's crisis of faith in a particular metaphysical tradition than of the status of history as such. As Judith Roof has noted, such a strategy does not undermine intellectual authority so much as reinscribe it; the truth that there is no truth, the knowledge that history no longer exists, becomes the new locus of the certainty, identity, and will to power that is ostensibly being displaced.[14]

Conclusion

This in turn brings me back to my starting point: the figure of transsexuality or transgenderism as the site of deeply invested and symbolically charged rewritings of history and time. In counterposing the differing temporalities shaping the work of Baudrillard and Haraway, I do not seek to make them represent "male" versus "female" versions of the postmodern; any such move would oversimplify diverse and often conflicting representations of history on both sides of the gender divide. Yet particular cultural affiliations and identifications undoubtedly shape our imaginings of temporal processes; the obsessive relationship to a past historicity that marks the texts of Marxist and post-Marxist theorists such as Baudrillard, Jameson, Lyotard, and Vattimo engenders a narrative of loss that is by no means as universal as these writers often assume. Thus even a cursory glance at recent feminist writings reveals an array of rather different temporalities when it is woman, rather than man, who is envisioned as the imaginary subject of history. Even as they call into question existing Oedipal stories, such texts insist on the relevance of history as an ongoing concern rather than a defunct problematic for many women. Furthermore, as evidenced by my discussion of Haraway, the questioning of sexual difference does not inevitably signal a waning of the historical imagination; rather, it may help to generate powerful new feminist stories of possible futures, fueling imaginative projections of new worlds and alternative genealogies.

Such a claim itself, of course, paradoxically undermines the trope of transgenderism by drawing attention to the particular gender-political affiliations shaping the formation of cultural narratives of beginnings and ends. The end of sex is an idea whose truth is self-evidently symbolic rather than literal, yet even as metaphor it captures only one aspect of the contemporary cultural imaginary. Not all social subjects, after all, have equal freedom to play with and subvert the signs of gender, even as many do not perceive such play as a necessary condition of their freedom. As Arjun Appadurai has argued in a different context, we cannot grasp the complex cultural dynamics of our own time in terms of a single logic of either increasing homogeneity or heterogeneity; rather, we need to consider the diverse and often simultaneous movements between de-differentiation and re-differentiation that are played out across the force fields of cultural worlds.[15] Thus even as gender distinctions are irrevocably denaturalized through economic, political, and technological changes, so in turn the very question of women's specificity and difference has come to the fore as never before. The erosion of gender remains indissolubly linked to the affirmation of particular gendered identities, such that a conventional opposition of "equality" and "difference" feminism reveals itself as an illusory and misleading antithesis.

In this sense, transgenderism remains a necessarily ambiguous figure for feminist theorists. I have questioned the view that symbols of gender crisis are inextricably linked to a loss of historicity and agency; in both the last fin de siècle and our own, this seems much more true of the feminized male than of the masculinized woman, whose ambiguous gendering is frequently charged with historical purpose and an exhilarating sense of new possibilities rather than with decadence and exhaustion. Thus the remarkable influence and impact of the Harawayan cyborg on the feminist imaginary undoubtedly bears witness to a widespread desire for inspiratory icons which do not simply reproduce extant images of idealized femininity. Yet Susan Bordo introduces a useful note of caution into the feminism/postmodernism debate, suggesting that such celebrations of multiple and shifting identities may merely serve once again to elide the particularity of women and to deny the specificity of gendered embodiment. Furthermore, the very prominence of metaphors of transvestism and cross-dressing within contemporary feminism has been called into question by Eve Sedgwick and Michael Moon, who argue that this often careless appropriation works to elide the particularities of actual transvestite cultures and practices, including their intimate and ongoing linkage to the history of homosexuality.[16] The same is of course true of transsexuality; its elevation to the status of universal signifier ("we are all transsexuals") subverts established distinctions between male and female, normal and deviant, real and fake, but at the risk of homogenizing differences that matter politically: the differences between women and men, the difference between those who occasionally play with the trope of transsexuality and those others for whom it is a matter of life or death.

Gender, in this sense, remains both essential and impossible for feminism, which shifts between a radical questioning of the ontology of femininity and an insistence upon its real effects. Neither the idealization nor the demonization of recent theories of transvestism and transsexuality, it seems to me, does adequate justice to feminism's always already conflictual relationship to the male/female divide. A similar oscillation between affirmation and negation also typifies the condition of history, which flickers persistently on our horizon in a movement of simultaneous doing and undoing. Clearly, our present imaginings of time differ markedly from nineteenth-century depictions of the purposeful unfolding of the laws of history. Yet in conceding the demise of Victorian evolutionism we do not negate, but rather affirm, our own sense of historicity, our recognition that certain assumptions and vocabularies are now no longer possible. The waning of nineteenth-century models of history does not necessarily signal a loss of locatedness in time or of the desire to imbue cultural phenomena with meaning by locating them within larger temporal frames. The distinction lies, perhaps, in the fact that we have become more aware of the speculative nature of our stories, and of their inevitable plurality, rather than in the fact that we have gone "beyond" them. Narratives of the end of history are, I have suggested, in this sense symptomatic of the very historicity they seek to disavow.

To put it another way, the signifier "history" has more than one referent. Often, as in the case of Baudrillard and Jameson, the proliferation of diverse histories in our own era is acknowledged only in order to be negated. It is only because we no longer have access to a true history, the argument runs, that we are increasingly surrounded by impoverished simulacra of the historical. Quite apart from the epistemological problems posed by such sweeping distinctions between authentic and inauthentic forms of representation, this nostalgic narrative works to erase the power-laden logics of previous histories, including, I would insist, their problematic relationship to women and questions of gender. In renouncing this unilinear trajectory from the presence to the absence of history, we leave ourselves free to ask other kinds of questions. How do current apprehensions of historical time either appropriate, transform, or contest those of earlier eras? To what extent do these diverse apprehensions bear witness to conflicting visions of the politics of history on the part of particular cultural groups? How can we remain attentive to disjuncture and nonsynchrony in the experience of temporality while simultaneously acknowledging systematic connections and relations among discrete cultural practices? From such a standpoint, the thesis of the end of history merely repeats rather than subverts the ongoing myth of a universal history.

Notes

[. . .]

1   Jean Baudrillard, *The Transparency of Evil* (New York, 1993), pp. 20–21; hereafter cited in text as *TE*.
2   Cited in Will L. McLendon, "Rachilde: *Fin-de-Siècle* Perspectives on Perversity," in *Modernity and Revolution in Late Nineteenth-Century France*, ed. Barbara T. Cooper and Mary Donaldson-Evans (Newark, Del., 1992), pp. 52–61.
3   Jean Baudrillard, *Cool Memories* (London, 1990), p. 149.
4   Donna Haraway, "A Manifesto for Cyborgs: Science, Technology and Socialist Feminism in the 1980s," in *Feminism/Postmodernism*, ed. Linda Nicholson (London, 1990), p. 191; hereafter cited in text.
5   Sandy Store, "The *Empire* Strikes Back: A Posttranssexual Manifesto," in *Body Guards: The Cultural Politics of Gender Ambiguity*, ed. Julia Epstein and Kristina Straub (New York, 1991), p. 294, I am grateful to Andrew Parker for providing me with a copy of this text.
6   Arthur Kroker and Marilouise Kroker, *Body Invaders: Panic Sex in America* (New York, 1987) and *The Last Sex* (New York, 1993).
7   Arthur and Marilouise Kroker, "Scenes from the Last Sex: Feminism and Outlaw Bodies," in *The Last Sex*, pp. 18–19.
8   Gianni Vattimo, *The End of Modernity: Nihilism and Hermeneutics in a Postmodern Culture* (Baltimore, 1988).
9   See Gianni Vattimo, "The End of (Hi)story," in *Zeilgeist in Babel: The Postmodernist Controversy*, ed. Ingeborg Hoesterey (Bloomington, Ind., 1991), pp. 132–41.
10   See Rita Felski, *The Gender of Modernity* (Cambridge, Mass., 1995), ch. 6.
11   M. J. Devaney, "'Since at Least Plato' and Other Postmodernist Myths," unpublished doctoral dissertation, University of Virginia, 1994.
12   Susan Bordo also makes this point. See her "Feminism, Postmodernism and Gender-Scepticism," in *Feminism/Postmodernism*, pp. 133–56.
13   Gianni Vattimo, *The Transparent Society* (Baltimore, 1992), p. 3.
14   Judith Roof, "Lesbians and Lyotard," in *The Lesbian Postmodern*, ed. Laura Doan (New York, 1994), p. 59.
15   Arjun Appadurai, "Disjuncture and Difference in the Global Cultural Economy," in *The Phantom Public Sphere*, ed. Bruce Robbins (Minneapolis, 1993), pp. 269–95.
16   Bordo, "Feminism, Postmodernism and Gender-Scepticism," pp. 144–45; Eve Kosofsky Sedgwick and Michael Moon, "Divinity: a Dossier, a Performance Piece, a Little Understood Emotion," in Eve Sedgwick, *Tendencies* (Durham, N.C., 1993), pp. 219–24.

CHAPTER 40

Elizabeth Deeds Ermarth

"BEYOND THE 'SUBJECT'" (2000)*

In the following extract from Elizabeth Deeds Ermarth's "Beyond 'The Subject'", the author (until recently Professor of English Literature, University of Edinburgh) brilliantly rehearses and goes beyond the concerns that were most lengthily expressed in her *Sequel to History* (Princeton: Princeton University Press, 1992). Those concerns led her not so much to argue for the end/death of histories, as simply to assume it in order to examine the creative possibilities in the theoretical/ideological spaces that modernist histories had once fully (but now only partially) occupied. For Ermarth, postmodernity/postmodernism changes everything: postmodernity is everything that modernity can never be. Things run differently now. Just how differently, only a reading of the extracts given here will begin to indicate, but at least a few pointers can be given in preparation.

In "Beyond 'The Subject'", Ermarth argues that what distinguishes modernist 'historical timings of time' is not its linearity or its chronology, but its alleged *neutrality*. Modernist histories – developed with a vengeance in the nineteenth century and casting their shadow over the twentieth – claimed a universal status for just one kind of timing: a neutral, infinitely receding medium in which everything exists ('we live *in* time . . .'), thus simultaneously proposing and legitimating the 'idea' of time as homogeneous and unproblematic. Modernist historical narratives thus work through the simple conceptual gesture (as Steedman in Chapter 37 also points out) of 'once upon a time', and then makes time 'produce' – produce results, explanations, directions, lessons; produce all kinds of unproblematical (objective) 'cultural capital'. This infinitely receding history produces 'common' past horizons that serve to maintain the 'continuity' of the 'past' with the present and the future: 'even the remote "pre-historic" past can contribute: nothing escapes'. This contrived 'nature' of historical time thus bequeaths to us the idea that time is natural, is common sense: time is the same for all of us everywhere and always has been and we are all inescapably in it.

Postmodernism's breaking with universals, its stress on the particular, the local, the petite narratives that produce differential timings, exposes modernity's sleight of hand. There are many ways of explaining how this works, but Ermarth draws on the differential linguistics of Saussure as a useful short-cut to an understanding of what is going on and its implications for modernist histories. Here, pulled together into a single quote, are some of these consequences:

> Saussure's ideas have radical implications for the possibility of 'doing' history, personal and otherwise . . . For example, instead of thinking of myself as an individual agent picking up signifying tools in a neutral space, Saussure . . . invites me to think of myself as a moving site of discursive specification . . . a simultaneous plurality of subject positive because I inhabit semantic systems in multiples simultaneously . . . I am indistinguishably teacher, thinker, musician, colleague, parent,

* Elizabeth Deeds Ermath (2000) "Beyond the 'Subject'", *New Literary History*, 31 (3): 195 and 200–15.

scholar, friend, driver, voter and so on. I am invited to recognise the obligation for constant negotiation among the many . . . discourses that constitute my context of meaning . . .

There are costs. I must sacrifice my idea of romantic individuality and of heroic, world historical action to which the infinities of modern space and time invited me, and instead I must confine 'my' subjectivity to that moving nexus where I can make this or that particular specification of whatever semiotic systems are available to me. 'The past' is a function of a present discursive opportunity, not a launching stage well lost. In the 'discursive [postmodern] condition' the production of meaning and value does not 'originate' with individual agency, human or divine, but instead occurs in-between potential and practice . . . In the indefinite gap between that potential and its specification lies the arena of freedom . . .

Time in the discursive condition is [therefore] never the neutral medium produced by historical conventions . . . discursive time is a *function* of sequences . . . it is thus not possible . . . to speak, as history does, of 'time'. Discursive times are finite. They are periodic. They come to an end and know nothing of the infinite horizons and heroic potentials of modernity and history's neutrality.

In this condition, postmodernism reconfigures individuality and agency. It doesn't do away with them, but it opens them up for new configurations, new acts of the imagination. And postmodernity doesn't get rid of time; what it does is to point to the arbitrary way that modernist histories have timed time — and the 'historicising' implications thereof.

WHEN *RETHINKING HISTORY* invited me to write this essay using the mode of personal history, I was delighted. Having been neglected all these years by David Frost and Oprah Winfrey, at last comes my opportunity to tell my story to a candid world. But almost immediately a problem arises from the disparity I find between what is personal, which in that never-to-be-had TV interview could be mere gossip, and what might be 'history' in the sense that term ordinarily implies. That is, 'history' as a universal sequence of events motivated by causalities so efficient that, even when individuals do not perceive them, they operate anyway, rather like the ineffable rules of that related, often dysfunctional fiction, The Market. History was a format congenial to the revolutionary new ideas of, among others, the Enlightenment philosophers who, building on the achievements of three centuries, theorized a new politics for a common 'human' world of rights, equality and progress: a world accessible to all and sustained by all; a world literally held in common, incompatible with secretive privilege which extinguishes candour, consensus and mutuality, which forecloses on democratic institutions and substitutes for them a shadow realm of coded recognitions and secret handshakes. Historical conventions uphold this candid world but, at the turn of the twenty-first century, that unified vision seems almost a dream and its founding subject largely a myth. The personal history of intellectual development turns out to be more problematic than first appears.

[. . .]

My intellectual 'development' has really been an exfoliation under influences from a motley lot of interdisciplinary and practical sources: art of all kinds especially contemporary and experimental art in drama, dance, theatre, architecture and above all in language; democratic politics in theory, and in practice; science from empiricism and Newton to relativity and quantum theory, the galvanizing argument about social justice collected under the term 'feminism'; philosophy from Plato – may he rest in peace – to phenomenology and post-structuralism. A handful of texts have been seminal for me but my tastes may be idiosyncratic and not easily transferable. Foucault has been a substantial influence even though I probably would not sign on to most of the particular statements he made; the same could be said for Derrida, and for feminist theory: all especially useful because they were relentlessly interdisciplinary and operated beyond the same old same old. Hayden White's willingness to think beyond the confines of academic history has been a perpetual sign of possibility. Two delightful little books on art history inspired the early and formative stages of my thinking about history, *Art and Geometry* (1964) and *The Rationalization of Sight* (1973) by the late William Ivins, Jr, a curator of pots at the Metropolitan Museum during the mid-twentieth century who occupied hours of Aegean crossings by making notes on interdisciplinary cultural history. His books still seem to me the epitome of simplicity and elegance. But what was seminal for me might not be for others, and anyway my so-called 'secondary' reading always took place in tandem with other reading, of narratives, or artworks and buildings and cities, of social relationships and of other discursive writing without words. In all this reading, history has been the troublesome, enabling language for threading together some possible thoughts about personal and cultural meaning and value. Even the finding of interdisciplinary similitude is the gesture of an historian. And still, it was not enough.

When I first turned away from unquestioning use of the historical conventions with which my education had been saturated, it was through my discovery as a postgraduate student of phenomenology, which questions the distinction between subject and object, and thus the possibility of 'objectification' that, as I was later to explain to myself and in print, was the main business of representational conventions, chief among them history. So I pursued it, through the work of Bachelard, Merleau-Ponty (Heidegger came later) and Hillis Miller, and I wrote my dissertation on George Eliot using it as a methodology. This deeply offended the reigning narrative theorists at University of Chicago where I had (I now think stupidly) transferred from Berkeley after my first marriage. My effort was dismissed; 'Too much influenced by Hillis Miller' was the comment reported to me. Thus was the aspiration represented by phenomenology reduced to one more small-minded, internecine, academic conflict.

But when did the connections between all these sources kick in, and what accounts in the first place for my apparently constitutional inclination away from methodological business as usual or for my sense that the available maps didn't account for what was obviously there in my peripheral vision? Like many in my time, I was aware that the political and ecological catastrophes of the twentieth-century suggested the presence of unacknowledged limitations on the long-standing assumption that knowledge of the past can improve the future. Like many I recognized that even the physical description of nature had changed so that different 'inertial systems' could be recognized where once only a single system had been. Like many I recognized that Picasso and Braque, Bergman and Godard represented encouraging, generous new departures in method and ideas. Like many I was, as I continue to be, deeply influenced by feminism. In an era of professional feminists, I should also say that I am a professional and a feminist, so that my grasp of the civil rights issues that animate the women's movement among others, has played a significant role in my choice of formulation. My long-standing feminist commitments have not been left at the office, nor trotted out for rallies, nor used as a template for measuring others, but instead factored in as part of a wider intellectual adventure. (The term 'feminism' means entirely different things in the UK and the USA, so I have no doubt this brief comment will leave everyone dissatisfied, but then, what formulation would not when it comes to matters of social equality?) Did my particular use of all this have anything to do with my valiant mother's lifelong effort to maintain independence, or her professional attachment to music, or her assumption of universal social equality? Did it have something to do with my father's genius for diagnosis, his ability to go far beyond the usual explanations, or with his talent with the trumpet? Did it have to do with their lack of reverence for the Big Bow Wow? Did my shyness or my strength have anything to do with their long unhappy contest, or with my own experience with the institutionalized smugness of provincial 1950s social cliques, or with the relative freedom and privilege of my early childhood where I learned what it was possible to expect?

But here I must pause because this is threatening to become a history and there was more to it than that. The 'more to it' cannot be explained through personal history. In order to explain this impasse, I revert to the more theoretical explorations which, it seems to me, are necessary guides to personal definition and even conduct: theoretical explorations that are intimately important, but not intimate. What resulted from my dual interest in history and its discontents was a lot of writing and lecturing, but in particular the two books and related articles written over two decades that represent my central arguments concerning what is at stake between modernity and postmodernity, and between history and whatever lies beyond history. In them I confront an entire shift in Eurocentric societies across the range of practice, away from classical and medieval paradigms to modernity, and then again, away from modernity to whatever is 'post' modernity. In this frame the term 'modernism' applies to a profound but relatively local event at the turn of the twentieth century, a phoenix fire of modernity, and 'modern' applies to a much longer epoch. The theoretical arguments involve revision of long-standing and deeply personal beliefs about identity and about sequence, and thus about what actually constitutes the 'personal' and 'history' in the first place.

Realism and Consensus outlines the emergence and mutation of what I later began calling 'the culture of representation': that is, the culture that succeeded the middle ages in Europe and that developed across the range of practice some powerful new formulations and values that produced representation resulted in the development and dissemination of the idea of history, the social form of representation. *Realism and Consensus* explores the way, the Renaissance objectified and unified the world. We can call this the One World Hypothesis (Ermarth 1998b; 2000). That hypothesis posits a world of agreement, not about this or that idea but about the formal possibility of agreement itself: about the possibility of a world held in common, a common or 'candid' world. Such a world first appears fully fledged and disseminated in the spatial neutrality achieved by Renaissance painting and architecture; their production of single, potentially unanimous arenas undivided by Manichean contests and unsusceptible to pluralizing discursive systems. The spatial neutrality of those Renaissance artefacts – encapsulated in the grammar of single-point perspective – announces and validates the power to make mutually informative measurements among widely separated instances: a power available only within a single comprehensive system of universally applicable measurements. It is not too much to say that without this production of conditions favourable to mutually informative measurement, modern science and technology would have been impossible and, as Ivins says, *was* impossible to the middle ages.

In writing this first book I taught myself how to use disparate materials in ways that we were not superficial but not timid either. This methodological effort was essential for locating the central motivating cultural values that would otherwise remain invisible to narrower disciplinary vision. I have the greatest respect for discipline, but I also know that it is a preliminary, not an end in itself: especially, if I want to get anywhere close to the springs of practice. For example, the formal assertions of potential union discoverable in Renaissance perspective systems produce the value of neutrality, a value most crucial to representational conventions not only in art, but in politics and science and history as well; neutral space is the main product of the formal consensus of Renaissance perspective systems. A similar formal consensus appears after the Enlightenment, when history came into its own; neutral time is the main product of the formal consensus produced by modern historical writing. History, in other words, is a version of the perspective grammar of Renaissance painting. But to see this connection at all, it was necessary to go outside disciplinary bounds. Temporal neutrality acts in narrative just as spatial neutrality does in painting: as a common-denominator medium, infinite and unconfigured, containing all culture, all theory, all physical events across the potential range from a supernova to a ringing telephone. While the neutral time of history only became fully deployed and disseminated in nineteenth-century narrative, it had already been codified by seventeenth century empirical science, politics and philosophy.

These related forms of perspective grammar were widely separated in time but shared a primary agenda: nothing less than the objectification of the world. The perspective grammar of realism – in painting or in history – transformed the physical cosmos from one riven by competition between good and evil and divided hierarchically and qualitatively to one unified as a single arena of explanation and measurement. Once the world is a single, thus objective arena of possibility, mutually informative measurement becomes possible. And because these enabling realist conventions are nothing if not circular, the reverse is also true: because mutually informative measurement is possible, the world is a single, thus objective arena of possibility.

The nineteenth-century neutralization of time and its antecedents back to the Renaissance neutralization of space, seem to me to belong to the most astonishing accomplishment of the culture of representation as it has existed over five centuries. I am still pursuing its implications and I certainly have used its methods in making mutually informative comparisons among widely separated instances in order to discover the emergent forms of history. This complex, extensive cultural event reflects a rationalization of faculties that belongs to modernity: it stems from the late-medieval, early Renaissance, and Reformation roots of modern Eurocentric societies, and it is much older than the Enlightenment though not as old as Plato, notwithstanding the claims made in some recent French analyses. It is a cultural achievement born from the late middle ages and one with an importance that is difficult to overestimate. It has supported such common-denominator projects in the culture of representation as empirical science, realist art, democratic politics and even, to an extent, capitalism and socialism; it still vastly influences our most fundamental conceptions of identity and sequence. We are well beyond 'master narratives' here, to the very structures of experience, the tools of thought, the discursive sets that make and foreclose possibilities.

This objectifying effort contains a hubris that can lead to colonial atrocities; but it is a hubris that also has inspired much of what Eurocentric societies value. It is the hubris of the explorers who sought the Orient and the cartographers who supported them, the architects of representational government, the international peacemakers, the champions of 'human' rights, the scientists mapping the human genome, the historians charring the obscure course of cultural change. And if there is hubris, there is also charity in the One World Hypothesis that history maintains: a kind of potential generosity that Meyer Schapiro once called 'the immense, historically developed capacity to keep the world in mind' (1937: 85).

Such capacity cannot belong to individuals, however. Instead, it thrives only as a complex function of collective agreements, most of them tacit and inexplicit. Too often the power to keep the world in mind has been mistaken or an individual achievement and has become the enabling 'optical illusion', as Herbert Butterfield once put it, for a certain class and culture (1963). How these issues produced their political and social implications in nineteenth century England I have taken up in an interdisciplinary book on the use of 'history' in that era as the primary form of social narrative (Ermarth 1997). History came into its own rather suddenly after 1848 in Britain, changing almost overnight from a marginal practice to a universally disseminated narrative format to be found in the work of the brilliant and original Sir Walter Scott and his many heirs (e.g. George Eliot, Trollope, Virginia Woolf), in Darwinian biology and in earth sciences, in cultural and social histories, and in the stalwart three-decker novel which most broadly disseminated a new kind of narrative for a revolutionary age. By the 1860s history in England has become the ruling convention of a particular social order. Dissemination of this idea of time was the work of the nineteenth century right down to the synchronization of clock time for the railroads that was a symptom and consequence, not a cause, of the temporal neutralization produced by history.

The fact that historical conventions exist primarily to establish neutrality is a thought that can be difficult to keep in focus, precisely because it goes to the heart of so many enterprises. Nevertheless, what distinguishes historical time from either mythic or post-modern constructions of temporality is its neutrality. Not its linearity – all sequences are linear, even circular or zig-zag ones. Not its chronology – the Anglo Saxon Chronicle is chronological, sort of, but it is not a modern history. But its neutrality – in other words history by virtue of a certain perspective grammar or consensus apparatus that I analyse as a temporal instance of realism – claims universality for one kind of time: the neutral, infinitely receding, universal medium 'in' which everything exists, a kind of metaphysical ether that justifies mutually informative measurement between 'now' and 'then' over a vast range of comparison. 'History' is the inscription of that temporal medium. All details – this battle, that marriage – are secondary carriers of this main feat, just as the pictorial details of the Madonna or saints were secondary carriers of a similar feat in the Renaissance production of neutral space.

From scientific to cultural narrative, and backed up by more than three centuries of preparation, this unprecedented idea of time took hold after 1800 and remains for most of us an almost automatic pilot. This kind of time has become the only conceivable kind: homogeneous, infinite, unproblematic, unconfigured by exotic influences like furies, or gods or wormholes in space. And the key to this kind of time is its neutrality as produced by the particular perspective grammar of history that aligns 'then' and 'now' into a single system of explanation and measurement. To establish the optical illusion of history, narrative must formulate events so that they require mediation. Hence the fascination with chronological indicators which in themselves are insignificant carriers of the main discursive event. The fundamental narrative strategy, familiar across the narrative range from histories of war and culture to popular romances and detective novels, involves mediations, crossings from place to place, and from time to rime, that literally establish and maintain the neutral time 'in' which alone objectivity is possible and mobility can be productive.

And productive it has been. Historical narrative works through the apparently simple gesture that says 'once upon a time' and then makes time produce: produce results, explanations, knowledge, capital. In fact, production is a necessity, and a way of reconciling us to present lack for the sake of future completion. The horizon of history is maintained by 'the future'; even the remote 'pre-historic' past can contribute; nothing escapes. The more we dig back then, the more we reinforce now the value of 'the future' and its enforced deferrals and deflections. the more we sustain the hope, even the expectation maintained by historical conventions that such inadequacy is only incompletion. Implicitly present losses, failures or separations are only temporary stakes on the way to 'the future' toward which we can proceed in reasonable hope and expectation of eventual recovery, success, reunion.

The problem with all this, including my own comparative historical methodology, is that, along with the entire culture of representation including empiricism and presumably representational (democratic) political institutions, history is having to face its own historicity. My early and continuing exploration of the postmodern challenges to modernity convinced me that the challenges to its 'objectivity' are too many simply to dismiss or ignore. The emergent causalities of history do not allow for the operation of chance or luck, even though those forces manifestly operate in ordinary affairs. The description of nature's laws has modified those established by Newton. It has been nearly a century since neutrality all but disappeared from time and space in art; and more recently neutrality has stood by in blue berets helpless to prevent bloodbaths in Europe and the Middle East. In 'A Brief History of History' (1998) I explore ways in which the search for causes, along with other historical usages, may themselves have become part of the problem in the difficult effort to understand exactly what it is we are doing culturally, now that the lights have changed and the possible explanations are multiplying. In general a multitude of symptoms across the range of cultural practice reveal that the founding assumptions of history have reached a point of mutation or reformation – a liminal condition that requires us to recognize the historicity of history. It, too, is a cultural production, a discursive function. Some recognize these symptoms of cultural change with delight; others are brought kicking and screaming to the work that reveals incontrovertibly the symptomatic evidence that history belongs to what (improving on Lyotard) I call 'the discursive condition' (Ermarth 2000: 408). Some seem to fund this recognition excessively trying and can be seen running away in an opposite direction, as, for example, with the tiny souls who write on the postmodern for the *Times Literary Supplement*. But wishing it away will not make it so, and Mr Podsnap has been gone these 150 years.

When I considered historical conventions as historically finite, it was easier to see the full extent to which they appear elusively paradoxical. The very act of moving attention, of creating gaps to be mediated, actually constructs the very neutrality that supposedly enables the mediation in the first place. The mediation is what causes neutrality to materialize. And that mediation is implicitly saturated with consciousness which does raise questions such as 'whose consciousness?' But historical narrative makes a point of masking its mechanisms; that is the irresistible appeal of its 'objectivity' – it masks the fact that it is an 'objectification'. Perhaps my interest in unmasking its mechanisms comes from some dim awareness that, as Borges likes to demonstrate in his stories, inattention to the mechanism can be fatal. In any case, historical mediation literally produces neutral time; that is above all what history 'represents', its 'objects' functioning only as markers or carriers for the larger project of objectification, just as the 'objects' of Raphael or Piero were only carriers for the more powerful generalization about space and the objectifiable world.

In historical narrative, quantitative distance-markers are especially conspicuous; they are easy to visualize in terms of pictorial representation, thanks to our deep cultural familiarity with the perspective grammar that Renaissance architects, painters and theorists have disseminated. In temporality, the most obvious distance markers are chronological indicators; these are especially familiar in academic contexts where 'periods' and 'centuries' seem almost to constitute the building blocks of intellectual life. We teach courses and read books with titles such as 'Twentieth-Century History' and *The Novels of the 1840s*. Scholarly attention respectfully stops at chronological 'period' boundaries. Publishers, libraries and universities reinforce these tendencies and collude in the elision, even suppression of work undertaken in broader discursive horizons that do not fit the existing categories, the preservation of which seems to have become a sacred duty.

When history has to face its own historicity, recognitions are involved that are potentially threatening, so recoil from the critique is understandable. Still, it is ironic that history, once an emancipatory and anti-dogmatic device, has nearly reversed its function when academic institutions and publishers reinforce history as dogma. Furthermore, its central value of 'neutrality' has become increasingly suspect in an era of intractable tribal conflict where its consensus mechanism can be seen as a 'terrorist apparatus' (Lyotard 1984: 63–5) because it can only suppress what does not formally agree. There are other problems. The 'future' does not appear to live up to its promises, sometimes not even when that future is only the next quarterly report; rationality does not seem to govern events; outcomes often do not justify sacrifice. There simply is too much that cannot be explained historically and that yet has value. And there is too much repetition of the same old historical stories the romantic, the patriotic, the righteous – that too often function only as alibis. My students have always understood that instantly and implicitly. The worthy dreams of reason and of the *demos*, as the Greeks knew, involve the repression of certain powers that only perpetuate themselves negatively, haunting and hampering it. History is having to face its repressions.

My study of modernity and of history as a consensus apparatus comparable to Renaissance painting was guided from the outset by my awareness of postmodernity in the margins. My agenda has always been to discover what modernity was capable of so that I might better understand the competition. Throughout I have been aware that the postmodern challenge to historical conventions offers more than mere negatives, but instead, openings for new, possibly even more enabling definitions of identity and sequence, for new kinds of relationship with the past, and above all for a new politics, possibly even a renewed politics. Activating such opportunities, however, requires a willingness to move beyond the nostalgia evident in so much discussion of the 'postmodern'. Just as modernity succeeded the medieval, bringing paradigm shifts with it, so post-

modernity has succeeded modernity bringing paradigm shifts with it. It is merely movement, and not movement that can be denied. Even if representational conventions are to
be defended against the postmodern challenge, and there are good reasons to attempt it,
the defence will be weak that has no grip on the opposition. Basic codes have changed
across the range of cultural practice, in science, in art, in politics. It is time to stop flinging
epithets and start considering, in as much consensual spirit as we can muster, the immense
practical implications of those changes.

My exploration of this broadly implicit critique of modernity, present from the beginning of my research, finally found its way into print as *Sequel to History* (1992), 17 years
after I starting thinking about the challenges of postmodernity and after I had published
a promised book on one of the most widely and wilfully misunderstood radicals of the
nineteenth century, *George Eliot* (1985). *Sequel* approaches the subject of time in the postmodern condition just as *Realism and Consensus* took up time in modernity. *Sequel* explores
what postmodernity is capable of, especially with regard to the deformation of modernity in general and its historical and representational values in particular. What is at stake
in this transition is definitely personal, but what, exactly, is at stake?

Once across the threshold of postmodernity — and most of us already have crossed
it here and there whether we like it or not — history in its traditional sense, along with
its founding unitary subject, are no longer possible simply because the postmodern world
is not one system but many. 'The discursive condition' is nor congenial to the One World
Hypothesis, nor to the assumed value of neutrality, nor to the project of objectification
with its emphasis on individual viewpoint and emergent form. With this recognition of
postmodern complexities, neutrality and the rest of the values associated with history do
not necessarily become lost, but neither can they remain universally applicable and, therefore, immune from choice or rejection. They are properties of some systems and not
others, and the choices between them are vexed and difficult ones.

The threshold of postmodernity has no simple location any more than the Renaissance
did. Eurocentric societies have been tipping away from modernity for nearly two
centuries. Non-Euclidean geometry was invented before the mid 1800s, and the linguistic
model for knowledge was invoked in England before 1870; Freud and Marx circumvented
the idea of irreducible entities, be they personal or social and the entire nineteenth century
in France, according to André Breton, denounced the 'ridiculous illusion of happiness and
understanding' that the Enlightenment had bequeathed it. By the end of the first decade
of the twentieth century, phenomenology had sought to override the distinction between
subject and object, painters and writers had abandoned the neutrality in space and time
upon which representation and history rested, Saussure had redefined language as a differential system, and Einstein had published the Special Theory of Relativity. By 2001 nobody
but Mr Podsnap would attempt to disregard all that. Like the Renaissance or the
Reformation, postmodernity belongs to a cultural event of such magnitude that to insist
on assigning it a simple chronological location is to render it almost entirely invisible.
Recognition or denial, however, are not my business here. I am addressing readers of
Rethinking History who certainly will have recognized already that something has happened
to the conventions of historical writing. The question now is what becomes of the past?
And what becomes of the founding subject of history, that individual viewpoint and recol-
lection that I am supposed to be tracing here and that, taken collectively with all others
has sustained the One World Hypothesis and its productions for centuries of European
achievement including its adventures in the new world?

In order to answer the central question about new relationships with the past, I turned to narratives that depart from the historical understanding derived from the Renaissance: from the understanding that the past is past and different from us and thus, for that very reason, a basis for mediation. That understanding, now seemingly so simple and obvious, was not obvious before the Renaissance and was crucial to the Renaissance birth of history. Erwin Panofsky's formulation of this thought remains one of the best because it includes both full respect for, and also the grain of critique of the birth of abstraction that arose from the newly invented historical relation to the past:

> The Middle Ages had left antiquity unburied and alternately galvanized and exorcised its corpse. The Renaissance stood weeping at its grave and tried to resurrect its soul. And in one fatally auspicious moment it succeeded. This is why the medieval concept of the Antique was so concrete and at the same time so incomplete and distorted; whereas the modern one, gradually developed during the last three or four hundred years is comprehensive and consistent but, if I may say so, abstract. And this is why the medieval renascences were transitory; whereas the Renaissance was permanent.
>
> (Panofsky 1960: 113)

The distanced abstraction required by historical conventions of description and explanation always puts particulars into a systematic and rational horizon, the generalizations of which are more important than the particulars which are only stepping stones to them. Take, for example, the generalization that classifies whales as mammals despite their obvious similarities to fish. Because the culture of representation does not allow for diversity in identification – something that prior modes of identification did allow – the creature must be either a mammal or a fish, and so the poor fish becomes one of us. History and associated representational conventions all dissolve particulars with abstraction – for good reasons but with sometimes fatiguing effect. When all particulars exist mainly as evidence, that is, as instances of developing forms and conditions that are abstract and accessible only through a sequence of cases, there is little savour left for the moment, unless it is snatched ahistorically from this relentless 'reality.'

Postmodernity re-introduces diversity, even contradiction, back into the process of identification; it lets inflection back into sequence. Postmodern identities consist of multi-level and sequential inflections that produce pattern without consensus, and sequential linkages liberated from the fatal forward motion of historical causality. This renewed inflection, formerly suppressed by scientistic hankerings for mere accuracy, renews emphasis on the slack, the 'play' available in the discursive element that allows for more than one kind of practice. Poets have always understood this. Poetry can be defined as precisely the demonstration of that play in language that interferes with productive mechanisms, that makes room for imagination, that contains contradiction without irritable, trivializing insistence on resolution. Postmodernity encourages recovery of that amplitude in the discursive element. This is partly why postmodernity brings back to the centre the artistic practices that modernity marginalized: because, as Bill Paulson has argued, literature is the 'noise of culture', its medium of possibility.

The 'discursive condition' contrasts utterly with (I may as well call it) 'the modern condition' because the postmodern medium is never neutral, always 'semiotic' in the Sense empowered by Saussure. In order to understand the role of 'the past' in postmodernity I rely on Saussure's most suggestive ideas about language. First, that languages function reflexively, not referentially (this is obvious to anyone who knows two languages). Second, that languages generate meaning negatively through recognition of their differential internal functions (this is considerably less obvious). And third, that verbal languages represent only one kind of semiotic system and that we 'speak' in many different sign systems that function as verbal language does, reflexively and differentially, but that are not verbal — for example, body language, garment language, the sign systems for traffic or fashion, the sign systems implicit in tea ceremonies or the world of wrestling, on the soccer field, in the boardroom, at the club, and so on. The term for such a system has come to be 'discourse' because the term 'language' tends to invoke verbal systems. The term discourse' lies behind my phrase, 'the discursive condition'. Saussure's ideas, presented in University lectures at Geneva c. 1906–11 and after his premature death published from notes as *Cours de linguistique génèrale* (1915) and translated into English in 1959, inspired his students at Geneva and have inspired creative thinking ever since.

Saussure's ideas have radical implications for the possibility of 'doing' history, personal or otherwise and also for the definition of individual practice. For example, instead of thinking of myself as an individual agent picking up signifying tools in a neutral space, Saussure and his heirs invite me to think of myself as a moving site of discursive specification, a subject position or, more accurately, a simultaneous plurality of subject positions because I inhabit semiotic systems in multiples simultaneously, not one at a time; I am indistinguishably teacher, thinker, musician, colleague, parent, scholar, friend, driver, voter and so on. Instead of thinking that language is only language and the world is 'real', I am invited to recognize that everything is language at every moment: a text, a readability, a writing, an inscription. Instead of thinking of myself as 'individual' (i.e. non divisible entity) engaged in a consensus apparatus that obliges me to discard much of my knowledge and sensibility, I am invited instead to recognize the obligation for constant negotiation among the many semiotic systems or discourses that constitute my context of meaning and value as a sort of environmental possibility. In such ideas the semiotic complexity of my day begins to find an intellectual model adequate to it.

There are costs. I must sacrifice my idea of romantic individuality and of heroic, world historical action to which the infinities of modern space and time invited me, and instead I must confine 'my' subjectivity to that moving nexus where I can make this or that particular specification of whatever semiotic systems are available to me. 'The past' is a function of a present discursive opportunity, not a launching stage well lost. In the 'discursive condition' the production of meaning and value does not 'originate' with individual agency, human or divine, but instead occurs in-between potential and practice: between the not-speakable general powers of a semiotic system (Saussure's *langue*) and the finite specifications of it (Saussure's *paroles*). In the indefinite gap between that potential and its specification lies the arena of freedom and the opportunity of 'the past.' Personal identity can be construed only in terms of the complex trajectory of such specifications, what Nabokov calls 'the unique and unrepeatable poetry of an individual life.' The 'discursive condition' *is* this linguistic in-between. There is no outside to it; we are born into it and into the codes that have been made available to us, either by effort or by default, and that were present long before we were and will survive us. Individuality consists of that trajectory of specifications by which one selects from the range of available semiotic systems and (necessarily) excludes the rest of the vast range of possibility as momentarily useless and thus mere 'noise' – although, as information theorists explain, 'noise' is just someone else's message. In short, each of us performs a continuous daily semiotic juggling miracle just so that we can communicate about the simplest things, stay on the functional side of the road, and generally stay out of harm and earn a living. It is not nothing. However, the intellectual models of modernity, particularly those of history, have told us it was nothing.

Postmodernity reconfigures individuality and agency; it certainly does not do away with them. But beyond the few indications already given I do not want to repeat here arguments made elsewhere about individual agency (Ermarth, 2000: 405–13). I will concentrate instead on the postmodern reconfiguration of time and thus of temporal sequence and our relationship to the past. Postmodernity does not do away with the past either, but neither does it use the past to sustain the universal claims, among them Truth claims, implicitly made by modern historical writing through its objectifying agendas.

Time in the discursive condition is never the neutral medium produced by historical conventions. Like discursive subjectivity, discursive time is a function of sequences, all of which are finite specifications of finite systems of potential. What is realizable are particular specifications of systemic potential, not the system itself which is never and can never be specified any more than 'English' can. It is thus not possible in the discursive condition to speak, as history does, of 'time'. Discursive times are finite. They are periodic. They come to an end and know nothing of the infinite horizons and heroic potentials of modernity and history's neutrality.

While it has always been obvious to most grownups that personal time comes to an end, modernity makes it easy, perhaps seductively easy, to lose sight of that determining fact within the infinities and neutralities of historical conventions. In the discursive condition time is a dimension of events not a containing medium for them: hence the impossibility for a neutral time acting as a common denominator for collective events at the level of history. History implies a totalized collectivity including all and everyone and it suggests that whatever does not participate in the collective sums, does not exist. We see this implication played out daily in the middle east, and on less dramatic scales nearer to home. Furthermore, modern history goes on forever, whereas discursive times are only as long as the given finite sequences of specification of particular potentials by a particular agent.

What then are the possibilities for writing histories once the consensus apparatus supporting modernity has been dismantled? This is the question currently engaging me and, while I attempt no simple answer, I can say that I find promising opportunities in the anthematic ambits of experimental narrative sequences that now are familiar from all kinds of fictions, films, even internet jokes that disrupt the explanatory machinery of history. This new narrative sequence has nothing to do with getting rid of so-called 'facts'; postmodernists are not loonies unable to kick a stone. In 'fact' postmodernity is much more respectful of detail than was modernity, in something like the same way quantum theory is more precise just as it becomes less secure in the familiar empiricist terms. But postmodernity does involve a key move away from objectivity to construct where the past has new functions. Such new relations for 'the past' can be sought in the experimental sequences 'written' in words of steel or sound or stone: in the narratives of the nouveau roman or Nabokov, in Frank Gehry's buildings, in Steve Reich's music, or in the ribbon of stone in Washington, DC bearing the names of Vietnam War dead. Such work demonstrates in practical terms precisely the power to turn convention aside, to reform the act of attention, to ground and limit the very formulation that is prior to any discussion at all whether practical or philosophical. Most important of all such work allows for a plurality of possible even contradictory 'readings' and 'meaning.' Artistic creations, so often marginalized by the objectifications of modernity, are nevertheless the most highly achieved cases of the kind of discursive specification that I engage in every day. They provide a range beyond what is conventionally imaginable. Language that emphasizes its own associative volatility – for example, poetry from Shakespeare to Stoppard – has its counterparts in the street and perhaps even, one hopes, in the boardroom where 'writing' takes place just as surely as on the poet's or novelist's desk or in the painter's studio.

New temporal habitations have been explored more by artists than by theorists despite the latter's use of the term, 'time'. Early examples can be found in Dada, Kafka or absurd theatre. A later, British example is Virginia Woolf's *The Waves*:

> Time lets fall it drop [says Bernard]. . . . Time tapers to a point; it is not one life that I look back upon; I am not one person; I am many people; I do not altogether know who I am. . . . How tired I am of stories, how tired I am of phrases that come down beautifully with all their feet on the ground! . . . I begin to long for some little language such as lovers use, broken words, inarticulate words, like the shuffling of feet on the pavement. . . . What delights me is the confusion, the height, the indifference. . . . Of story, of design I do not see a trace. What is the true story? That I do not know. Hence I keep my phrases hung like clothes in a cupboard, waiting for some one to wear them.
> (1931: 184, 277, 238–9, 218)

The thread of meaning breaks, but (scandal!) without catastrophe. Half a world away Julio Cortázar, another genius of the revisionary sequence, especially admired *The Waves* for daring to stick its hand outside of history. Later still, the narrator of Marguerite Duras's *The Lover* recapitulates the theme:

> The story of my life doesn't exist. Does not exist. There's never any center to it. No path, no line. There are great spaces where you pretend there used to be someone, but it's not true, there was no one.
> (1985: 8)

In place of 'the story' is 'writing' which Duras describes as either the most powerful adventure – it is either 'all contraries confounded, a quest for vanity and void' – or else it is nothing more than 'advertising.' These few writers testify, from different parts of the twentieth century and from different cultures and continents, to the presences of a new kind of sequence in which the past has intense value but history does not, and where temporality belongs to a digressive and paratactic order, not an historical one.

Such sequences depend on digression, or 'a formality of sustained interruption' (Ermarth 1992: 145): a digressive formality foreign to the emergent forms of historical conventions but completely at home in contemporary films such as *Pulp Fiction*, *The Double Life of Veronique* or *The Big Lebowski*. Instead of producing history and meaning, they exfoliate, digress, embedding any meanings in patterns of repetition and variation that mutate in the course of the sequence and often stop arbitrarily. The volatility of association takes precedence over the production of historical causality. We get a sequence defined by its peripheral visions as much as by its forward motion: a sequence by comparison with which conventional historical sequence, moving like a good Aristotelian plot toward its increasingly inevitable end, seems to have blinkers on. Modern history may be plot-like and form-like, but in 2001 it is not life-like.

The past is not past in postmodern narrative sequences, but a present reiteration, a constitutive element of the series. Such a 'past' does not resemble the collective formalities of history. Instead the elements of memory are part of a continuing, personally marked recognition – 'anthematic recognition' alter the 'anthemion' or interlaced narrative pattern described and practiced by Nabokov among many others (Ermarth 1992: 198; 2000: 415). Whereas history has been weeping at the grave of the past for five centuries and attempting to resurrect it, postmodernity simply refuses to declare it dead and thus dispenses with the necessity for burying it. Instead the past is ever-present in the contested patterns of linguistic and discursive recognition. And these patterns always belong to finite individual sequences that replace the grand rationalizations of history. The unique and unrepeatable poetry of an individual text or life does not serve as a basis for the commanding consensus that established the conditions of history and of so much else. What is gained for the sequence is amplitude and inflection, even quality perhaps. What is lost is the power of generalization that unifies absolutely everything according to the terms of a single system of measurement. The objectified universe has lost its (Newtonian) certitude and finality; but then, as George Eliot long ago remarked, finality is but another name for bewilderment and defeat.

Acknowledgments

Some passages and phrases in this essay have been taken or modified from my review article, 'History Speaking', in *History and Theory* (February 1998), and from my article 'Beyond the Subject', in *New Literary History* (2000; listed below). My thanks to the editors of those journals for letting me take liberties with my own words.

References

Butterfield, Herbert (1963) *The Whig Interpretation of History*, London: G. Bell and Sons, Ltd.
Duras, Marguerite (985) *The Lover* (*L'amant* 1984), trans. Barbara Bray, New York: Random House.
Ermarth, Elizabeth Deeds (1985) *George Eliot*, Boston: G.K. Hall.
—— (1992) *Sequel to History: Postmodernism and the Crisis of Representational Time*, Princeton: Princeton University Press.
—— (1995) 'Ph(r)ase Time: Chaos Theory and Postmodern Reports on Knowledge', *Time and Society* 4: 95–110.
—— (1997) *The Novel in History 1840–1895*, six volume new-historical series, (general ed.) Gillian Beer, London: Routledge.
—— (1998) 'A Brief History of History', in Raymund Borgmeier, Herbert Grabes and Andreas H. Jucker (eds), *Angliestentag 1997*, Trier: WVT Wissenschaflicher Verlag Trier, pp. 327–36.
—— (1998a; 2nd edn of 1983) *Realism and Consensus in the English Notel: Time, Space and Narrative*, Edinburgh: Edinburgh University Press.
—— (1998b) 'Time and Neutrality: Media of Modernity in a Postmodern World', *Cultural Values*, Special Issue on 'Time and Value' 1: 355–67; in book form as *Time and Value*, Oxford: Blackwell.

—— (2000) 'Beyond the Subject: Individuality and Agency in the Postmodern Condition', *New Literary History* 31: 405–19.

Ivins, William J. Jr. (1964) *Art and Geometry: A Study in Space Intuitions*, reprint of 1946 book, New York: Dover Publications, Inc.

—— (1973) *On The Rationalization of Sight, with an Examination of Three Renaissance Texts on Perspective*, reprint of 1938 Paper no. 8, Metropolitan Museum of Art; New York: Da Capo.

Lyotard, Jean-François (1984) *The Postmodern Condition: A Report on Knowledge*, trans. G. Bennington and B. Massumi. Theory and History of Literature, Vol. 10. Minneapolis: University of Minnesota Press.

Panofsky, Erwin (1960) *Renaissance and Renascences in Western Art*, 2 vols, Stockholm: Almqvist and Wiksell.

Paulson, William R. (1988) *The Noise of Culture: Literary Texts in a World of Information*, Ithaca and London: Cornell University Press.

de Saussure, Ferdinand (1959) *Course in General Linguistics* (lectures c. 1906–11), trans. Wade Baskin from 1915 French first edition, New York: McGraw-Hill.

Schapiro, Meyer (1937) 'Nature of Abstract Art', *Marxist Quarterly* 1: 77–98.

White, Hayden (1973) *Metahistory*, Baltimore: Johns Hopkins University Press.

—— (1978) *Tropics of Discourse*, Baltimore: Johns Hopkins University Press.

Woolf, Virginia (1931) *The Waves*, New York: Harcourt Brace and Jovanovich.

CHAPTER 41

David Harlan

THE DEGRADATION OF
AMERICAN HISTORY (1997)*

In 'A Choice of Inheritance' from David Harlan's *The Degradation of American History* (1997) the author (Professor of History at California State University, San Luis Obispo) draws on the works of Hayden White and Richard Rorty to devastating effect (in our minds) as he draws a line under modernist histories as we have come to know them. An engagement with the idea of the end of history more in keeping with Steedman than Ermarth, perhaps, his essay calls for such a radical rethinking of conventional, academic/professional histories, that their modus operandi are fatally compromised: after Harlan, histories – if something is to travel under that name – will not be fellow travellers of the epistemological, of objectivity and/or truth.

Drawing on Richard Rorty for his more radical arguments – a Rorty who has travelled too far down the postmodern road to stop – Harlan argues that his importance for history is twofold: his devastating, anti-foundational critique of objectivity and, growing out of this, his belief that history (and especially intellectual history) is not a matter of studying the past 'in and for itself and on its own terms', but for ourselves and in our terms. For Rorty – and for

* David Harlan (1997) *The Degradation of American History*, Chicago: University of Chicago Press, pp. 127–30, 153–7, 209–13.

Harlan – the point of going to 'the before now' is not to discover what really happened back there, but how 'stuff' taken from back there to suit current purposes might help those purposes; the idea is to raid and to ransack the past for anything – images, metaphors, ideas – that will cast new light on the present and help us to imagine new futures. In the Epilogue to his book – also reproduced here – Harlan summarises what Rorty's (and his) sense of the past might mean – namely, the end of academic history as popularly understood and the beginning of something 'that has not yet been'.

This 'newness' has, for Harlan, three constituent parts. First, it would *not* include any claims for objective truth ('it is not so much that the arguments against historical objectivity seem convincing (though there is that); it is that we do not *need* a theory of objectivity'). Second, it is the value we get out of stories which is important (including those articulated in the past tense and referring to a once actually – albeit one characterised by Steedman's 'double disappearance') and not the truth claims made on their behalf: 'It is [Walt Whitman's] "Song of Myself" that moves us . . . not the personal life of the purportedly racist and bigoted little man who is reputed to have written that great poem. If we are told – as the historian David Reynolds recently told us – that "the real Walt Whitman did not, in fact, live up to the vision of America he gave us" . . . all we can do is shrug our shoulders and say "Too bad for the real Walt Whitman". The only Whitman that matters to us is the Whitman who emerges from his poems'. And third, the task of the raider of 'the before now' is to transform some of the things that happened back then – that had significance back then – into something of significance now; a mode of moral reflection; 'a way of curing up life into meaning'. That none of this, comments Harlan, 'gets taught in graduate school goes without saying', but it ought to be taught if the 'uncured before now' can become what the putative neutrality, the putative third person objectivity, the putative disinterestedness and the putative academic (non-worldly) practices of professional history prevents it from being: a primary form of emancipatory, empowering, moral reflection: old modernist-type histories fade away and die here.

H AYDEN WHITE WAS ONE of the first historians to grasp the importance of linguistic theory for historical writing. In several books and dozens of articles he tried to make historians *look* at the language they use, rather than pretending to peer *through* it, at something presumed to lie beyond it. Moreover, in the 1960s and early 1970s, when historical realism and covering law theory were all the rage, White was urging historians to think of historical writing as an interpretive art. And at a time when Whiggish assumptions about history had been reduced to the status of curios and the individual had all but disappeared from historical explanations, Hayden White was insisting that human history has always been the story of human choice, that men and women have always chosen who they *are* by choosing who they *have been*, and that "no amount of 'objective' historical work pointing out the extent to which this *chosen* ancestry is *not* the *real* ancestry can prevail against the choosing power of the individuals in the system." A liberal humanist in the finest sense of the word, White has spent nearly thirty years trying to convince his fellow historians that they can use contemporary philosophy of rhetoric to write good, liberal history—that is, history that not only strengthens our understanding but nourishes our possibilities.

But White was unprepared for the transition from structuralism to poststructuralism. Having bent structuralist theory to his own classically liberal ends, he was unable to do the same with poststructuralism. Steeped in the long, benevolent tradition of linguistic humanism, he hated poststructuralism's destabilizing strategies and its glacially cold anti-humanism. Deconstruction in particular appalled him; he called it a "fascinating and at the same time cruelly mutilating activity" that seemed to tear at the very fabric of our humanity. Finally, in the late 1980s, challenged by epistemological conservatives to account for the transparent horrors of the Holocaust, he seemed, even to his most sympathetic readers, to have retreated. Where he had earlier insisted that "there are no grounds to be found in the historical record itself for preferring one way of construing its meaning over another," he now seemed to argue that the Holocaust—and presumably such other moral abominations as the genocide of Native Americans, the enslavement of black Africans, the terrors of Soviet collectivization, the bombing of Hiroshima and Nagasaki, the French and American war against Vietnam, and so on—simply could not be emplotted as comedy. But by appearing to make this crucial concession—that a series of historical events determines, *in and of itself*, the forms of emplotment that historians may use to interpret it—Hayden White seemed to cut the heart out of his own philosophy.

It is precisely at this point that Richard Rorty became important, especially for those historians who were intrigued by postmodernism and had lost all faith and confidence in history's increasingly dubious claims to objective knowledge (however defined), but who nevertheless thought of themselves as traditional, even culturally conservative historians. For these scholars Rorty seemed to pick up where White left off. Like White, he is a liberal humanist with a volunteerist and progressive vision of history. And for all his talk about antifoundationalism, his philosophy is firmly established on a foundation of traditional liberal assumptions: that human beings are inherently outgoing and creative; that they have the capacity to continually expand their range of emotional identifications; that they are capable of mastering their own history; that with a modicum of luck they just might create a more free and equitable society. And like White he continues to defend a classically liberal vision of individual autonomy and self-creation. Finally, and again like White, Rorty thinks philosophers and historians should give up their narrow and increasingly sterile professionalism and help the rest of us come to terms with "the blind impress that fate has stamped on our foreheads." In other words, for Rorty as for White, history is a classically humanist discipline, deeply ethical and powerfully redemptive.

But Rorty has traveled much further down the postmodern road than White was willing to venture. [. . .] White harbored a strong metaphysical urge to touch bottom, to make contact with something real and authentic, something more ultimately satisfying than the rattle and hum of historical contingencies, something more permanent and enduring than the endless proliferation of new meanings and novel interpretations. White longs to escape what Derrida somewhere calls "the epochal regime of quotation marks." But for Rorty there is no escape, simply because there is no place to escape to, no natural order of things lying concealed behind the flux of daily appearances, no "intrinsic nature" or "real essence" waiting to be discovered just below the surface of life—not by the priest, not by the philosopher, and surely not by the historian. Indeed, he thinks it is precisely this Parmenidean yearning for something deep down in the nature of things that keeps us imprisoned in antiquated and ineffectual habits of thought. Thus when White seemed to retreat to the comforting assurance that the Holocaust can be described only in certain predetermined and sharply circumscribed ways, Rorty stuck to his grim conviction that "*anything* can be made to look good or bad by being redescribed."

What makes Rorty's work so important for historians is that he tries to use this ethically empty insight to support a set of deeply ethical beliefs. He thinks he can use postmodern theory—that garret-spawned world of superreflecting surfaces and endlessly circulating images—to reinforce what is in fact a remarkably traditional humanism.

[. . .]

Rorty's importance for historians rests on two central points: his critique of objectivity and, growing out of that, his belief that intellectual history is mainly a matter of finding intellectual predecessors and lining them up in chronological order. But what are we to make of all this?

Concerning Rorty's denial that historians can produce reliable, objective knowledge about the past, when all the arguments are laid on the table it finally comes down to this: historians who defend the possibility of objective knowledge are saying, "Look, we *can* hold the world steady in our gaze—or at least steady enough to count as steady." But to many of us, historians and others, the world just does not seem steady; indeed, the very ground seems to be quaking and trembling beneath our feet, even as we listen to all this healthy-minded, Vaseline-impregnated, responsible-sounding professional Methodism. And we suspect—especially if we have made the mistake of reading too much Adams and not enough Dewey—that things will get worse before they get better, that only skulls will be grinning at the final awards banquet. For many of us, William James hit it right on the head: "We stand on a mountain pass in the midst of whirling snow and blinding mist, through which we get glimpses now and then of paths which may be deceptive, if we stand still we shall be frozen to death. If we take the wrong road we shall be dashed to pieces. We do not certainly know whether there is any right one."

But the pragmatic purveyors of "historical method" and other household gods rush in to reassure us, once again, that things are not as bad as they seem: "Here is the path, here in front of us. True, there is a precipice over there, but right here is solid ground. Trust me." But even the seemingly solid ground seems to be riddled with appalling enigmas:

> Here is a story that is going around the desert tonight: over across the Nevada line, sheriff's deputies are diving in some underground pools, trying to retrieve a couple of bodies known to be down in the hole. The widow of one of the drowned boys is over there; she is eighteen, and pregnant, and is said not to leave the hole. The divers go down and come up, and she just stands there and stares into the water. They have been diving for ten days but have found no bottom to the caves, no bodies and no trace of them, only the black 90° water going down and down and down, and a single translucent fish, not classified. The story tonight is that one of the divers has been hauled up incoherent, out of his head, shouting—until they got him out of there so the widow could not hear—about water that got hotter instead of cooler as he went down, about light flickering through the water, about magma, about underground nuclear testing. . . . What does it mean? It means nothing manageable.

What does it mean? What could it *possibly* mean? Maybe every event really does contain some certain significance, as Ishmael wanted to believe and as the authors of *Telling the Truth about History* continue to believe. But the rest of us can only wonder. For the truth is that God grinds us round his mill as he will, and all our professional procedures will no more save us than the Royal Navy's measured forms could save Billy Budd.

So Rorty gives up any pretense of discovering "what really happened" in the past. He does not want to explain the origins of Dewey's ideas; he wants to employ them—along with Hegel's and Nietzsche's and Freud's and Heidegger's and anybody else's he can use to fabricate a new angle of vision. He is not trying to explain how the past flowed into the present; he is trying to ransack the past for images, metaphors, ideas—anything that may cast new light on the present. Someone once called the past a foreign country; for Rorty it is more like a huge warehouse, stuffed to the rafters with political essays, philosophical treatises, religious tracts—uncountable at tempts by various and sundry people to make sense of their lives; scribblings and musings written and hoarded out of fear or cunning or the need to establish a small fund of minor consolations—a fund that Rorty thinks we should pillage and plunder.

Historians do not like this sort of thing very much. The labor historian Daniel T. Rodgers probably spoke for most of his colleagues when he berated the "postmodernists" for portraying the past as "a vast attic of referents and motifs open to a multitude of ransackers, not just those pledged to historical rules of sequence and context." And indeed, Rorty's way of doing history—especially his rejection of historical objectivity, and thus of objectively discernible "sequence and context"—may be just what Rodgers thinks it is: an attack on professional standards. But Rorty is probably right when he claims we can learn more than most of us have wanted to admit by giving up our claims to objective knowledge and embracing the perished past for what it obviously is: an anarchy of discontinuous images and thoughtless clamor, a theater of shattered ciphers, all glimmering and sparkling with an appalling brilliance.

Which brings us to the second issue: as we have seen, Rorty thinks history is largely a matter of adopting intellectual predecessors and lining them up in chronological order, so they seem to constitute intellectual tradition. He thinks we should spend less time trying to reconstruct historical contexts and more time trying to assemble genealogies of predecessors. He is right, of course, for all the obvious reasons, but here we need mention only one: the seemingly simple act of adopting a particular predecessor is freighted with moral consequences, not all of which are immediately apparent. We historians do not talk about this very much, but it is just here, in this always complicated and often impenetrable business of arguing with our adopted ancestors, that history comes into its own as an essential and indispensable form of moral deliberation.

Literary critics tend to leave the room when anyone starts talking about ethical criticism. They think it is simplistic and dogmatic, that it deadens the reader to the purely literary qualities of the text, to its incessant play of images and signifiers, its hidden complexities and ironies. They read literature because they like what it does for them, and what they can do with it, rather than for any normative function it may perform. Harold Bloom is a good example: if you asked him what he thinks about ethical criticism, he would probably say that literature teaches us how to talk to ourselves rather than how to deal with other people. Literature opens the door to "that polar privacy / a soul admitted to itself."

This is essentially what Rorty says about intellectual history. After all, to adopt a particular thinker as an intellectual predecessor is to adopt a particular patterning of thought and desire. What Rorty values in intellectual history is pretty much what Bloom values in literature: they both teach us how to talk to ourselves. The books we read, the characters we learn to care about, the thinkers we admire, the predecessors we adopt—

they all color our perceptions and shape our desires. They teach us what to want, what to value, who to admire. In a very real way, they define the kind of persons we are— and the kind of persons we hope to become.

But getting to the point where we can seriously think of ourselves as working in a line of descent that begins with, say, Emerson may be more more difficult, more personally bedeviling, than Rorty has so far admitted [. . .]. And as if that were not enough, it turns out we need a *multiplicity* of genealogies, a plurality of traditions. Nothing less will work in this polyglot America, composed, like Melville's *Pequod*, of "mongrel renegades and castaways and cannibals." Arthur Schlesinger Jr. and some others insist that what they call "the American creed"—always and unambiguously singular—must become "the common possession of all Americans." He wants us to transform our immigrant diversity into an American unity. But as Henry Louis Gates has pointed out, this is "to dream of an America in cultural white face, and that just won't do." Those who see merely a trendy multiculturalism in Gates's caution need only remind themselves that Gates is saying pretty much what Randolph Bourne said three-quarters of a century ago. In "Transnational America" (1916) Bourne warned us, "We shall have to give up the search for our native 'American' culture. . . . There is no distinctively American culture; it is apparently our lot rather to be a federation of cultures." Melville, of course, had suggested as much sixty years earlier.

The difference between Melville, Bourne, and Gates on the one side and Schlesinger on the other is this: Schlesinger thinks the various cultures and traditions of this compound America can be trimmed and shaved till they fit what he calls "a common American culture." But Melville, Bourne, and Gates are thinking of *opposed and competing* traditions, traditions that are constantly jostling and clashing with one another, traditions we can use to confront and challenge other, more deeply held traditions. They think we should concentrate on learning to negotiate our way *between* and *among* these opposing traditions; that we should teach ourselves how to play them off against one another, how to use one tradition to see what cannot be seen—and ask what cannot be asked—with the others.

This is what the historian John Patrick Diggins seems to have done in the best of his many books, *The Lost Soul of American Politics* (1984). Like William Carlos Williams, Diggins wants a criticism deeply embedded in the American grain. And he thinks he has found the essential components in New England Calvinism and the American liberal tradition. Most of us tend to follow V. F. Parrington's lead when it comes to Calvinism and liberalism: they are ideological opposites—the two mutually repelling poles of American political thought. And so they are in many respects. But Diggins wants us to see that the Calvinist tradition can be made to serve as the conscience of American liberalism, giving it the psychological depth and moral content that it otherwise lacks.

Moreover, he argues that the greatest thinkers of nineteenth-century America— Abraham Lincoln and Herman Melville—did just this. Thus Lincoln, apostle of Lockean individualism and defender of "the sacred rights of property," knew instinctively what Locke could never had known, even had he lived through the American 1860s: that it was God himself who unleashed the terrible horrors of the Civil War, and that he did so as just and fitting punishment for the sin of claiming other men as property:

> Woe unto the world because of offences! For it must needs be that offences
> come; but woe to that man by whom the offence cometh! If we shall suppose
> that American slavery is one of those offences which, in the providence of

God, must needs come, but which, having continued through His appointed time, He now wills to remove, and that He gives to both North and South, this terrible war, as the woe due to those by whom the offence came, shall we discern therein any departure from those divine attributes which the believers in a living god always ascribe to him? Fondly do we hope—fervently do we pray—that this mighty scourge of war may speedily pass away. Yet, if God will that it continue until all the wealth piled by the bond-man's two hundred and fifty years of unrequited toil shall be sunk, and until every drop of blood drawn with the lash shall be paid by another drawn with the sword, as was said three thousand years ago, so still it must be said, "The judgments of the Lord are true and righteous altogether."

Many historians continue to insist that history is "an accumulative science, that it gathers truth through the steady, if plodding efforts of countless practitioners turning out countless monographs." What is at issue in American history, however, is not our ability to know the past but our ability to find the predecessors we need—to think with their thoughts, to work through our own beliefs by working through their beliefs. Only thus does history become a mode of moral reflection.

[. . .]

Epilogue

> Where do we find ourselves?
> —Ralph Waldo Emerson, 1842

A sense of the past is a way of being in the present. At its best it is a way of arguing with ourselves, a means of rethinking who we might become by rethinking who we once were. As Tolstoy never tired of insisting, history and literature are essentially forms of moral reflection, tested and accredited means of pondering what we should value and how we should live. Since the early 1960s this traditional vision of history has been driven into exile, first by the professionalization of American historical writing, then by the expanding influence of the social sciences. But as early as 1966 Hayden White was warning his colleagues that these developments would eventually leave history isolated from the main currents of American intellectual life—currents that were even then transforming the rest of the humanities. "The most difficult task which the current generation of historians will be called upon to perform," White explained, "is to preside over the dissolution of history's claim to autonomy among the disciplines, and to aid in the assimilation of history to a higher kind of intellectual inquiry. . . . The burden of the historian in our time is to reestablish the dignity of historical studies on a basis that will make them consonant with the aims and purposes of the intellectual community at large."

Nothing remotely like this happened, of course. And now, as the century's terminus looms ahead of us, the historians who dominate the profession—the men and women who occupy the endowed chairs, run the professional organizations, and preside over the distribution of academic patronage—are more fiercely committed to the professionalization of history and its reduction to a social science than their predecessors in the early 1960s. Thirty years after White wrote "The Burden of History," the discipline has become just what he feared it would: the great reactionary center of American intellectual life. At the end of the 1990s, as disciplinary boundaries blur and the disciplines start bleeding into one another, historians have risen up to insist on the autonomy and intellectual integrity of historical studies. At a time when disciplinary paradigms have become increasingly decentered and irrevocably plural, they reassure one another that we must have "the courage of our conventions"; just when anthropologists discover the virtues of cross-cultural comparison—of placing Balinese cockfighting, for example, or West African carving or New Guinea palm-leaf painting in interpretive tension with our own cultural practices, our own sense of how things stand in the world, so as to form a commentary on them—historians pound the table and insist that artifacts can be interpreted only in their proper historical contexts. This last obsession has been especially crippling. For all their apparent willingness to follow cultural anthropologists like Clifford Geertz, historians stop dead in their tracks when Geertz talks about using the imaginative products of other cultures to deepen and enrich our own moral lives. That the emergence of history as the reactionary center of the humanities has been presided over by historians who consider themselves liberal pragmatists will surprise only those who mistake the wan theology of John Dewey for the autobiography of God.

All but lost in the compression of ideas that inevitably accompanies the formation of such reactionary centers is a deeply ironic possibility that can now be glimpsed only from the margins of contemporary historical practice: the possibility that we could go all the way with contemporary theory and come out the other end with a reinvigorated but nevertheless traditional vision of history, that is, history as a form of moral reflection.

What would such a history look like? First and most important, it would not include a renewal of history's traditional claim to objective knowledge about the past [. . .]. It is not so much that the arguments against historical objectivity seem convincing (though there is that); it is that we do not *need* a theory of historical objectivity—and that all our efforts to come up with one have only obscured issues far more pressing and important. Just as students of religious behavior have learned to bracket the ontological status of the religious experiences they study, so we historians must learn to bracket the ontological status of the historical narratives we read and write. That does not mean we should treat them as fictions; it simply means we accept them as historical narratives without pressing too hard on the question of their ontological status. Peter Novick must have had something like this in mind when he wrote the following:

> Those who think as I do . . . want to offer what we hope will be fruitful— perhaps even edifying—new ways of looking at things in the past, without aspiring to any higher claims. Others are, in a sense that seems to me deluded but not pernicious, concerned with "moving toward the truth" or "getting it right." My friends and I can find the work of these historians suggestive and/or fruitful and/or edifying, while disregarding the far-reaching and, to us, irrelevant claims that are made for them. . . . Just as in matters of religion, non-believers feel that they can get along without a god, so we who are called historical relativists believe we can get along without objectivity. . . . To say of a work of history that it is or is not objective is to make an *empty* observation, to say something neither interesting nor useful. . . . Although the term "a-objectivist" is clumsy and difficult to pronounce, it would, I think, be more accurate, by analogy with "amoralists" and "agnostics" who aren't against

morality or religion—they just don't think it very interesting, important, or relevant to their lives.

All of which is simply to say, it is the stories that interest and sustain us, not the truth claims made on their behalf.

Second, it is the values we find in those stories that count for us, not the context in which they were written or the details of their authors' often wretched lives. It is "Song of Myself" that moves us, that nurtures and nourishes our best hopes for democracy in America, not the personal life of the purportedly racist and bigoted little man who is reputed to have written that great poem. If we are told—as the historian David Reynolds recently told us—that "the real Walt Whitman" did not, in fact, live up to the vision of America he gave us In "Song of Myself," all we can do is shrug our shoulders and say, "Too bad for the real Walt Whitman. The only Whitman that matters to us is the Whitman who emerges from his poems.

Contemporary theorists call this "the strong textualist position." In fact, it is an utterly traditional way of reading history, as the outspokenly conservative historian Gertrude Himmelfarb has (more than once) reminded her colleagues:

> The Victorians even while relishing the scandals about their heroes, knew them to be scandals about their *lives*, not about their *work*. Byron's poetry was not thought to be less great because his morals were less than admirable. Nor were George Eliot's novels tainted by her long-standing extramarital affair with George Lewes. Nor was John Stuart Mill's philosophy discredited by his relationship with his great and good friend Harriet for the twenty years while she was still Mrs. John Taylor. Nor was Carlyle's reputation as a moralist diminished by the revelations of his sexual "irregularities," as the Victorians delicately put. it. Nor was Gladstone's political career jeopardized by his well-known habit of prowling the streets at night, seeking prostitutes and lecturing them on the evils of their ways, sometimes bringing them home, where his wife dutifully served them tea—or hot chocolate, according to some accounts.

Third, it is in trying to make Whitman's hopes and Tocqueville's fears and Du Bois's tragic vision our own—trying to make them grow in our own minds, transforming them from something that merely existed in the past into something we have made ours—that history comes into its own as a mode of moral reflection, a way of curing up life into meaning. As Geertz puts it, "The passage is from the immediacies of one form of life to the metaphors of another." But this act of appropriation, this attempt to use other people's cultural expressions to reflect on our own, to unsettle our moral lives, to "turn our impoverishing certitudes into humanizing doubts," is of course deeply problematic. For Whitman, Tocqueville, Du Bois—or any other thinker worth spending time with—will almost always resist our attempts to appropriate them. And if they come to us at all they come later rather than sooner, almost as if unbidden. Over the years you simply find that a thinker you have come to know—a way of grasping life that you have come to admire, a sensibility you think worth cultivating—not only has stayed with you but has become part of your own internal patterns of perception and reflection. Trying to figure out what all these chosen predecessors may or may not have in common, trying to perceive affinities and attractions between them, trying to arrange them in chronological order so you can think of yourself as the latest in a long line of such thinkers—this is pretty much what people used to mean when they talked about acquiring "a sense of the past."

That none of this gets taught in graduate school goes without saying. But that is beginning to change, if for no other reason than because the whole tired debate about the ontological status of historical narratives—a debate that has preoccupied us and bored our students for how many years now?—has finally exhausted itself. If the entire body of American historians ever gathered in one place—say, at the Whaleman's Chapel in New Bedford, Massachusetts, presided over, even unto this day by Father Mapple himself—one would hear a single anguished cry rise up from the assembled multitude: "Dear, God, please spare us yet another wearisome treatise on pragmatism and objectivity." If God does judge it meet and right to grant that prayer, then perhaps this particular fin de siècle will be the moment when American history sets out to become what it once was: not one of the social sciences in historical costume, but one of our primary forms of moral reflection.

CHAPTER 42

Dipesh Chakrabarty

"THE DEATH OF HISTORY? HISTORICAL CONSCIOUSNESS AND THE CULTURE OF LATE CAPITALISM" (1992)*

Dipesh Chakrabarty's "The Death of History: Historical Consciousness and the Culture of Late Capitalism" (1992) explores the possible death/end of history in the capitalist West but not necessarily in countries such as India. Chakrabarty's proposition is this: history is about studying social change over time. But perhaps 'advanced' Western societies, developing as rapidly as they are and losing those fixing coordinates that are so essential for measuring developments, can no longer be studied historically 'for the meaning of change, is destroyed in the process'. On the other hand, a slower-paced India makes all of its internal changes far more visible such that 'change' can indeed be examined. Yet this situation prompts Chakrabarty to pose another question – namely, that although today practically all the governments in the world sponsor historical study – and although he thinks it has indeed become, to use a Foucauldian expression, a universal way of thinking of the self – what would be lost if 'there were nothing called "history" as we, the professional historians, understand and practice it? Why cannot countries that, even as late as the early nineteenth century, did not have anything called "history", do without it today?' In other words, can India especially live (as for most of its 'history' it has lived) 'outside of history'?

As might be assumed from the way that Chakrabarty poses these questions, that answer will be that, in the end, a history of some kind is needed; that his engagement with the end

* Dipesh Chakrabarty (1992) "The Death of History? Historical Consciousness and the Culture of Late Capitalism", *Public Culture*, Durham, NC: Duke University Press, pp. 56–65.

of history concludes positively. But his way of arriving at this conclusion is the result of an argument that twists and turns in illuminating and thoughtful ways, ways that the final reading of this Part, by Kerwin Klein, will pick up under the name of memory. But between these readings there are two more, the first from Jean François Lyotard, the second from Jean Baudrillard.

[IN THIS PAPER] I want to take a trajectory that cuts across certain positions the Australian cultural critic Meaghan Morris traverses in her stimulating article "Metamorphoses at Sydney Tower." I should make it clear that my invocation of "the death of history" has nothing to do with Francis Fukuyama's well-publicised but nevertheless vulgar Hegelianism I find it more productive for my purpose to engage with the interesting way Morris raises the question of history as a problem of method in studying "popular culture,' which is where her interests intersect with those represented in *Subaltern Studies* (committed to studying the "popular" in the context of South Asia).

If I can translate Morris's interests into mine, then the question that arises (via Morris) is something like this. History is about studying social change over time. But perhaps a slow-paced society like India makes all its internal changes far more visible to the observer than do late-capitalist, consumerist, fast-moving countries? "What do you do," asks Lawrence Grossberg (whom Morris quotes in formulating her own problem),

> when every event is potentially evidence, potentially determining, and at the same time changing too quickly to allow the comfortable leisure of academic criticism?

It is possible that "history" has died in the advanced capitalist countries in a sense quite different from Fukuyama's. Societies running in the fast-forward mode cannot any longer be studied — this is how the argument would run — for even the evidence, the memory of change, is destroyed in the process. History exists in Third World societies precisely because it has not yet been devoured by consumerist social practices.

I should emphasise that this is not Morris's position. The quote from Grossberg is what her essay takes off from. But her discussion helps us to renew and open up a question that many of my colleagues in university history departments usually treat as a problem long solved (by Messrs. Coingwood and Carr) and hence permanently closed: What is History?

[. . .]

Critique(s) of history

My "Indian" history tells me that writing history (in its modern, secular sense) is neither a "natural" nor an ancient activity in India. I only have to transport myself mentally back to the eighteenth century to know that there is nothing inherent in the logic of being an "educated" person (in India) that should make historical consciousness or even an encounter, somewhere in the process of schooling, with a subject called "history" an inevitability. Yet there is today something compulsive about this subject. All governments insist on it. It is impossible to imagine a country now where history would not be part of a person's education at some point in his or her progress through educational institutions. I want to ask: What is at stake in doing History — its teaching, writing, methods, evaluative procedures, etc. — that has allowed it to become, to use a Foucauldian expression, such a universal technique of the self? What would be lost if there were nothing called "history" as we, the professional historians, understand and practice it? Why cannot countries that even as late as the early nineteenth century did not have anything called "history," do without it today?

A book like E.H. Carr's classic text *What is History?* will not answer this question; it treats "history," the discipline, as something given and, in that sense, entirely "natural." This sense of the past that we practice in the universities as "history" has, to follow Peter Burke, three foundations: a sense of anachronism (the idea that things can be out of date, something that in Europe's case Burke dates back to the Renaissance), rules of evidence, and causality as a major means of explanation. We could add a fourth element to all this: a sense of anachronism would require for its own survival a sundering of secular time from sacred time, the City of Man from the City of Gods, that is, a banishment of gods and other unworldly creatures from narratives about the world of humans. This is what is often referred to as the "humanism" of the discipline of history.

I do not need to argue in detail here the connection between nationalism and history or that between modernity and history. Suffice it to say here that "history" was absolutely central to the idea of "progress" (later "development") on which colonialism was based and to which nationalism aspired. If the capitalist mode of production and the nation-state were the two institutions that nineteenth-century Europe exported to the rest of the world, then it also exported two forms of knowledge that corresponded to the two institutions. "Economics" embodies in a distilled form the rationality of the market in its imagination of the human being as *homo economicus*; "history" speaks to the figure of the citizen. "History" is one of the most important ways in which we learn to identify ourselves with the nation and its highest representative, the state.

Once we grant this connection between positivist historical narratives (causal explanations strung together through a liberal and strategic sprinkling of "coincidences") and the social organisation of the modern (nation-)state, we realise that there is no escaping "history." Historical narratives are integral to the institutions and practices of power of the modern bureaucracies we all are subject to, particularly those of the state. Just consider how the court of law functions. It wrings positivist historical narratives out of you. Can we ever even imagine winning a case, however simple, by flouting the rules of evidence (often shared between judicial and historical discourses) by employing, say, the narrative techniques of a Nambikwara myth or those of a postmodernist Dennis Potter play? A critique of history is therefore not a sentimental plea against history. I am not talking about history as "cultural imperialism." It once surely was that for many, but to deny now, in the name of cultural relativism, any social group — peasants, aboriginals, Indians — access to the "post-Renaissance sense of the past" would be to disempower them. History could die only if these institutions of power that feed upon it were to disappear. No one, not even a Baudrillard, is yet promising that.

This is not to suggest, however, that these institutions have not changed with time. The sovereignty of the nation-state is now at least a debated topic. The nation is no longer a sacrosanct concept. It now has to contend with factors that, for a certain subject/reader of history, have indeed become global — the environment, for example, or even the idea of a "world heritage." Nor could one deny what technology and consumerist practices have done to make us question modernist constructions of time, a questioning that is inherent in the postmodern gesture of "junking" history, in the insistence (after Heidegger) that "time has ceased to be anything other than velocity, instantaneousness and simultaneity, and [that] time as history has vanished from the lives of all peoples." Morris's quotation from Grossberg that I cited in the first part of this essay returns us to this very problem, the so-called death of history.

It is not difficult to accept the proposition that in a land of pure consumerism, if such a land could ever exist, history — perhaps even memory — would die, for the subject of pure consumption would have no use for the historical construction of temporality, i.e., for what Burke calls the (modern) sense of anachronism. This would be the kingdom of pure capital (I am following Marx's use of this term as an abstract and universal logico-philosophical category) in pursuit of its own aim of erasing difference, whether spatial or temporal. Capital, as a category, does not require history. This is how Marx put it in the *Grundrisse*:

> while capital must on one side strive to tear down every spatial barrier to intercourse, i.e, to exchange, and conquer the whole earth for its market, it strives on the other side to annihilate this space with time, i.e., to reduce to a minimum the time spent in motion from one place to another. The more developed the capital, therefore, the more extensive the market over which it circulates, which forms the spatial orbit of its circulation, the more does it strive simultaneously for an even greater extension of the market and for greater annihilation of space with time.

It is obvious that in this passage Marx anticipates the currently fashionable statements about "the death of history," with the difference that he locates this "death" as a tendency within the pure category of "capital" itself. For the temporality with which Marx says capital strives to kill space (i.e., space as difference) is also one that aims to "reduce to a minimum the time spent in motion from one place to another." This time must also kill historical time, the narrative of "progress" that deploys temporality as a marker of difference. If the world were to be entirely at the mercy of capital, then it would presumably be held together by a chain of simulacra in an eternal consumerist simultaneity. In such a Baudrillardian paradise of lotus-eaters (the starving cannot consume), history would indeed be an unwelcome distraction, for its grand narratives of the state and power would sound like a siren call, to labour, the hard toil of class, gender and other kinds of struggle without which there can only be a capitulationist acceptance of the world we find ourselves in.

But capital exists in history, i.e., in contradictory and uneven relationship with another series of structures that need the representational system we in academia call "history" (the sense of anachronism, secular time, the narrative of progress) — these structures are the nation-state and its attendant institutional formations. To quote Marx once again:

> Capital drives beyond national barriers and prejudices as much as beyond nature worship, as well as all traditional, confined, complacent, encrusted satisfactions of present needs, and reproductions of old ways of life. . . . But from the fact that capital posits every such limit as a barrier and hence gets *ideally* beyond it, it does not by any means follow that it has *really* overcome

> it, and, since every such barrier contradicts its character, its production moves
> in contradictions which are constantly overcome just as constantly posited.

One of these contradictions of "capital *in* history" is that we are citizens and consumers at the same time, and I want to suggest that "history" survives the cultural logic of late capitalism" through this tension — the sometimes hostile and sometimes collusive relationship between citizenship and consumerism. Which means that the empirical subject of consumption does not have to be a posthistoricist subject. The sense of anachronism constitutive of historical time can, does, and will find interesting, albeit contradictory, accommodations with the anti-historical tendencies of consumerism. And this is where I get back to my reading of Meaghan Morris.

What I read with Morris's help is an anecdote that I have to relate in an autobiographical mode. An experience in Melbourne once brought home to me the important role our "modern" sense of anachronism plays not only in fabricating the story of "development" or "progress" (that marks both imperialist and nationalist thought) but even in our consumerist social practices. It also indirectly helped me to think about what might be at stake for the Indian ruling classes for them to want to teach peasants "history" — i.e., to give them, *à la Burke*, a sense of anachronism. The answer came to me one day in a flash when I had just started lecturing at the University of Melbourne in the middle of the 1980s. One of my second-year students, when she felt free to be friendly, said to me one day coming out of the class, "You're such a dag, Dipesh. You still wear flares!" — "dag," in Australian slang, standing for a person who is a source of amusement for others, a "character," in short. "And what's wrong with that?" I said, giving my Indian trousers a general, and somewhat embarrassed, looking over. "They're so seventies, don't you see?" was her answer.

There I was, I felt, face to face with a sense of anachronism, an extremely acute one, a hyper sense of history without which, it seemed to me, there would be no consumerism and nothing of the kind of (narratives of) prosperity and economic expansion of the First World that have now seized the imagination of the ruling classes of my country and of many others. So this, I thought, was what was at stake in doing history, in Indian peasants having a historical consciousness: it made it a lot easier for some people to make money from them!

But I caricature. Even though as a cultural artifact it is something that Indians borrowed only relatively recently from the West, I know from experience the importance that "history" had in my own Indian/Third World upbringing. If I could continue to treat myself as a "case in point" for a little longer, I should mention that I personally came to history through my involvement in Maoist political movements in Calcutta in my undergraduate years in the late sixties, when I was pursuing an honours degree in physics. While the movement failed in achieving its emancipationist aims and turned out to be both violent and tragic, it did succeed in persuading me that I was simply not brave enough to face the repression that the Indian "democratic" state was capable of unleashing on people who opposed it. I left the movement but not without a certain sense of failure that was itself rooted in a particular "historical" sensibility. By the time I left the life of an activist, I had read enough party literature to know that the likes of me belonged to the "garbage heap of history."

Setting out to go where I thought my destiny was — a "garbage heap," but I guess a nice one! — I joined one of the two business schools the government had set up in the country. Strange though it may appear, it was during my studies in business administration that I had my first serious intellectual encounter with "history" (at school it was just one of those boring subjects). History was a compulsory subject at this business school. With hindsight, I know why the authorities at this public institution insisted that the future managers of the country should know history. The course we studied was Marxist in its orientation and was called "Historical Roots of Economic Backwardness." What it sought to transmit to us was a Marxist political-economic critique of India's colonial past and its consequent (or so the course argued) experience of underdevelopment. The lecturer was a well-known Marxist historian of the country. Obviously, this national institute had decided that such a critique of colonialism should form part of the common historical memory that the new nation and its managers should have. At a personal level, I might add parenthetically, I was delighted to discover Marxist history in a professional form. It helped to purge myself of my troubling feelings of failure and guilt. The "garbage heap," this history told me, was itself a result more of the impersonal forces of history than of individual choices. Moreover, I discovered that the particular "rubbish dump" where I found myself was inhabited by some interesting people, including the professor who had introduced me to history. So when I graduated and my professor asked me if I would be interested in pursuing a career in history rather than the one in personnel management that I had just been offered by a Scottish firm in Calcutta, I had no difficulty in making up my mind. Life, it seemed to me then, would be meaningless if I did not study "history."

I offer this story to illustrate the conclusion I draw from it: that "history" was, and has been, important to not only the process of identity-formation of an individual middle-class Indian like myself but to that of the Indian "nation" as well, which is why a government-funded MBA course insisted on the students learning some history. The contemporary universal importance of "history," the discipline, is thus tied up, as I have already argued, with another universal of our times: the nation-state and its companion institutions (run by economic and bureaucratic rationality) that dominate all our lives irrespective of where we are on this planet.

Reading Morris on the Sydney Telecommunications Tower, however, has given me a sharper appreciation of what was at issue in that cross-cultural encounter in Melbourne over my Indian flares and their status as historical objects. Meaghan Morris studied a small death that "history" died in Sydney Tower between 1981, when she first "read" the Tower, and 1989, when she went back to it for a diachronic, post-bicentennial snapshot. In 1981 the Tower portrayed and stood for, among other things, a clichéd "narrative of Progress," "as an annunciation of modernity":

> The lower deck proclaimed the transformation of Sydney as a locale; . . . the upper deck celebrated the history of towers, lookouts, and associated tourist activities. The theme linking the two levels . . . was the overthrow of . . . "the tyranny of distance" . . . enabling Australia's integration into the age of global simultaneity.

All this was gone in 1989. "Worse," writes Morris,

> it was as though none of the representations I had studied had ever been there. I asked questions about the renovations, but no one who was working there had been around long enough to remember the decor of the Tower having

ever been different from the way it is today. So there was a crazed culture
critic staggering round the turret saying "What have you done with the
evidence?"

The lower deck "had become a cafeteria," its old photographs replaced by "plastic bas-
reliefs with a wildflower motif," and the upper level had lost most of its historical
references. "With them, the whole linking discourse to the history of Sydney as a 'site'
had disappeared." The work of consumption had left the Tower with no "historical"
memory of its older self.

I say "*historical* memory" advisedly, for I am not talking about just any use of the past
tense (such as those made in fairy tales, legends, or "myths"). I am discussing a particular
form of memory (i.e., History, the discipline) which regulates itself by appealing to what
Peter Burke calls its rules of evidence, the kind of "evidence" that Morris had in mind
when she referred to the destruction of it in the Tower. Constructing "evidence," I want
to argue, is a project of preservation, of making "monuments" of certain objects that are
actually contemporaneous with ourselves. For them to acquire the status of "historical
evidence," however, we have to be able to deny them their contemporaneity by assigning
them to a specified period in a calendrical past, an act by which we split the "present"
into the "modern" and the "traditional" or the "historical," and thereby declare ourselves
to be modern. This denial of the contemporaneity of certain objects is what constitutes
the historical sense of anachronism. Without it there is no evidence, and without evidence,
there is no "history." History is therefore a practice of "monumentalising" objects — from
documents to sculptures — of simultaneously acknowledging and denying their existence
in our "own" time. What allowed my Melbourne student to express her sense of anachronism about my flares (and about their wearer, the "dag") was that they existed as tangible
evidence in the same time as the one she inhabited at the time of speaking. I had kind of
monumentalised my anachronistic, Indian/Third World sense of style!

Monumentalising, preserving, making a "heritage" out of assorted objects is essential
to the politics of both nationalism and the nation-state. This is where history becomes
the business of the citizen, the subject of the grand narratives of Freedom and Progress
that, ultimately, legitimise both the nation-state and the modern market. As an activity,
monumentalising can only live in tension with consumerist practices. This is the contradiction that marks the historic life of capital, the tension between the citizen and the
consumer. And to the extent that consumption has dominated the productive side of capitalism in its self-representations since the Second World War, this tension, it would seem,
has been far more obvious in this period than ever before in the history of capitalism
(though, as we know from Berman's astute reading of Marx and modernism, this tension
was something Marx saw as a defining characteristic of capital). It points us to a deeper
contradiction between capital and the nation-state.

When I say "contradiction," I mean a contradictory relationship. For the collusion
between consumerism and "heritage," i.e., between the consumer and the citizen, reveals
itself in the discourse of tourism. This is the discourse of "heritage industry" which some
historians now see as the side of the bread that is buttered. The relationship, however,
is inherently fraught with conflict, as so many cases of heritage litigation would suggest.
Besides, with the heightened sense of commodification of history that assails the historians (who are preservers after all) as the heritage and the travel industries increasingly
expose "history" to the vagaries of the marketplace and to the fickleness of a media-

influenced public culture, a tension develops between what is now called "public history" and what has until now constituted the "high culture" of the historical profession.

The heritage industry is new in India but shows all the symptoms of this tension between the citizen and the consumer. I quote a recent report:

> In 1988 the pre-Mughal Chaumachi Tomb in Mehrauli on the outskirts of Delhi almost joined the ranks of vanished monuments. Enthusiasts of a citizens' group known as the Conservation Society of Delhi (CSD) were horrified to find a developer, armed with a written decree, about to demolish the tomb. The developer had apparently found a loophole in the uncoordinated zoning laws, but the CSD, with the support of an alert press, succeeded in getting a stay order from the Supreme Court. Examples of this type could be multiplied. In Bombay, when the navy proposed demolition of the historic clock tower in its dockyard, various citizens' groups including the Bombay Environmental Action Group, the Save Bombay Committee, and the Indian Heritage Society intervened and saved the structure.

The same report, of course, by its discussion of "conservation" and "tourism," reminds us of the flip side of this relationship, the collaborative side which gives the otherwise oxymoronic expression "heritage industry" some meaning.

History will die when this contradiction between the citizen and the consumer, between the nation-state and capital, is resolved (exclusively or overwhelmingly) in favour of the consumer and capital. But until that has happened — and there is no a priori reason why it must be resolved this way — postmodernity will remain, as Lyotard puts it, primarily a condition of knowledge. On the other hand, as the concept of the nation-state loses the sanctity it once had for both imperialists and nationalists (one has to remember the close connection between these two apparently contradictory ideologies), postmodern critiques of the grand narratives of "nation" and "progress" can converse fruitfully with Third World experiences of modernity. It is possible that one day the nation-state will become (at most) a purely practical arrangement unadorned by passions or sentiments of nobility. But even this cannot happen without struggle, nor is such an end in any sense a "given" in history. In the meanwhile, however, we will need "history as critique" in order to develop "critiques of history" as part of our understanding of both capital (the narratives of production/consumption) and the state (with its narratives of progress and freedom). In this we need dialogues between intellectuals who locate themselves in the First World — where consumerism has been "naturalised" — and those who speak out of their experience in the Third World, where much of both capitalism and the modern state remains, to return to Guha's creative invocation of Gramsci, dominant but not hegemonic.

I therefore do not read Lyotard's claims about the death of the grand narratives (of the state) as realist description. For me, the dead of Baghdad (or those of Kuwait) will always be far more dead than the lethal grand narratives of Freedom and Progress which killed them.

CHAPTER 43

Jean François Lyotard

THE POSTMODERN EXPLAINED
TO CHILDREN (1992)

Jean François Lyotard's 'Missive on University History'* (taken from his *The Postmodern Explained To Children* (1992)) poses the question of whether today it is still possible to organise the plenitude of the past (for at one time certain metanarrative theorists thought they had done so), the sublime (unpresentable) past, in forms 'referring them to the Idea of a universal history of humanity'. Lyotard's answer is 'no' for reasons revealed in his closely argued essay.

To those who know the work of Lyotard (not least *Libidinal Economy*, *The Postmodern Condition*, *The Differend* and the many essays such as those that make up *The Inhuman*), his negative response should not be unexpected. There are many reasoned arguments for this, but basically Lyotard always accepted the old fact-value problematic – namely, the impossibility of drawing, in a logically entailed sense – value(s) from fact(s). Thus, from the facts/events of the past, no entailed meaning or significance (no sense of progress or regress, etc.) could be drawn, which means that whatever the point of studying the before now might be, the drawing of ethical/moral lessons could not be one of them. And, moreover, given that values are, precisely, ungroundable beliefs (ungroundable either in facts or in some unproblematical/undeconstructible ethical system – for the latter doesn't exist), then opposing 'belief systems' are, ultimately, incommensurable. And Lyotard happily accepts this, for the reason that the non-totalisability of thought, the impossibility of grounding – 'once and for all' – a mere way of seeing and believing such that it could be dogmatically asserted as *the* truth, means that totality – and hence totalitarian thought – are ruled out forever: there are no rules, no algorithms, no certainties, no truths beyond peradventure. And this is precisely a good thing for Lyotard since it ensured that the future, the 'to come', was always open, an invitation, an 'open invitation' to make up new rules in the absence of rules in ways that 'will never have been good enough'. And if the future is open to interminable writing and rewriting, and if in that future histories of the past are interminably written and rewritten, then until such history writing itself comes to an end, the past is always subject to endless interpretation/appropriation: the written-up past is always determined by the future.

Does this mean – the question is raised in the last few lines of the above paragraph – that histories will not end? Lyotard seems clear on this. Certain types of history – metanarratives – have already died; towards them we can only have a sense of incredulity (this is the message of *The Postmodern Condition* and the extract offered in the following pages), while academic histories can never provide, in their 'empirical' inadequacies, their facticity, an opening to an ethics or a morality. So what use is the historicised past? The answer is indeterminate; logically, one can draw any 'lesson' one likes from the 'before now', or none at all; logically, the study of the past is a useless passion. And in fact, what might be useful would be that we developed the capacity to forget; that we learnt to unburden ourselves of

---

* Jean François Lyotard, 'Missive on University History', in *The Postmodern Explained to Children* (1992) London: Turnaround, pp. 35–47.

the weight of the before now and gazed, in totally ungroundable yet highly desirable ways, towards an emancipatory future. This is an ungroundable choice, an undecidable decision, but one that Lyotard recommends we think about, and through.

I**T IS INADVISABLE TO** grant the narrative genre an absolute privilege over other genres of discourse in the analysis of human, and specifically linguistic (ideological), phenomena, particularly when the approach is philosophical. Some of my earlier reflections may have succumbed to this "transcendental appearance" ("Presentations", *Instructions païennes*, even *The Postmodern Condition*). On the other hand, an examination of "histories" might help us to address one of the great questions presented by the historical world at the end of the 20th century (or beginning of the 21st century). For if we claim that this world is historical, we necessarily intend to treat it narratively.

The question that concerns me is this: can we today continue to organise the mass of events coming from the human and non-human world by referring them to the Idea of a universal history of humanity? I don't intend to deal with this question philosophically here. Nonetheless its formulation calls for a number of clarifications.

1. I start out by saying: can we *continue* to organise . . . The word implies that previously we could organise these things. And here I am in fact referring to a tradition: that of modernity. Modernity is not an epoch but a mode (the word's Latin origin) within thought, speech, and sensibility. Erich Auerbach saw its emergence in the writing of Augustine's *Confessions*: the destruction of the syntactical architecture of classical discourse and the adoption of a paratactic arrangement of short sentences linked by the most elementary of conjunctions: the *and*. Like Bakhtin, he also encounters this mode in Rabelais, then in Montaigne.

For my part, and without trying to justify this view here, I see a sign of it in the genre of first-person narration chosen by Descartes to explain his method. The *Discourse* is also a confession. But what it confesses is not the dispossession of the "I" by God but the effort of the "I" to master every given, including itself. Descartes tries to graft the finality of a series directed towards the mastery and possession of "nature" onto the contingency that the *and* leaves between sequences conveyed by phrases. (Whether or not he succeeds is a different matter.) This modern, mode of organising time is further developed in the 18th century in the *Aufklärung*.

The thought and action of the 19th and 20th centuries are governed by an Idea (in the Kantian sense): the Idea of emancipation. It is of course framed in quite different ways, depending upon what we call the philosophies of history, the grand narratives which attempt to organise this mass of events: the Christian narrative of the redemption of original sin through love; the *Aufklärer* narrative of emancipation from ignorance and servitude through knowledge and egalitarianism; the speculative narrative of the realisation of the universal Idea through the dialectic of the concrete; the Marxist narrative of emancipation from exploitation and alienation through the socialisation of work; and the capitalist narrative of emancipation from poverty through techno-industrial development. Between these narratives there are grounds for litigation and even for differends. But in all of them, the givens arising from events are situated in the course of a history whose end, even if it remains beyond reach, is called universal freedom, the fulfilment of all humanity.

2. Second clarification. When one says: "Can we continue to organise . . .?" one at least assumes — even if the answer (intended or not) is negative (that we cannot) — one

assumes the persistence of a *we* capable of thinking or experiencing that continuity or discontinuity. The question also asks: what constitutes this *we*? As the pronoun in the first person plural indicates, it concerns a community of subjects, you and me, or them and me, depending on whether the speaker is addressing other members of the community (you/me) or a third party (you/them + me) for whom these other members – represented by the speaker – are designated by the third person (them). The question asks whether this *we* is or is not independent of the Idea of a history of humanity.

In the tradition of modernity, the movement of emancipation is one in which the third party, initially external to the *we* of the emancipatory avant-garde, will end up joining the community of speakers, whether actual (first person) or potential (second person). There will be only you and me. In this tradition the place of the first person is in fact marked by the control of speech and meaning: let the people have a say in politics, let the worker have a say in society, let the poor have a say in economics, let the particular assume the universal, and let the last also become the first. Excuse me for simplifying.

It follows that, caught between the actual situation of minorities (where there are many third parties and not many of *you and me*) and the unanimity still to come (when every third person will be banished by definition), the *we* of my question exactly reproduces the tension humanity must experience in its vocation for emancipation, a tension between the particularity, randomness and opacity of the present and the universality, self-determination and transparency of the future promised by emancipation. If this tension is exactly the same, the *we* asking the question – "Shall we continue to think and act in the name of the Idea of a history of humanity?" – this *we* is also raising the question of its own identity as established by the tradition of modernity. And if the answer to the question should be *no* (no, human history is no longer credible as a universal history of emancipation), then the status of the *we* asking the question will also have to be revised.

The *we*, it seems, will be condemned (but only in the eyes of modernity) to remain particular, to be you and me (perhaps), to leave many third parties on the outside. But since this *we* has not forgotten (yet) that third parties were once potential and even promised first persons, it will have to resign itself to the loss of unanimity and find another mode of thought and action, or else sink into incurable melancholy for this lost "object" (or impossible subject): liberated humanity. In either case we are affected by a sort of grief. The work of mourning, according to Freud, involves recovering from the loss of a loved object by transferring the investment in the lost object to the subject – from them to us.

Still, there are other ways of dealing with it. One is secondary narcissism. According to many observers, it is now the dominant mode of thought and action in developed societies. I fear it may be no more than the blind (and compulsive) repetition of an earlier bereavement – the loss of God – which in truth gave rise to the mode of modernity and its project of conquest. Such a conquest today would do no more than perpetuate the conquests of the moderns, differing only in its renunciation of a search for unanimity. Terror would no longer be exercised for the sake of freedom but for "our" satisfaction, the satisfaction of a *we* permanently restricted to its particularity. Would it still be too modern if I were to find this perspective intolerable? The word for it is tyranny: the law "we" proclaim is not addressed to *you*, fellow citizens or even subjects, it is applied to *them*, the third parties, those on the outside, without the least concern for legitimating it in their eyes. As I recall, this was Nazism's way of dealing with emancipation and its way of exercising a terror whose logic, for the first time in Europe since 1789, was not in principle accessible to all and whose benefits could not be shared by all.

A different way of dealing with the universal emancipation promised by modernity would be to "work over" (in the Freudian sense) not just the loss of this object but the loss of the subject to whom this goal was promised. It would not only be a matter of recognising our finitude but of elaborating the status of the we, the question of the subject. That is, of escaping both an unrevised renewal of the modern subject and its parodical or cynical repetition (tyranny). Such elaboration, I believe, can only lead to an immediate abandonment of the linguistic structure of communication (I/you/he) which the moderns, whether consciously or not, held up as their ontological and political model.

3. My third clarification will concentrate on the words *can we* in the question: "Can we today continue to organise events according to the Idea of a universal history of humanity?" As understood by Aristotle and linguists, the modality of the *possible* [*pouvoir*] applied to a notion (here the pursuit of universal history) contains at once its affirmation and negation. That this pursuit is possible does not imply either that it will take place or that it will not take place, but that what certainly will take place is the fact that it will or will not take place. There is uncertainty about the contents, the dictum (the notion's affirmation or negation), but necessity regarding the subsequent fact, or *modus*. We recognise here Aristotle's thesis of contingent futures. (They still have to be dated.)

But the expression *can we* does not only connote possibility, it implies capacity as well: is it in our power, our strength and our competence to perpetuate the project of modernity? The question suggests that to be sustained, such a project would call for strength and competence, and that these things may have failed us. Such a reading would have to spark an enquiry, an enquiry into the failing of the modern subject. And if this failing should be a matter for dispute, then we must be able to produce evidence for it in the form of facts or at least signs. The interpretation of this evidence may well engender controversy, and at the very least it must be submitted to cognitive procedures for establishing facts or speculative procedures for validating signs. (I am referring, without further explanation, to the Kantian problematic of hypotyposes that plays a major role in his historico-political philosophy.)

Without wishing to decide here and now whether it is constituted by facts or signs, the evidence which we can collect on this failing of the modern subject seems difficult to refute. In the course of the past fifty years, each grand narrative of emancipation – regardless of the genre it privileges' – has, as it were, had its principle invalidated. *All that is real is rational, all that is rational is real*: "Auschwitz" refutes the speculative doctrine. At least this crime, which is real, is not rational. *All that is proletarian is communist, all that is communist is proletarian*: "Berlin 1953", "Budapest 1956", "Czechoslovakia 1968", "Poland 1980" (to name but a few) refute the doctrine of historical materialism: the workers rise up against the Party. *All that is democratic is by the people and for the people, and vice versa*: "May 1968" refutes the doctrine of parliamentary liberalism. Everyday society brings the representative institution to a halt. *Everything that promotes the free flow of supply and demand is good for general prosperity, and vice versa*: the "crises of 1911 and 1929" refute the doctrine of economic liberalism, and the "crisis of 1974–1979" refutes the post-Keynesian modification of that doctrine.

The investigator records the names of these event-, as so many signs of the failing of modernity. The grand narratives have become scarcely credible. One is then tempted to give credence to a grand narrative of the decline of the grand narratives. But as we know, the grand narrative of decadence was already in place at the beginning of Western thought, in Hesiod and Plato. It follows the narrative of emancipation like a shadow. So nothing would have changed – except that extra strength and competence will be needed to face the task at hand. Many believe this is the moment for religion, a moment to rebuild a credible narration where the wounds of this fin-de-siècle will be recounted, where they will be healed. They claim that myth is the originary genre; that in myth the thought of origin is present in its originary paradox; and that we must raise myth from the ruins to which it has been reduced by rational, de-mythologising and positivist thought.

But this course of action, it seems to me, is far from being just. Besides, we should note that in this brief description the expression to be able [pouvoir] has undergone a further modification, signalled in the way I have used the word just. To the question: can we perpetuate the grand narratives? the answer has become: we ought to do this or that. Being able also implies having the right; in this sense, the expression draws thought into the universe of deontics: the slippage from right to duty is as easy as that from the permissible to the obligatory. The issue here is the contingency of the linkage to the situation that I have described as the failing of modernity. Many types of linkage are possible, and one has to decide. Deciding nothing is still deciding. Remaining silent is still speaking. Politics always rests on the way one phrase, the present phrase, is linked to another phrase. It is not about the volume of discourse or about the importance of the speaker or addressee. From the different phrases which are actually possible, one will be actualised; and the actual question is: which one? The description of this failing does not give us any clue to the answer. This is why the word postmodernity is able to embrace such conflicting perspectives. These few remarks are simply meant to indicate the anti-mythologising direction I think we should take in "working over" the loss of the modern we.

Now to the topic indicated by my title. I wonder if the failing of modernity – in the form of what Adorno described as the collapse of metaphysics (for him, concentrated in the failure of the affirmative dialectic of Hegelian thought in the face of the Kantian thesis of obligation or the event of senseless annihilation named Auschwitz) – I wonder whether this failing could be connected to a resistance on the part of what I shall call the multiplicity of worlds of names, the insurmountable diversity of cultures. Taking this approach to the question in conclusion, I want to go back and reappraise several of the issues I noted earlier regarding the universality of the grand narratives, the status of the we, the reason for the failing of modernity, and finally the contemporary issue of legitimation.

As child or immigrant, one enters a culture through an apprenticeship in proper names. One must learn the names that designate near relations, heroes (in a general sense), places, dates and also, I would add (following Kripke), units of measure, space, time and exchange value. These names are "rigid designators": they signify nothing or at least can be laden with various and conflicting significations; they can be attached to phrases belonging to altogether heterogeneous regimes (descriptive, interrogative, ostensive, evaluative, prescriptive, etc.) and included in incommensurable genres of discourse (cognitive, persuasive, epideictic, tragic, comic, dithyrambic, etc.). Names are not learnt by themselves – they are lodged in little stories. Again, narrative's strength lies in its capacity to hold together a multiplicity of heterogeneous families of discourse – so it has to be "inflatable", if I can put it that way. Narrative arranges these families of discourse into a sequence of events determined by the culture's proper names.

The great coherence of this organisation is reinforced by the narrative's mode of transmission, most visibly in what I shall call, for convenience, "savage" societies. André Marcel d'Ans writes: "Among the Cashinahua, every interpretation of a miyoi (myth, tale, legend or traditional narrative) opens with a fixed formula: 'Here is the story of . . . as I have

always heard it told. It is now my turn to tell it to you. Listen!' And the recitation invariably closes with another formula which goes: 'Here ends the story of . . . He who told it
to you is . . . (Cashinahua name), known to the whites as . . . (Spanish or Portuguese
name)'." The ethnologist tells us, the whites, how the Cashinahua storyteller tells the story
of a Cashinahua hero to a Cashinahua audience. He can do this because he is himself a
(male) Cashinahua listener – and he is a listener because he bears a Cashinahua name. So
a ritual using strict denominations defines the narration's audience and recurrence. All the
phrases contained in such narrations are, as it were, fastened to named or nameable
instances in the world of Cashinahua names. The universe presented by any one of these
phrases, regardless of its regime, refers to this world of names. The hero or heroes and
places presented, the addressee and lastly the addressor are all meticulously named.

To hear the narratives, you have to have been named. (All males and girls prior to
puberty can listen.) The same applies to telling them (only men can). And to having your
story told (to be the referent) as well (all the Cashinahua can, without exception). By
putting names into stories, the narration keeps the rigid designators of its common identity sheltered from events of the "moment" and the danger of what could be linked to it.
To be named is to be narrated. There are two aspects to this: every narrative, even ones
which seem anecdotal, reactualises names and the relations between names. In reciting
its narratives, the community reassures itself of the permanence and legitimacy of its
world of names through the recurrence of this world in its stories. As well, some narratives are explicitly stories of naming.

When we directly raise the question of the origin of tradition or authority among the
Cashinahua, we come up against the usual paradox in such cases. If we suppose that a
phrase cannot be authorised unless the addressor holds some authority, what happens when
the addressor's authority results from the meaning of the phrase? The phrase, in legitimating the addressor presented by its universe, legitimates itself in the eyes of the
addressee. The Cashinahua narrator draws the authority to tell stories from his name. But
his name is authorised by his stories, particularly by stories which tell of the genesis of
names. This *circulus vitiosus* is typical.

We see here the discursive procedures of what might be called "a very large-scale
integrated culture". Identification reigns absolutely. Being self-enclosed, it eliminates the
debris of the narratives – unassimilable events by making sacrifices, drug-taking (in the
case of the Cashinahua) or fighting border wars.

Mutatis mutandis, this is the mechanism of a culture's self-identification. Its disintegra-
tion in situations of servile dependency, colonial or imperialist, spells the destruction of
cultural identity. But in struggles for independence, this mechanism becomes the gueril-
las' major asset, since narrative and its transmission give the resistance an immediate legitimacy (or right) and logistics (means of transmitting messages, coordinates of sites and of
times, use of knowledge about natural phenomena in the cultural tradition, etc.).

As I have said, legitimacy is secured by the strength of the narrative mechanism: it
encompasses the multiplicity of families of phrases and possible genres of discourse; it
envelops every name; it is always actualisable and always has been; both diachronic and
parachronic, it secures mastery over time and therefore over life and death. Narrative is
authority itself. It authorises an infrangible we, outside of which there is only *they*.

This kind of organisation is absolutely opposed to the organisation of the grand narratives of legitimation which characterise modernity in the West. These narratives are
cosmopolitical, as Kant would say. They involve precisely an "overcoming" [*dépassement*]

of the particular cultural identity in favour of a universal civic identity. But how such an overcoming can take place is not apparent.

There is nothing in the savage community to lead it to transform itself dialectically into a society of citizens. Saying that it is "human" and that it already prefigures a universality is settling the issue in advance: having assumed a universal history, the humanist inscribes the particular community into it as a moment in the universal becoming of human communities. This is also, *grosso modo*, the axiom of the grand narrative of speculative thought applied to human history. But the question is whether there is a history of humanity. The epistemological account is the most cautious but also the most deceptive: anthropologists use the rules of the cognitive genre to describe the narrations of savage communities and their rules, without claiming to establish any continuity between the rules they are describing and the rules of their own mode of discourse. In the Lévi-Straussian account, anthropologists are able to introduce an identity of functioning, a so-called structural identity, between myth and the explanation of myth – but only at the expense of abandoning any attempt to find an intelligible passage between them. There can be identity but no history.

All of these difficulties are well known – and trivial. I remind you of them only because they may make it easier to assess the extent of the present failing of modernity. It is as though the enormous effort, marked by the name of the Declaration of Rights, seeking to deprive peoples of their narrative legitimacy (shall we say lying upstream in the course of time) and make them take up the Idea of free citizenship (lying downstream) as the only legitimacy – it is as though that effort, which has taken so many different paths over the past two centuries, had failed. A premonitory sign of this failure might be seen in the very designation of the author of this Declaration of universal import: "We, the French people".

The workers' movement is a particularly telling example of this failure. In theory, its internationalism meant that the legitimacy of the class struggle did not derive from local (popular or labour) traditions but from an Idea to be realised the Idea of the worker emancipated from the proletarian condition. Now we know that, from the time of the Franco-German War of 1870–1871, the International was deadlocked over the issue of Alsace-Lorraine, and that in 1914 both German and French socialists voted for national war budgets, etc. Stalinism as "socialism in one country", and the suppression of the Komintern, openly proclaimed the superiority of the nation's proper name over the universal name of the Soviets. The spread of struggles for independence since the Second World War and the recognition of new national names seem to imply a consolidation of local legitimacies and the vanishing of a universal horizon of emancipation. New "independent" governments either fall in line with the market of world capitalism or adopt a Stalinist-style political apparatus – "leftists" with their sights set on that horizon are eliminated without mercy. As the current slogan of the far right in France would have it: put the French first (implying: leave freedoms until later).

You could argue that these retreats into local legitimacy are reactions of resistance to the devastating effects which imperialism, and its malaise, have had on particular cultures. That is true, and it confirms the diagnosis, or makes it even worse. There is no trace of a cosmopolitan perspective to be found in the way the world market reconstituted itself after the Second World War, or in the intense economic and financial battle now being conducted for domination of this market by multinational banks and companies – with the support of national States. Even supposing the parties to this game still prided themselves on achieving the goals set by economic liberalism, or by Keynesianism in the modern era, it would still be difficult to give them any credit on this score. Obviously their game, far from reducing the inequality of wealth in the world, exacerbates it and, far from breaking down barriers, exploits them for commercial and monetary speculation. The world market does not constitute universal history in the modern sense. Moreover, cultural differences are promoted at every opportunity in the guise of tourist and cultural commodities.

What, finally, is this *we* that tries to reflect on this predicament of failing if it is no longer the core, minority or avant-garde which anticipates today what liberated humanity might be tomorrow? By trying to reflect on this predicament, are we condemning ourselves to be no more than negative heroes? It is at least clear that a certain image of the intellectual (Voltaire, Zola, Sartre) is caught up with this failing. This was an image sustained by the acknowledged legitimacy of the Idea of emancipation, an image which shadowed the history of modernity through thick and thin. But the violence of the critique mounted against schooling in the sixties, followed by the inexorable erosion of teaching institutions in every modern country, is enough to show that learning and its transmission no longer command the authority which once made us listen to intellectuals when they moved from the lectern to the podium. In a world where success means gaining time, thinking has a single but irredeemable fault: it's a waste of time.

That, in general terms, is the question I am posing – or rather the question which I believe poses itself. I did not intend to answer it, just to discuss it. When we meet, we will be able to discuss more fully the aspects of its elaboration that I have not considered in this missive. After the age of the intellectual, the age of the party, it would be interesting if, on each side of the Atlantic, without presumption, we could begin to trace a line of resistance to the failing of modernity.

CHAPTER 44

Jean Baudrillard

'THE END OF THE MILLENNIUM
OR THE COUNTDOWN' (1997)*

In Jean Baudrillard's short essay 'The End of the Millennium or the Countdown' (1997), the author – who, until his retirement, was for many years Professor of Sociology at the University of Paris (Nanterre) – rethinks many of the themes expressed in *The Future of An Illusion* (Cambridge, Polity Press, 1994).He also draws on a corpus of works that, in their inventive and highly original arguments, make him one of the world's most (in)famous 'postist' writers. Such is the density of the essay and the presumed familiarity with the general position Baudrillard assumes, a brief resumé of his piece may be less useful than a more general

* Jean Baudrillard (1997) 'The End of the Millennium or the Countdown', *Economy and Society*, 26 (4): 447–55.

'contextualisation' of it vis-à-vis his *oeuvre* – or at least parts of it. So, in terms that we hope may be helpful, Baudrillard's position with regard to the 'end of history' might be put skeletally in three ways.

First, we have come to the end of history in metanarrative forms; in those Hegelianised Marxist formats; in those various linear (generally progressive) fables that believed that the end – towards which we are moving – was given in the beginning and that the decipherment of that beginning and its necessary end could inform us as to its various stages of development and furnish us with ideas as to how we could (generally) facilitate their passage. As with all teleological thinking, this is a theory of (final) closure, of totality. In this act of the imagination, the end is always in the process of becoming 'nigh', and Baudrillard has no time for this fable.

Second, Baudrillard believes that our sense of history (in the sense of perceived change, of significant shifts) has also died because, in our contemporary world, we have become bereft of 'Events'. An 'Event' should be something that makes things run differently after its occurrence, thus opening up the future in ways that could not have been envisaged and thus prepared for. But 'Events' don't happen like that nowadays: the fall of the Berlin Wall, the Gulf War, September 11, for example, might as well not have happened. This is not to deny that they did happen, but it is to deny that, unexpected as in many ways they were and having the potential, therefore, of changing everything, they were, in fact, able to be rapidly recuperated into various systems that nullified them. Bereft of such history-making 'Events', 'history' has become just more of the same, causing an attendant lack of 'historical sense'.

Third, given that history as a discourse is clearly the product of historians' theories and methods, the resultant (academic) discourse is the creator, the constitutive agent of the past *as if* it were really 'history'. This attention to language as constitutive of 'reality' thus points to the problematical nature of all modes of representation that seek to assure us that there is not only something out there to represent (which Baudrillard freely admits there is), but that their mode of representation accurately represents it. But that is, as all anti-representationalists 'know', impossible. 'Too bad for representationalists', then, but this 'fact of life' doesn't lead Baudrillard to despair (he accepts a certain kind of nihilism), but rather to an attitude of expectation and adventure: unrestrained by the 'radical alterity of the world' we can create our own worlds in the way we have always done: linguistically. The 'world' can thus be made, as it always has been made, to obey our syntax – our grammars, our verb tenses. The question this raises for Baudrillard is whether we need to burden our present or future imaginative leaps with the past tense. Thus Baudrillard toys with the idea (especially in the closing chapters of *The Illusion of the End*) with new tropes, new metaphors, new conceptualisations such that the future might be formed in ways that have not yet been or, indeed, even imagined. Here histories of both a metanarrative and academic kind seem superfluous to radical emancipation.

Consequently, historians and their productions scarce seem to figure in this process of rethinking the point of historicisations if the practices of historians are so antithetical to future thinking and acting, to praxis. In *Postmodernisms*, an interesting recent publication (Blackwell, 2002), Hans Bertens and Joseph Natoli have compiled a list of theorists who they consider to be the most crucially important for the current of thought that arguably best raises to consciousness the conditions of our cultural moment. The list comprises the names of over fifty theorists of which only one – Hayden White – is a historian. Does this not point graphically – in the suggestive way that Baudrillard likes to think in – to the marginality of historians in our culture and to the end of their influence?

In the Millennial countdown the time remaining is already past, and the maximal utopia of life give way to the minimal utopia of survival. This is the paradox of the achieved utopia which puts an end to the utopian dimension. It creates an impossible situation, in the sense that it exhausts historical possibilities.

Keywords: time; history; utopia; hyperspace; extreme phenomena

HOW CAN WE JUMP over our shadows when we no longer have any? How can we pass out of the century (not to speak of the millennium) if we do not make up our minds to put an end to it, engaged as we are in an indefinite work of mourning for all the incidents, ideologies and violence which have marked it? The remorse that has been expressed and the – more or less hypocritical – commemorations and recantations give the impression that we are trying to run the events of the century back through the filter of memory, not in order to find a meaning for them – they have clearly lost that *en route* – but in order to whitewash them, to launder them. Laundering is the prime activity of this *fin de siècle* – the laundering of a dirty history, of dirty money, of corrupt consciousnesses, of the polluted planet – the cleansing of memory being indissolubly linked to the – hygienic cleansing of the environment or to the – racial and ethnic – cleansing of populations. We are turning away from history 'in progress', with none of the problems it poses having been resolved, and plunging into a regressive history, in the nostalgic hope of making a politically correct one out of it. And in this retrospective, necrospective obsession, we are losing any chance of things coming to their term. This is why I advanced the idea that the Year 2000 would not take place: quite simply because the history of this century has already come to an end, because we are reliving it interminably and because, therefore, metaphorically speaking, we shall never pass on into the future. Our millenarianism – for we are, the same, on the eve of a millenarian dateline – is a millenarianism with no tomorrow. Whereas the coming of the Year 1000, even though it was experienced with dread, was a prelude to *parousia* and to the advent of the Kingdom of God, and hence the prelude to an infinite promise, the point of reckoning which stands before *us* is a closed, involuted one. All we have left of the millenarian dateline is the countdown to it. For this century – which can do nothing more than count the seconds separating it from its end without either being able, or really wanting, to measure up to that end – the digital clock on the Beaubourg Centre showing the countdown in millions of seconds is the perfect symbol. It illustrates the reversal of the whole of our modernity's relation to time. Time is no longer counted progressively, by addition, starting from an origin, but by subtraction, starting from the end. This is what happens with rocket launches or time bombs. And that end is no longer the symbolic endpoint of a history, but the mark of a zero sum, of a potential exhaustion. This is a perspective of entropy – by the exhausting of all possibilities – the perspective of a counting down to infinity. . . . We are no longer in the finalistic, historical or providential vision, which was the vision of a world of progress and production. The final illusion of history, the final utopia of time no longer exists, since it is already registered there as something potentially accounted for, in digital time, just as mankind's finalities cease to exist at the point where they come to be registered in a genetic capital and solely in the biological perspective of the exploitation of the genome. When you count the seconds separating you from the end, the fact is that everything is already at an end; we are already beyond the end.

In the countdown, the time remaining is already past, and the maximal utopia of life gives way to the minimal utopia of survival. We are experiencing time and history in a kind of deep coma. This is the hysteresis of the millennium, which expresses itself in interminable crisis. It is no longer the future which lies before us, but an anorexic dimension – the impossibility of being finished and, at the same time, the impossibility of seeing beyond. Prediction, foresight being the memory of the future, it diminishes in exact proportion to the memory of the past. When everything can be *seen*, nothing can be *foreseen* any more. What is there beyond the end? Beyond the end extends virtual reality, the horizon of a programmed reality in which all our known functions – memory, emotions, sexuality, intelligence – become progressively useless. Beyond the end, in the era of the transpolitical, the trans-sexual, the transaesthetic, all our desiring machines become little spectacle machines, then quite simply bachelor machines, before dying away into the countdown of the species. The countdown is the code of the automatic disappearance of the world, and all our little humanitarian machines, by way of which we anticipate that disappearance – the Telethons,[1] Sidathons[2] and all the rest of the Thanatons – are merely the promotional Sales Event for the misery of this *fin de siècle*. But – and this is even more paradoxical – what are we to do when nothing really comes to an end any more, that is to say, when nothing every really takes place, since everything is already calculated, accounted for, expired and realized in advance (the simulacrum taking precedence over the real, information taking precedence over the event, etc.)? Our problem is no longer: what are we to make of real events, of real violence, but what are we to make of events which do not take place? Not: what are we to do after the orgy? But: what are we to do when the orgy no longer takes place – the orgy of history, the orgy of revolution and liberation, the orgy of modernity? Little by little, as the hands of the clock move around (though, sadly, digital clocks no longer even have hands), we tell ourselves that, taking everything into account – taking everything into a 'count-down' – modernity has never happened. There has never really been any modernity, never any real progress, never any assured liberation. The linear tension of modernity and progress has been broken, the thread of history has become entangled and the last great 'historic' event – the fall of the Berlin Wall – signified more an immense repentance on the part of history which, rather than heading off towards fresh perspectives, seems rather to be splintering into scattered fragments and reactivating phases of events and conflicts we had thought long gone.

All that we believed past and finished, left behind by the inexorable march of universal progress, is not dead at all, but seems rather to be returning to strike at the heart of our ultra-sophisticated, ultra-vulnerable systems. It is a bit like the last scene of *Jurassic Park* in which the modern (artificially cloned) dinosaurs burst into the museum and wreak havoc on their fossilized ancestors preserved there, before being destroyed in their turn. Today, we are ourselves, as the human species, trapped in this same way between our fossils and our clones.

So, the countdown extends in both directions: not only does it put an end to time in the future, but it also exhausts itself in the obsessional revival of the events of the past. A reverse recapitulation, which is the opposite of a living memory – fanatical memorization, commemorations, rehabilitations, cultural museification, listing of sites of memory, extolling of heritage. In fact this systematic obsession with re-living and reviving everything, this obsessional neurosis, this forcing of memory is equivalent to a non-occurrence of memory – equivalent to a non-occurrence of current history, of the non-occurrence of the event in the information space. This amounts to making the past itself a clone, an artificial double, and to freezing it in a sham exactitude, which will never actually do it justice. But it is because we have nothing else now but objects in which not to believe, nothing but fossilized hopes, that we are forced to go down this road: to elevate everything to the status of a museum piece, an item of heritage. Here again, time reverses: instead of things first passing through history before becoming part of the heritage, they now pass directly into the heritage. Instead of first existing, works of art now go straight into the museum. Instead of being born and drying, they are born as virtual fossils. Collective neurosis. As a result, the ozone layer that was protecting memory becomes frayed; the hole through which memories and time are leaking out into space expands, prefiguring the great migration of the void to the periphery. . . .

Closing down, closing down! It's the end-of-the-century sale. Everything must go! Modernity is over (without ever having happened), the orgy is over, the party is over – the sales are starting. It's the great end-of-the-century sale. But the sales do not come after the festive seasons any longer; nowadays, the sales start first, last the whole year long and the festivals themselves are sold off everywhere. The stocks have to be used up, time-capital has to be used up, life-capital has to be used up. Everywhere, we have the countdown; what we are living through in this symbolic end of the millennium is the prescribed term, whether it be that of the planet's resources or of AIDS, which has become the collective symptom off the prescribed term of death. It is all these things which hover over us in the shadow of the Year 2000, together with the delicious, yet terrifying enjoyment of the period of time left to us. But, ultimately, perhaps the Year 2000 will not take place? Perhaps, on the occasion of the Year 2000, we shall be granted a general amnesty?

There is no finer parable to describe this countdown than Arthur C. Clarke's story, 'The nine billion names of God'. A community of Tibetan monks has been engaged from time immemorial in listing and copying out the names of God, of which there are nine billion. At the end of this, the world will end. So runs the prophecy. But the monks are tired and, in order to hasten the work, they call in the experts at IBM, who come along with their computers and finish the job in a month. It is as though the operation of the virtual dimension were to bring the history of the world to an end in an instant. Unfortunately, this also means the disappearance of the world in real time, since the promise of the end of the world associated with this exhaustive counting of the names of God is fulfilled, and, as they go back down into the valley, the technicians, who did not actually believe in the prophecy, see the stars going out in the firmament, one by one.

This parable depicts our modern situation well: we have called in the IBM technicians and they have triggered the code of the world's automatic disappearance. As a result of the intervention of all the digital, computing and virtual-reality technologies, we are already beyond reality; things have already passed beyond their own ends. They cannot, therefore, come to an end any longer, and they sink into the interminable (interminable history, interminable politics, interminable crisis).

This is the fulfilment of Canetti's vision that:

> as of a certain point, history was no longer real. Without noticing it, all mankind suddenly left reality; everything happening since then might well not have been true; but we could not be aware of that . . . As long as we didn't [find] . . . that point, we would be forced to abide in our present destruction.

And, in effect, we persevere, on the pretext of an increasingly sophisticated technology, in the interminable deconstruction of a world and of a history unable now to secrete anything by way of which it can abolish itself. Everything is free to go on infinitely. We no longer have the means to end processes. They unfold without us now, beyond reality, so to speak, in an endless speculation, an exponential acceleration. But, as a result, they do so in an indifference which is also exponential. Endless, is also desireless, tension-less, passionless, without any real events. An anorexic history, no longer fuelled by real incidents, and exhausting itself in the countdown. Exactly the opposite of the end of history, then: *the impossibility of finishing with history*. If history can no longer reach its end, then it is no longer properly speaking a history. We have lost history and have also, as a result, lost the end of history. We are labouring under the illusion of the end, under the posthumous illusion of the end. And this is serious, for the end signifies that something has really taken place. Whereas we, at the height of reality – and with information at its peak – no longer know whether anything has taken place or not.

Perhaps the end of history, if we can actually conceive such a thing, is merely ironic? Perhaps it is merely an effect of the ruse of history, which consists in having concealed its end from us, in having ended without our noticing it. So that it is merely the end of history that is being fuelled, whereas we believe we are continuing to make it. We are still awaiting its end, whereas that end has, in fact, already taken place. History's ruse was to make us believe in its end, when it has, in fact, already set off back in the opposite direction.

Whether we speak of the end of history, the end of the political or the end of the social, what we are clearly dealing with here is the end of the *scene of the political*, the end of the *scene of the social*, the end of the *scene of history*. In other words, in all these spheres, we are speaking of the advent of a specific era of *obscenity*. Obscenity may be characterized as the endless, unbridled proliferation of the social, of the political, of information, of the economic, of the aesthetic, not to mention, of course, of the sexual. Obesity is another of the figures of obscenity. As endless, unbridled proliferation, as the saturation of a limitless space, obesity may stand as a universal metaphor for our systems of information, communication, production and memory. Obesity and obscenity are the contrapuntal figure of all our systems, which have been seized by something of an Ubuesque distension. All our structures, end up swelling like red giants which absorb everything in their expansion. Thus the social sphere, as it expands, absorbs all the political sphere on its way. But the political sphere itself is obese and obscene, while at the same time becoming increasingly transparent: the more it distends, the more it virtually ceases to exist. When everything is political, that is the end of politics as destiny, it is the beginning of politics as culture and the instant poverty of that cultural politics. It is the same with the economic or the sexual spheres: as they dilate, all structures infiltrate and submerge all the others. Such as the extreme phenomena: those which occur behind the end (extreme = *ex terminus*). They indicate that we have passed from growth to excrescence, from movement and change to stasis, ek-stasis and metastasis. They countersign the end with excess, with hypertrophy, with proliferation, with chain reaction, with an overstepping of the mark. Not with lack, but with precisely the opposite.

Ecstasy of the social: the masses. The more social than social.
Ecstasy of the body: obesity. The fatter than fat.
Ecstasy of information: simulation. Truer than true.

Ecstasy of time: real time, instantaneity. More present than the present.
Ecstasy of the real: the hyperreal. More real than the real.
Ecstasy of sex: porn. More sexual than the sexual.
Ecstasy of violence: terror. More violent than the violent
etc.

All this, by a kind of potentiation, a kind of raising to the second power, of pushing to the limit, describes a state of unconditional realization, of total positivity (every negative sign raised to the second power produces a positive), from which all utopia, all death, all negativity has been expunged. Hence also a state of the extermination, the cleansing of the negative, which is a corollary to all the other forms of purification or cleansing. Thus, freedom has been obliterated, liquidated by liberation; truth has given way to verification; community has been liquidated and absorbed by communication; form gives way to information and performance. Everywhere we see a paradoxical logic which puts an end to an idea by its very realization, its excessiveness. And in this way history itself comes to an end, finds itself obliterated by the instantaneity and omnipresence of the event.

This kind of acceleration by inertia, this exponentiality of extreme phenomena, produces a new kind of event: strange, random and chaotic events which Historical Reason no longer recognizes as its own. Even if, by analogy with past events, we think we recognize them, they no longer have the same meaning. For the reason that the same incidents (wars, ethnic conflicts, nationalisms, the building of Europe) do not have the same meaning depending on whether they arise as part of a history in progress or as part of a declining history. Now, we are in a history which is declining – this is why they appear ghostly to us.

But is a declining history still a history?

We have not only lost utopia as an ideal end, but historical time itself in its continuity and its unfolding. Something like a short-circuit has occurred, a switching of temporal dimensions – effects preceding causes, ends preceding origins – and this has led to this paradox of achieved utopia. Now, achieved utopia puts an end to the utopian dimension. It creates an impossible situation, in the sense that it exhausts the possibilities. From this point on, the problem in hand is not one of changing how life is lived, which was the maximal utopia, but one of survival which is a kind of minimal utopia.

So today, with the loss of utopias and ideologies, we lack objects of belief. But, even more perhaps, we lack *objects in which not to believe*. For it is vital – doubtless even more vital than to believe – to have things in which not to believe. Ironic objects, so to speak, detached perspectives, ideas in which one can believe and not believe, totally freely. Ideologies performed this ambiguous function pretty well. All this is now jeopardized, vanishing progressively into extreme reality and extreme operationality.

Other things are emerging: retrospective utopias, the revival of all earlier or archaic forms in what is, in a sense, a retrospective or necrospective history. For the disappearance of avant-gardes, those emblems of modernity, has not brought about the disappearance of the rearguards. Quite the opposite. In this process of general retroversion (has history perhaps gone down with a retrovirus?), the rearguards find themselves once again in pole position.

We are familiar with the parodic, palinodic event, the event Marx analysed when he depicted Napoleon III as a grotesque stand-in for Napoleon I. In this second event – a debased avatar of the original – a form of dilution, of historical entropy set in. History presented itself as though it were advancing and continuing, whereas it was actually col-lapsing. The current period offers numerous examples of this debased, extenuated form of the primary events of modernity. Ghost-events, [. . .] cloned events, farcical events, phan-tom events – a little bit like phantom limbs, those phantom extremities which hurt even when they are no longer there. Spectrality – of communism in particular.

Events which are more or less ephemeral because they no longer have any resolution except in the media (in the sense in which we speak of the resolution of an image); they have no political resolution. We have, in a sense, a history which is no longer in the making, but remains at the virtual acting-out stage, and retains a spectral air of *déjà-vu*. Sarajevo is a fine example of this unreal history, in which all the participants have impo-tent walk-on parts. It is no longer even an event, but the symbol of an importance specific to history. Everywhere, virtuality – that of the media hyperspace and the hyperspace of discourses – develops in a way diametrically opposed to what one might call, if it still existed, the real movement of history.

In the past, the virtual had actuality as its end, its destination. Today, it is the func-tion of the virtual to proscribe the actual reality. In the absence of real history, virtual history is here, and provides the sanction, in the guise of information, for the definitive absence of that real history. Hence the absence of responsibility – both individual and collective – for the consequences, since we are already, by virtue of information, beyond the event, which has not taken place.

We might speak here of a kind of 'event strike', to use Macedonio Fernandez's expression. What does this mean? That the work of history has ceased to function. That the work of mourning is beginning. That the information system is taking over the baton from History and starting to produce the event in the same way that Capital is starting to produce Work, so that labour no longer has any significance of its own, just as the event produced by information has no historical meaning of its own.

This is the point where we enter the transhistorical or the transpolitical, that is to say, the sphere where events do not really take place precisely because they are produced and broadcast 'in real time', where they have no meaning because they can have all possible meanings. We have, therefore, to grasp them now not politically, but transpo-litically, that is to say, *at the point where they become lost in the void of information*. The sphere of information is like a space where, after emptying events of their meaning, an artificial gravity is created for them; where, after deep-freezing them politically and historically, they are re-staged transpolitically, in real – that is to say, perfectly virtual – time. We might speak in the same way of the transeconomic sphere, that is to say, the sphere where classical economics gets lost in the void of speculation, just as History gets lost in the void of information.

But, in the end, perhaps we have to pose all these problems in terms other than the hackneyed ones of alienation and the unhappy fate of the subject. And there is precisely the Ubuesque side of this technological excrescence, of this proliferating obscenity and obesity, of this unbridled virtuality and virality which invites us to do so. Our situation is a wholly pataphysical one; that is to say, everything around us has passed beyond its own history, has moved beyond the laws of physics and metaphysics. Now, pataphysics is ironic, and the hypothesis which suggests itself here is that, *at the same time as things have reached a state of paroxysm, they have also reached a state of parody*.

Might we advance the hypothesis – beyond the heroic stage, beyond the critical stage – of an ironic stage of technology, an ironic stage of history, an ironic stage of value? This would at last free us from the Heideggerian vision of technology as the effectuation and final stage of metaphysics; it would free us from all retrospective nostalgia for being, and we would have, rather, a gigantic objectively ironic 'take' on all this scientific and technological process which would not be far removed from the radical snobbery, the post-historical, Japanese snobbery Kojève spoke of.

An ironic reversal of technology, similar to the irony of the media sphere. The common illusion about the media is that they are used by those in power to manipulate, seduce and alienate the masses. A naive interpretation. The more subtle version, the ironic version is precisely the opposite. It is that, through the media, it is the masses who manipulate those in power (or those who see themselves in such terms). It is precisely at the point where the political power thinks it has them where it wants them that the masses impose their clandestine strategy of neutralization, of destabilization of a power that has become paraplegic. At the very least, let us agree that matters are undecidable here; that both hypotheses are valid; and that, at any event, any interpretation regarding the media is reversible. It is precisely in this reversibility that the object of science – of the most sophisticated of current sciences. Through the most subtle procedures we deploy to pin it down, it not the scientific object itself toying with us, presenting itself as an object and mocking our objective pretension to analyse it? Scientists are not far from admitting such a thing today, and this irony of the object is the very form of a radical illusoriness of the world, an illusion which is no longer physical (of the senses) or metaphysical (mental or philosophical), but pataphysical, to use the term Jarry applied to the 'science of imaginary solutions'.

Let us extend the hypothesis to all our technologies, to the technical universe in general, which is becoming the ironic instrument of a world which we believe we transform and dominate whereas in fact it – the object – imposes and asserts itself through all the interposed technologies, which we merely operate. Such is, here again, the form of the illusion. Not the illusion of error (we are not wrong about technology – there is no sense perpetually reviving that unfounded accusation), but the illusion of a game – it is simply that we do not know the rules.

The ironic hypothesis – that of a transcendental or technical irony – being by definition unverifiable, let us content ourselves with the undecidable, with the mere possibility of that hypothesis, which is in itself more subtle and exciting than all the others. We are faced in the end with two irreconcilable hypotheses: that of the perfect crime or, in other words, of the extermination by technology and virtuality of all reality – and equally of the illusion of the world – or that of the dome play of technologies, of an ironic destiny of all science and all knowledge by which the world – and the illusion of the world – are perpetuated. Let us content ourselves with these two irreconcilable and simultaneously 'true' perspectives. There is nothing that allows us to decide between them. As Wittgenstein says, 'the world is everything which is the case'.

Notes

This lecture was given at the ICA, 8 May 1997, as part of the Big Thinkers series.

1   The French equivalent of 'Children in Need'.
2   TV event for World Aids Day.

CHAPTER 45

Kerwin Lee Klein

'ON THE EMERGENCE OF MEMORY IN HISTORICAL DISCOURSE' (2000)*

The final reading of this Part is taken from Kerwin Lee Klein's 'On the Emergence of Memory in Historical Discourse' (2000) in which he argues – tentatively – that the recent rise of 'memory studies' may well signal, if not the end, then at least a reconsideration of history:

> It is no accident that our sudden fascination with memory goes hand in hand with postmodern reckonings of history . . . as an oppressive fiction. Memory can come to the fore in an age of historiographic crisis precisely because it figures as a therapeutic alternative to historical discourse.

The reasons for this alternative way of figuring the past are thus fairly recent, for although the phrase 'collective memory' was coined in 1902 and Maurice Halbwachs's *The Social Frameworks of Memory* was published in 1925, the scholarly boom in 'memory' began in earnest in the 1980s, an earnestness which, by the late 1990s, ensured that it brimmed with such titles as 'Sites of Memory' or 'Cultural Memory' or 'The Politics of Memory'. As a result, history's hegemonic primacy as *the* way to 'grasp the past' is arguably being subverted, as it becomes 'the leading term in our new cultural history'.

And, for Klein, this may, be an indication of a major shift in the potency of history, for history, as he explains, finds its meanings 'in large part through its counter-concepts and synonyms, and so the emergence of memory promises to re-work history's boundaries . . . increasingly [functioning] as antonym rather than synonym, contrary rather than complement and replacement rather than supplement'. Klein remains uncertain as to the possible outcome of this opposition, but he considers that, at least, the use of memory as a frequent replacement for history reflects both an increasing discontent with historical discourse and a desire to draw upon some of the oldest patterns of linguistic practice.

These considerations on memory and history bring Part Four to a close. It seems, as might be expected, that everyone we have considered has a feeling of 'incredulity toward metanarratives' and that, for some, the fall-out from their collapse is impacting upon academic histories. Whatever the views of the 'historians' featured in this Part, no consideration of the current state of 'the nature of history' can leave out of the discussion the possible end of that interesting experiment of historicising the past, modernist style and, maybe, postmodern style too.

---

* Kerwin Lee Klein (2000) 'On The Emergence of Memory in Historical Discourse', *Representations*, 69, Winter: 127–50.

WELCOME TO THE MEMORY industry. In the grand scheme of things, the memory industry ranges from the museum trade to the legal battles over repressed memory and on to the market for academic books and articles that invoke *memory* as key word. Our scholarly fascination with things memorable is quite new. As Jeffrey K. Olick and Joyce Robbins have noted, "collective memory" emerged as an object of scholarly inquiry only in the early twentieth century, contemporaneous with the so-called crisis of historicism. Hugo von Hofmannsthal used the phrase "collective memory" in 1902, and in 1925 Maurice Halbwachs's *The Social Frameworks of Memory* argued, against Henri Bergson and Sigmund Freud, that memory is a specifically social phenomenon. But outside of experimental psychology and clinical psychoanalysis, few academics paid much attention to memory until the great swell of popular interest in autobiographical litera-ture, family genealogy, and museums that marked the seventies.

The scholarly boom began in the 1980s with two literary events: Yosef Yerushalmi's *Zakhor: Jewish History and Jewish Memory* (1982) and Pierre Nora's "Between Memory and History," the introduction to an anthology *Lieux de mémoire* (1984). Each of these texts identified memory as a primitive or sacred form opposed to modern historical conscious-ness. For Yerushalmi, the Jews were the archetypal people of memory who had adopted history only recently and then only in part, for "modern Jewish historiography can never replace an eroded group memory." For Nora, memory was an archaic mode of being that had been devastated by rationalization: "We speak so much of memory because there is so little out left." Despite or perhaps because of their elegiac tone and accounts of memory as antihistorical discourse, these works found an amazing popularity and were quickly joined by others. In 1989 the translation of Nora's influential essay in a special issue of this journal and the founding of *History and Memory*, based in Tel Aviv and Los Angeles, showed the crystallization of a sell-conscious memory discourse. A decade later the schol-arly literature brims with such titles as "Sites of Memory" or "Cultural Memory" or "The Politics of Memory."

The emergence of memory as a key word marks a dramatic change in linguistic prac-tice. We might be tempted to imagine the increasing use of *memory* as the natural result of an increased scholarly interest in the ways that popular and folk cultures construct history and the past. Such a reading would be too hasty. For years, specialists have dealt with such well-known phenomena as oral history, autobiography, and commemorative rituals without ever pasting them together into something called *memory*. Where we once spoke of folk history or popular history or oral history or public history or even myth we now employ memory as a metahistorical category that subsumes all these various terms. Indeed, one of the salient features of our new memory talk is the tendency to make fairly sweeping philosophical claims for memory or even to imagine memory discourse as part of what is vaguely hailed as the rise of theory in departments of litera-ture, history, and anthropology.

Recent works on memory often tie the rise of the word to the waves of theory that had washed over American human sciences by the 1980s. In its most popular (if simplistic) understandings, theory talk—variously figured through high "structuralism," "poststruc-turalism," "postmodernism," "deconstruction," "*posthistoire*," and a host of other often confused labels—was imagined as a devastating critique of the totalizing aspects of histor-ical discourse. And yet by the end of the eighties, we were awash in new historicisms that took memory as a key word. These seemingly antithetical trends, the discourse of memory and the antihistoricist vocabularies of postmodernity, converged in the "new

cultural history" as historians began borrowing from semiotics and scholars in traditionally formalist fields—literature, art, and anthropology—began venturing into historicism.
I am not much interested in trying to define "new cultural history" let alone "postmodernism." Many of the scholars popularly associated with postmodernism do not even use
the word. Nor am I interested, here, in trying to separate out the ways in which certain
poststructural texts may radicalize rather than escape historicism. But I am very interested in the common sense that "memory" is the new critical conjunction of history and
theory or, as Alon Confino and Allan Megill put it, that *memory* has become the leading
term in our new cultural history.

   Memory is replacing old favorites—*nature, culture, language*—as the word most commonly paired with history, and that shift is remaking historical imagination. It is not as if
History or *history* or *historicity* or *historical discourse* denoted unproblematic realms of experience that now face an alien memorial invasion. *History*, as with other key words, finds its
meanings in large part through its counter-concepts and synonyms, and so the emergence
of *memory* promises to rework *history*'s boundaries. Those borders should attract our interest, for much current historiography pits memory against history even though few authors
openly claim to be engaged in building a world in which memory can serve as an alternative to history. Indeed, the declaration that history and memory are not really opposites
has become one of the clichés of our new memory discourse. In preface after preface, an
author declares that it would be simplistic to imagine memory and history as antitheses
and then proceeds to use the words in antithetical ways in the body of the monograph.
Such disclaimers have little effect on the ways in which the words work. Where history is
concerned, memory increasingly functions as antonym rather than synonym; contrary
rather than complement and replacement rather than supplement.

   [. . .]

   We have, then, several alternative narratives of the origins of our new memory discourse. The first, following Pierre Nora, holds that we are obsessed with memory because
we have destroyed it with historical consciousness. A second holds that memory is a new
category of experience that grew out of the modernist crisis of the self in the nineteenth
century and then gradually evolved into our current usage. A third sketches a tale in which
Hegelian historicism took up premodern forms of memory that we have since modified
through structural vocabularies. A fourth implies that memory is a mode of discourse natural to people without history, and so its emergence is a salutary feature of decolonization. And a fifth claims that memory talk is a belated response to the wounds of modernity.
None of these stories seems fully credible.

   A different way of reckoning with the rise of memory discourse is to place it within
the cultural context of the postsixties United States and attribute it to identity politics.
Charles Maier has warned of the "surfeit of memory" and the politics of victimization. In
his view, memory appeals to us because it lends itself to the articulation of ethnoracial
nationalisms that turn away from the cosmopolitan discourses of history. Allan Megill has
gone further and offered a falsifiable proposition: if identity grows problematic, then will
memory become more important. But as semantic history that proposition is not very
helpful. Identity is part of memory discourse; as Philip Gleason recounted back in 1980,
identity was virtually unknown in the social sciences and humanities prior to the 1950s.
Erik Erikson's work in the sixties publicized the term, and it took off in the seventies,
little more than a decade ahead of *memory*. The two words are typically yoked together;
to mention the one is to mention the other. Richard Handler, at a recent conference on

history and memory, warned that the enthusiasm for *identity*—the key word of bourgeois subjectivity—undercut the claims of memory work to deconstruct the Western self. Since Handler's cautions seem to have gone unheeded. I doubt that retelling the story here will do much good, but I reference it as evidence of the circularity that marks so much of what we flatter ourselves is postmodern reflexiveness. I will go so far as to agree with this aspect of Maier's concern: we should be worried about the tendency to employ memory as the mode of discourse natural to the people without history.

If we limit ourselves to academia, another way of thinking of the rise of memory talk in the eighties is as a response to the challenges posed by poststructuralism. Viewed from a certain deconstructionist perspective, Memory looks like a reaction-formation. Faced with the threat of linguistic anarchism, the conservatism of the academy has asserted itself by assimilating a few empty slogans and offering up a "new" cultural history effectively purged of real intellectual radicalism. Here one might cite the litany of dangers of Memory: The reification of bourgeois subjectivity in the name of postmodernism, the revival of primordialism in the name of postcolonialism; the psychoanalytic slide from the hermeneutics of suspicion to therapeutic discourse; the privatization of history as global experiences splinter into isolated chunks of ethnoracial substance; the celebration of a new ritualism under the cover of historical skepticism. I have some sympathy for such an account; certainly one of the reasons for memory's sudden rise is that it promises to let us have our essentialism and deconstruct it, too. Even when advertised as a system of difference, memory gives us a signified whose signifiers appear to be so weighty so tragic—so monumental—that they will never float free. But can we credibly imagine a "pure" postmodernism untainted by mystical tendencies? Can we even imagine a coherent narrative of postmodernism as a cultural movement? If the skeptical moments of Jacques Derrida belong to postmodernism, so do the mystical enthusiasms of Blanchot.

[. . .]

A fuller account of memory talk will need a detailed reckoning of the interweaving of popular and technical vocabularies, since our scholarly usage is so tightly bound up with the everyday. Memory serves so many different scholarly interests, and is applied to so many phenomena, that an inclusive history of its origins would indeed approach the universal. But having begun with the wider interpretive horizons of popular culture, we should conclude with them as well, for it is our position within broader publics that makes this genealogy of interest. Here, I am less interested in origins and more in effects. Were academic discourse as hermetically sealed as we like to believe, the benefits of memory talk might outweigh the risks. If it were a simple matter of a handful of progressive and predominantly secular academics reclaiming "piety" as an epistemic concept, we might, if only through appeals to strategic essentialism, make a case for sacralizing portions of the past out of respect to the worldviews and experiences of colonized peoples, or victims of child abuse, or the survivors of the Holocaust. But that is hardly the case, and the insistent association of memory with semireligious language not only undercuts the claims of memory to critique metaphysics, it also opens troubling vistas.

Aura, Jetztzeit, *Messianic, trauma, mourning, sublime, apocalypse, fragment, identity, redemption, healing, catharsis, cure, witnessing, testimony, ritual, piety, soul*: This is not the vocabulary of a secular, critical practice. That such a vocabulary should emerge from the most theoretically engaged texts, and that it should advertise itself as a critique of metaphysics, is all the more remarkable. Were we to attend closely to the more numerous studies in which scholars simply appropriate such words without any careful discussion, the tendencies would appear far more pronounced. And we should remember that our scholarly language circulates within popular discourses saturated with religiosity. Many academics may live in enclaves of irony, but most Americans believe in angels. As I write this essay, the State of Kansas has just announced that it will eliminate all references to evolution in its standards for science education. Whatever its intentions, Memory will not deconstruct neoconservatism.

The clustering of quasi-religious terms around *memory* suggests some conclusions about the effects of our new key word. I do not believe that our recycling of archaic usage is a simple matter of some primordial essence shimmering through a postmodern surface. Our use of memory as a supplement, or more frequently as a replacement, for history reflects both an increasing discontent with historical discourse and a desire to draw upon some of the oldest patterns of linguistic practice. Without that horizon of religious and Hegelian meanings, memory could not possibly do the work we wish it to do, namely; to re-enchant our relation with the world and pour presence back into the past. It is no accident that our sudden fascination with memory goes hand in hand with postmodern reckonings of history as the marching black boot and of historical consciousness as an oppressive fiction. Memory can come to the fore in an age of historiographic crisis precisely because it figures as a therapeutic alternative to historical discourse.

Guide to further reading

Part One: Reconstructionism

Texts on the nature of history abound, and a good many of them have been written in defence of reconstructionist approaches to it. Because reconstructionist historians view history as essentially a methodology rather than an epistemology, there is a surfeit of handbooks and 'how to do it' texts. We have included two extracts from such texts in this book, the most well known being Geoffrey Elton's *Return to Essentials* (Cambridge: Cambridge University Press, 1991). In addition, Deborah A. Symonds's chapter 'Living in the Scottish Record Office' from Elizabeth Fox-Genovese and Elisabeth Lasch-Quinn's *Reconstructing History* (New York and London: Routledge, 1999) comes from a book collection that attempts to defend such an approach. Two classic examples of reconstructionist barnstorming of the past thirty-five years are Geoffrey Elton's now somewhat antiquarian *The Practice of History* (London: Methuen, 1967) and Jack Hexter's *The History Primer* (London: Allen Lane, 1972). By definition, such texts defend the belief in the correspondence of past event and present word, and are usually written in the assumptive mode, following the example of long-lived history methodology texts that reflect the nineteenth-century obsession with telling the past as it really was. The most notable example is *Introduction to the Study of History* by C.V. Langlois and C. Seignobos (New York: Barnes & Noble, 1966). Most recently, we find Arthur Marwick's *The New Nature of History: Knowledge, Evidence, Language* (Houndmills: Palgrave, 2001), which is the latest incarnation of his book *The Nature of History* (London: Macmillan, 1970). Marwick is reconstructionism personified.

Any reasoned defences of empiricism would also, of course, include Carl Becker's 'Everyman His Own Historian' (*American Historical Review*, 1931, 37: 221–36), Charles Beard's 'Written History as an Act of Faith' (*American Historical Review*, 1933, 39: 219–31) and his 'That Noble Dream' (*American Historical Review*, 1935, 41: 74–87). However, while Becker and Beard accepted the relativism of history, acknowledging that history is written in the here and now, both ultimately tried to salvage empiricism and its association with objectivity and truthful telling. More recently, reconstructionist attitudes have been defended by James T. Kloppenberg in his 'Objectivity and Historicism: A Century of American Historical Writing' (*American Historical Review*, 1989, 94: 1011–30) and by Andrew P. Norman in 'Telling It Like It Was: Historical Narratives on Their Own Terms' (*History and Theory*, 1991, 30: 119–35). This defence continues up to the present and is well illustrated by Chris Lorenz's responses to postist assertions in 'Historical Knowledge and Historical Reality: A plea for "historical realism"' (*History and Theory*, 1994, 33: 297–327) and 'Can Histories be True? Narrativism, Positivism, and the "Metaphorical Turn"' (*History and Theory*, 1998, 37: 309–29). The most recent bulwarks of reconstructionism are two articles by Perez Zagorin, 'Historiography and Postmodernism: Reconsiderations' (*History and Theory*, 1990, 29: 263–74) and 'History, the Referent, and Narrative: Reflections on Postmodernism Now' (*History and Theory*, 1999, 38: 1–24).

The rise of anti-representationalism in particular has produced a sustained realist counter-offensive in the past twenty years or so. For the defence of agent intentionality – one of the elements of reconstructionist thinking – see Mark Bevir's debate with Frank Ankersmit in 'Exchanging Ideas' (*Rethinking History: The Journal of Theory and Practice*, 2000, 4 (3): 351–72) and Bevir's *The Logic of the History of Ideas* (Cambridge: Cambridge University Press ([1999] 2000). Geoffrey Roberts's review, 'Postmodernism versus the Standpoint of Action', of *On 'What is History?'* by Keith Jenkins (*History and Theory*, 1997, 36: 249–60) is a robust response from a reconstructionist to the emergence of the new postist genres of history. The most recent introduction to the core belief of the genre – empiricism – is to be found in Stephen Davies's *Empiricism and History* (Houndmills: Palgrave, 2003). Martin Bunzl in *Real History* (London: Routledge, 1997) offers a particularly coherent support of realism in historical practice. He acknowledges that the epistemological debates that we think have created the four main genres underpin all our questions about history as a form of knowing that goes beyond the simple primacy of the empirical. Such questions inevitably become more overt and as such constitute the defining feature of the next genre – constructionism.

Part Two: Constructionism

Two of the extracts in our collection are worthy of consideration as full-blown introductions to the mainstream of historical thinking and practice today. These are Peter Charles Hoffer and William W. Stueck's *Reading and Writing American History: An Introduction to the Historian's Craft* (two volumes, Lexington, MA: D.C. Heath & Company, vol. 1, 1994) and John Tosh's *The Pursuit of History: Aims, Methods and New Directions in the Study of Modern History* (Harlow: Longman [1984] 2000). The most detailed study of the nature of history from an empirical, analytical, constructionist perspective can be found in C. Behan McCullagh's *Justifying Historical Descriptions* (Cambridge: Cambridge University Press, 1984) and *The Truth of History* (New York and London: Routledge, 1998). The most detailed examination (although restricted to the US context) of objectivity and its history in a conceptually and epistemologically sceptical world is Peter

Novick's *That Noble Dream: the 'Objectivity' Question and the American Historical Profession* (Cambridge: Cambridge University Press, 1988).

In the past decade or so, several vigorous restatements of the constructionist genre have been published – see, for example, Joyce Appleby, Lynn Hunt and Margaret Jacob's *Telling the Truth About History* (New York and London: Norton, 1994), Lynn Hunt's 'Does History Need Defending? (*History Workshop Journal*, 1998, 46: 241–49) and her *The New Cultural History* (Berkeley: University of California Press, 1989); see also Richard Evans's *In Defence of History* (London: Granta, 1997) and Mary Fulbrook's *Historical Theory* (New York and London: Routledge, 2002). As we have suggested, most 'how to do it' primers are cast in defence of the constructionist genre – see, for example, Jeremy Black and Donald M. MacRaild's *Studying History* (Houndmills: Palgrave ([1997] 2000) and the collection edited by David Cannadine, *What is History Now?* (Houndmills: Palgrave, 2002).

Possibly the most able defender of the empirical-analytical position is Georg Iggers – see his *Historiography in the Twentieth Century: From Scientific Objectivity to the Postmodern Challenge* (Hanover and London: Wesleyan University Press, 1997) and 'Historiography between Scholarship and Poetry: Reflections on Hayden White's Approach to Historiography' (*Rethinking History: The Journal of Theory and Practice*, 2000, 4 (3): 373–90). Michael Bentley's edited *Companion to Historiography* (London: Routledge, 1997) is a major showcase for mainstream history today. A very helpful introduction to the diversity within constructionist history is Anna Green and Kathleen Troup's *The Houses of History: A Critical Reader in Twentieth Century History and Theory* (Manchester: Manchester University Press, 1999). The most prolific student of constructionism is Peter Burke – see his edited *New Perspectives on Historical Writing* (University Park, PA: The Pennsylvania University Press, 1992), *History and Social Theory* (Ithaca, NY: Cornell University Press, 1993) and *Varieties of Cultural History* (Oxford: Polity Press, 1997).

There are four leading advocates for social science history. They are Christopher Lloyd, *The Structures of History* (Oxford: Basil Blackwell, 1993); Clayton Roberts, *The Logic of Historical Explanation* (University Park, PA: The Pennsylvania University Press, 1996); Graham Snooks, *The Laws of History* (London: Routledge, 1998) and Miles Fairburn, *Social History: Problems, Strategies and Methods* (Houndmills: Macmillan, 1999). Wearing his ideology on his sleeve is the Marxist Alex Callinicos in his *Social Theory: A Historical Introduction* (Cambridge: Polity Press, 1999). Gender and women's history are well represented by Gisela Bock in 'Women's History and Gender History: Aspects of an International Debate' (*Gender and History*, 1989, 1: 7–30), Joan Scott, 'Gender: A Useful Category of Analysis', *American Historical Review*, 1986, 91: 1053–75 and *Feminism and History* (Oxford: Oxford University Press, 1996).

While the four genres of history as we have described them are epistemologically distinct, there are texts that lead us from one to another through their subject matter. The following are three examples that lead us from constructionism to deconstructionism. The first is Roger Chartier's *Cultural History* (Cambridge: Polity Press, 1988), in which he moves us from the *Annales* tradition (of Braudel *et al.*) into symbolic anthropology and a philosophical discourse on history. The second is Bryan Palmer's *Descent into Discourse: The Reification of Language and the Writing of Social History* (Philadelphia, PA: Temple University Press, 1990) in which he, a Marxist, defends historical materialism against the encroachments of critical theory and the linguistic turn. Third, in George C. Bond and Angela Gilliam's edited collection *Social Construction of the Past: Representation as Power*

(London and New York: Routledge, 1994), contributors explore the alternative constructive (deconstructive?) intersections between the past, history, ethics, domination and
resistance. In other words, all three texts move us into the next genre that reflexively
examines not just the past and the historian's methods and concepts for getting at its
presumed truth, but at the idea of truth itself.

Part Three: Deconstructionism

Although Jacques Derrida's notion of deconstruction is very different from the one
informing the *genre* categorisation of this Reader, nevertheless, few serious students of
history can avoid (well they, can but they ought not to) coming to grips with his ideas.
Excellent introductions, at various levels of difficulty, are: Geoffrey Bennington's *Jacques
Derrida* (written with Derrida) (Chicago: University of Chicago Press, 1993) and his
Interrupting Derrida (London: Routledge, 2000). Nicholas Royle's *Jacques Derrida* (London,
Routledge, 2003) is, says Derrida himself, 'Excellent, strong, clear and original', and he
should know. Royle's book has a wide-ranging Further Reading section, usefully anno-
tated. Martin McQuillan (ed.) provides a very useful introduction to an extensive set of
readings pulled together under the title of *Deconstruction: A Reader* (Edinburgh: Edinburgh
University Press, 2000). The 1987 volume, edited by Derek Attridge *et al.*, *Post-
Structuralism and the Question of History* (Cambridge: Cambridge University Press), although
now old, contains several essays on Derrida's work that are related to history. *Philosophies
of History: From Enlightenment to Postmodernity* (Oxford: Blackwell, 2000), edited by Robert
Burns and Hugh Rayment-Pickard, puts postmodernism into a lengthy and wide-ranging
'perspective'; another Reader, this time edited by Geoffrey Roberts (*The History and
Narrative Reader*, London: Routledge, 2001) assesses the impact of – and resistances to –
the kind of 'narrativisation' advocated by Hayden White and Frank Ankersmit; it is an
excellent volume.

Hayden White's work is obviously a must for anyone trying to understand anything
about the contemporary condition of historical theory; his *Metahistory* (Baltimore, MD:
The Johns Hopkins University Press, 1973) and his latest collection of essays *Figural Realism*
(Baltimore, MD: The Johns Hopkins University Press, 1999) are examples of a truly original mind; White is the most important philosopher of history in the later twentieth century. Frank Ankersmit – White's European counterpart – is also a crucially important and
original theorist in his own right; his most recent book, *Historical Representation* (Berkeley,
CA: University of California Press, 2000) pulls together – and extends – three decades of
historical philosophising. Ewa Domanska's edited volume entitled *Encounters: Philosophy of
History After Postmodernism* (Charlottesville, VA: University Press of Virginia, 1998) is a
series of interviews with a string of postmodernists or those engaged with it – namely,
Hayden White, Hans Kellner, Frank Ankersmit, Georg Iggers, Jerzy Topolski, Jorn
Rusen, Arthur Danto, Lionel Gossman, Peter Burke and Stephen Bann. Frank Ankersmit
and Hans Kellner have edited an excellent volume of essays, entitled *A New Philosophy of
History* (London: Reaktion Books, 1995), informed by 'the linguistic turn'.

Books by Alun Munslow, *Deconstructing History* and *The Routledge Companion to
Historical Studies* (London: Routledge, 1997 and 2000 respectively), and Keith Jenkins's
Why History? (London: Routledge, 1999) have useful Further Reading sections. Jenkins's
text lists works by, or on, Derrida, Baudrillard, Lyotard, White, Ankersmit, Ermarth

and Harlan. Alun Munslow's latest examination of history today, *The New History* (Harlow: Pearson Education, 2004), has as extensive reading list to complement the one included in this Reader. Readers interested in experimental histories and the debates issuing from their existence should read practically any of the issues of the journal *Rethinking History: The Journal of Theory and Practice*, which Routledge have been publishing since 1997. Much older and interested very much in analytical and the history of ideas approaches, the journal *History and Theory* (Blackwell) has, over the past few years, published many fine articles on the impact of 'postist'-type discursive incursions into the rather staid world of the professional historian. Thus, as one example, theme issue no. 41 (December 2002) was on 'innovative histories', and future volumes are sure to keep revisiting the problematic nature of history after 'deconstructionisms'. Other history journals carrying articles engaged with the 'nature of history' under the impact of deconstructionist approaches include *New Literary History*, *Clio*, *Gender and History*, *Representations*, *Journal of Women's History*, *Women's History Review*, *New Left Review*, *Past and Present* and *Textual Practice*.

Part Four: Endisms

The thematic of Endisms also has a considerable literature. One of the arguments as to the end of history, that of Francis Fukuyama, should perhaps have been examined in this Reader, but in our view Fukuyama's books and articles are – in their rethinking of a sort of metanarrative when such a phenomenon is well past its sell-by date – curiously old-fashioned and thus dated at birth. Nevertheless, Fukuyamas's thesis – still best outlined and developed in his *The End of History and The Last Man* (London: Penguin, 1992), has attracted the attention of historians and theorists since it first appeared, from Perry Anderson's 'The Ends of History' critique (in his *A Zone of Engagement* (London: Verso, 1992), through Jacques Derrida's *Specters of Marx* (London: Routledge, 1994) to the last chapter (on 'the end of history') in M.C. Lemon's very recent *Philosophy of History: A Student Guide* (London: Routledge, 2003). Although very different and, again, in our view now marginal to contemporary debates as understood in this Reader, L. Niethammer's *Posthistoire* (London: Verso, 1992) recalls now older concerns. Gianni Vattimo's 'The End of Hi(story)' in *Zeitgeist in Babel* by J. Hoestery (ed.) (Bloomington, IL: University of Indiana Press, 1991) is a short statement of Vattimo's position on history, more extensively outlined in his *The End of Modernity* (Baltimore, MD: The Johns Hopkins University Press, 1985). Gertrude Himmelfarb's *On Looking Into The Abyss* (New York: Knopf, 1994) is a rather sour series of critical engagements with varieties of 'new history', including postmodern ones, and she engages, *inter alia*, with its 'endist' possibilities. Tamsin Spargo's edited volume *Reading The Past* (Houndmills: Palgrave, 2000) contains some interesting readings and includes the essay 'Why Bother With History?' by Keith Jenkins which first developed (in the journal *Rethinking History*) some of the ideas embodied in this Endisms section.

There are, of course, many texts that contain discussions of deconstructionist and endist/postist-type concerns in general terms, often running arguments that revolve around the phenomenon of 'postmodernism'. Examples are Robert Berkhofer's *Beyond The Great Story* (Cambridge, MA: Harvard University Press, 1995) and two brilliant texts by Sande Cohen which take readers into a different world compared to that inhabited by most historians of whatever stripe: *Historical Culture, On the Recoding of an Academic Discipline* (Berkeley: University of California Press, 1988) and *Passive Nihilism* (London:

Macmillan, 1998). *Postmodernism in History: Fear or Freedom?* by Beverley Southgate (London: Routledge, 2003) is an excellent polemic. Ernst Breisach's *On the Future of History: The Postmodernist Challenge and its Aftermath* (Chicago: The University of Chicago Press, 2003) casts a survey-like eye over debates on 'the nature of history' under the impact of the postmodern in ways all students should find illuminating.

Apart from a few incursions into 'endist' debates, most feminist historians work under the banner of constructionism and deconstruction. Over the years, there has been much discussion about the possible consequences of adopting a radical 'postist'-type discourse vis-à-vis concerns over subject(ivities) agency, emancipatory narratives, culturalism, etc., some of which are exemplified in the following: Judith Butler and Joan Scott, *Feminists Theorize the Political* (London: Routledge, 1992); K. Canning, 'Dialogue: The Turn to Gender and The Challenge to Post-Structuralism', *Journal of Women's History* (5 (1), Spring, 1993); Joan Hoff, 'Gender as a Postmodern Category of Paralysis', *Women's History Review* (3 (2), 1994) with a response by Susan Kingsley Kent and Caroline Ramazanogau, in *Women's History Review*, 5 (1), 1996. Wendy Brown's 'Feminist Hesitations, Postmodern Exposures', in *Differences: A Journal of Feminist Cultural Studies*, 3 (1), 1991, is a strong critique of those who fear postist incursions into feminist concerns. Susan Standford Friedman's 'Making History: Reflections on Feminism, Narrative and Desire', in *Feminism Beside Itself*, edited by D. Elam and R. Wiegman (London: Routledge, 1995), pulls a lot of recent thinking together. A general overview that comes up to debates in the late 1990s is Johanna Alberti's *Gender and the Historian* (London: Longman, 2002).

Bibliography

American Historical Association (1995) *Guide to Historical Literature,* 3rd edn, New York and Oxford: Oxford University Press.

Ankersmit, Frank (1983) *Narrative Logic: A Semantic Analysis of the Historian's Language*, The Hague: Martinus Nijhoff.

Appleby, Joyce, Hunt, Lynn, Jacob, Margaret (1994) *Telling the Truth About History*, New York: Norton.

Atkinson, R.F. (1978) *Knowledge and Explanation in History: An Introduction to the Philosophy of History*, London: Macmillan.

Attridge, Derek, Bennington, Geoff and Young, Robert (1987) *Post-Structuralism and the Question of History*, Cambridge: Cambridge University Press.

Bann, Stephen (1984) *The Clothing of Clio: A Study of the Representation of History in Nineteenth-century Britain and France,* Cambridge: Cambridge University Press.

Beard, Charles (1934) "Written History as an Act of Faith", *American Historical Review*, 39 (2): 219–31.

Beard, Charles (1935) "That Noble Dream", *American Historical Review*, 41 (1): 74–87.

Bentley, Michael (ed.) (1997) *Companion to Historiography*, London: Routledge.

Berkhofer, Robert (1995) *Beyond the Great Story: History as Text and Discourse*, Cambridge, MA: Harvard University Press.

Black, Jeremy and MacRaild, Donald M. ([1997] 2000) *Studying History,* Houndmills: Macmillan.

Breisach, Ernst (2003) *On the Future of History*: *The Postmodernist Challenge and its Aftermath*, Chicago: University of Chicago Press.

Bunzl, Martin (1997) *Real History*, London: Routledge.

Callinicos, Alex (1995) *Theories and Narratives: Reflections on the Philosophy of History*, Cambridge: Polity Press.

Carrard, Philippe (1992) *Poetics of the New History*, Baltimore, MD: The Johns Hopkins University Press.

Chamberlain, Mary and Thompson, Paul (1998) *Narrative and Genre,* London and New York: Routledge.

Chartier, Roger (1997) *On the Edge of the Cliff: History, Language and Practice*, Baltimore, MD: The Johns Hopkins University Press.

Coleman, B.I. (1973) *The Idea of the City in Nineteenth-Century Britain*, London and Boston: Routledge & Kegan Paul.

Collingwood, R.G. (1994) *The Idea of History* (revised edn, edited by Jan van der Dussen), Oxford: Oxford University Press.

Croce, Benedetto (1960) *History: Its Theory And Practice* (new edn translated by Douglas Ainslie), London: Russell & Russell.

Curthoys, Ann and Docker, John (1997) "The Two Histories: Metaphor in English Historiographical Writing", *Rethinking History: The Journal of Theory and Practice*, 1 (3): 259–74.

Danto, Arthur C. (1968) *Analytical Philosophy of History*, Cambridge: Cambridge University Press.

Davidson, Donald (1984) *Inquiries into Truth and Interpretation*, Oxford: Oxford University Press.

Domanska, Ewa (1998) *Encounters: Philosophy of History After Postmodernism*, Charlottesville, VA: University Press of Virginia.

Dray, William H. (1957) *Laws and Explanations in History*, Oxford: Oxford University Press.

Dray, William H. (1964) *Philosophy of History*, Englewood Cliffs, NJ: Prentice Hall.

Elton, G.R. (1991) *Return to Essentials,* Cambridge: Cambridge University Press.

Evans, Richard J. (1997) *In Defence of History*, London: Granta.

Evans, Richard J. (1997) 'Truth Lost in Vain Views', *Times Higher*, 12 September: 18.

Fiumara, Gemma C. (1995) *The Metaphoric Process: Connections Between Language and Life*, London: Routledge.

Fox-Genovese, Elizabeth and Lasch-Quinn, Elisabeth (eds) (1999) *Reconstructing History: The Emergence of a New Historical Society*, New York and London: Routledge.

Gallie, William B. (1964) *Philosophy and the Historical Understanding*, London: Chatto & Windus.

Gardiner, Patrick ([1952] 1961) *The Nature of Historical Explanation*, Oxford: Oxford University Press.

Gardiner, Patrick (1959) (ed.) *Theories of History*, Glencoe, IL: The Free Press.

Goldstein, Leon (1976) *Historical Knowing,* Austin: University of Texas Press.

Goodman, Jordan (1997) 'History and Anthropology', in Michael Bentley, *Companion to Historiography,* London: Routledge, pp. 783–804.

Harlan, David (1997) *The Degradation of American History*, Chicago: University of Chicago Press.

Hempel, Carl G. (1965) *Aspects of Scientific Explanation*, New York: The Free Press.

Hexter, J.H. (1991) "Carl Becker, Professor Novick, and Me: or, Cheer Up, Professor N.!" *American Historical Review* Forum, 96 (3): 675–82.

Hindess, Barry and Hirst, Paul (1975) *Pre-capitalist Modes of Production*, London: Routledge.

Hoffer, Peter Charles and Stueck, William W. (1994) *Reading and Writing American History: An Introduction to the Historian's Craft* (2 vols), Lexington, MA: D.C. Heath & Company.

Hollinger, David A. (1989) "The Return of the Prodigal: The Persistence of Historical Knowing", *American Historical Review*, 94 (3), June: 610–21.

Hollinger, David A. (1991) "Postmodernist Theory and *Wissenschaftliche* Practice", *American Historical Review* Forum, 96 (3), June: 688–92.

Hunt, Lynn (ed.) (1989) *The New Cultural History,* Berkeley, CA: University of California Press.

Jameson, F. (1991) *Postmodernism, or, The Cultural Logic of Late Capitalism*, London: Verso.

Jenkins, Keith (1997) *Postmodern History Reader*, London: Routledge.

Jenkins, Keith (1999) *Why History?*, London: Routledge.

Jordanova, Ludmilla (2000) *History in Practice,* London: Arnold.

Kearney, Richard and Rainwater, Mara (eds) (1996) *The Continental Philosophy Reader*, London: Routledge, pp. 289–464.

Kellner, Hans (1989) *Language and Historical Representation: Getting the Story Crooked*, Madison, WI: University of Wisconsin Press.

LaCapra, Dominick (1983) *Rethinking Intellectual History: Texts, Contexts, Language*, Ithaca, NY: Cornell University Press.

LaCapra, Dominick and Kaplan, Steven (1982) (eds) *Modern European Intellectual History: Reappraisals and New Perspectives*, Ithaca, NY: Cornell University Press.

Lloyd, Christopher (1986) *Explanation in Social History*, Oxford: Basil Blackwell.

Lorenz, Chris (1994) "Historical Knowledge and Historical Reality: A Plea for 'historical realism'," *History and Theory*, 33 (3): 297–327.

McCullagh, C. Behan (1984) *Justifying Historical Descriptions*, Cambridge: Cambridge University Press.

McCullagh, C. Behan (1991) "Can Our Understanding of Old Texts be Objective", *History and Theory*, 30 (3): 324–38.

McCullagh, C. Behan (1998) *The Truth of History*, London: Routledge.

Mandelbaum, Maurice (1977) *The Anatomy of Historical Knowledge*, Baltimore, MD: The Johns Hopkins University Press.

Marwick, Arthur ([1970] 1989) *The Nature of History*, third edn, London: Macmillan.

Marwick, Arthur ([1993] 1998) "'A Fetishism of Documents'? The Salience of Source-based History', in Henry Kozicki, *Developments in Modern Historiography*, Milton Keynes: The Open University, pp. 107–38.

Marwick, Arthur (2001) *The New Nature of History*, Houndmills: Palgrave.

Megill, Allan (1985) *Prophets of Extremity: Nietzsche, Heidegger, Foucault, Derrida*, Berkeley, CA: University of California Press.

Mink, Louis (1987) "Narrative Form as a Cognitive Instrument", in R. Canary and H. Kozicki (eds), *The Writing of History: Literary Form and Historical Understanding*, Madison, WI: University of Wisconsin Press.

Munslow, Alun (1997) *Deconstructing History*, London: Routledge.

Munslow, Alun (2000) *The Routledge Companion to Historical Studies*, London: Routledge.

Munslow, Alun (2004) *The New History*, Harlow: Pearson Education.

Norman, Andrew P. (1991) "Telling It Like It Was: Historical Narratives on Their Own Terms", *History and Theory*, 30 (2): 119–35.

Oakeshott, Michael (1933) *Experience and Its Modes*, Cambridge: Cambridge University Press.

Poster, Mark (1997) *Cultural History and Postmodernity: Disciplinary Readings and Challenges*, New York: Columbia University Press.

Ricoeur, Paul ([1975] 1994) *The Rule of Metaphor: Multi-Disciplinary Studies of the Creation of Meaning*, London: Routledge.

Ricoeur, Paul (1981) *Hermeneutics and the Human Sciences*, Cambridge: Cambridge University Press.

Ricoeur, Paul (1984) *The Reality of the Historical Past*, Wisconsin-Alpha Chapter of Phi Sigma Tau, Marquette University.

Ricoeur, Paul (1986) *The Rule of Metaphor: Multi-disciplinary Studies of the Creation of Meaning in Language*, trans. Robert Czerny, London: Routledge.

Roberts, Clayton (1996) *The Logic of Historical Explanation*, University Park, PA: The Pennsylvania State University Press.

Roberts, Geoffrey (1997) "Postmodernism Versus the Standpoint of Action", *History and Theory*, 36 (2): 249–60.

Roediger, David (1998) *Black on White: Black Writers on What it Means to be White*, New York: Schocken Books.

Roediger, David (2002) *Colored White: Transcending the Racial Past*, Berkeley, CA: University of California Press.

Rorty, Richard (1997) 'Introduction', in Wilfred Sellars *Empiricism and the Philosophy of Mind*, Cambridge, MA: Harvard University Press, pp. 1–12.

Rosenstone, Robert (1988) *Mirror in the Shrine: American Encounters with Meiji Japan*, Cambridge, MA: Harvard University Press.

Rosenstone, Robert A. (1995) *Visions of the Past: The Challenge of Film to Our Idea of History*, Cambridge, MA: Harvard University Press.

Rosenstone, Robert A. and Munslow, Alun (2004 forthcoming) *Experiments in Rethinking History*, London: Routledge.

Scott, Joan W. (1988) *Gender and the Politics of History*, New York: Columbia University Press.

Scott, Joan W. (1989) "History in Crisis? The Others' Side of the Story", *American Historical Review* Forum, 94 (3), June: 680–92.

Strawson, Peter F. (ed.) (1974) "Imagination and Perception", in *Freedom and Resentment and Other Essays*, London: Methuen.

Symonds, Deborah A. (1999) 'Living in the Scottish Record Office', in Elizabeth Fox-Genovese and Elisabeth Lasch-Quinn, *Reconstructing History: The Emergence of a New Historical Society*, New York and London: Routledge, pp. 164–75.

Topolski, Jerzy (1991) "Towards an Integrated Model of Historical Explanation", *History and Theory*, 30 (3): 324–38.

Trachtenberg, Marc (1999) "The Past under Siege", in Elizabeth Fox-Genovese and Elisabeth Lasch-Quinn (eds) *Reconstructing History: The Emergence of a New Historical Society*, New York and London: Routledge, p. 9.

Turner, F.J. (1961) "The Significance of the Frontier in American History", reprinted in *Frontier and Section*, edited by R.A. Billington, Englewood Cliffs, NJ: Prentice Hall.

Walsh, W.H. (1958) *An Introduction to the Philosophy of History*, London: Hutchinson.

White, Hayden (1973) *Metahistory: The Historical Imagination in Nineteenth Century Europe*, Baltimore, MD: The Johns Hopkins University Press.

White, Hayden (2000) 'Response to Iggers', *Rethinking History*, 4, (3): 391–406.

Windschuttle, Keith (1995) *The Killing of History: How Literary Critics and Social Theorists are Murdering Our Past*, New York: The Free Press.

Index

Numbers in **bold** type indicate articles.

eBooks – at www.eBookstore.tandf.co.uk

A library at your fingertips!

eBooks are electronic versions of printed books. You can store them on your PC/laptop or browse them online.

They have advantages for anyone needing rapid access to a wide variety of published, copyright information.

eBooks can help your research by enabling you to bookmark chapters, annotate text and use instant searches to find specific words or phrases. Several eBook files would fit on even a small laptop or PDA.

NEW: Save money by eSubscribing: cheap, online access to any eBook for as long as you need it.

Annual subscription packages

We now offer special low-cost bulk subscriptions to packages of eBooks in certain subject areas. These are available to libraries or to individuals.

For more information please contact webmaster.ebooks@tandf.co.uk

We're continually developing the eBook concept, so keep up to date by visiting the website.

www.eBookstore.tandf.co.uk